SYRIA AND LEBANON UNDER FRENCH MANDATE

SYRIA AND LEBANON UNDER FRENCH MANDATE

STEPHEN HEMSLEY LONGRIGG

Here were the end, had anything an end. . . .
The act, over and ended, falls and fades:
What was once seen, grows what is now described,
Then talked of, told about, a tinge the less
In every fresh transmission; till it melts,
Trickles in silent orange or wan grey
Across our memory . . . .

R. BROWNING, *The Ring and the Book*, xii.

Issued under the auspices of the
Royal Institute of International Affairs

OXFORD UNIVERSITY PRESS

LONDON NEW YORK TORONTO

1958

Oxford University Press, Amen House, London E.C.4
GLASGOW NEW YORK TORONTO MELBOURNE WELLINGTON
BOMBAY CALCUTTA MADRAS KARACHI KUALA LUMPUR
CAPE TOWN IBADAN NAIROBI ACCRA

PRINTED IN GREAT BRITAIN

PREFACE

THE formal historian of a very recent period, however conscientious, must labour under great disadvantages. These concern his materials, still largely unassimilated or unpublished: his own power of perspective, the more liable to distortion as the objects viewed are nearer, or too near: and his own human tendency to prejudice in a field in which he has himself observed, with emotion and doubtless some partiality, the unfolding of the events described. Nor can he, after researches of some years duration, expect as many readers, or the same rewards, as the visiting journalist, political pamphleteer or imaginative gossip-writer. These are highly deterrent considerations and may explain why no reasonably satisfying history of the French Mandate in Syria and the Lebanon seems yet to have been published.

I have been led to undertake the present work partly by personal interest in the territory (to which I paid many and sometimes prolonged visits between 1925 and 1950) and by my acquaintance there with a considerable number of French, Syrian, and Lebanese residents or officials: partly as a devoted admirer (outside the political sphere) of the French genius and achievement, and at the same time a friend of Arabs for more than forty years: and partly because, as an official for some years in another and neighbouring Mandated Territory ('Iraq), I believed that I could appreciate fairly well the difficulties and possibilities of the mandatory relationship. And, apart from the remembered gleanings from innumerable conversations with French and Syrian friends on these and similar problems, a fairly wide range of written sources in French, Arabic, Italian, and English was available.

The episode of the French Mandate ended twelve years ago and, *tant bien que mal*, can be seen now as a completed whole. As such it seems to offer an interesting and not profitless subject for historical treatment, and one upon which a tentative judgement can be passed. Some at least of current misconceptions can be corrected and a sounder factual basis offered for the use of popular writers, journalists, politicians, and the like than is at present available. This may be the more useful since the annals of the Levant from 1920 to 1945 well illustrate the earlier working of certain persisting forces (notably that of Arab nationalism) in that region, and to some may seem to throw light also on the scarcely less persisting French attitude to their other dependent—or till recently dependent—Islamic territories. My own conclusion, as will be seen in these pages, has been that the French Mandatory conferred for twenty years considerable material and practical advantages on the territory entrusted to it, and performed without reward services which have been on the whole unduly depreciated by the recipients, and by the world: but that France's handling of political issues was generally, indeed surprisingly, maladroit and destined, through its persistence in inappropriate and anachronistic policies, to end in disillusion and failure.

It was no doubt unfortunate, and prejudicial to the position of France, that the armed forces of my own country, each time in association with a much smaller French contingent, were twice compelled by the exigencies of global war to occupy the territory which in 1918 was shortly to be placed, and in 1941 had for twenty years been placed, under a French Mandate. On each occasion, as will be seen, a measure of misunderstanding or even acrimony resulted as between the two Powers. In so far as this was due to tactlessness or to unauthorized local action on either side, to natural minor clashes of immediate interest, to a differing attitude to Arab aspirations, or, far more, to the profoundly dissimilar temperament and mind of the two peoples, a degree of such misunderstanding was no doubt inevitable; but I have found difficult to explain the curious and persistent obsession of the French at all levels that the British themselves cherished ambitious or malicious designs on Syria, or desired to replace the French there. It is a matter of indisputable general history that this was never the case; nothing could, at any period, have induced the British Government to accept in Syria the responsibilities—or anything remotely resembling them—which the French had assumed and so tenaciously retained.

I can make no claim to have consulted all, or nearly all, the possible sources of information on my subject. These are almost infinitely copious and varied, and the writer of a general history must, if he wants ever to publish, be content with less. Nevertheless, the bibliographical note attached to this book as its Appendix E will show that its author has not been entirely neglectful; certainly no one version of events—that of the High Commissioner's report-writers, or of French or Arab publicists, or of Italian critics or British or American observers—has been accepted without critical reference to others, or without due allowance for the elements of prejudice, self-congratulation or *suppressio veri*, of which few are wholly innocent. I myself have aimed above all at complete objectivity and sober truth, with moderation in such judgements as seemed unavoidable; and my narrative must thereby lack, I realize, the bright colours, the sweeping condemnations and eulogies beloved by many readers. Firm supporters of a partisan French or Arab position will, if they read these pages at all, doubtless approve whatever in them appears to favour their own case or claims, and reject what is damaging. I shall be surprised, however, if my critics, from whatever quarter, convince me that they are more objective than I; if they correct my facts, or suggest valid considerations which I have overlooked, I shall be grateful: as will, I hope, the future historian who, some years hence, will retell the story with greater fullness and more penetration than mine.

S.H.L.

CONTENTS

NOTE ON TRANSLITERATION

Arabic names have been, for the most part, transliterated upon recognized lines, except that (i) vowel-quantity signs are omitted: (ii) *hamza* has usually been omitted, except when medial: (iii) ذ is transliterated as dh, ض as ḍh, ظ as dh.

The English version of many common place-names (Damascus, Aleppo, Beirut, Alexandretta, Sidon, Tyre) is retained, in the interest of the general reader. French versions (Hasatché, Alep, Beyrouth, Aley, Merdjayoun, etc.), are not used, since these are strange to English readers. In certain cases, however, the western (or French) rendering of family names (Eddé, Chamoun, Tabet, Trad) is used, when the holders of these names themselves habitually speak and write French, and use this form.

I

TURKISH PROVINCE

I. COUNTRY AND PEOPLE

THE name of Syria has, in ancient and modern history, designated varying areas; it has never been the title of a single, independent state including all 'Syrian' and no other territory. As a defined geographic unit it is bounded southward by desert, eastward by the steppe country which separates it from central 'Iraq, north-eastward by the upper Euphrates (though Syrian claims to the northern Jazira, and to Mosul itself, were and are not unknown), and westward by the sea. On its northern and north-western face the Amanus range, the Cilician plain beyond, and the Anatolian regions of 'Ayntab and Mar'ash, Urfa, and even Diyarbakr have at times been claimed as Syrian. The inclusion of Palestine in any geographic or historical, ethnic or cultural Syria is, at least since later antiquity, beyond question; on the other hand, the Roman province of Syria, the Turkish *Wilayet* of Damascus, and the Syrian Republic of today, each contained or contain no more than a fraction of Syrian territory. The country, an episode in whose fortunes is to be the subject of these pages, is that part of historical and geographical Syria which fell under French Mandate after the First World War.

It is one of the most interesting countries in the world. In contrast to the drab aridity of much Asian and Arab territory, Syria with the Lebanon possesses not only a long Mediterranean coastline, often of striking beauty, but a hinterland varied by mountain ranges of scenic majesty and bearing historic names—Amanus, Lebanon, Anti-Lebanon, Hermon, and the rest: by rich intermontane plains and valleys, high or marshy: by famous rivers—the Orontes (Nahr al-'Aṣi), the Liṭani, the sources of the Jordan, the Euphrates itself: and by broad fertile uplands and arid steppes, merging eastward and southward into desert. To each of these regions belongs its characteristic air and climate, its humidity or dryness, at their best admirably healthy and inspiring, at their worst tolerable: to each its own vegetation and fauna in unusual variety over a wide range of species: to each its own great and famous cities. If these pages fail to interest their readers, the fault will never lie with the country where the scene is laid: a scene which offers the magic of ancient historic and prehistoric eminence, and within it contains the sites, or the survivors, of cities among the oldest in the world, with place-names and natural features which connect the present day with the great empires and most famous personalities of antiquity and the Middle Ages. A region fascinating for its fusion (sometimes incomplete) of races and of cultural contributions from East and West spread over 5,000 years, Syria cannot but be a paradise of the archaeologist and scholar, historian and sociologist, dear equally to the student and devotee of early and medieval Islam, Christianity, and Judaism. At no epoch from the dawn of history until the conquest by the Ottoman Turk in the sixteenth century of our era has the Syrian scene been uninteresting or insignificant; many a time it has afforded the stage upon which the best that contemporary civilization could offer—in imperial status, in art and culture, in material progress—was displayed. Nor, even in the four duller centuries which followed the victories of Salim the Grim, was there lack of striking personalities and the living seeds, at least, of future re-emergence.

The territory lies open in each direction to a varied succession of physical and cultural invasions. It forms a vital area in the land-bridge between three continents, whereby its fortunes have inevitably partaken of the histories of greater neighbours and of world movements. It has been profoundly influenced by the Mediterranean Sea, its western boundary and route to Europe, and equally by the presence to eastward of a living and inexhaustible desert world. It has found livelihood and wealth not only in its own resources but in controlling the passage of merchandise across its territory: and, with this traffic, that of ideas and cultures. It has attracted immigrants by its waters and climate, empires by its strategic advantage, conquerors by its cornfields, forests, and gardens. The immemorial routes ran and run by sea to Europe, by the coast road through Acre and Gaza ('Akka and Ghazza) to the Nile Delta, by mid-desert or by northern desert-fringes to the Euphrates and 'Iraq, by way of Cilicia to central and western Asia Minor, by the northernmost Jazira to eastern Turkey-in-Asia, by the Ḥawran and east of Jordan to the Ḥijaz and the Holy Cities, and by the Wadi Sirḥan to Central Arabia through deserts which have at no time been barriers to folk movement. Free passage both ways along all these routes has been, for millennia, an element fundamental to the fabric of the Syrian people and its fortunes.

The highly differentiated regions into which the country itself is divided owe their character in part to variation in land surface due to mountain uplift, to inter-mountain plain or depression, and to flatness of the hinterland, in part to varying rainfall which follows generally the elevation of the ground and its nearness to the cloud-bearing sea. It results from these natural accidents that different areas of the country vary greatly both in their power to support life and in their openness of access; and these features have in some measure determined not only the way of life of regional communities, but the degree to which they have been conscious of a partial separateness. But it is important to notice that no river, or desert, or mountain range in Syria is impassable, or even difficult to cross or penetrate; none has been or could be an effective barrier. As far as the population has desired, there has always been (though not with uniform facility) interregional movement throughout the territory. Its internal variations increase its interest and in some measure diversify its civilization, but detract nothing from its essential physical unity which (in its true limits of geographical Syria) is marked with unusual clearness.

The population of the Syria of the early twentieth century had, in its racial mixture, varied little for some centuries past. It consisted, then as now, of an amalgam whose constituent elements included a contribution from most of the races of western Asia, attracted at some period towards the conquest of, or infiltration into, so favourable and so accessible a land. To whatever Mediterranean and Alpine-type human stock had first possessed it invaders had been added from each direction through the ages, a process begun long before the dawn of history and continued, in its earliest and later light, by arrivals of Amorites and Aramaeans from the steppe, Hittites and Kurds from Anatolia, Greeks and Romans and Crusaders from the West, Mongols and Turks from the East; and, most persistently over the latest two millennia, Arab tribesmen from the barren lands of the south and east. The digestion of these and other incoming elements to form a substantially homogeneous whole—not without its half-assimilated enclaves—was aided by centuries of time, close interpenetration, and identity of living conditions; by these, as its end-product, it fashioned a Syrian people, differentiated by dialect, outlook, and a score of minor peculiarities from its Arab neighbours, in spite of common language, faith, conditions of life, and a body of shared tradition. Syria in 1914, like its sister-countries, had been, in respect of at least nine-tenths of its people, self-consciously an Arab country for a thousand years, thanks to the Arab-Islamic conquest, to the subsequent accretion of Arab population through the centuries, and to the unquestioned dominance achieved by that culture and tradition; but it had retained within the world of Arab culture, which stretched from ‘Iraq to Aden and to Morocco, its own character and individuality.

Its formative elements, innumerable and largely beyond analysis as in all human societies, included the no longer distinguishable residue of all that the various racial and cultural contributions had offered, and most notably those of the great religions between which the population was divided; they included also the influences of the country itself, its particular living conditions, and its orientation amongst the nations. But to these age-long factors had been added, especially during the past century, another of great significance: that of the influence of European thought, method, and aspiration. The geographical position of the Levant, and its varied forces of attraction, had indeed at all periods ensured it against isolation from Europe; in early modern times it was better known to, and more frequented by, Europeans than perhaps any part of Asia or Africa. A period of yet more frequent traffic began with the dawn of the nineteenth century. The means of European penetration were various; they can be here briefly dismissed as the processes and agents of trade, industry, and shipping, the great improvement in communication by sea and land, the diffusion of news, the presence of consular agents of the Powers, the emigration of Syrians in thousands to foreign countries, the visits of pilgrims and scholars to southern Syria (that is, Palestine), the relations between local Christian communities and the Churches in Europe, and the establishment of foreign schools and universities on Syrian soil. Indeed, the total of foreign effort in the country (of which some detail will be given in later pages) exceeded in intensity that made in any other eastern land, and the Syrian civilization of the early twentieth century largely, though unevenly, reflected this. Foreign influence, which was but faintly operative among the rural masses of the country, was felt in varying degrees and forms in the towns; it had by no means displaced the traditions or loyalties of Islam, and indeed its claims and ideologies had gained little entrance in some still powerful circles. But its impact had, through the years, modified or transformed not only much of the urban scene and atmosphere—the appearance, housing, equipment, and social habits of the citizens —but had profoundly (though far from uniformly) affected the ways of thought of the leaders in every community, and set standards and created demands to which nothing corresponded in the shabby, transitional conditions, material or administrative, of the Syria of those years. The extent of the variety, both in degree and in kind, with which different communities within the country responded to the calls of 'westernization' will appear in later pages; of Syria as a whole it can be said that it had received, for better or worse, a greater injection of the elixirs or poisons of the West than had any comparable territory, and that these, too often ill-selected and ill-digested—and indeed in many cases quite unintentionally administered, as a by-product of other action—had had deep effects, more disturbing than satisfying, on the bodies and minds of its inhabitants.

The social classification of the people is, in very general terms, easy to establish. A characteristic element at one extremity of the range was the body of camel-owning *badu* (nomadic) tribes on the eastern and southern fringes of the territory: migratory tribesmen—and nominal Sunni Muslims—concerned with little save their own pride, feuds and raiding, their dependence on grazing and on the outpost market-villages, and their avoidance of Government. Next to these come the half-nomadic inlying sheep-owning tribesmen, based on villages in the cultivated zone; their organization and leadership, like those of the *badu*, were on strictly tribal lines unvaried for centuries. Next, the folk of the settled villages of plain, mountain, valley, and sea-coast were numerically the greatest element in the population, since perhaps three-fifths of all Syrians derived their living from their work in their (or their landlords') open cornfields, orchards, or market gardens. In some such areas a tribal organization survived, others were part of the great estates of absent landowners, others but fewer were divided into smallholdings; but in all the dominant features of their outlook were a deep rural conservatism, a devotion to the immediate all-important interests of rainfall and pests, crops and their prices, a natural regionalism based on strong local attachments and suspicion of the world outside, and, towards Government, an attitude of pessimistic resignation.

The lower orders in the towns—day-labourers, artisans, small shopkeepers, transport workers—had less of conservatism in daily scene and habit and less indifference to—and more demands from—Government, with a greater exposure to multiform modern influences, and to the impact of ready leadership. Finally, at the top of the social structure (the governmental hierarchy apart) stood the varied ranks of the upper-middle and upper classes of the larger towns. In the less eminent but larger part of these appeared the merchants, larger shopkeepers, contractors, managers, officials, and petty industrialists, while in the highest element stood the superior men of religion of all the communities, the richer property owners, a few outstanding men of business, and those writers, publicists, and lawyers who formed the specifically political element.

These social cleavages, not more marked, after all, than in other countries, did not destroy the important element of homogeneity which was permitted by the blurred dividing lines between them, and was encouraged by close mutual familiarity and the identity of the general, age-long Syrian conditions of life. All shared in a deep background of Arabism, nearly all in the satisfying tradition of Islam; all were at one in enduring a foreign Government, and in their places in the international world; and all, save a small prosperous class, were afflicted with the pervasive lowness of living standards which characterized all contemporary Turkish territory, and indeed most of the East.

For all the danger of such generalizations, a suggestion of some fundamentals in the Syrian character must be attempted, since, while each social level and each community had its own features, some basic elements seemed common substantially to all. None were without quickness of perception and response, humour and social gifts; the historian of Syria nowhere deals with primitive minds, never with dull stupidity. But the age-long acceptance of social stratification, the long denial of education to the poor, and an element also of Islamic resignation, had divided the public into two unequal groups. Of these, the one, greatly (at least twenty times) the larger in size, was profoundly ignorant of modern knowledge, thought, aspirations, or standards. The other, far more evolved in modern ways and sophistication, was capable, as the masses could not be, of leadership: the leadership, that is, of landowner or rich townsman, of the intelligentsia, or (notably in the minority communities) of the divines. The smallness of the dominant class must be emphasized, and the wide evolutionary gulf which separated it from the deeply ignorant, easily inflamed, and irresponsible masses for which the leaders claimed, nevertheless, to speak: and, equally, the already visible shortcomings of the 'evolved' class itself for which often brilliant qualities of intellect and personality could not easily compensate. These defects were (with notable individual exceptions) those of an over-emotional approach to public affairs, an acquiescence in incomplete study of conditions, a lack of the faculty of sustained, objective thought: and, with these, an inveterate refusal to compromise, or to treat politics as 'the art of the possible'—an art calling for patience and self-abnegation.

2. MUSLIM AND CHRISTIAN

The Sunni Muslim community, by far the greatest in size and ubiquity in the territory, embraced the mass of the population in every area, except in those islands or enclaves which we shall in turn consider. Members of the Sunni community, central to the main body of Islam and closely bound to their brothers in neighbouring lands, were in the religious field at one with their Turkish governors, and by this and by their respect for the Sultan-Caliph were loyal to, though not uncritical of, his régime in all save rare individuals of the 'enlightened' class. They formed the mass of and for whom government existed, and to whom all other communities were tolerated sectarians. By their greatly preponderant numbers and, in a manner fundamental to the Islamic-Turkish system of government, by their relation to the State, and perhaps also by the superiority-complex which these things had engendered, the Sunni majority must necessarily provide the force for any countrywide movement. Meanwhile, in the Administration everywhere (save in autonomous Lebanon) they held nine-tenths of the posts, the official schools were theirs, and they almost alone supplied officers to the Army and Gendarmerie, and judges to the Courts. Their Awqaf (pp. 17–18) were everywhere, with hundreds of employees and thousands of beneficiaries. Socially, they could reckon in scores the 'best families' of every township, with lands and tenants in every village. With less predominance—or, locally, none at all—in the coastal strip, and showing in general a lesser penetration by western influences than that which had transformed their Christian compatriots, the Sunni majority, some 2 million strong, could show nevertheless many members well instructed on western as well as on traditional lines, many households inclining to modern ways.

This majority was, by overwhelming preponderance, Arab; little political, though locally a strong social, significance seemed to attach to the small non-Arab groups present in the body of Sunni Islam. A few Turkoman villages, partly tribal in organization, existed in the northern marches and gave no trouble to their rulers; speaking Turkish, they were survivors of pre-Ottoman streams of Turkish incursion. The Syrian Kurds were of more, but not much more, significance. They supplied an element in the population of Damascus, where they had been partially assimilated to the Arab majority and had learnt Arabic as their second language; and great numbers of their race lived in the foothill region north of Aleppo, where, retaining their tribal loyalties and Kurdish speech, they had for some years been adopting an ordered cultivating life in place of their original nomadism. They had little connexion with the mass of Kurds elsewhere in Turkey. One more non-Arab element, the Circassian (Charkes) villagers settled in Syrian outposts in Ḥamidian days, had resisted all assimilation with Arabs, to whom their foreign ways and unknown language made no appeal. These were law-abiding folk, not unwilling to give service to the Turkish (as later to the French) authorities.

The Sunni community so far described did not include the whole of Syrian Islam. The latter covered also Islamic communities not only doctrinally and socially distinct, but bearing also to the dominant Sunnis a varying relation of solidarity or of dissidence. To the Christian or Jew, these were equally Muslims; to the Muslim orthodox they were, in the normal traffic of life, suspect and inferior, even though in the broader pretensions of Arabism they were treated as securely within the fold and their leading spokesmen could find an assured hearing on public affairs. These sects, thus sited on the fringes of Syrian Islam, were those of the Mutawalli (pl. Mutawila) and the Isma'ili sects of Shi'i belief, the heterodox 'Alawi (or Nuṣayri) villagers, and the Druzes (Duruz).

Of these, the Mutawila, who kept the strict doctrine of Persian or 'Iraqi Shi'ism, were divided between the Biqa' plain, the townships southwards from Beirut, and the southern Lebanon. In the first and last of these areas they formed a local majority; but they were generally a poor and backward folk with little land of their own, and could boast no more than a half-dozen of leading families. Their relations with neighbours were varied, from fear and inhibition to shortlived alliance; their own clan-sense was extremely strong. The strength of the Mutawila was in 1914 some 80,000–100,000. The Isma'ilis, found to the number of perhaps 12,000–15,000 in the Ḥamah area, with a lesser group under Ladhqiya (Latakia), adhered to a creed derived centuries earlier from the main body of Shi'ism but with some mixture of non-Islamic elements. They gave no trouble to their rulers, and little to neighbours.

The 'Alawi or Nuṣayri sectaries, who in their mountain homes behind the Ladhqiya coast-line and west of the Orontes may represent a distinctive blood-mixture as well as a self-conscious culture-group, spoke Arabic (with a small minority of Kurdish-speakers) and lived the life of the most backward Syrian rural masses. Their branch of Shi'ism was heavily mixed with pre-Islamic and possibly Christian elements; outwardly they were distinguished by their extreme veneration for 'Ali, the Prophet's son-in-law. They numbered perhaps 175,000–200,000 souls, were organized in villages, obeyed their feudal leaders, and cultivated the estates of these and of Sunni landowners. The latter formed an important minority in the 'Alawi territory and indeed, with substantial Christian elements, mustered easily a majority among the coastal townsfolk.

The Druzes were collected in three main concentrations: the one, in that part of the Lebanon mountains which they had shared for centuries with the Maronites: a second, on the slopes of Hermon: the third, in the hill-massif called by their name Jabal al-Duruz, which lies east of the inland grain-growing Ḥawran district, to which, increasingly, they had moved since the troubles of 1860. Their beliefs show (in so far as they are known) heavy non-Islamic accretions, and indeed their claim to stand within Islam itself has been widely doubted. But their social habit was closely similar to that of their neighbours, their outlook and way of speech are substantially Islamic, and their racial origins are probably as authentically Arab as those of any Syrian community. The events of 1925–6 were to show how closely their leaders could be identified with the main body of Syrian Muslims, and even before 1914 spokesmen from their Lebanese villages were not absent from the debates of nationalist progressives; but as a community they maintained, in close subordination to a dozen 'noble' families, an unusual isolation, and were ill regarded by all save themselves. The Druze character, dour, unfriendly to strangers, and inclined to savagery, was capable also of loyalty and tough endurance. Educationally, for all their small, secretive class of the religiously 'instructed', they shared with the 'Alawis and the *badu* the most backward place in Syria. Their numbers in the Jabal did not exceed 50,000.

The Turkish Government had, towards these dissident Muslims, no such formulated policy as it had evolved towards the Christian *millets*. Nuṣayris, Druzes, Mutawila, and Isma'ilis were permitted no status as separated sects, their 'personal status' suits and formalities were dealt with perforce by the Sunni Qadḥis, their religious hierarchies were unrecognized, no seats on the Administrative Councils were theirs, and the sense in which it was true that the Christian *millets* formed not only social-religious communities but political parties also, was untrue of the Muslim minorities. The days in which regional enclave-independence could have been claimed or effectively maintained were over; the 'Alawi territory had been militarily subdued and administratively incorporated—though not without its lawless areas or periods—in the mid-nineteenth century; the Druzes in their isolated Mountain had been repeatedly chastened by Turkish forces, and the claims of their dominant families and religious hierarchy had been somehow reconciled with those of normal government. The Jabal al-Duruz enjoyed, indeed, exemption from military service, as a reward for holding the bedouin at bay; and the central Government had long acquiesced in its failure to collect taxes from the Jabal villages. But these privileges, permitted with increasing reluctance, were not due to the status or merits of a religious minority, but to the isolation and strength of the Druze terrain and the sullen tenacity of its people. In general, the future of the Muslim minorities could in 1914 have been prophesied as one of decreasing isolation, progress towards normal government, and full or fuller incorporation in the machine and privileges of the State.

Of the minorities who professed neither Islam nor Christianity, none is here of high significance. The Jews, town-dwelling and Arabic-speaking in Syria, in all some 20,000, were, except in religion, assimilated to the Arab population save in a greater westernization of mind and habit. With self-management of their own community under their *millet* status, and with their own schools with those of the Alliance Israélite Universelle, and conscious of little feeling against them save the normal Muslim (and indeed Christian) attitude of innate superiority, they were neither molested nor dissatisfied, and knew always that they possessed powerful friends abroad.[1] Of the Kurdish-speaking Yazidis in Jabal Sinjar and a few north Jazira villages, with their wild ways and mysterious religion, nothing need be said here; they play no part in Syrian history.

If the same were true of the Christian sects, the story of modern Syria would, if the poorer, be one of less strain and conflict. In point of race the Christians, except the clearly foreign Armenians,[2] differed little from the Muslim majority, unless indeed the compact concentration of the Maronites can indicate some forgotten ethnic separateness: or unless it be accepted that the sects, or some of them, survive from different waves of immigration. All save the Armenians (and many of these) were Arab-speaking, all in manner of life as in environment were closely assimilated to the Muslims. Agriculture was less usually their livelihood, except among the Maronites, while their share in the skilled handicrafts and in modern-type business exceeded the Muslim. Their preference for town-dwelling was due partly to traditional aptitudes, partly to their enjoyment thus of greater security. The general picture of the Christian minorities was in 1914 that of close-knit groups held in some measure to each other by similarity of status and by common distinctness from Islam, but divided by the internal autonomy jealously preserved by each, by social exclusiveness, by doctrinal cleavage, by differing centres of education and worship, and by their varying attitudes to the Government and to foreign friends. They were for the most part scattered widely over the range of (mainly the larger) towns; a congregation of some or most was found in urban centres from Anatolia to the

[1] In the sanjaqs of Jerusalem, Nablus, and Acre, the small surviving Jewish communities (perhaps some 25,000 strong) were since the 1880's, and particularly since 1900, in process of being greatly reinforced by the immigration of European Jews sponsored and financed by patriotic or religious Jewish bodies—a considerable incursion of alien Europeans into Arab territory which attracted at the time little attention elsewhere in Syria.

[2] Except the immigrant elements (Armenian, Nestorian) the local Christians represented substantially that part of the seventh-century Syrian population which, while Arabized with the rest, had for various reasons resisted conversion to Islam.

confines of Egypt; and even the Maronites, the most compact, formed a majority only in a small area of the Lebanon. Each of the major 'nations'—for such, in a certain sense, they were—was officially a *millet* of the Turkish Empire, enjoying thereby the status bestowed by the Ottoman Government since its earliest days, with remarkable liberality, on the communities of 'people of the Book' scattered locally among the Muslim majority: the status of a community autonomy which included jurisdiction in some civil and all personal-status cases, the full control of their properties and schools, and the right to be heard by the Sultan himself through their appointed heads. They enjoyed exemption from military service, until 1909. Each was represented on all local Administrative Councils, and each could contribute a few minor officials. In each the priesthood was highly influential, organized and unified the community, and supplied the secular leadership. Members of each, familiar as fellow townsmen and often well liked, could gain an acceptable place in trade and affairs, could be represented in cultural circles by outstanding spokesmen, and could play an even predominant part in the political thinking of these years. The Syrian Christians, in fact, for all their sophisticated discontent with Turkish methods, and for all their flirtations with foreign friends, had at least until 1909 little cause for complaint against an administration which not merely tolerated but specifically favoured them. Except for the compact Maronite community, the scattered and unformidable Christians need call, it seemed, for no special attention (unless their particularist ambitions should ever clash with the Sultan's Government), while the details of their relation to Ottoman religious and family law could be gradually revised.

The oft-drawn picture of Syria as a 'mosaic of minorities' can be misleading, and this not only by ignoring the immense preponderance of the Sunni Muslim population, but also by unduly emphasizing the elements which separated this majority from the rest, and minimizing the wide common ground which all shared. If there was room for policies of Christian particularism there was room also for thinking on pan-Syrian lines which, without trespass on legitimate community pride and liberties, would express the essential unity of the territory, the ages of familiar coexistence, the shared racial origins, and the great common legacy of Arabism.

That at this time the Christian communities had temporarily outstripped the Muslim in the ways, the skills, and the mental attitudes of the West, could not be doubted. This was due to the orientation given to their interests first by their religion, then by their residence in the towns most open to cosmopolitan traffic, and again by the example of some outstanding pioneers, by the active interest in the Eastern Churches shown by the Governments, ecclesiastics, and publics of the West, and by the influence of schools founded and sustained in Syria by these latter. The Christians had, it is obvious, no monopoly of westernization in contemporary Syria, since this had spread also far and deeply into upper and middle-class Muslim society; but, with a lesser force of traditional religious-social thinking among the *millets* to be overcome, it had advanced further and more deeply in the Christian and Jewish communities than elsewhere.

All or almost all the Christians of the territory had participated in the striking phenomenon of emigration from Syria, notably from the coastal areas and the Lebanon ranges, to the countries of South and North America, West Africa, Egypt, and even Australia. The motives for this persistent movement were those of poverty and land-hunger at home, an unprogressive Government, Christian hatred (after 1909) of conscription, and the need felt by gifted traders for wider business opportunities. By 1914 nearly half a million Syrians lived abroad, enriching their home-staying kinsmen with remittances which saved many a needy family in its village and built many a red-tiled house.

No political importance was likely to attach to the small remnant of Nestorian (or Assyrian) Christians found in northern Syria, and not much more to that part of the Catholicized (or Uniate) ex-Nestorian community known as Chaldean. Each numbered a few thousand, each was an exiled splinter from a greater Church abroad. The tiny Protestant communities (Presbyterian, or rarely Anglican) were all the product of American and British missions, and were significant only by the personal distinction of certain of the converts. The same is true of the few hundred Catholics of the Latin Rite.

Still without serious weight in the society or politics of the territory, were the Syrian Orthodox (or Jacobite) monophysites, of whom under their Patriarch resident at Mardin some hundreds lived in Beirut, Ḥamah, and the Biqa‘, some thousands in Ḥumṣ (Homs), the northern Jazira, and Aleppo. These, distinct in doctrine as in community organization, mixed easily with their neighbours and could claim distinguished spokesmen. Their Catholic counterpart—that is, the part of their community converted to the Roman faith—was controlled by another Patriarch, also resident at Mardin. It was represented by groups of a few thousand faithful in each of Damascus and Aleppo wilayets, and a few hundred elsewhere.

The Armenians in Syria, a community far less numerous than later events were to make it, had known no more than glimpses of the terrors of persecution which elsewhere in Turkey had horrified the world; even in periods of fear and alarm they had in Syria been as well treated, and had enjoyed the same condescending freedom, as other Christians of the country. They were prominent in business, admirably industrious, excellent artisans, often wealthy, and led by a highly cultivated upper class. Most retained the use of their own language, but commonly understood Arabic also. Their largest colony was in Aleppo, with smaller groups in Beirut and other towns. The majority of these were members of the Gregorian, or national, Church with its wide international organization under regional Patriarchs; but a large minority had been converted to Catholicism. These formed the Armenian Catholic Church, whose chief strength was in the Aleppo wilayet.

A similar process of partial secession had sundered the Eastern Orthodox (or Greek Orthodox) Church, most ancient of the Churches independent of Rome; a considerable minority of these also had been detached to form the important Greek Catholic Church. The still Orthodox majority, under their (Arab) Patriarch, retained in 1914 little of the original Greek either in their liturgy or (except in Jerusalem) their priesthood; it was an Arab Church, generously befriended by Russia to secure a Russian hold in the Holy Land. Its numerous congregations were scattered throughout the territory, with strong representation in Ladhqiya and its coastal villages, in central Syria and Aleppo, in the northern and central Lebanon, and in Beirut; they were strengthened by men and families of high standing and by well-organized institutions. The Uniate Church of the Greek Catholics, or Malkites, could boast lesser numbers but with an equal dispersion, not less progress in western education, greater wealth, and many distinguished sons. Their largest concentration was at Damascus, with others in villages of Lebanon and the Biqa', Aleppo, Beirut, Ḥumṣ, and the Ḥawran.

The Greek Catholics, like the other Uniate Churches, were in their social and political thinking the most likely allies of the important sect yet to be considered, the Maronites. This ancient community, which had entered the Roman fold centuries earlier while retaining no little of its own ancient ways, was domiciled almost solely in the Lebanon, Biqa', and coastal towns. Their virile character and strong community self-consciousness, their record of centuries of valley-fighting and even of local empire, and their domination by a powerful priesthood under their redoubtable Patriarch, combined to give the Maronites something of the character of a miniature nation. This, with its ancient faith and its leanings to the West led by able scholars and patriots, and the sympathy evoked by its earlier sufferings at Druze and Turkish hands, had gained for the central region of its territory the privilege, without parallel in Turkey, of autonomous status under the Sultan (pp. 21 ff.). The Maronites, some 250,000 strong and consolidated by history, present privilege, and close geographic concentration, were likely to pose a problem to whoever should try thereafter to normalize their status as Syrian subjects.

3. TURKISH GOVERNMENT

Something has been indicated of the attitude of the Turks in their administration of Syria both to the majority and minority sects of Islam and to the tiny Christian 'nations' who formed a small proportion of the population. It remains to review more generally the tone and capacity of latter-day Ottoman rule in this Arab province, and to assess whatever could be bequeathed by it to a successor Government, including the training in statecraft derivable from it by the Syrians who participated, or who were eager to replace it.

Syria had in 1914 been for 400 years a part of the Ottoman dominions: a period forming, no doubt, the least glorious and the least interesting of its history. During the first seven-eighths of these years, until the middle of the nineteenth century, the territory had witnessed almost no material development; the mass of its people, in its age-long feudal and stratified organization, had inclined more to the stagnation of medieval Islam than to the quickly changing phases of society in contemporary Europe. In spite of a measure of 'western' penetration through the traffic of the ports, the pressure of Frankish traders, missionaries, and consuls, the growing effects of modern communications, a decade of Egyptian occupation, and latterly some stirrings of well-intentioned modernity in the Turkish army and administration itself, Syria during this long period endured, with many interruptions by the uprising of local potentates, the rigours and liabilities —with few of the blessings—of government as the remote province of a foreign Power. Pasha succeeded Pasha at Aleppo, Damascus, Tripoli, Sidon, Acre; tenures of office were usually brief, promotion or permanence obtained commonly by bribes, the higher offices rarely held by Syrians; taxation was capricious and unequal, order was maintained fitfully in the more accessible areas, public services scarcely existed, justice was archaic or unobtainable. Yet this régime, forming the normal and not unacceptable background to the life of the Muslim masses—to whom, indeed, no other form of State or society was easily imaginable—was congenial enough to the upper and upper-middle classes at least of the Sunni-Muslim community, was supported by the powerful clique of its own functionaries, was criticized only in whispers by the minorities, and was on the whole tolerated by the foreigners whose Capitulations[1] saved them from its worst features.

In contrast to these earlier centuries the Turkish Government of the later nineteenth and early twentieth centuries represented a compromise between the primitive conceptions and flagrant abuses of the earlier age and the modern type of government which the statesmen of Europe—and indeed the irresistible pressure of world exigencies—were pressing on the Ottoman Empire. Upon a public in Syria much of whose upper stratum was rapidly becoming aware of western ideas was now imposed a semblance of controlled and departmentalized government. With little pretence at other than foreign and authoritarian rule, the territory was at least divided under the 'wilayet system' into regular administrative units—the wilayet under its Istanbul-appointed Wali, the sanjaq with its usually Turkish but sometimes Syrian Mutaṣarrif, the qadḥa with its usually local Qa'immaqam, the naḥiya with its local Mudir—and the familiar provinces and districts[2] (which still in substance hold the field) came into existence. With them, and with half a century of fitful and fumbling progress in reluctant and too often misconceived and ill-applied 'reform', came all the familiar phenomena of latter-day Ottoman government.

Amid all the criticism which Ḥamidian and 'Young Turk' efforts in government have aroused, it is to be remembered that, much like its unreformed precursor, the newer régime, not unacceptable to the great majority of its subjects, and not easily replaceable, enjoyed considerable advantages. The first of these was the almost universal prestige of the Sultan-Caliph, the Islamic sanction implicit in his government, and the continuity it had enjoyed for four centuries. Next came a profound knowledge of local psychology and conditions, unapproachable by at least any western successor. Thirdly, a considerable (but generally underrated) skill was exercised in day-by-day administration by dint of great elasticity, ready expedients unknown to law or regulation, and acquiescence in the lowest tolerable standards. A valuable weapon too in a government so unambitious was possession of the sole

[1] The Capitulations granted by successive Sultans of Turkey to foreign governments were essentially the grant of the privilege of Christian non-Turks to be judged according to their own laws while living in Turkish territory. The first such grant was made to the French in 1536. Subsequent capitulatory grants followed this pattern and were normally renewed by incoming sovereigns. The French privileges were many times renewed and restated, and similar grants were made to the British in 1583 and thereafter to Holland in 1613, Austria in 1718, Russia in 1784, and to almost every other major Power (including the U.S.A.) in that century or the next. Every foreign colony in Turkey became thereby, in a measure, a 'State within a State'.

[2] A table in Appendix A (i), p. 369 below, gives the administrative units in 1914.

'fountain of honour'—the gifts, privileges, appointments by which a measure of goodwill and obedience could be bought: and, with this, an equal monopoly of military power.

Such were the advantages which permitted Turkish rule to survive, never effectively questioned, in spite of its abiding poverty and defective equipment, its ill-trained, ill-paid personnel, the difficulties created for it by European creditors and critics, the ceaseless wars and secessions which were currently distracting the Empire and diverting its resources, and the frequent acts of unwisdom by the ruling clique. It is indeed remarkable that, in spite of all these, Syria—largely by reason of the strong foreign element in its cultural life, and the material development of 1880 to 1914—was reckoned the most advanced of Ottoman provinces; and although criticism of the Turkish administration by its intelligentsia grew more outspoken with each succeeding decade, the régime could on the whole point to considerable and continuing improvement, not least under the Ḥamidian autocracy itself. The latter could claim, indeed, to be notably favourable to Syria; Sultan 'Abd al-Ḥamid II surrounded himself with an Arab (largely Syrian) bodyguard, employed Syrians in high places, built the Ḥijaz Railway, settled Circassian refugees on the eastern fringes, increased army garrisons, appreciated the importance of the land route to Egypt via Syria after the construction of the Suez Canal in 1869, and permitted foreign railway-building.

But the picture of the territory in the latest Turkish period is, on the whole, drab and uninspiring enough. The legislation imposed upon it was, however well intentioned, often unsuitable or barely applicable, and in practice largely ignored. The Administrative Councils in districts and municipalities were at best representative only of a small upper class, and chosen by scarcely concealed official nomination; the higher officials were usually Turks; and in spite of the presence of many competent and honest officials the standards of administration were low, corruption widespread, delays inordinate, confusion general.

If the Army[1] had indeed been modernized earlier than any branch of the civil administration, and if, thanks to the high Turkish military qualities, it had considerable fighting value, it was in Syria none the less ill equipped, ill paid, and ill treated, its units used or misused for widely varying purposes, its transport and supplies roughly improvised as occasion demanded, its specialist departments primitive, its officers widely ranging from the excellent to the deplorable. The troops in Syria, four-fifths Syrian by race, were recruited by conscription from Muslims (and from

[1] Under the current system, Damascus was the Headquarters of the Fifth Army.

Christians after 1909) and habitually detested their period of service.

Law and order were normally maintained with fair reliability, but violent breaches of the peace were still not infrequent and called for yearly punitive columns. These, not always successful, were conducted with great severity against disturbers of tranquillity or reluctant tax-payers among the tribes of the eastern fringe, the Nuṣayris of the Ladhqiya hinterland, or the dour Druzes in their Mountain; but of protracted insurgence, or the régime of the 'valley lords' of previous centuries, there was no longer question. The Gendarmerie, an effective force in spite of many inadequacies, were ubiquitous on roads and in small-town posts, and alone made out-station government a reality.

Administering codes of law of which part had been modernized but much remained archaic and confused, the Courts[1]—other than the Mixed or Capitulatory Courts[2]—were of two types. Issues of personal status, and all matters[3] covered by the Shara' (Islamic law and usage) or by the codes of the Christian or Jewish communities were dealt with by the Shar'iya Courts under their Qaḍhis or, with full discretion,[4] by the heads of Councils of the Christian sects, whose decisions the Turkish Execution department would carry out on demand. Cases of normal civil, commercial, or criminal type were within the competence of the Niḏhamiya Courts (of the Peace, of First Instance, and of Appeal), and were judged under codes based usually on French models but amended and confused by an inextricable series of later legislation. Though on paper comprehensive, the system was in fact inadequate in its contradictory basis of law, in its procedural confusions and delays, and by its employment of a personnel entirely inadequate in instruction and, too often, in character. Execution was capricious and uncertain. The jails were filthy and grossly maladministered.

The administration of the Muslim Awqaf—Religious Endowments, or Pious Bequests—calling in their various categories[5]

---

[1] The Niḏhamiya (Regular) Courts were instituted throughout Syria in 1879.
[2] The Capitulatory Courts included the Mixed and the Consular Courts. The former, which were Turkish Courts, dealt with commercial and all civil suits between a Turk and a foreigner; the latter dealt with all cases—civil, commercial, or penal—between two foreigners, and derived their authority from that of the foreign State concerned.
[3] These were marriage, divorce, nullity, alimony, affiliation, guardianship, succession, and allied matters.
[4] The competence of the 'Community Courts' of the Christian and Jewish *millets*, under their Patriarchs, Bishops, or Rabbis, varied slightly according to the privileges granted to the *millet*. This competence did not usually include matters of succession, for which reference had to be made to the Shara' Courts.
[5] The Awqaf Maḏhbuṭa (that is, 'attached' to the Government) were administered by the Directorate of Awqaf: the Awqaf Mulḥaqa ('controlled') were administered by a trustee under the supervision of the Directorate. Awqaf Mudawwara ('transferred') were controlled by the Finance authorities: and Awqaf Mustathnat was administered by trustees, without supervision.

for various degrees of official control, was conducted by Muslim jurists under rules of great rigidity; but these were unadapted to serve modern social purposes, and were applied with little liberality. By result the Awqaf in Syria presented a deplorable picture of neglected properties and institutions, wasted funds, outdated or misleading records (if records at all), and a host of parasitic employees.

The fiscal system was at once simple and despairingly inept. Apart from Customs revenues, charged uniformly *ad valorem* at rates[1] for whose amendment the agreement of the creditor Powers was necessary, the main sources of revenue were the traditional tithe[2] on agricultural produce values, collected in cash by tax-farming in the more accessible areas: the tax on buildings and other (unbuilt) real property: and the tax on animals, based on some semblance of annual count. Lesser sources of revenue—the professional or (in certain cases) income tax, road and vehicle taxes, and a number of 'fees for services'—contributed little but could be highly vexatious. Certain revenues had long since been allotted to the service of the Ottoman Public Debt, a monopolistic joint-stock company[3] which supported its own administration for collection; these were the taxes on alcohol, tobacco,[4] silk, salt, and skins, with a stamp-duty and various licence-fees and the proceeds of a 3 per cent. surcharge on Customs duties. Throughout the field of tax-collection, whether for the Turkish treasury or for its European creditors, inefficiency and corruption were ubiquitous; but the system continued in spite of all to operate, was deeply rooted, and its replacement was to prove difficult. The currency itself was stabilized, in spite of widespread forgery, by the use of gold coins and an adequate silver and copper issue; paper money, issued under monopoly by the Imperial Ottoman Bank, was almost unknown in Syria before 1914.

Where missionary enterprise was so widely developed, it would have been idle to expect from an impoverished State much achievement in services of Public Health or Education. These in fact made, in Turkish Syria, no attempt to meet even minimum needs. The State educational effort was limited to a few primary schools in the large towns, attended chiefly by poor Muslim

[1] Charged at 8 per cent. until 1908, thereafter till 1914 at 11 per cent. In 1914 the rate was raised (without the Powers' concurrence) to 15 per cent., and next year to 30 per cent.

[2] The tithe was not collected in the Lebanon.

[3] The O.P.D. was administered by a Board of seven members representing the countries and banks interested; the original French share (1881) was 40, the British 28, per cent.

[4] The Tobacco Monopoly was ceded in 1883 to the 'Régie Co-interessée des Tabacs', which paid the Ottoman Public Debt a fixed annual sum. The first agreement, for thirty years, was renewed in 1913 for fifteen more years.

children: a very few colleges for the training of teachers, and secondary schools or *lycées*: and a Faculty of Medicine at Damascus. Teaching in the secondary schools and the Faculty was in Turkish; French was the usual foreign language taught. Teachers at all levels were ill trained and ineffective, and less than 2 per cent. of wilayet revenues were devoted to State education. The Turkish law of 1913, making primary education compulsory, was in practice ignored—as were its other provisions. The remarkable ancient sites and buildings of the territory, nominally protected by law, were in fact exposed to ruinous dilapidation and illegal theft, and no public museum testified to enlightened interest.

State hospitals, small, dirty, and ill-equipped, existed only in the largest towns, and a few ill-provided dispensaries elsewhere. The quarantine services, rendered important by Syria's entrepôt status, depended on an internationally-composed Council; this was served by foreign and Turkish doctors and maintained a rudimentary but not inadequate administration in main centres.

The staple industry of the country, agriculture, was aided by no government action, whether by a cadastral survey or specialized education, or by works of irrigation, or by a prudent taxation system or (except for an almost inoperative Agricultural Bank) the supply of credit, or the provision of roads; all these were equally to seek. Even the Land Registry, or Tapu Department, boasted no tolerable cadastral maps. The State did nothing to aid exploitation of natural or mineral resources. Potential water-power was unused, forests far advanced in the process of slow destruction. Town-planning, in spite of some local pride, was starved of funds, was confined to traditional standards, and was helped by no considerable plans[1] for drainage, street improvement, or conservancy. Services of light, water, and tramways, where installed, were the work of foreign companies. Almost the entirety of road, railway, and port development was equally the work of European (in effect French) enterprise, except for certain military roads and for the tracks which were kept open by free labour demanded from villagers in the form of road tax[2] paid in kind. Only the telegraphs[3] were a state concern, and, even so, a telephone service for private subscribers was unknown. A postal service, slow and insecure, served internal needs, while mails for abroad were handled by French, Austrian, British, German, and Russian post offices.

[1] Certain schemes initiated or completed at Aleppo, Antioch, Ḥumṣ, Beirut, and Damascus were exceptions to this rule.

[2] Under Turkish law men aged between 16 and 60 must offer, at most, 30 days work every 5 years. The tax could be paid in cash or by the corvée.

[3] Cables for abroad were sent by land-line to Istanbul or to Egypt. A submarine cable linked Ladhqiya and Cyprus.

It was to be expected that the Turkish revolution of 1908–9, destroying the régime of 'Abd al-Ḥamid and inaugurating that of determined innovators, would change Ottoman administration and public life as greatly as, or more than, the Reforms of seventy years earlier had done. Its effects were, in fact, considerable but little beneficial to the Syrian public. They included indeed, the disappearance of some of the worst features of Ḥamidian rule—spies, tale-bearing, the grossest nepotism, illegal arrest, arbitrary action by concealed agencies; and, bringing a more modern approach to administration, the Revolution inspired high hopes among the politically-minded. Its parliamentary institutions at Istanbul, the election of Deputies in Syria, and the partially reformed local Councils in every wilayet and sanjaq, gave at least the hope of a less brazenly authoritarian régime, in which popular voices could be heard, grievances be discussed, scandals exposed. Inspectors toured the provinces, revised the cadres of officials, and dismissed the worst. Instructions from the capital showed some consciousness of the obligations of a modern Government, and there appeared, indeed, some practical signs of improvement. It was certain that less tolerance would be shown to outworn privileges, to local disorder, and to areas of virtual non-government; less tolerance, too, for such resented anomalies as the separate status of the Lebanon (pp. 21 ff.) and the favoured position of foreigners with their Capitulations, inviolable missions, monopolist industrial enterprises, and pervasive creditor status. Of the characteristic all-Turkish policy of the Committee of Union and Progress, which dominated the Government, and the directness of its clash with Arab hopes of decentralization or home rule, more is to be said (pp. 27–9); this apart, and for all the eager patriotism of many of its champions, the Young Turks' deposition of 'Abd al-Ḥamid, and their open indifference to the Faith and tradition, could not but scandalize the Muslim masses and many of their older and natural leaders, and could tend, at least temporarily, to diminish both social and governmental stability. In Syria, certainly, the new régime (partly through its many distractions elsewhere in the Empire) made disappointingly little administrative or social contribution, and its initial popularity, where this existed, survived but a few months. Syrian society was disturbed and apprehensive, punitive expeditions in the remoter countryside continued on habitual lines, and election-time squabbles were an added source of disorder, while no major administrative reforms, no redress of grievances, and but limited improvement in the public services, were yet to be seen. The revitalized Ottoman Government directed by the Committee had, by 1914, done little to facilitate the task of those whom destiny had designated as its successors. Moreover, the Syrian people at every level, including the modern-minded élite from whom any local statesman or administrator must be drawn, had been habituated for generations past only to low or the lowest standards in administration; and, while more than competent in the arts of destructive criticism, had lacked all initiation into those of constructive government.

4. MOUNT LEBANON

If the direct subordination of the Dayr al-Zur and Jerusalem sanjaqs to Istanbul was due, respectively, to the exigencies of a tribal wilderness and to the jealous politico-religious rivalries of Christian Powers, the curious phenomenon of the separate status of the Lebanon in the later nineteenth century had other origins, and other effects.

The conditions which led to the European intervention on the Syrian coast in 1860, and the establishment of the autonomous sanjaq, dated only from the two or three decades immediately preceding that event. For many generations before that, the mixed communities inhabiting the Lebanese mountain-massif—the virile, compact, stoutly Catholic, and priest-fearing Maronites, the tough, half-secret, and feudally (as also religiously) stratified Druzes, and some scattered villages of the other Christian sects—had agreed together in tolerable amity. They had seen the ascent and fall of dynasties arising from each or any of their communities, had acted as close and accepted neighbours, had been indifferently landlord or tenant or worker on estates of every ownership; they had sustained, in community of interest, scene, language, livelihood, and familiar friendship, a scarcely troubled symbiosis. This régime, perhaps always precarious after the first penetration of disturbing influences from without, showed in the second quarter of the nineteenth century clear signs of corruption. These were due to significant changes in Maronite society, destruction of their old feudal leadership, the deep disturbance caused by ten years of Egyptian occupation, and growing Ottoman jealousy of suspected foreign 'interference'. Factions appeared among the mountaineers, which inevitably followed community cleavages; French consular and missionary prestige, and the leadership of a too-masterful priesthood, gave new pretensions to the Maronites, and in reaction against this an added Druze self-consciousness declared itself—with the certainty of Turkish support, if not their actual instigation, against foreign protégés. The traditional inter-community peace of the Mountain was threatened, then broken, and turned finally to bitter intrigue and violence. A climax of strife and bloodshed was reached in 1860, followed by a massacre of Christians in Damascus, and by the landing of a French (but internationally authorized) force at Beirut. After weeks of inter-Power and Turco-European consultation, in which the French pressed a strong occupationist policy, agreement was reached on the institution, with a five-Power guarantee and Turkish acquiescence, of an autonomous régime for Mount Lebanon, with the professed design of securing the Maronites thereafter from the malice of Druze neighbours and Turkish Pashas. The special régime, drafted in 1861, was established in final form in September, 1864. It lasted until 1915. The area[1] covered, which excluded the city of Beirut, was small; it omitted not only the major ports of Tripoli, Sidon, and Tyre but also the inlying plain of the Biqa'; and its narrowness, contrasting with the historic (if always ephemeral) conquests of Lebanese amirs, was at times resented by ambitious Maronite spokesmen. The Biqa' was especially coveted; Sidon, it was said, had itself applied for admission. But such additions were all refused, and many Lebanese were themselves opposed to any extension, which would have been resolutely declined by the Sultan and his ministers.

The government of the Mountain, without subordination to the adjacent sanjaqs, was under its statute vested in a Christian[2] Governor appointed by the Porte, but in effect chosen by the Powers. He was always elevated to the high rank of Mushir, or Marshal, and was assisted by a small elected[3] Council, each of the Qa'immaqams of the seven qaḏhas being similarly provided; but in fact these had little weight, and the Governor was all-powerful. His official headquarters was at Dayr al-Qamr, his own residence not infrequently at Beirut.

The Courts of Justice in the Mountain were, after 1879, framed closely on the Ottoman model and administered Turkish law; commercial cases alone must, until 1913, be heard at Beirut. The Police Force, under a Maronite commander, was wholly recruited in the sanjaq, where no Turkish soldier was permitted to set foot, and where compulsory service in the Ottoman armies was not demanded. A Customs barrier separated the Lebanon from the rest of Syria; Customs dues, if in excess of local needs, were to be remitted to Istanbul, whose treasury in return was bound, in theory, to make good the deficiencies of Lebanese revenue against

[1] The sanjaq contained some 1,600 square miles, but was never precisely delimited on the ground.

[2] The Governors, in four cases Europeans who had adopted Turkish nationality and service, belonged to the Latin, Armenian Catholic, or Greek Catholic branches of the Church.

[3] By two-stage village voting, so as to represent the Maronite, Druze, Orthodox, Greek Catholic, Sunni Muslim, and Mutawalli communities by respectively 4, 3, 2, 1, 1 and 1 members.

its requirements. Other fiscal arrangements were simple; a tax on buildings and some lesser dues were collected, but not the crop tax or tithe. Schools and dispensaries being almost entirely the concern of the local communities and foreign missions, few governmental village schools were provided; but in its early construction of roads, and its substantial villages with pleasant communal amenities, the autonomous Lebanon far surpassed other Syrian districts.

The Statute of 1864 was amended once only, in 1912, when certain requests of the Lebanese were in part granted by the Porte, and a new Protocol was signed. Local election procedure was thereby amended; the jurisdiction of the Lebanese courts was extended to commercial cases, the powers of the Governor were curtailed, the Police augmented. Permission was given for the use of two more seaside villages for steamship calls, adherence to an annual published budget was prescribed, and certain fiscal changes were permitted. The imperfect satisfaction of these demands increased the chronic ill feeling between the Mountain and the central Government in the years immediately before 1914; nor was this improved by the refusal of Istanbul to provide funds for increasing the wages of the Police (who went on strike), nor by the mountaineers' refusal to take part in elections for the Imperial Parliament. Lebanese complaints were many that the Turkish Government was—had long been—dishonouring its engagements under the 1864 Statute, and trespassing on the Mountain's cherished autonomy; it is, on the other hand, doubtful whether the chauvinism of the Young Turks would much longer have tolerated the humiliating anomaly which this status presented.

Although the régime from 1864 to 1915 prevented recurrence of the horrors of 1860, and secured a half-century of tranquillity, the position was not without its defects, which time was not diminishing. It had been installed in the sole interests of a single Syrian community, the Catholic and French-protected Maronites; this alone must ensure its ill-favour with the mass of Muslim and most other non-Maronite Syrians. The power of the clergy among the Maronites, which during the nineteenth century had substantially replaced that of the old feudal leaders, was unchecked and, for the community as citizens, must be counted unfortunate. A due balance of power as between the central and local Governments was never established, suspicion and mutual aversion always prevailed. In the tiny world of the Mountain itself, there was no end to the intrigues and struggles for office and position, nor to rival approaches to Turkish officialdom and the foreign Consuls in Beirut. The area was too small, too unfertile, and too isolated to offer a career to the many enterprising young men born in its valleys; this encouraged Christian emigration, while the Druzes in thousands left for their stronghold in the Ḥawran. More serious than any of this was the support implied, by this emphasized Maronite privilege, to the sectarian separatism which must, if encouraged, fatally obstruct the even and equal government of the territory. The formation of autonomous Lebanon by armed foreign intervention, overriding the Sultan's sovereignty and serving the interests of a single sect, was well-intentioned to save Christian lives; but it was retrograde as a move in modern national government, was quite unearned by any freedom-seeking struggles of the Maronites themselves, and could be justified solely by the impotence or malice of the then existing rulers. Under a better government of Syria, competent to defend its own subjects from outrage, there would be good reason to reconsider the continuance of the régime.

5. THE FIELD OF POLITICS

Some outline has now been given of the elements and stratification of the Syrian public of 1914, and of their government; it is now necessary, for a proper appreciation of the task undertaken by the French in 1920, further to consider the contemporary political currents discernible among part of the upper (potentially the governing) class: the economics of the country: and the position or ambitions of foreign Powers whose interest it had attracted.

If by 1914 influences of 'westernization' in Syrian society had produced not only social and some administrative progress but also an interesting political movement, the latter must be less considerable than a more unified or more advanced population would have made possible. But with a large Muslim majority to whom a Sultan-Caliph and his rule, however defective, were inevitable and unquestionable, and a mass of population to whom government itself meant little save tax-gathering, conscription, and oppressive exigencies, it was impossible that, until more years of 'enlightenment' had played their part, the great bulk of Syrians should be other than politically apathetic. Among the masses, whatever might be claimed by eager speakers in their name, there was before the First World War no trace of concerted political action or aspiration; and how readily this backward public would be susceptible of political incitement by the 'enlightened' was for the future to show.

The masses apart, there was meanwhile, even among most of the small literate class, little else to be seen than half-acquiescent criticism of the existing régime. Many of the 'educated' worked in the Administration itself, and stood or fell with the massive, and not disloyal, Turkish bureaucracy; many more were not unhappy in an easy-going régime of low standards. Some were genuinely devoted to the sovereign, or the Empire, or the Army, or all of these; some, untouched by the first stirrings of Arab nationalism, believed the direction of true progress to lie in economics rather than politics. Older men, strong in family influence, were little in sympathy with restless youth, with its foreign conceptions and uncomfortable demands; and numbers of the comparatively advanced Christian minorities could find all the outlets they needed within their own communities. Some even hoped vaguely for a solution of their difficulties by a western, foreign intervention rather than by any dubious and dangerous struggle towards political self-help.

But even if almost no part of the Syrian masses, and few enough even of the superior class, took part in politics before the war—if, therefore, there could be no claim as yet that a national movement existed—yet much more than nothing had happened in this field since the mid-nineteenth century. Modern influences had produced the beginnings of a critical spirit and increasing world-knowledge, which had not left even the backward masses wholly untouched. Its geographical situation continued to expose Syria to a complex of foreign relations; the Arab tradition and sense of ancient and still recognized unity remained as a potential, in some contexts an actual, rallying-ground. The course of history, the increasing tempo of change, the crystallization of political conceptions in Europe and the dominance of nationalism among these, the successful struggles of the Balkan nations to escape from the Ottoman Empire—all these were not unobserved in the Levant; and from nearer at hand came accounts of militant nationalism in Egypt or India or Persia. Finally, the existing régime of foreign government in Syria, against which any political movement would be directed, must be felt as ever more anachronistic; there was at home plenty to complain of, evils to remedy, reforms to demand.

It was inevitable that in this territory, so long a Turkish province, a specifically political class should come finally into existence. Years of increasing western contact and western educational effort had by the later decades of the century created a class capable of supplying a very different leadership, and towards very different ends, from that of Turkish Pashas, Turkish-trained officialdom, or old-school Islamic functionaries. This class could not but react from the old régime of subjection and apathy; they had been taught to feel the frustration of powerlessness, the need for self-assertion in new and wider fields. Their quick brains, ready sympathies, excellent powers of speech, were gifts necessary to politicians; and the conditions of their lives offered, except to Army officers and some few officials, no adequate outlets for their energies in such other activities as sport, the arts, or industry. Not all could be successful writers, lawyers, or men of business; the great field for the active and the advanced was bound to be that of politics—which would not be those of conservatism.

In all phases of the nascent Arab national movement there can be seen a mixture of elements and objectives among fellow workers who were bound anon to be revealed as standing for quite different ambitions. Their programmes were drafted with little sense of their implications, and no great expectation, usually, of fulfilment. But each phase of the movement left, not always visibly, some legacy to the next. Thus the period of Egyptian rule, though it failed as the Arab Empire imagined by Ibrahim Pasha, reoriented some perceptive minds; the governorship of Midḥat Pasha, with his advocacy of decentralization and the full equality of the non-Turkish races, was again suggestive. Still more important because touching profounder springs of thought and emotion, the revival of the Arabic literary language, Arab history, and Arab culture from the middle of the nineteenth century, was served by outstanding Arab-Christian scholars, and contributed forcibly to the emergence of modern Arabism as a focus of loyalty. This work persisted, was echoed and repeated in Damascus, Aleppo, Ḥumṣ, Nablus, Jerusalem; and though its political content was still small, and such political voices as were raised fell on unheeding ears, yet it indispensably prepared the soil for a later political harvest, and in its creation of a diffused national feeling it could appeal powerfully to Muslim intellectuals as well as Christian. By 1890 traces of an Arab self-consciousness were found by travellers in every Arab wilayet, but particularly in Syria.

During the long reign of Sultan 'Abd al-Ḥamid, who conciliated many by his skilful use of Arab materials and who by his formidable spies could prevent all overt activity against the régime, the movement made slow progress. It was the period in which revulsion against undifferentiated passive membership of a foreign Empire moved insensibly from the merely sentimental and literary field to the political: and in which also the first major division appeared between differing elements within the movement. The main body, later to become the nationalist movement—itself composite—had as its inspiration an inconstant blend of Arabism (with or without an Islamic colouring) and feeling for the Syrian fatherland conceived as possessing some form of autonomy. The smaller body, with its centre in the coastal area and its heart in the compact Catholic and naturally separatist Maronites, looked no farther than its own community and immediate neighbours; it glorified in its French connexion, turned its back (for all its own Arab speech) on the Islamic and Arab-conscious hinterland, and dreamed of a future in which security from Turkish pressures would be achieved by a foreign (necessarily a French) intervention. Spokesmen of both groups found abundant common ground in anti-Turkish indignation and their shared secular culture; the narrower separatism of the Lebanon, though crystallized already in the autonomous sanjaq, did not emerge widely from its own mountain; and there were Catholic publicists, even, who preferred the larger conception and breathed the still thin air of all-Syrian nationalism. But the conflict of objectives was there, and the future was to show its deep reality.

Meanwhile, the value of the Ḥamidian period lay in the politically-tending ferment operative in educated urban society: the strength of which movement (as yet unworthy of the name) lay in the questionings, the indignations it aroused in private conversation, and the half-formulated thoughts for the future to which the continuing work of the European schools in Syria, the world press, foreign visitors, and the writings of Arab journalists all contributed. And the Syrian *émigrés* in the Americas and in Paris formed their clubs and committees where, in safety, Arab or Syrian or Lebanese patriotism could run riot. The 'League of the Arab Fatherland' of Najib 'Azuri, founded in Paris in 1904, attracted some European interest; an Arab Club, with political implications, was founded at Istanbul immediately before the 1908 revolution and, with its branch at Damascus, contained members destined to be future political leaders[1] of their country.

The developments of the years following the Turkish revolution were rapid and significant, even if still confined to a small social class; and if leadership passed for a time to other centres than Syria, none followed events with more keenness than Syrian Muslims and Christians, who were fully represented in every coterie in Istanbul, Cairo, or Paris.

In Paris, a short-lived Ottoman-Arab Brotherhood was founded in September 1908, with a programme of the equality of races, the use of the Arabic language in administration, and greater Arab representation.[2] Another ostensibly literary, but in part political, Arab Club was founded in 1909 with branches in the Syrian cities. Neither of these long survived the realization that the 'equality for all' of the Young Turks was to mean equality

[1] These included Mud͟hhir al-Raslan, Shukri al-Jundi, Jamil Mardam Bey, Zaki al-Khaṭib, Luṭfi al-Ḥaffar, Rafiq al-'Ad͟hm.

[2] The Turks, with two-fifths of the population of the Empire against three-fifths of Arabs, had more than double the number of deputies in the Chamber, and 37 (as against 3 Arab) Senators.

solely as Ottoman subjects, with no consideration for Arab racial or cultural separateness; hopes for home rule in the Syrian wilayets were dashed by the rigid centralization which was the Committee of Union and Progress's sole theory of government, and by their explicit jealousy of Arabism. In Istanbul also was born the secret Qaḥṭaniya Society, picked in membership and ambitious in programme; its founders envisaged the Arab wilayets as forming half of a Dual Monarchy under the Sultan. The Qaḥṭaniya, which as such did not survive a year, was reborn in secrecy among Arab army officers in 1913 under the name al-'Ahd, the Covenant; as such it adopted a sweeping plan of Arab independence and, with this, was to join forces with al-Fatat (the Young Arabs) in Damascus late in 1914.

The movement gained a strong foothold in Cairo where, in spite of a separate loyalty to Egypt as such, Arabism was followed by a small intelligentsia with keen interest. An 'Ottoman Party for Decentralized Administration' was founded there late in 1912, containing eminent Syrians[1] among its members. Its programme was one of substantial home rule for the Arab wilayets.

In Paris, Syrian and Lebanese residents lived from 1908 onwards an eager life of societies, meetings, and publications which reflected, on the one hand, the formulation of a convinced Lebanese (as distinct from Syrian) movement, and, on the other, the rapid failing of early hopes in the liberalism of the Turkish revolution and a resulting aspiration, ultimately, towards a wholly different régime in the Arab provinces. The Ottoman League,[2] founded in France in 1908 in support of the new régime in Istanbul, did not survive the early disclosure of true Young Turk intentions; and in June 1910 a leading *émigré* spokesman, Shukri Ghanim, published in Paris the full Arab claims for more representation, more authority, more high appointments, and the official use of Arabic. A year later, also in Paris, seven young Muslims[3] of Syria formed in great secrecy the Young Arab Society,[4] a group which, removed in 1913 to Beirut and later to Damascus, lasted until, in 1918–20, its objectives seemed on the point of achievement. It aimed at complete Arab independence.

The programmes and fortunes of these societies indicates that the progress was, year by year, from lesser to greater demands—

[1] Rafiq and Ḥaqqi al-'Adhm of Damascus, Rashid Ridha of Tripoli, Iskandar Ammun (a Lebanese Christian), Fu'ad al-Khaṭib (Lebanese Muslim), Na'if Tallu (Muslim of Damascus), and three Muslims of the Jerusalem sanjaq.

[2] Containing mainly Lebanese Christians—Georges Samné (a historian of these events), Alfred Sursok, Najib Trad, and Shukri Ghanim.

[3] These were Jamil Mardam Bey of Damascus: Rustum Ḥaydar (a Mutawalli of Ba'lbek): 'Awni 'Abd al-Hadi of Janin: Rafiq al-Tamimi of Nablus; and Tawfiq al-Naṭur, Muḥammad al-Miḥmisani, and 'Abd al-Ghani al-'Uraysi, all of Beirut.

[4] Jam'iyat al-'Arabiya al-Fatat, or briefly al-Fatat.

from a minimum of considerate government, through decentralization, to at last a total separation from the Empire. At the same time the manner of such separation, and the régime which would follow it, were left relatively vague. Currents of half-formed opinion flowed through the conference-rooms in favour of an independent pan-Arab Empire, a Syrian Kingdom or Republic, a Lebanese State, a federation of Arab provinces, and other lightly visualized and seemingly unattainable possibilities. Political writings, such as, notably, those of ‘Abd al-Raḥman Kawakibi (1849–1903) inspired or solidified the movement. From the Turkish side it may well be felt that some form of home rule satisfactory (at least temporarily) to this tiny minority of malcontent Arab subjects could at any time have been offered—and loyally observed—with no loss, but great profit, to the Empire. But Turkish policy remained rigid, insensitive, and unwise.

A last chance of understanding was given when, late in 1912, the group of known reformers in Beirut were invited by the Wali himself to present their considered proposals. These were formulated as the official use of Arabic, more and better posts for Syrians, the control of some departments by elected local bodies, military service on regional lines, a measure of local financial authority, and the appointment of foreign advisers. These proposals were published by their authors in February 1913. But the final victory of the C.U.P. in Istanbul over their Liberal rivals destroyed all hope that such reforms could be accepted; instead, the Reform Committee was dissolved, its appeals to Istanbul rejected, and six of the reformers imprisoned for some weeks. A revised wilayet Law issued in May as a measure of appeasement contained no more than a derisory fulfilment of the demands.

The last attempt by the same Arab, substantially Syrian, reforming elements was the holding of a conference in Paris in June 1913, by invitation of the Young Arab Party. It was attended by twenty-four delegates, all Syrians save four, and it secured wide recognition from the French press and public. The resolutions were moderate. None suggested secession from the Empire; they repeated, in fact, no more than the Beirut demands for Arab rights in the constitutional and administrative fields; and they were conveyed by their authors to the leading Powers of Europe, though these could not consider intervention in a strictly Turkish affair. Istanbul agreed further to consider the proposals, and welcomed three of the Arab delegates to the capital; but in mid-August a Decree appeared containing, after all, but little of substance. It was profoundly disappointing to the expectant Arab committee men, who, it seemed, must now despair of such concessions as would give, in acceptable substance, the desired home rule within the Empire. Even if a political movement had been widespread among their population (which it was not), the Arab subjects of the Sultan had no force, no effective weapons save that of passive resistance—and, *au fond*, had still an imperfect unity of conception as to their objectives.

In view of what the future held for Syria, within no more than a half-dozen of years—its explicit demand for full independence, and the foreign Mandate imposed upon it—it is right at this stage to emphasize three features of the political scene of this period, implicit in what has been recorded above. First, the sole political activity open to the intelligentsia at this stage was that of *demanding*: that is, of meeting, talking, and writing in support of their claims. Such activity, conducted with emotion against a common enemy, called for none of the restraints, the compromises, the responsibilities of normal politics, and still less contained any awareness of administrative complexity. It was, in fact, the worst of educations for governing a difficult and heterogeneous country.

Secondly, how far favourable or important was the impression conveyed to foreign countries by this Syrian (or wider Arab) demand for home rule? In general, such demand could scarcely be unsupported in sentiment by all liberal circles in Europe, where few illusions about Turkish government remained. But few newspaper readers, and few Governments, were disposed to rate Arab practical abilities highly; many observers felt, and some baldly prophesied, that the last state of the Arab territories might well, under their own rule, be worse than the first. Moreover, a strong Arab movement must carry with it implications possibly embarrassing to European Powers; whichever of the latter gave it countenance must expect the suspicion of the others, and every nation's attitude to it must involve also its attitude to Turkey and to its own Islamic subjects.

But, thirdly, of the reality and vigour of the demand for Arab self-government, and the intelligence and tenacity of its authors, no doubt could well exist; these Syrians, it seemed, had perhaps the ability, and certainly the will, and sought also the occasion, to govern their own country. Whatever the backwardness of the general population, whatever 'rights' might be claimed by foreigners, a self-selected and ambitious local governing class already existed, and would not easily be displaced.

6. THE MEANS OF LIVING

The favoured situation and climate of Syria and its historical past rendered its actual poverty the more paradoxical; yet in fact the country's standard of material life was, in these years, amongst the masses low by any standards. In spite of its broad acres and industrious populace, in spite of a half-Europeanized commercial class and the provision of facilities for commerce—railways, shipping, banks, foreign agents, modern techniques of trading—more complete than elsewhere in all Asiatic Turkey, the masses equally in town and country were poor to subsistence level, the middle class shabby and ill found, and the upper landowning or trading families rich, with rare exceptions, only by comparison with the prevailing indigence.

Admitting this, it was still believed by Syrian (largely Lebanese) *émigrés* in the New World, and by well-wishers in France, that this could all be changed; potential wealth was there, the country could emerge into fruitful prosperity, when once under wiser rule advantage had been taken of a central position on world routes, good communications, a favourable climate, abundant river water and fertile soil, a profusion of agricultural products, silk, olive oil, forests, fish, and sponges, minerals, livestock, a tourist industry—and an outstanding commercial acumen. Such agreeable visions played some part in the policy of France, and would play it again in that of Syrian nationalism.

The position of Syria on routes between Europe and Asia must always offer the chance to maintain, in a well-organized entrepôt area, a managing, servicing, and perhaps financing class of merchants and middlemen, and to realize a national source of income from rendering these services. Apart from this aspect, the commercial life of Syria consisted essentially in the distribution of foodstuffs grown in the fertile areas: the bulk import[1] of manufactured goods and some raw materials[2] from Europe,[3] and the distribution of these throughout the country. The great centres of import and transit were Beirut, Aleppo, and Haifa.

The exports of the territory never equalled the imports in value, and an adverse visible balance of trade was habitual; in 1910, a typical year, imports were valued at 170 million francs, exports at 85. The latter consisted normally of small surpluses of natural produce. In good years a moderate tonnage of cereals was available for shipping, with consignments of oil-seeds, sheep-skins, sponges, wool, dried fruit, oranges and lemons, nuts, liquorice, and raw silk. Among processed products the most notable were silk, olive oil, tobacco, wine, and local fabrics. The foreign trade was managed and financed largely by European firms and by local

[1] The main imports of the period were sugar, rice, coffee, tea, some flour, petroleum: cement and tiles: machinery: hardware, china, glass, paper: and, above all, textiles and clothing.

[2] Especially wood, iron, and other metals.

[3] Great Britain was the leading supplier, followed by France, Austria-Hungary, Italy, Germany, Russia.

merchants acting with these. Dependence on foreign capital was in general as complete as elsewhere in Turkey. All insurance was foreign, carried out through local agencies. Banking facilities were offered by the (Anglo-French) Imperial Ottoman Bank, the nominally Turkish Banque de Salonique, and in 1913 the Crédit Lyonnais, with agencies of other European and many small local banks. Chambers of Commerce existed at the three greatest towns, but with little effect. Trade union organization was unknown, though bazaar craftsmen could at times combine.

The communication system was well in advance of Turkish-Asian standards. Wheeled vehicles (including half a dozen motor cars) could move over most of the rough unmetalled routes as well as the better-kept highways of the Lebanon and the towns, though wide areas remained unpenetrated. The two highways in greatest use—Beirut–Damascus and Beirut–Tyre—had been constructed by French companies. None of the Syrian rivers are navigable. In contrast to the worse than indifferent postal and telegraph system (p. 19), the ports and shipping services of the country were adequate to its current needs. The port of Beirut[1] ranked third in the Turkish Empire and was adequately equipped with a sea-wall, lighters, and sheds; it served all central Syria, though the rise of Haifa after 1906 seemed to threaten its primacy. Haifa itself and Jaffa and Tripoli were destined, by Turkish agreement with France in 1913, to be transformed by the latter into modern ports, and meanwhile took appreciable traffic. The port of Alexandretta, originally conceded to French enterprise, was under German development in 1911–14 as part of the Bagdadbahn project. Suwaydiya, Ladhqiya, Sidon, and Jaffa welcomed an occasional steamer. The other coast towns[2] with their open roadsteads dealt, with rare exceptions, only with local sailing craft. The ports and coastal waters were used by regular services[3] of French, Austrian, British, Italian, and Russian lines, and by occasional other seasonal sailings to deal with special crops or cargoes, or with pilgrims. Coastal lights were the concern of the French concessionary Administration des Phares.

The railway system was, for a Turkish province, unusually complete. Except for the Ḥijaz Railway and the Bagdadbahn, it was entirely French in its finance and management. Following the

[1] The Concession for the construction and operation of Beirut harbour was given to the (French) Compagnie du Port de Beyrouth, in 1888; in 1903 it was assigned to the Régie Générale des Chemins de Fer.

[2] Baniyas, Ṭarṭus, Jubayl, Juniya, Nabi Yunis, Tyre, Qayṣariya.

[3] These consisted of the (French) Messageries Maritimes: the Austrian-Lloyd: the (British) Khedivial Mail Line: two Italian lines: the (Russian) Steam Navigation and Trading Co.; and occasional sailings of other British lines, and of Rumanian, German, Turkish, and Bulgarian steamers.

pioneer Jaffa–Jerusalem line, finished in 1892, the narrow-gauge[1] Beirut–Rayaq–Damascus–Muzayrib line was finished in 1895; it was managed by the Régie Générale on behalf of the D.H.P. (Chemin de Fer de Damas, Hama et Prolongements), itself a nominally Turkish but effectively all-French concern. A French-owned light railway, of the Société des Tramways Libanais, ran from Beirut to Ma'malatayn and was destined for later prolongation. Broad-gauge lines were those of the main D.H.P. system; the line Rayaq–Ḥumṣ–Ḥamah was opened in 1902, Ḥamah–Aleppo in 1906, and Ḥumṣ–Tripoli in 1911. Shortly before the war Franco-Turkish and Franco-German agreements on railway building prepared the ground for further French enterprise; lines eastward to the Euphrates, southward to Lidd (Lydda), and eastward from 'Afula were envisaged. The Syrian sections of the Baghdad Railway,[2] whose recent construction had keenly interested Syrian observers, were likely to reorient much of north Syrian traffic; they were those of Iṣlaḥiya–Muslimiya–Aleppo, Muslimiya–Jarablus, and (in 1914) Alexandretta–Ṭopraq Qal'a (Toprakkalé). Sections of the Ḥijaz Railway[3] (p. 16) were opened for traffic at dates between 1903 and 1908. It ran southward from Damascus by Dar'a, Ma'an, and Mudawwara to Medina, and its connected lines in southern Syria, or Palestine, were important as opening new routes from the hinterland to the Mediterranean.

The industries of the country were, before the First World War, exiguous but not uninteresting. The most obvious, that of tourism, pilgrim traffic and *estivage*, was most developed in southern Syria, but already active also in the central areas, with their great beauties and variety of interest; and towards this the improved communications and semi-European hotels of recent years assisted, with the nostalgic propaganda of prosperous Syrians abroad, whose own homeward remittances were an important national asset. The scarcity of useful raw materials, the lack of any industrial tradition, the feebleness of local buying power, and inability to compete in foreign markets necessarily limited Syrian manufactures to a minor role. The chief of such industries was that of silk[4] spinning and weaving, mostly unmechanized and largely financed by firms of Lyons and Marseilles; but this industry, like others, seemed in

[1] Narrow-gauge is 105 cm., normal or broad-gauge is 1·435 m.

[2] The Taurus and Amanus tunnels were incomplete in summer 1914, the Euphrates bridge at Jarablus unfinished, and the line east of Euphrates still in the early stages of construction.

[3] This enterprise, a political project of Sultan 'Abd al-Ḥamid, was organized as a Sunni Muslim waqf.

[4] Much of the Lebanese and 'Alawi silk, however, was exported as cocoons or raw silk, almost all to France.

1914 already to have passed its best days, thanks to the competition of imported products. The same was true of the home-woven cotton and woollen-garment industry which, based largely on imported yarns, supplied clothing to the nearer wilayets and to Egypt: and of those of knitted garments, lacemaking, and embroidery. A concrete factory worked at Aleppo, and two more in southern Syria; brick and lime were burnt at many places; modern-type furniture and woodwork was produced at Beirut and elsewhere. The carved and inlaid work of Damascus was still made, but in little volume. Small industries of pottery, baskets, glass-making, rope and string, rugs and hair-tents, saddlery and leather-work, sweets, and 'oriental fabrics' maintained themselves. A paper-making enterprise started at Beirut had failed; a small chemical factory had been established near the same city. Oil was extracted from flowers for scent, and sesame oil for food. Cigarette manufacture from local tobacco—a Régie monopoly—was carried out in half-modern factories at Damascus and Aleppo; a score of small tobacco workshops existed in the Lebanon, outside Régie control. Wines of fair quality were made for export under French tuition, and *'araq* for local consumption. Flour mills working mainly by water-power were ubiquitous, and a modern mill had been established at Beirut. The extraction of olive oil, in part by modern methods, was, with the silk industry, the most important of industrial activities; it fed the many small soap factories which supplied the local market.

Few of these varied but humble industries used mechanical power, or occupied greater workshops than a single room. To the rare exceptions—some spinning and weaving 'factories', a chemical works, a cement factory, a few oil-presses, flour mills and irrigation pumps—energy was supplied by oil-engines. Power for the public services was provided by a powerhouse at Damascus and another at Beirut; modern hotels had each its own generating plant. A French concern had obtained in 1906 a concession for tramways and power supply for Beirut, and maintained three tramway services in 1914; another company equally French had, even before that, installed some gas and electric lighting. In Damascus, a similar French Company for Tramways and Electric Light gained a concession in 1902. No other city was lighted by electricity before the First War.

Mineral wealth was of the scantiest, in spite of hopeful assertions or prophecies to the contrary. Some working of asphalt took place at Ḥaṣbaya, on the slopes of Hermon, and traces were known also at Jazzin, and near Ladhqiya, and on the Dead Sea. Lignite was found in Lebanon, but was almost totally unexploited. Traces of petroleum attracted a measure of interest from British and American companies: a season's prospecting was carried out, but no deposits located. Salt was worked by the Ottoman Public Debt, notably at the Jabul Lake east of Aleppo. Chrome had been mined for a time near Ladhqiya, but was later abandoned. A concession was given in 1911 to a Turco-Italian company for the extraction of phosphates, but no field work followed. Good building stone existed widely, and low-quality marble. The basalt rock of the Ḥawran was fashioned into millstones, and plastic clay into pots; the presence of iron was confidently reported, but it was extracted only, and on the minutest scale, at Kasrawan in the Biqa'. The hopeful or credulous spoke also of copper, lead, nickel, and antimony, but no commercially valuable deposits of these were brought to light.

With mineral wealth so derisory, other natural resources could afford little compensation. The lakes and rivers of the country were rich in fish, but this without specialized transport could be of no more than local value; sea-fishing for mullet, mackerel, and sardines was primitive in method, though potentially a resource not to be ignored. The sponge fisheries, equally unaided by modern techniques, had lately declined; the purple dye industry, famed in antiquity, was no more. On land, the world-famed forests of earlier days had been almost wholly destroyed by neglect, fire, goats, and excessive cutting; and the poor remainder was let by Government annually to contractors to cut further for immediate gain: timber and wood for building and industry were commonly imported. The liquorice root was collected by an American company; various wild grasses, reeds, and fibres were used in cottage industry. The produce of the bedouin herds and the cultivator's livestock—camel-hair, wool, hides and skins, chickens and eggs, cheese, clarified fat—could not contribute seriously to export; nothing had been done to improve breeds, products, or processes. Animal husbandry was treated wholly on traditional lines; animals—sheep, goats, cattle—were small in size and in productivity. Hides, roughly treated, were reckoned as of poorish quality, and the local wool too coarse for any purpose but carpet-making. Dairy-farming as an industry was unknown.

Agriculture, greatest of Syrian resources and occupations, afforded the livelihood of two-thirds, perhaps three-quarters, of its people. It embraced a wide variety of cultures, methods, conditions, and environments, and seemed to offer a fair prospect of future if no great immediate wealth. In fact the peasantry were, in their fashion, skilled and undaunted agriculturists; and, blessed with advantages great as compared with barren Arabia, they had evolved techniques of cultivation which had for centuries seemed adequate to their fields and needs. The coastal plain was temperate, watered, and intensely cultivated, the mountains closely terraced by generations of villagers. The inland valleys were fertile and favourable, the nearer steppe country was sown extensively to the limit of the sufficing rain-belt, and its oases were rich with gardens. The olive and mulberry provided for the soap and silk industries, and for some export, and neither had reached its limits of expansion. The mountain-grown tobacco, including the world-famous 'Latakia' type, was closely supervised by the Régie authorities, but could doubtless be extended by more flexible administration, new varieties, and better processes. The vines were of good quality, their wine acceptable. A beginning had been made with short-staple cotton. The date, sugar-cane, and banana had been introduced. Hemp and flax sufficed for the local rope industry. All types of vegetables were grown, and the varied fruits of the coast-strip and the inland oases were of excellent quality. The leguminous crops were important for food and fodder; rice where possible, millet and maize more generally, were established crops. But in extent and value the rain-grown spring cereals, wheat and barley, of the valleys and the inland plains (notably those of Aleppo–Ḥamah and the Ḥawran) by far exceeded all other crops, and provided for the basic needs of the country with, in most years, a small surplus for export.

But this favourable account has omitted, so far, those persistent elements in Syrian agriculture which, for all its attractive variety, had prevented it from raising the population out of poverty: elements which before 1914 were commonly ignored, and which later years of European control could not overcome. The renowned specialities of the mountain zone and the rainfed plains—the olive, mulberry, vine, tobacco plant, and fruit-tree—could be further improved only within the limits imposed by the smallness of the congenial area, the high proportion of rock and cliff within it, and in some districts the dense over-population which must make for poverty—and had already made for emigration; nor, with the exception perhaps of raw silk, was the quality of the local products such as to lead them to an assured place in foreign markets. And output, from plant or tree or unit of land area, was well below even a fair world average.

Of the main agricultural crops, especially the spring cereals, more must be said. These can be grown either by rain, or by systems of irrigation which must greatly increase their cost and are anyhow limited by available river water and by the supply of capital. Irrigation was before 1914 little practised,[1] from lack of

[1] There were limited areas of free-flow irrigation at Damascus, in the Biqa', and on the Orontes. Other irrigation was achieved by the water-wheels of Ḥamah, and a few mechanical pumps and water-lifts. The country contained no major irrigation works.

capital, security, or spirit of enterprise; the Syrian grain-lands were by vast majority rain-watered. This at once restricted their possible maximum extent to about one-third of the country if all land be considered as 'cultivable' which could possibly, in a year of exceptional rainfall, be economically cultivated: but restricted it to about one-sixth, if cultivable land is taken, more realistically, as that *usually* capable of growing crops:—land, that is, with a fairly assured rainfall of 8–10 inches a year, and a total area of approximately 8–9 million acres. This maximum area contrasts with the 2½–3½ million acres actually under cultivation before the First World War;[1] and these latter figures themselves include the area, equal to nearly half the total, customarily left fallow every year. By reason of sheer rainlessness, therefore, in all but an inexorably limited proportion of its surface, Syria could never without extensive irrigation possess really spacious crop-growing areas; and the rain alone, seasonal and uncertain, could never unaided produce much more than cereal spring crops.

Thus narrowly limited, Syrian agriculture showed other discouraging features. In the wide desert-fringe there was imperfect security from nomad marauders. Taxation was heavy and capricious. Productivity was lower than in any comparable country. The use of land was wasteful, crops were of mixed or inferior type and commanded low prices, cultivation methods were primeval and unprogressive, improvement by capital works almost unknown. The prevailing system of land tenure, elsewhere than in the highly-populated smallholding areas, was such as to discourage all development and to keep the peasants impoverished. Crop-sharing with absentee town-dwelling landlords[2] was the rule over most inland areas, and resulted for the fallah in perpetual indebtedness and insecurity of holding. Landlords existed, indeed, who cared for their peasants, or contributed to agriculture by works or loans or expert knowledge; but these were uncommon. Nor were conditions greatly better on lands held undivided by whole communities, and debarred thereby from improvement by the year-by-year reallotment of plots: nor even on the slightly better administered State Domains which, till 1909, had been the private estates of the Sultan.

Enough has been said to show how illusory was the view that

[1] The area reached some 4½ million just after the Second World War, and 7 million, or more, in 1955.

[2] These held their lands, usually unmapped, from Government under the 'Tapu system' by heritable leasehold. Estates often included the whole of many villages and their lands; the village cultivators had no legal status or rights *vis-à-vis* the 'tapu owner', and received in kind a share of the crop varying from 60 to 40 per cent.

Syria could soon or easily become the economic paradise sometimes lightly prophesied. A reforming Administration, such as destiny reserved for Syria after 1918, might find indeed many possibilities of development—in agriculture, stockbreeding, fisheries, industry, communications, and possibly mineral exploitation. But it would be compelled to acquiesce in the abiding adverse conditions of the country: adverse to agriculture, to industry, to any foreseeable rapid increase of wealth. It would be unable to produce rainfall or minerals or industrial raw materials which nature had denied; it could not control the policies of other countries, nor the economic climates of the world. It would not easily achieve, in a divided and backward country, either an atmosphere of social harmony or a general effective desire for economic progress on untraditional lines. It would find the speed of advance despairingly slow, blocked by ignorance, conservatism, and vested interests; nor would its best efforts be rewarded, probably, by the gratitude of the beneficiaries.

7. THE FOREIGNERS

The penetration of Middle Eastern countries by western influences has been mentioned already in these pages as affecting the Turkish Government of Syria, commercial activity, social and intellectual life, and the local political movement. But since the deep interest of one European Power in the Levant was soon to lead to its assumption there of heavy responsibilities, it concerns us further to examine the nature of that interest. The pages here following will deal first with the part played in Syria, up to 1914, by other foreign Powers, and conclude with that of the French Republic.

The Syria of the nineteenth and early twentieth centuries had, indeed, its place in the attention of every western nation. Apart from its role in history, archaeology, and religion, few governments could ignore the various modern aspects of Turkish-Asian affairs—Armenian massacres, palace revolutions, proclaimed reforms, the Baghdad Railway—or could fail to speculate on the future break-up (or the just possible revitalization) of the Ottoman Empire—or to watch, meanwhile, each other's moves and penetrations in that field.

Many nations, thus far interested, had no part of significance to play in Syrian affairs. Such was the case of Spain, with little consular representation and a scattering of Franciscan and Capuchin monks, and such also that of the Scandinavian countries, each with a Consul or Vice-Consul and a modicum of trade. The Danes had in addition a mission at Damascus and some schools in the hinterland. Greeks contributed some households of seamen, shopkeepers, and artisans, while their Government watched the fortunes of the local Orthodox communities whose higher priesthood had, until recently, been of Greek nationality. The Netherlands and Belgium maintained small consular staffs; both had some share in commerce and shipping. The Belgians had, besides, some subjects among the Catholic Orders, a share in commerce and shipping, and a share in earlier activity in railway construction. Austria-Hungary had its part in trade and shipping, hotel-keeping, and the religious communities.

The Italians could recall a past when the trade of Pisa, Amalfi, Genoa, and Venice had dominated the Levant, when Italian communities had held primacy among Europeans, and when their language was that of the best partly-westernized society, and of commerce. Those days were past, but in 1914 the Italians were still a considerable and possibly a growing element. Their shipping and trade (in commodities directly competitive with the French) took a leading place among the European nations. Italian decorations were awarded to Syrian notables, and money from Rome was spent judiciously among them; their policy had, since 1880, marked the eastern Mediterranean as a possible colonial field. Italian anti-clericalism was not reflected in their activities in the Levant, where rich missionary societies and their Government itself sustained Catholic missions and the schools of many Orders. Italy might well, to a Syrian patriot, rank as potentially formidable.

Of United States activities, the opposite was truer. Their commercial interest in the territory was limited to a single liquorice-exporting firm, their consular representation was on a small scale, political motives were non-existent. But the philanthropic interest of American Protestantism was sincere. It was represented by a 'Colony' at Jerusalem and by the enterprises, elsewhere, of important missionary bodies. These, which had amicably divided 'spheres of influence' with the British, maintained at many towns since 1845 mission stations and schools, a Seminary, dispensaries and orphanages, a printing press, churches which gradually formed small Protestant congregations and, above all, the Syrian Protestant College. The latter, founded in 1846, was moved from 'Abayh to Beirut twenty years later, and by the wise administration of outstanding Presidents had built up an eminent educational position in the country, indeed in the whole Middle East. If the majority of pupils were Christians, and by majority Orthodox, yet the westernizing influence of the College was not confined to these; it was, through its hundreds of alumni, considerable and continuous in the upper circles of all Syrian communities, including the Muslim.

The British missionary effort, alive since 1840, had been a forerunner of the American, but was both smaller and limited to a definite area. Within this, and responsible for some thirty schools (including girls' schools) and a hospital, worked English, Scottish, and Irish missions of various Societies, and small local Anglican and Presbyterian communities formed around English churches at Beirut and Damascus. The British share of shipping and import was greater than that of any nation, her methods and goods were admired, her prestige high; but no efforts were made at social or cultural eminence. British higher policy regarded Syria as a staging area on the eastern land route, and as one from which a threat to Egypt might develop. Plans for an eastward trans-desert railway had at times been mooted by British writers, and found occasional support in official circles; and some interest in the population was shown by British representatives in Egypt. Great Britain, more consistently[1] than France, had always supported the Ottoman Empire—but would, in default of this, be anxious to stand well with any Arab successor-State that might arise. The territory was central to Arabism and Islam, and therefore not to be ignored by an Empire with many Arab and Islamic contacts and interests; but it was at no time an actual or a desired British sphere of interest.

Russia was by 1914 a less apparently significant factor in Syrian affairs than might have been supposed from her long record of expansion at the expense of Turkey. Few Russians lived in the territory, their language was spoken by no Syrian, and their small commerce with the country consisted mainly in the supply of petroleum products. Her consular representatives were mainly concerned with the annual pilgrim traffic to the Holy Places, which was organized on grandiose lines and reflected the closeness of Russian interest in the Orthodox communities; the same feeling had prompted financial help to many boys' and girls' schools and colleges throughout the wilayets. The great bulk of such expense and effort was, indeed, expended in the Palestine sanjaq, not much in central Syria; Russian interest in the former remained especially strong for the familiar nexus of political-religious reasons centred on the Holy Sepulchre.

The position of Germany was very different. This nation had no traditional connexions with Syria, stood close to no community in it, had no Muslim subjects, and was a newcomer to the Eastern world. But imperialist ambitions which developed late in the nineteenth century, the desire for expansion and trade in any quarter, and the impetuous ambition of the sovereign, had by the

[1] With lapses in Gladstone's anti-Turkish speeches, and in British sympathies for the Christians in Balkan countries.

early twentieth century brought the German flag to Syrian ports, followed by its commercial travellers, its banking and insurance agencies, its hotels. German dominance at the Porte (interrupted but temporarily in 1908–10) was firm between 1911 and 1914, and extended to the Army and to ubiquitous commercial projects. The most famous of these, the Bagdadbahn, deeply affected northern Syria. Intended to form part of a German economic empire in Asia Minor, it had led meanwhile to a rapid increase in German residents. Both Catholic and Protestant German missions and missions schools were at work. The quarter-century-long vigorous incursion of Germany into Turkish-Asian, and especially Syrian, affairs was a portent of clear significance.

The position of France in the territory on the eve of the 1914–18 War had been earned by centuries of diplomacy and effort, and, for better or worse, far exceeded that of the other Powers. It was marked by a massive array of French religious, charitable, and educational institutions, by the wide use of the French language, and by French social and cultural influence in considerable sections of the population; and it was considered in France itself as justifying a keen and traditional interest in the country—and an ambition to play a further part there if and whenever circumstances should allow.

To trace the long stages whereby French influence in Turkey was established does not belong to the present narrative. It arose in part from France's eminent position as the outstanding representative of the West, and of Christendom confronted by Islam: in part from her own need for an eastern ally—an ally far more formidable in the sixteenth than in the nineteenth century—against European rivals: and in part from her own desire for expansion, in and beyond the Levant, for general reasons of prestige and commerce. To the Capitulations, which she was the first Power to obtain (p. 15), and which secured her early commercial penetration of Anatolia and Syria, she added in the seventeenth century the honorific role of Protector of Latin Catholicism; and this cherished privilege, though never left long unchallenged by other Catholic Powers and imitated soon by Russia on behalf of the Orthodox, was easily though never officially extended to an exclusive right of protection of—or at least accepted spokesmanship for—the local communities of Uniate Catholics, with whom (and, above all, with the ever-favoured Maronites) it enabled France to achieve an intimate position. Her appeal to such communities was indeed fourfold. She appealed as the leader of Catholicism, and the local priesthoods were her faithful clients: a relationship which survived the irreligion of the French Revolutionary era, the strong advent of anti-clericalism in

France itself a century later (largely concealed[1] from the Uniate congregations), and the separation of Church and State in 1906. She appealed, secondly, as a Great Power, a status which survived the blows suffered in the Napoleonic Wars and in 1870. Thirdly, she was accepted as the exponent of a great 'civilizing mission'—her own favourite and not unjustified claim through the ages—and this role was visibly supported by her fruitful efforts in the cultural field. Finally, it was France who had carried out almost the totality of physical works of development on Syrian soil, and was known to be planning more; who had landed an army on the Lebanon coast in 1860; and whom circumstances might one day compel, not unwillingly, to land another. Meanwhile, the closest terms of friendship, tutelage, and familiar acquaintance on every level bound the French to Syrian Catholicism, and signs of the French cultural occupation were ubiquitous.

To the Turkish Government the French attitude had been for centuries that of firm supporter, if not without periods of inconsistency; and if by 1914 her position in Turkish councils had fallen below the German, British, or Russian, this was not yet reflected in Franco-Syrian relations. French activity in the country's economic life was unapproached by that of any other Power. She had taken more than her share of Turkish loans, supplied experts to many posts, controlled the Imperial Ottoman Bank, administered the Public Debt and the Régie des Tabacs. French capital and enterprise had built and exploited the main railways of the territory, and the earliest roads. Hers were many of the major municipal enterprises of tramways, gas, and electricity, hers the work of port development and the coastal lights. French shipping in the ports exceeded even the British, she was the greatest buyer of Syrian exports, and second only to Great Britain as an importer. French capital was widely spread in the growing, spinning, weaving, and marketing branches of the silk industry, had initiated factories for chemical products and scent, owned or participated in minor enterprises in many towns, and dominated some branches of the import trade. The hopeful tourist industry was mainly French in character as in language.

French cultural influence was spread by the circulation of French-language books and papers, by exchanges of visits, by social and business interchange continuous over decades, and, very substantially, by the help given by French money, interest, and personnel to the schools of the Uniate communities. But as formative of the local cultured Christian class, and as vitalizing all

[1] The often-quoted remark of Gambetta that 'anti-clericalism is not an article for export' was exemplified by the visible correctness or piety of the French in Syria, religious and lay; a French Consul remarked that at home it would be fatal for him to go to Mass, in Syria fatal to keep away.

educational effort, the direct contribution of French religious orders was outstanding. The Jesuits, well established in Syria since the seventeenth century, maintained important schools, a Seminary, and the famous University of St. Joseph at Beirut. The last-named, founded in 1875, started with a secondary school and a faculty of Theology, added Medicine and Pharmacy, Dentistry and Midwifery, an Oriental faculty, and in 1913 Schools of Law and Engineering. It administered the important Catholic press, and maintained an observatory.

The Franciscans maintained a dozen mission stations in north and central Syria, using monks of whom a majority were French. The Lazarists had five major missions in the country, including the famous college of Antura in the Lebanon and an important college at Damascus. The Carmelites had houses at Tripoli and at Bisharra, as well as their monastery at Haifa. The Capuchins (in part Italian) were represented at Beirut and elsewhere. The Marist brothers, and those of Christian Teaching, had schools in many towns. The Dominicans, the White Fathers, the Benedictines, Trappists, Salesians, Priests of Zion, Assumptionists, and others were represented at Jerusalem and elsewhere in that sanjaq. The teaching of girls, with its great power of propagating French influence, was in the hands of Catholic, mainly French, sisterhoods widely spread throughout the country. These were the Franciscan Sisters, the Dames de Nazareth, the Daughters of Charity, the Sisters of St. Joseph, of Nôtre Dame des Douleurs, of the Holy Family, of St. Vincent de Paul, of Besançon, and others; they taught in some dozens of admirably conducted schools, and maintained also other institutions of charity, orphanages, dispensaries, and workrooms.

To the work of these religious enterprises, which in some cases an annual subsidy from Paris helped to maintain, can be added that of the Lay Mission with its ostentatiously non-Catholic boys' and girls' schools, and the institutions of the Alliance Israélite Universelle, which used French teachers for its work among Syrian Jewry. It is claimed that, of 90,000 children attending school (other than the primitive Mosque schools) in Syria in 1914, not less than 50,000 were pupils at one or another of French or French-aided mission schools and colleges. And, with few but conspicuous exceptions,[1] the medical care and hospitalization of the public (including the Muslims) was chiefly to be found in the hospitals and dispensaries maintained by French or Catholic charity, and aided by the French Government.

[1] Notably American, Danish, and British (Scottish) hospitals and dispensaries: those, on a humble scale, of the local Christian communities: a few private hospitals, and the two or three of the Turkish Government. A number of European and Levantine doctors had small private clinics.

The attitude of the Syrian public to this multifarious and culturally valuable French effort was various. To the Maronites and Greek Catholics, France was above all others the friend, civilizer, and protector, French citizenship a favourite dream, her intervention a conceivable means of liberation from Turkish rule. To the other Catholics she was, if familiar and benevolent, less attractive by reason of inter-community jealousies, but still dominant and august. To the non-Catholic Christians, especially the large Orthodox community and the Gregorian Armenians, France was rather the age-long favourer of their Maronite doctrinal opponents and social rivals. To the Druzes, even more, France was suspect as the great Maronite supporter. To the Sunni Muslim majority she was, by her obvious Christian championship and her suspected interventionist ambitions, the most feared of the Powers; indeed, the dread of foreign intervention, involving a change of masters—and Christian for Muslim, at that—was a specific if unemphasized element in the home-rule movement of the time. Although numbers of non-Catholics and even Muslims attended the French colleges, and French was widely spoken among the Muslim as well as Christian intelligentsia, yet such visible signs of French influence outside the ranks of the Catholics were in great part illusory; they did not truly indicate devotion to France,[1] though they widely deceived, in that sense, the French public and Government. The great and largely unrealized weakness of France's traditional position in Syria was that its vital roots lay only in the minority communities, or part of these.

This truth, known to the best-informed of realistic Frenchmen, was hidden from their general public and Government. To the wide Catholic element at home, the French achievement in Syria was incomparable; 'The Faith and the Flag' had gained the Levant, had won triumphantly lands where for centuries France had been known, had served, had been revered; the 'civilizing mission', claimed as wholly disinterested and non-acquisitive, must continue and prevail. And to the voices of religion and tradition, which drowned easily those of the left wing and the anti-clericals, were added the calculations of the business men, who hoped for trade and colonial riches: the strategists, who valued Syria's place on vital routes: of colonialists, who would fly the tricolour as high in eastern as in western Mediterranean, and who claimed that the Arab cities of the Levant were of paramount importance as centres of Islamic influence: and of statesmen who foresaw the collapse of the Ottoman 'sick man' and who, innocent

[1] The Indian intelligentsia, of the second and later decades of the twentieth century, schooled in England and highly appreciative of English culture, yet in politics vigorously anti-British, offer in some measure a parallel.

of territorial ambitions for the moment, would later claim insistently their part of his belongings.

Syria, Lamartine had said, was 'an admirable French colony—waiting for France'! No foreign territory had so cherished a place in French imagination: the country was theirs already! In December 1912 the French premier emphasized in the Chamber the 'rights' of France in Syria, and confirmed that Great Britain, on her own admission, claimed none. Enthusiastic circles and societies in France looked for the early establishment of a French naval base at Beirut. The Sultan of Morocco, on a visit to Syria, pronounced that its occupation by France was inevitable and not distant. More and more distinguished Frenchmen, though never their Government, expressed similar views; Maurice Barrés was prominent among them.

And the French Republic was in a mood not averse from expansion. By internal revival and by foreign alliance the nation had recovered its strength, its pride, and its ambitions since the debacle of 1870. Claiming particular gifts for the uplifting of backward peoples, France in the nineteenth century had added to her new Empire one territory after another in Asia and Africa. The acquisition of Algeria in 1830 had been followed by that of Tunis (by Treaty) in 1881, and that of Morocco effectively in 1911. The complicated structure of French Indo-China came into existence progressively in the second half of the century, the Somali Coast became a colony in the 1880's, Madagascar passed from protectorate to colony ten years later, vast areas of west and central Africa were united as a French Governorate-General in the same years. No doubt in due course—does one ever know?—Syria, the 'France of the East', would take its due place beside them.

II

WAR AND VICTORY

1. TURK AND ARAB

In the early summer of 1914 the Syrian wilayets could afford, to an observant prophet, material for much erroneous forecasting. The country seemed, socially and economically, not less but rather more stable than its wont. No irritant features disturbed the normal relations between its diverse communities; the dominance of the Sunni majority was entirely assured, the ancient privileges of the minorities not overtly threatened, Zionism in the south scarcely noticed. The Turkish Government, with peace in Europe and with some realization of the imperative need for internal reform, was likely to press on as best it could with administrative changes, better public services; it would tolerate less and less the Druze, 'Alawi, and bedouin areas of precarious or refused subordination; and it would move further towards conciliating, by suitable mimimum gestures, the few but insistent Syrian spokesmen now claiming forms of Arab autonomy. If it could succeed in disrupting the outward unity of these claimants, or in convincing them of their powerlessness, and if foreign Powers continued to abstain from interference, then nothing thereafter need hold back the Syrian wilayets from accelerated progress. In a further atmosphere of better administration and less complaint, an end might come, perhaps, to anachronistic Lebanese privileges and to the Capitulations themselves. Meanwhile, German influence in Syria would increase with the operation of their Baghdad Railway, their economic penetration, and their general dominance in the councils of Turkey. Neither British nor Russians were likely to burst into activity in Syria, though more might be heard of the former's trans-desert railway to 'Iraq, and perhaps of her friendships with Arab potentates: in which case French suspicions would be proportionately strengthened. The latter themselves, the most pretentious and active of strangers within the Syrian gates, would proceed no doubt with further projected railway and port improvements, would lend yet more money to the Ottoman treasury, would play a certainly undiminished part in local enterprise, and would benefit from the new privilege, granted in 1914, whereby their missions would be safeguarded and tax-free.

The outbreak of the European War in the first week of August 1914, however uncomprehended by the backward Syrian masses, signified already to the educated class and Turkish officialdom that incalculable events were at hand. Under German leadership, the early involvement of Turkey was certain; the state of war declared between the latter and the Allies (France, Russia, Britain) on 29 October made this explicit, and hastened tendencies and events already visible to observers in Syria. The country, a province of Turkey and of the Mediterranean, took its place as an immediate element in strategy. German officers[1] arrived in numbers to take up positions in the IV Army which, consisting of five and later six divisions, was mobilized and concentrated even before the declaration of war.[2] Troop movements, the collection of stores, gifts of gold to powerful tribesmen, and urgent work on roads and railways were signs of the times. They were followed, in November 1914, by the full descent on Syria of a wartime régime. Its leader, surrounded by a Turco-German staff, was the Commander-in-Chief of the IV Army, and effective dictator of Syria until January 1918, the notorious Aḥmad Jamal Pasha,[3] Minister of Marine and one of the supreme triumvirate[4] of the Committee of Union and Progress.

The history of the Turkish armies[5] in Syria during the war is inglorious; but they remained in being (as perhaps few armies in the circumstances could have done) and could at times fight well in spite of shortage of all supplies, constant desertion, variable leadership, little pay, and harsh treatment. Turco-German relations were indifferent or bad, and the proclamation of Jihad—Holy War against the Christians—in November 1914 did little to raise the morale either of troops or public; in spite of parades, ceremonies, and copious propaganda, it was generally ignored. The attempt by Jamal Pasha to seize and occupy the Suez Canal, in January 1915, was a failure. A second attack under German leadership in August 1916 had no greater success. Street widening and demolition of buildings in the Syrian towns, for military convenience, added to the unpopularity of the Turkish forces and Government. The requisition of stores from the public was a

[1] The use of these in many capacities (command, intelligence, propaganda, supply, &c.) was a feature of the Turkish Army of 1914–18. Marshal Falkenhayn himself commanded (mid-1917 to March 1918) and was succeeded by Liman von Sanders from March 1918.

[2] From early August onwards orders in this sense were received by the IV Army Command.

[3] Anti-German in feeling, Jamal was considered mildly Francophile. He was a practising Muslim, amiable and accessible in society, a shrewd politician, mediocre general, and competent administrator. He has left his own account of events (see bibliography, Djemal Pasha).

[4] The others were Enver Pasha and Tal'at Pasha.

[5] The IV Army was reinforced later by the VII and VIII Armies.

constant hardship, sheer looting was not unknown, and the destruction of mulberry and other trees for fuel was a grievous blow at village industry. The Tripoli–Ḥumṣ and Damascus–Muzayrib sections of railway were largely stripped for materials needed elsewhere, and the condition and rolling-stock of the lines still in use deteriorated to the lowest level.

With internal order maintained by ubiquitous military dominance, the civil administration continued; indeed, elements of fear and hope among the Governors led to some improvement, at Aleppo, Beirut, and elsewhere, in both local and central (including educational) services. The closure of foreign institutions compelled the opening of more government schools. Many high officials were suspected not only of normal corruption but of dispatching fortunes abroad; their quality and attitude, as ever, was widely variable. The autonomous status of the Lebanon was abolished in October 1915, and its administration adapted to that of a normal sanjaq; the capitulatory rights of foreigners had been already revoked, in November 1914. In 1917 the Turkish Government abolished by law the judicial powers of the heads of the *millets*, thus depriving these of their time-honoured privileged status. The debasement of the currency, by the issue of great quantities of unacceptable and therefore valueless notes, was ruinous to the local economy.

Among the civil population conditions never became intolerable in the inland, and especially the grain-growing, areas. Crops were of average abundance, except in 1915 when a locust visitation was among the severest remembered. Although thousands of military deserters were harboured among the tribes, and conscription was rigorously applied in the towns (though largely inapplicable in remoter areas),[1] the masses, accustomed to the lowest standards, had little more than their normal quarrel with their rulers.

In the Lebanon and on the coast, it was otherwise. From the first hour of the war shipping ceased to arrive, imported goods grew rarer and finally unobtainable. Isolation from the outside world was nearly complete. Remittances from abroad, so vital to Lebanese economy, fell to a low level, and a small incoming trickle could be distributed only by stealth through the surviving foreign residents.[2] The men of the coastal plain and towns were conscripted and marched away. Rumours of Allied landings, a prayed-for deliverance, led always to disappointment; restrictions

[1] It was not applied in the Lebanon, even after the 'normalization' of the sanjaq.

[2] The American missionaries showed great ingenuity and devotion in this work.

on movement, and the nightly 'blackout' were obnoxious novelties. But these were minor horrors compared to the conditions first of food shortage, later of sheer famine, that supervened after the first year of war. The coastal and mountain folk, always dependent on food from the hinterland, were deprived of almost the whole of their supplies by persistent hoarding by growers and merchants, the Allied blockade of the coast, the paucity of freight trains, the commandeering of pack-animals, and by a government policy which reflected increasing Turkish anti-Christian feeling and belief in their disloyalty. If the accusations of 'deliberate extermination' brought by Lebanese spokesmen and later writers are overstated,[1] it is certain that Turkish malice as well as their military exigencies (and sheer inefficiency) was largely to blame in a long-drawn tragedy which cost the Mountain perhaps a fifth of its inhabitants, and Beirut and the coastal towns a large though a lesser proportion. Disease multiplied amid the emaciated survivors, and drugs were unobtainable; hundreds died in the streets, villages were abandoned to decay, the cemeteries were wholly inadequate to the demands for space.

The declaration of war was followed by the closure of most foreign consulates and by steps to remove enemy subjects from the country, and closely to supervise those still within it. The majority of French, British, and Russian subjects were interned, partly in Damascus, partly at places in remote Anatolia; some few were permitted to leave for Europe, and a number of older persons were allowed to continue philanthropic work. Foreign schools, except the German and American, were closed, and their buildings requisitioned. The fortune of foreigners left provisionally at liberty, and the activity of the neutral consulates, depended on the varying moods of Turkish officialdom, and on their own ingenuity. American missionary enterprises, since the United States were never at war with Turkey and broke off diplomatic relations only in April 1917, continued to operate, and the American Red Cross and the Armenian Syrian Relief Committee did much for an oppressed and starving public; viewed with suspicion by the Turks, and with little sympathy by the Catholic Christians, their efforts saved thousands of lives of every local community, including the Muslim, and were limited only by the quantity of stores they could secure from abroad.

In the small and secret political world of the Syrian towns, the last weeks of 1914 were filled with eager speculation. The

[1] It was subsequently denied by Syrian nationalists that the coastal area (meaning in particular the Christians) had suffered worse than the hinterland; Shakib Arsalan (p. xii of his Introduction to Rabbath, *L'Évolution politique*), speaks of the 'legend of Lebanese famine'.

Lebanese[1] debated their future status—and boundaries—in the event of general changes, and were in communication with their large communities abroad. Inland, members of the secret Youth Society (al-Fatat) and the Covenant (al-'Ahd), with their centre at Damascus, believed that the hour of Arab liberation was near; and, seeking means to ensure it, they addressed in January 1915 a letter of inquiry to the Sharif[2] of Mecca as to one—doubtless the only—who might with unquestionable authority lead an Arab revolt with British assistance, and thereby realize Arab independence. The circles in Syria where some form of political Arabism was discussed in low but urgent tones, and none but a tepid loyalty was felt to the Turkish war effort, grew wider in succeeding months. As in the secret inner circle, so in ever larger sections of the Muslim (and some Christian) upper and middle classes, desire to break from the Turkish Empire was restrained not by lack of Arab enthusiasm but by two other factors: the one, a certain continued veneration for the Caliph: the other, dread of a European—which must mean French—intervention in Syria, made possible by the collapse of Turkey. Two month-long visits to Syria by the Amir Fayṣal,[3] second son of the Sharif, instructed him effectively for the first time in the sentiments of the Syrian political world, and served to establish a significant connexion between the keen but powerless independence movement in that country and the policies and events now impending in the Ḥijaz (pp. 54 ff.). From the second of his visits (May–June 1915) the Amir took back secretly to his father a paper, known later as the Damascus Protocol, setting forth the terms[4] on which the Syrians now visualized a possible Anglo-Arab agreement to secure the independence of the Arab lands.

The policy of Jamal in his administration of Syria was initially one of conciliation and the cultivation of sentiment loyal to the Caliph and his sacred cause. But, after his failure on the Canal, and in view of the largely Arab composition of nearly all his military units, he felt that the time had come to change a

[1] A number of Maronites and Malkites approached the French Consulate-General at Beirut for permission to join the French Army. This, since they were Turkish subjects, was necessarily refused.

[2] Ḥusayn bin 'Ali, installed by the C.U.P. at Mecca in 1909, after years of exile at Istanbul. His religious authority was of great consequence in the Islamic world. Ḥusayn himself was pious, cautious, shrewd within limits, and generally well-intentioned: but also domineering, obstinate, and often unrealistic.

[3] This Prince, born at Ṭa'if in 1883 and educated by Arab and Turkish tutors, accompanied his father to Istanbul in 1891 and lived there until the appointment of Sharif Ḥusayn to Mecca. He had seen aspects of military and political work in western Arabia, and was elected to the Turkish Chamber in 1913.

[4] A defensive alliance would be made between the Arab States and Great Britain; in return for sponsorship and protection the latter would have 'economic preference' (Antonius, pp. 157–8).

mild for a 'strong' policy. He secured the replacement of many Arab by Turkish units, thus scattering the officers busily plotting in al-'Ahd. Although the secrets of this society and of al-Fatat were unknown to him, his agents had discovered, in the French consulates of Beirut and Damascus, papers[1] which incriminated a number of leading citizens. Beginning with the execution of a Maronite priest, a series of arrests was ordered, a court martial was assembled at 'Aliya (Aley) in the Lebanon in July 1915 and, after a grossly improper trial, fifty-eight of the leading citizens of Syria were sentenced to death for treasonable acts or writings against the state: that is, for association with an Arab nationalism disloyal to Turkey, or for an alleged guilty connexion with the French. Forty-five of these were abroad or had succeeded in avoiding arrest; 2 were reprieved; 11 (all Muslims except one) were publicly executed[2] in Beirut on 21 August. These steps were followed some months later by the adoption of a new policy of repression, whereby hundreds were removed from their homes and interned in remote places whence they never returned: and this again by a series of further arrests, early in 1916, for 'plotting against the state'. After another prolonged and brutally-conducted trial at 'Aliya, the public hanging was carried out early in May of twenty-two more of the leading professional and learned men of the country. Seventeen of these were Muslims, the rest Christians. Many, probably a large majority, were innocent of anything which could justify such a sentence; some of them, it was claimed, had never touched politics at all. The victims, dying undaunted, revealed nothing of the secret societies to which some had belonged. The Amir Fayṣal who, publicly as his father's envoy to Jamal Pasha but secretly to concert plans with the Syrian nationalists, was in Damascus at the time, tried whole-heartedly but in vain to influence Jamal to mercy. A grievous blow had been suffered by Syrian society—and an immense impulse given to the plans of Syrian politicians for liberation.

The outbreak of the revolt in the Ḥijaz in June 1916 was at first concealed from the Syrian population, which had long been fed on stories of Muslim solidarity; later, when admitted, it was belittled and distorted, with venomous attacks upon its leader. The next stage was one of further arrests by Jamal Pasha of leading Syrians.[3] A number were flogged and otherwise brutally

[1] The French Consul-General (F. Georges Picot) had omitted to destroy these dangerous papers before he left; Fabre-Luce (*Deuil au Levant*, p. 32) speaks of 'une liste oubliée au Consulat'.

[2] The Turkish viewpoint is given in an official IV Army publication, *La Verité sur la question syrienne* (Istanbul, 1916).

[3] They included Shukri Pasha al-Ayyubi, 'Abd al-Ḥamid Pasha Qaltaqchi, Zaki al-'Adhma, Faris al-Khuri, and Shukri al-Quwatli.

ill-treated; their lives were saved and their release secured only by a letter to Jamal from the Amir Fayṣal, threatening instant reprisals against Turkish prisoners. The Pasha continued to rage against the treachery of the Sharif, and to govern the country with the sullen hatred of an enemy, until his transfer from Syria in January 1918. He was succeeded as Commander of IV Army by Muḥammad Jamal Pasha.

Yet another visit by the Amir[1] to his friends at Damascus, paid in the utmost secrecy in May 1917, completed the solidarity of conception between the Arab Army[2] by now operating in the Ḥijaz and the surviving leaders of Syrian nationalism; their loyalty to the Amir was assured, and his appearance as deliverer in Syria would herald the liberation of the country. Meanwhile, desertion from the Turkish forces was redoubled, an understanding was reached with desert-fringe tribal leaders, and ever wider circles in the Syrian towns became aware of impending events. In such circles, which were essentially those of Sunni Islam, time-honoured fears of French intervention were widespread, and indeed were shared—perhaps in some part inspired—by the known views of Fayṣal himself.

2. THE PROMISES

If vital elements in future Syrian politics were taking shape during the war in that country itself, and notably among such elements the Arab nationalism which has held the field ever since, other powerful forces were in the same years becoming explicit in the Chancelleries of Europe, and in the deserts of Arabia. These forces, in part allied, in part antagonistic, to the forces of Arab nationalism, were to involve their principal artificers, France and Great Britain, in serious disagreement, and the Syrians in high hopes followed too soon by cruel disillusion.

In France it was felt in the weeks following the outbreak of war that the hour for the realization of her hopes and projects in Syria was at hand, even though a major French military effort in that area could scarcely be envisaged. To eager colonialists and missionaries, and to circles in or near the Government, not only all Syria but Cilicia, part of central-south Anatolia, and even the

[1] He was accompanied by one of his British staff-officers, Major T. E. Lawrence, a wayward and egocentric but brilliant and courageous young archaeologist, with a flair for Arab contacts and desert operations. The Amir stayed in a village near Damascus with the Bakri family, and met Riḍha Pasha al-Rikabi, the Turkish Commander of the city.

[2] This, apart from a small British and smaller French contingent, consisted of Arab regiments under ʻIraqi and Syrian officers, with miscellaneous Ḥijazi tribal forces. The supply services and most Staff functions were supplied by the British.

Mosul[1] wilayet, would form part of a French inheritance. France stood, from the outset, for the complete realization of all her 'rights' in the Levant. It was natural that a proposal made by an Arabophile enthusiast for the proclamation of 'an independent Arab Empire under Allied supervision' should win no serious hearing; natural also that a French 'Naval Division of the Levant' should move to eastern Mediterranean[2] waters and stay there throughout the war, and that the guns of French warships should help to repel Jamal Pasha's forces from the Suez Canal. Many Syrians were accepted in the Foreign Legion, and a number, later, in other units, while steps were taken to train infantry companies from Middle Eastern elements in Cyprus and Port Said early in the war, a force later to appear in the field, from early 1918, as the Légion d'Orient. A British project for an Allied landing at Alexandretta was treated by the French with suspicion, and was acceptable only on terms of French participation and command; the fear of some measure of supersession in the Middle East by the British, with their forces on the spot and with a freer hand in strategy,[3] was already evident. Some comfort could be derived from the resolutions and enthusiasm of Syrian and Lebanese Committees in the great cities of Latin and North America, West Africa, Australia, Egypt—and above all those in Paris,[4] which stood throughout the war, close to the Quai d'Orsay.

An early exchange of views between France, Britain, and Russia revealed that the last-named refused to support French aspirations to a sole Catholic control of the Holy Places, nor, with her own Orthodox pretensions, would she tolerate a Protestant monopoly. Russia's own positive claims in the Turkish Empire lay elsewhere; these were covered by the tripartite Constantinople Agreement of 18 March 1915, as those of Italy were satisfied by the Pact of London of 25 April. In British Government circles, Kitchener's term of office at Cairo, his Arab leanings, and some approaches[5]

[1] The Christian elements in Mosul had long been within the claimed French cultural sphere: the Chaldean community, an interesting minority, was considered as a 'faithful client of France', and its scale was strangely exaggerated by French opinion into actual majority status in the wilayet (Gontaut-Biron, p. 23).

[2] It was frequently at or off Arwad Island, which became thereby an important information post.

[3] Since there were already a British base and forces in the Middle East (Egypt); and since France was, and Britain was not, invaded by German armies.

[4] In 1917 the Comité Central Syrien was formed in Paris, almost entirely from Lebanese and Catholic elements, to unify the activities of the *émigré* committees throughout the world. Though composed of elements not always harmonious, it was of course overwhelmingly Francophile in sentiment and programme, and opposed to Arab claims.

[5] In the form of conversations sought in February 1914 by the Amir 'Abdullah (second son of the Sharif) with Lord Kitchener and Ronald Storrs in Cairo. Kitchener's attitude to this approach was discouraging; he listened but could promise nothing.

to him by the Sharif of Mecca early in 1914, had increased their interest in a possible anti-Turkish movement in Arabia; the attack on the Canal showed that mere desert wastes were an inadequate defence. The control of Palestine was felt in Great Britain to be more and more specifically a British concern. The widening strategic views natural in a world war revived interest, also, in a British railway from the Mediterranean to the Persian Gulf, especially after the invasion of 'Iraq by British-Indian forces; and the recent Turkish promise, in June 1914, of an oil concession to a British-German company covering the wilayets of Mosul and Baghdad might one day lead to trans-desert pipeline requirements and a Mediterranean oil terminal. A Cabinet Committee in Whitehall in 1915 concluded that Palestine must be internationalized: a decision in which a considerable element was, no doubt, the pressure of Zionist spokesmen on British ministers.

In the autumn of the year new elements came forcibly into the Arab scene. The outbreak of a world war involving Turkey had given new immediacy to Anglo-Ḥijazi relations; the Sharif could see new possibilities of independence, and indeed of a grandiose Empire; and Great Britain could see wartime value in a major Arab rebel and ally. By renewed liaison in Cairo in the last weeks of 1914 the two sides had moved nearer; and the British High Commissioner,[1] instructed from Whitehall, declared early in 1915 that his country would, when the Turks were overthrown, recognize the full independence of peninsular Arabia, and an Arab Caliphate if such were established. The Sharif Ḥusayn was by this time in secret touch with Damascus (p. 50); the Amir Fayṣal on his behalf had become a sworn member of the Syrian secret societies, and had carried the Damascus Protocol to Mecca; and the Sharif's hesitant or negative attitude to the Holy War was an outward sign of his feelings.

The correspondence[2] between the Sharif Ḥusayn bin 'Ali in Mecca and Sir Henry McMahon in Cairo was inaugurated by the former's letter of 14 July 1915 carried to Storrs from the Amir 'Abdullah. The series of exchanges continued until the end of January 1916. The Sharif stated and restated the Arab demands which were to be secured to them by Great Britain, as their ally, in return for immediate armed rebellion against the Turks. These demands were those, unchanged, of the Damascus Protocol—independence for the Arab countries, and British recognition of an Arab Caliphate. The British High Commissioner, reluctant at first to be explicit in his promises, came in his second letter, dated

[1] Lord Kitchener's successor in Cairo in 1914 was Sir Henry McMahon, who was succeeded by Sir Reginald Wingate early in 1917.

[2] The (English) text is in Antonius, Appendix A, pp. 413–27 and in Cmd. 5957 of 1939.

24 October 1915, to closer quarters with the all-important question of the extent of the Arab territory whose independence was proposed. He accepted the frontiers as suggested, but with important exceptions. The excluded areas (over which Arab independence was thus specifically *not* promised) were the districts of Alexandretta and Mersin, and 'portions of Syria lying to the west of the districts of Damascus, Homs, Hamah, and Aleppo', their exception[1] being due to the presumption that they were 'not purely Arab' and that Great Britain was not free to engage herself regarding them 'without detriment to the interests of her ally, France'. The Sharif accepted the exclusion of the wilayet of Adana[2] (containing Mersin), but not that of Alexandretta (which lay in the wilayet of Aleppo) or of any part of Syria whatsoever. Agreement was not in fact reached in the correspondence as to Arab rights on the Syrian littoral and coastal ranges; the Sharif abated nothing of his claim, while McMahon refused to treat these areas as covered. The only solution was for each side to maintain its position, but to postpone further argument until after the war. This was done; and on the basis of agreement covering the rest of the Arab world in Asia—an agreement for British specific recognition of Arab independence—the Sharif was prepared wholeheartedly to throw his influence on the Allies' side, and to launch his armed revolt against the Turks. He assumed the title of King[3] in October 1916.

The correspondence, extraordinarily ill drafted on both sides, ended in January 1916. The Sharif maintained touch with the British over questions of supply, armament, and synchronization, urged an Allied invasion of Syria simultaneously with his own Ḥijaz revolt, and with caution admitted his entourage and leading Ḥijazi tribesmen into the secret. As soon as the Amir Fayṣal, sickened with Turkish brutalities in Syria, had returned to Mecca, the revolt was proclaimed on 5 June 1916. Mecca was captured from the Turks by Arab forces, and a new era in Arab politics had begun.

[1] A further exception was made for the wilayets of Baghdad and Baṣra, where because of admitted British interests a special régime would (said the High Commissioner) be needed; this was, in vague terms, agreed by the Sharif. The sanjaqs of Jerusalem, Nablus, and Acre, were not excepted, nor mentioned, in the correspondence; it has been, therefore, an unvarying Arab claim that this part of southern Syria was covered by the promise of independence. The contention is, in terms of the text, irrefutable; it is nevertheless certain that McMahon, if asked at the time whether his intention was to hand Palestine (with its unique international status and strong non-Arab and non-Muslim interest) to unrestricted Arab independence, would have replied No; and in fact he stated, in 1939, that he had *not* intended its inclusion. The Sharif would in 1915 probably have agreed to some form of special régime for that area of Syria, though never to one which would threaten Arab sovereignty.

[2] The wilayet of Adana was almost completely non-Arab, and could be claimed as 'part of Syria' only by uncritical enthusiasts.

[3] He announced himself as 'King of the Arab countries', but was recognized by the Allies only as King of the Ḥijaz.

The British commitments *vis-à-vis* the Sharif, which had led to this result, had been the subject of no day-by-day discussion with the French; but since they involved the striking of an important blow at the common enemy, and since the British negotiator had punctiliously reserved the French position (whatever it was) in western Syria, the nature of these commitments was revealed to a French representative[1] in London in November 1915, even before the Sharif–McMahon correspondence was complete;[2] and M. Georges Picot, for France, specifically accepted[3] the project of Arab government to cover Damascus, Ḥumṣ, and Aleppo.

But the new engagements towards the Arabs raised or revived, in French eyes at least, broader questions regarding the future of the Levant territories, whose formulation and solution could wait no longer. An internationalized Palestine, and these promises to the Sharif Ḥusayn, involved trespass on French monopolistic claims in central and northern Syria. With nothing yet settled about Cilicia or Anatolia or northern 'Iraq, it seemed to Foreign Ministers high time to seek agreement on this sensitive and important area: to establish a programme which, while consistent with an independent Arab régime over most of it, would give satisfaction to the claims, or 'rights', of the Powers in these territories which their armies were to detach from a vanquished Turkey.

The negotiations on these matters were carried out in London, St. Petersburg, and again London in February to May 1916. Authority within limits to bargain and to draft had been given to Picot by the French, to Sir Mark Sykes[4] by the British. The resulting agreement, known (perhaps unjustly to its authors) as the Sykes–Picot Agreement, was signed by both on 16 May 1916, after the content of the Anglo-Russian and Franco-Russian clauses had been agreed between the Governments. Ratifications as between Sir Edward Grey and M. Paul Cambon were signed on 9 and 16 May.

[1] M. Georges Picot, ex-Consul-General and now the recognized French authority on Syrian affairs. A compatriot (Fabre-Luce, *Deuil au Levant*, p. 31) describes him as 'un vrai coq gaulois, qui fait valoir en toute occasion ses privilèges de demi-souverain'. His conversations on this occasion were with Sir Arthur Nicolson.

[2] The persistent story current in French polemics and propaganda that France was 'never told', or 'told only in outline' (Gontaut-Biron, p. 307), of the McMahon commitments, is unfounded. Antonius (p. 244) is here in error (see Poincaré, vii. 206).

[3] E. L. Woodward and R. Butler, eds., *Documents on British Foreign Policy, 1919-39*, 1st series, vol. 4, no. 334, p. 481.

[4] A young ex-officer, with considerable earlier study of Asiatic Turkey to his credit. No orientalist, and a lighthearted amateur diplomat, his integrity, charm, and excellent intentions could not compensate for lack of judgement.

SKETCH MAP SHOWING SYKES-PICOT ALLOTMENT OF TERRITORY AND ULTIMATE MANDATE BOUNDARIES

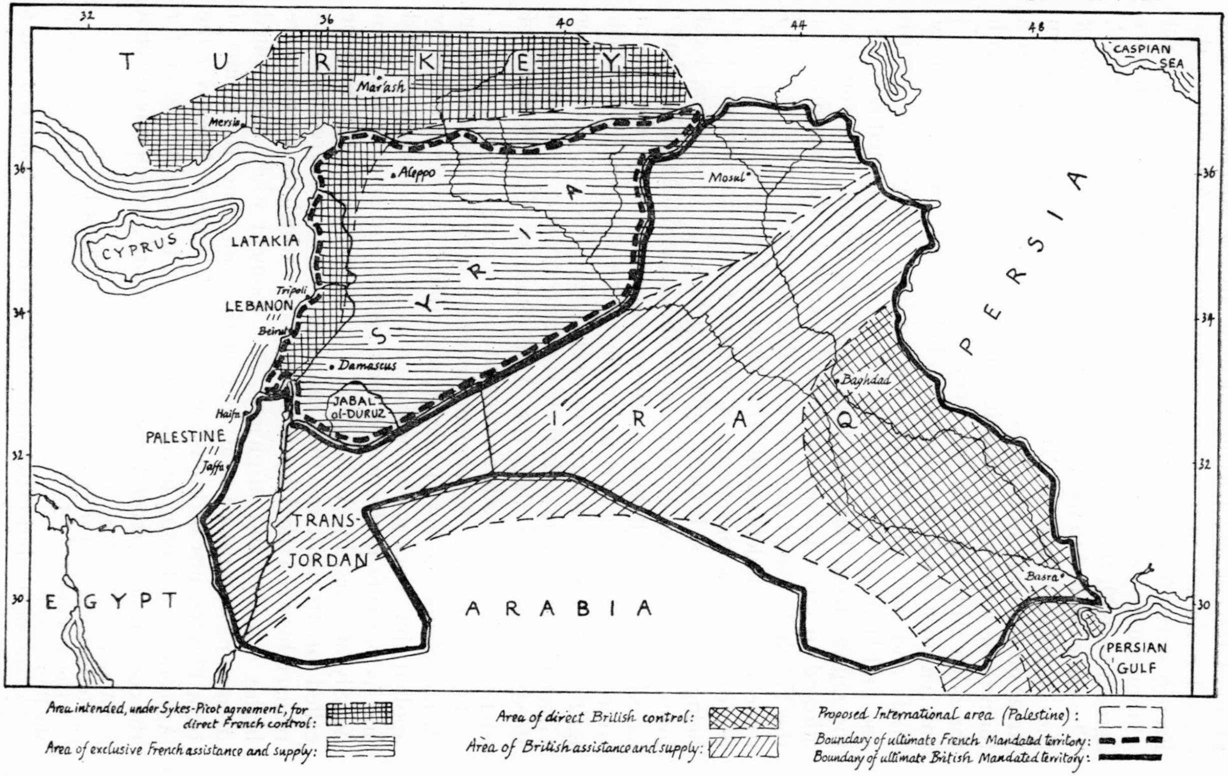

The Agreement,[1] as far as it concerns this work, covers the Fertile Crescent and part of Anatolia. In the 'excepted' area of coastal Syria and in a wide area of Cilicia and Asia Minor, the French were given *carte blanche* to set up 'such direct or indirect administration or contol as they may . . . see fit to establish after agreement with the Arab State or Confederation of Arab States'. The same applied to the British position in the Baṣra[2] and most of the Baghdad wilayet in 'Iraq. Palestine, indicated as a Brown Area[3] on the map, was to have an international administration in a form to be approved by Russia 'after subsequent agreement with the other Allies and the representatives of the Sharif of Mecca'; and within it Great Britain was to hold, as her own, the ports of Haifa and Acre. Alexandretta was to be a free port for British use, and Haifa for French, with free access to connected railways; the railway from Haifa to 'Iraq would be British, and would be allowed to cross French-controlled territory. The remainder of the Fertile Crescent and north Arabia was to be 'recognized and upheld' as an independent Arab State or Confederation of Arab States 'under the Suzerainty of an Arab Chief', the northern half[4] being subject to a French right of priority in enterprises, local loans, and the supply of advisers or officials, and the southern half[5] carrying a similar British privilege. All areas except the Brown were to form a Customs union, in which the existing Turkish tariff would remain in force for twenty years. Neither France nor Great Britain were to cede their rights in any part of the area to a third Power 'other than the Arab State or Confederation of States' without each other's consent.

The Sykes–Picot Agreement, in which both France and Great Britain claimed to have made great sacrifices, was never integrally applied; but since it was held after 1918 by the French as valid and as partially protective of their rights, and since it has been heavily attacked by Arab opinion, some comment on it may be called for. Its merit was that, under its provisions, agreement was realized between the Allies in a matter over which the French were highly sensitive and suspicious, at a moment when inter-Allied disagreement must be fatal; and, at the same time, the claims of both Powers, just or unjust, were at least defined. Moreover the Agreement took pains to allow, to a large if incomplete degree, for the commitments recently made to the Sharif: his specific consent

[1] Antonius, App. B, pp. 428–30.

[2] Including Kuwayt and some of the Persian Gulf littoral.

[3] The area destined for direct French government was the Blue, and that of the British the Red.

[4] Mosul and its district (excluding Kirkuk), the northern Jazira, and eastern Syria.

[5] North-central 'Iraq, with Kirkuk, the central Jazira, western 'Iraq, the present-day Kingdom of Jordan, and southern Israel.

to future régimes in the Blue, Red, and Brown areas was to be sought,[1] while the remaining areas were to be under direct Arab rule. On the other hand, critics of the Sykes–Picot Agreement urged the neglect of the wishes of Arab populations thus arbitrarily placed, in coastal Syria and southern 'Iraq, under European rule with no regard to their own views or ambitions; they indicate the departure in spirit, even more than in letter, from the McMahon commitments. Arab independence appears indeed in the Agreement as little more than a necessary evil to be tolerated by the Powers (paradoxically, rather in the more backward regions than in the more advanced) after France and Britain had selected the areas they preferred for themselves. The actual or potential force of Arab nationalism is seriously underestimated, and no provision is made for that Arab sense of unity which was already linking Damascus with Mecca, Baghdad, and Jerusalem. The Agreement, in fact, had outstanding defects not only moral but practical; it was from the first unworkable, created heterogeneous zones and inapplicable restrictions, and ignored geographical as well as political and psychological facts. It was withheld from the Sharif[2] until he became aware of it from Russian sources in November 1917, and was then explained to him by British spokesmen with a minimum of frankness.

Whether they took the restrictions provided in the Agreement seriously or not, the prospect of Arab government in hinterland Syria could not but be a blow to French aspirations; and so also was the internationalization, instead of French and Catholic supremacy, proposed for the Holy Land. But the situation in the latter was, before the war ended, to be further modified, and the separation of southern Syria from the rest to be made more than ever irreparable, by the introduction of a new element in Palestine, that of acknowledged and advancing Zionism. The immediate background to the issue of the Balfour Declaration was one of pressure on the British Cabinet from British and American Jewry[3] to secure for them their National Home while this seemed possible;[4] but it is obvious that considerations additional to those of sympathy with the scattered Jewish race (though this too was real and operative) or of desire to gain Jewish goodwill in the worst days of war, lay behind this gesture. It was approved, indeed, in advance not only by the American but by the French

[1] In the event it was, of course, never so sought.

[2] Also from the Italians.

[3] German Jewry was in 1916–17 making similar overtures to the German Government.

[4] Earlier in the war the Russians, still a factor, were anti-Zionist, and Asquith as Prime Minister till 1916 also opposed it. Lloyd George, as well as Balfour, strongly supported it.

Government,[1] after conversations between leading Zionists and the Quai d'Orsay; but the consolidation of the British position in Palestine by way of a British-sponsored Jewish National Home (whatever that might mean) was certainly a main British motive, such position being designed to ensure the defence of Egypt and the East, to cover railway and oil-line projects, and perhaps to serve as a bridgehead in the Arab world. In the event, a letter was addressed by Balfour as Foreign Secretary to Lord Rothschild on 2 November 1917, stating that his Government 'view with favour the establishment in Palestine of a National Home for the Jewish people, and will use their best endeavours to facilitate it', providing that nothing be done to 'prejudice civil and religious rights of existing non-Jewish Communities'. Specific French approval, conveyed in a letter from the Foreign Minister to a leading Zionist, was forthcoming on 14 February 1918.[2]

The importance of the Balfour Declaration to Syrian history is profound. It led, by stages, to British dominance in Palestine from 1918 to 1947, to a partition of Syria, and ultimately to the loss of Palestine's millennary Arab character and population. A judgement on this document, and the policy which inspired it (most insufficiently explored or considered at the time) does not belong to the present work. It need only be said here that too little seems to have been realized of the overwhelming preponderance (over 90 per cent.) of the Arab inhabitants of Palestine so lightly dismissed as 'non-Jewish communities', and that a naïvely optimistic view was taken of the possibility of creating the National Home without the gravest prejudice to Arab rights. Few of the inevitable results of the Declaration were anticipated by its authors, including its permanent and disastrous effect on Arab opinion and attitude throughout the Middle East. The Declaration had, in the event, little influence on the conduct of the war, and was an immediate as well as a lasting embarrassment to Great Britain both in all her Arab dealings and in her relations with the French. Even the remaining possibility, that the execution of the promise might be restrained on lines consonant with the actual conditions of Palestine, was not to be realized: the pressure of Jewry on successive British Governments was sufficient fatally to preclude the adequate acknowledgment of Arab rights. Meanwhile, in and after 1917, it was to lead to Arab disillusion in British promises and, generally, in western integrity. It created a permanent element of bitter anti-Zionism in Arab politics, and a rallying point against the Powers who had given that movement its entry (otherwise than as exemplified by the interesting but limited Jewish villages founded in Palestine before 1914) into

[1] This is often ignored by French writers.

[2] Hunter-Miller, v. 20.

Arab territory. And it involved a bitterly resentful Syria, in and after 1947, in its share of the full tragedy of Arab Palestine.

Meanwhile the Arab Revolt, with its British supply of munitions, officers, and strategic leadership, was playing its part from June 1916 onward in the war against Turkey by the weakening or immobilization of Turkish forces, the destruction of their communications, and the effect of its operations and spirit on the inhabitants of Syria. In the Arab forces, led by the Amir Fayṣal with an Arab and British staff, the 'Iraqi and Syrian officers considered themselves as the spearhead of visible, dynamic Arab independence, with Syrian liberation as the first objective. The contribution of Arab forces to the Palestine-Syrian campaign can be variously assessed; excessively disparaged by some French[1] or other Catholic writers, it has perhaps been over-valued by some British and most Arab opinion. It was by any standard considerable,[2] and was effective in creating Arab pride and encouraging immediate pretensions. The forces of the Amir became an integral part of the Egyptian Expeditionary Force after July 1917. A small French detachment had, with natural motives of flag-showing, been attached to the Sharifian Army, a French Military Mission was maintained under Colonel Brémond at Jidda beside the British Mission, and some French munitions were supplied; and to the main British force by now emerging from Egypt for the invasion of Palestine a 'French Palestine-Syrian Detachment' of approximately brigade-group strength had been added. These, although *faisant petite figure* beside the massive divisions of General Allenby, were of good quality and played a creditable part.[3] Georges Picot, who in 1917 paid visits to Cairo and Jidda to assert French interest, was deputed to represent the French Government[4] with the British Command as the armies entered Palestine, and was at Allenby's side to uphold the claims of his country. His suggestion for the setting up of a half-French civil administration in Palestine was not, however, accepted by the Commander-in-Chief.

3. THE ENTRY INTO SYRIA

Some idea of the conditions within Syria during the war has been given; it was a period of extreme misery in part of that

[1] e.g. Gontaut-Biron, p. 44; or Lammens (*La Syrie*, ii. 243), who makes great play with 'l'inactivité, l'incapacité militaire de Faisal et des Bédouins'.

[2] Both Lord Allenby and his biographer Lord Wavell regarded the Arab effort as very valuable. Allenby (dispatch dated 28 June 1919) speaks of the Amir as 'a bold and skilful leader' who 'has always co-operated wholeheartedly'.

[3] Notably at Ṭul Karam and Nablus, 19–21 September 1918.

[4] His appointment as High Commissioner of France in the Levant dates from April 1917.

territory, of disquiet and apprehension in it all. If a conservative element in the population would gladly have seen the Sultan-Caliph triumphant and the foreigners discomforted, the bulk of the more 'evolved' classes, whether awaiting Arab independence or (as in Maronite circles) the intervention of France, expected with impatience, but could not hasten, the day of Allied victory which would bring them deliverance.

That day was inexorably approaching, in general through the gradual weakening of Turkey and in particular through the slow advance of General Allenby's forces from the south. The story of the Palestine Campaign of 1916–18 has often been told, and does not belong to the present narrative. After the failure of the Turkish attacks on the Canal the concentration of powerful forces in Egypt seemed to the British Cabinet a needful strategic precaution, especially after Turkish divisions were released by the British abandonment of Gallipoli. With Sir A. Murray as Commander-in-Chief in Egypt, and a Cabinet under Lloyd George in London seeking paths to victory in eastern fields, the British Army in the Nile Delta turned late in 1915 from a defensive to an offensive role. An invasion of Palestine was decided, an advance through the Sinai desert was begun, and al-'Arish was taken from the Turks on 21 December 1916. The decision to press forward was based on the desire to distract the enemy, to demoralize the Turkish forces with their large proportion of Arab troops, and to take Jerusalem with its vast moral significance. In January 1917 Rafaḥ was taken, in March British forces were approaching Gaza; but two failures there in April and May led to a pause, and to the replacement of General Murray by Sir Edmund Allenby. The Arab forces of the Amir Fayṣal came under his command, for use as a mobile right wing or screen. He was ready for a further advance in October 1917, occupied Beersheba late in that month, and entered Jerusalem on 9 December. In spite of orders to dispatch troops to Europe, where the war was now in its most critical phase, Allenby next launched two expeditions into the sanjaq of Ma'an, in order to achieve with Arab help the complete isolation of Turkish forces farther south; these failed, but incessant railway destruction and raiding by Fayṣal's half-regular, half-tribal forces[1] combined to embarrass the Turks.

[1] Father Lammens (*La Syrie*, ii. 236–7), with his powerful anti-Arab bias, relies upon a story passed by Jamal Pasha to Liman von Sanders (*Funf Jähre*, pp. 330-8) to the effect that early in 1918 Fayṣal, disappointed at the course of events, 'se tourna de nouveau du côté des Turcs', offering to take the place of the Turkish IV Army against the British, on condition that the Turkish Government would guarantee him the formation of an Arab State. The idea that Fayṣal would, with brazen perfidy, consider changing from the obviously winning to the obviously losing side, and in so doing would be followed by his British-supplied and largely British-led forces, is scarcely imaginable.

During 1918 the Ottoman forces, in spite of all the efforts of Liman von Sanders and his German staff, and many good and loyal Turkish officers at every level, slowly disintegrated through the action of low morale, constant desertion, disease, lack of supplies and transport, and the scantiness of reinforcements from a higher command now largely uninterested in the Syrian front. The British, in contrast, were well supplied, well led, plentifully reinforced from India, possessed of complete air superiority—and fully informed of conditions behind the Turkish lines. Allenby's plan aimed at a final battle of annihilation. Its first phase was to sever Turkish southward communications from Damascus by the capture of Dar'a, which task he entrusted to the Arabs. This was to be closely followed by a mass ride of his 15,000 cavalry to contain and isolate practically the whole of the enemy forces. The operation started on 19 September, and was abundantly successful. The break-through was complete, Nazareth entered, the 'Afula–Beisan valley overrun, and in the ensuing Battle of Megiddo almost all the Turkish forces west of Jordan were destroyed or captured, while those in Ma'an and 'Amman areas east of Jordan, in full retreat, were harried and largely scattered by the Arabs and by a British mounted brigade. The Navy occupied Haifa, whence the railway inland could bring supplies. 'Amman was occupied by British forces on 25 September, Dar'a by Fayṣal's Arabs on the 25th, and exulting tribesmen seized Azra' and Ghazala, and prisoners in thousands. All pressed their advance, against dying opposition, towards the north. By the evening of 30 September a senior Sharifian representative (the Amir Naṣir), with tribal escort, reached the outskirts of Damascus. Led by the 'Iraqi officer Nuri al-Sa'id, Arab forces entered the town early on 1 October, followed a few hours later by British troops,[1] whose appearance was greeted with manifestations of joy.

Among the leading citizens of the occupied capital there were two parties. One, smaller and less representative, followed the two brothers, the Amirs 'Abd al-Qadir and Muḥammad Sa'id, of the Jaza'iri family,[2] and had been in close touch with the Turkish commander before he left Damascus; the other was the committee of Fayṣal's adherents, who in almost continuous session had been awaiting his arrival to acclaim him as their head. The Amir Naṣir and Colonel Lawrence found, at mid-morning on

[1] Of the 3rd Australian Light Horse. These and other units accepted the surrender of thousands of Turkish troops in Damascus and its villages. There does not seem to the writer to be adequate foundation for the often-repeated story that the entry of troops into Damascus was purposely delayed so as to enable the Amir to have the honour.

[2] Descendants of the famous 'Abd al-Qadir, the Algerian patriot exiled to Damascus by the French in 1856.

1 October, that the Jaza'iris claimed already to be in power as heads of a Government: a claim intolerable to the Sharifians and odious to the Arab forces who were even now entering the town and relieving British troops of their police duties. The Jaza'iris, after furious argument, were required to stand aside: the immediate governorship was (under long-standing arrangement) conferred by Lawrence on behalf of Fayṣal on 'Ali Riḍha Pasha al-Rikabi,[1] who was already in contact with the British forces, and for whom, for a day, Shukri Pasha al-Ayyubi deputized. Amid violent protest by the Jaza'iri brothers their 'civil government' of the city was pronounced abolished, and military government was established, deriving its authority from the Army. The Arab flag was hoisted[2] over Damascus, amid transports of enthusiasm; and two days of intensive organization of the public services—police, street lighting, water-supply, relief-work—followed, with rapid delegation of control branch by branch, to whichever of the notables or higher officials was available. Riḍha al-Rikabi assumed duty as Military Governor. A sudden and fanatical revolt, led by the Jaza'iris during the first night and second morning of the occupation, was quickly suppressed; it cost 'Abd al-Qadir his life and Sa'id, temporarily, his liberty. Shukri Pasha was dispatched on a mission to Beirut and the Lebanon, not yet occupied. More Sharifian as well as British troops moved in.[3] On 3 October the Commander-in-Chief arrived in person, and confirmed the arrangements made for the temporary administration of hinterland Syria under Rikabi; and here for the first time he met the Amir Fayṣal, whose own entry had been delayed (through his absence at a distance) and whom the population of Damascus now greeted, as he galloped in, with an emotion long remembered.

The local problems of the Damascus oasis being temporarily solved, the Amir and the Pasha installed with British and French liaison officers, and the surrender of further thousands of Turkish troops accepted, it remained for General Allenby to complete rapidly the occupation of central and northern Syria. British troops, flanked and at times preceded by Arab forces,[4] began this northward movement from the Damascus area early in October, in the face of great supply difficulties, fatigue, and illness. Ḥumṣ

[1] p. 52 above. A senior Turkish officer (but by family and sympathy Syrian) who had been from the beginning a member of the movement which looked for liberation under the Amir Fayṣal. He had, simultaneously, commanded the Turkish forces in Damascus.

[2] An Arab flag (black, white, green, and red) had indeed been flying since 30 September.

[3] Also the small French detachment (p. 61) under Captain Pisani: 'the good soldier', says Lawrence, 'bewildered by the political hubbub'.

[4] The Amir's forces, soon to shed their tribal auxiliaries, were increased in their early days in Syria by the recruitment of Arab ex-Turkish soldiers.

was occupied without opposition on 11 October by Fayṣal's men, Ḥamah on the 17th. Aleppo was defended by none other than Muṣṭafa Kamal Pasha,[1] future dictator of a reborn Turkey; but combined Arab-British attacks reduced the city on the 25th and 26th and fought off a counter-attack. The Muslimiya railway junction was reached and occupied on 29 October. During the same four weeks British troops advanced northwards along the coast from Haifa. Acre, Tyre, and Sidon were taken without opposition. On 8 October Beirut was entered by the troops of the British XXI Corps, including most of the French Détachement Français de Palestine-Syrie;[2] a small landing party from French ships[3] had made its appearance the day before, and other units from the east and south now flowed into the city. Tripoli was reached by British troops immediately before the Armistice.

This, whose terms were those[4] of complete Turkish surrender, was signed on the island of Mudros on 30 October by a single Allied plenipotentiary, Admiral Sir S. Calthorpe; French participation, for which Clemenceau and Pichon had pressed resentfully, was rejected by Lloyd George. The Armistice, which ended Turkish armed opposition, was followed by the gradual occupation of the remaining towns of northern Syria, and by the regrouping of Allenby's forces for garrison duty, in anticipation of their rapid reduction.[5]

The territory thus occupied, accustoming itself with mixed feelings to the sight of foreign garrisons and troop-movements, and to the immense mental and economic upheavals which these involved, showed from its first hour of occupation that it would present problems in plenty.

In Beirut, the earliest political act of the British was to reverse a hopeful initiative by the new Damascus authorities, who had immediately, and with nobody's (unless Lawrence's) authorization,

[1] Later, Kamal Ataturk. He commanded the VII Army, and assumed command of the remnants of the IV, VII, and VIII Armies from Liman von Sanders on 1 November.

[2] The D.F. P-S appears in General Allenby's Order of Battle, 1 September 1918 as attached to the 54th (East Anglian) Division. The detachment was commanded by Colonel P. de Piépape.

[3] Some British ships were in company with the French, but did not land a party.

[4] The terms included the demobilization of all Turkish forces, except in so far as necessary to keep order; the disposition of remaining troops was to be determined by the Allies. The latter were to occupy such strategic points as they might select. Turkish forces were to be withdrawn from N.W. Persia and Trans-Caucasia. All Turkish garrisons still in Arabia, Syria, and 'Iraq were to surrender, and all were to withdraw fron Cilicia unless essential to maintain order.

[5] By the end of 1918 withdrawals from Syria included the XXI Corps with 10, 53, 54, 60, and 75 Divisions. The need of increased forces in Egypt was felt in and after March 1919, when conditions there became seriously disturbed.

sent Shukri Pasha al-Ayyubi (p. 64) with a token force to assume Arab authority in Beirut wilayet: or rather, to support in the Amir's name the Arab Government already proclaimed there on 1 October by 'Umar Bey Da'uq,[1] who took over authority from the outgoing Turkish Wali, Isma'il Ḥaqqi Bey. He had assembled the Muslim and some Christian notables and hoisted the Sharifian flag on 4 October, thus to forestall the still-awaited British troops by a *fait accompli*. But the status of Beirut city and wilayet, as that of Damascus and Aleppo, could not at present be other than that of Occupied Enemy Territory, and many considerations, legal, practical, and international, seemed to the Commander-in-Chief to preclude the installation of Syrian, or Arab, authority in the coastal area of Syria. The flag was removed by Allenby's orders, Shukri Pasha and his entourage retired, and only his resuscitation of the Council of the Lebanese sanjaq was allowed to hold good.[2] The Commander-in-Chief appointed the senior French officer present, Colonel de Piépape, as Military Governor of Beirut, and ignored the strongly-worded anti-French petitions from some sections of the public which followed this appointment and the appearance of French officers as administrators. The arrival of the latter as Military Governors, or Town Commandants, at Tyre, Sidon, and elsewhere was greeted with minor disturbances by Arab nationalist elements. These were repressed.

Authority in the territory could, in international law as in common sense, belong at this stage solely to the Commander-in-Chief of the occupying Army. His delegation of such authority to a semi-civilian administration had been among the subjects of a consultation held between the French and British Foreign Ministers in London on 19 September. The results of this meeting were contained in the instructions issued by Allenby's Chief of Staff on 24 October, whereunder three Occupied Enemy Territory Administrations were set up in Syria: administrations whose boundaries reflected, as best they could, the commitments made already to the Arabs and those of the Sykes–Picot Agreement. These administrations were to be of neither British nor French nor Arab nationality, but would derive their authority strictly from the Commander-in-Chief as such; the nationality of the local Chief Administrator or garrison would in no way prejudice forthcoming Peace Conference decisions. Military Commanders, including the Amir Fayṣal himself, were to keep strictly to their

[1] It appears that 'Umar Bey's initiative was due to a suggestion from the Amir Sa'id al-Jaza'iri (at Damascus) on 30 September; a similar suggestion made by him to the Maronite Patriarch was not adopted.

[2] He visited Ba'abda, convened the old Council, hoisted the Arab flag, and appointed Ḥabib Pasha al-Sa'd as Governor of the Lebanon in the name of King Ḥusayn. This action greatly shocked Maronite opinion.

military role. O.E.T.A. South, under a British Chief Administrator, covered the sanjaqs of Acre, Nablus, and Jerusalem: that is, Palestine (the Brown Area of Sykes–Picot), with which henceforward the present history is not concerned.[1] O.E.T.A. North covered the coastal strip and ranges from a point midway between Tyre and Acre to Alexandretta, inclusive; a French Administrator (Colonel de Piépape) was appointed, and addressed himself immediately to his tasks, while M. Georges Picot[2] remained as High Commissioner. O.E.T.A. East contained the rest of Syria north and east of O.E.T.A. South, thus including the territory east of Jordan—and covering also, to the indignation of the French, the inter-mountain Biqa' plain which they claimed to belong to the Blue Area. In O.E.T.A. East, 'Ali Riḍha al-Rikabi figured as Chief Administrator, ostensibly responsible to the Commander-in-Chief and instructed, doubly to ensure this, to accept a British and a French liaison officer at his side. But the Arabs, to whom these arrangements represented a severe disappointment and surprise, were no students of international protocol; they could see only that this was an administration staffed by Arabs in an Arab country,[3] in the presence of an Arab prince to whom independence, no less, had been recently and specifically promised. The Amir Fayṣal and his Syrian and 'Iraqi officers and ministers considered themselves, and acted, as the rulers of a territory whose true boundaries, to them, must be those of full unpartitioned Syria. They felt but a minimum and momentary obligation towards a foreign military Commander outside it; and indeed with passing weeks it became less and less realistic to regard the Arab Administration as an O.E.T.A. of normal pattern. Lawrence left Damascus, and the Arab scene, immediately after the installation of Fayṣal's Government.

[1] The northern boundary of the Brown Area had been indicated, without exactness, after Franco-British argument and consultation with Russia. It dissatisfied Zionists when, late in 1917, they became aware of it. Whereas the French demanded the Ṣafad area, which their O.E.T.A. North (later West) did not include, the Jews asked for a wide area of southern Lebanon, the whole Liṭani river and southern Biqa', Hermon and the sources of the Jordan, and the Ḥawran and Transjordan. In terms of the Balfour Declaration there was no applicable criterion whereby to establish boundaries for 'Palestine', and the Jews not unnaturally claimed everything within reach. At the same time, the French claim to annex territory which included Palestine-Jewish settlements was clearly inappropriate.

[2] M. Coulondre acted during Picot's absence, and was the first to protest against the 'Sharifian' Government of Beirut.

[3] The Amir Fayṣal's proclaimed Decree of 6 October created a Council of State with powers of legislation and administration on all subjects; it contained from five to fifteen members, with the Chief Administrator (or, in Syrian eyes, Chief Minister) at its head. The Proclamation, which emphasizes the Arab character of the new Government, was specific upon the subject of 'complete independence' and the authority of King Ḥusayn.

Some sense of the impending problems had been felt by both sides in the course of the Franco-British consultations of 19 September, with the probability that O.E.T.A. arrangements would disappoint the too-eager Arab politicians; and indeed the Amir himself expostulated with the Commander-in-Chief at the division of Syria into three zones. This, and the appearance (immensely popular with their old friends and protégés) of the French in authority at Beirut, and pervasive signs that Arab independence was by no means yet an accomplished fact, led to immediate symptoms of uneasiness. The Franco-British proclamation of 11 November[1] was intended to reassure the doubters and authoritatively to assert Allied policy. It did so in the most unequivocal terms; it promised to the peoples so long oppressed by the Turks a 'complete and final liberation'; it promised 'the setting up of national governments and administrations that shall derive their authority from the free exercise of the initiative and choice of the indigenous populations' in Syria and Mesopotamia; it promised that the Allies' 'only concern is to offer such support and efficacious help as will ensure the smooth working' of the Governments 'which those populations will have elected of their own free will'.

The effect of these fair words was immediately sedative; it remained to be seen what type of action would follow by Allies whose own conceptions of the present situation were, as will be seen, already widely divergent.

[1] Text in Antonius, pp. 435–6.

III

THE FRENCH AND THE AMIR

I. FACTORS IN A SETTLEMENT

A NAÏVE observer might have supposed that an acceptable settlement of Syria would present little difficulty. The country, though blessed by no great assets, and now prostrate with after-war exhaustion, was essentially viable. It was well known, and favourably regarded, by the greatest and now victorious nations of the world. It inherited no serious debts, no clashing interests, no ill will. Its people were intelligent, progressive, and industrious, with highly attractive qualities; and though in the masses largely illiterate and backward in political conceptions, they possessed a class capable of leadership. Yet the events of the twenty-two months following the Armistice were to show how complicated, in fact, were Syria's problems, how protracted and embittered were to be the debates designed to establish its future; while the twenty years thereafter would demonstrate how little success, in political terms, was to attend the solution ultimately enforced.

Apart from the territory itself and its inhabitants, what, late in 1918, were the necessarily dominant elements in the case? First of these was the fact of British military occupation: an occupation to be carried out within the restrictions of international usage, in Turkish provinces whose sovereignty until renounced still belonged to the Sultan. The Commander-in-Chief of the occupying Power must ensure order and the public services, but must otherwise abstain from all but minimum alterations in the régime of its predecessor; and to the limitations thus implied was added the less usual element that (as the British Government made fully clear from the first) the occupying Power had no intention whatsoever of continuing to occupy. Meanwhile British prestige stood high, thanks to recent overwhelming victory and to the ubiquitous presence in the territory of a large army which dwarfed the small French and Arab contingents.

The second major element present can be mentioned briefly, since its cogency is already familiar to readers of these pages; it was the voice of France, insistent, at every level, in support of its traditional 'rights' in Syria. It was foredoomed to clash tragically with the third force to be mentioned, that of Arab or Syrian nationalism. This found its ready spokesmen in the survivors of the pre-war nationalist movement, which brutal Turkish suppression, wartime contact with the Ḥijaz and ʻIraq, the fact of victory, and the appearance of an Arab prince in their midst, had now immensely strengthened and inspired. It is true that the bulk of the rural and much of the urban populations were habitually uninterested and apathetic: true, that in considerable enclaves non-government rather than Arab government was the ideal: that, even among the politically conscious, parochial or community loyalties could be stronger than national: that lingering pro-Turkish feeling still had power over not a few of the old Sunni families, the ex-officials, the naturally conservative, and those who distrusted the young, self-selected protagonists of Arabism. Moreover, the warmest Arab nationalists could be divided by personal allegiances, by varying ideas of tempo or priority, and by the particular leadership they favoured. Thus the incoming Amir himself, with his great qualifications as their leader, could not and did not command universal acceptance; there were, to the end, circles in which his family (rebel against the Caliph), or his non-Syrian origin, or his bedouin contacts, or his too-great friendliness to Europeans, or his calm, unfanatical statesmanship, were elements adverse to his acceptability. But, with all this, Syrian nationalism had since 1914 made immense strides forward, and could now appeal for general support. Whether or not its objectives were limited to the Syrian nation, and whatever constitutional form (unitary or federal state, monarchy or republic) its various spokesmen might favour, and whatever the motives, ideals or ambitions of individuals among these, the nationalists were not far at present from carrying all before them; and the months and years following would show—what indeed all but the wilfully blind could see already—that the movement was by far the strongest political force in the territory and would stand, with whatever variations, for the uniting of all Syria and its complete independence. Meanwhile, the earnest immediate wish of the nationalist movement was to impress the outside world with its power and reality.

The fourth element to be reviewed, smaller in scale than Syrian nationalism, was not less keenly upheld. The separatism of the Catholics in the Lebanon rested upon three bases: one, its historical validity since 1861: next, its fear of Muslim domination, or more generally its non-participation, except linguistically, in the Muslim heritage, and its sense of belonging primarily to Europe: and, thirdly, its strong leaning to France. Lebanese spokesmen, ignoring or misrepresenting the considerable non-Catholic or non-Christian proportion in the area for which they spoke, varied in their demands from mere perpetuation of the old autonomous sanjaq to the establishment of a Greater Lebanon, and from close attachment to the rest of Syria to complete detachment from it; but all stressed the separateness of their community from the Muslim majority, all were well placed to be heard in Europe as in Beirut, and almost all called for French protection.

If the peacemakers were aware of these elements in the Syrian scene, others of strong potency outside the territory were not less effective, and serve to show that the statesmen of Versailles, San Remo, and Sèvres had no *carte blanche* for their treaty-drafting. The conception of self-determination for liberated peoples had, since its formulation by President Wilson early in 1918, already gained a remarkable dominance in European Cabinets as the official touchstone for the settlements now imminent; and Syrians among others could appeal to this accepted principle. The victorious nations had renounced 'territorial acquisitions'; colonization, even in its more enlightened modern forms, was unfashionable; control of dependent territory would be exercised instead by the now evolving Mandate system whereunder a Mandatory, chosen by the mandated themselves, would acquire no sovereignty, seek no selfish advantages, keep an Open Door, and help but never exploit the people confided to it by the League of Nations.[1] The case of Syria was, indeed, precisely covered by provisions written into the Covenant of the League, and thereby into the Versailles Treaty: provisions under which its existence as an independent nation could now 'be provisionally recognised subject to the rendering of administrative advice and assistance by a Mandatory' until such time as Syria and the other communities formerly belonging to the Turkish Empire 'are able to stand alone. The wishes of these communities must be a principal consideration in the selection of the Mandatory.' How far these provisions were consistent with Arab independence, or with the Sykes–Picot Agreement, and how far they would in the event be observed even by the Powers who drafted and ratified them, remains to be seen.

Among the peace-making nations, the directness of their interest in Syria varied. Russia had disappeared from the international scene, Germany and Austria-Hungary were defeated and powerless. Italy, though not uninterested, had nothing to urge about the disposal of Syria at this stage, since her own war

[1] The mandatory system, formulated in particular by General Smuts and President Wilson, was accepted by the principal Allied representatives at Versailles in the first weeks of the Peace Conference, as applicable to certain territories which included those now to be detached from Turkey. The principles involved were drafted (by a Commission appointed on 25 January 1919) as part (Art. 22) of the Covenant of the League of Nations. See Appendix C, p. 347 below.

prizes were to come from elsewhere in Asiatic Turkey. The United States had no ambition but to continue her educational and humanitarian work; the State Department desired neither territory nor political power, and rumours in French and Syrian circles that America would accept—or even was seeking—a Middle Eastern Mandate were baseless. At the same time, American observers in the country (and more especially the circle round Dr. Howard Bliss in Beirut) were acute because disinterested students of Syrian opinion, and American views, generally sympathetic to Wilsonian ideas, could not but be a factor at the conference tables of Europe.

Great Britain, in spite of inveterate French suspicions—in spite, too, of the *obiter dicta* of unauthorized Englishmen,[1] and the doubtful offers made by equally unauthorized Syrians—had no desire, in all of Syria other than Palestine, but to leave it to its own devices. She was committed to support a Jewish National Home in Palestine; she was concerned to maintain a position in that southern Syrian province as a neighbour of Egypt and as a gateway to the West; but she was interested in the rest of Syria solely as a post-war responsibility for immediate order-keeping until peace should be concluded with Turkey, a process whose long delay[2] was a grave embarrassment to all concerned with the Levant. But for the rest, Lloyd George could assure Clemenceau emphatically, as Grey had assured Poincaré in 1912, that Great Britain had from November 1918 onwards no ambitions whatsoever in Beirut, Damascus or Aleppo, but had, on the contrary, at least from mid-1919 onwards, every objection to spending more money or undertaking new commitments. She remained, however—and herein lay a major element in her embarrassed post-war diplomacy—under an obligation to respect the pledge given to the Sharif Ḥusayn in 1916, for Arab independence in stated areas; and these included, beyond question, the whole of inland Syria.

That this pledge must clash seriously with traditional French ambitions was certain from the attitude of spokesmen in Paris throughout the war, and notably after the Armistice. Wilsonian self-determination was a doctrine accepted reluctantly by French statesmen and publicists, and indeed repudiated by some as unneeded, unpredictable, dangerous, and ill accorded with the

[1] For instance, T. E. Lawrence, a consistent disparager of the French and at times capable of naïvely imperialistic views.

[2] A peace treaty between the Allies and Turkey was drawn up at San Remo (April 1920), signed by the then-recognized Turkish Government at Sèvres on 10 August, and rejected by the Ankara Government a few weeks later. A final Peace Treaty was not concluded until 24 July 1923 (p. 109). The conclusion of peace with Turkey occupied nine months longer than the entire course of the war.

French *mission civilisatrice* in a territory whose backwardness and needs were more obvious to her than its own aspirations. With the McMahon promise of Arab independence, they professed little concern; it was never a French promise, and its partial echo as a limiting factor[1] in the Sykes–Picot Agreement (itself claimed as having involved grievous French sacrifices) was to be minimized. Arab independence, hailed as a British manœuvre at French expense, responded to no necessity, and would surely find dangerous echoes in North Africa; Arab nationalism was the agitation of a few xenophobic hot-heads. Later pages of this book will show that the French underestimate of Arab nationalism as a political force was serious, her overestimate of her own acceptability in three-quarters of that country not less so; and to these errors, caused by a blindness due less to factual ignorance than to obstinate 'wishful thinking', must be ascribed a great part of the disappointment which France was to encounter in the years to follow.

Meanwhile her claim, stated and restated from November 1918 onwards, was in effect for a free hand in the whole of Syria: a Syria to include not only Palestine but also northern[2] 'Iraq, Cilicia, and a large area of Asia Minor: and a free hand, with minimum restrictions from any cause or quarter, to enjoy all her traditional 'rights'. The latter[3] were, as ever, based on her ancient Capitulations, her protectorate of Catholics, her educational and philanthropic work, her economic effort in the territory, and on the affection in which, as she believed, France was held by the Syrian people. The objectives other than cultural which she sought in Syria—prestige, strategic advantage, commercial opportunity—could, she was certain, be obtained best, or only, by completing the moral right already enjoyed by a political right which 'should logically accompany it',[4] that of actual administrative control. The desire to continue cultural work in good conditions was, indeed, unexceptionable, nor need other advantages be precluded if freely given by the authorities of the country itself; it would be reasonable to assert political 'rights' if such were accepted as valid by a majority of the people. But they were not so accepted,

[1] Because any French administration in coastal Syria was to be established 'after agreement with the Arab State or Confederation of States', while in hinterland Syria French rights were limited to a priority in the supply of loans, advisers, &c., to an independent Arab State.

[2] The Sykes–Picot Agreement had placed part of Mosul wilayet in Zone A.

[3] For a very different analysis of the French 'mystique' in the Levant, Rabbath (*L'Évolution politique*, p. 399) quotes from Admiral Castex (*Théories stratégiques*, p. 280). 'Mystique faite de plusieurs facteurs: de souvenirs historiques inadaptables au présent: de sentimentalisme sans rapport avec le réel: de clichés legués par les générations qui nous ont précédés: enfin, d'un point de snobisme.'

[4] Gontaut-Biron, p. 2.

and it was the moral and logical weakness of the French position that it based a claim to political dominance on voluntarily-given past services of a wholly different and non-political type—services whose 'completely disinterested character' never ceased to be alleged—while minimizing, or effectively ignoring, the proclaimed principle of self-determination. How persistently this French claim was to be pressed will appear in the present chapter; but behind it lay also, it must be realized, a sincere belief that France had in this field a great and humane contribution to make.

These weaknesses in the French position did not diminish the fervour with which it was held by the Government and four-fifths of the people of France, including, of course, her representatives in Syria itself. The long strain of the war: the bitterness of seeing others (the British) advance in military triumph into a long-fostered French preserve: the sense of undeserved subordination and material inferiority displayed before the appraising eyes of the Syrians: an irritated willingness to believe the worst about the intentions of Allies who were also age-long rivals, and who were now sharply offending by their divergence from the French viewpoint in Middle Eastern policy: erroneous estimates of the political forces now in play in the Levant: all these together were to lead not only to an attitude towards Arabism which time was to prove disastrous, but also to that curious outbreak of bitter Anglophobia in the Western Zone of Enemy Occupied Territory, which was a sad feature of the next twenty months. Among anti-British accusations made in Beirut and Paris alike (made not indeed by all, but by most, Frenchmen) were those that Britain 'less occupied than France during the war' had scored triumphs of intrigue instead: had maliciously created an anti-French Arab nationalism: was using 'a bedouin and his horde of bandits' as their instruments in Syria: was pro-Protestant and anti-Catholic: failed to appreciate the sacred rights (and the total disinterestedness) of France: and lost no opportunity to humiliate the French, with the evident intention of replacing them. To such charges profound differences of national character, age-long rivalries, and imperfect understanding made their emotional contribution.

Such, in the contrasting viewpoints of Arabs and Europeans, and in the difficult circumstances of the time and place, were elements which were in play among, and can largely explain, the events next to be recorded.

2. THE COASTAL ZONE, 1919

The full military occupation of the coastal, or French, Zone was not achieved in a day; it was delayed not only by Turkish reluctance to withdraw their troops, who in the northern cities sought to stay behind in the guise of gendarmes, but also by the wretched state of communications, and by the tenacity of 'liberating' Arab forces who at Antioch and Ḥarim had taken possession before French detachments could arrive, and were dislodged only by General Allenby's categorical orders. Possession was completed, in the last days of 1918, by the occupation of Alexandretta and Antioch; but although strong British and slowly increasing French military forces could be seen everywhere, and a beginning of administration was established, the Nuṣayri mountain zone was still unpenetrated, the southern Lebanon was insecure, the Arab-administered areas to the east were uneasy neighbours, and echoes from disturbed Cilicia affected the northernmost districts of the Zone. In Cilicia itself, which became Zone N[1] in December 1918, the Armenian troops first sent by the French were a sad failure, by reason of their own indiscipline and the angry resentment they aroused; it became necessary to relieve them by British troops. The Turkish II Army had completed its withdrawal west of Bozanti by 26 December; but Colonel Brémond, appointed Chief Administrator with a skeleton staff, could do little to administer the territory, thanks to the lawless recalcitrance of Turkish villagers, hastily-formed 'irregulars', and even, to an increasing extent as 1919 went on, Turkish regular troops. It was necessary to use Turkish administrative personnel, to tolerate a bad or largely non-existent administration, and to concentrate on securing communications; and even this called for military reinforcement by French troops who were badly wanted elsewhere. Meanwhile, east of Cilicia, the Commander-in-Chief was forced, from the first days of 1919, to occupy the main towns[2] of a wide area of central-southern Anatolia, in order to ensure a minimum of control and to forestall threatened massacres. This area, however, was never included in an O.E.T.A.; Turkish administration continued.

In the coastal Zone[3] of Syria, the scene from mid-October 1918 onwards of an exacting and harassed French effort, their most urgent task was the relief of hunger and misery among the people whom war and maladministration had reduced to dire

[1] It consisted of the wilayet of Adana, minus the qadha of Salefka (Ichili). Anglo-French relations in Cilicia were considered cordial.

[2] 'Ayntab and Killis were reached by British troops, and garrisoned, on 24 December, Birijik and Mar'ash in February, and Urfa in March 1919.

[3] Zone W consisted of the old wilayet of Beirut, minus the sanjaqs of Nablus and Acre: the Lebanon sanjaq: the qadhas of Alexandretta, Antioch, Ḥarim, and Baylan (the four grouped as the sanjaq of Alexandretta), and Jisr al-Shaghur (placed under Ladhqiya). The qadhas of Rashaya and Ba'lbek, in the Biqa', were treated as part of Zone E, though claimed by the French as belonging to the Blue Area.

extremities; in the last year of the war the missionaries, belonging to states at war with Turkey, had not been permitted to continue their work in the towns and villages afflicted, in many cases almost depopulated, by famine and disease.

The effects [says George Antonius] were only too visible when the British forces entered Bairut, and a tribute is owed them for the speed and the efficacy with which they distributed food and clothing from their own stores of supplies. The crews of the French destroyers who had entered Bairut harbour . . . were equally helpful. Still more creditable were the efforts made in the months that followed to provide necessities on a larger scale to the destitute population of the inland districts, when French, British and American relief agencies sprang up, that vied with each other in a humane and honourable competition.[1]

The Commander-in-Chief formed a Directorate at his Head-quarters to deal with relief and to co-ordinate all public and private efforts. The French authorities of O.E.T.A. West, using both their own personnel and the Jesuit and other Fathers who had hastened to reoccupy their former places, instituted and perfected schemes of emergency food supply on a basis of paid, half-paid and unpaid allotments. In the Mountain they could profit from the existing machinery under the restored Council of the sanjaq,[2] and elsewhere also could act through the heads of communities. Some supplies of food were found in the granaries of local hoarders, far more were brought in from Port Said, Mersin, and the Syrian hinterland. Depots were established for distribution, soup kitchens were opened in the worst areas. With the distribution of rations went the establishment of orphanages,[3] under missionary supervision, for the thousands of abandoned children. To care for these, houses were requisitioned, clothes and furniture obtained or improvised. Vagrant or destitute women were collected and cared for. Workshops were organized for the production of required equipment, and to find work for enfeebled hands. Dispensaries and public assistance institutions were urgently established. Works of cleansing and incineration, drainage and rehabilitation were organized. With these steps, which it was not possible to discontinue until after the winter of 1920–1, went the collection from all sources (including the inland cities and the nomadic tribes) of Armenian refugees who, in tens

[1] Antonius, p. 242.

[2] The Government of the Lebanon, and its Council, under Ḥabib Pasha al-Sa'd, hastened to change from an Arab to a French allegiance, and greeted MM. Coulondre and Piépape with enthusiasm.

[3] Sixteen were founded or refounded by the French during 1918–19, and 13,000 children dealt with; in mid-1922 4,000 were still so housed. The French Sisters at Beirut, Sidon, Ḥammama, Batrun, Ghazir, Damur, and Baḥasif played a major part.

of thousands, had during and since 1915 escaped from massacre in Asia Minor. These were now traced or presented themselves, their quarrels with Muslim neighbours were composed, repatriation camps were formed for their reception, workshops established, orphanages set up, and some hundreds of able-bodied men recruited into the Armenian battalions which already formed part of the Détachement Français de Palestine-Syrie. The intention, for the main body of refugees, was not absorption but repatriation: or rather, concentration in Cilicia, where an Armenian 'home' for this ancient nation could perhaps (for the second time in history) be formed. To this end, convoys by sea taking 8,000 repatriates, in French and British ships, were dispatched to Mersin; far more, however, remained in Syria, with a future of gradual acclimatization.

The establishment of health services was a first objective of the O.E.T. Administration and of the reviving missions alike. Hospitals were opened in their own or requisitioned buildings, as fast as equipment could be collected; training classes for nurses were organized, doctors dispatched to every qaḍha. Quarantine and disinfection measures were taken which successfully averted the danger of epidemic disease, and laid the basis for future medical services. The opening or reopening of government schools, attended mainly by poor Muslim children, devolved upon the O.E.T. Administration and the townships, and some dozens had been established in the Zone by the end of 1919; that of the (far more numerous) private schools was the concern of the Christian communities to whom they belonged, and of the foreign missions. On M. Georges Picot's initiative, priorities for supply and equipment were arranged at a general conference of all concerned. The missionaries, returned from France, Asia Minor, or America, quickly reoccupied their buildings (unless requisitioned for other purposes, as could happen), and pupils thronged to fill classrooms for which teachers, equipment, and books, in replacement of all that war had destroyed, were slow to arrive. By March 1919 fully 150 private schools under varying sponsorship were open and busy, those under French influence substantially predominant; a year later they numbered more than 1,000, and by mid-1920, 1,400. The French Jesuit University of St. Joseph and the (American) Syrian Protestant College struggled gladly back into life. An Antiquities Department came into existence during 1919.

While by these means town and countryside could gradually return to some semblance of their normal conditions, the French Administration was setting its house in order. Its military forces, reduced by the dispatch of units to Cilicia, were reinforced by arrivals from France: arrivals, however, whose fewness and deficiencies were deplored by the watchful French civilians in Beirut, already embittered by the too-visible British preponderance. The force was in January 1919 renamed the Troupes Françaises du Levant. The indiscipline of the Armenian units, marked by mutiny, desertion, and brigandage, was deplored by the French Command, and damaging to its prestige. The O.E.T. civilian Administration likewise struggled initially against grave disabilities. It was ill supplied with metropolitan personnel, whether from France or from Army ranks locally available; and even these, in the opinion of responsible Frenchmen, were too often of indifferent quality. Less than half the number of French executives required could be produced in these early months; administrators of experience were rare, specialists unobtainable, transport deficient, every sort of material lacking. Military-civil friction, of the familiar type, manifested itself; the civil departments complained of the tactlessness of the military commanders, both French and British, and not less of the prevalence of anti-French feeling in the Zone, which they readily attributed to British and Arab propaganda. They resented equally the British refusal to permit the freedom of legislation or reform which they felt to be necessary. Regulations, of which under a Military Government the permissible scope was strictly limited, were confined to matters of immediate concern; these included, for example, the moratorium proclaimed on 26 November 1918, and limitations on the permitted increases in house rents. Meanwhile, M. Georges Picot was sending many and bitter telegrams to the Quai d'Orsay alleging anti-French activities by British Intelligence officers—whose attitude was, indeed, evidently more pro-Arab than pro-French.

Supported by the Commander-in-Chief[1] and his services to the best of their ability, the Chief Administrator of Zone W was assisted by a headquarter staff led by four expert advisers, and gradually evolved an administrative machine. French *administrateurs* were appointed to Beirut city and to the sanjaq of Lebanon, Military Governors to the outlying sanjaqs. Each qadha was administered by a Lebanese Qa'immaqam if available (with a Frenchman in attendance), or directly by a French officer. The Administrative Councils of the units were restored, and were allowed most of their old functions; for the rest, no régime but one of direct French control was, at this stage, conceivable, though the forms and nomenclature of Turkish administration were retained. The Turkish law of 1917, depriving the Christian heads of

[1] It was the policy of General Allenby to interfere to the least possible extent in the administrative zones, whether S, W, or E.

communities of their powers, was ignored, and their ancient *millet* privileges were restored.

In the administration of justice, the work of the Shara' Courts and of the Christian hierarchy could continue or restart. All cases other than of personal status were heard, in the early weeks, by military courts until early in 1919, after patient overhaul of the Turkish judicial personnel, regular civilian Courts could be cautiously restarted. Amnesty for old offences was freely given. A Lebanese Bar was created, a system of judicial records was formed, a Commercial Court was established in Beirut, three Courts of Appeal was set up at Beirut, Ba'abda, and Alexandretta, and a Court of Cassation inaugurated. The Awqaf properties and records were discovered to be in the last stages of decay. In the administration of finance, tax-collection was attempted sparingly at first, but orthodox budgeting on regional lines[1] was introduced; the inevitable deficit was, as in the other Zones, made good from British funds.[2] Turkish currency having lost all value, the void was filled by the temporary use of Egyptian money,[3] until the creation of a Syro-Lebanese currency early in 1920. The French banks established before 1914 reopened, joined by the Banco di Roma and the Anglo-Egyptian Bank; but economic life was slow to revive. Normal foreign trade was impossible, civilian shipping was scanty, and the Syrian ports were still administered, or almost monopolized, by the Army. Industry was inanimate, and internal trade exiguous. Nevertheless, the relief works organized by the Administration, and the money spent by the occupation forces, infused some life. Loans were given to cultivators, the silk industry was brought back into being, a long-term plan for its restoration was drawn up, and confident hopes for the future could be felt by an Economic Mission sent out by the Chambers of Commerce of Lyons and Marseilles.[4] Road work was carried out under French control, especially on coastal routes. In Beirut, clearance and rehabilitation proceeded, drains were constructed, and the new Turkish streets, begun but abandoned, were completed. The railways, which lay mostly in the Arab-held Eastern Zone, remained for the time inaccessible to the impatient French engineers; these, however, started on the restoration of the Tripoli–Ḥumṣ line. Postal services were

[1] Separately for Lebanon, the wilayet of Beirut, and the sanjaq of Alexandretta.

[2] The Troupes Françaises du Levant were, of course, maintained from French funds.

[3] This annoyed the French, who wished to introduce their own currency; apart from loss of prestige, it was inconvenient and costly for them to use their francs (which depreciated rapidly after 1918) to buy Egyptian pounds.

[4] It followed the important Congrès français de la Syrie, held at Marseilles in January 1919.

restarted before the end of 1918. Efforts were made throughout 1919–20 to rehabilitate the port of Beirut, encumbered by Turkish wartime sinkings and neglect; the same was true of the small port of Tripoli. The construction of a harbour at Alexandretta was entrusted to a French company in supersession of the Germans.

Order was generally well maintained: the territory was, until the end of 1919, heavily garrisoned, the inhabitants suffered largely from lowered vitality, and most were content to watch events. A selection was made from the remnants of the Turkish *polis* and Gendarmerie, and a training school inaugurated. Severe Armenian–Muslim fighting in Beirut in November 1918 did not spread, cases of banditry were easily suppressed, and frontier episodes with 'Sharifian' outposts were primarily of political import even when the local clash was severe. Trouble in the wild 'Alawi hills was more prolonged; the highlands were, indeed, entirely out of control and attacks on French posts and detachments on the coast, organized notably by Shaykh Ṣaliḥ al-'Ali (an 'Alawi headman understood to be in close touch with Damascus), were frequent[1] and often unpunished.

Throughout this initial phase of French administration the predominance of British garrisons, and the inevitable subordination of O.E.T.A. West to a British Commander-in-Chief were, not surprisingly, galling to French pride and pretensions. Anglo-French personal relations were in many cases cordial, in a few the reverse; some French officers accepted philosophically the frustrations of a transitional phase, others did not. To the latter, cases of British 'interference' were not hard to find. Limitations which seemed necessary to the Commander-in-Chief were applied to French initiatives, and were resented; transport, including the French-owned railway system, was still almost monopolized by military needs; the French-constructed port of Beirut could not at first be placed at their free disposal; the opening of a British bank, and the temporary use of Egyptian money, were viewed with exasperation. British and American participation in relief work and repatriation was accepted with reluctance, and was sometimes ungenerously decried.[2]

More serious was the genuine divergence of opinion regarding the Arab Question, reflecting as it did a similar cleavage at the

[1] The post of Babanna, twenty miles east of Ladhqiya, was relieved by French troops, after fierce assaults and a short siege, in April 1919; and at Muraykib near Ṭarṭus, in July of that year, a French column barely repelled a heavy attack by armed villagers. In August, consultations between an Anglo-French mission and a party of 'Alawi notables produced a short period of peace; but in December Dandashli tribesmen attacked Tall Kallakh, repulsed a first French relieving column and were driven off by a second, which was followed up by a punitive expedition.

[2] Gontaut-Biron, pp. 87, 256.

council-tables of Europe. The Arab occupation of hinterland Syria, which to the British seemed a minimum conformity with the McMahon undertaking, was to the French unnecessary, provocative and, they hoped, temporary. They saw themselves deprived of the widest areas of their own 'France of the East'; their garrisons were excluded even from the Biqa'! Their liaison officers in Syria were treated, they complained, as of little authority. Their best Syrian friends—the Amir Sa'id al-Jaza'iri himself—could, it seemed, be arrested by the British. They felt bound to show courtesy to the Amir Fayṣal on his passages through Beirut,[1] and must witness with disapproval the enthusiasm of the Muslims of their Zone for his cause. They could not prevent Arab nationalist fervour from showing itself even in Mount Lebanon and its Council, while Muslim delegates from the Zone braved prohibitions, risked arrest, and made their eager way to Damascus. During the visit of M. Picot to that city early in 1919, and indeed at all times and levels, the fundamental difference between French and Arab conceptions of the Syrian future was evident; yet, like the British themselves, the French were paying meanwhile, until the spring of 1920, a subsidy to a 'Sharifian' Administration which did not cease by its spokesmen and propaganda, its pinpricks and frontier episodes, to provoke French annoyance and dismay. In all this, M. Picot and his collaborators were convinced, the British, frank supporters of Arab aspirations, were hand-in-glove with Fayṣal's agents and determined to embarrass (ultimately, no doubt, to supersede) the French occupation. These suspicions, which aroused a bitter Anglophobia, were unfounded save in so far as British sympathy with the Arab cause was sincere and British assessment of the French 'rights' in Syria was considerably lower than their own. Of active anti-French intrigue there could be, in fact, no probability and no motive; nor was British support of Fayṣal either immoderate or blind.

The decision taken in Europe in September 1919 (p. 94), providing for the relief of British by French troops in the West Zone and by Arab troops in the Eastern, with the replacement of a British by a French Commander-in-Chief at Beirut, seemed likely to reduce many present irritations. Though treated as greatly overdue, and as still too partial a cure, it was well viewed by the French administrators. The French Troupes du Levant, on whose services Cilicia was making heavy calls, were substantially reinforced, while British units concentrated for withdrawal. By the end of 1919 the latter had divested themselves of both military

[1] He visited Beirut, after a tour in northern Syria, on 16 November 1918, and was received with great enthusiasm by Muslim and some Christian elements, with coldness by the French and Maronites. Five days later he left for Europe.

and civil authority throughout Syria, and left the stage free for the French—and the Arabs. General Gouraud, a picturesque, gallant, and distinguished military figure and devout Catholic, quite unversed in problems of civil government or politics or the Islamic world, landed in Beirut on 21 November 1919, and assumed the posts of High Commissioner and Commander-in-Chief. His great prestige, his strongly Christian bias,[1] and his inaugural assertion that all French rights would be upheld, gave immediate confidence to the Catholic elements, and made clear to all Muslim or Arab nationalist sympathizers that the hour for decision could not now be far distant. The General was accompanied, in the capacity of Secretary-General, by a scholar, publicist, and political writer of some standing, M. Robert de Caix, a warm upholder of every French claim, and unfriendly alike to alleged British transgressions and to Arab claims;[2] his influence on French policy, for the next four years, was of the strongest.

Political activity in the French Zone could in this period take but one of two forms: one, the dispatch of missions to Paris to press the views of the senders on members of the Peace Conference or the Supreme Council: the other, the expression of opinion, by meetings, deputations, and propaganda, in the territory itself. The many Syrian and Lebanese Committees in countries of both the western and eastern hemispheres continued to telegraph to Paris or London views which represented the dreams and memories of these long-emigrated exiles as the burning realities of Syrian aspiration. Within the Zone itself, the population of the extreme north, Alexandretta and Antioch, in spite of the pressure of Christian minorities and trans-frontier Turks, hoped by considerable majority for early inclusion in the Arab State. The sanjaq of Ladhqiya (or that part of it which was effectively controlled) was remote equally from Sharifian or pan-Syrian or Lebanese aspirations, though its substantial Sunni-Muslim minority could not but side with Damascus. The sanjaq of Tripoli, predominantly Muslim, was of the same complexion. Beirut city was divided between a majority Christian and a minority Muslim sentiment, with the former group far from homogeneous; the Beirut sanjaq, largely Muslim and Druze, though with important Christian elements, could speak with no single voice, and the same was true of the Biqa‘ with its Christian, Mutawalli, and mixed population.

[1] M. Gabriel Puaux (High Commissioner, 1939–40) speaks (*Deux années au Levant*, p. 29), of 'le Général Gouraud, dont le regard d'aigue-marine ne connaissait point la fraude ni même la simple prudence'. Cf. Fabre-Luce, *Deuil au Levant*, p. 69: 'son regard bleu et tendre: on y lit sa pureté, et l'on oublie . . . les limites de son intelligence. C'est un homme simple'.

[2] He held his office until the end of 1923, and thereafter remained a principal French spokesman, notably at Geneva, on Syrian affairs.

Mount Lebanon itself, the Maronite stronghold, and the Christian communities closely adjacent to it, were divided on different lines: to many, perhaps most, of the dwellers in the old autonomous sanjaq, the perpetuation of its privileges was all, while to others a Greater Lebanon, more spacious and viable, was an idea of long standing and with some elements of historical justification based on the past (but always ephemeral) conquests of the Lebanese amirs. In either case a measure of French control, varying from direct administration to mere sponsorship, was assumed. To still other Christians a federal Syria, in which Lebanon would be a privileged or autonomous element, was the desideratum—probably with, but just possibly without, a 'special position' for France as guide and supporter. To Sunni-Muslim opinion overwhelmingly, and to Mutawalli and Druze by majority, a single, free, independent Syrian State was the only tolerable solution, and from this attitude orthodox Muslim opinion was not to vary for the next full generation. But whatever could be urged in support of these and other views, as expressed on the spot to whatsoever civil or military officer or visitor would listen, and exposed in Paris and Versailles by successive delegations, there was no doubt for what policy Gouraud, and behind him France, stood firm: it was one of French control or protectorate, under whatever guise and title, over the whole of Syria. This, with any *ménagements* of Arab claims or British obstructions that might be necessary, it remained for the High Commissioner to bring about.

It is necessary next to turn to the Arab Government of inner Syria to which, for all its triumphant establishment and its promised permanence, the stars in their courses were to prove ineluctably adverse: and to the debates and compromises of peace-making in Europe.

3. DEBATE AND INQUIRY: VERSAILLES–DAMASCUS

Apart from the immense political difficulties, at first ill realized but finally insoluble, which confronted him on his assumption of authority in Syria, the Amir Fayṣal with his Chief Administrator, 'Ali Riḍha al-Rikabi, his group of loyal officers and his thronging Syrian welcomers, was faced by formidable administrative problems. The country, less desolated by famine than the Lebanon, was profoundly disorganized and impoverished, its whole machinery of government fragmented, its security uncertain, its trade stagnant, its currency worthless. And, though the British Army could help in some measure with the provision of military stores and transport, and could prevent large-scale disturbance, the task of governing, from such beginnings, an extensive, difficult, and factious country devolved, with no such foreign advisers or specialists as later Arab governments would enjoy, on the largely unskilful hands immediately available to the Amir.

The confusions, delays, and impotence, even the insubordinate acts, which marked the first weeks of Arab government could not be taken as typical of the intentions or powers of the new régime. Fayṣal's initial proclamation, issued with Allenby's consent on 6 October (p. 67, n. 3), while ignoring the subordination of an Enemy Territory Administration to its (in this case British) Commander-in-Chief, and treating it rather as a national Government set up by the Amir on behalf of King Ḥusayn, at least stressed that Arab worthiness of its new independence must be shown by its acts. The Amir and his staff realized, moreover, that whatever constitutional link with the Kingdom of the Ḥijaz might survive (and there were here differing conceptions), a clearly Ḥijazi complexion in his Government of Syria was unthinkable;[1] to be acceptable, and indeed to be workable, it must be staffed by Syrians with such 'Iraqi[2] help as was available in his entourage, and with a few imported Syrian-Egyptians. Moreover, Fayṣal's own position was that of an Arab prince of international status rather than that of a visiting Ḥijazi; and his personal followers in Syria, already many, rapidly multiplied under the influence of his success, personality, and obvious irreplaceability. From the first, therefore, the Administration was Syrian; it continued to be called 'Sharifian' only through habit, ignorance, or the pejorative malice of its critics. (Persistent denigration of the prince himself—young, handsome, intelligent, socially charming, admirably intentioned—was a feature of the propaganda of the coastal Christians, the Lebanese émigrés—and the French.)[3] The aim of the Administration was from the first day, without heed to the niceties of protocol or the debates of European statesmen, to consolidate an Arab State of Syria.

Governors, each in his grade, were installed in every administrative unit. In outlying areas a suitable local candidate (such as Salim al-Aṭrash in the Jabal al-Duruz) was installed as Governor. Turkish law and practice were, inevitably, retained throughout,

[1] Compare Lawrence, *Seven Pillars*, p. 649: 'Rebels, especially successful rebels, were of necessity bad subjects and worse governors. Feisal's sorry duty would be to rid himself of his war-friends.'

[2] The number of 'Iraqi officers in the Turkish Army in general, and in the Ḥijazi forces of 1916–18 in particular, was high. They included men of excellent quality; Ja'far al-'Askari, Nuri al-Sa'id, Yasin al-Hashimi, Jamil al-Madfa'i were all future Prime Ministers of 'Iraq, and at least 150 more were loyal and capable officers, such as Ra'uf al-Kubaysi, Mawlud al-Mukhliṣ, Rashid al-Khawja, and many more future ministers and mutaṣarrifs.

[3] The judgement of the comparatively few French who met the Amir was quite otherwise: e.g. Mme. Georges-Gaulis, *La Question arabe*, pp. 123–4: 'un caractère, une personnalité. Il est intelligent et fin, assimilateur à l'extrême, sans vanité, travailleur acharné. . . . Il ne ment jamais . . .'; p. 129: 'L'on ne peut méconnaître ses facultés persuasives, son sens de la direction, son tact et sa finesse.' These qualities became very familiar to the British in 'Iraq, 1921–33.

though military and civil powers were commonly amalgamated. Courts of law were opened, often under their old incumbents. Municipalities were everywhere restarted, with their Presidents and elected councillors. The local qaḍha or sanjaq Administrative Councils were reassembled. Revenue, under Turkish law, was collected. At the capital, the Chief Administrator, acting in effect as Chief Minister, presiding over a Council of Directors,[1] each of whom was charged with a major department; and the Council issued, after the Amir's ratification, decrees with the force of law, and sanctioned the State budget. The Amir's Civil List was on a scale eloquent of the gulf between this administration and O.E.T.A. orthodoxy. In all the circumstances, indeed, it could not but be Allenby's policy to leave the Eastern Zone substantially to itself, until guidance should appear from London or Versailles. Meanwhile, the Administration, whose shortcomings in personnel and efficiency were serious and pervasive, and which could not hope at this stage to surpass (if indeed to equal) the long-despised Turkish standards, enjoyed a financial subvention equally from French and British funds. The Amir's position as virtual monarch, while viewed askance by most of the scattered Catholic communities, and accepted coldly by some circles in northern Syria and in the Jabal al-Duruz,[2] was supported nevertheless by a greater mass of favourable opinion than any ruler of Syria had enjoyed since the Middle Ages. To these Fayṣal was the incarnation of Arab freedom and pride, and among them he commanded a warm devotion at once nationalistic, social and, by reason of his family, religious. The Arab Club, founded at Damascus soon after the occupation, was the political vehicle of these feelings, and was soon to dominate public life; its tone was hotly nationalist, and its propaganda was mainly directed against France which was felt to be—and which in large measure her own utterances declared her to be—the most dangerously acquisitive of the Powers. The foundation in Damascus early in 1919 of an Arab Academy showed the awareness of Fayṣal's Government of the great cultural inheritance behind the nationalist movement.

While the wheels of government began to turn, trade and normal life could also revive. The bedouin elements in Fayṣal's forces quickly melted—not before some regrettable lapses of behaviour in the too-tempting settled districts—and normal buying-parties from the tribes could throng the bazaars. British and Indian garrisons, scattered from north of Aleppo to Ma'an,

[1] Those of Interior, Finance, Justice, War, Health, Sûreté, Education, Intelligence, Public Works, Agriculture, and the Tribes.

[2] Certain of the Druze leaders made overtures to the French, as a measure of insurance, and M. Picot in 1919 obtained a *madhbaṭa* (round-robin) from a number, professing devotion.

waited impatiently for repatriation, which in fact they achieved in October-November 1919; but meanwhile they spent freely. Foreign goods could enter the country for the first time for five years, and were distributed to every village. The D.H.P. railway was somehow operated, and the Ḥijaz line was entrusted to a Muslim Director-General. Urban security was generally preserved, save for isolated brawls involving the disliked Armenians, as at Aleppo in February 1919. The sedentary tribes were quiet, routes little disturbed. A few governmental or municipal schools reopened, while those of the Christian communities and the foreign missions hastened to re-establish themselves.

Much of this progress was made in the Amir's absence, since late in November 1918 he left[1] Beirut, in a British ship, for Europe and the Peace Conference. In France his reception—that merely of a distinguished visitor, not of a national spokesman—was courteous but cool; he and his father were blamed for not seeking the prior approval of the French Government, and he was accounted Francophobe and a stumbling-block to French ambitions. He received a decoration from the hand of General Gouraud, was shown the battlefields and correctly fêted before crossing to London. Lawrence, who joined him in France (in Arab dress), was asked to leave and did so; his crude Francophobia was unfortunate both for his Arab friends and for his own country. In England, which the Amir reached on 10 December, his welcome from personal friends as well as from the British Government was warm and intimate. But his ignorance of the language and unfamiliarity with the ways of western diplomacy did not prevent his early awareness that there were limits—those of ultimate French opposition—to the support he could expect; the essential dilemma of British policy was already apparent.

Meanwhile, some Franco-British decisions had been reached. In conversations during December between Clemenceau and Lloyd George the former had insisted on the validity of the Sykes–Picot Agreement, and on full realization of French rights in Syria and Cilicia; but he was willing, in return for British help elsewhere at the forthcoming Peace Conference, to renounce the Mosul area[2] and any share in an internationalized Palestine:

[1] With him were Nuri al-Sa'id, Fa'iz al-Ghuṣayn, Rustum Ḥaydar, Taḥsin Qadri, and Dr. Aḥmad Qadri.

[2] At this period (*a*) no commercially usable oil had yet been discovered in the Mosul area; (*b*) the great Kirkuk oilfield, discovered in 1927, lies for the most part *outside* the Zone A in which Sykes–Picot gave France the privilege of 'assisting' an Arab State if so requested; (*c*) the retention of Mosul in Zone A could not in any case have affected the shareholding in the Turkish Petroleum Company in which French interests had hitherto no part. In fact, it was agreed by the Bérenger–Long conversations (1919) that France should inherit the German share (25 per cent.) in the Turkish Petroleum Company; and this was ratified at San Remo in April 1920 (cf. Longrigg, *Oil in the Middle East*, p. 44).

a renunciation which, later confirmed by letter, saved France from an infinity of future troubles,[1] and strengthened by implication her claim to the rest of Zone A. This claim, stated to be based on 'history, agreements, contracts and the aspirations of the people', was again proclaimed by M. Pichon, Minister of Foreign Affairs, on 29 December 1918.

Fayṣal, who had already exposed his viewpoint in *Le Temps*, re-crossed to Paris in the second week of January 1919, and submitted a memorandum to the Peace Conference, whose sessions had begun early in the new year. In it he asked, as representing King Ḥusayn (to whom the McMahon promise had been made), that the Arabic-speaking populations south of a line Alexandretta–Diyarbakr should be recognized, under League of Nations guarantee, as independent sovereign peoples, within boundaries to be fixed later on a basis of self-determination. This written argument, based strictly on President Wilson's principles,[2] was followed on 6 February by his personal appearance, in the face of initial French opposition, as one of two delegates for the Kingdom of the Ḥijaz[3] to the Peace Conference. He then, again accompanied by Lawrence, amplified his claim for Arab self-determination, for adherence to the McMahon promise, and for execution of the clear and categorical Anglo-French Declaration of 11 November 1918. He was willing to except Aden, an acknowledged British possession; Palestine, it was admitted, could call for a special régime; 'Iraq or part of it would 'accept help' from Great Britain, and Mount Lebanon the same from France. For the rest, the Amir demanded independence; and a telegram to Paris from a mass meeting of his leading supporters at Damascus confirmed his authentic spokesmanship. His proposal that the Peace Conference should take formal means to discover the wishes of the concerned populations was highly acceptable to the American delegation; and in subsequent inter-Power discussions the suggestion of President Wilson that a French-British-Italian-American Commission should visit the Middle East, and report on public opinion there, was accepted by all on 25 March. The joy of the Amir, entirely confident of its results as certain to confirm Arab near-unanimity, was immense. Apart from his own people he was by now conscious of American support, the highly respected Dr. Bliss[4] of the Syrian Protestant College of Beirut being a chief

[1] The matter was, however, in retrospect hotly debated among French statesmen, notably in the Chamber on 25 June 1920.

[2] As enunciated in his Mount Vernon speech of 4 July 1918, and repeated in subsequent speeches.

[3] This was the representation due to a (smaller) belligerent country: Syria as such (a Turkish province) had obviously no such right.

[4] French propaganda against Bliss as an 'American propagandist' was singularly misdirected.

adviser of the President, on lines critical of the French claims: and aware also of at least cordial goodwill from the British, freely expressed by Lloyd George who repeatedly assured Clemenceau that Britain's word had been given and that the promises to the Arabs must stand. The Amir could count also, it seemed, on some Zionist co-operation; seeking allies where they could be found, he had on 3 January 1919 initialed an agreement[1] with Dr. Weizmann in which the latter, in return for Arab tolerance, welcomed an Arab State as Palestine's neighbour.

Against all this, the French claims were, so far, immovable; and in their support they could produce at the Conference spokesmen[2] of the Central Syrian Committee. This, claiming to speak for all Syria as well as for dozens of Syrian committees throughout the world, consisted mainly of Christian Lebanese; its proposal was for a Syrian State, with wide boundaries, under a French Mandate. The C.S.C., whose policy was to turn, a year later, to one of Lebanese separatism, remained highly active in Paris, where its views carried weight in spite of the quite contrary assertions of French (minority) opinion which either was better aware of true Syrian opinion, or would gladly shun the whole Syrian enterprise. A delegation[3] from the revived Council of the Lebanon also arrived at Versailles under French auspices, with a programme of Greater Lebanese independence under French protection; and this, scornful of Fayṣal's pretensions and of 'bedouin' backwardness, was supported some weeks later by a second delegation of Maronite Lebanese (conveyed in a French warship), headed this time by their Patriarch. The latter, Mgr Élie Pierre Hoyeck (Elyas Butrus Hawwayik), dominant in his own community and venerated in France as a powerful friend, demanded specifically a Lebanese State within its 'historic and natural frontiers'; and he could feel satisfied, after conversations with Clemenceau and Pichon, that he had obtained a promise, in principle, that his wishes would be met. The Patriarch's delegation returned to Lebanon early in October 1919; a second Maronite party under Bishop 'Abdullah Khuri was dispatched early in February 1920, and continued to bring pressure to bear on the Quai d'Orsay. A spokesman of the Chaldeans of Mosul district, claiming for themselves a considerable northern-'Iraqi and northern-Jazira State, was fortunately without effect on the peacemakers.

[1] This agreement (Antonius, App. F, pp. 437–9) was, however, strictly conditional on Arab effective attainment of independence; it therefore never became operative.

[2] The chief speaker was Shukri Ghanim—whose own absence from Syria had so far lasted thirty-five years.

[3] It contained two Maronites (Da'ud Ammun and Émile Eddé) and one of each of the Greek Orthodox, Druze, and Muslim communities.

The decision of the Big Four to send a Commission of Inquiry to the territories concerned was unlikely to point the way to a clear-cut solution, since all positions already established were sure to be upheld whatever its verdict; but it was the best the Peace Conference could do, and it shelved the whole question for six months. No progress was attempted throughout the summer of 1919, even though delay must serve only to exacerbate the situation. The Americans at least, however, lost no time in naming their delegates for the Commission, Dr. H. C. King and Mr. Charles Crane; the British nominated Sir Henry McMahon and Dr. David Hogarth. But the French, for obvious reasons disliking the whole enterprise, decided after all, late in May, to boycott the Commission, and the British, on second thoughts,[1] followed them in their non-cooperation. The Italians had nothing to gain by membership, and equally withdrew. The Commission therefore, which arrived in the Levant on 10 June, was to consist of Americans only.[2]

The Amir Fayṣal returned to Beirut late in April 1919. He was received with enthusiasm and, whatever his private doubts, spoke freely of forthcoming independence. But he managed to retain a correct tone towards the French, even after conversations with Picot had again confirmed the wide gulf between French and Arab conceptions which his repeated exchanges with Clemenceau and Pichon had failed essentially to diminish: a fact which he could not but emphasize in conversation, on 12 May, with General Clayton and Colonel Cornwallis at Damascus. At the latter capital he found the Arab Government stabilized, its departments operating, the provincial administration largely a replica of Turkish officialdom (but without its foreign language and personnel), and the public services within humble limits advancing. His thoughts and those of his politically-minded supporters—notably the newly-formed pan-Arab Independence Party, overt successor of al-Fatat (pp. 28–9, 50 f.), and the Syrian Union Party—turned at once to the need both to provide a constitutional basis for the régime (its nominal status as a mere Occupied Territory Administration being generally ignored), and to organize the country for the coming Commission of Inquiry. This was to involve the immediate formation of a Representative Assembly, and orders were issued to all areas, including the Western and Southern Zones, to arrange for elections

[1] Also influenced by doubts as to the desirability of the Commission proceeding also to 'Iraq (upon which the French very naturally insisted) and by some degree of Zionist pressure, since the unpopularity of that movement in Palestine was known to be growing rapidly.

[2] The official designation was the 'American Section of the International Commission on Mandates in Turkey'. The two commissioners were accompanied by an advisory and secretarial staff.

and to send their delegations to Damascus. The Commander-in-Chief, seriously alarmed by the Franco-Syrian situation, directed that the Assembly when 'elected' should deal with no issues other than that of giving evidence to the Commission, and that no delegate from the south or west should attend; but his instructions were, as was foreseeable, ignored. In the choice of Deputies, some show of adherence to Turkish electoral procedure was made, strict compliance being anyhow impracticable. The delegates, who included more than their due proportion of Christians, were no doubt effectively representative of the great majority of Syrians; they were elected in all areas of Zone E, while a few, reasonably qualified to speak for majority opinion, appeared also from Palestine and from the coastal Zone. The resulting National Congress, so called, met on 20 June 1919, and declared itself to be the legally representative body for all Syria; and on 2 July it passed resolutions from whose content orthodox Syrian nationalism was never to vary. They repudiated equally the Sykes–Picot Agreement and the Balfour Declaration; they demanded sovereign status for a united Syria–Palestine, under the Amir Fayṣal. Rejecting the imputation of immaturity, they refused all political control from foreign Powers, but would accept a measure of American (or, *à la rigueur*, British) assistance—but never, in any circumstances, French. These resolutions, angrily rejected by the Lebanese Catholics (and by the Syrian Committee in Paris), were published throughout the country and enthusiastically acclaimed. To British observers, they and the genuine if ill-disciplined political force which they represented came as no surprise; that such were, for better or worse, the opinions of the strongest political elements in Syria was already appreciated. By the French, in Beirut and Paris alike, they were condemned as the bombast of a self-chosen minority.

The King–Crane Commission finished its inquiries in Palestine[1] by the fourth week of June, and thereafter spent four weeks in the Western and Eastern Zones of Syria. Men of integrity and good sense, and representing a nation totally devoid of ambitions[2] in the Levant, they spent the most patient efforts in discovering the

[1] The Commissioners' ultimate recommendation for this territory was in favour of a great reduction in the Zionist programme, which they saw to be quite inconsistent with the rights of the Arab inhabitants (Section E of Part 1 of their Report: Antonius, pp. 448 ff.).

[2] Isolated Syrians professed to believe the possibility of (or even to advocate) an American Mandate over Syria; and an occasional embittered Frenchman was able to discover either United States veiled ambitions or, more probably, those of Great Britain to be realized behind an American screen. Count R. de Gontaut-Biron, with his extreme Anglophobia, accuses the British of 'bribing whole villages' to give anti-French verdicts, and the Commission itself of concentrating on Protestant interests.

facts of public opinion in every community. They visited almost all townships of any pretension, received hundreds of petitions, heard repeatedly the views of every group. In the Western Zone, they found considerable support for the acceptance of French aid, or protection, or Mandate. In Beirut, the Municipal Council (elected, however, in Turkish days) stood by majority for an American or British Mandate, if Mandate there was to be; the Maronite and Greek Catholic communities were unhesitatingly for France. The Greek Orthodox community was divided; all claimed a united Syria, but did not agree on the Mandatory. Islamic opinion was, without complete unanimity, hostile to a French connexion: all, or almost all, were Syrian unionists. The small Protestant groups asked for American or British protection. The spokesmen of Mount Lebanon declared for the French, though a Syrian-unionist minority was not lacking. In Sidon, Ladhqiya, Alexandretta, and Tripoli the same Muslim-Christian cleavage—never precise, and always shaded by intensive rivalries and *arrière-pensées* locally variable—was a foregone conclusion. In the Biqa' it was the same; Catholic Christianity favoured the French with near-unanimity, other Christans were hesitant and divided, Sunni Islam was ranged with rare exceptions against all French pretensions, heterodox Islam was the same but with more waverers or dissidents.

In the Eastern Zone the case could not be otherwise. The demand was everywhere for a united Syria, embracing its old southern sanjaqs; it was for a French Mandate or effective connexion with France only in the small and scattered Catholic circles, and in some groups also among the non-Catholic Christians, the Druzes, and a few families of Aleppo and the north. These sectional and minority preferences could not affect a majority verdict, that of eight-tenths of the dominant Sunni-Muslim community, and probably seven-tenths of the whole population, in favour of the policy already formulated *ad hoc* by the Syrian Congress.

The course of the King–Crane inquiries was claimed by French observers,[1] and by some later French writers, as grossly ill conducted but as nevertheless by no means invalidating their claims;[2] to others, in Syria and outside, the very opposite appeared to be true. The final Report[3] of the two Commissioners was indeed almost wholly destructive of French claims to be an

[1] For example, General Brémond (*Le Hedjaz dans la guerre mondiale*, p. 327): 'la sinistre bouffonerie de la commission américaine . . . une odieuse comédie . . . dirigée exclusivement contre la France'.

[2] The recommendations do in fact support French contemporary claims in asserting the need to re-unite Palestine with the rest of Syria.

[3] Antonius, App. H., pp. 443–58.

acceptable Mandatory, if weight were to be given to the wishes of the population consulted. But the Report in any case had no influence upon the decisions to be taken in Europe; submitted by its authors in Paris on 28 August, it was studied (as far as appears) by nobody and was completely ignored by all statesmen among the responsible peacemakers.[1] First published in 1922, it favours the application of the mandatory[2] system, for a limited period, to a united Syria–Palestine, with the old Mount Lebanon to continue as autonomous, and the whole to be placed under a constitutional monarch, the Amir Fayṣal. The Mandate (a conception generally disliked and repudiated by Syrians, said the Commission, in favour of 'assistance') should, according to majority opinion, be allotted to the United States or, failing that, to Great Britain, but not to France. A French Mandate, unless restricted to the unenlarged Lebanon enclave, could lead, they believed, to Arab–French hostilities.

During and after the Commission's visit, the movement towards revised and modernized constitutional forms in the Damascus Government continued, and an Organic Statute was drafted providing for only a minimum of strictly temporary control by the Commander-in-Chief. The latter, however, took exception to the new Council of Ministers, directed their reversion to Directorate status, and asked also that the powers given by the Statute to the Amir should revert to the Chief Administrator; His Highness was to take no part in the administration. A further warning to the Amir was necessitated by the increasing scale of street demonstrations in Damascus, by the multiplication of tiresome border incidents, and by the improper comments of his followers on Allied policy; and a British political officer, with a spokesman of the French High Commission, M. Laforcade, waited upon Fayṣal to explain that the British were resolute to proceed with the National Home in Palestine, would in no circumstances themselves accept a Mandate for Syria,[3] but would feel bound to suppress 'trouble' there if the politicians or the mob went too far. Such warnings could do little, however, to stop the march of events or the growing tensions of the time. Months were passing, nothing had been settled, Arab claims had not been met; Syria, truncated and cut off from the sea, had no present status and a threatened future. The politicians of Damascus, uneasy,

[1] This might possibly have been otherwise but for President Wilson's sudden breakdown in health on 26 November 1919.

[2] The recommendations dealing with 'Iraq (which the Commission did not visit) were, in effect, in favour of a united 'Iraq under British Mandate.

[3] This entirely truthful assertion, conveyed to the Amir (as well as to the French) repeatedly both in Damascus and in Paris, was to be confirmed by the subsequent thirty years of history; but it puzzled Fayṣal, who failed to understand how Great Britain could abandon what she had just liberated.

emotional, and too little realistic, pressed for greater firmness, or for aggression. A Committee of National Defence was formed in Damascus, recruitment for the Amir's army was pressed forward. Yasin Pasha, his Chief of Staff responsible for these steps—and, it was said, for plans for the invasion of the coastal areas—was ordered to Cairo and interned; but military activity in Syria did not diminish, and a force designed to attain a strength of three divisions was under active training.

4. THE KING OF SYRIA

During the spring and summer of 1919, British and some French forces maintained uneasy garrisons and a French-directed Administration (p. 97) in Cilicia, faced by the hostility of the population and harassed by Turkish irregular, and some regular, troops. The national movement in Anatolia was daily gaining strength in opposition to the effete Government in Istanbul. A successful and inspiring National Assembly was convened at Ankara late in July; news came in August that British forces were withdrawing from Caucasia; and prominent personalities of Kamalist sympathy escaped from the capital to join the new movement. Propaganda on Islamic and Turkish traditionalist lines was not only fostered in Cilicia, but was injected far into Syria; and in the latter, apart from the survivals of Ottoman sentiment, many partisans of Arab nationalism could already regard Turkish support as a not impossible counterweight to European pressure. The National Congress of the Kamalists held at Sivas on 13 September further consolidated this movement, which had now all the elements of a genuine national uprising, strong with the enthusiasm of despair, admirable leadership, considerable armaments, and a unanimous popular following. Its emergence in a field where peacemaking with a helpless enemy had in 1918 seemed an easy task for the Allies was henceforward greatly to complicate the Middle Eastern picture, and to embitter Franco-British relations.

These relations had already been fitfully deteriorating. To the grievances of the French in coastal Syria, and the persistent allegation of a British part in 'Sharifian' propaganda, was added the growing wrath of French publicists against alleged British evasions or delays in handing to France what they still claimed with resentful passion—a free hand in the whole of Syria. The many bitter spoken and written words in the Paris of 1919 could not be unheeded in London, where they were taken as indicating the limits within which, in the last resort, Anglo-French differences must be confined. Moreover, the British desire to curtail after-war expenditure must apply to the Levant as it was doing simultaneously in 'Iraq. Everything pointed, therefore, to a gesture which would at least provisionally satisfy the French, and would please public opinion in England. It was decided to ask the French to take over, as from 1 November 1919, the military Command and the provision of garrisons in western Syria and Cilicia, without alteration, for the moment, of existing boundaries[1] between Zones, and without prejudice to permanent peace arrangements. In eastern Syria, Arab forces would relieve the British.

French acceptance of this proposal, made on 15 September, was immediate; Clemenceau and his Government had indeed been pressing for such a step for months past. The Ministry of War proceeded to the dispatch of reinforcements to Syria and Cilicia, consisting of French African troops, and that of Foreign Affairs selected General Gouraud (p. 82) to command them and to become France's supreme representative in the Levant.[2] Clemenceau used the occasion to address to the Syrian nation a promise that a régime of 'liberty, order and progress according to the wishes and interests of its people' would be theirs. To French opinion, the arrangement was an instalment, on acceptable lines if greatly overdue; but it was no comprehensive settlement, and seemed ominously to leave the Amir more free than ever to oppose the full attainment of French 'rights'.

Fayṣal himself had in August been invited to London to be told of these decisions, and to receive advice. He arrived on 19 September. Acquainted with the position, he protested strongly against provisions which seemed significant of future French plans, against which he must be helpless; and he urged again the summoning of a three-Power Conference finally to decide Syrian questions on lines of the wartime promises and Wilsonian doctrine. It was refused; the British defence of Arab Independence (now placed, in Syria, specifically at the mercy of France) was effectively at an end; Whitehall could only hope that French action hereafter would not prove too far inconsistent with the McMahon and Sykes–Picot understandings, nor turn its back too completely on self-determination. There was, from this viewpoint, little that was encouraging in the bitter tone of M. Clemenceau's dispatches to London, and the Amir was advised to make the best terms he could. He proceeded to Paris, shocked and apprehensive, and there held many conversations, and exchanged memoranda, with French officials, generals, and ministers. These, though their course cannot be completely reconstructed, resulted

1 French forces would, therefore, have no right to enter the 'four towns' of inland Syria, nor the Biqa', nor (since it lay in Zone B) Trans-Jordan.

2 In this capacity he relieved M. Georges Picot, who proceeded on mission to Turkey.

in a provisional agreement (or, others would say, a draft or proposed agreement) whereby Arab rule in inland Syria was assured, the Amir would recognize a separate and mandated Lebanon, the Druzes would be autonomous within Syria, the Biqa' would form a neutral zone, Syrian diplomatic representation abroad would devolve on France, and French priority was confirmed in the provision of any 'assistance' accepted by the Amir's Government. The agreement was probably the best for which either party could, at the moment, hope; but it could work peacefully only if both showed the rarest qualities of restraint. These, in the event, were not forthcoming, and the agreement, if such it was, was never accepted in Damascus.

The Amir returned to his country in mid-January, and to a Government now released from even nominal subordination to a British Command. His four months of absence, during which the Amir Zayd had acted for him, were marked by increasing political tension,[1] more unrealistic ambitions of the politicians, more bitterness against the French (and, in some measure, the British), growing economic difficulty, and an increase of frontier clashes. The 'Alawi country was largely beyond French control (p. 80)—thanks to arms and propaganda, it was said, from Damascus. A telegram to Fayṣal in London had alleged a French eastward advance in the Biqa' shortly after Gouraud's landing (21 November), and this was hotly disputed;[2] the Syrian Congress, still in session, were barely pacified by Riḍha al-Rikabi's[3] assurance that such trespass would be temporary. The Amir Zayd, announcing the forthcoming relief of the British troops by French and Arab, had stressed the need for patience and discipline; but such were not the methods of the National Congress, which received with consternation the news of the Fayṣal–Clemenceau Agreement, claimed that its own members alone were the true spokesmen for the nation, and once again addressed to the Powers its demand for full immediate independence. The temporary dissolution of Congress on 4 December, at the Amir's suggestion, produced a few weeks of comparative calm; but with the visible departure[4] of British garrisons nationalist fervour re-awoke, and

[1] The 'Iraqi element in the Syrian Administration, confined as it was almost entirely to military functions, was from about this period onwards increasingly unhappy, and relations with Syrian colleagues deteriorated; some leading 'Iraqis had already decided to leave Syria as soon as opportunity offered.

[2] General Gouraud frankly informed General Allenby of his intention to occupy the Biqa': nor did the latter dissuade him. The British Foreign Office, to whom Fayṣal appealed, expressed its complete inability to interfere with French operations.

[3] Rikabi was forced to resign on 14 December, and was replaced for a few days by 'Abd al-Ḥamid Pasha.

[4] It was complete in both Zones by the end of December; the last British troops left Beirut on 20 January 1920.

the need for increased defensive power was realized. Late in December conscription was introduced and Committees of Defence were formed in the main towns.

Fayṣal, shrewd and moderate, and by now fully aware of the doubtful possibilities and stark impossibilities of the situation, realized that he must identify himself with an 'extremist' policy or retire; nevertheless, he pleaded with his supporters for patience, for realism, for time. But he could not persuade them that his arrangement with Clemenceau was other than a derogation from the country's unity and independence, to which they were wholly committed; and to retain any support, the Amir's own attitude must needs harden with theirs. He himself assumed the duties of President of the Council and added new members to it. He daily received notables and party leaders, who pressed upon him extreme views which at heart he knew to be vain and unrealistic. Compulsory recruitment of all men from twenty to forty years of age was forced on, though its non-application in outlying areas was tacitly accepted. Preparations were made to pay companies of irregulars. Tribesmen and villagers formed bands for incursion and pillage in the Western Zone, which could combine looting with patriotism.

Meanwhile, an initial personal interview and later exchanges between the Amir and General Gouraud were correctly conducted. French troops were withdrawn from Ba'lbek, where clashes at Christmas 1919 had been serious, though they remained at Rayaq and elsewhere in the Biqa'. But in spite of the Amir's undertaking to restrain his followers, key posts in his Administration were reported still to be given to perfervid enthusiasts, wild speeches were increasingly delivered, French use of the Rayaq–Aleppo railway (essential for their supplies to Cilicia) was maliciously restricted. Supplies from hinterland to coast were withheld, a partial blockade of the French Zone established. In northern Syria, forces of Fayṣal's Government launched a successful attack at Ḥammam, and severe fighting followed between them and a French column. An attempt was made to blow up a Liṭani bridge, another near Ṭarṭus was attacked. Raids occurred on the Acre–Sidon road and nearby villages, and order had to be restored by two French columns which visited the area. Acts of violence recurred on the Ḥumṣ–Tripoli highway, on roads inland from Alexandretta, and at the latter town itself. The French post at Harim was attacked and blockaded till relieved by Senegalese troops. Nor were these the only cases alleged of aggressive provocation by authorized Syrian agents and forces, though for other attacks the Damascus authorities disclaimed responsibility. Great Britain, against whose forces and occupied territory in north-western 'Iraq similar tactics were being employed in the same months by armed bands[1] and propaganda from Aleppo, decided as from January 1920 to cease her subsidy to the Damascus Government. France did the same a month later.

As the unquiet winter of 1919–20 gave way to spring General Gouraud toured the coastal Zone, studied its problems, and in March announced that French 'control' would henceforth be substituted for direct administration: a reform, however, which produced little visible effect. French forces and administrators multiplied in the coastal cities and the Lebanon and, in spite of many heavy commitments in Cilicia,[2] faced the probability of an eastward expansion not long delayed. In Damascus, it was the Amir's policy first to stabilize his Government, then with the *fait accompli* of a Syrian State behind him, to return to Europe with a national mandate. To recall the dissolved National Congress was a first step; it was taken in February 1920, and a majority of the members, with a number of unelected *remplaçants*, and strengthened by representatives of the political parties, the al-'Ahd society, the Arab Club, and the ranks of the lawyers, shaykhs, and men of religion, met in conclave as the 'Palestine Conference' on 27 February to debate and resolve on the position of Palestine. They declared it to be part of Syria, emphatically rejected Zionism, and claimed a United Syria fully independent. The resolution was conveyed to the capitals of Europe.

On 6 March a plenary meeting of the National Congress heard an inaugural speech of the Amir. After quoting President Wilson, recapitulating the McMahon and subsequent promises, and praising Arab wartime services, the Amir demanded the decision

[1] Inspired or led by 'Iraqi officers, members of al-'Ahd in Fayṣal's service, and by border tribesmen: Longrigg, *'Iraq*, pp. 116, 119–20.

[2] The French position in Cilicia and southern Anatolia, following the relief of British by weaker French garrisons late in 1919, was full of difficulty. The Turkish nationalist movement was fully in action, its influence paramount, its forces active in Cilicia in an atmosphere of xenophobia, anti-Christian emotion, and pillage. Little attempt could be made to administer the territory, and communications were barely preserved; it was an exhausting, uphill campaign of survival, until a Franco-Turkish armistice, signed on 30 May 1920, gave temporary relief. In the first five months of that year, during which two improvised French divisions tried to sustain the position and communications, the main episodes of the desperate and mainly adverse hostilities were (*a*) the loss of Mar'ash after a siege, persistent attempts at its relief, and a final retreat to Iṣlaḥiya (21 January to 13 February 1920): (*b*) the siege of Bozanti, March to May 1920, followed by gallant but unsuccessful attempts at relief, and an evacuation which led to the loss of the whole garrison: (*c*) the siege of, assaults upon, resolute defence and final abandonment of Urfa (9 February to 11 April 1920), which it had proved impossible to relieve: an episode ending with shocking Turkish treachery: (*d*) the first and second sieges of 'Ayntab (1–16 April, and 1–25 May). These and other defensive operations, including the defence of the Taurus–Amanus railway by a series of static posts, made great calls on the scanty forces of General Gouraud and were a cause of delay in his moves against the Damascus Government.

—that of the Syrian people—on the future national régime and the Constitution which should embody it. Kamil al-Qaṣṣab, for the Committee of National Defence, bade Congress declare a parliamentary, constitutional, and decentralized régime for all-Syria, with the Amir as King. A committee of nine sat to prepare a reply to the speech; but there could only be one. The session of 7 March, directed by Hashim al-Atasi, rehearsed the usual arguments on Unity and Independence, resolved on the immediate formation of an all-Syrian National Government (to include a Palestine freed from Zionism, and a Lebanon guaranteed a special position), and with unanimity offered the throne to the Amir. His proclamation and the rendering of homage took place, amid great enthusiasm, on 8 March. The heads of the Christian communities were prominent among the swearers of allegiance, and Muslim members of the Council of the Lebanon braved French ill will, and earned a prolonged incarceration, by hurrying to Damascus. Syria was a Kingdom,[1] and the *Khutba*, in the Friday prayers of every mosque, included the name of King Fayṣal I.

The Council of Directors, formed as a stop-gap under military auspices, gave way immediately to a Cabinet[2] under 'Ali Riḍha al-Rikabi. This, with the intention not least of reassuring the Powers, issued a ministerial programme which spoke not only of the defence of Syrian independence and maintenance of order, but also of universal equality before the law, the protection of foreign interests, aid to be offered (if need be) to the Allies in keeping order in the Levant, and economic development; and the King himself in a letter to Gouraud[3] showed willingness to accept, from an Allied nation, all help consistent with complete independence. Turkish laws, necessarily, remained in force, and the administration and Courts continued unchanged; but the decision was maintained to resist a foreign currency, such as the French were even now introducing[4] into the coastal Zone. A Committee was appointed to draft a Syrian Constitution, and after ten weeks

[1] A meeting of a number of the Amir's 'Iraqi officers resolved, simultaneously, that 'Iraq should be an independent Kingdom, under the Amir 'Abdullah.

[2] Its composition:—President, 'Ali Riḍha al-Rikabi: President of the Council of State, 'Ala al-Din al-Durubi: Interior, Riḍha al-Ṣulḥ: Foreign Affairs, Sa'id al-Ḥusayni: War, 'Abd al-Ḥamid al-Qalṭaqchi: Commerce and Agriculture, Yusif al-Ḥakim: Justice, Jalal al-Din Zuhdi: Finance, Faris al-Khuri: Education, Saṭi' al-Ḥuṣri (author of a valuable account of these eventful days, *Yaum Maysalun*).

[3] The General replied courteously, though without accepting the new position. The Amir had almost certainly warned him in advance (*Daily Telegraph*, 16 March 1920).

[4] The Imperial Ottoman Bank had established in 1919 a subsidiary, the Banque de Syrie, to which in March 1920 the High Commissioner entrusted locally the exclusive rights of note issue: the Syro-Lebanese pound equalled 20 francs, irrespective of all fluctuations of the latter. The note issue was covered by credits in the Caisse centrale du Trésor Public in Paris, and by French National Defence Bonds.

produced a text, modelled on the democratic structures of European states. It was prudently silent as to the boundaries of Syria, and indicated in its terms no movement towards a pan-Arab conception, or a federation of Arab States.

Nothing, however, which the Syrians in Damascus or King Ḥusayn[1] in Mecca could now say or do could stop the execution of the decisions which France had long regarded as predestined, and which Great Britain had ceased to resist. The resolutions of the Syrian Congress and the enthronement of King Fayṣal were alike rejected as untenable by Paris and London. Lebanese Christian indignation ran high, all 'Sharifian' claims were repudiated, and on 22 March representatives of the various communities in the Lebanon met at Ba'abda and with cordial French encouragement proclaimed their own independence from Syria.[2] King Fayṣal, whether so styled or not, was invited by telegrams from London to return to Europe for further consultation, and meanwhile the Allied Supreme Council was convened at San Remo on 25 April. Here the assembled statesmen decided to offer a Mandate for 'Syria and the Lebanon' to the French Republic, and for 'Iraq and Palestine with Transjordan to the British. The Mandates were, in principle, accepted by the Powers concerned; and France, subject only to such interpretation as she might herself adopt to mandatory obligations or restraints, had thenceforward a free hand in the whole of central and northern Syria: coast, hinterland, and desert.

News of the conferment of the Mandate, published on 5 May,[3] was received with horror rather than surprise in Damascus, but with satisfaction[4] in dominant circles in the Lebanon. In spite of the menace of the growing French forces, the attitude of Gouraud in Beirut and of the French Government in Paris, and the intransigence of the new King's own followers, he himself had since mid-March made such efforts as were within his power to maintain tolerable relations with his western neighbours. But his suggestion first of official Syrian representation in the coastal Zone, then of the assumption of 'control' of the claimed western areas of his kingdom, were alike and not unnaturally rejected. The San Remo decisions, when these were announced, did not of themselves preclude the existence of some sort of Arab State in inland Syria;[5] but they were met in Damascus, in terms of the

[1] He telegraphed to Lloyd George, on the now invariable lines.

[2] In mid-May the Lebanese Delegation, then in Paris, was reassured by Millerand that the creation of a separate Lebanon formed part of French policy.

[3] It was notified by General Allenby, in Cairo, to Fayṣal on 27 April.

[4] The Central Syrian Committee in Paris reacted similarly; in the U.S.A. the 'Syrian-Lebanon League of North America' protested to the President against a 'Moslem Arab theocratic monarchy'.

[5] As the British were shortly to prove by their handling of their own Mandate in 'Iraq.

National Congress resolution of 8 May, by a demand for full sovereign independence and the absolute rejection of all mandatory tutelage (though without rejection of a modicum of French aid *en ami et allié*) and of a separated Palestine; and they led more than ever to truculent attitudes, and acts of frontier violence, by Syrian patriots. The King refused, indeed, the demand of many of his followers that he should declare war on France; but he could not, perhaps would not, restrain his officers and bands of irregulars from provocation.[1] What confidence he retained was based still on fond hopes of a settlement to be reached in Europe; but he realized imperfectly that the Americans had lost all interest,[2] that the British were confining themselves to urging a *modus vivendi* with France, and that in Turkish help, despite some Kamalist overtures, there could be no solution. Meanwhile popular feeling led to a change of Cabinet; that of Rikabi, thought too moderate, gave way on 3 May to another under Hashim al-Atasi, who combined the premiership with the Ministry of the Interior.[3] The Administration, starved for funds and everywhere subordinated to the prevailing political excitement, declined in efficiency and control to a low level. The King tried, with all his force and eloquence, to maintain the morale of his people.

General Gouraud, keenly alive to the French tradition in Syria and moved by the eagerness of his officers and the French public to assert it, was impatient also of the unrealism, the indiscipline, the insults of 'the Sharifians'. He was assured that, in spite of the extravagant claims and emotions of politicians, the real Syria desired and awaited France and all that she could bring. His country had at last her Mandate; and neither the General nor his entourage could in these days of tension and impatience conceive any such interpretation of it as would satisfy both themselves and the Arab politicians. By the second week of July all hope of compromise and possible *bon voisinage* had disappeared. An armistice with the Turks in Anatolia, signed on 30 May, permitted the distracted General, while it lasted, to set his Syrian house in order. He was certain of immunity from British or American intervention. His plans took shape, his troop movements began. Two towns in the Biqa', Ḥaṣbaya and Rashaya, threw off allegiance

[1] Some at least of these acts, unauthorized by their Government, were merely vindictive or acquisitive; they were most active in the extreme south (Palestine border), in the Biqa', and in the sanjaq of Alexandretta.

[2] The last of the American Peace Delegation left Paris on 11 December 1919, and strong isolationist forces at home were preparing to sweep aside their President's idealistic, though never interventionist, plans.

[3] The other ministers (in part unchanged) were 'Abd al-Raḥman Shahbandar (Foreign Affairs): Faris al-Khuri (Finance): Riḍha al-Ṣulḥ (President of the Council of State): George Bey Rizqullah (Commerce): Jalal al-Din Zuhdi (Justice): Saṭi' al-Ḥuṣri (Education): Yusif al-'Adhma (Defence).

to Fayṣal and invoked the French. A letter to Gouraud from the King announcing that he intended now, as invited, to visit Europe met the reply, given to his envoy Nuri al-Sa'id on 9 July in Beirut, that a significant message was about to reach him. This letter, handed to the King on 14 July, was in fact an ultimatum. It stated that the Mandate would not, in the French view, be inconsistent with Syrian self-government; it would involve the bestowal of aid and collaboration, without colonization; and meanwhile it was, for its detailed application, to be studied in eastern Syria forthwith by a French committee of specialists. The letter then formulated a series of complaints against the acts of the Damascus Government, and made specific demands, failure to comply with which within four days would liberate the French from all previous restraints. These demands were that the Mandate must be accepted: the Arab Army must be reduced, conscription abandoned: the Rayaq–Aleppo railway must be handed over for French operation, with military garrisons at the principal stations; the new French currency must be introduced in Syria; and the worst anti-French offenders must be punished for their crimes.

Even before the arrival of Gouraud's letter at Damascus on the 14th, its substance was known. It aroused fierce indignation. The situation was immediately made known by the King to the European Consuls in Damascus, with the urgent request that they should intervene. At the same time, Fayṣal telegraphed to the capitals of the principal Powers and to Geneva. All this could be of no avail; and there was little hope of moderate councils in the Syrian Congress, from which all sense of reality, and particularly of their own total military ineffectiveness,[1] had by now departed; it went, indeed, so far as to attack, for hesitation or cowardice, its own Government and King, and to insist, against all facts or probabilities, on its full sovereign rights. This outburst, at the Congress meeting on 19 July, led to its dissolution by the King's orders. But angry mob demonstrations, in part directed against the King in person, created an ugly and dangerous situation in the city, and their suppression was not without serious loss of life. Fayṣal himself and his ministers could better appreciate the situation. They realized that non-acceptance of the ultimatum could lead to nothing but early extinction, and they hoped that, after all, second and more liberal thoughts might yet prevail in Europe. Personal telegrams of acceptance in principle had already been sent by the King to Gouraud on 18 and 19 July, and, though not accepted as tantamount to compliance with the French terms, secured at least a three-day respite. The official agreement of the

[1] This was of course well realized by senior (almost entirely 'Iraqi) officers of the Army.

Syrian Government was sent, by telegram, on the afternoon of the 20th, and orders for general demobilization were issued in Damascus.

But the decisive telegram failed to arrive in time, owing to the destruction of telegraph lines, doubtless by Syrian irregulars or villagers; and on the 21st, contrary to expectation, the forward movement of French troops towards the Anti-Lebanon was reported. The King, having consulted his French liaison officer, Colonel Cousse, dispatched his Minister of Education, Saṭi' al-Ḥuṣri, urgently to intercede with Gouraud, whom he found at 'Aliya early on the 22nd, in a mood of irritation,[1] obduracy, and suspicion of all Syrian protestations. Granting a further delay of one day only the High Commissioner returned al-Ḥuṣri to Damascus with a list of further demanded 'guarantees'. Pausing at the headquarters of General Goybet, in command of the French forces advancing on Damascus, and obtaining from him a further twenty-four hours grace (until midnight on 23 July), al-Ḥuṣri reached the capital late on the 22nd.

The Cabinet met early the next day, and considered the new demands contained in General Gouraud's letter; this called, not discourteously, for a radically changed Syrian attitude and a frank acceptance of the Mandate and of all French demands. But the French determination to occupy Damascus, and all Syria, was now clear.[2] Even before Fayṣal's delegate could return from the meeting of foreign Consuls, which he had hastily summoned, the population had become aware of the desperate position and, amid great confusion and divided councils, were preparing to seize whatever weapons were available and take the field under the Minister of War, Yusif al-'Adhma. No more than a hasty note was secured by Colonel Cousse, late in the evening, from the King, and forwarded to Gouraud: it refused to concede the latest 'guarantees', alleging that acceptance would lead inevitably to

[1] A further cause of the General's determination (for such it now was) to occupy Syria without more delay was, probably, the recent action of the Council of the Lebanon. This or part of it on 10 July met secretly (that is, without the usual French supervision) and resolved to demand or proclaim its own complete sovereign independence, without French tutelage but with Syrian fraternal co-operation. This resolution, detestable to the French, was passed by an easy majority of Council members present. These, however, were arrested by the French (the proceedings having 'leaked') at Zaḥla on their way to join the King at Damascus and, as they hoped, to proceed to Europe with him to plead their cause. The High Commissioner, with angry accusations against the King of bribing the Lebanese Councillors to sell their country, caused telegrams of loyalty to be sent to Paris by the Maronite Patriarch and others, and took the drastic action of banishing the arrested Councillors from their country. The Council was instantly dissolved.

[2] During the Cabinet meeting on the morning of the 23rd, news arrived that French forces, alleging shortage of water, had already advanced towards Khan Maysalun, contrary to the undertaking given by General Goybet.

civil war. News of the main French advance by way of 'Ayn Jadida caused a rush of some hundreds of demobilized soldiers and civilians under the Minister of War, in defiance of the King's restraining orders, to join the small regular Arab forces[1] guarding the Maysalun Pass. Here the French troops, mainly Algerian and Senegalese with metropolitan units, met a spirited if ill-organized and hopeless resistance. The action, in which French aircraft and tanks participated, lasted for six hours. Severe heat and thirst afflicted both sides. The French, better led, disciplined, and equipped, forced[2] the pass and continued their march on Damascus, while the Syrian force fell back and disintegrated. The city was entered without further opposition, public buildings were occupied by French troops, the initial proclamations were drafted, and contact was established with the townsfolk and such of their leaders as bowed, at last, to the inevitable.[3]

The King with his ministers withdrew from the city on the afternoon of the 25th, to Kiswa, a village on the Ḥijaz Railway line south of Damascus. There he waited: and, encouraged by a hopeful message from Nuri al-Sa'id, who had stayed in the city on his behalf, ventured to appoint a new Cabinet designed to render possible, after all, a tolerable collaboration with the French. It was headed by 'Ala al-Din al-Durubi.[4] The King himself returned for a few hours to Damascus, but, after a further exchange of messages with General Gouraud, was compelled to leave the city on the 28th by train to Dar'a. Two days later, urged by telegrams from al-Durubi in Damascus and by French threats to bombard the village, he proceeded to Haifa, where he was received with every courtesy, and thence to Italy and a new life elsewhere. Although his last message to General Gouraud was in a tone of indignation, all his subsequent statements in Europe were remarkable for their dignity and restraint. An incalculable loss to Syria was thereafter to open the way for transcendant services at his hands to its sister country, 'Iraq.

[1] The *Livre d'Or* speaks of Arab forces in strength of approximately one division, but it is difficult to accept so high an estimate. Ḥaddad mentions 4,500 men, including tribesmen and volunteers. The impression gained from al-Ḥuṣri (p. 343) and from Fayṣal himself is of a lower figure than this (*Morning Post*, 6 September 1920).

[2] Their losses are given in the *Livre d'Or* as 24 killed, with 30 other casualties; the Arabs sustained far more, including Yusif al-'Adhma himself.

[3] The French claimed that their reception in Damascus was warm and friendly; the Arab accounts give the opposite impression.

[4] The other members (in part survivors from the existing ministry) were Faris al-Khuri, Jalal al-Din Zuhdi, Yusif al-Ḥakim, Jamil al-Ulshi, 'Aṭa al-Ayyubi, 'Abd al-Raḥman Yusif, and Badi' al-Mu'ayyid.

5. THE FRENCH INSTALLED

The occupation of Damascus by French troops was synchronized with that of Aleppo, after a brief skirmish with Arab troops at Muslimiya, and that of other principal cities. They were received with outward calm, and in places with expressions of welcome of which by no means all were insincere; and if certain regions of the country—areas round Aleppo, the Ḥawran, the Nuṣayri hills—were still in turmoil, there was no sign of a resistance which would offer serious difficulty to French arms.

The terms imposed by General Goybet, less upon the country at large than upon overtly Francophobe elements in Damascus, were such as might be expected. The Syrian Army was disarmed and disbanded, when not transferred with modifications to gendarmerië duties; war material was delivered to the French; an indemnity of 10 million francs was imposed. Courts martial were assembled to try some three-score offenders[1] accused of crimes against life or property; most of these, however, including the thirty-four sentenced to death, had already escaped and were tried in absence. Use of the Arab flag was forbidden. The new collaborationist Cabinet formed by King Fayṣal on 26 July was accepted by the French, and 'Ala al-Din and his colleagues entered immediately upon their duties; but the Prime Minister and one of his colleagues, Shaykh 'Abd al-Raḥman al-Yusif, were dragged from their train and murdered while on a visit to the disturbed Ḥawran country three weeks later. General Gouraud paid his first visit to Damascus on 8 August, and was greeted suitably by representatives of all communities. His staff proceeded urgently to the reorganization of the territory, the collection of arms, and the establishment of comprehensive French control.

The relation between the Government of King Fayṣal and that now installed by the Mandatory-elect could furnish an interesting problem in constitutional law. If the Syrian monarchy be taken as having enjoyed no valid sovereign status, then it could be no other than a prolongation, or perhaps a usurpation, of the Occupied Enemy Territory Administration set up, in an occupied Turkish province, by General Allenby as Commander-in-Chief; and in that event the French themselves (their Mandate not yet in force, nor Turkish sovereignty yet renounced) were for their first months in a like position. But can King Fayṣal's Administration, claimed as that of a sovereign monarchy, be so dismissed? It had been acknowledged as such by no foreign Power; it had exercised

[1] These included well-known personalities—Aḥmad Muraywid, Fu'ad Salim, Shukri al-Quwatli, Sa'id Ḥaydar, Amir 'Adil Arsalan, Iḥsan al-Jabiri, Riyaḍh al-Ṣulḥ, Bahjat al-Shihabi, Nabih al-'Adhma, Khalid al-Ḥakim, and a number of officers who had served in the desert campaign of 1916–18.

authority over by no means all the territory which it claimed: and the *de facto* detachment of Syria from Turkey could lead to no legally admissable change of sovereignty until the ex-sovereign himself renounced his rights. On the other hand, changes of sovereignty have not, in history, always been sanctified by treaties or by the approval of lawyers; the position in Syria, since mid-March 1920, had been one of the effective exercise of power by an authority based on at least the forms of an election, and certainly on a majority support so strong as to be unquestioned within the territory. There was a Constitution, due forms of law and administration, and a series of sovereign acts whose validity was admitted by practical acceptance and perpetuation, even by the French successors; Fayṣal's laws and regulations, and the assets and liabilities of his Administration, were treated by the incoming Mandatory as valid until changed.

The government of Syria as an Arab State had lasted for nearly two years, in spite of the lamentable initial conditions of the territory, its inland isolation and hampered commerce, its economic weakness, its lack of active help from outside—in spite, indeed, of the ill will of powerful outside interests. Never stable nor truly efficient, never in the prevailing conditions able to do much for its subjects, the Administration had nevertheless shown abundant vitality, an excellent comprehension of local conditions, a willingness to decentralize, toleration of all communities without rancour or fanaticism, and the possession of a considerable number not merely of competent military officers but also of civil administrators. Moreover, the Arab national movement upon which the State and monarchy were based was a strong political force, which had been gathering pressure for a generation, enjoyed all the powerful appeal of emotional patriotism, was conversant with the spirit of the times in other countries, had been strengthened by its wartime martyrs, was fully confident in its own capacity, and had had good reason, based on the Allies' wartime and post-war promises, to expect that its claim to independence would not be opposed.

These assets were not enough. Apart from the unequivocal French demand for Syria, which alone as between a very great and a very weak nation was sufficient to condemn all Arab hopes, the national movement in Syria suffered, itself, from serious weaknesses: the weaknesses, in effect, which for at least the next full generation were to prove a major element in its political misfortunes. The movement, as a serious and potent motive, was still limited to a small political class and to such following as this could partially or temporarily inspire; it did not include—and King Fayṣal's own supporters did not include—the totality even of the Muslim instructed classes, since a proportion of these were for varying reasons tepid or hostile to his cause, while a proportion felt also that a temporary foreign mandate in some form was necessary to the consolidation, progress, and enrichment of their country. Thus restricted, the Syrian nationalists, sole basis of King Fayṣal's throne and state, suffered further from an incomplete knowledge of the politics, forces, and methods of the international world; they lived in a closed and emotional region of hopes, general principles, and enthusiasms; they had by temperament and training no adequate conception of the necessary gradualness, the indispensable compromises, the need for the conciliation and retention of friends, the recognition of politics as truly the 'art of the possible', by which alone the weak can hope for political success. King Fayṣal's officers and congress members, journalists and speakers, had no just idea of the magnitude of the difficulty by which they were confronted: that is, by French ambition and the unwillingness of the British[1] to go beyond certain lengths to restrain it. They possessed, to meet it, no technique more effective than provocation and insult.

The French themselves, in their invasion of inland Syria, have been heavily criticized. It was an area in which (unlike the contemporary British position in 'Iraq) they had no obligation to keep order, no existing responsibilities, no requirement to maintain an Administration they had already set up: an area in which they had specifically committed themselves to supporting an independent Arab State: in which they had declared, with full solemnity, that they would be guided by the principles of self-determination: and in which a forcibly-imposed foreign régime, under whatever title or sponsorship, must face the most difficult and unfavourable inauguration when it stepped in to take the place of a national State and monarchy. The reasons, therefore, which led the French Government, supported by probably four-fifths of French public opinion, to invade Syria and impose its authority by force of arms, must have been powerful. There was in these reasons an element of anger, against the unhelpful (if not indeed unfriendly and supplanting) British, and against disrespectful Arabs; there was an element of indignation that the 'sacred rights' of France should be questioned. There was error, perhaps self-deception, in the French estimate of two things. One of these was the degree of popular support they enjoyed or would enjoy in Syria, which (as the future was to show) they seriously overestimated; the other was the strength of the

[1] Nor did the nationalists aid their own cause by open hostility to the British (pp. 96–7) when these were (and had proved at the Peace Conference to be) their only European friends.

nationalist movement, which for all its faults and weaknesses they gravely undervalued. It was the French conviction that they would be welcomed by the mass of Syrians, that they had a great and worthy task to fulfil in that country, and a historic right to fulfil it on their own terms. Self-determination, they believed, could mean little among so backward and mutually contradictory a population; or, at the least, its procedures could be postponed, with advantage to all, for some years. If an Arab State was the desideratum, then there should be, in due course, an Arab State —not that of Fayṣal, imposed and unwanted, but another to be somehow, at some period, patiently evolved, even if, through no fault of France, that State would not include the southern Syria which Great Britain had, for her own or Zionist ends, cut off. Meanwhile, none could analyse mandatory obligations more lucidly than French lawyers, none could take a higher view of them than her heroic Catholic generals and eloquent statesmen. Of self-interest or colonization, there was to be no question; there was confidence that time would show one more French work of humanity, civilization, and statecraft.

The question is here inevitable: If the British could, a few months later, invite the Amir Fayṣal into 'Iraq and use him —chastened, admittedly, by his painful eviction from Syria— as a chief instrument in constructing a sovereign Arab State, was it impossible for the French, in the summer of 1920, to make such terms with his Syrian kingdom as would consolidate and assist this while giving to France all that she required of cultural supremacy and political advantage? The adoption of such a policy, if in practice attainable, would have been evidently the best solution of the problem as thus posed. But its adoption was in fact precluded, to an almost equal extent, by both of the two contending elements: by the irritation and impatience of the French, and by the provocative intransigence of the Arabs. It would have been a possible solution only if calm goodwill and mutual appreciation had been present; but these qualities were absent from the scene, and the strong and largely emotional forces engaged brought matters, instead, to an outcome which was by then no longer avoidable.

The Syria which emerged from the war was far from the Syria of geography, of natural economics, or of national claims; it had been truncated by the loss of Palestine and Transjordan, a loss for which the French were not responsible, but for which Arab and especially Syrian statesmen were, throughout a long future, to blame the unwise or selfish policies of the European Powers— especially, and with reason, Great Britain. A Syrian State including the whole of geographical Syria would from the outset have enjoyed important advantages, and Europe would have been spared at least one reiterated and not ill-founded reproach.

The larger question remains, that of the possibility in 1919 of realizing the single Arab State which King Ḥusayn, in the days of the McMahon letters, had conceived as including (with possible limited exceptions) the whole of Arabia and the Fertile Crescent and beyond. In this wide Arab territory there were, certainly, important elements of unity: a common language, a common pride and tradition, by vast majority a common religion, a common self-consciousness as participators in a glorious past and an imagined future. But was there among these elements, and was there in the Arab populations as they existed from the Taurus to the Arabian Sea, material for the construction of a single State? It has been a recurring accusation by Arab statesmen that selfish and uncomprehending Europe deliberately divided the Arab world into a group of separate states when its desire and right was to form a single empire conterminous with the 'Sons of the Arabs'. As a weapon in political controversy, the accusation has value; it embodies much of the emotional unrealism dear to all but the best Arab publicists; nor can it be pretended that in the divisions actually made—'Iraq, the lesser Syria, Palestine, Transjordan—the interests of European Powers played no part, nor that self-determination was practised to determine these divisions, nor that they corresponded to logical or natural units of area. But if the facts of 1919 are to be faced objectively, it must appear that no Arab authority existed, or was remotely in sight, which could be capable of holding together the various and far-flung Arab territories as a single State. There did not exist the sense of political (as distinct from sentimental) cohesion; local and regional loyalties were infinitely stronger than those of generalized Arabism, communications even between the various potential capitals were slow and but half-explored, standards of past administration and of society—indeed, the whole conception of government and of life—differed within the widest limits between the various areas, and no vestige existed of a ruler or a governing class capable, with general acceptability, of setting up tolerable regional administrations and of unifying these. The conception belongs, indeed, to the dreamland of early Arab nationalism; and if the western Powers prevented, as effectively as they did, any attempt to turn the dream into physical fact, they doubtless saved the Arabs thereby from grave embarrassment and certain failure.

IV

FIRST YEARS OF THE MANDATE

I. THE MANDATE

THE award of a Mandate to France for 'Syria and the Lebanon', made by the Principal Allied Powers on 28 April 1920, was accompanied by no detailed provisions; these remained to be drafted to the satisfaction of the Council of the League, by whom the award itself must be confirmed. The Treaty of Sèvres, signed on 10 August 1920, provided in its Articles 94 and 95 for the application of Article 22 of the League Covenant (p. 374) to Syria and the other ex-Turkish provinces; but this Treaty was never ratified by Turkey. A drafting committee worked on the text of the Mandate, mostly in London, in the summer and autumn of 1920, and a text was placed before the Council on 21 February 1921. But its consideration was postponed; conditions in the Near and Middle East were still disturbed, and the United States Government was unhappy at the lack of specific provision for an Open Door policy in mandated territories. It was nevertheless the wish of the Council that the Mandatory Powers-elect should act henceforward, as from 1 March 1921, as though the Mandates were in force; and this they did. Draft Mandates for Syria–Lebanon, Palestine with Transjordan, and 'Iraq were published in August 1921, but were not resubmitted to the League Council until July 1922. The final text, which did not differ significantly as between territories save for the provisions covering Zionism in Palestine, was approved by the Council on 24 July 1922. But further discussions were still to be held between France and Italy, regarding the latter's rights[1] in the territory, before the Mandate could be declared, on 29 February 1923, to have become effective: by which date all Turkish rights to Syria had been renounced under the Treaty of Lausanne, which was signed on 24 July.[2] The last American scruples were removed by further Franco-American exchanges, ending with a Convention signed on 4 April 1924, and ratified on 13 July, covering American

[1] The principal Italian demand was for foreign judges in cases involving Italians, in the absence of the Capitulations. The French-Italian agreement was signed on 23 September 1923.

[2] It came into force on 6 August 1924.

rights and the Open Door. Germany, Austria, and Belgium having undertaken to recognize whatever régime in Syria should be established, 13 July 1924 became the date upon which vanished the last diplomatic obstacle to the full exercise of the Mandate.

This document as published after its acceptance by the League Council—which thus superseded the Principal Allied Powers as granter of the Mandate—was the 'specific definition' thereof by the League itself. Disputes arising between France and any other League member regarding its interpretation were to be submitted to the Permanent Court of International Justice, and meanwhile the Mandatory was to report annually to the Council. The latter provision linked the Mandatory with the specialized body of which the establishment is foreseen in Article 22 of the Covenant, and which was duly set up by the League at Geneva, for the specific purpose of supervision of the territories so placed: that is, the Permanent Mandates Commission. This, established as early as 1921, was composed initially of nine members selected by the Council from various (and mainly non-mandatory) nations, who were to sit as individuals and not as governmental spokesmen. Its task was to study and criticize the Reports placed before it: to question the Mandatories' accredited representatives: and to examine petitions addressed to the League by interested parties. From the high quality of the Commission's members, and the essential nature of their task *vis-à-vis* the mandatory conception, it could be expected that the institution would be valuable or, indeed, indispensable; and in the practice of the next twenty years this was, within limits, confirmed. The Commission's proceedings were characterized by frankness, goodwill, and considerable shrewdness; it by no means always accepted the Mandatories' official reports[1] as the final word, could indicate gaps, remark inconsistencies, and ask searching questions. The comments and judgements of the Commission could not but be taken seriously by a Mandatory, since they were in effect those of the most advanced nations of the world. Nevertheless, apart from the slow tempo of its biannual meetings, the Commission could do little immediately to influence events; it had no direct dealings with the territories, could obtain no information which a Mandatory withheld, and had no power save that of suggestions and reporting. That League States-members with little direct interest in a mandated territory should risk French displeasure by undue criticism was unlikely; France was 'the man on the spot', was

[1] The Annual Reports by the French High Commissioner, as submitted to the League, form one of the most important sources for the present work. Admirably clear and full for most departmental activities, they offer an incomplete and necessarily a one-sided picture of the political scene.

eminently a Great Power, was pursuing her tasks with great assiduity—and could expect to be left alone.[1]

The terms of the Mandate (Appendix D) covered the duty of framing a Constitution for the territory within three years: the 'rights, interests, and wishes' of the inhabitants: their progressive development as independent States: and the encouragement of local autonomy, as far as circumstances permitted. It sanctioned the retention of the Mandatory's own troops in the territory 'for its defence': the use by these troops of the country's means of communication 'at all times', and the raising of local militia. Foreign affairs, and local relations with foreign Consuls, were to devolve solely on the French. Extradition treaties between France and other Powers would apply to Syria. No part of the territory could be ceded, in any manner, to a foreign Power. A complete judicial system, guaranteeing all foreign and 'native' rights, was to be instituted. Capitulations would not be applicable in favour of foreigners, and the Consular Courts would continue to act only until superseded by new arrangements; but capitulatory rights would (unless voluntarily surrendered) be again exercisable on the expiry of the Mandate. The Awqaf would be administered in strict accordance with religious law. Freedom of conscience and worship, and non-discrimination between communities, were to be ensured; public instruction would be carried out in the local languages, all communities continuing to maintain their own schools; their existing privileges would be maintained. Foreign religious missions were to enjoy full freedom 'provided that their activities are confined to the domain of religion'. In economic matters, freedom was given to the Mandatory to develop the territory, while avoiding harmful monopolies and keeping an Open Door for all League members. Necessary taxation could be levied. The Mandatory would adhere on behalf of Syria–Lebanon to international conventions, and to 'measures of common utility' to combat disease. An Antiquities Law would be drafted and put into force. French and Arabic would be official languages.

Though critics have not been lacking of certain of its terms, the text reveals that the provisions of the Mandate had been carefully drafted, and covered all the essential aspects of a novel relationship. It is, nevertheless, at once apparent not only that the Mandatory was invested with virtually unlimited powers, but that its whole policy could depend upon what sense it cared to give to certain important phrases in the text, such as 'native

[1] These considerations did not prevent keen interest in events in Syria by independent Italian observers, who produced a considerable literature critical of French policy. British opinion was less copious, but was generally aware of Syrian discontent. American writers expressed similar views, with less realization of the Mandatory's very real difficulties.

authorities', 'the wishes of the population', 'as far as circumstances permit', and so on. It was clear, indeed, that the mandatory conception, as here formulated, had already moved far from that suggested at its first appearance in Article 22 of the League Covenant. The latter describes Syria as one of the territories whose 'existence as independent nations can be provisionally recognized, subject to the rendering of administrative advice and assistance by a Mandatory' for a time; the Mandate itself suggests, instead, a derelict territory over which the Mandatory was, for an unlimited time, to exercise complete control over every activity, and to perform the normal functions of sovereignty. There is little suggestion of partnership, or of a backward nation enjoying the temporary assistance of one more advanced. There is no Article prescribing that 'the Mandatory shall ensure that the national self-respect of the population shall not be offended, nor their full exercise of sovereign rights retarded more than may prove strictly necessary'; and the desideratum that the Mandatory should be the people's own choice had been blatantly unfulfilled.

The acceptance of the task by France had, from the outset, its critics in that country; it would, many Frenchmen felt, be a thankless burden, and was widely understood to be contrary to the popular will of Syrians. To others the Mandate was a needless or insulting impediment to full French freedom of action; a Protectorate, or direct annexation, would have been greatly preferred. Others, in part sharing such views, saw compensation in expected strategic or economic advantages to be gained. To a majority however—in contrast to the cynical view held by Arab nationalists, that the French were, first and last, actuated by mere 'imperialism'—the task appeared to be one not only essential to a lofty French tradition and to enlightened patriotism, but in truth a trusteeship and a civilizing mission; and it was true that the French, while not indifferent to the advantages their country herself might derive, were prepared sincerely to put forward their best efforts, to spend life and treasure, and to face local unpopularity, in order to produce in the mandated territory a régime which they and the world could approve and admire.

To the Arab Muslim majority in Syria–Lebanon the Mandate wore an appearance very different from that presented by the eloquence of French spokesmen. Arab opinion had not indeed been unfavourable, a year earlier, to the acceptance of administrative, technical, military, or financial help from a western Power, as long as this would involve no political control. But the diplomatic and military history of the period, which ended with full and forcible French occupation, had led the Arab leaders progressively to adopt quite other views: the Mandate, they believed now and henceforward, was a device whereby, amid the complacency of western nations, *carte blanche* had been given to France to enter their country by force and to dispose of it to her own advantage. A French refusal to 'unify' the territory or to grant immediate full independence would be hailed not as cautious and benevolent state-building, a first phase indispensable to political education and a conscientious compliance with mandatory duty, but as a self-interested policy of divison and exploitation. This bitter and emotional attitude was of necessity blind to much of the true position, and was unjust to the elements of good sense and of idealism which in fact existed in French policy; but it was irremediably the attitude of the strongest political force in the territory. Elsewhere among the population there was, of course, room for other and varying views of the Mandate imposed upon them. Among the Maronites and most other Uniates there was lively satisfaction and welcome, among other Christians, a divided attitude. In some respectable Muslim circles there was willingness hopefully to await results, and to profit meanwhile by what the French could unquestionably offer. Among the Druzes and Nuṣayris, judgement was generally suspended, until their own place in the new order should become more clear. But of the nationalist attitude there was from the first no doubt.

2. TASKS AND PROBLEMS

The general purposes of the Mandate, and most of the particular political, administrative, economic, and financial tasks that would be involved, were clear at the outset of the French mandatory endeavour. Given only the goodwill, the active help, of the majority of the population, and of its highly influential if not always adequate political leaders, then by collaboration towards agreed ends these purposes could doubtless be achieved; but no energy, devotion, or astuteness on the part of the Mandatory could avail, unless the Syrians felt, and showed, that their interest lay in sharing in the common effort. The problem here was not only that of agreeing forthwith the main objectives of the Mandate and the timing for their achievement; it was that of maintaining an atmosphere of friendliness and mutual confidence, and this could be created only by a French attitude of genuine sympathy with Syrian aspirations, with careful consideration for their highly sensitive *amour propre*. How far would the French effort succeed in this?

Two more specific problems which first confronted the incoming Mandatory were, indeed, both closely connected with the

French prospects of acceptability, or the reverse, in their exercise of the Mandate. One concerned the general structure which France was to devise for the country as a whole, the other concerned the means she would adopt for its day-to-day government. Since the Mandatory's attitude in both regards was made plain from the earliest days of their occupation, it can here, by slight anticipation, be described. The problem of exercising control presented no difficulty to the French administrators; fundamentally unfriendly to Arab nationalism and its impatient aspirations, and dreading a too rapid evolution which might attract envious North African eyes, they believed their duty to include the cautious bestowal of minimum (if inevitably increasing) powers on the Syrians and the Lebanese, while themselves retaining authority on every detail of constitutional and administrative life. Amid all the emphasis of their publicists on the need to educate, guide, and 'assist' the weaker nation, it was felt to be not only a clear right but an evident duty for the Mandatory to retain in every sphere the power to supervise, check, and if need be prohibit, all and every local initiative.[1] The months of 1918–20 already spent in the Western Zone had shown, and the period now opening was to confirm, that while willing to take some account of local preferences and methods, the French conception of a Syrian Administration was perfectionist; they were habitually to exalt administrative efficiency over political acceptability, and in the process to ignore or offend popular feelings which they felt to be trivial or perverse. They preferred sound meticulous government to far less competent self-government. They entered upon their mandatory duties prepared to serve Syria, as they saw it, sincerely and arduously, but strictly upon their own terms. Between such terms and those upon which Syrian goodwill and co-operation could have been gained, there lay a great gulf which twenty uneasy years would fail to bridge.

The French, in spite of post-war exhaustion, avoided from the outset at least one possible ground for criticism: no objector could complain that they failed, by economy or negligence, to provide for Syria an elaborate and costly machinery of French representation and control. This machinery, still embyronic in mid-1920, assumed during succeeding months the form which it was, with slight variations, to retain for twenty years, during which the ubiquity and authority of French officialdom was the leading

[1] M. de Caix at the Permanent Mandates Commission, 5th session, October–November 1923, remarked that 'it was possible that certain minor decisions, especially by provincial authorities, might to some extent escape the control of the mandatory Power. But these could only be exceptions. France remained fully responsible for what was done in the countries entrusted to its care. This responsibility was the very essence of the mandate.'

feature of public life. At the head stood the High Commissioner, responsible[1] to the Ministry of Foreign Affairs for the administration of the Mandate. He acted for the Syrian and Lebanese States in all foreign relations, and carried out, *vis-à-vis* local authorities, all the duties of supervision, initiation, and veto. His extensive headquarters, housed in the Grand Sérail of Beirut, contained his personal offices, those of his Secretary-General,[2] and those of the specialized branches dealing with Intelligence, the press, propaganda, and the Sûreté Générale; the Bureau Diplomatique, the Personnel Branch, the Archives, and the subordinate services were grouped under the Secretary-General. The same headquarters came shortly to include also offices to deal at the highest level with all questions of departmental interest to, or emanating from, the States. Separate services thus existed in the Grand Sérail for Finance, Justice, Public Works, Education, Legislation, Archaeology, Agriculture, Customs, Posts and Telegraphs, Lands, Awqaf, and Public Health; and to these were added Inspectorates for the Mercantile Marine, Monopolies and Mines, a Copyright and Royalties Office, Veterinary Services, and the Control of Concessionary Companies.

These all-French services of control had their counterpart at each stage in the regional organization of the Mandate, with a machinery of complete French control in all areas. At headquarters, the significance of the enormous bureaucratic machine of the Grand Sérail lay in its formidable extent, its cost (borne by the French treasury),[3] its inevitable slowness of movement, and its psychological remoteness from the world of Arab politics and countryside administration. (It forms a curious contrast to the scale of operations of the half-dozen British officials who, from the winter of 1920–1 onwards, formed in Baghdad the office of the High Commissioner for 'Iraq.)[4]

Long before their assumption of authority the French were aware both of the framework of the Turkish organization of the territory as a single, comprehensive system with minimum departures from uniformity, and also of the strongly unifying policy of King Fayṣal and of all Syrian nationalist spokesmen. The loudest cry, from all that was articulate in the population (other than in a part of the minorities), was the cry for Unity;

[1] His specific powers derived from a Decree of 23 November 1920.

[2] This post was divided into two in November 1927.

[3] In theory, recoverable from the territories; but in practice France did not recover these 'civil expenses of the Mandate'.

[4] A keen nationalist, E. Rabbath (*L'Évolution politique*, p. 76), says 'Dans le domaine des impondérables . . . la méthode britannique, souple et élastique, ménage les susceptibilités et rehousse la dignité des peuples mineurs, tous sentiments particulièrement vifs en Orient'.

and to ignore this must be to ignore not only the strongest visible political force, but also the essentially Arab character of the whole population in its language, culture, and way of life. There was in July 1920 a strong, or overwhelming, case for accepting, as a living and valuable asset, the conception of a single Syrian State already evolved under Fayṣal: a State economically viable, supplied with adequate sea outlets, and capable of settling down into a tolerably satisfied régime. Such a State could have been formulated and fostered by the French with infinitely less opposition—that, indeed, only of small, diehard elements—than must greet the solution which in fact they were to adopt; and the minorities' opposition to Unity would be far less formidable if discouraged or overruled from the outset than if allowed full scope, and indeed encouragement, for years before the final and much more painful unification which time, for a number of foreseeable reasons, must and did bring about. The chance to avoid all accusation of 'divide and rule'—a charge always repudiated by official French spokesmen, but admitted with great frankness by unofficial—and those of 'favouring Christian minorities', was freely given to the Mandatory in its earliest days of policy-making; no overriding necessity existed in 1920 to create small, weak, non-viable States which must always depend upon the Mandatory for their existence, and each of which contained a considerable minority dissatisfied because denied unification with Syria. Even in the case of Mount Lebanon, the tiny autonomous enclave created by foreign intervention sixty years earlier, it might well have seemed desirable to limit rather than to extend its necessarily invidious privileges,[1] with a view to the earliest achievement of a uniform status and government for all Syria; and indeed the sole *raison d'être* of Maronite autonomy ceased to exist from the moment when a new and enlightened Government assumed control.

That the French rejected a clearly feasible and popularly demanded policy of unification in favour of partition was due to their evaluation of quite other considerations. For the Maronites, they found themselves unable to resist the emphatic expositions of the aged Patriarch[2] and the numerous Maronite hierarchy, and simultaneously of the strong Jesuit forces interested in Syria, in favour, not only of the perpetuation of the Mountain's privileges, but of the wider, more ambitious Lebanese State which had long been the dream of many Maronites. They were glad to gratify loyal friends, and were persuaded that no harm or outcry would

[1] Which, also, had been abolished by the Turks in 1915 (p. 48).

[2] Guarantees in the required sense were obtained by the Patriarch from MM. Clemenceau and Pichon on his visit to Paris in 1919. The forthcoming foundation of a 'Great Lebanon' was confirmed in a letter from M. Millerand to a Maronite Archbishop, Mgr 'Abdullah Khuri, on 24 August 1920.

result from the incorporation of the non-Christian areas; they were happy to consolidate friendly districts and communities—and to secure for France the best part of the coastline.

Emphasizing the evident differences between the communities—Maronites, Nuṣayris, Druzes, Antioch Turks, bedouin—but ignoring their greater fundamental similarities, the French planners could assert that by their policy they were merely yielding to the actual facts of heterogeneous Syrian society: were preventing the subordination, perhaps the ill-treatment, of weak by stronger elements: were giving the more backward (or, in Lebanon, the more advanced) a better chance of evolution in comparative isolation than they could enjoy as engulfed parts of a Syrian State: and were reserving for them a later day of self-determination when they could, if they wished, join the main body. These were, indeed, arguments of considerable apparent cogency: and with them it could be claimed that the French, in defiance of the politicians, were rightly carrying out the last words of Article 1 of the Mandate:[1] that is, by granting 'local autonomy' to the communities which desired it. It has, indeed, been well and often pointed out, by other than the French, that the protection of minorities was among the fundamental duties of a Mandatory.

Whatever the strength of these arguments, the French decision, adopted with little hesitation and later maintained with tenacity, in favour of a multi-statal structure for Syria, greatly increased Syrian discontent and their own difficulties. The fragmentation of the territory was a convenient, superficially attractive, and not indefensible policy, and it was greeted at the time by the smiles of France's best friends in the territory. But, as time would show, it was a policy deficient in broad wisdom and vision, it ignored the basic facts of Syrian ethnography and culture, and the strength and convictions of the majority community. Thirty years later friends of Lebanon may well regret the bestowal on that fragment of Syria of a never justifiable national status, and may believe that it would today be more advantageously placed as part of a united country, to which it could have made a valuable, stabilizing contribution. And if concessions made in 1920 to Druze or Nuṣayri separatism had been limited to some degree of local privilege, inoffensive to Syrian statesmen, a host of subsequent troubles would have been avoided.

A third problem for solution, or acceptance, was that of confessionalism. The representation of every sect proportionately on all governmental Councils and in public employment was not

[1] 'The Mandatory shall, as far as circumstances permit, encourage local autonomy'; it was, on the contrary, urged by Syrian Muslim statesmen that the 'local' here meant 'Syrian', and not the localism of small enclave communities.

only a usual and applauded feature of Turkish institutions, but was accepted as a matter of course in a society where the privileged religious group took, in a measure, the place of nationality itself in the public mind. Under the Mandate, the system was perpetuated as an acknowledgment of inalienable rights, a recognition of the strongest of social bonds; and in fact loud outcry habitually greeted all seeming departures from it. But a minority of the intelligentsia, claiming more 'modern' views and exalting national over archaic sectarian loyalties, pressed (and today still presses) hotly for the abolition of the confessional basis. The French, in this matter, accepted the facts and loyalties of society as they found them, and could scarcely have done otherwise.

3. PACIFICATION

The territory which France occupied in July 1920 resisted her in arms to an extent quite insignificant when compared with the protests of its politicians. Military resources for serious opposition were lacking; but even when such efforts were made by countryside patriots, applauded in Damascus as heroic, they lacked all substantial support, and were poorly synchronized. They attracted to their service none of the major communities of the territory, very few of the armed forces of ex-King Fayṣal, and yet fewer of his political adherents. The only area where the French found serious trouble was that in which disturbance was the work of a neighbouring Power, Turkey, which stood for anything but Arab nationalism. The task of establishing law and order, as the first condition for mandatory blessings, was therefore of no insuperable difficulty; most areas, and almost all considerable towns, passed easily under the new authorities. These were wisely careful to preserve the familiar forms of government and to maintain, *faute de mieux*, the great majority of existing officials.

In the northern frontier Zone, no peace was in sight. The French troops in Cilicia were hard pressed from the moment when the armistice of 30 May 1920 lost its effect; isolated detachments were surrounded, communications cut, and the re-establishment of traffic between Adana and Mersin was achieved only by a difficult operation which culminated in a successful engagement at Yenija on 27 July. A fortnight later, a mere fifty miles from Aleppo, a savage attack was launched by Turkish irregulars on a Senegalese post guarding a railway viaduct; the post succumbed, the garrison were butchered. Meanwhile the fortunes of war around 'Ayntab, to the north-east, entered a new phase. Late in July the Turks attacked the French force encamped near the city; but a successful defence permitted a *sortie* to be made, and the troops lately besieged could join those advancing under Colonel Andréa. Within a few days the combined forces had surrounded 'Ayntab and its Turkish garrison, and could act as supply centre for a wide area of detached posts. In mid-November part of the division of General Goubeau joined the force, and the siege could be pressed; but this operation was weakened by the need to detach troops for operations south of Aleppo (p. 121), and to deal with Turkish reinforcing columns. Nevertheless, pressure on 'Ayntab was maintained during the severe weather of early 1921, and the Turkish garrison surrendered on 8 February: an important success for the French forces, well timed to correspond with the opening of the London Conference[1] later in the month.

The resulting lull in local fighting made easier the Agreement of 20 October 1921 between M. Franklin-Bouillon, the French diplomat who visited Ankara, and the Kamalist Government.[2] It was followed by the withdrawal of French forces from Cilicia (accompanied by thousands of Christian refugees) behind a new frontier which was still more favourable to the Turks than that provisionally agreed in London. It involved the abandonment of the districts (previously within the Aleppo wilayet) of 'Ayntab, Rum Qal'a, Killis, Mar'ash, and Urfa, and of the whole Baghdad Railway along the south face of Asia Minor.[3] The sanjaq of Alexandretta–Antioch, with its partly Turkish population, was to remain in Syria under a special régime.[4]

Neither this Agreement, however, nor the subsequent conclusion of peace between France and Turkey[5] secured tranquil conditions in northernmost Syria. The French complained of incessant raids on Syrian villages, carried out partly by villagers

[1] Following the Allied occupation of Istanbul in March 1920, and the move of the Kamalist Government to Ankara, British policy continued (with a loyal but self-damaging persistence) to back the Greeks in Asia Minor, with the increasingly tepid support of France who rightly saw her interest to lie in an understanding with Turkey. At the London Conference M. Briand, behind the backs of the British, reached an understanding with the Turks for the establishment of a new boundary with Syria, and for the grant of economic privileges to France. These terms were rejected by the Grand National Assembly; but they stopped Franco-Turkish overt hostilities in Cilicia, and prepared the way for the Franklin-Bouillon Agreement.

[2] This Agreement (Cmds. 1556 and 1570, of 1921), following a period of mutual criticism between the British and French over their respective policies towards Turkey, was condemned by the former as highly improper: in fact, as a separate peace with the enemy. It was no less severely criticized by circles in France who saw in it a needless sacrifice, by victors to vanquished, of a valuable province capable of enriching France and defending Syria.

[3] Except the sector where the railway is deflected southward so as to touch Aleppo: that is, between Maydan Akbas and Choban Bey.

[4] The Turks of Antioch–Alexandretta were to have 'all facilities for the development of their culture', and Turkish was to be an official language; see pp. 126, 211.

[5] Armistice of Mudania, 11 October 1922: Treaty of Lausanne, signed 24 July 1923, effective from 6 August 1924.

and tribesmen from the Turkish side, but partly also by gangs of Turkish irregular troops or *chetehs*. These created insecurity almost continuously from 1922 to mid-1924 on the frontier and indeed deep into Syria, where unrest and violence were encouraged by Turkish example if not initiative. Such acts of aggression called for defence works and for constant activity by French aircraft, locally-raised militia companies, and the Syrian Gendarmerie. General Weygand (p. 132) complained that false or exaggerated accounts reached the European press; but the situation was in fact highly embarrassing, the Turkish attitude malevolent, and regular officers of their Army sometimes involved. The most serious of the affrays was that of Ḥajjilar in the early spring of 1924, when regular French troops were called in. Thereafter, the Turkish attitude improved, and steps were taken to patrol the frontier and erect observation posts.

In the steppe-desert of eastern Syria, no early attempt could be made to impose order on the nomads, who enjoyed a congenial anarchy until the first camel (*méhariste*) companies were formed during 1921, under French officers. Dayr al-Zur was visited by a French mission late in 1920, and in June 1921 a small detachment was established there. This was attacked two months later by tribal forces of the ʻUqaydat. The situation was restored by a column from Aleppo, which compelled surrender and the restoration of loot; but men of other tribes remained in the field until, after further and costly operations, peace and general submission were secured. General de Lamothe visited Dayr by air in October and received full surrender. The incorporation of the Euphrates area in the sphere of government was by December 1921 provisionally complete, and the presence of French officers, with the *méhariste* companies, kept a light administration in existence. Ḥasaja,[1] then a small village, was occupied in May 1922, and in that year and the next north-eastern Syria, including the Bec-de-Canard, was assiduously patrolled. The *méhariste* companies met, however, frequent opposition from the Kurdish[2] and mixed inhabitants of this peripheral territory, as well as from invaders from Turkey and from the Shamiya bedouin; a patrol which visited Baḥandur in July 1923, following the murder of the local Qa'immaqam, was attacked while temporarily divided, and lost nearly all its effectives. Good order was maintained in the towns except when, in April 1922, politically-inspired disorders consequent on the Crane visit (p. 147) broke out in Dayr and Jarablus.

The situation in parts of the Aleppo area was, in the autumn of 1920, widely disturbed. Armed Turkish bands supported

[1] Correctly, Ḥasaka: French version, Hassetché.

[2] Kurdish infiltration into this area dated from before 1914.

those formed from malcontent or marauding elements among the local population; anti-French propaganda was active; and the north Syrian nationalist leader Ibrahim Bey Ḥananu, a man of authority and attainments,[1] could place himself at the head of former or fugitive Turkish soldiery and concert operations with the regular troops of Badri Bey. The capture of the French post at Jisr al-Shaghur roused the districts south-west of Aleppo, and a threat to Idlib and Ma'arrat al-Nu'man, and even to Aleppo seemed imminent. General de Lamothe collected, with difficulty, the material for two columns which formed at Idlib and Ḥammam; a third was planned but did not materialize. The northern column, involved in fierce fighting with Ḥananu's followers, disengaged successfully; its constituent of Syrian gendarmes deserted. Through difficult country, and intermittently attacked and counter-attacking, the column secured Ṭallina, Ḥarim, and finally Jisr al-Shaghur. Their positions here were violently attacked during Christmas week; but a relieving column effected junction on 29 December, and the major military task was at an end. Order was gradually restored during the spring and summer of 1921 while insurgent forces melted and disappeared; but conditions around Aleppo were still unsafe, and local or Turkish bands (supplied by well-wishers in the city) were still active until the autumn. Ibrahim Ḥananu, escaping capture, made his way to Transjordan in July; he was arrested by the British, handed to the French, brought to trial—and set at liberty. The normal restlessness of the Aleppo tribes made its contribution to disorder; the Muwali, who winter athwart the Ḥamah–Aleppo road, rose in the late spring of 1921, attacked sedentary tribesmen, and cut the railway. The ensuing operations by a French column were of unusual violence, involving the burning of tribal settlements, the driving off of flocks, and severe casualties. The same tribes were again disturbing the peace by mutual raiding two years later.

In the wild hills of the Nuṣayri (or 'Alawi) sectaries, French control had never since 1918 extended far beyond the coast and main road. The overthrow of King Fayṣal's Government increased the ill will of the Nuṣayri protagonist, Shaykh Ṣaliḥ al-'Ali, and his liaison with Ḥananu and the Turks. His bold attacks on French posts called in April 1921 for military operations against him. These involved the movement of two columns from north to south, beginning in early May. The campaign was marked by opposition which included a number of costly engagements spread over two months. The operations, sustained by the personal authority of Shaykh Ṣaliḥ, decreased in scale during the later

[1] In Turkish times, a senior official (*maktubchi*) at wilayet headquarters; he was destined to become the outstanding nationalist leader of northern Syria.

summer of 1921, and virtually ended with the surrender of their leader in October. Thereafter the *Territoire des Alaouites* was afflicted by no more than normal episodes of lawlessness. The appearance late in 1923 of a sixteen-year-old 'prophet' in a Nuṣayri village, with supernatural claims and reported miracles, led to his temporary detention for fear that the enthusiasm of his quickly-growing following might lead to fanatical violence; but he proved docile, and no disturbances followed his release.

Within the Great Lebanon, disorder was isolated and local. In the towns its inspiration was normally political, as repeated episodes or demonstrations showed; on the roads it was mere banditry, of which a series of bad cases under a notorious leader, Mulḥim Qasim, were reported from the Biqa' in 1924: and as between villages it represented a regrettable survival of the inter-community violence of former days. The outbreak of Druze-Christian fighting in the Shuf area in the spring of 1923 led to many casualties and called for vigorous government intervention, with the establishment of a special court to try offenders.

In the extreme south, a period of indecision in the Jabal al-Duruz followed the retirement of King Fayṣal, whom the local clan leaders had accepted as overlord; and these could not be indifferent to propaganda which reached them from 'Sharifian' sources, or, more precisely, from the entourage of the Amir 'Abdullah, who in January 1921 had advanced northward from the Ḥijaz into Transjordan with the declared intention of avenging his brother. Such plans were effectively forbidden by the British, who filled the vacuum in south-eastern Syria by installing him as Amir of Transjordan, subject to their own Mandate and to his good behaviour. Nevertheless, enough threat of invasion by tribal forces from that area, and irritant intrigues by Syrian exiles, was in the air to call for French vigilance on the southern borders, the mission of aircraft, and the preparation of counter-measures. But a more restrained attitude[1] of the Amir (though not always of all his subjects) and the opening of friendly French negotiations with the Druze leaders averted the danger, and French troops could enter and garrison the Jabal without opposition in mid-summer 1921. In the adjacent Ḥawran a slight show of French military power was necessitated by initial unrest from July to October 1920, with Ibrahim al-Ḥariri as leader of a would-be Ḥawrani rebellion. But the Druzes and other neighbours remained unaffected, and no more resulted than three months of confused non-government and some railway-line destruction. An

[1] The accusation by some French critics that the Amir 'Abdullah was permitted, or even encouraged, by Great Britain in his anti-French activity at this (or any other) stage is entirely baseless.

attempt to assassinate General Gouraud on 23 June 1921 at Qunayṭara, which cost the life of his interpreter, was the work of isolated fanatics (believed to be Lebanese Mutawila) in an otherwise tranquil countryside. An abortive rising in 1922 in the Jabal 'Amil, of southern Lebanon, under Kamil Bey al-As'ad was easily suppressed.

4. THE STATES OF THE LEVANT

The constitutional plans of the Mandatory were put into effect a bare six weeks after the entry into Damascus. On 30 August 1920 the High Commissioner published a Decree establishing the new State of Great Lebanon; and the following day witnessed a picturesque ceremony of inauguration, conducted with eloquence[1] by General Gouraud. A second Decree was issued containing a provisional Statute.[2]

The new State was to be governed by a French official,[3] assisted by a representative Advisory Council nominated by the High Commissioner. Great Lebanon was divided into four sanjaqs (North Lebanon, Biqa', Mount Lebanon, South Lebanon), containing twelve qadhas; the major municipalities of Beirut and Tripoli had independent status. The territory was thus, besides the original sanjaq of Lebanon, to include the half-Christian, half-Muslim city of Beirut: most of the sanjaq of Tripoli (natural gateway to Syria) with its overwhelming Muslim majority: the whole of the fertile Biqa' where the Sunni, Mutawalli, and Druze villagers were nearly double the Christian: and the hilly and coastal districts inland from Tyre and Sidon, where Christians formed about two-fifths of a predominantly Mutawalli population. The new State has lost therefore, as compared with the old sanjaq, all its homogeneity; the newly included districts were in some cases Muslim-dominated, in others were shared in various proportions between Muslims and Uniate or Orthodox Christians. No single area boasted a uniform population, and by no manipulation of frontiers could the tangle of interlaced minorities be unravelled. The Maronites still formed the largest single community, but were less than half of the whole; they were followed, in order of total strength, by the Sunni Muslims, Greek Orthodox, Mutawila, and Druzes, all scattered in residence and varied in political colouring.

[1] The High Commissioner's reference in his speech to the Government of King Fayṣal as 'la puissance néfaste qui prétendait vous asservir' seems a needless affront to Syrian opinion; but he spoke as a staunch Catholic to Catholics.

[2] *Oriente Moderno*, April 1922, pp. 654 f. (hereafter referred to as *Or. Mod.*)

[3] The first Governor was Captain Trabaud, a naval officer; he was relieved in April 1923 by M. Privat Aubouard.

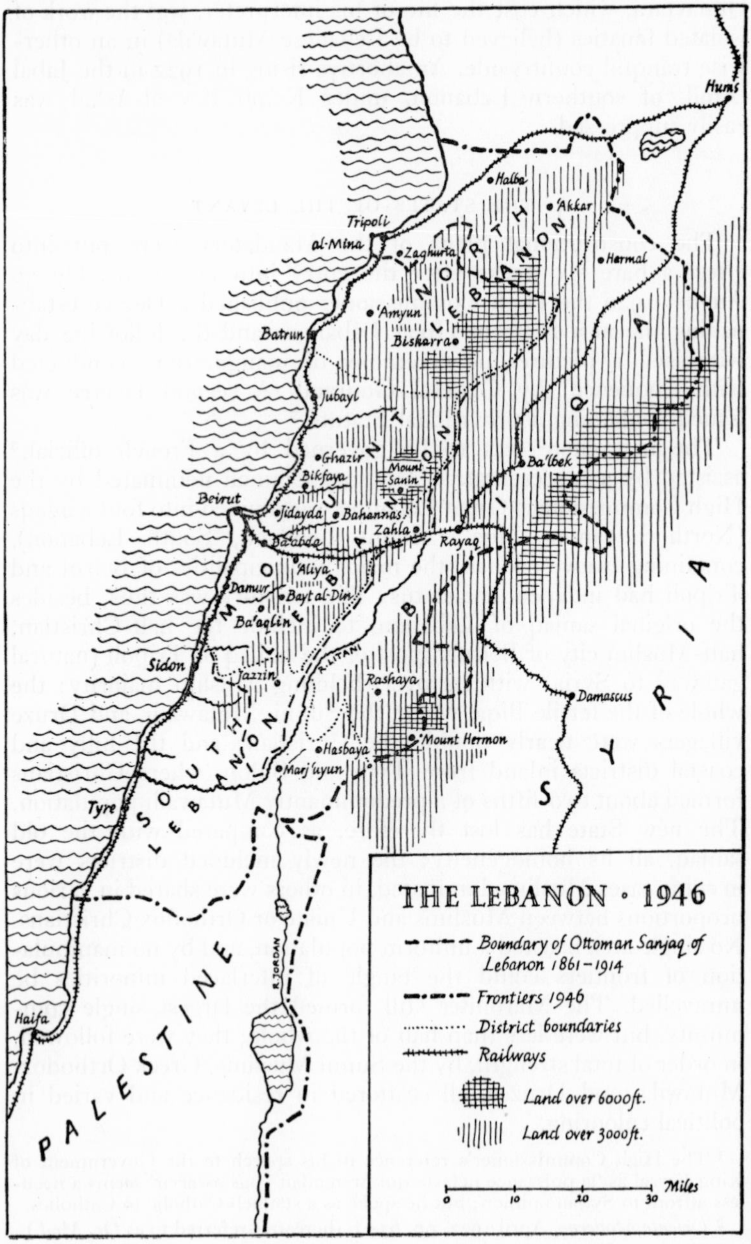
THE LEBANON · 1946
Boundary of Ottoman Sanjaq of Lebanon 1861-1914
Frontiers 1946
District boundaries
Railways
Land over 6000ft.
Land over 3000ft.
0 10 20 30 Miles
Hums
Halba
'Akkar
Tripoli
al-Mina
Zaghurta
Hermal
'Amyun
Batrun
Bisharra
NORTH LEBANON
Jubayl
Ghazir
Mount Sanin
Bikfaya
Beirut
Jidayda
Bahannas
Zahla
Rayaq
Ba'lbek
Ba'abda
'Aliya
Damur
Bayt al-Din
Ba'aqlin
MOUNT LEBANON
BIQA'
Sidon
Jazzin
R. LITANI
Rashaya
Damascus
Mount Hermon
Hasbaya
Marj'uyun
Tyre
SOUTH LEBANON
SYRIA
R. JORDAN
Haifa
PALESTINE

The Governor was to preside over a full range of state services, each administered by a Lebanese official nominated by the High Commissioner and supervised by a French Adviser and technical helpers. In each sanjaq the Mutaṣarrif was accompanied by an Adviser, and at each sanjaq and qaḍha headquarters were to be found French inspectors, technicians, and Intelligence Officers. The old Administrative Council was revived in each sanjaq, but on a basis of nomination instead of election.

Thus inaugurated, the new and heterogeneous State, to the delight of some of its subjects and the consternation of others, began its constitutional and administrative career under the high favour and meticulous supervision of the Mandatory.

Elsewhere, units similar in form were being established. The coastal and mountain country of the Nuṣayri or 'Alawi villagers, formerly the two sanjaqs[1] of Ladhqiya and Ṭarṭus, was by Decree of 2 September formed into a single separate 'Territory'.[2] The justification for its detachment from the main body of Syria lay, if anywhere, in the backwardness of these mountaineers, the fear of their oppression by Sunni rulers, their actual distinctness in religion, and the expressed desire of most of their own spokesmen (encouraged, no doubt, by resident French officials), to be granted a separate and protected status; and it was, in fact, probable that they would, under direct French administration, enjoy initially a better chance of material progress. Nevertheless, all the objections to the creation of non-viable and dissident enclaves (p. 117) apply with full force to this erection of the 'Alawi country into a separate unit of government: a unit capable of permanence only under specific French protection, and one whose reintegration with Syria must grow yearly more difficult. Moreover, the 'Alawi hillmen had by no great margin the majority in the Territory; the Sunni and Greek Orthodox landowners and town-dwellers could boast some two-thirds of their numerical strength, far exceeded them in wealth and education—and were, almost to a man, strongly in favour of union with Syria.

The administration of the Territory, since trained officials of local origin scarcely existed, was necessarily one of direct French rule, even though the forms and Councils[3] of the Turkish (and Occupation) Government were retained. The earliest French Governors were all military officers,[4] and the equally military

[1] The new Territory was enlarged by the detachment of the two qaḍhas of Ṣafita and Ḥuṣn from Tripoli sanjaq, and that of 'Umraniya from Aleppo.

[2] It became a 'State', on 1 July 1922.

[3] These were constituted by nomination on strictly confessional lines.

[4] Colonel Niéger, followed for a time by General Billotte, under whom the main pacification took place.

Intelligence Officers were ubiquitous at every out-station. Once pacification had been completed, the Territory settled down to a régime of zealous colonial administration, and unquiet political disunity.

The decision to govern by dividing was applied no less to the former Kingdom of inland Syria. The old wilayet of Aleppo (its northern frontier still stormy and unsettled) became by Decree of 1 September 1920 the separate State of Aleppo: a measure the more surprising since Aleppo–Damascus form so compactly the main body of inland Syria, but seeking justification, presumably, in the jealousy often observable between them. At the head of the new state was placed an ex-Major-General of the Turkish army, Kamil Pasha al-Qudsi. He was supported by a Council of Government composed of heads of services, by the usual Administrative Council, and by a Délégué of the High Commissioner with a staff of experts and specialists. The out-station administration maintained with but slight changes the existing administrative units and procedures, but with the addition of vigilant and authoritative Intelligence Officers at the more considerable stations. The qaḍha of Alexandretta was promoted to the status of a sanjaq, with the attachment to it of the qaḍhas of Antioch and Jisr al-Shaghur, and two frontier naḥiyas; and the new sanjaq, while placed under Aleppo, was given from the first a measure of administrative separateness[1] in view of its frontier position and Turkish element. The sanjaq of Dayr al-Zur was also placed nominally under Aleppo.

Damascus, after the first uneasy weeks of occupation, received by Decree a Statute similar to that of Aleppo. A Syrian Governor, Ḥaqqi Bey al-'Adhm, was placed at the head, supported by a French Délégué and by the usual Councils and staffs of advisers, experts, and Intelligence Officers. Though the forms of Syrian executive authority were partly observed, almost the entirety of effective power belonged to the Délégué, and behind him to the High Commissioner; these exercised all legislative, financial, and administrative control above the levels of mere formality or routine.

While these States were coming into existence, to the chagrin of all who saw in them only disunion and dependence when union and independence were sought, negotiations were proceeding with the spokesmen of the ruling families in the Jabal al-Duruz. A meeting at Qanawat was attended by Colonel Catroux in November 1920, and bases of agreement were reduced to treaty form[2] and

[1] This 'special régime' was accorded even *before* the Franco-Turkish Agreement of 20 October 1921.

[2] *Or. Mod.*, September 1925, pp. 472 f.

signed by M. de Caix on 4 March 1921. These amicable negotiations and Treaty, which contrast remarkably with the mere imposition of régimes in the other States, seemed likely to lead to a relatively liberal form of control; the Druzes, under an elected local Governor, Salim Pasha al-Aṭrash, and an annual Congress with a permanent Committee, were to form a unit specifically distinct from the State of Damascus, to control (under French advice) their own administration and finances, and to enjoy their traditional right of carrying arms. A French Administrative Adviser was to act as a link with the Délégué at Damascus. Druze 'independence' was formally announced in March 1922, and steps were taken to delimit the Druze-Syrian boundary. A French garrison had already moved into the Jabal in June 1921.

Thus, subject to the results of war or diplomacy on the northern frontier, and to pacification elsewhere, the Mandated Territory emerged, early in 1921, into the strangely fragmented pattern described. Great Lebanon, a complex of heterogeneous accretions, was a State; so also were the relatively uniform units of Damascus and Aleppo. From the latter, Alexandretta was partially detached with a special administrative régime; from the former, the Jabal al-Duruz had been completely severed. The country of the Nuṣayri villagers, with its Muslim and Christian seaside towns, had become the separate 'Territory of the 'Alawis'. The desert tribes and the remoter north-east could be considered as still French 'military territory'.

But it was not intended to leave the new States either devoid of representative institutions, or completely dissociated from each other; the first would have been both illiberal and against local usage, the second would have clashed too blatantly with pan-Syrian sentiment. The nominated Administrative Councils were never meant, therefore, to persist; to be even as liberal as their Turkish predecessors they must rest upon some sort of representative basis. This called for elections, and these for a census. For the Lebanon, the High Commissioner decreed[1] on 8 March 1922 that an elected Representative Council should be set up, and a few days later enacted[2] an electoral procedure. The census produced[3] was highly imperfect, for the reasons (those of concealment, misunderstanding, falsification, conjecture, and motives peculiar to the communities) which in such countries always prevent accurate personal registration; but, *faute de mieux*, elections for the Council were held during April 1922, though not without the declaration of a boycott by many of the Muslims and a thousand mutual

[1] *Or. Mod.*, May 1922, pp. 710 ff. [2] Ibid., pp. 723 ff.

[3] It gave totals, in Great Lebanon, of 330,000 Christians, 275,000 Muslims, 43,000 Druzes, 3,500 Jews, and 20,000 Syrians and foreigners.

accusations of pressure and intimidation. The Council met first on 25 May 1922, the distribution of seats being on confessional lines.[1] The first President was the veteran Maronite politician and official Ḥabib Pasha al-Sa'd, with a Vice-President and secretaries of other sects. The part of leader of the opposition was played by Fu'ad Arsalan, a Lebanese *évolué* of a leading Druze family.

In the other States, progress towards representative institutions was slower, and the preliminary census[2] not more accurate. Soon after the arrival of General Weygand as successor of Gouraud in April 1923, a popular and hopeful appointment, the High Commissioner's Decree[3] for elected Councils in the States was issued in June 1923; and after elections, from which there were wholesale abstentions in protest, with shutting of bazaars and emptying of streets, the Councils met in Ladhqiya, Aleppo, and Damascus in November 1923, not without demonstrations of protest, threatened boycott, and bitter criticism of the Councils and their derisory powers. That of Ladhqiya still contained a high proportion of nominated members; the other Councils were chosen by the familiar double-stage procedure of primary and secondary elections, and all included Deputies, for their two-year term of office, were in such proportions as to secure the due representation of all communities.[4] It was claimed in French circles that a great majority of Francophile deputies were returned.

The Representative Councils were, in the eyes of their French mentors, a first means of associating the people with the conduct of their public affairs—a 'première ébauche de régime parlementaire'.[5] The Councils were free to discuss matters referred to them by the French authorities, could pass resolutions on matters of health and public works, could offer suggestions on any subject within their purview, could discuss their budget; and no Decree affecting their State was to be published without their previous cognizance. The facts, however, appeared quite otherwise to the local political world. The nationalists pronounced the elections to have been improperly conducted, with undue exercise of French influence in favour of 'tame' candidates and with a wide resulting gap between the voices of the 'representatives' and those of the authentic public. The Councils moreover were without powers; they could initiate nothing, their views could be (and commonly

[1] Christians 16 seats (Maronites 10, Greek Catholics 2, Orthodox 4), Muslims 11 (Sunnis 6, Mutawila 5), Druzes 2, lesser denominations, *en bloc*, 1.

[2] It gave totals of 1,019,000 Sunnis, 8,800 Shi'is, 190,000 'Alawis, 47,000 Druzes, 14,000 Isma 'ilis, 10,600 Jews, 167,600 Christians, and 15,000 foreigners (including Lebanese).

[3] *Or. Mod.*, January 1924, pp. 2–14.

[4] Voting was not, however, 'by rite' but so arranged that 'chaque électeur, quelle que soit sa réligion, vote pour tous les députés sans distinction'.

[5] High Commissioner's Report for 1923–4.

were) corrected, reversed, or ignored by the French, and they possessed no power of legislation other than on petty issues; and they were a thousand miles from the spirit of (for instance) the Anglo-French Declaration of November 1918, or of the often-quoted Article 22. These shortcomings did not, however, prevent the Councils from showing considerable vigour in debate or even from affording, at times, a platform for outspoken views critical of French policy;[1] sometimes indeed, by their evident lack of experience, they seemed to confirm the French contention that greater powers could not at present be wisely allowed.

In the interrelations of the States, their mutual isolation was not intended to persist; the question was rather how soon, and in what form, to allow some degree of joint constitutional life. General Gouraud (or M. de Caix)[2] had from early days envisaged a Federation of States, as the natural compromise between rival conceptions; and it was easy to find, in the expressed views of 'moderate' notables, some support for the establishment of such a structure. In June 1921 the High Commissioner unofficially announced his intentions, and a year later issued a Decree[3] establishing a Federal Council for the three States of Aleppo, Damascus, and the 'Alawis. The Lebanon and the Druzes were significantly omitted; the former through its Council proposed instead the negotiation, by the High Commissioner's mediation, of formal Agreements between itself and the other States. The Federal Council of Syria was to consist of five members from the Administrative Council of each State, and these at their first meeting elected as President of the Council an outstanding notable of Antioch—more Turk, indeed, than Arab in descent, career, and language—Ṣubḥi Bey Barakat. The Council, after two formal meetings, met first with elected members emanating from the statal Representative Councils at Aleppo on 12 December 1923. Certain of the State services, it was resolved, were to be 'federalized', initially those of Justice, State Domains, Land Registry, the Court of Cassation, the Awqaf, and inter-State Public Works, to which were later added, at least in intention, the Gendarmerie, Higher Education, and Posts and Telegraphs; the unification of most of these did not in fact, however, proceed far or did not begin. Resolutions were passed to give the three constituent States the reduced status of wilayets, to send a delegation to

[1] For instance, in the Lebanese Council, over questions of gambling, of archaeological research by foreigners, of the rights granted to the Radio-Orient Telecommunications Company, and to the Régie des Tabacs.

[2] Decisions on political matters were generally believed to be those of M. de Caix as Secretary-General, the two High Commissioners whom he served being both Generals unversed in such matters.

[3] *Or. Mod.*, II, pp. 283–7.

Geneva (which the High Commissioner did not permit), and to abolish the Régie des Tabacs (p. 18 n.). It was the statutory function of the Federal Council, in its two meetings annually,[1] to deal with its own budget, to consider legislation common to all three States, and to debate any issues that the States desired to bring before it. Federal Directors[2] of the shared Departments were appointed.

Federation, except in its omission of the Lebanon, could be regarded as a progressive step, and was hailed by French apologists as the true answer to Syria's problem. But in fact it pleased no one, never came fully to life, and looked quite unlikely to supply an effective government. To the States of Damascus and Aleppo it was unsatisfying; their leaders, except for a separatist party at the northern capital, demanded full integration, not a secondary status under a nerveless superior body. The Federal Council itself lost no time in voting its own replacement by a unitary system. The 'Alawis were, as ever, disunited; the Nuṣayri population[3] cherished its special status, and claimed to prefer attachment to the Lebanon itself rather than to Syria, while the Sunni Muslims and many Christians called for all-Syrian unity. The 'Alawi Representative Council twice in 1924, by majority, resolved its withdrawal from the Federation. These moves weighted the scales again in favour of a policy of plain dismemberment. General Weygand, on a visit to Ladhqiya in June 1924, sounded the knell of Federation, and was to follow it by a Decree of 5 December 1924 establishing a unitary State of Syria, from which Great Lebanon, the 'Alawis, and the Druzes were all omitted. The new State, which came into existence on the first day of 1925 (and in the process of birth suffered a loss of territory in favour of both Lebanon and the 'Alawis) was to keep its form and boundaries (and its grievances) for the next twelve years.

The Decree[4] establishing the State prescribed Damascus as the capital. A President was to be elected by the Representative Council, and a Cabinet of five ministers appointed by him. He had power to nominate all senior officials, subject always to the agreement of the High Commissioner.[5] French advisers were

[1] They were held in December 1923, and April and December 1924. A permanent Federation Office dealt with current business between meetings.

[2] Among these, Ḥasan 'Izzat Pasha, an ex-Turkish General: Muḥammad 'Ali Bey al-'Abid (p. 192): 'Izzat Pasha: and Naṣri Bakhash, director of Economic Affairs at Aleppo.

[3] The census taken in 1923 showed a less decisive Nuṣayri majority than the French had earlier supposed; the figures, in thousands, were 'Alawis 101, Sunnis 94, Isma'ilis 5, Christians 34.

[4] Text in *Or. Mod.*, January 1925, pp. 3 ff.

[5] The appointments of lesser officials were subject always to the concurrence of the Délégué.

attached to all high local officials. The Representative Council—in effect an amalgam of the Councils of the two constituent states—was given powers which wholly failed to satisfy the local political world; it could debate (but could not render executory without the President's and High Commissioner's counter-signature) the Budget, fiscal proposals, draft legislation,[1] and other matters. The High Commissioner maintained a Délégué[2] at Damascus, and Délégués-Adjoints at Aleppo, Dayr al-Zur, and Alexandretta. The territory of the State was divided into one wilayet (Aleppo) and six sanjaqs, Damascus, Ḥumṣ, Ḥamah, Alexandretta, Dayr al-Zur, Ḥawran. Out-station administration followed the familiar lines. The Aleppo wilayet, for its greater wealth and seniority, enjoyed a privileged position in the spending of its own revenues; the Alexandretta sanjaq, now independent of Aleppo and furnished with a Statute of its own, fell directly under the State of Syria.

The re-separated State of the 'Alawis[3] retained its French Governor,[4] assisted by a French and local staff and its Representative Council. Its directorates, of Justice, Posts, and Customs, all administered by Frenchmen, depended on Beirut. In the Jabal al-Duruz, predominantly isolationist in feeling (and an asylum for the criminals of all neighbouring areas), the governorship of Salim al-Aṭrash was made uneasy by the indiscipline of the other Aṭrash leaders, notably the Amir Sulṭan. The latter, offended by the arrest of a criminal[5] who sought (in his absence) asylum at his village of Quraya, raised a force of his followers in July 1922, and tried to rally the countryside; but he attracted no major support, his house was bombed from the air, and a small French column was sent to remove the arrested prisoner. The column, at first thrown back, was later reinforced and restored the position; and Sulṭan, having entered Transjordan and found no welcome there, was thankful to make his submission at Suwayda in May 1923. A severe fine was imposed on the Jabal. Salim Pasha resigned his charge, was persuaded to resume it, but died in September of that year; and the Druze Council preferred, amid all the Aṭrash candidates for the post, to appoint the French

[1] But in fact the High Commissioner continued to issue, often without prior consultation, the bulk of new legislation.

[2] The first of these was M. Schoeffler, of the Colonial Service, till July 1925: then M. Aubouard till December 1925, followed by M. Pierre Alype until, in July 1927, he was succeeded by M. Delelée-Desloges.

[3] Text of the Decree in *Or. Mod.*, January 1925, p. 4.

[4] General Billotte was succeeded as Governor in 1922 by M. Léon Cayla, of the Colonial Service, and he in 1925 by M. Schoeffler, who remained in that post for twelve years.

[5] A Lebanese Shi'i implicated in the attempt on General Gouraud in May 1921.

Adviser, Major Trenga, as temporary Governor. He was succeeded, by the same choice, and no less provisionally at first, by Captain Carbillet,[1] of whose régime in the Jabal more will be said later (p. 152 ff.). The Druze State, equipped now with an elected Council and free of attachment to the State of Syria, could enjoy outward peace until July 1925.

5. PHASES OF GOVERNMENT

Simultaneously with these attempts at constitutional advance the internal administration of each State devolved upon the large body of local officials who worked willingly enough for the new régime, and their very numerous French colleagues. With the eradication of some members of pre-existing officialdom on grounds of inadequacy, the administrative machine began to operate, under the meticulous thoroughness of French control. At each main headquarters, the Délégué and his staff were all-powerful; at lesser centres the Délégué-Adjoint, and the sometimes over-zealous Intelligence Officers,[2] dominated the local administration and the public. The efforts of all these were effective during these early years in improving perceptibly the level of Turkish or 'Sharifian' administration; but the duplication of channels, language, and methods, and the looming presence of the heavily-staffed High Commission itself, made also for delay and frustration. The quality of the French officials, of whom few spoke or learnt Arabic, was variable; many were of the highest class, many more were full of goodwill but deficient in specialized knowledge, some imported too much of the methods of West Africa, some failed in tact, a few were by any standards inadequate. The average quality, if sometimes judged too harshly by many Syrians and by some Frenchmen, was certainly not the best that France could have produced. At their head, General Gouraud as High Commissioner for three years gave every proof of his highmindedness and admirable intentions, if with an undisguised leaning to men of his own religion. He was succeeded in April 1923 by his exact contemporary,[3] General Maxime Weygand, a military commander of equal eminence, and superior as an impartial administrator and statesman. General Weygand, no less a Catholic, held his position with distinction for twenty months, as acceptably to Syrians as was permitted by the French policy

[1] Described by Fabre-Luce (*Deuil au Levant*, p. 93) as 'un prognathe, avec des yeux fixes, des cheveux plats et noirs'.

[2] These were officers of the French Regular Army, seconded for these mainly civilian duties, but paid from French funds.

[3] Both were born in 1867.

which he carried out, until his abrupt supersession by an officer of entirely different type, and eleven years older.

Of the administrative achievement of these years, which was considerable and in its aggregate forms the best defence of French mandatory policy, something may suitably be said at this stage, notably the foundations now being laid in matters of legislation, finance, justice, and the armed forces.

In the first-mentioned of these, little call was made upon Syrian collaboration. Though in theory the High Commissioner legislated by Decree only on matters common to all states, or particularly concerning the Mandatory as such, in practice laws and regulations on every subject were the close concern of the legal branch of his headquarters. Local resentment was felt at the scarcity of consultation with Syrian opinion; there were cases indeed when the absence of such consultation led to the non-application of a Decree as impracticable. Of the abundant supply of new decrees and regulations by the States, no part was executory without the French counter-signature.

In the financial field, the French initial task was of particular difficulty. The expenses of the High Commission and its services, and of the French forces, devolved naturally upon the French treasury; but it was necessary meanwhile to render each of the States viable,[1] to clear up an infinity of wartime problems, to control spending, and to strengthen the means of assessment and collection of revenue. The task of the French financial advisers was especially arduous. A Decree of January 1921 created a General Budget for all the States. Its revenues were those of the Common Interests, from which it paid the costs of the Services, certain other interstatal charges, and the subventions to the States' budgets. The insistence of the Lebanon on being excluded from pan-Syrian organization led, however, to the early replacement of the General Budget by other, not dissimilar, arrangements whereby certain of the joint services became financially autonomous while the bulk was covered by two *ad hoc* Budgets. The whole financial as well as administrative operation of the Common Interests was reserved for the High Commission and its dependent services. A joint Lebanese-Syrian Commission having failed, in September 1923, to agree on a division of the Common Interests surplus as between the States, the High Commissioner ruled that 47 per cent. should go to the Lebanon and 53 to the Syrian States—a decision, inevitably, acceptable to neither.

The State budgets, in their first year, had no hope of self-sufficiency; they could, even with the aid of the Common Interests surplus, be balanced only by a substantial direct grant from the

[1] As from 1 January 1921, when their independent financial life began.

High Commission. From 1922, however, all States, except those of the 'Alawis and Alexandretta, were able by rigorous economy to balance their budgets without help from the French treasury. In 1923 and thereafter they were able not only to balance unaided, but to place excess sums to a reserve account for major works and emergencies. In spite of the permissive terms of Article 15 of the Mandate, the Mandatory took no steps towards recovering its expenditure directed to the 'organization of the administration, development of natural resources, or execution of public works'. These considerable expenses, and those of the French War Office, were the subject of frequent reference in the French Chamber and press.

The system of direct taxation, uniform[1] throughout the territory, with minor local variations, was preserved intact in spite of its unsatisfactory features. Tax-farming of the tithes was, however, discontinued, and a lump sum imposed instead on every village. Certain fiscal peculiarities of the old Lebanon were brought into line. Conservatism among the public was an obstacle to the smooth introduction of the new currency (p. 98), but it became as from January 1921 the sole legal tender. Following the franc, it depreciated rapidly in these years, became unpopular because unstable, and was even accused,[2] without justice, of being an instrument of French exploitation. The position of the Banque de Syrie (p. 98) was regularized for a term of fifteen years from April 1924, in spite of loud protests by the Representative Councils and the political world.[3]

The important Customs administration, greatest of the Common Interests, was supervised at every level by French experts. The rate of duty, previously 11 per cent. on imports, was raised in 1924, for most[4] commodities, to 15 per cent. for goods originating from League members, the U.S.A., or Turkey, but 30 per cent. for all others. The administration of this important department showed great improvement on Turkish standards.

The Ottoman Public Debt, and its subcontractor the Régie des Tabacs, raised questions of peculiar complication which must be solved by the Mandatory on behalf of the States. Both these organizations were unpopular with the Syrian public, who had done nothing to incur the debts thus due for repayment, and

[1] The direct taxes were those levied on built property: on unbuilt property: the *temettu*' or occupation-tax: the tithe: the animal-tax: the vehicle tax: and the road (or forced-labour) tax.

[2] Equally baseless was the popular charge that the French were 'draining Syria of all its gold'.

[3] The Permanent Mandates Commission, also, were critical of the Bank's privileges; it noted that the Administration made a point of collecting its own fines not in the local currency but in gold.

[4] Most foodstuffs remained at 11 per cent.

who suspected manœuvres on behalf of the French bondholders; the extension of the Régie's contract after 1914 was, moreover, criticized as illegal because unratified. The Debt was entitled, under the Treaty of Lausanne, to its allotted revenues as from March 1920; and these, from mid-June 1923 till the end of 1925, were temporarily consigned to a 'blocked' account. The determination of the proportion of the total Debt due from Syria–Lebanon occupied some years of calculation, negotiation, and protest between Beirut, Paris, Geneva, and Ankara; it was finally fixed at £T11 million (gold), payable in eighty-seven annual instalments. In 1926 all Public Debt agencies in Syria and Lebanon were closed, the collection of Debt revenues being handed to the local revenue authorities. In the yet more complicated questions of Régie claims and liabilities, the High Commissioner sought in vain for an acceptable solution; meanwhile even the complete separation of its operations and accounts in Syria–Lebanon from the rest of the ex-Turkish Empire, in March 1923, was compromised later by transactions between the Régie and the Ankara authorities which ignored the rights of the successor-States. The Régie began in 1924, nevertheless, to feel its way towards an ultimate extension of its monopoly in Syria (due otherwise to expire in 1929), in the face of an unfriendly public opinion. The latter was itself divided over the question of regulating this important industry, as between state control, a monopolistic company, and complete *laissez-faire*.

In the Courts and codes of justice, few early decisions fell to be taken by the Mandatory. The Turkish system had already been continued in the West Zone with suitable modifications due to severance from Istanbul, and had equally persisted in Fayṣal's Syria. It was not unsuited to the territory; and the French authorities lost no time in confirming existing Courts in the new States, creating new Courts of Appeal and of Cassation, and proceeding to a careful overhaul of the magistrature. The premises and equipment, records and subordinate staff of the Courts were simultaneously improved, and their procedures expedited and simplified. No alteration was made at present in the working of the Shara' or the Courts of the non-Muslim communities. A beginning was made with the formidable task of preparing[1] new codes of law. In 1922 a provisional 'Conseil du Contentieux' was instituted in the Lebanon, and two years later a Council of State, concerned with the working of the public services, was established in the same State. Similar bodies were established in the 'Alawi State and in Syria in the same year. Finally a 'Tribunal

[1] A Commission of jurists sat in Paris in 1921–2, with the collaboration of Lebanese and Syrian lawyers.

des Conflits' was set up by the High Commission in 1924 to deal with cases of conflict of jurisdiction between judicial and administrative bodies, and the High Commission itself.

In spite of these numerous reforms and improvements, the retention of a modified state of siege from 1920 to 1925, with arbitrary arrest and banishment as normal measures against political offenders, could not but diminish the prestige of French justice; and the same was true of the favour alleged to be shown to foreigners, whose rights in the mandated territory created a vexed question. Capitulatory privileges continued to be enjoyed, and Consular Courts to sit, until the promulgation of the Mandate on 1 November 1923, the legislation prepared earlier in replacement of these not having been enacted because of popular outcry against it. Capitulatory rights were however expressly suspended under the Mandate, and in July 1923 decrees were issued establishing the Courts which would deal thenceforth with cases involving foreign subjects. All Courts when trying such cases were to be presided over by a French judge; the prosecuting officer would, or could, be French, and either party could claim a majority of French judges. These Courts were to form an integral part of the regular judicial system of the country, the French judges were functionaries of the States, and the normal law of the country would be administered. The French staff necessitated by these provisions was recruited in France, and the new Courts first sat in March 1924. The Mixed Courts, however, though they operated in fact with efficiency and probity, provoked continuous outcry from the press, the politicians, and the barristers (who went on strike when the Decree was first published, and again a year later) as being a derogation from national sovereignty, an insult to their own competence and a favouring of the foreigner: an outcry which no French explanations or defence could diminish, and which ignored the extent to which such a system was forced upon the Mandatory by the pressures of the ex-capitulatory Powers. The right of foreign 'juristic persons' to own real property, denied by Turkish law, was accorded in 1923.

Other steps taken in the same period by the High Commission, though unquestionably productive of improved standards in the judicial field, were liable no less to nationalistic objection and the displeasure of the local Bar. The senior French judges became *ex-officio* Inspectors of all Courts, and as such exercised a powerful and a resented force of supervision and discipline. In Lebanon the use of French judges was so far extended in 1925 by a process of 'fusion' that they participated in all (save the lowest) courts even in purely local suits; no judgement in Lebanon could be given thereafter without the concurrence of a French judge. This provision, however educative in intention, was hampered by shortage of interpreters, and by the disfavour of some local judges; it was never extended to the Syrian States.

The detachment of Syria from the Ottoman Empire involved loss of the Muslim governmental control of the Awqaf, as exercised by the concerned Ministry in Istanbul. Rather than see these important properties deteriorate, the High Commissioner in March 1921 set up, under his own final control, an organization, wholly Muslim in personnel, to link the Awqaf with the Government. A High Council of the Awqaf was given powers of policy-making, interpretation, and control; a General Commission became the supreme administrative agent. Finally, a Controller General was for all purposes the executive arm of the Commission and the legal representative of the Awqaf and had direct responsibility to the High Commissioner, by whom he was appointed. The latter could ratify or reject all acts of either the Council or the Commission, except on matters of Muslim law. All these arrangements, with their country-wide network of dependent offices, assured better control and maintenance, and fewer abuses, than had been known for centuries; but the patent fact of ultimate non-Muslim control was unfortunate.

The provision of armed forces to ensure peace in a largely discontented country was an urgent task for the French occupiers. Troops of the metropolitan French Army were, indeed, few but essential: battalions of the Foreign Legion and a few artillery and specialized units were, with the staffs and command, the chief contribution from France itself. Moroccan, Algerian, and Tunisian regiments, with Madagascans and Senegalese—the latter bitterly resented by Syrian opinion, as an offence to their own higher civilization—formed, with the Aviation, the bulk of the French forces from overseas. Their strength, more than 50,000 in 1921, did not exceed 15,000 early in 1925.[1] The organization, armament, and training at all levels were those normal to the French Army. The highest military command, held by the High Commissioner as long as he was himself a General, was in practice exercised by a General whose authority covered also the Syro-Lebanese troops raised locally as an integral though distinct part of the Army of the Levant.

In the incessant operations of the armed forces in these early years, essential help was given by these Syrian and Lebanese auxiliaries, whose recruitment began in 1921, and whose strength had by 1924 reached some 7,000 of all ranks. Closely supervised by

[1] The official handbook *Syria* (2 vols. Damascus, 1955), vol. 1, p. 149, speaks of the French régime as 'backed by an army which was estimated in 1924 at 70 thousand men, and which was considerably enlarged during the following two years'. This is misleading: see below, p. 149.

French officers and N.C.O.s, discipline was generally good, the personnel intelligent and active if of still uncertain reliability. Great efforts were made to improve the type, training, and standards of the local officers, and to divorce these from politics. The function of the force was to assist the French Army in military operations, and the Gendarmerie in dealing with smaller-scale disorder; its cost was borne, for the most part, by the funds of the Common Interests, with a limited subsidy from the French Treasury.

As in the military, so in the Police–Gendarmerie structure, it was not possible for the French to build upon Turkish foundations; a higher type of officer, and a new attitude in the rank and file, were essential. The work of recruitment and training, begun in the Lebanon and the ʻAlawis in 1919, was continued in the other States after August 1920; officers and instructors were borrowed from the metropolitan Gendarmerie, professional standards were improved, inferior elements eliminated, and efforts made to free the force from political and social pressures. The training schools at Damascus and Baʻabda were revitalized, and in 1923 a French mission arrived, at Lebanese request, to assist the Gendarmerie of that State. Organization and distribution in each State followed, in general, the outline of the sanjaqs and qaḍhas.

The Police, a small body in each State intended for urban and traffic duties, and strictly separate from either mandatory or gendarmerie forces, were under French command in the Lebanon and French advice elsewhere. The services of the Sûreté Générale were, throughout the territories, the concern not of the States but of a Directorate under the High Commission; they covered the supervision of foreigners and suspects, political and other inquiries, expulsions and extraditions, passports and movements, migration and pilgrims, counter-espionage, control of 'artistes', hotels, and the cinematograph.

One other activity of these years, highly creditable to the French effort, remains to be mentioned: the disposal of tens of thousands of Christian refugees from Anatolia. The costly efforts made in 1919–20 to resettle Armenians in Cilicia proved fruitless when the evacuation of that province by French troops in December 1921 led to an influx of 30,000 penniless fugitives into north Syria and the Lebanon. A further wave of exiles was set in motion late in 1922, 15,000 more Armenians reached Aleppo, and in mid-1923 another 30,000, of whom a third were Greeks,[1] the rest Armenians. By the end of 1923 some 120,000 had entered Syria, of whom more than two-thirds were to remain there.[2] The efforts

[1] Repatriation of these to Greece was, with difficulty, arranged.

[2] The numbers on 1 January 1925 were—Armenians 89,000, Chaldeans 4,000, Jacobites 1,800, Greek Orthodox 900, Syrian Catholics 250.

immediately necessary to shelter and feed these refugees in a country already economically depressed, and resentful of economically competitive newcomers, was but the beginning. Reception areas were provided, anti-epidemic measures taken, rations of food ensured, dispensaries opened. The work, first of relief and later of settlement devolved in part upon the mandatory authorities, in part upon the States, in part upon French, American,[1] and British missions who all laboured with generous persistence. Camps and suburban settlements were constructed, necessaries provided, local employment encouraged, schools organized, orphanages founded. By 1925 the position, still distressing, had become largely static; a much enlarged Christian element had entered the Syro-Lebanese body politic.[2] The energy and frugality of the newcomers, and their contribution of cheap labour and new industrial skills to the labour market, did nothing to reconcile the Syrian public to their advent; but no overt anti-Armenian violence resulted.

6. ACROSS THE FRONTIERS

The League of Nations and its Permanent Mandates Commission enjoyed in this period no very high consideration among either the Syrians or the French. To the former, these bodies were remote, unresponsive, and ineffective; to the latter it was a nuisance, if not a humiliation, to be compelled to report to an international body, and to be (however courteously) questioned regarding French action in a territory where France claimed a unique position and age-long rights. It was, however, already clear that petitions in plenty regarding Syria would find their way to Geneva, to be referred thence to the French Government—almost never (as the Commission's *rapporteur* was to comment) with any visible results. To political Syrians, the League was the heartless instrument of the Great Powers who had appropriated their country; but it was still not hopeless to bombard it with petitions.

In France itself, the bulk of conservative opinion in the Church, the Army, and circles interested in strategy, commerce, and the traditional French 'mission' and prestige, was in full support of the Mandate; and while official policy was scrupulously correct in its theory of self-denying mandatory service, most of the public regretted only that Syria was not frankly a Protectorate.

[1] The American provision of charitable funds and workers for this purpose exceeded the French or the British: it represented a great and continuing work.

[2] The largest settlements were at Aleppo and its vicinity and at Beirut, with major or lesser groups at or near Damascus, in Alexandretta and its villages, and up and down-stream from Dayr al-Zur.

They applauded all that they were told of French achievement, believed in the loyalty of the Syrians, saluted military feats, minimized difficulties, and blamed these, which they imperfectly understood, as due to minority ingratitude or British intrigue. In spite of the beginnings of disillusion, they felt that France had a great task to perform; her prestige in the world was at stake; Syria must be retained, organized, developed. But contrary opinions were represented also by elements of the left wing: that the Mandate was a profitless burden and should be abandoned or heavily restricted—perhaps to a merely diplomatic or advisory relationship—and retained only for a limited period, with its strong Catholic content diminished in favour of laicism. The Mandate became an issue in French politics; to propose reduction of the budget allotments for Syria was an annual move; and the advent to power of M. Herriot as Prime Minister in June 1924 presaged appointments of close interest to the mandated territory.

Much of French opinion remained the victim of the curious obsession of a British malignity shown, it was averred, in every Syrian political claim or anti-French demonstration. This persistent myth gave rise to written and spoken words of extraordinary bitterness[1] whenever it seemed possible to allege a fresh example of British ill will. It was true, indeed, that the stringency of French control, and the reported misdoings of this or that French official, evoked some unfavourable British comment; true also that anti-French movements or writings occurred in countries —Transjordan, Egypt, Palestine—in which the British were present. The attitude of the latter was in fact interested, at times critical, never malevolent, and still less ambitious; it was entirely in their interest that the French in Syria should succeed in their task, which nothing, then or later, could have induced Great Britain to undertake.

The interest of Italy, when once its subjects' rights had been assured (p. 109), was limited to watching events and maintaining her old contacts; but she felt increasingly that the Levant could be a scene for Italian peaceful expansion, that 'the French monopoly' was improper, and that visible sympathy to Arab aspirations was worth the showing. Neither Germany nor the United States had in these years any new part to play. The latter resumed their philanthropic work and their trading activity, watched the Open Door, and noted the scores of critical resolutions passed by the Syrian Committees in every American city. Their long-standing educational effort in the territory was fully

[1] Cf. for example, Pierre Benoit's popular novel *La Châtelaine du Liban, passim*; or Mme. Georges-Gaulis, *La Question Arabe*, p. 210: 'la campagne menée contre nous par nos alliés d'hier'; p. 220: 'l'implacable rivalité des coloniaux britanniques'. Such is the normal view expressed by French (unofficial) writers.

maintained, and among the Armenian refugees American charity played a generous part.

Of Syria's neighbours, Turkey took by far the most significant place, and this for more reasons than that merely of the incessant trans-frontier disturbances which the Turks fomented. The Franco-Turkish Agreement of October 1921,[1] though its substance was duly incorporated in the Lausanne Treaty, sadly failed to produce good-neighbourly conditions. The new boundary was not for the present demarcated; the hopeful Customs Agreement negotiated in September 1922 remained long unratified; and Ankara spokesmen, referring to the Alexandretta sanjaq still as 'our Alsace–Lorraine', welcomed petitions and delegations from the Turkish element in it, and sometimes from Damascus itself. The prestige of Muṣṭafa Kamal stood high in Syria; propaganda in the Turkish interest was noticeable in the principal cities, and it spread even to Lebanon, where a noisy demonstration round a Turkish flag took place in Beirut in November 1922. The bad-neighbour policy of Turkey in these years,[2] and accusations by Syrians that France in her Turkish frontier settlement had abandoned their rights and territory, were among the unmerited French difficulties of the time. In fact, the 1921 frontier (the best, no doubt, then obtainable without war) was a reasonable approximation to the Turco-Arab racial divide,[3] and its establishment and defence might well have earned Syrian gratitude.

Compared with all this, Syria's other neighbours had little to contribute. Palestine, now under a British Mandate complicated and frustrated by the implications of the Balfour promise, could not but maintain the closest connexions with Syria–Lebanon with which hitherto it had formed a single and substantially homogeneous territory. The frontier, fixed in December 1920 by a Franco-British Agreement,[4] did not prevent the use of Palestine as a refuge for fugitive Syrian politicians, nor the Palestinian Arab press from eagerly espousing Syrian nationalism, nor the visits of leading Zionists to Syria to assure themselves that Jewish rights there were intact. Syrian (and all Arab) opinion of the Zionist experiment was strongly, indeed passionately, opposed to

[1] It was bitterly attacked by military and right-wing writers in France as an abandonment of the rich prize of Cilicia, of Christian friends, and of the true defence line of Syria.

[2] Until the de Jouvenel Agreement of 18 February 1926 (p. 173).

[3] In spite of small Arab minorities in some of the surrendered areas.

[4] Cmd. 1195 of 1921. It was slightly modified later, after scrutiny by a Boundary Commission whose report was ratified in March 1923 (Cmd. 1910 of 1923). This modification in detail of the Sykes–Picot boundary line, with the object of including in Palestine all the Jewish settlements was resented by French and Lebanese observers.

British policy in Palestine, from which the French could happily dissociate themselves:[1] a policy which declared itself, even in its relatively mild earlier form, as a tragically damaging element in Anglo-Arab relations. Syro-Palestine official dealings, on matters of police, travel, and border co-operation were satisfactory. A Customs Agreement was made late in 1922.

Transjordan, where the Amir 'Abdullah ibn Ḥusayn was installed as ruler under British guidance, and later Mandate, in April 1921, maintained a correct attitude as far as the Mandatory could ensure this; but in tribal and unofficial circles, permeated by Sharifian influences and resentful Damascene exiles, Francophobe talk and exhortation were rife; and this was not without disturbing effects in Syria, while the extreme lightness—or non-existence—of British control in remoter parts of Transjordan permitted the easy passage of the lawless or proscribed across the frontier. A Customs Agreement was made with the 'Amman Government in May 1923.

With the Amir's father, King Ḥusayn of the Ḥijaz, Syrian connexion was limited to mutual visits, the sending of telegrams, and the making of periodical protests by the King to Geneva, Paris, or London. The Sharifian faction lost ground in Syria, and the self-proclamation of Ḥusayn as Caliph, on 5 March 1924, aroused little interest in Syria.

From 'Iraq, where the enthronement of King Fayṣal in August 1921 was viewed with displeasure by French opinion, Syria remained at this period largely isolated. Foolish or malicious rumours that the King was 'planning to recover the Syrian throne' could be ignored by all intelligent men. The cross-desert motor route, inaugurated in 1923, was still in its infancy. Trade and transit, regulated by a Customs Agreement of 1924, were still small in volume. Liaison between the authorities of each country over desert tribal movements and quarrels, past and continuing, led in May 1923 to a conference of officials and tribesmen at al-Qa'im on the Euphrates, followed by a second at Dayr al-Zur in September. These failed to agree, but a Court of Arbitration held at Albu Kamal in September 1924 composed most of the outstanding tribal claims. The Syro-'Iraqi boundary, roughly established[2] in May 1920 as between the Arab Government of Damascus and the British in 'Iraq, was the subject of a provisional Anglo-French Agreement of 23 December 1920: an Agreement which, extraordinarily, provided for the bisection of both Albu Kamal and the Jabal Sinjar. By mutual consent the earlier boundary retained its

[1] Though France had in fact supported the Balfour promise at the time, pp. 59–60.

[2] It gave the whole Jabal Sinjar to 'Iraq, and Albu Kamal to Syria.

force on the spot, and the demarcation of a workable boundary was to await the appointment of a Commission.

There remains, still beyond Syrian or Lebanese boundaries, one type of activity to be mentioned, both as typical of the world-wide dispersal of their citizens and as exercising a perceptible influence: that is, the busy and numerous Committees formed by the Syro-Lebanese *émigrés* in Egypt, Palestine, France, and other west European countries, and in a score of cities in North and South America. All these, composed of active and successful men, ceased not to judge, usually on fragmentary and biased information, the public affairs of their old homes, and to send telegrams to Geneva, Paris, or Beirut in advocacy of any or all of the possible policies for Syria and Lebanon. But the aggregate of these did not compare in importance with the Egypt-based 'Syro-Palestine Congress' and its Executive Committee, which a General Syrian Congress[1] at Geneva in August 1921 had set up on the initiative of the Amir Michel Luṭfullah,[2] and Shaykh Rashid Riḍha.[3] The Congress, financed mainly by Luṭfullah, met frequently in Cairo in and after 1922, issued manifestos in favour of Syrian unity and independence, intervened at Geneva and at every capital concerned with Syrian affairs, bitterly criticized current French actions, and kept up the closest communication with politicians in the country. The *dirigeants* of the Committee varied slightly from year to year; its most important members included, in 1922, Shakib Arsalan,[4] Musa Kadhim Pasha al-Ḥusayni,[5] 'Abd al-Qadir al-Mudhaffar, Sulayman Bey Kin'an, and Iḥsan al-Jabiri.[6] Many protests were made by Maronite and other non-nationalist spokesmen, and by the Representative Council in Beirut, against the views of the absentee and, as they claimed, unrepresentative Congress.

7. PHASES OF POLITICS

The first five years of mandatory government were a period of increasing mutual knowledge, accompanied by some disillusion, as between French and Syrians, and one in which contact was made with tough administrative problems. If fair progress was made in solving these, and in material improvement, little advance was visible towards solving the main political problem,

[1] The list of constituent bodies is given in *Or. Mod.*, December 1921.

[2] A wealthy Greek Orthodox Syrian, resident in Egypt; his title was bestowed by King Ḥusayn.

[3] A Syrian scholar and divine of oustanding prestige, resident in Cairo.

[4] A (Lebanese) Druze scholar, writer, and nationalist.

[5] Head of the Ḥusayni family of Jerusalem.

[6] Of the well-known Aleppo family, brother of Sa'dullah.

which indeed the French occupiers seemed, even by 1925, still to have incompletely realized.

The masses in the countryside continued to ignore politics (except when specifically incited thereto by their landlords or visiting strangers), and to find the conditions of their lives, as of their minds, but little changed; but in the towns it was more evident that in modernity of atmosphere, in new possibilities of progress and enterprise, a new era had dawned. If much of this was displeasing to the conservative, or the jealous, the visible fact of emergence from the shabby obscurity of an Ottoman province was at first widely welcomed; and that this, so largely due to the French presence, led to so little articulate gratitude, is explicable on various grounds. The new conditions were soon taken for granted; they would have been achieved anyhow—equally without a Mandate—in so fast-changing an age! Moreover, the mere man in the street was conscious of adverse features in his new daily life; the prices of goods were capricious, the French-established currency seemed to buy less and less, and the new age did not preclude, evidently, economic hard times such as developed in and after 1922. Official regulations were as exacting as in the old days, but their higher exponents were now foreigners who spoke only French, and who dominated all the haunts of officialdom. These same foreigners, with their separate lives and manners, were sometimes in conduct and attitude not above criticism; and to them was due the alleged favouring of Christians, the welcome given to a mass of disliked Armenian strangers, the continuance of the high taxes to be paid to the creditors of the old Turkish Sultans.

Such homely grievances among the mass did not preclude the continuance of a considerable body of opinion tolerant of the Mandate and its visible fruits: a body which included, besides the fatalistic poor, much of the official and trading classes, and that part of the urban middle and upper class which saw real advantage in the (admittedly imperfect) régime as it was, and had little confidence in nationalist politicians. And among the favoured Maronites and other Catholic Uniates, and a fair part also of the non-Catholic Christians, Jews, and Muslim minorities, the sense of particular mandatory favour, of freedom from Sunni dominion, still outweighed the criticisms, never difficult to formulate, against the French.

With the Sunni majority and a part of the Christian and dissident Muslim sects it was otherwise; and these were dominated by political leaders of great activity and conviction, who claimed to speak for the Syrian nation—a claim which the French, after dismissing it for years as the irresponsible agitation of a small minority of self-seekers, were in the end reluctantly to acknowledge as valid. These, the nationalists, themselves divided inexactly into moderate and extreme groups, did not deny the benefits of European assistance; they continued to value the French culture which they shared, were often on cordial terms with individual Frenchmen and would at times accept office under French auspices. But on the whole the divergence between their own and French views, and their tenacity and impatience, prevented the collaboration on which all success in the mandatory experiment must rest and, in fact, deprived the French of any chance of successful state-building in the fashion and tempo which they adopted in this period.

Many of the criticisms launched against the régime by militant nationalism have been suggested on previous pages. France, they asserted, was an unwanted, empire-seeking foreign Power thrust by military force into an Arab land. It had abandoned northern Syria to the Turks, to ease its own bargain-driving. Barriers divided the new 'Syria' from every neighbour. The unity of the truncated territory itself had been shattered; a number of small States, framed on archaic confessional lines, had been substituted. Syrian and Muslim areas had been detached and joined to a Great Lebanon created solely to please the Maronites. Powers given to the Councils or officials of the States were derisory, elections manipulated by the French; French officials (rarely Arabic-speaking) were everywhere in charge, and often of low quality. French was too often the language of the administration and the Courts; the latter favoured foreigners and humiliated the local bench and bar. Even the Awqaf, and the Ḥijaz Railway, were French-controlled. Confessionalism as a basis of government, abandoned in Europe, was preserved in Syria. Christian interests, and French commercial advantage were unduly favoured. A depreciating currency had been forced on the country, to its heavy loss. Little economic progress had been made since 1918. The Syrian claim to war reparations from Turkey was rejected; they were, it seemed, only Turks themselves, after all! Tens of thousands of unwanted Armenians had been ushered into Syria, to undercut Syrians and take work from them. The press was muzzled, deportation without trial habitual, personal liberty precarious, a state of siege continually in force, no national army permitted.

To many, perhaps most, of such accusations a prudent observer could and can see sometimes a complete, often a partial, defence. No adequate credit was given to the generous goodwill, or indeed devotion, of much of the French effort, nor was the inevitability of error in some parts of so novel a field sufficiently realized. Certainly, the initial French conception of mandatory tutelage appears in retrospect too perfectionist and too heavy-handed, their constitutional policy too changeable, the treatment of majority opinion too cavalier, the delegation of power too reluctant, the deference to Maronite (or 'Alawi) opinion excessive, blows dealt to local *amour-propre* too common, and French staff too often ill chosen and ill supervised; but many of the defects urged in detail against the régime were due in reality to conditions of the world and the times beyond the power of France to control, some were matters of doubtful opinion in which the French choice or policy had strong arguments to support it, and some arose from the very persistence of local non-cooperation.

The last-mentioned feature was manifested in varying degrees among a political public still evidently immature and too apt to adopt methods of irresponsibility or even violence at clear variance with its claim to be *imperii capax*. The press, extremely abundant in its representation of every sect and attitude, and often the work of skilful pens, was by majority disorderly and intemperate, preferring political diatribes to any semblance of a news service, and distinguishing little between criticism and crude incitement to violence. As, in spite of the prevailing 'state of siege' and the still valid Turkish press regulations, the press gained confidence and abandoned restraint, the patience even of General Weygand was exhausted, and he caused, amid loud outcry, a new Press Law to be enacted early in 1924. Under this, or indeed before it, the suspension of newspapers was common. Since freedom was grossly abused, a free press could not be permitted; nevertheless, the papers, while they lasted, formed the chief outlet for political activity.

Political parties did not exist in Syria, save for the unofficial but active groups in the diwans and coffee shops, and surviving traces of the parties of the war period and before. In the Lebanon, a National Party stood for Lebanese integrity, but was critical, in its newspaper, of French policy; and in the same State the Churches (notably the Maronite, under its dominating Patriarch) served largely the purposes of political parties and pressed constantly for their own community interests with admirable organization of interviews, petitions, newspaper articles, and sermons. Deputations to the High Commissioner and his Délégués conveyed the demands of politicians or the aggrieved on every subject. Manifestos and telegrams to the French President or ministers, the League of Nations, or Whitehall, by any group or individual urged their hopes or protests. Discussions in the Representative Councils ranged freely over all current topics—national unity, the reallotment of territory, the Mandate itself, the Public Debt, the Régie, the Armenians, concessions, the Press Law, amnesty for exiles, the missionary schools, election scandals, the powerlessness of the Councils; and the attempt to withhold budget allotments from unpopular institutions, such as the Mixed Courts, was not unknown. Elections were boycotted as a protest by dissatisfied nationalist voters, fierce denunciations were levelled at election procedure. Threats were uttered to boycott French goods—or the too-amenable Deputies themselves. Shops were shut in protest against an ill-chosen Representative Council, and against the Mixed Courts; the latter issue led also to a strike of barristers. Noisy, sometimes violent demonstrations were easily organized from the city mob or the students on any pretext. The private visit of Mr. Crane (p. 120) to Damascus in April 1922 led to repeated demonstrations not only in that city but in Ḥumṣ, Ba'lbek, Dayr al-Zur, Jarablus, and elsewhere, violent enough to necessitate military intervention, and marked by bloodshed; long sentences of imprisonment were passed on the instigators,[1] and these in turn led to the shutting of bazaars. These serious episodes were pronounced by General Gouraud, surprised and shocked, to be (one knows not how) the fault of the British. The Director of the Interior in Lebanon, As'ad Bey Khurshid, a confirmed Francophile, was murdered on the same occasion.

To so much hostility in the political field the French reply was to continue to act as they thought right: to expound their policy by official announcements, by press articles,[2] by interviews: to reiterate the essential objects of the Mandate: to invite attention to French sacrifices, financial and humanitarian: to reason with political leaders: and to grant amnesty to the condemned or detained[3] as freely and early as seemed safe. Meanwhile, no move was visible to remove the essential cause of the many troubles: that is, the explicit and sustained dissatisfaction of the most active and articulate classes among the public at French mandatory policy and method.

[1] Notably Dr. 'Abd al-Raḥman Shahbandar, 20 years. He was an English-speaking Beirut University-educated medical practitioner, and life-long nationalist.

[2] The charge that some local papers were 'bought' by the French can be neither substantiated nor denied; doubtless certain subsidies were paid.

[3] The usual place of detention for politicians was Arwad Island: Palmyra was also used. Banishment from the country was less common.

V

REBELLION AND PROMISE

1. GENERAL SARRAIL

THE sudden recall of the vigorous, respected, and generally popular High Commissioner, General Weygand, in December 1924, to a less eminent post, came as an unwelcome surprise to the French in Syria and to the local political world; a loyal Catholic, he had made every effort at impartiality, was not without liberalism, and had found such acceptance as his Government's policy made possible. His removal was due to the desire of the left-wing, anti-clerical Government in France, which under M. Herriot had achieved power in June 1924, to give effect to their views not only at home but—a departure from the French tradition—also abroad: a desire which, with the eager willingness of their nominee, the ageing,[1] authoritarian, and impatient General Sarrail, led them to ignore, in favour of ideological considerations, the basis of the French position in a territory where their only reliable support was Catholic. It was anyhow improbable that the General would successfully administer, on lines of laicism or indeed on any other, a complex area calling for patient and expert handling. His appointment was, in fact, almost the most unhappy imaginable.

But there appeared in Syria, at the outset of 1925, no special cause for apprehension. The political situation, if *au fond* unsatisfactory, was not critical. The centres of discontent were well appreciated, armed opposition did not exist. The French dominance in the fields of administration, justice, and finance was pervasive and unquestioned. The Great Lebanon, with all its factions, gave the appearance of a vigorous political life, and General Weygand had in October 1924 promised it constitutional advance. The State of Syria had come into being, the sanjaq of Alexandretta seemed well content with its accepted régime, the 'Alawis had their separate State, the Druzes were believed to be passing gratefully through a period of accelerated progress. The early establishment of a formal Statute for each State was expected; the terms of the Mandate called for these within three years from 29 September 1923, and had led the French Government to send

[1] Born in 1856, he was now 69—eleven years older than each of his predecessors.

an expert, M. Auguste Brunet, to Syria during 1925 to help the High Commissioner in his consultations and to report his conclusions to a Committee set up in Paris under M. Paul-Boncour. French garrisons in the territory had been reduced to less than 15,000 men, costs to the French Treasury were falling, and criticism of the Syrian régime in the Chamber was not immoderate. The new High Commissioner, if prepared for moderate political concessions, might feel hopeful of a peaceful and fruitful tenure of office.

Landing at Beirut on the second day of 1925, General Sarrail plunged with full energy into the execution of his policy. On his first day he called for the resignation of the Governor of Lebanon, General Vandenberg,[1] a popular officer of traditionalist views, and informed the Representative Council of the Lebanon that a Lebanese Governor would replace him. The announcement, disliked by a considerable minority among the local communities, was followed by the holding of an extraordinary meeting of the Council on 12 January, to make its selection from candidates approved by the High Commission. The desire of the Deputies for some discussion of candidatures was, however, abruptly refused; the Délégué left the meeting, which broke up; and Decrees issued by the High Commissioner the next day dissolved the Council itself and appointed an anti-clerical Frenchman—M. Cayla, governor of the 'Alawi State—as temporary governor of Lebanon with power to legislate single-handed. Still in January, a High Commissioner's Decree abolished, in the cause of liberalism, the restrictive payment of caution-money by newspaper proprietors, and allowed a number of banned sheets to republish. Nevertheless, a leading paper, *L'Orient*, was suppressed a few days later, journalistic indiscretions were viewed with no less intolerance than before, and the unpopular law governing these was not only retained but reinforced in April by stronger sanctions. The state of siege, maintained in Syria–Lebanon since the earliest days, was abolished on 10 January, and the maintenance of order (except for offences against the Army) became the concern of the State governments alone; but under a second simultaneous Decree the military were still empowered to intervene in case of trouble with full authority, including that of search, requisition, disarming, and banishment. These powers were repeatedly exercised.

If these events showed both the liberal intentions and the despotic impatience of the General, he had already shown his damaging tactlessness in another field. He gave bitter offence by refusing to attend the symbolic and time-honoured reception offered by the Latin community of Beirut in his honour, as

[1] Appointed by General Weygand in 1924, in replacement of M. Aubouard.

representative of France the Protector of Catholicism: a pointed rebuff to the Church, which led to questions in the Chamber in Paris, to adverse notice at the Vatican, and finally to an apology by M. Herriot himself to the Apostolic Delegate in Beirut. The ceremonial visit paid to General Sarrail in his first week by the octogenarian Maronite Patriarch was returned, after more than two months, only with an ill grace and on specific instructions from Paris. Cayla in turn provoked Maronite episcopal wrath by a public reference to the virtues of laicism in education, and pointed counter-action by the Archbishop of Beirut, in withholding from the governor the usual invitation[1] to Easter celebrations, led to an apologetic visit of recantation by the chastened Governor to the Patriarch.

In Lebanese political life, meanwhile, the same unsuccessful efforts were being made to break with the confessionalism which, accepted by most but resented by a few, permeated all public affairs. The introduction, by Decree,[2] of a new system of administrative units in the Lebanon—eleven districts[3] each under a Muḥafiḏh (*administrateur*), divided into thirty-four naḥiyas—was primarily a measure of economy; but the Decree published on 27 March—after no local consultations, to the general indignation—abolishing both two-stage elections and the confessional allotment of seats in the Chamber, was so unpopular that it was soon replaced by two others whose effect was to retain both confessionalism and two-stage election, and merely to adjust election procedure and units to a new distribution into five electoral[4] districts. This provision was intended to fuse the communities into more composite, less sectarian units.

The arrival of M. Brunet gave Lebanese patriots a new audience for their hopes and grievances, which included the abolition of 'fusion' in the Courts (p. 136), the early summoning of a Constituent Assembly, the abolition of the Régie, a Tripoli–Jaffa railway, and a high protective Customs tariff. A new political party, the Progressive, was formed; new appeals against French policy were launched by Lebanese *émigrés* to the League of Nations. The first-stage elections for a new Representative Council—free, unlike those of 1922, from Muslim boycott—took place late in June.

[1] Lack of solidarity between the Maronites and the Greek Catholics was indicated by the invitation extended to Cayla by the latter.

[2] *Or. Mod.*, June 1925, pp. 274 ff.

[3] Also one autonomous naḥiya, Dayr al-Qamr. The districts were those of Tripoli, Batrun, Kasrawan (H.Q., Juniya), Matn (H.Q., Baḥannes), Beirut, Shuf (H.Q., Ba'aqlin), Ba'lbek, Zaḥla, Ṣayda, Ṣur, Marj'uyun.

[4] The distribution of seats among the communities was: 10 Maronite, 7 Sunni, 5 Shi'i, 4 Greek Orthodox, 2 Greek Catholic, 2 Druze, and 1 for lesser sects. The five electoral districts were those of Beirut, Tripoli, Baḥannes, Sidon, Zaḥla.

They were contested by all communities, with keen personal rivalries and the usual mutual accusations of corruption and 'undue influence'. The secondary voting resulted in the election of thirteen ex-Deputies and of seventeen new ones, with supporters and opponents of the existing Cabinet well divided. The closing stages of election time were marked by rioting in Beirut by noisy crowds. Shooting and stone-throwing caused some casualties. The new Representative Council met on 16 July, when its first act was to confirm M. Cayla as Governor.

In the State of Syria, one-day old on the day of Sarrail's arrival, the President, Ṣubḥi Bey Barakat, accepted without demur his Délégué's suggestions for the portfolio holders[1] in a first Cabinet. These settled to their work, and the State of Syria to its functions; but the administration appeared to be improved neither by the new statehood nor by the wider latitude expected from the new High Commissioner: nepotism and bribery, the weapons too often employed by Ṣubḥi Bey to strengthen his position, increased perceptibly, and the tone and morale of the public services suffered.

A strong deputation of Syrian politicians waited on General Sarrail in his second week in Beirut and presented a list of their demands, which covered the whole political and administrative field; it was joined by further parties from Ḥumṣ and Ḥamah, and by a Sunni and Christian delegation from the 'Alawi State once more demanding union with Syria. The General's ready permission for the formation of political parties allowed the amalgamation of existing nationalist groups in a People's Party, formed in February and conspicuous with fervid oratory in the months following; headed by Dr. 'Abd al-Raḥman Shahbandar, it included most of the political leaders except the professed 'moderates', and with a programme of national sovereignty and unity, full personal liberty, and judicial and many other reforms, it constituted a vigorous opposition to the Administration of Ṣubḥi Barakat, and easily outshone the second new-formed party, that of Syrian Unity. Various episodes were utilized to fan the flames of opposition, and a visit to Damascus on 8 April by Lord Balfour, signatory in 1917 of the letter which had given birth to the new Zionist position in Palestine, led to serious, indeed fanatical, rioting in the city which endangered the visitor's own life and

[1] To Interior was appointed the lawyer and former judge, Naṣri al-Bakhash: to Justice, 'Ata Bey al-Ayyubi, an ex-Mutaṣarrif of high standing: to Education, Riḍha Bey Sa'id, a medical doctor and professor: to the Council of State, Ḥaqqi Bey al-'Adhm (p. 126): to Finance, Jalal Bey Zuḥdi, who had been Minister of Justice under King Fayṣal: and to Works, Ḥasan 'Izzat Pasha, a general of the Turkish army, barely Arabic-speaking. In August, 'Ata Bey resigned and Ḥamdi Bey al-Naṣr joined the Ministry.

called for military repression. Order was not restored without casualties, and the usual rancorous complaints of over-severity.

When the Representative Council of the new State assembled for its first session[1] as such on 16 April, considerable elements among the highest and lowest in the city and countryside were already restless and discontented. A new and severe Press Law showed, as did his outspoken comments on local journalists, that the High Commissioner had already lost patience with their vagaries. Another *arrêté* forbade the growing evil of student street politics. Economic conditions were gravely depressed, poverty acute. All the grievances long felt against the French dispensation were unredressed. Stories of French troubles in the Rif were repeated, and the effective strength of their troops in Syria was known to have reached the lowest level since the Mandate began. Constitutional demands, in the now usual sense, were made from M. Brunet when he visited Aleppo and Damascus in June.

The 'Alawi State, save for its normal Sunni-Nuṣayri difference of attitude and the reappearance of its rustic Prophet (p. 122) in the early summer, remained tranquil. In the Jabal al-Duruz, Captain Carbillet, a zealous, well-meaning officer with West African experience, devoted to his Druze subjects but blindly insensitive in his handling of them, had by Druze request assumed the governorship temporarily in July 1923, permanently in October 1924. He held his position for twenty months, during which he conducted, with tireless energy, a régime intended to bestow on the population a whole series of unexpected and largely inappropriate blessings. He improved roads, dug channels, established more law courts, cleaned the villages, founded municipalities, opened a score of schools under imported Catholic teachers, established a museum, revised the land-tenure system to encourage planting, and by two-stage elections convened a new Council in terms of the 1921 Franco-Druze Agreement. That such a programme, carried out with heedless enthusiasm, must bewilder rather than please the inhabitants, and would seriously alarm the feudal leaders whose position it ignored, was little appreciated; no superior authority in the French hierarchy appeared to supervise the activities of the Jabal Governor, though brief visits to it were paid by Weygand in 1924, and by Sarrail himself in April 1925. Forced labour was employed on an unprecedented scale. Taxes were, for the first time in Druze history, collected in full. Rigid control of personal movement was established. The use of the schoolmasters as informers was everywhere practised. Punishments, for offences sometimes trivial, were arbitrary and

[1] The mandates of the deputies, elected in their respective states late in 1923 (p. 127), were due to expire in November 1925.

even capricious. The sensitiveness of Druze pride was repeatedly offended. And such power as did not belong solely to the Governor was visibly passing from the hitherto all-powerful chieftains to the newly-elected Deputies and the officials.

It was not surprising that in April 1925 a Druze delegation asked for audience with the High Commissioner, both to complain of the Carbillet régime and to remind him that under the 1921 Agreement their governor should be a Druze. General Sarrail replied with eulogies of the Captain and dismissed the Agreement as now valueless save as a historical document. Carbillet proceeded on leave to Europe late in May. His successor at Suwayda, Captain Raynaud, was at once approached by the Aṭrash faction with the same insistent protests against the Carbillet régime, upon which he himself reported adversely. A second Druze delegation to Beirut was refused audience by the High Commissioner as being unrepresentative and self-seeking, since certain Druze factions, outside the Aṭrash following, were known to be supporters of Carbillet; the delegates managed only to see M. Brunet, who took no action. Captain Raynaud again in mid-June had to fine the townsmen of Suwayda and arrest trouble-makers for a brawl and rifle-firing[1] at 'Id al-Adḥḥa celebrations. His reports in this sense being unwelcome, Raynaud was then abruptly replaced, under the High Commissioner's orders; but his successor, Major Tommy Martin, was in turn greeted by a monster anti-Carbillet petition. This he sent to Beirut, where it was ignored. Yet another Druze deputation to Beirut could gain access only to the Chief of the Intelligence Service.[2] On 11 July General Sarrail ordered that five Druze leaders should be summoned to Damascus 'on the pretext', as he directed, 'of receiving their demands', and should there be summarily arrested and despatched to Palmyra. This sad act of ill faith was carried out in respect of three of the chieftains, in spite of the protests of the Délégué, who correctly assessed it.

The most bellicose of the Aṭrash chieftains, Sulṭan, was decided by this treatment, or still more by the recent course of events in the Jabal and the explicit threat to all Aṭrash influence—and by the certainty that he himself was now in incurably bad standing with the French—to risk all on an armed outbreak. His followers, mobilized and inflamed, fired on French aircraft on 18 July: occupied, looted, and largely burnt Ṣalkhad on the 20th: and the following day, at Kafr, cut to pieces a French column nearly 200 strong who had left Suwayda to rescue some stranded airmen.

[1] A French lieutenant was wounded, probably by mistake.

[2] Major Dentz, later (1941) to be the most unfortunate of High Commissioners.

Barely 70 could return to Suwayda, where Sulṭan's forces besieged them the same evening in their barracks: a siege which, though never complete, was to last for two months.

It was still little appreciated in Beirut that more than a local incident had occurred. There seemed to be no general rally of Druzes to Sulṭan's standard, the factions in the Jabal remained divided, the religious leaders held aloof; and the High Commissioner allowed a battalion of *tirailleurs marocains* to leave for Africa on 30 July. But a serious reverse was at hand. The relieving column for Suwayda organized and commanded by General Michaud, some 3,000 strong (a third French, two-thirds Syrian and half-trained Madagascan), left Azra' on the Ḥijaz Railway on 2 August, disposed as a striking force and a supply column. These, under attack, lost contact. A night assault near Mazra'a by strong Druze forces led to complete demoralization of the Madagascan and Syrian elements, the capture of nearly the whole convoy, and the precipitate retreat of the survivors to Azra' with a loss of over 800 men and officers by death, wounds, capture, or desertion. The Colonel of the Madagascans committed suicide on the battlefield, and General Michaud was recalled to France. Two thousand rifles, a battery of artillery, and a large quantity of ammunition and supplies fell into the hands of the incredulous and triumphant Druze commander.

2. THE DRUZE REBELLION, EARLY MONTHS

The rebel success against the Michaud column changed, in a day, the character of the rising. Enriched by munitions and prestige, Sulṭan al-Aṭrash could now assume a confident though never undisputed[1] leadership of the Jabal, and could gain recruits in hundreds from the enthusiastic, the hungry, or the intimidated; smaller contingents came from the Ḥawran and Hermon areas, and from among the Druzes of Lebanon. He could count on the elements always radically anti-French, and on those whom the Carbillet Administration or the High Commissioner had offended: and not less on the considerable class always ready for a congenial rising against Government as such. The hesitation which followed the victory of 3 August soon ended; the appeals to moderation conveyed to Sulṭan by Raynaud could not, in such an atmosphere, succeed. Druze demands for an Aṭrash-dominated independent and privileged State provoked an enthusiasm with which no French invitations to submission and fine-paying could compete, and attempted mediation by an eminent Lebanese Druze was no

[1] A considerable Druze element, hostile to Aṭrash leadership, never joined his bands in spite of much intimidation.

more successful. Bold and ambitious raids began, within a fortnight, to move far beyond the Jabal. The 'rebellion' had begun.

That a movement started with such *éclat* should spread into other parts of Syria was unavoidable. There was no tradition of stability or peace, no prejudice against civil uprising, little loyalty to the Government. For reasons elsewhere indicated there was widespread discontent among the more vocal classes, and little sign that redress was at hand. There were political leaders—those of the People's Party—disposed to urge extreme policies, to which was easily given an aura of idealism. Emotion among the intelligentsia and the mob alike was quickly aroused, and impetuously diffused. The times were bad, poverty and unemployment widespread. French troops had been visibly reduced. A lead had been given, from however unexpected a quarter; an opportunity, which might never recur, had been suddenly offered. The appearance of a nation-wide movement in arms might do wonders in Geneva and Paris. The decision was taken in Damascus to utilize to the fullest, by an alliance without precedent, the amazing sudden success of a community whom the Syrian leaders had previously regarded as alien, inferior, and predominantly separatist.

The rebellion, if rightly so called, was to spread in some degree over a considerable part of Syria and a limited area of southern Lebanon, and it produced insecurity and apprehension even in the far north, where the rebels secured no firm hold. The rank-and-file participants, who at no time exceeded a thirtieth part of the manpower of the country, were predominantly villagers, peasants, and town-workers led by poverty and frustration to hope for better times somehow attainable by uprising; their leaders, varied in motives as in character, and declaiming the slogans of patriotism, infected the movement with an enthusiasm in which idealism, sectarian zeal, anti-foreign resentment, cupidity, and the impossibility of turning back, all had their part; but the normally political class, in the upper ranks of townsmen, failed with few exceptions to take the field. That the unemployed, the ruined, and the criminal should be well represented was not surprising; they had as companions a proportion of genuine patriots, brave men, and doughty fighters, while hundreds more were in their ranks through intimidation or the destruction of their homes. It is the less strange that a wide gulf should be discernible between the named objectives of the rebellion and its course and methods.[1]

[1] A close parallel is afforded by the mixed participants and mixed motives in the Resistance movements in occupied countries of Europe in 1940–5, when the noblest and the lowest fought sometimes side by side. But this is true of every rebellion in history.

This was no national uprising. A small minority of Syrians participated, the majority played the role of victims or spectators. Wide areas were undisturbed. The professed nationalists, except for a few dozen individuals, played no part save that of exhortation. The funds spent came largely from Egypt or Palestine, less and unwillingly from the pockets of the rich in Syria. Much of the rebels' energy was expended on gaining a living from the countryside and on inter-community strife. No statesman with a truly national appeal, no considerable military leader appeared, no central organization controlled events, little correlation of effort or timing was visible. The Government of Syria—ministers, officials, departments—gave no countenance to the rebellion, those of Great Lebanon and the 'Alawis still less; and the greatest part of the public abstained, if it could, from overt help to a movement which damaged and alarmed it. The regular Syrian armed forces, if they fought half-heartedly and frequently deserted, at least did not, unless rarely, join the rebels. But, for all this, the 'Syrian rebellion'[1] expressed something authentic in the spirit of the country, appealed greatly (especially in retrospect) to its countrymen, and could show its veritable heroes and martyrs. It became and remains a heroic episode in the Syrian national tradition.

The aerial bombardment of Druze villages suspected of sheltering rebels after the Michaud disaster did nothing to stop the course of events; it increased, instead, the spirit of resentment and violence. Parties of Druzes sallied forth to raid villages and flocks nearer and nearer to Damascus, and on the slopes of Hermon. In the capital, apprehension grew, foreign and some local Christian families were evacuated westwards, French troops occupied strategic points, and political meetings grew more tense; but a rising of the population, for which some clamoured, was prevented by the fears of the majority. A close approach of the forces of Sulṭan al-Aṭrash, on 24 August, was located by air observation and successfully attacked by a force of Algerians. It was followed by the arrest of eminent townsmen believed to be in touch with the Aṭrash leaders. Six leaders of the People's Party were detained and sent to Arwad; Dr. Shahbandar made his escape and joined other nationalists in the Jabal itself. In the proclamation there of a Syrian National Government by the Druze clan-leaders and the nationalist *émigrés* together, was seen the effective *rapprochement* between Damascus and Suwayda, a phenomenon new in history which was to give the rebellion its character. Under the flag of Fayṣal's Kingdom of Syria, and with

[1] Like the ' 'Iraq rebellion' of 1920, which has much in common with it in its partial scope, mixed motives, lack of organization, and the politicians' and urban middle-classes' abstention.

al-Aṭrash as President, a programme of all-Syrian unity, independence and democracy, a national army and the withdrawal of the foreigner, was addressed to the Syrian nation.

While rebel action grew wider in raids in the Ḥawran and southern Syria, restless tribesmen harried the villages in the north, and did not spare the suburbs of Aleppo and Antioch. Sarrail's dispatches to Paris were curt and uninformative, but a certain menace in the situation was appreciated, and French reinforcements began to arrive from Europe late in August. These increased the still meagre forces at the General's disposal, some of poor quality and some (the Syrian auxiliaries) unwilling to leave their own districts. Early in September he dispatched General Gamelin[1] to restore the position in the Jabal al-Duruz. With newly-arrived tanks and aircraft the latter advanced from Azra' and occupied Musayfira on 14 September, held it against a powerful rebel attack, and in the face of further opposition relieved Suwayda on the 24th. But, from shortage of supplies and manpower, it could not be held; after the destruction of some buildings it was evacuated, and the column with the released garrison returned to Musayfira. Based on this, the troops visited various parts of the Jabal and surrounding country, not without brushes with Druze parties and reinforcements trying to reach those from Transjordan. The French force was withdrawn to Damascus early in November, leaving the Jabal still unsubdued and rebel morale heightened. A High Court established with summary powers in Damascus, to try offenders against public security, could do little enough towards pacification.

October brought no alleviation to conditions which were now miserable, for the law-abiding, over an increasing area. The dense quarters of Damascus itself were full of uneasy fears, open insurrection was discussed, and the infiltration of active rebels increased. Trans-desert motor convoys were repeatedly attacked in the Shamiya desert and were forced to abandon that route.[2] The main Beirut–Damascus road itself became unsafe, the railway was attacked both in the Damascus–Rayaq and the Dar'a sections. Police posts were assaulted at Qunayṭara and Ba'lbek. Villages and garden settlements in the Ghuṭa were daily raided by marauding bands—or heroic but hungry patriots?—who defied capture and increased their forces by recruitments from the terrified and half-ruined inhabitants. Sallies into the dense fruit-gardens by the Damascus garrison could do nothing to restore a hopelessly

[1] Future Commander-in-Chief of the French Armies in Europe, 1939–40. He assumed command of the forces in Syria (but under the High Commissioner) on 2 September 1925.

[2] They adopted instead the route Jerusalem, 'Amman, Azraq, Ruṭba. The present writer travelled in the first of these diverted convoys.

deteriorated position; and this was only exacerbated by the burning of villages (themselves the helpless victims of rebel requisitioning and violence) and by the exhibition in the public squares of Damascus of the bodies of dead 'bandits'[1] brought in by the returning troops. This gruesome exhibition, ordered by General Sarrail though disliked by most French officers,[2] served none of the intended deterrent purpose; the mobile Druze bands with their accretions easily avoided capture and left the sedentary to suffer. The latter would have preferred, but could not expect, protection by the forces of the Mandatory.

Early in the same month the town of Ḥamah fell for forty-eight hours into the hands of invading tribesmen and of its own nationalist population, led by a deserter captain in the Syrian Legion. All communications were cut, and great damage was done to the government offices and bazaars by arson and pillage. Legitimate authority was restored only after the urgent arrival of troops from Rayaq and Aleppo and a bombardment which caused further damage.[3] Three days later a similar threat of 'combined operations' by tribesmen without and resentful townsmen within was made at Aleppo; but here the French were able by great efforts to prevent entry or concerted rising, though the countryside and roads remained for some time insecure; the impunity of the rebels or bandits gained them many recruits in a countryside already impoverished by the serious crop failure of 1925. The railway station at Kawkaba was burnt down, Ma'arrat al-Nu'man surrounded but rescued, attacks on Idlib and Ḥamdaniya repelled. Nearer its source the rebellion was simultaneously spreading by way of the Wadi 'Ajam across the slopes of Hermon. The Druzes of Qal'at al-Jindal had refused French orders to disarm, had raised the standard of revolt and driven out Christian householders, and set the example for the Druze village of Majdal al-Shams to do the same and evict their gendarme post and their Christian neighbours. The infection was spreading westward.

Infiltration into the bazaars of Damascus, where looting and armed clashes had already occurred, reached a new point of danger when on the afternoon of 18 October a strong band was able to enter the city already on the point of outbreak if opportunity should offer. Reinforced from the mob and by the entry of

[1] These, and most of the men killed or captured in the Ghuṭa orchards, were mainly villagers who, suspected of harbouring rebels, were in fact guilty only of being forced to provide food and shelter: a common phenomenon in this type of war.

[2] M. de Caix, at the Permanent Mandates Commission (Rome, 1926) did not conceal his disgust at 'these procedures'.

[3] Accurate (or even approximate) figures for casualties cannot be given: on this occasion the Syrians alleged 200 dead.

other parties from without, the rebels easily disarmed such gendarmes as they encountered, surrounded the Palais 'Adhm[1] and set it on fire. An Armenian camp on the outskirts of the city was attacked and burnt, and twenty of the inmates killed. The French Command at this stage ordered the withdrawal of all troops from the turbulent Maydan quarter, a half-detached intricate area south of the main town; and proceeded next, without notice or declaration of martial law, and without warning to foreign residents other than French, to bombard from the citadel first the inlying gardens and then the Maydan itself and the quarters of the city adjacent to it on the north. Another area, in the centre and north-west of the city, was protected by French troops throughout; yet another was first protected, then abandoned, and in the latter the task of saving Christian lives fell to a number of courageous Muslim leaders, and notably the Amirs Sa'id and Ṭahir al-Jaza'iri. The bombardment lasted, in slow time and with small projectiles, till noon on 20 October, in spite of the urgent intercession of Christian and Muslim notables with General Gamelin. It was stopped, and the exhausted and mutilated city fell silent, when the city spokesmen agreed to pay a collective fine of £100,000 (Turkish gold) and 3,000 rifles: a fine never, in fact, exacted. During the bombardment military and gendarme posts in the town had been overwhelmed and disarmed, and the work of looting and arson by rioters and rebels had continued, so that the damage done by these and by French gunfire could not thereafter be distinguished. The bombardment itself, heavily criticized from many quarters at the time and afterwards, appeared to the military authorities not only to be morally and practically justified by the rebel tactics, but also to be the most effective (perhaps the only) answer to the immediate military problem of clearing armed insurgence from the packed and impenetrable city—and equally, as was urged by some,[2] to solve the humanitarian problem of saving Christian lives from Muslim mob violence.[3] The judgement of the world, however, has been in general that the bombardment, however militarily desirable, was neither legally nor morally justified by the conditions, and was bound to do lasting damage (including damage to Franco-Syrian relations) out of proportion to the immediate ills which it might cure.

No reliable estimate could be made, then or later, of lives lost

[1] The beautiful Arab-style palace built by As'ad Pasha al-'Adhm (a former Governor), and in 1925 used partly as a museum and partly as the High Commissioner's Damascus residence.

[2] Including General Sarrail himself.

[3] Anti-Christian feeling had increased, due in part to their suspected Francophile sentiments, and partly to the flagrant misconduct of Armenian and Circassian volunteer auxiliaries.

among combatant rebels, looting mobs, or terrified townspeople, nor of the material damage done to the ancient and beautiful city and its monuments by French gunfire, the mêlées in the streets, or the destructive violence of the rabble.

The tragic episode was followed by the arrival at Beirut of two American destroyers, by the exodus for the coast of as many frightened (and in many cases ruined) Damascenes, Christian and Muslim, as the roads and trains could carry, and by lively apprehension that it all might well happen again. In fact some rebel infiltration continued, and gangs moved on the outskirts of the city; but the town leaders had learnt their lesson and refused co-operation with a major force led to the neighbourhood of Damascus, on 26 October, by Zayd the son of Sulṭan al-Aṭrash.

A blow of different type awaited the harassed but unrepentant author of the bombardment. In view of the simultaneous outcry of the world's press and opinion, and the grave harm done to French relations with Islam, the support which General Sarrail had hitherto enjoyed from M. Herriot and his group against the attacks of M. Briand and the Right, could not be maintained; the agitation for the removal of a High Commissioner whose own reports had been misleading, and whose impatient lack of judgement had for ten months been gravely and patently damaging to France, must now be satisfied. He was recalled by a Cabinet decision of 30 October, sailed from Beirut on 8 November, and made his report to the Committees of the Chamber ten days later. On 6 November the name of M. Henri de Jouvenel, a senator and editor of *Le Matin*, was announced as his successor. Meanwhile the High Commission was entrusted *ad interim* to General Duport, lately arrived in Syria on a military mission of inquiry.

The events of 18 to 20 October, hailed as 'methods of barbarism' by Syrian patriots, increased the impetus of the rebellion. Aleppo had renewed fears of tribal invasion, and the roads and railways of central Syria were chronically insecure since Nabq had, late in October, become the headquarters of well-led bands of the patriotic, the adventurous, and the hungry, who harried the countryside. Damascus remained uneasy, with complete stagnation of business, daily clashes in the streets, and aggressive sallies by troops into the rebel-infested fruit-gardens. Martial law, with a curfew, was proclaimed late in November. Beirut itself, its economic life seriously damaged and its streets filled with frightened refugees, was depressed and apprehensive, and the establishment of French gun-positions on the hills above the town was little reassuring. The existing Circassian and Armenian volunteer companies—admirable fighters on occasion, but truculent, brutal, and detested by the Muslim-Arab public—were increased and freely used; but they spoiled their record of valuable service to the French Command by needless ferocity and shameless looting[1] (which French courts martial had on occasion to punish), and proved a disastrously irritant factor in the bad days of mid-October in Damascus. The free use of these detachments, under French officers who highly valued them, has been severely criticized; yet in a time of crisis, with such virile manpower available and eager to serve, and with a desperate shortage of any other, it would have required uncommon self-denial by the French Command to refuse for 'political' reasons to employ them. Politically still more unhappy, and more encouraging to inter-community bitterness which the Mandate existed not to foster but to minimize, was the adopted French expedient of giving arms to Christian civilians, whether in the streets of Damascus or in the villages of southern Lebanon; whatever the admitted shortage of regular troops, and the urgent pleas of defenceless Christians, the result could never be to produce effective or reliable auxiliaries, but always to prejudice the future by increasing ill-feeling, and sometimes vendetta, between Christian and Muslim, from which the former must be the greater sufferers.

The main operations in November took place in the southern Lebanon, an extension of those begun by the Druzes a month earlier. In the second week of the month a strong body of Druzes and Ḥawranis, under Zayd Beg, occupied Ḥasbaya on the western Hermon slopes. The garrison of the town retired to Marj'uyun. On the 11th the rebel force occupied Kawkaba, a Christian village, and on the 15th Marj'uyun itself. A detachment proceeded thence to attempt the capture of Nabaṭiya, a Mutawalli village, while on 20 November Zayd with the main body assailed and besieged Rashaya. The latter commander could, if victory attended him, hope for help from the main body of the Lebanon Druzes, and he sought the favour of the Christians by proclaiming tolerance and fraternity, to such effect that he was seen in some cases even to return looted property to its owners; but his followers were less enlightened, and episodes of Druze–Christian violence at Kawkaba and elsewhere drove terrified Christians in thousands from their village homes. The capture of Rashaya would have given Zayd a free hand to dominate the Biqa' and to threaten Beirut; it was the more desperately and gallantly defended by its small garrison of Tunisians and the Foreign Legion. The siege of Rashaya, fiercely pressed, was relieved on 24 November by a great French effort. The position in south Lebanon was thereby, for the moment, saved; and the timely landing and deployment of

[1] The property of villagers in the Ghuṭa settlements and elsewhere was habitually seized by these troops and sold openly in the bazaars of Damascus.

French reinforcements made possible a considerable operation of concentration and converging advance. The Nabaṭiya garrison, which had successfully resisted, marched on Kawkaba and Marj'uyun, while columns moving simultaneously from Rashaya and Qunayṭara met at Ḥaṣbaya and, after stiff fighting, expelled the Druze occupiers. Their bands, deprived of local bases, were thenceforward confined to the less accessible hill country and to minor raids; and their brothers in the Lebanon decided, in mid-December, to announce their loyalty to their legitimate Government and the new High Commissioner. The Christians, reassured, could return to their half ruined villages, and the Mutawila were deaf thenceforward to appeals for solidarity.[1] This partial restoration of the position in the Hermon and south Lebanon area, even though villages in both northern and southern Hermon were still rebel-held, was a turning point in the fortunes of the rebellion.

3. THE DRUZE REBELLION, LATER AND LAST PHASES

If conditions in much of Syria at the turn of the years 1925–6 were still those of misery and disturbance, there were now solid reasons to hope for better times, in which Syrian nationalists and the Mandatory alike would stand more chance of realizing their aims. The rebel forces were unlikely to gain more ground; five months had shown that their appeal to the Syrian public had been largely rejected, their hope of military victory must be illusory, and they could offer nothing, save distant hopes, to compensate for the widespread destruction which their outbreak had caused. Moreover, M. de Jouvenel, the incoming High Commissioner, was from his first day vigorously pursuing a policy of peace. This had initially some effect in inducing isolated submissions, and stabilizing the still uncommitted part of the public; but since his attempt at a political settlement did not succeed, it will be well to follow the later course of military and guerrilla operations to their end, before passing to the political and constitutional scene.

In the first days of 1926 a threat developed on the northern frontier, where the Aleppo nationalist Iḥsan al Jabiri had formed on Turkish soil an 'Army of the North'; but he failed to create serious trouble when coldly welcomed by the north Syrian public and resisted by locally raised detachments under French officers. The Anti-Lebanon, however, was for a time solidly and much of the Biqa' intermittently in rebel hands, to the grave damage of the

[1] They were rewarded, early in 1926, by the passing of a statute in Lebanon giving for the first time official recognition to the Shi'i (Ja'fari) rite, and to their status as a *millet*.

villagers, especially the Christians. The rebel 'Government' of Nabq and its raiding parties were still active. The villages of the Ghuṭa were still occupied at will by Druze and mixed bands which consumed their goods and drew upon them undiscriminating punishments—bombardment, burning, fines—from the punitive columns sallying from Damascus. The latter city itself was distracted by rebel infiltrations, French reprisals, frequent shooting, occasional arson, and the levying of tribute by the insurgents from the wealthier Damascenes. In the Hermon area much remained to be done in clearance and restoration. The Jabal al-Duruz was still inaccessible to the forces or authority of the Mandatory.

M. de Jouvenel entered on his task with confident enthusiasm. He brought to it a liberal viewpoint, diplomatic skill, great social gifts, and a personal habituation to success.[1] A rapid journey to London had convinced him of British benevolence, which General Sarrail and many Frenchmen had professed to doubt. But his earliest attempts to make peace were fruitless. Realizing the considerable influence of the Syro-Palestine Committee in encouraging the rebellion (from the comfort of Cairo), he conferred with its members on his way from Paris to Beirut; but the terms of settlement which they conveyed to him were tantamount to a surrender by the French of their most cherished convictions—and their Mandate. M. de Jouvenel rejected mediation by the Committee on such terms; but he authorized an attempt at peacemaking by a mission of well-meaning Syrians and Lebanese[2] who visited the Jabal late in December. He received on 22 December a deputation from Damascus of notables influential (to say the least) with the rebels, and two days later proclaimed an amnesty for all insurgents (other than leaders or criminals) who should lay down their arms before 8 January. To the Druzes he promised their own constitution and government. The rebels, however, were still dominated by their Aṭrash leaders, and demanded, at a National Assembly convened late in February, terms quite unacceptable: unity for all Syria (including the districts embodied in Great Lebanon by General Gouraud), an immediate Franco–Syrian Treaty, complete home rule, and the withdrawal of French forces.

With both sides unyielding in their claims, no submission could be expected at present from the rebels or their political leaders, and mid-winter conditions precluded major military

[1] Mme Georges-Gaulis (*La Question Arabe*, p. 149) comments that by his gifts 'ce proconsul-né . . . se fait pardonner certaines vivacités d'homme aimé de la chance et des femmes'.

[2] The leader was a respected Lebanese Druze, the Amir Amin Arsalan.

operations. The early attempts by General Andréa at systematic purging of the Ghuṭa by the clearing of through-roads, the erection of blockhouses and barricades, and frequent disciplinary visits by military columns, proved a failure. They brought ruin to the villagers, and the indiscipline[1] of the locally-raised auxiliaries, Circassian and Armenian, left a trail of angry bitterness and endangered the lives of the already disliked Armenian inhabitants of Damascus. The clearance and pacification of the Ghuṭa was still, in April 1926, a remote prospect.

The outlying Maydan quarter offered a scarcely easier problem, haunted as it was by mobile and truculent rebels who used it as a base for their disorders in the city, and whom the inhabitants were powerless to eject. In mid-February a series of battles in street and garden, conducted with savage indiscipline by the auxiliaries and followed by wholesale looting, cleared the quarter of most of its inhabitants. A few weeks later, however, it was still used as a rebel rallying area, and early in May the French Command decided on its further destruction by shelling,[2] air-bombing, renewed ground operations, and the diversion of its water-supply. Only in August was comparative quiet restored to the remnants of the Maydan area, and its garrison withdrawn. The inhabitants returned, restoration could begin. Meanwhile in the Ḥawran, on the fringes of which the rebellion had gained some ground, representative chiefs thought it well in mid-February to declare their loyalty to the Government.

In the extreme north, conditions deteriorated early in 1926, with renewed invasions of Kurdish and Turkish-sponsored parties, and more movement by tribal and bandit forces who claimed the status of patriots. The Turkish Government, contrary to specific agreements and obsessed by the Mosul controversy[3] then at its height, monopolized the lines of the Baghdad Railway and was not unhappy to add to French embarrassment. The situation improved after the visit of de Jouvenel to Ankara in February, when a degree of border collaboration[4] was achieved, at the cost of a minor sacrifice of territory. Thereafter organized patrols on both sides of the frontier kept the peace, though the Syrian Gendarmerie were recognized as unreliable. The admirable General Billotte returned for some weeks to his former post at Aleppo; air-bombing scattered tribal concentrations which had been menacing on the outskirts

[1] General Andréa took severe disciplinary measures against at least fifty offenders.

[2] No even approximate estimate of damage or loss of life due to these and similar operations can be given; they were naturally exaggerated by the Syrian and minimized by the French official accounts.

[3] Longrigg, *'Iraq*, p. 156.

[4] The Convention is in *League of Nations Treaty Series*, vol. 54, pp. 195 ff.

of that city, and loyal or wavering shaykhs were secured by payments in cash. Insurgent bands remained in being, however, for some months more in the Jabal al-Zawiya, east of Aleppo.

In the area of Ḥamah–Ḥumṣ, no operation of policy or war availed fully to restore peaceful conditions during 1926. The towns were victimized by blackmail and kidnapping, the countryside insecure. The (Christian) Mutaṣarrif of Ḥumṣ himself was murdered in July—and unavenged. The capture of Nabq by French forces in March did not wholly correct the position. The bandit-patriots, among whom was the guerrilla leader Fawzi al-Qawuqchi,[1] terrorized the open country astride the Damascus–Ḥamah road and the northern Anti-Lebanon. Parties appeared briefly in an area previously untouched, the North Lebanon province, not far from Tripoli; and although they were here unwelcome the country inland from Tripoli and 'Akkar, and the northern Biqa' also, were badly disturbed for many weeks during the summer. Ba'lbek was looted by rebels, and Tripoli itself called for barbed-wire defences and a larger garrison. In this region only small-scale punitive operations were attempted, and these were successful in keeping open, intermittently, the north–south railway and the roads in the Biqa'; but the ultimate disappearance of rebel forces in the area was due less to military defeat than to time, wastage, and discouragement.

Elsewhere, with the spring of 1926 larger operations could be carried out, and more troops were available. In March, columns in the north Hermon area, where ground had been regained in the late autumn of 1925, succeeded in clearing the district of Druze and allied parties, but only after repeated fighting. The submission of rebels gained in impetus; the tide, locally, was turning. In the south Hermon area, still rebel-occupied with its centre at Majdal al-Shams, two French columns co-ordinated their movements from Marj'uyun and Qunayṭara and after concentration began their advance on 1 April. A number of villages including Banyas were entered against opposition, and Majdal al-Shams itself was taken by storm on 3 April. The operation was followed by many surrenders and the pacification of an important area. The disarmament of the south Lebanese villages and the exaction of fines in rifles from them led, it was alleged (notably by the Maronite Patriarch), to great hardship.

The original centre of the rebellion could be dealt with by General Gamelin now that the southern Lebanon was safe and his forces untroubled from the west. Two columns, of which the

[1] He had served under the French as a captain in the Syrian auxiliary forces, and had deserted. He was later employed by the 'Iraq Army, and led gangs in Palestine in 1936–9 and 1947–8.

greater was commanded by General Andréa, were synchronized to move by separate routes to Suwayda, starting from Azraʿ on 22 April. The resistance of the Druzes, who ignored invitations to surrender in leaflets dropped from aircraft, was in places stubborn but everywhere unavailing; Suwayda was entered on the 25th, Shahba three weeks, and Ṣalkhad five weeks later, and thereafter these severe blows to rebel morale were followed by the dispatch of French light columns to all parts of the Jabal. The followers of Sulṭan al-Aṭrash, thus hunted from their homes, were weakened by many submissions and desertions. The majority of the peasantry, the adventure over, returned to their crops, diminished by hundreds of casualties, and ruined by the loss of their possessions. But a strong nucleus remained under arms, and a true pacification and disarmament of the Jabal was still to occupy many weeks. A French Governor was installed and an administration restarted, after ten months of anarchy; but Sulṭan, though deserted by many of his lieutenants, remained at large as a powerful force leader able at will to cross into (but not allowed to stay in)[1] Transjordan. Dr. Shahbandar, with considerable Druze elements, transferred his headquarters to the Ghuṭa, whence they could enter or harry the outlying quarters of Damascus. The loot taken from the Colonne Michaud was in part recovered, its dead properly buried. The Druzes still in arms moved increasingly into the desert, volcanic area of the Lajah, south-east of Damascus, where French aircraft constantly pursued them in the later months of 1926. The remnant was attacked with ground troops in March 1927 and evicted. Thereafter the Aṭrash forces, with no longer a semblance of 'national' character, were reduced to personal followers of Sulṭan and his nearer kinsmen, and could do no more than launch an occasional raid from whatever remote refuge they had found. Sulṭan was driven by British aircraft and cars from al-Ạzraq, in Transjordan, crossed back into Syria, and finally withdrew at midsummer 1927 to be welcomed as an exiled patriot into Najd territory.

If the rebels' loss of the Jabal presaged the end, its immediate effect in the summer of 1926 was the aggravation of trouble in Damascus and the Ghuṭa, already described. The destruction of the Maydan suburb, followed by its permitted reoccupation, occupied the spring and summer of the year; the earlier half of the same period saw the long, costly, and unsuccessful efforts of General Andréa to clear the Ghuṭa. Late in April a change of method was adopted to meet a situation in which a self-appointed 'Government' was now administering the oasis, with its financial

[1] The Chamberlain–de Jouvenel talks (London, November 1925) had included agreement on this among other provisions.

and judicial branches and a well-organized system of military defences, tank-traps, supplies, and telephone lines. After due warning and time allowed for the evacuation of women and children,[1] villages believed to be harbouring rebels were bombarded and in some cases destroyed; flying columns of troops were harassed by rebel elements, intangible and almost invisible in the dense gardens. Not until 18 July was the long-planned main operation launched. Its 6 columns, with an alleged total of 8,500 men supported by artillery, tanks, and armoured cars, converged on a thick planted area 14 miles long and 11 wide, with intent to drive all rebels concealed within it against the prepared barrage surrounding Damascus. The operation, carried out with great resolution, was substantially successful in its essential task of *nettoyage*; the rebels were with few exceptions driven from the Ghuṭa, some to seek other fields of action north of Damascus, others south, but never again to coalesce in the same single force, nor to reduce the suburbs of the capital to the same helpless misery. One large rebel party, escaping from the gardens, provoked savage reprisals by an attack on Senegalese troops, who for some hours killed every Syrian they saw; another managed temporarily to surround a considerable French column north of the city. Other French columns entered and searched abandoned Ghuṭa villages, shooting summarily dozens or scores of the inhabitants as rebels or harbourers of rebels, and taking more as prisoners to Damascus: whither the less-disciplined elements among the soldiery took also an abundant loot for sale in the bazaars. Even after these operations troops bivouacking in the gardens were subject to sudden attack, and had to defend themselves in bloody encounters. The device of diverting some of the Ghuṭa irrigation canals was adopted, and provoked the rebels in turn to tamper with the Damascus water-supply. Fines, payable in gold and rifles, were exacted with stringency from all villages.

From late July until early October the slow and painful process of eradicating rebel resistance, constantly reinforced from outside and ceaselessly exhorted by Shahbandar and his friends, continued throughout the Ghuṭa oasis. Many episodes could still prove that the reign of violence was not yet over, and rebel bands could in August attack French details, capture a supply train, and penetrate destructively into the capital. But towards the end of the year such incidents grew fewer, road and rail communication was safer, and traffic more dense. In the first months of 1927 the rebellion died down and, except for the occasional raids and highway crimes of the desperate, ceased to be; and at midsummer the military régime imposed in September

[1] The great majority, however, refused to leave their homes.

1925 could give way to the forms of normal administration. Comparative peace descended at the same time on the anarchic Ḥumṣ–Ḥamah region, with the disappearance of Qawuqchi and his followers.

The Druze families who moved late in 1926 to Qaṣr al-Azraq in the lava desert of Transjordan were accepted as residents there only under assurances of good conduct, and were closely watched by the Amir ‘Abdullah's police and British detachments.[1] During 1927 some hundreds were peacefully repatriated, the remainder with Sulṭan al-Aṭrash were dispatched into Najd. These steps could not, however, preclude some frontier restlessness as between Druze outlaws and the local tribes of Syria and Transjordan, along a border not yet demarcated.

The rebellion had lasted for two years. Against the resolution of the French nation and forces it could have, evidently, no prospect of success unless by creating a movement in the political field in Europe capable of radically altering French policy. How far the policy which de Jouvenel's successor was to carry out had in fact been modified by the rebellion, in the sense sought by Syrian politicians, cannot be precisely determined; the latter would claim great gains from it in return for the shed blood of patriots and martyrs, while orthodox Frenchmen would deny that Syria had by this malevolent violence achieved anything to compensate[2] for its grievous losses. That Syria gained from it neither unity nor independence is certain, and it seems difficult to establish that the course of Franco-Syrian negotiation, or the general treatment of the latter by the former, was affected favourably by the two years of costly disturbance. In any case, the rebellion had confronted the French with a military problem of great intricacy, at a time of weakness and preoccupation. That it was unexpected, and its considerable scale too slowly recognized, was due in part to the habitual French underestimate of the force and resources of local nationalism—or more generally to their imperfect grasp of the essentials of the Syrian problem—and in part to poor military leadership in the first weeks. Once tackled, with slow accession of reinforcements from overseas, the task of restoring order still proved to be one of extreme difficulty, by reason especially of the intangible mobility of the enemy, the dozen areas in which he could simultaneously operate, and the ease with which the towns could be corrupted by infiltration. The full narrative of the campaign, as seen from the French side, reveals it as one of grave difficulties surmounted by resolution and professional skill, and

[1] Of the Royal Air Force and the Transjordan Frontier Force.

[2] The same question produces equally contradictory answers in the case of the ‘Iraq rebellion of 1920; cf. Longrigg, *‘Iraq*, p. 126.

enriched with the record of a score of episodes of great gallantry.[1]

The French forces of repression, apart from their unhappy but almost inevitable use of ill-disciplined auxiliaries, have been accused of excessive severity and of too little discrimination between enemy forces and the victimized public. A strong case can indeed be alleged in favour of both of these charges, whose substantial truth was (and is) believed not only in Syrian circles but by many European witnesses. It is certain that in bombardment and burning, in summary execution, and in destruction of property much was done which belongs to the most hateful phases of war, such as the repeated punishment of the innocent for the crime of being compelled to shelter and feed the rebel bands. But it must be equally realized that no one could be less desirous of taking such action, for its own sake, than the French Command;[2] in no army did higher standards, normally, prevail; and the conditions, in which a pitiless severity seemed to local commanders to be demanded, were entirely the creation of an enemy who, by his chosen tactics and with open eyes, habitually brought ruin and death to the villages and countryside of his fellow countrymen.

4. M. DE JOUVENEL

The extent to which the rebellion fell short of the status of a national uprising is well shown by the vigour, almost the normality, of political life throughout its length: and, in some cities, for much of the period, of commercial life also. To study the moves and countermoves of the High Commissioner, the States, and the politicians is almost to forget the disordered conditions still widely prevalent during the same months. We return now to the early days of M. de Jouvenel as High Commissioner, and to his buoyant and optimistic policy—as liberal, he believed, as that of Sarrail, but less inept[3]—which, with an almost naïve over-simplification, aimed at an early political settlement of Syria's troubles while still resolute on claiming respect for all French interests.

He turned first to the Lebanon where, in spite of all the harm done by his predecessor's unwisdom, wavering loyalty had, since the Druze invasion (p. 161), found an ally in fear; and to reinforce

[1] See, *passim*, the *Livre d'Or des Troupes du Levant, 1918–1936* (Beirut French Army Press, 1937).

[2] It is highly unjust to allege (as does the official handbook of the Syrian Government, vol. 1, p. 154) that 'the French authorities allowed their forces to kill, loot, and burn indiscriminately in a desperate effort to terrorize the in-inhabitants of the country into submission'.

[3] Mme Georges-Gaulis (*La Question Arabe*, p. 142) speaks of the General as 'las, vieilli, parfaitement ignorant des difficultés syriennes . . . violent, brutal'.

this by immediate favour was de Jouvenel's first care, and his first lesson to Syrian disloyalists. On landing he was greeted by an exemplary resolution of the Representative Council, elected only five months earlier; and in his first speech he announced that he would treat it forthwith as no less than a Constituent Assembly entitled (subject only to France's own mandatory prerogatives) to draft its own Constitution.[1] The Council met in mid-December, invited the views of a number of professional organizations, and formed a drafting committee. The occasion was seized by (mainly Muslim) apostles of pan-Syrian unity to protest against the proposed consecration for ever of a Lebanon which notoriously included unwilling Muslim-Syrian accretions. Telegrams in this sense reached Beirut from Tripoli, Ba'lbek, and elsewhere, the press fulminated, Lebanese unionists conferred with Syrian, and Muslims of Beirut refused to serve in a Constituent Assembly thus oriented. But the agitation led, perforce, to nothing; steps were, indeed, taken by the High Commissioner himself to suppress it and to curb the press, and the work of drafting proceeded. The French reservations[2] were announced as providing for their own continued control of foreign relations, for a right of veto of 'fundamental' laws and the dissolution of Parliament, and for the prerogative of arbitrating as between different States. In spite of the unpopularity of these restrictions on their independence the Council had no difficulty in accepting, with slight amendment, the text offered by their drafting committee, in which French influence[3] had been predominant; and on 24 May 1926 the Constitutional Lebanese Republic was proclaimed. The High Commissioner named twelve Senators, who with the Representative Council (now the Chamber of Deputies) elected an eminent Greek Orthodox lawyer and ex-editor, M. Charles Dabbas, as President of the Republic in place of M. Cayla, who had resigned ten days earlier.

A Ministry was formed[4] on 31 May under Auguste Adib Pasha,

[1] The Representative Council had in October 1925 claimed to be heard as a body (as distinct from M. Brunet's personal consultations) on constitutional questions, and its President had presented a report to M. Paul-Boncour in Paris.

[2] Published, as applying to all the States of the Levant, on 22 May 1926. They refer to Article 22 of the Covenant of the League, and were to be invoked on critical occasions in 1932 and 1943.

[3] The resulting constitution was, indeed, accused by Lebanese critics, then and later, of being no more than a French imposition. N. A. Ziadeh, *Syria and Lebanon*, p. 50, states categorically that 'the Lebanese Constitution was drafted in Paris and imposed on the Representative Assembly'.

[4] The ministers were: Prime Minister and Finance, Auguste Adib: Interior, Bishara al-Khuri: Justice, Najib al-Qabbani: Education, Najib al-Amyuni: Works, Yusif effendi Ephthimios: Agriculture, 'Ali Naṣrat al-As'ad: Health, Dr. Salim Talḥuq. This Cabinet contained two Maronites, and one each of the Sunni, Shi'i, Druze, Greek Catholic, and Greek Orthodox communities.

a Maronite of high standing with long financial experience in Egypt. Having published its Utopian programme, it weathered a storm raised by angry unionists over a speech by President Dabbas, emphatic on the unchangeable integrity of the Republic. The High Commissioner, rejecting a nationalist suggestion that the Lebanon boundaries be fixed on a basis of local self-determination, declared the time unsuitable for changes; but agitation continued on that issue, proponents of a Smaller Lebanon were arrested, and a number of newspapers were suppressed.

The Lebanese Constitution, which provoked Syrian and unionist dismay by declaring its present territory unalterable, provided for a two-Chamber Parliament, the collective and individual responsibility of ministers, two-stage universal (male) suffrage, representation in the familiar confessional proportions, and nomination by the President of 7, out of 16, Senators. The latter were to serve for 6 years, the 30 Deputies for 4, and the President, elected by both houses in joint session, for 3 with the possibility of re-election. The President was given, besides ceremonial duties and powers, the right to name the Prime Minister and, after a vote of three-quarters of the Senate, to dismiss the Chamber. The Constitution was soon to prove too elaborate for so small a State, and too easily mishandled by politicians to the detriment of good administration; meanwhile it failed also, as every nationalist and the Maronite Patriarch himself indicated, with some asperity, to confer any real independence. It perpetuated, instead, all the reality of French control.

The first weeks of constitutional life in the Republic showed already serious weaknesses. Apart from the continued objection by some of the Deputies to the undefined but all-pervasive French powers of interference, relations between ministers, the Chamber, and the Senate were from the outset unhappy. A sense of financial realism was lacking, ambition for costly enterprises accompanied the outcry for reduced taxation, and the omnipresence of personal and confessional interests and *pistonnage* embarrassed the Administration. By the end of 1926 the need for revision of the Constitution was already clear.

In spite of the persisting disturbances in Syria, and of the wide gap outstanding between French and Syrian conceptions of a tolerable *modus vivendi* (as a delegation from Damascus to the Grand Sérail in mid-December made plain), M. de Jouvenel had no intention of limiting constitutional advance to the more amenable Lebanon. On 21 December 1925 he ordered the holding of elections for new Representative Councils to replace those now time-expired both in the 'Alawi territory and in the parts of Syria not under martial law: elsewhere, that is, than Damascus, the

Ḥawran, and the Jabal al-Duruz. The Deputies for the districts in which elections could be held, including the 'Alawi State, were then to confer as to their constitutional desiderata and their conception of inter-unit relations: a provision which seemed to Syrian unionists to presage a still further parcellation of their country, though this was not intended. Meanwhile a number of *détenus* were released from arrest.

The elections held in March, in areas where they could be held, gave results generally unsatisfactory to the High Commissioner's plans. The 'Alawis, with the abstention of many from the Sunni and Christian minorities, declared through their new Representative Council that they clung to their 'independence' and separation, but would welcome an inter-State economic commission. A drafting committee was set up at Ladhqiya to frame a Constitution, and made progress in the face of the usual forms of opposition; a proposal to call the citizens of the State 'West Syrians', as a face-saving compromise, effected little. In the Alexandretta sanjaq the Deputies, in part under Turkish influence, voted for total separation from Syria; and in March the Representative Council proclaimed independence, voted a Constitution, asked the High Commissioner for the continued exercise of his supervisory services, and demanded the appointment of their present Délégué-Adjoint, M. Durieux, as President. But this régime, unacceptable to the Arab party and undesired by the French, was short-lived; the Syrian Government was able, by a mission of two ministers, to persuade the separatists to reverse their policy, and in June they agreed to remain as before within the Syrian framework. Nationalist accusations that the Délégué-Adjoint himself, or the High Commissioner, played some sinister part in these tergiversations seem groundless.

The representatives at Dayr al-Zur, meeting in March, desired that all Syrian and Lebanese Deputies should form jointly a single Constituent Assembly. In the Ḥawran, although martial law was abolished on 11 February, no elections were held at present, and some signs of a separatist spirit were visible. The Aleppo Deputies met in February after sparsely-attended elections marked by rowdy demonstrations, at least one bloody street fight, and the arrest (and dispatch to Arwad) of anti-election agitators. The most eminent of these, Ibrahim Bey Ḥananu (p. 121), escaped from the town and joined rebel bands outside; the danger to the city represented by these was met by the recruitment of more Kurdish irregulars by the French Intelligence Officers. The Council thus formed, which consisted of minor personalities, nevertheless telegraphed at its first meeting to the High Commissioner in favour of a unitary Syro-Lebanese State, with provision for decentralization; and meanwhile they demanded the release of their arrested friends. At Ḥumṣ and Ḥamah no elections could be held; the boycott announced by the People's Party was strictly observed.

In Damascus, still in the grip of martial law and barricades, and the scene of frequent street affrays, the Syrian Head of State, Ṣubḥi Bey Barakat, resigned on 21 December 1925 an office which he was no longer capable of filling to reasonable public satisfaction;[1] he had, moreover, lost the confidence of the High Commission by his self-identification with the demands of the recent Syrian deputation to Beirut. To replace him, de Jouvenel's choice fell on Shaykh Taj al-Din al-Ḥasani, a judge and divine respected for his personal character and as the son of an eminent father, and, though never himself a rebel, sufficiently a nationalist to be acceptable to that faction. In spite, however, of the moderation of his own views he was forced by pressure from the People's Party to offer the High Commissioner a programme of general amnesty, unification of Syria, membership of the League of Nations, reduction of the Lebanon to its original sanjaq, and evacuation of French troops; and since much of this was clearly unacceptable, the appointment was not made. No other local candidate satisfied the High Commissioner's requirements; but conditions in Damascus, as de Jouvenel saw during a visit early in February, were such as to call imperatively for the restoration of orderly government. He felt bound to reimpose, temporarily,[2] direct mandatory rule, and charged M. Pierre Alype, a senior member of his own staff, with the duties of Head of State. Some progress in the normalization of public affairs resulted, while the process of wearing down the rebellion continued outside.

M. Alype installed in Damascus, the High Commissioner decided to pay a rapid visit to Ankara both to secure Turkish abstention from trouble-making on the border, and to deal with the deadlock which the Frontier Commission, set up in 1921 but convened only in 1925, had already reached. His visit was successful. An agreement initialed on 18 February, and signed on 30 May,[3] provided for the arbitration of disputes as between Turkey and France (acting for Syria), for 'benevolent neutrality' by each in case of outside attack on either Power, for frontier co-operation,

[1] He spoke Arabic with difficulty, was known to favour Aleppo as the capital, and filled public appointments with his 'Turkish' friends. Against these defects his intelligence and charm could not prevail.

[2] From 9 February to 27 April.

[3] Signature was delayed by the Turkish reaction to (highly correct) French unwillingness to permit the Baghdad Railway to be used by Turkey in the event of hostilities (which at that time appeared possible) between Turkey and Great Britain over the Mosul wilayet.

and for other outstanding matters.[1] M. de Jouvenel was forced to agree to minor adjustments of the frontier in the area of Killis and of Payas; these involved a loss of territory to Syria which was both condemned by local nationalists, and questioned also by the Permanent Mandates Commission as contrary to the terms[2] of the Mandate. Conditions on the frontier markedly improved (p. 164–5). M. de Jouvenel followed his Turkish visit by another to the High Commissioner for Palestine on 30 March.

His success in Turkey, the recent improvement in Damascus since the partial clearance of the Maydan, and the now impending reoccupation of the Jabal al-Duruz, led the High Commissioner to take further steps towards establishing constitutional life in Syria.[3] Little which commended itself to him could be based on the recent and incomplete Syrian elections, even though his staff could claim that 31 out of a potential total of 38 Deputies had been duly elected in the areas available for polling. M. de Jouvenel proceeded, therefore, on 28 April to appoint as provisional Head of State a son-in-law (therefore known as Damad)[4] of 'Abd al-Majid, the last of the Ottoman Caliphs. Aḥmad Nami Bey, by race a Circassian, now aged 48, was the son of a high official who had made Lebanon his home; he himself had held senior appointments, was rated as Francophile, and had sons in France. Accepting the office in Damascus, the Damad reached a working agreement with the High Commissioner on the basis of an early Franco-Syrian Treaty,[5] a Constituent Assembly to be convened forthwith, and collaboration, if no more, between the existing States to secure a sea outlet for Syria. A Cabinet was formed containing three members of the People's Party, the rest of the ministers[6] being 'moderates'; no Ministry failing to include

[1] Extradition of criminals, river-water distribution (the Quwayq and the Euphrates), and use of the Baghdad Railway.

[2] Under Article 4 the Mandatory was responsible for seeing 'that no part of the territory of Syria and the Lebanon is ceded or leased or in any way placed under the control of a foreign Power'. The French, however, represented the adjustment, reasonably enough, not as a surrender but as a long-waited demarcation.

[3] As it proved impossible to satisfy the conditions of the Mandate (Art. 1) by completing a Constitution within three years (as had been done in the Lebanon) the French Government applied to the League Council on 20 September 1926, and again on 12 March 1927, for an extension of the period.

[4] The word, meaning (in Turkish) 'son-in-law', was regularly used as a title by and of those who married the Sultan's daughters.

[5] Although such a treaty (evidently on the Anglo-'Iraqi model) had not yet been declared as part of the official policy of France, it was tacitly understood to be in prospect. This was stated by de Jouvenel at the Permanent Mandates Committee, which he attended, in June 1926.

[6] In Interior, Agriculture, and Education were installed the three nationalists, respectively Ḥusni al-Barazi, Luṭfi al-Ḥaffar, and Faris al-Khuri. The others, in Finance, Works, and Justice were Shakir al-Na'ama, Wathiq al-Mu'ayyid, and Yusif al-Ḥakim.

the former element could hope for adequate support for whatever programme might be evolved. Even in this better atmosphere, however, spokesmen of the People's Party, the new ministers among them, continued to demand concessions obviously unacceptable to the French: a general amnesty, a National Army, the evacuation of French forces, a short-term treaty, a plebiscite for the Lebanese border districts, and a unified Syria. The High Commissioner, rejecting most of this, consented to a ministerial programme published on 16 May on the more moderate lines already agreed with the Damad—a Constituent Assembly, a Treaty to be ratified by the Syrian Parliament, consultation between Lebanon and the other States on their interrelations, an Army, a rebased currency, eventual League of Nations membership, and indulgence to political *détenus*.

But the temporary alliance within the Cabinet was insecure. The nationalist ministers led, rather than abstained from, opposition to a moderate programme; the shutting of bazaars and organization of street demonstrations were not discouraged by them; and when on 11 June they declined to sign a declaration repudiating rebel activities they were arrested and, with other more or less open sympathizers with the rebels, were dispatched once again to Arwad Island. The vacant places in the Cabinet were filled by more amenable figures,[1] and the official programme reiterated.

But in truth the essential conditions for co-operation and progress did not yet exist. The gulf between French and nationalist conceptions was still at its widest, far wider than a too-hopeful High Commissioner had imagined, and unbridgeable by his blandishments. The French were not prepared to make sweeping concessions, which they felt to be unsuitable to the moment of anticipated military victory, unwelcome to the favoured minorities, and contrary to the very bases, as they saw them, of a well-conducted Mandate. They intended to uphold Greater Lebanon, to retain Maronite and Catholic support, to remain in effective control of all the States, to liberate and to unify in their own time and fashion—or not at all. Deadlock, in fact, had been reached; and after one more public collision between Beirut and Damascus on the question of the Lebanese boundaries, and one ill-advised Decree by the High Commissioner on Muslim and other personal status, which aroused universal opposition,[2] M. de Jouvenel,

[1] The second Syrian Ministry contained: in Interior (with Agriculture and Economics) Wathiq al-Mu'ayyid: Justice, Yusif al-Ḥakim: Finance, 'Abd al-Qadir al-'A<u>dh</u>m: Works and Commerce, Shakib Mayṣar: Education, Shakir al-Ḥanbali.

[2] The Decree withdrew all personal-status questions from the confessional (including the Shara') Courts. It was the subject of protest by all Christian Patriarchs, and the Muslim dignitaries. A month later its application was, wisely, 'postponed'.

still confidently hopeful that all was well, returned to France. He gave his account of events at Geneva on 17 June, and resigned his office a month later. His mission, superior in merit as in fortune to that of his predecessor, had failed: not this time so much through personal shortcomings as through insufficient advance from a policy which made success impossible.

5. M. HENRI PONSOT

As probable successor to M. de Jouvenel the name of General Weygand was freely canvassed in France and in Syria;[1] but the opposition of the Cartel des Gauches (who having nominated Sarrail had been forced to acquiesce in his recall) was decisive against another[2] military High Commissioner. The choice fell instead on M. Henri Ponsot, a professional diplomat, aged 49, without political affiliations but widely experienced; he was at the time Deputy Director of the African and Levant section at the Quai d'Orsay. Appointed on 27 August 1926, he arrived in Beirut on 12 October; and, characteristically, he made no statement on landing.

Unlike his predecessor, he was in no hurry. He devoted four months to patient touring of the country and discussion with the representatives of every interest. He found the territory in a demoralized, nervous, and disturbed condition. Rebel bands and some eminent leaders were still at large, roads locally unsafe; a military régime and strict censorship prevailed, and the economic condition of markets and of homes was greatly depressed. A sign of this was the prolonged strike in Beirut during July and August against the charges made by the concessionaire company on the local tramways, and for electric light and power. The strike called for police intervention and lasted for twenty days: and almost simultaneously a printers' strike largely paralysed the press. The unsolved political problems of the country early showed themselves to the new High Commissioner through a memorial submitted to him by Beirut Muslims, in favour of the truncation of Greater Lebanon: by continual press criticism of the present régime in Lebanon—its cost, inefficiency, narrow confessionalism, and lack of real self-government: and by the now familiar protests from unionist elements at Ladhqiya. Rumours were current that conversations (denied *in toto* by the French) were in progress between the Quai d'Orsay and Syro-Palestine Congress spokesmen. On the other hand, the Mixed Tribunal of Justice in the Lebanon was helping to cure the surviving evils of banditry and

[1] A petition to this effect was received in Paris from the Lebanon.

[2] General Gamelin was thought a likely candidate.

inter-community fighting, submissions of ex-rebels were increasing, and a measure of stabilization was visible. The fine on the city had been remitted, funds were provided for rebuilding the ruined quarters, and Alexandretta had been recovered for the Syrian State (p. 172). And when in November a crisis arose in the Damad's Cabinet, due to personal quarrels, a new Ministry could be quickly formed.[1]

M. Ponsot followed an early visit to Damascus by another to the Jabal al-Duruz. Here he found evidence—it had reached him already in round-robins addressed to the Grand Sérail—of an anti-Syrian separatism now easily prevalent over the pan-Syrian unionism by which Sulṭan al-Aṭrash had been beguiled as a means of gaining wider support. A new Administration was installed in the Mountain under a French Governor, Colonel Henry, with a nominated advisory Council (consisting half of officials) and with Druze Directors of Interior, Justice, and Finance, a volunteer army of some 600 men,[2] Qa'immaqams at Ṣalkhad and Shahba, and a Municipality at the capital, Suwayda.

Most of the fines levied on the Druze villages were set aside to be spent on rehabilitation, and to finance an Agricultural Bank. A spur of railway was constructed from the Ḥijaz line near Azra' to Suwayda. Druze rebel bands still venturing into the Jabal from outside were driven off, or destroyed; the biggest of these, under 'Abd al-Ghaffar Pasha, submitted with some hundreds of men in August 1927. Shahbandar betook himself to 'Iraq in December 1926, and later to Egypt. But, in spite of a now universal wish for tranquillity, the endless quarrels between Druze chiefs made precarious even the restoration of a régime resembling that of the favourable 1921 Agreement.

Elsewhere, the High Commissioner's chosen role was for the moment that of listener. From every quarter he was pressed to declare amnesty for the detained rebels or the obstructors of the recent elections, and to ease the press censorship. In Beirut he heard the grievances of the Maronite Patriarch, the Armenians, the Muslims, the Mutawila of the Biqa', and the Jews. In Damascus, Aleppo, Ḥumṣ, Ḥamah, he received both formally by deputation and informally in many private conversations the now unvarying demands of the main body of the nationalists, still undaunted and confident that better times lay ahead. All demanded amnesty, compensation for 'victims of the rebellion', a Constituent

[1] The distribution of portfolios was: Interior, Ra'uf al-Ayyubi: Justice, Yusif al-Ḥakim: Finance, Ḥamdi al-Naṣr: Education, Shakir al-Ḥanbali: Works, Rashid al-Mudarris: Agriculture and Commerce, Naṣuḥ al-Bukhari.

[2] One company of these, who were all under French officers, acted as the Gendarmerie of the Jabal.

Assembly freely elected, a provisional, to be followed by a permanent, National Government, the unification of Syria (with a plebiscite to be held in the border qaḍhas of Lebanon), a national Army, freedom of speech and the press, abolition of the Mixed Courts, and a satisfactory Franco-Syrian Treaty. Senior French officials and Syrian dignitaries met together for consultation at the High Commissioner's office on 9 January 1927; but he still gave no hint of his intentions, and left for conversations in Paris on 27 February.

Political activity conducted outside Syria, but concerned with that country and conducted by Syrians, was as active as it had ever been. A Lebanese Committee in Paris submitted its complaints to the Quai d'Orsay. Syro-Lebanese *émigrés* in France sought to profit from their many contacts there, and founded a new Arabic-French magazine. The permanent Commission of Syrians at Geneva hurried to the banks of the Seine whenever a possible opening occurred. In Berlin a Lebanese committee roundly condemned French methods; in Detroit an imposing Syrian-American Congress was held in March 1927, and resolutions were passed with exalted unrealism. The Syro-Palestine Congress in Egypt lost no single opportunity of representing, urging, protesting to Paris, Geneva, London, or Washington, and published in Cairo an illustrated book, *The Syrian Calamity*. But its authority was, later in 1927, to be diminished by a prolonged schism in its own ranks, which now included many eminent Syrians recently banished, or escaped, from their own country. The points at issue were partly practical, partly of policy, partly of discipline. The position, which for a time defied reconciliation, led to the foundation of a shortlived rival, the Syrian Nationalist Association, with the exiled statesmen nicely divided between the mutually recriminating bodies.

While M. Ponsot was still absent, the embarrassments of the Lebanese Cabinet between the hammer and anvil of the Chamber and the Senate led to its resignation on 2 May, in despair of a situation which allowed it no executive power. A seven-minister Cabinet[1] was formed in its place, with the understanding that this should, for economy, be later reduced in numbers. It was destined to last only for seven months; but during its life the much-needed first changes in the Lebanese Constitution were carried through. The reform, supported by much local and all French opinion but furiously attacked by sections of the press, the Deputies, and the

[1] Prime Minister and Minister of Education, Bishara al-Khuri: Justice, Shukri Qardaḥi: Interior, Georges Tabet (Thabit): Finance, Khalid Shihab: Works, Aḥmad al-Ḥusayni: Health, Dr. Salim Talḥuq: Agriculture, Alyas Fayyaḍh. These belonged respectively to the Maronite, Greek Catholic, Sunni, Shi'i, Druze, and Greek Orthodox communities.

émigrés abroad, was proposed to Parliament by the President and, in spite of outcry, easily[1] passed into law in October 1927. Its effect was to confer increased authority on the President, who was given power to expedite a lagging budget and (with later parliamentary sanction) to add to a defective one, to call for reconsideration of unwise legislation, to direct executive action to be taken on proposals interminably delayed in the Chamber, and, for stated reasons and on Cabinet advice, to dismiss the Chamber. These provisions, which made possible the reasonable dispatch of business, were accompanied by others: the Senate was abolished, the Chamber was increased by fifteen members to be nominated by the President, and its power to increase proposed budget allotments was withdrawn. Cabinet solidarity was enforced, and half its members must be Deputies. As President of the new Chamber a Sunni, Shaykh Muḥammad al-Jisr, was elected. The budget for the next year (1928) was voted with exemplary speed; but the seven-man Ministry was still top-heavy, and refused to face the need for immediate economy. It was replaced late in January 1928 by a three-member Cabinet,[2] pledged to reform; its programme was one of the abolition of unneeded posts, reorganization of the administrative districts, reduction of the number of deputies. The initial vote of confidence which it obtained was almost unanimous.

M. Ponsot returned from France in June 1927, to find conditions in Damascus and its neighbourhood considerably nearer to normal. A month later he ordered the abolition of the military 'special régime' of the last years, and normal administration could be restored. Some of the most prominent leaders still in *résidence forcée* were given greater liberty of movement. On 27 July, after consultations with Governors and ministers, the High Commissioner issued a declaration of policy evolved, in outline, during his stay in France. He affirmed a continuance of the Mandate, to be applied as ever with full regard to the people's wishes, which would be paramount in framing the Constitution. The Mandatory reserved its right to arbitrate between States, and to maintain order. Separatism would not be encouraged, both political and economic development would be fostered. The Common Interests would continue to be administered by France. Local troops would gradually replace French.

The declaration was greeted by the Syro-Palestine Congress in Cairo with savage bitterness, in Syrian nationalist circles

[1] Nationalists alleged, as usual, that pressure was brought to bear on Deputies by the French, to secure a favourable vote.

[2] Prime Minister and Minister of Justice and Education, Bishara al-Khuri: Interior and Health, Ayyub Tabet: Finance, Works, and Agriculture, Ḥusayn al-Aḥdab.

with some but not excessive disappointment on the grounds of its vagueness, its uncertain application, and its silence on such issues as amnesty for the condemned or fugitive, personal and political liberty, the future boundaries of Lebanon, judicial reform, and the terms of the future Treaty. The Nationalists' counterstroke was the convening on 20 October of a Congress where a programme was formulated not, indeed, all in terms acceptable to the High Commissioner but avoiding emphasis on the more intractable issues and showing the intention of collaborating to some degree with France, for the first time, over the forthcoming elections and Constitution. The forces of opposition in Syria had, indeed, for some months been busiest in their combination not so much against the French as against the Government of the Damad. The latter, in the changed times, had few friends. Early in February 1928 he was allowed to resign after his twenty months in office, and was thanked by M. Ponsot for his efforts. He was succeeded as Prime Minister of a 'Provisional Government' by Shaykh Taj al-Din, and on 15 February a new Cabinet of distinguished but not extremist members was announced.[1] The relatively moderate programme which it published contained important claims and demands, but made also friendly references to the French and to the need of interstatal consultation. The High Commissioner, announcing in his turn the imminence of elections for a Constituent Assembly (with an 'Agreement' with France to follow later), removed the restrictions on personal liberty imposed since 1925, lightened the press censorship, and proclaimed amnesty for all insurgents except thirty-nine named persons:[2] all this, as a means of securing free elections and as marking, incidentally, the end of the rebellion. The return of many nationalist leaders from *résidence forcée* was uneventful. A further statement by the Government of Shaykh Taj reaffirmed the reciprocal nature of French and Syrian rights and duties, called for early free elections, hoped for Syrian representation on the Common Interests, and wished for the preparation of a Franco-Syrian Treaty which Parliament would approve.

March 8, the anniversary of Fayṣal's proclamation as King of Syria eight years ago, passed quietly. Shaykh Taj was well received on his northern tours. The more extreme nationalists, temporarily tolerant of the present ministry, pressed for fewer exclusions from the amnesty, and in this were in part gratified a month later. In face of the High Commissioner's decree of 20

[1] Prime Minister, Shaykh Taj al-Din: Interior, Sa'id al-Muḥaysin: Justice, Ṣubḥi al-Nayyal: Finance, Jamil al-Ulshi (p. 103 n.): Education, Muḥammad 'Ali Kurd 'Ali: Works, Tawfiq Shamiya: Agriculture, 'Abd al-Qadir al-Kilani.

[2] Eighteen were Syrians, 13 Druzes, 6 Lebanese, 2 'Alawis. These were political offenders; criminals were not pardoned.

March, unifying the election procedures for all parts of Syria, they demanded representation by sanjaqs (liwas) rather than qadha by qadha, finding the latter principle cramping to People's Party candidates. They complained of the right to vote being given to alien Armenians, and later were to bring charges of interference with the vote-counting by district officers and by the Minister of the Interior. The Prime Minister on 4 April announced the distribution of seats in the Chamber among the religious bodies.[1]

The primary elections were held, with a minimum of demonstrations and recriminations, on 10 April, the secondary on the 24th. In the country districts local notables, largely conservative, were usually elected; in the towns, success went to the candidates of the Nationalists, whose leaders all secured seats. A majority for the forces of co-operation seemed to the French authorities to be assured, even though the People's Party proclaimed the exactly opposite view. The Constituent Assembly met at Damascus on 9 June 1928.

Its success in providing a Constitution, eight years after the fatal day of Maysalun—and, more than that, in providing the basis for an acceptable *modus vivendi* between Mandatory and mandated, whereby at last the spirit of Article 22 of the Covenant could be made manifest—must now depend on nationalist willingness to accept less than their full programme, and that of the French to soften or lighten the rigours of control and the exercise of their own 'rights'.

[1] To the Sunnis, 52 seats: 'Alawis, 3: Greek Orthodox, 2: Armenian Orthodox, 3: bedouin tribesmen, 4: Isma'ilis, Syrian Orthodox, Greek Catholics, Armenian Catholics, Syrian Catholics and Jews, 1 each.

VI

ADVANCE AND RECESSION

1. THE SYRIAN CONSTITUTION

THE period from mid-1928 to the end of 1935 was shadowed in Syria by a continuous economic depression which, the fault not of the French or Syrians but of world conditions, contributed to the restless unhappiness of the country. Not infrequently used by the politicians for their own ends, it necessarily slowed down the pace of desired progress in the material field and the public services. In the Administration, whose structure and procedures were almost unchanged in these years, little advance was made in the 'Syrianization' of the higher posts or in the passing of greater responsibilities to that Republic; but many departments were successfully overhauled, some abiding questions settled—the Ottoman Debt, the control of the tobacco trade—judicial reform was advanced, a machinery for the Common Interests was established, and both French and Syrian officials gained in experience.

No solution was found during the period to the political issues which, to local eyes, far transcended in interest the course of either administration or economics, and which persistently divided the Mandatory from the mandated. The French enjoyed, on the whole, the not uncritical support of the Permanent Mandates Commission[1] at Geneva, and clung with great tenacity to their policy of separating the 'Alawi and Druze territories from the Syrian State, of maintaining intact the Greater Lebanon, of controlling closely the whole administration and judiciary, including the *troupes spéciales* and the financially all-important Common Interests. These were the features of French policy particularly repugnant to the statesmen and parties of Syrian nationalism. The simultaneous handling of strictly similar issues by the British Mandatory in 'Iraq,[2] on lines less insistent on

[1] Its meetings, usually biennial, were attended by M. Robert de Caix (who annually visited the Levant to collect his material) and frequently also by the High Commissioner. The proceedings were closely watched by Syrian statesmen.

[2] The temptation to apply a separatist policy—to govern by dividing—could have been no less considerable in 'Iraq, with its well-marked Kurdish, Shi'i, Yazidi, and Assyrian minorities, and its regionalism as between north and south. Such a policy was resisted by British as well as 'Iraqi authorities, with a broad wisdom which even the tragic Assyrian episode of 1933 (Longrigg, *'Iraq*, pp. 231 ff.) does not discredit. The transfer of real powers to the local Government

mandatory 'rights' and more acceptable to the local politicians, forms a contrast to the uneasy course of events in the Levant. Meanwhile the Syrian people continued to be represented in the political field by a small 'evolved' class which claimed to speak for the normally apathetic and conservative mass of taxpayers—and occasional rebels; and Syrian politics continued by their instability, their tone of irresponsibility, and their ready recourse to violence, to show an immaturity which, rightly or wrongly, seemed to many both in Syria and in Europe to justify the cautious or negative attitude of France. Though the ostensible objectives of the nationalist leaders were, on a broad view, far from ignoble, and their intelligence was high, their refusal of all compromise with their Mandatory and of all acceptance of interim solutions was, though entirely characteristic of Middle Eastern politics—perhaps, indeed, of all lively peoples held reluctantly under tutelage—an apparent disservice to the present welfare and tranquillity of the country.

The Constituent Assembly which met in Damascus on 9 June 1928 contained a clear majority of the small-town and country-side 'notables' almost unquestioningly chosen as Deputies by the rural voters—or, complained the nationalists, imposed upon these by the anti-nationalist local officials of the district; but these 'moderates' had no organization, stood for no programme save a vague conservatism, and were easily intimidated. The Syrian Reform Party founded in 1929 by senior ex-Turkish officials[1] survived, with little real influence, a bare two years: the Liberal Constitutional Party, founded in northern Syria in 1930 by Ṣubḥi Barakat, was too nepotistic (and too friendly to the French) to be effective when opposed by a livelier nationalism. The Syrian Liberal Party of Shakir Na'ama al-Sha'bani, founded in the early days of the Mandate, contained able men but could play no dominant part. If these organizations failed to provide acceptable leadership, it was all too probable, though by the French largely unexpected, that the unorganized rank-and-file Deputies should

established in December 1920, and transformed into a constitutional monarchy in August 1921, was from the first a feature of the mandatory régime; nor (in spite of French suggestions to this effect) did the 'Iraqi public services suffer by comparison with the Syrian. The 'Iraqi Army and Police were from the first under direct 'Iraqi command. Provincial administration was 'Iraqi from 1920 onwards, with a minimum number of British 'administrative advisers'. The first Anglo-'Iraqi Treaty was concluded in 1924, amended in 1927, and replaced in 1930. Admission to the League was achieved in 1932. A treaty was concluded between Britain and the Amirate of Transjordan in 1928 and amended in 1934; British control there was even lighter than in 'Iraq. A similar development in Palestine was hopelessly precluded by the presence there of the Jewish National Home, to which it was realized that an Arab Government, otherwise so clearly indicated, would be fatal.

[1] Ḥaqqi Bey al-'Adhm, Naṣif al-Ayyubi, 'Awni al-Qadhamani, &c.

yield all initiative to the numerically fewer enthusiasts of the Nationalist movement. This, under the leadership of outstanding politicians, was now feeling its way towards the creation of a loose but countrywide group to include such smaller parties as that of Istiqlal (Independence), the survivors of the People's Party, the old 'Ahd and Fatat groups (p. 28), and coteries of prominent lawyers, teachers, writers, and publicists. Members of these, immediately after the suave and hopeful opening speeches of the High Commissioner and Shaykh Taj al-Din, secured their own election to the posts of President of the Assembly (Hashim Bey al-Atasi) and the other official positions in it, and that also of president of the Drafting Committee to which, with its majority of eager nationalists, was entrusted the preparation of the Constitution.

Less than two months sufficed to produce a draft Constitution, inspired by the most advanced western forms. It was that of a parliamentary republic, with a single Chamber to be elected, for four years, by universal suffrage exercised in two stages. Executive power belonged to a President (who must be a Muslim) and a responsible Ministry; the former could, in certain circumstances, adjourn or dissolve the Chamber. A High Court was established, to try ministers for treason. Equality as between citizens of all sects was prescribed, with freedom of religious observance and for the community schools. The promised Electoral Law was to provide for the specific representation of the religious minorities. The draft was, in most respects, inoffensive to the High Commissioner, who had left its preparation to Syrians; but, although it was passed *en bloc* by the Assembly on 7 August and was next to be debated article by article, it contained nevertheless elements to which the French could not be indifferent. It ignored, in fact, both the actual course of Syrian history since 1918, and the existence of a Mandate. It declared 'Syria', including Transjordan, Palestine, and the Lebanon, to be one and indivisible; it gave the Syrian Government power to organize the armed forces, and to the President the power to conclude treaties, grant pardons, appoint ambassadors, and proclaim martial law—all functions considered by the French as peculiar to the Mandatory as long as such existed.[1]

On 9 August, therefore, the High Commissioner informed the Assembly that Articles 2, 73, 74, 75, 110, and 112 could not be accepted, and suggested a 'separation' of these from the rest of the text. The Assembly, in spite of the plea of Taj al-Din and a few moderates in favour of compromise, rejected this suggestion,

[1] The Permanent Mandates Commission in June 1928 expressed the hope that, until self-government in Syria had been established, 'the Mandatory will retain such a measure of authority as will fully enable it to continue to direct and superintend this evolution, and to fulfill all its obligations to the League of Nations'.

claiming to be uninterested in France's unilateral obligations; and, in order that immediate deadlock should not result, found itself adjourned by the High Commissioner for three months as from 11 August, and for a further three thereafter. M. Ponsot visited France (followed thither by more than one Syrian statesman) and on his return proposed[1] in December that Article 2 (the indivisibility of 'Syria') should be suitably reworded, and an Article 116 added to the Constitution in such terms as to secure, for the mandatory period, both internal security and the due execution of France's international obligations. Articles affecting France's obligations in regard to Syria were, in terms of the new Article, to be applicable 'only under conditions to be determined by agreement between the two Governments', laws affecting such matters being promulgated only after such agreement; and French-made 'decisions of the nature of laws or regulations' could be modified only with French concurrence. The Assembly, among whose members threats and persuasion, street demonstrations, and the mere passage of time, had increased the Nationalists' dominance, rejected the offered formulae, and stood by the intransigent manifestos issued by the nationalist groups during December. Shaykh Taj, informing M. Ponsot that he could not secure his friends' agreement on the lines proposed, offered instead an Article[2] specifying that the provisions held by France as objectionable 'should be carried out in accordance with special agreements to be made between France and Syria, pending conclusion of a Treaty to define relations between the two'. But the High Commissioner found that this wording presaged too clearly the establishment of a régime in which the Mandate as a whole, with its implied universal control, would be unworkable. He rejected the suggestion; and in spite of a number of meetings between him and nationalist leaders, and the apparent possibility (as it seems in retrospect) of finding an acceptable formula, M. Ponsot, while expressing to Shaykh Taj his regrets at Syrian intransigence, felt bound to prorogue the Assembly *sine die* on 5 February 1929. This was in effect to renounce the hope of an agreed Constitution, and the step was followed by the usual indignation meetings, angry speeches and press articles, street and student demonstrations, and telegrams to Paris and Geneva.[3] The twelve months following the High Commissioner's initiative and the change of Government in Syria in February 1928 (p. 180) had failed, after all, to produce the expected step forward in Syrian development.

The year 1929 and early 1930 was, by Syrian standards, a

[1] *Or. Mod.*, March 1929, p. 119. [2] Ibid., March 1929, p. 120.

[3] The Syro-Palestine Committee at Cairo, and its representatives at Geneva, were loud in their denunciation of French impolicy and 'colonialism'; but their authority was the less by reason of the deep split in their own ranks at this time.

period of calm. The national celebration of Martyrs' Day at Maysalun, and even the anniversary of the Balfour Declaration, were conducted peaceably, though the latter was marked by the shutting of bazaars. The events in Palestine of midsummer 1929 were echoed in Syria by signs of national solidarity on the Zionist question; bazaars were closed in protest, demonstrations occurred in the towns, and the Palestine frontier was closed for some weeks. The many conferences held by political parties during the year produced no more than the usual affirmations and condemnations. Leaders of the nationalist movement, and particularly Hashim al-Atasi, took pains to keep the High Commissioner informed of the unchangeability of their views. These they restated in August 1929 and again, following a National Conference in Damascus, in October, continuing to demand a Franco-Syrian Treaty as the sole acceptable expression of the Mandate. But what sort of treaty, was M. Ponsot's rejoinder, with an adversary whose desired Constitution denied the Mandate itself? One further meeting of Atasi with the High Commissioner late in April 1930 produced no agreement or *détente*; that conditions were, on the contrary, deteriorating was already clear in January 1930 from the series of strikes in Damascus by the public against municipal taxation and by high-school students against the withholders of their diplomas or allowances. An impressive 'Manifesto to the Nation'[1] was issued by Atasi and the nationalists in April. A few newspapers were, as usual, suppressed by the President of the Republic or the High Commissioner; the violence and frequently the sheer mendacity of the journalists was, indeed, extreme and incorrigible. A demand by the local Circassians for a National Home of their own could not be taken seriously. Resolutions by a congress of the exiled Druzes at Nabq in Sa'udi Arabia had no longer any relation to Syrian realities; chronic restlessness on the northern frontier had considerably more. An interesting Industrial Exhibition was held in Damascus, but could only for a moment distract from the serious and still growing economic depression.

In terms of politics, these months were notable for an attempt, half-hearted and inconclusive, to revitalize the 'moderate' elements; it was the work of the Reform Party, that of two Liberal Parties, and that of the Monarchists. Directed against the Government of Shaykh Taj, the resulting programme, whose execution was entrusted to a nine-man inter-party Committee, was distinguishable from that of the Nationalists only by its quieter tone and tempo, and its lack of anti-French fanaticism. It called for independence and unity, a Constitution, material development in every field, and the improvement of judicial and financial administration. But though

[1] *Or. Mod.*, May 1930, p. 192.

centres of 'moderate' activity existed or were founded in many towns, no effective action resulted; the Cabinet was able to survive the assaults both of the *cartel modéré* and of the more extreme nationalists.

The appearance of a specifically Monarchical Party dated from the summer of 1928, and was marked by public meetings and by telegrams to the High Commissioner and to Europe—but by little agreement as to the best candiate for the throne. Essentially a protest against present shortcomings, and a needed outlet for Arab loyalty, the movement gained considerable ground in diverse Syrian circles. The princes favoured for election to the Syrian kingship were the Amir Fayṣal, second son of ibn Sa'ud: or King Fayṣal of 'Iraq, or his brother Zayd: or the Sharif 'Ali Ḥaydar: or the ex-Khedive 'Abbas Ḥilmi: or Aḥmad Nami Bey Damad, or 'Ali Riḍha al-Rikabi, or some other member of one of the great Syrian families.

The untimely dissolution of the Constituent Assembly was among the causes which led at this period to the closer consolidation of nationalist groups to form a bloc under single control. This development was not, indeed, completed until 1936; but since 1927, when the People's Party was in decline, the need for integration had been apparent, agreement on policy and timing between rival centres in Aleppo and Damascus had been sought, and Nationalist representation in the Constituent Assembly had taken the form of a partly-solidified National Front. The nascent Bloc gained strength from the incorporation of Ibrahim Ḥananu's considerable organization in the north, and in June 1930 a Committee of National Concord grouped the leading regional leaders in a single body. It was as a National Bloc, thus achieved, that these patriots were to face the elections of 1932, though full Bloc organization or single command were not yet perfected.

By the beginning of May 1930 it appeared to the High Commissioner, after another visit to Paris and further talks with Atasi, that no hope remained of a modified nationalist attitude on the disputed articles. He decided to cut the knot, and at last to satisfy the terms of Article 1 of the Mandate, by imposing a Constitution which would confer on the Syrians substantially the form of government which their constituent representatives had chosen, with only such overriding modification as he found indispensable during the lifetime of the Mandate. By two Decrees dated 14 May he dissolved the Constituent Assembly and promulgated a Constitution for Syria.[1]

[1] Other Decrees signed and published on the same dates, dealing with the sanjaq of Alexandretta, the Druze and 'Alawi territories, and the Common Interests, will be referred to in later pages. These, and the Constitution, are given in *Or. Mod.*, August 1930. The High Commissioner's covering letter to M. Briand is in *Or. Mod.*, June 1930, p. 229.

The Constitution, of which the text was communicated to the League of Nations, was in almost all respects identical to that adopted by the Constituent Assembly: but the definition of 'Syria' in Article 2 was so altered as to become inoffensive,[1] certain minor changes of wording were made, and Article 116 presented those safeguards for the French position which the Constituent Assembly had rejected. The imposed Constitution was to take effect after the holding, at a date to be fixed by the High Commissioner, of elections to the Chamber of Deputies for which it provided; and that the mandatory safeguards which, to Syrian indignation, it now contained were not to preclude a broader subsequent Franco-Syrian Agreement was clear from words used by M. Ponsot at Geneva in June. He then declared to the Mandates Commission that France was still animated by the spirit of Article 22 of the Covenant, and still intended to 'guide these territories gradually towards complete independence, as soon as their populations are in a position to stand alone'.

The new Constitution, received with apathy by the mass of Syrians and with approval by a few, was in the nationalist camp the subject of immediate protest. The press condemned it as imposed, arbitrary, and 'of unknown parentage'. Changes in the Cabinet[2] reflected ministerial stresses. The Committee at Cairo and its permanent Delegation at Geneva reacted in their normal fashion. In Damascus, where the Committee of National Concord (p. 187) found it difficult to accommodate also the Monarchists, meetings in protest against 'dismemberment and servitude' were accompanied by threats of future non-cooperation, by telegrams from the principal Syrian cities to Geneva, by strikes (in which, however, an economic element was also present), and demonstrations. Nevertheless, law and order were not seiously threatened, and an uneasy peace descended on Syria with the hot weather of 1930. Amnesty for a number of *détenus* and offenders condemned by courts martial for their share in the troubles of 1925–6 was granted by the President of the French Republic on 14 July, and was extended by the Acting High Commissioner, M. Tétreau, by further acts of grace. Some of the more serious offenders, notably Dr. Shahbandar, remained in exile. No immediate action was indicated by the High Commissioner towards bringing the new Constitution into force.

[1] It became 'Syria constitutes an indivisible political unity'.

[2] This had been in office since 6 February 1938. The Minister of the Interior now resigned, Jamil al-Ulshi (Finance) took his place, and Tawfiq al-Shamiya (Public Works) took over Finance.

2. FRUSTRATED TREATY

In the event, two years were to pass between the proclamation of the Constitution and its coming into effect: a period of relative outward calm in the local political world, and of continuing severe depression in the economic.

The 'temporary régime' of government under Shaykh Taj al-Din continued. It was able to effect some economies in the Administration, to establish a special court for tribal cases, to form a separate sanjaq of the Jazira in the north-east by dividing the Euphrates province, and to benefit by the French abolition of some of their surviving 'military tribunals' and decreasing reliance on their Special Services. To meet economic difficulties, no ready cure suggested itself; nor could a visiting French economic mission do much more than to note the sad general stagnation. A prolonged boycott of the Belgian-owned electric-power company at Damascus, with an anti-foreign colouring, was settled by a reduction of the charges; but voices were raised also in favour of a general boycott of foreign goods.

The Ḥasani Cabinet maintained itself with little difficulty and a minimum change of personnel.[1] It continued to press the French for the amnesty of exiled patriots—whose return must add much to its own embarrassments—and to act as a bridge between the Mandatory and full-blooded local nationalism. Among the pardoned were Dr. 'Abd al-Raḥman Shahbandar (still practising medicine in Cairo) and Iḥsan al-Jabiri. But a general desire for change, the restlessness of politicians long unemployed, and the too-moderate views of Shaykh Taj's supporters, encouraged political activity in the Syrian towns, mostly with a strongly anti-Cabinet complexion. The nationalists met repeatedly in conclave, reformulated their position, and kept close contact with the unionist elements in Lebanon, the 'Alawi country, and the Jabal al-Duruz. At Damascus a new 'Party of the National Pact' produced a programme barely distinguishable from the standard nationalist position; and if the Monarchical Party (heartened by a short visit of ex-King 'Ali of the Ḥijaz, early in 1931) had some difference of aim, the other parties represented mere groups of personal followings more or less identical in policy and grouped together, though without precise integration, in the Bloc. Such parties were those of National Union, of the Liberals, of Independence, of the People, and of Reform, each with its officials, its meeting place, its manifestos, and newspaper polemics. The attitude of the leaders, among whom Hashim al-Atasi enjoyed

[1] Fu'ad al-'Adili, Minister of Public Works, resigned in June 1931, handing his functions to Badi' al-Mu'ayyid.

a pre-eminence based on his age, services, and qualities, was one of guarded co-operation with any Chamber which might be produced by genuinely free elections. They urged that parliamentary candidates should cease to be restricted by a local-residence qualification, and that both French and Syrian local authorities should abstain (as in fact they rarely did) from all interference. The publication of the Anglo-'Iraqi Treaty of June 1930 set a definite precedent for Franco-Syrian relations, and greatly influenced political thinking; but the absence of mutual confidence between the Mandatory and the Syrian leaders precluded optimism. Talk of an 'Iraqi-Syrian union was not unknown, and feelings of pan-Arab unity were strengthened by the reported severities of the Italians in Libya.[1]

M. Ponsot, for whom another 'career' diplomat, M. Jean Helleu, acted in his absence, returned to Beirut in mid-November 1931. After a year of inaction he produced on his arrival, to the general surprise, three Decrees[2] which gave the signal for a new burst of political activity. One established a Consultative Council[3] to supervise the putting of the Constitution into force; one regulated the 'provisional organization' of the Administration, under a representative of the High Commissioner, pending the appointment of functionaries under the new régime; and one dealt with the conduct of the elections themselves. At the first meeting of the Consultative Council M. Ponsot again expressed the preference of his country—a preference recently reaffirmed by the League Council—for the treaty method of conducting, and ultimately terminating, the Mandate; and steps towards this end could be hoped from the Chamber now to be elected. Meanwhile the régime of the interim Government, he said, was over; a firm, united, and truly national administration, able confidently to deal with France, was required.

To this approach the Nationalists' reply was hesitant, in places negative, but by majority cautiously co-operative. They emphasized their own position as sole true spokesmen for Syria, rehearsed their past grievances, and demanded to be told in advance the terms of the proposed treaty. Meanwhile a Decree of 7 December prescribed the allotment of Deputies to each constituency, and provided for representation of the minorities; Parliament was to consist of 70 members, including 52 Sunni Muslims, 14 members for the minorities,[4] and 4 for the nomadic tribes.

[1] The patriot 'Umar Mukhtar was hanged in September 1931.

[2] *Or. Mod.*, December 1931, pp. 575 ff.

[3] It was to consist of past Presidents and Governors of States, former Prime Ministers, and six senior officials.

[4] 2 Greek Orthodox, 1 Jewish, 1 Isma'ili, 3 Armenian Orthodox, 1 Greek Catholic, 1 Syrian Catholic, 1 Armenian Catholic, 1 Syrian Orthodox, 3 Shi'i.

The elections revealed Nationalist unanimity in the Ḥumṣ–Ḥamah area, some diversity in shades of nationalism in Aleppo (as well as the familiar personal or family divisions), and rival lists[1] in Damascus. The voting, on 20 December, was in most areas peacefully conducted and, as with the elections for the Constituent Assembly, it resulted, after the secondary elections on 5 January 1932, in the return of a Moderate majority. At Ḥamah considerable disorder occurred, and armed forces had to intervene while the elections were suspended. At Aleppo, fortune did not favour the more extreme party, that of Ḥananu and the Jabiris; its members in consequence withdrew after the primary elections and launched bitter attacks upon official interference and alleged tampering with the urns. A six-day strike, with noisy processions of demonstrators, was directed chiefly against the local Muḥafidh and the Chief of Police.[2] An attack was made on the house of Ṣubḥi Barakat, who as a Moderate leader had been elected, and stone-throwing by the mob, and shots fired by the Police, resulted in eight wounded. But the election results, though thenceforward intermittently condemned as invalid by Aleppo nationalists, were held to stand. Their aftermath was a personal assault on Ṣubḥi Barakat by two students in an Aleppo hotel, in April; one of the assailants committed suicide. In Damascus and Duma, as at Ḥumṣ, excessive violence led to the postponement of the election; demonstrators, as usual pleading Government abuses, tried to force entrance into the offices, attacked the Municipality, and wounded a number of policemen. Eight dead and fifty wounded were counted as a result of this violence and its suppression by the armed forces.

The High Commissioner, approached by al-Atasi who demanded the holding of fresh elections in all constituencies, rejected the plea. He believed, as did all French and much 'moderate' opinion, that extremist violence was a weapon used for purposes of intimidation to conceal lack of popular support; and he ordered first and second-stage elections to be held again, in the postponed areas only, in March and April. These were, this time, better conducted and resulted in nationalist victories, including those of six outstanding figures elected for Damascus city.[3]

Nationalist representation in the finally resulting Chamber was that of a numerical minority,[4] but, as before, a minority full of dynamism and talent. The bedouin members were solidly

[1] Those of the Nationalists and close Bloc supporters: of the Reform Party: and of a coalition of 'Moderates'.

[2] Respectively Wathiq al-Mu'ayyid, and Bahij al-Khaṭib, of whom more will be heard.

[3] Zaki al-Khaṭib, Iḥsan al-Sharif, Fakhri al-Barudi, Luṭfi al-Ḥaffar, Jamil Mardam Bey, Fa'iz al-Khuri.

[4] They had 17 seats against an amorphous majority of 54 alleged Moderates.

Monarchist and those of the minorities usually 'moderate', as were the bulk of rural and small-town notables.

The Chamber, hailed as the first Syrian Parliament to sit since that of Fayṣal in 1920, met on 7 June at Damascus for a one-week Extraordinary Session, and proceeded with sufficient decorum to elect its officers: Ṣubḥi Barakat as President of the Chamber, various notables as its Vice-Presidents and Secretaries, and Muḥammad 'Ali Bey al-'Abid—a wealthy 70-year-old ex-Ambassador, the son of 'Izzat Pasha (the notorious Secretary of Sultan 'Abd al-Ḥamid)—as President of the Republic.[1] The election of the Deputies was formally validated by the Chamber, not without acrimonious discussion,[2] and their salary rate and that of the ministers was fixed. The new President entrusted the respected aristocrat Ḥaqqi al-'Aḏhm with the formation of a Ministry, in which the latter prudently included two Nationalists,[3] as well as one[4] of his own school of thought; he himself kept the portfolio of Interior. The Chamber, after two days devoted to regional and personal issues and to the claims of the still unamnestied exiles, adjourned on 14 June.

During the summer and autumn of 1932 speculation concerned itself with the contents of the Treaty of which, it was understood, M. Ponsot would bring back the text with him from Paris. If this was to be acceptable, it would be necessary for the French to move far from their previous position as to the unification of Syria and as to genuine self-government and independence; and few nationalists expected this. The Ministry of Ḥaqqi al-'Aḏhm was the subject of press attacks from its first day. The out-of-office Aleppo extremists expressed themselves with great bitterness; a giant deputation from the north, specifically anti-French and anti-Government, brought far-reaching demands to the President and ministers as well as offering a number of suggestions of local north Syrian interest.[5] Early in August a strike at Aleppo of silk-dyers and of underpaid government officials was exploited by Communists (whose own secret printing-press was discovered), and led to clashes and bomb-throwing; at the end of the same month the alleged discovery of a nationalist plot was

[1] Other candidates had been the Damad, Ḥaqqi al-'Aḏhm, Hashim al-Atasi, and Ibrahim Ḥananu.
[2] The Syro-Palestine Committee, of Cairo, continued to deny validity to the elections, especially those of Aleppo.
[3] Muḏhhir al-Raslan (formerly Prime Minister of Transjordan) in Justice and Education, and Jamil Mardam Bey in Finance and Agriculture.
[4] Salim Bey Janbart (Greek Orthodox President of the Aleppo Chamber of Commerce) in Public Works.
[5] These concerned the Aleppo water-supply, the government offices, road and street improvement, increase of schools and agricultural education, reform of the law courts, and lighter taxation.

followed by many house-searches, a confession by an obscure Armenian, and the arrest of seventy leading citizens. A strike was declared in protest, armed forces patrolled the streets, petitions of remonstrance were handed in; but the expected support of the Damascus nationalists was for once not forthcoming. The Ministry appealed for calm, and the prisoners were released some weeks later. Two new but ephemeral political parties, the Constitutional Liberal in northern Syria and the Agrarian in southern, were formed. A central meeting of the National Bloc on 10 October decided that Nationalist Deputies should collaborate in the Chamber if, but only if, the French Treaty proposals were revealed in advance, and proved acceptable; there had for some months been among them groups both of collaborationists and of diehard objectors, with Aleppo, for the moment, providing the protagonists of the latter. After a postponement of the Chamber's ordinary autumn session for one month, the High Commissioner returned from France by way of Turkey on 21 October, bringing a French decoration for the President. The Chamber was opened on 29 October, re-electing Ṣubḥi Barakat as its President; but, since no revelation of the Treaty contents was made, the Nationalists decided to boycott the proceedings. They in fact abstained from the first and second meetings, but attended after an adjournment until 5 November; and they did not obstruct, though they did not participate in, an otherwise unanimous vote that the Ministry should be authorized to pursue its treaty negotiations. The Chamber then proceeded to its normal duties, including the consideration of next year's budget. The High Commissioner left again on 22 November for Paris and Geneva.

At the Palais des Nations, M. Ponsot explained French policy on the lines now familiar, indicated the continuing role of his country in the Levant (a role which seemed, indeed, to be inconsistent with any real local independence in the foreseeable future), and confessed to no early expectation of a unitary Syria; there would, on the contrary, he indicated, be a Treaty Zone and a Mandatory Zone, of which the latter would include the Druzes, 'Alawis, and Lebanon, thus effectively destroying Syrian unity and its access to the sea. This speech was officially reproduced by M. Ponsot on his return to Syria as a guide for the local public. It led, as was to be expected, to spirited attacks and the growing disillusion of the nationalists.[1] Talks with Shakib Arsalan and Iḥsan al-Jabiri at Geneva had left the High Commissioner unmoved.

It had further to be faced that the many petitions reaching the

[1] An official 'Reply by the National Bloc' was prepared and published in book form by Dr. 'Abd al-Raḥman Kayyali, of Aleppo.

Mandates Commission from Syria were in tenor so contradictory as to appear self-cancelling; there would, therefore, be no firm support from Geneva for the unitary conception. Indeed, the Commission was clear that, while Syria and Lebanon alone were separate units for which a Mandate had been granted, yet the Mandate did not exclude—indeed it could be read as calling for—the constitution of autonomous regions within the two mandated territories. The French therefore would, as far as the League was concerned, have a free hand in their treatment of the all-important question of Druze and 'Alawi status; and remarks by the French premier in Paris, late in March, stressed significantly the vast expenditure of his country in Syria, the continuance of her mission there, and her need to retain troops in the Levant.

In Syria, under pressure by the Chamber, the French allowed the President to pardon those still held in captivity for election-time offences; but such as remained of the political exiles of 1925–6 could be given amnesty only by direct French authority, and this was still withheld in spite of telegrams from Damascus to Paris pleading for visible signs of a 'new deal'. The last few weeks of 1932 saw the beginning of shorter-range exchanges between the High Commissioner and the Syrian Cabinet and President on the substance of the Treaty. These continued in the new year, in spite of evident intransigence in the political circles where this was endemic. Moderation was, in fact, losing ground; Nationalist meetings on 18 February, when their aims were again formulated, expressed views remote from all compromise, even while M. Ponsot and his staff were carrying the negotiations with the Syrian Cabinet to the stage of an agreed and almost completed text. On 18 April a Manifesto to the Nation was published by a group of Damascus nationalists, emphasizing the shortcomings of their present negotiators and the paramount need for the unity of the country; and this was followed by the resignation of the two Nationalist ministers, Jamil Mardam Bey and Mudhhir al-Raslan. Processions were formed around the Chamber building, and in other cities, with street violence as the probable next stage in public protest. French troops lined the streets of Damascus when on 22 April the Chamber was reopened. Only 38 out of 70 Deputies attended. The House adjourned till the 27th, when[1] in a Chamber surrounded by troops, and in a city on general strike, the Prime Minister asked for, and was granted, an adjournment until 8 May to give time 'to resolve the crisis' and to find new ministers. The Cabinet was in fact reconstructed on 5 May. On the 8th the Deputies, without Nationalist participation, agreed by 38 votes

[1] In the meanwhile a rapid visit had been paid to Damascus and Palmyra by the King of the Belgians, escorted by the High Commissioner.

out of 43 that treaty negotiations should be continued. The session ended on 31 May after three weeks of normal working, and the Deputies sent cordial messages to the High Commissioner, who had been taken ill. M. Ponsot left for France on 2 July. On his recovery, he was posted to Morocco, and did not revisit the territory to which he had given six years of patient and whole-hearted effort; success was denied by factors mainly beyond his control, and especially by the untimely rigidity of his country's policy.

His successor was announced as the Count Damien de Martel, formerly Ambassador in Tokyo, a shrewd and disillusioned diplomat, capable of facing the realities of politics as well as of enjoying the pleasures of life. Three months were spent by the Syrian political world in speculating upon what the new High Commissioner might bring or offer, and in reforming their own ranks. A general Nationalist Congress was held at Ḥumṣ, and the various groups (including the Masons, who were now showing activity as a political force) convened their committees, or their full membership, at Damascus. The minorities, particularly at Aleppo, were scared by the Assyrian massacre in northern 'Iraq into cherishing more than ever whatever French protection Nationalist policy would allow them. The latter party sent Ṣubḥi Barakat to Paris to do what good he could by canvassing his acquaintances there, who included leading ministers.

To suit the incoming High Commissioner, who reached Beirut on 12 October, the opening of the Syrian Chamber was postponed till 18 November. M. de Martel visited Damascus on 2 November. His introduction to that city was unfortunate; the events in Jerusalem in mid-October had excited Muslim opinion to the point of angry demonstrations, and the coincidence of 'Balfour Day' led on 3 November to an outbreak of mosque-inspired violence, with fiery speeches, an attack by a crowd 1,500 strong on a police post, and a menacing move against the British Consulate. One dead and a number of wounded were carried home. The prime mover, Zaki al-Khaṭib, was arrested but later released. Talks between the President, the Cabinet, and the High Commissioner began again on 22 November, with agreement apparently in sight on the outstanding issues; but the atmosphere in the city and in political circles was deeply unquiet, with feeling prevalent against a 'dismembering' Treaty. On 14 November Salim Janbart, a moderate statesman, resigned from the Cabinet, and was replaced.[1] Two days later his colleagues authorized the Prime Minister to sign the now completed draft, which, with Presidential permission and fortified by the authorization given by the Chamber on 8 May, he

[1] By Laṭif al-Ghanima, an Aleppo Christian.

did on the same day. The Treaty, with its many attachments and Exchanges of Letters, was forthwith communicated to the Chamber. The latter opened on 18 November, under heavy armed guard, with an attendance of 69 Deputies including the 17 Nationalists. Ṣubḥi Barakat was re-elected to the Presidency; his first act was to call for a two-minute silence in honour of Fayṣal, the first King of Syria, who had died in Europe ten weeks earlier.

It was immediately apparent that the Treaty had no chance of the ratification which stood as an item on the agenda for 21 November. Its publication by the High Commissioner on the 19th, with explanatory comment,[1] led immediately to the issue of yet another anti-Treaty manifesto by its opponents, and to a general strike in Damascus, with sporadic rioting. Pressure on the 'moderates',[2] both inside the Chamber and outside, grew every hour; Nationalist Deputies, when the Treaty was placed before the Chamber on the 20th, insisted on immediate general discussion, with the certainty of rejection, instead of the more normal consignment to a Committee. The French Délégué, under orders of M. de Martel, secured an adjournment for four days, in the hope of a *détente* and to prevent unconstitutional action; but no *détente* occurred, street agitation increased, and on the 24th the High Commissioner suspended the Chamber for the remainder of the session. Two days later he caused the President of the Chamber to withdraw the Treaty from its cognizance, and announced to the public that, as he saw no prospect of free and constitutional action by the Deputies, it would be improper to give them such responsibilities. The posting of troops in and around the Chamber thwarted the Nationalist attempts to hold a further session; some strikes and rioting, with one death, followed. The National Bloc, amid its many resolutions, declared the Ministry to have fallen, since it had acted against the national interest and against the will of 'the noble Deputies' (whose election the Nationalists themselves had repeatedly declared invalid). Plans were already in formulation for the dispatch of a strong mission to Paris. December passed calmly; the plan to call an 'extraordinary session' for 1 January 1934 failed for lack of support.

The Treaty[3] thus rejected had been modelled, with differences, on the Anglo-'Iraqi Treaty of 1930. It was one of 'close alliance'

[1] It was *not* simultaneously published in Paris, the public of which was informed through the London papers. In the French Chamber opposition was shown, even thus early, to signing a Treaty considered as 'tantamount to ending the Mandate'.

[2] These events strikingly recall those whereby, in the Baghdad of 1924, efforts were made by threats, violence, and assassination to prevent the passage of the Anglo-'Iraqi Treaty of that date, similarly favoured by a 'moderate' majority.

[3] *Or. Mod.*, December 1933, pp. 607 ff.

between France and Syria, and was given a life of twenty-five years to date from the admission of Syria to the League of Nations, whenever that should occur. The transfer of authority to the Syrian Republic was to be accomplished, under a contemplated series of military, financial, economic, and other agreements, within four years, the 'preparatory period'; thereafter, if all went well, and subject to satisfactory legislation being passed for the protection of individual and community[1] rights, the French would recommend the admission of Syria to the League; meanwhile they would progressively associate Syrians with their conduct of the country's foreign affairs, as a prelude to a régime of regular 'mutual consultation' after independence had been achieved. Each State would have diplomatic representation at the capital of the other. The French would be consulted on the identity, posts, and powers of European officials to be retained.[2] Syria would maintain the 'economic unity' of the territories now under Mandate: in other words, would retain the Common Interests organization, whereby the all-important Customs revenues were at present administered by the French. The latter would maintain forces in Syria (and not merely at named locations, as in 'Iraq), would assist in organizing the Syrian Army and Police, and would collaborate in defensive measures.

There were, in all this, enough continuing fields of French control to render the Treaty doubtfully acceptable to Syrian *amour-propre*; but the main objection was the preserved separation of the Druze and 'Alawi States from the Syrian Republic, a matter covered by an Exchange of Letters attached to the Treaty. In this direction, concerning which abundant signs of Syrian feeling had been given during the past fifteen years, the only progress marked by the draft Treaty was a stipulation that the Awqaf of the two States should henceforth be administered jointly with those of Syria, and that recourse from their higher courts should in future be to the Syrian Court of Cassation. The Syrian Prime Minister admitted that, although in his view the two territories formed part of Syria, yet they were entitled for a time to a special régime acceptable to them; and the High Commissioner agreed that their status should be re-examined at the time of Syria's own admission to the League, with the participation of the inhabitants themselves whose agreement would be a condition of any changes.

[1] The attack on the Assyrian community in 'Iraq could be taken as due, in part, to the omission of such stipulations in the Anglo-'Iraqi Treaty: or, more generally, to British over-confidence in future 'Iraqi treatment of this disliked and provocative minority.

[2] In the corresponding situation in 'Iraq, the Anglo-'Iraqi Treaty provided that the 'Iraqis were under no such obligation to consult their ex-Mandatory.

The two years following the rejection of this Treaty were in Syria a period of some administrative but no political progress. The Cabinet of Ḥaqqi Bey maintained itself for a further three months, in spite of intra-ministerial quarrels and lack of firm support in the Chamber. A National Rally at Ḥumṣ in February showed both the militant strength of that party's following, and the persisting divisions within it as between northern and southern Syria. The High Commissioner, on his return from France in the same month, felt bound to prolong the suspension of a Chamber from which he could hope for no orderly government; and this decided the al-'Adhm Ministry to avoid charges of 'collaboration' by resigning. The President of the Republic then called upon Shaykh Taj al-Din to form a Cabinet.[1] This, composed of experienced and respected men, was destined to last for two years. In the absence of the Chamber the administration, deriving little or no support from the feeble and leaderless Moderates, was harassed by attacks on every issue by the Nationalists, whose press was as usual immoderate in its violence and distortions. The Ministry was able nevertheless to keep ordered government in being, and to introduce a number of reforms and economies while working in fair harmony with the Délégué and French officials. The continuance of economic hard times, and the introduction of such controversial measures as the Tobacco Monopoly[2] (p. 206), with various embarrassing legacies from former Ministries, were adverse features which Shaykh Taj and his colleagues must strive to overcome. The Nationalists found material for protest in every act of the Administration, and of the French; the latter in turn gave offence by instituting a 'Committee for the Defence of the States under Mandate' with no Syrian membership, and, to the annoyance of ex-Turkish Generals and Colonels, excused this by remarking that no Syrian had sufficient experience for such studies. The repeated insistence of the High Commissioner that, in present conditions, economic advance should take priority over politics fell on the deafest of ears. In May 1934 a joint tour by the President and the Prime Minister in northern Syria was disturbed by lively demonstrations.[3] A mosque episode at Aleppo, insulting to the President, was followed by a campaign of inflammatory speeches, bomb-throwing, the shutting of bazaars, student strikes and riots, and police counter-action. Many arrests were made and

[1] The Ministers of Finance and Agriculture (Henri Hindiya and Muḥammad Yaḥya al-'Adali) were already Deputies: three ministers from outside were 'Aṭa al-Ayyubi (Justice), Ḥusni al-Barazi (Education), and Jamil al-Ulshi (Works). Shaykh Taj himself retained Interior.

[2] It was remarked that, two years earlier, nationalist leaders had themselves been urging a monopoly.

[3] The President had, perhaps unwisely, pardoned a man convicted of shooting at Ibrahim Ḥananu.

sentences passed; the Nationalists used every device to exploit these incidents by a frantic press campaign, and by communications made (with gross misrepresentation) to the foreign Consuls and to Arab rulers. Advocates hurried to Aleppo from all Syria to defend the accused. A further outbreak of disorder and stone-throwing marked the Prophet's birthday.

Such episodes, and the continuance of all the causes which had led to the suspension of the Chamber a year earlier, led M. de Martel to suspend it again,[1] this time *sine die*, early in November 1934. The communiqué which he issued blamed the Nationalist leaders for their attitude and methods, which he found entirely damaging to the cause of Syrian progress; he himself awaited a more reasonable and statesmanlike attitude. But he could find little hopeful in the tone of the brief outburst of protest and strikes which greeted his action, nor in the continuing Nationalist meetings—notably at Ḥumṣ in June 1935, and at Aleppo in September—, the celebrations of the Day of Maysalun (20 July), the visit of the resentful Mufti of Jerusalem, or the ostentatious *rapprochement* of extremists with the Maronite Patriarch and the latter's pointed excursion into Syrian nationalism (p. 206). The political situation in Syria in the autumn of 1935 was, if outwardly calm by local standards, one of repression and menace; the clash between French policy and national aspiration was unchanged, Syrian demands unsatisfied, their proponents unrepentant and determined. The events of the first weeks of the new year, 1936, which amid disorder and near-anarchy were to usher in a new phase of Franco-Syrian relations, are reserved for a later page.

3. THE LEBANON

In passing from a study of Syrian to one of Lebanese politics, one moves to a world closely similar yet variously different. There has been throughout history fullest familiarity and interchange between coastal and hinterland Syria, with the previous common bond of Turkish law, usage, and social legacy, and in each territory a greater or lesser representation of all the communities found in the other; there was now also their common current experience of the shared tutelage, administrative control, and personalities of the Mandatory. Yet, with all this, variations already existed sufficient to mark a real distinctness in Lebanese political life. Added to the difference of geography, land surface, and orientation was that of dissimilar social composition, with the lack in Lebanon of the overwhelming Sunni Muslim majority found in Syria. The Lebanese had achieved a more advanced social sophistication, and yet

[1] A further one-month suspension had already been ordered by the President.

showed greater subjection to specific local influences unknown in Syria, such as that of the Maronite Patriarch. None of the political leaders were common to both territories, and the qualities or weaknesses of Lebanese statesmen were not identically those of Syrian. The economic interests of the two territories were in some measure divergent. And, finally, the attitude of the French Mandatory, faced by less opposition in Lebanon and indeed enjoying a hard core of regular support, could be less uncompromising and was less resented in the heart of their ancient 'sphere of influence', where no indulgent régime could act, as it could in Syria, as a dangerous precedent for North Africa.

The Lebanese politics of these years showed, indeed, most of their abiding weaknesses: the lack of national solidarity, the devotion to sectarian or personal ends, the ceaseless squabbling for place and power, the interventions of religious dignitaries in the political fray, the difficulty of purging waste, abuse, and corruption. With all this, compensated as it was in some measure by the goodwill and ability of many Lebanese leaders and the high intelligence of their public, the leading element of Syrian politics was lacking in Lebanon: that is, the ceaseless clash with the Mandatory. Admittedly there was a numerous Muslim and a considerable Greek Orthodox element hostile to the Mandate; there were circles where disappointment and jealousy had produced anti-foreign resentment; and there were political parties with programmes incompatible with the French presence. But, with a more developed economic life, there could be satisfaction at the constitutional progress already made (in clear advance of that of Syria) and there existed the distractions of a more active, more satisfying public life within the close-knit minority communities which were the heart of Lebanon. The dominant Maronite community remained Francophile, if not without moods of disillusion and criticism, while to many others, including some Shi'i and Sunni Muslims, the existence of a separate Great Lebanon had by now become desirable; and this could be perpetuated, it was obvious, only by French determination.

The problems facing Lebanese politicians at the present stage were, in particular, two. One was the establishment of a suitable form of Constitution and Administration, with due regard to economy,[1] efficiency, and the excessive claims of confessionalism. The other was the need to create, if at all possible, an all-Lebanon loyalty from elements some of which, notably the Sunni inhabitants of the districts recently annexed to Lebanon, resolutely

[1] Figures produced in September 1929 showed that the percentage of the total State expenditure represented by officials' salaries was 75 in the Lebanon, as against 45, 40, and 35 per cent. respectively in Syria, the Jabal al-Duruz, and the 'Alawi Government.

refused such loyalty (though not unwilling to participate, meanwhile, in the Government of the State), and sought attachment to their own people in Syria.[1] The fatal step taken in 1920 to please the Maronites, by the flat refusal of self-determination in Tripoli, the Biqa', and south Lebanon, continued to present both in Syria and in Lebanon the most difficult and abiding of their problems.

The three-minister Cabinet which assumed office in Beirut in January 1928 conducted an adequate and not unprogressive administration, and made useful reforms, especially in the judicial branch;[2] but incessant agitation against it in the Chamber clamoured for representation of the communities now excluded, and for greater 'progress'. (Others proclaimed the need for *one* minister only—or none!—and a reduced cadre of officials.) It survived for a few months, but the opposition led by Fu'ad Arsalan, Shaykh Jisr, Musa Nammur, and others proved too strong, and early August 1928 saw a change of Cabinet and the accession to power, as Premier and Minister of Education and Health, of Ḥabib Pasha al-Sa'd with, this time, four more ministers.[3] Announcing an attractive programme, which included major irrigation projects, he obtained his vote of confidence. It was justified by good work in restoring war damage in southern Lebanon, but not by any of the desired economies; indeed, the budget for 1929, as submitted, indicated greater expenditure than ever before. In March 1929 Charles Dabbas was re-elected to the Presidency, against the candidature of the rich Egyptian Georges Luṭfullah, whose claim to Lebanese nationality was suspect.

In April of the same year a second amendment to the Lebanese Constitution was passed by the Chamber. It gave, most desirably, a six-year term and more power to the President (including authority, with Cabinet agreement, to dissolve the Chamber), and less to the Deputies. The Ministry of Ḥabib Pasha resigned on 8 May. The succession, refused by Emile Eddé and by Muḥammad al-Jisr, fell to Bishara al-Khuri, a genial Maronite lawyer and statesman who had been President of the Council of State. His Cabinet was of only three members,[4] and promised economy,

[1] A party of Lebanese Muslims visited Damascus at the time of the Constituent Assembly. It was strongly repudiated by the Lebanese Government, and the usual French reassurances were forthcoming.

[2] The Council of State (established in 1929) was abolished, its duties transferred to the Court of Cassation. Courts of First Instance and Peace Courts were reduced in number. The 'Special Courts' (for cases of crime involving intercommunity violence) continued in being.

[3] The other ministers were: in Works and Agriculture, Ḥusayn al-Aḥdab: in Justice, Shakir al-Qardaḥi: in Finance, Ṣubḥi Ḥaydar: in Interior, Musa Nammur.

[4] The Premier took the Ministries of Interior and Health, Ḥusayn al-Aḥdab those of Finance, Works, and Agriculture, and Najib abu-Suwan (President of the Court of Cassation) Justice and Education.

development, and impartially conducted elections for the renovation of the elected[1] portion of the Chamber. These were held early in June; they excited great interest, but disorder between rival factions occurred only at Tripoli and Zaghurta. But the Khuri Ministry was to last a bare five months. It resigned in August, stayed reluctantly in office for two more months, and was replaced on 10 October by a five-man Cabinet[2] with Eddé as Premier and Minister of the Interior. He added a non-political Under-Secretary for Economic Affairs, Gabriel Manassa. The Eddé programme was one of rigid economy, with reduction of administrative units, law courts, officials, and expenditure on government schools. The Prime Minister asked and obtained permission in December 1929 to legislate by decree-laws for the sake of speed and simplicity. In the short life of his Administration he wielded, in fact, an efficient but unpopular axe. He abolished half the existing tribunals, dismissed all mudirs of naḥiyahs, reduced the administrative units in the country from eleven to five muḥafadhas[3] (subdivided into qadḥas), and shut more than 100 government schools. The savings from these measures were, it was claimed, to be spent on productive works; but too many vested interests were damaged and scandals exposed, and too many of the poorer Muslims, who almost alone used the government schools, were deprived. The Cabinet failed to withstand the resulting outcry, and fell to an overwhelming vote of no-confidence. It was replaced[4] on 25 March by another Maronite ex-premier, Auguste Adib Pasha, with four colleagues[5] devoted to a strictly similar, but in the event more tactful, campaign of economy. The administrative reorganization was maintained, the powers of Peace Judges increased, and seventy-five of the schools reopened. Important legislation was passed dealing with Taxation, Pensions, and Agricultural credit. The turbulent Dandash tribe of the Biqa', which gave great trouble in 1928–9, was banished to the

[1] Thirty deputies were elected, 15 nominated. These respectively were distributed by communities as follows: Maronites, 10 and 5: Greek Catholics, 2 and 1: Armenian Orthodox, 1: Greek Orthodox, 4 and 2: Armenian Catholics 1: Sunnis, 6 and 5: Shi'is, 5 and 3: Druzes, 2 and 1.

[2] Other ministers were Abu-Suwan in Justice and Education, Aḥdab in Works, Nammur in Finance, and Aḥmad al-Ḥusayni (a Shi'i) in Agriculture and Health.

[3] The new major units were: North Lebanon (with qadḥas of 'Akkar (H.Q., Ḥalba), Zaghurta, Bisharra, Batrun, and al-Kura (H.Q., Amyun)): Mount Lebanon (qadḥas of al-Matn (Ba'abda), Kasrawan (Juniya), al-Shuf (Ba'aqlin), and Dayr al-Qamr): Southern Lebanon (qadḥas of Ṣayda, Ṣur, Marj'uyun (Judayda): Biqa' (qadḥas of Zaḥla, Ba'lbek, Harmal, Rashaya): and Beirut.

[4] After consultations in which the post was re-offered to Eddé.

[5] Education was given to Jibran Tuwayni (an Orthodox journalist), Works to Ḥusayn al-Aḥdab, Interior and Health to Nammur, Justice to Aḥmad al-Ḥusayni.

Euphrates. Death removed at least one stern critic of French methods, Fu'ad Arsalan. It was at Christmas 1931 to remove another, the venerable Maronite Patriarch, Mgr Pierre Hoyeck (Ḥawayyik), after a thirty-year tenure of his office. He was succeeded by an uncompromising and strongly political prelate, Mgr Arida ('Ariḍha).

The Adib Ministry lasted throughout 1931, in spite of all the usual sources of distraction, and a new one in Ḥabib Pasha's 'Republican Reform Party'. To these were added during 1931 industrial disturbances which, as in Damascus the same year, were not solely industrial. Early in March the students in Beirut agitated, in a manner calling for police intervention, for cheaper seats in the cinemas—and won the day. Late in the month a committee of merchants, townsmen, and students organized a truculent boycott of the tramways and the electric power supplied by the concessionary Company; the situation lasted for three months, and was restored late in June by a reduction of charges for which the Government was forced to press the Company; arrested demonstrators were then released. It was generally understood that Communist elements were at work behind these incidents, as well as behind anti-Italian riots, threats to their Consulates, and boycott of their schools and goods. Other distractions included a long-drawn struggle between rival bishops for the Patriarchy of the Greek Orthodox Church, marked by many inconclusive meetings of the Synod and finally by a schism which ended only with the death of one of the rivals. They included also fierce, at times bloody, quarrels between Armenian factions.

The reasons for the High Commissioner's intervention in May 1932, and his suspension of the already twice-amended Constitution, lay in the continued factions and extravagances of the Chamber, the excessive confessionalism which it encouraged —and which the forthcoming Presidential election[1] would but increase—and, above all, the continuance of the world-wide economic crisis which was currently afflicting the Lebanon. M. Ponsot by Decree suspended the Constitution and installed a 'temporary régime' in which President Dabbas was empowered to legislate by Decree (with the High Commissioner's concurrence), and to preside over a simple Council of seven Directors. In spite of the feeling in some quarters that the President, who had sworn to respect the Constitution, should resign when this was suspended by French direct action, he proceeded energetically with the tasks of a simpler and more effective Government. Meetings of protest against the suspension were forbidden; the strife of parties and

[1] Probable candidates, all Maronite, were Khuri, Eddé, Ḥabib Pasha, and Georges Tabet; Shaykh Jisr, though a Muslim, also had ambitions.

factions—in which the Unionists of Emile Eddé and the Constitutionalists of Bishara al-Khuri were perhaps the least ephemeral, though the basis of division between them was scarcely more than personal, and both were Maronites—rather diminished, for a time, than increased; and advantage could be taken of the real satisfaction felt at the change by a large part of Lebanese opinion. Reductions were made in overgrown officialdom, cuts in salaries imposed,[1] the Gendarmerie and Police reduced. A number of administrative and fiscal reforms were made, Directorates amalgamated, the powers of village headmen defined. The financial crisis forebade the tax reductions for which there was outcry; but sums were saved for public works, and progress was made in improving port facilities, in agricultural marketing, and in other fields. Cases of discovered corruption were taken to Court; but the slow progress made with these, and the President's general amnesty declared in September 1933, showed again the strength of family and confessional influences.

The twenty months of non-constitutional government in Lebanon was thus a period of consolidation and achievement in the face of grave economic troubles. But it could not last for ever. The forces either discontented with it, or with the difficult times in general, or with Charles Dabbas as President, showed themselves in the incursion of the Maronite Archbishop of Beirut, Ignace Mubarak, into politics with a destructive public speech which his Patriarch disowned, by the latter's growing preference for a restoration of the Chamber, and by evidence of other minority discontent, such as that of the Shi'is of Jabal 'Amil.

The restless beginnings of political organization among the youth of the Lebanon (pp. 225 ff.), the older but inconstant groupings of candidates for future power, and the radical Republican Reform Party with its friends in France, kept the ever-restless political world in uneasy movement. A strong body of opposition to the emergency régime declared itself, increasing after the High Commissioner's return from France in the autumn of 1933; and he himself came to believe that a partial restoration of the Constitution could now be allowed as a compromise between a fully authoritarian régime and the proved evils of the 1926 Constitution. On the second day of 1934, therefore, he published Decrees[2] accepting the resignation of Dabbas as President, and passing his functions to a French official (M. Aubouard) until the installation of a successor: revising the electoral procedure:[3] and appointing

[1] French officials of the High Commission also accepted a temporary 10 per cent. reduction of salary.

[2] *Or. Mod.*, February 1934, pp. 66 f.

[3] Single-stage elections were prescribed; 18 Deputies were to be elected, by Muḥafadhas, on a proportional basis as between sects.

Ḥabib Pasha al-Sa'd, now aged 75, to the Presidency, of which he assumed the functions on 31 January. The elections were peacefully conducted. Dabbas became President of the Chamber, to which seven more Deputies[1] were named by the Mandatory. The Chamber possessed, under the new régime, no power of initiating expenditure, nor of getting rid of the Secretary of State. 'Abdullah Bayḥum assumed the latter office, with responsibility only to the President; and five Directors acting as ministers (though without that rank) formed a Council. This procedure worked for a time satisfactorily and 1934, in spite of some outspoken criticisms by Mgr Arida (who spared the French no more than his own local opponents), was a quiet year of progressive government. Voices raised in favour of restoring the full Constitution were balanced by those of a courageous minority who sighed audibly for direct French rule. Dabbas resigned his charge late in 1934, and was to die in France less than a year later, a severe loss to his country. To avoid the factious excitements of a change in the Presidency, M. de Martel on the last day of 1934 prolonged the term of Ḥabib Pasha to cover the year 1935, Bayḥum remaining as Secretary.

The three well-remembered strikes which occurred in 1935 had each its political as well as economic motives, though in varying proportions; the long depression had frayed political nerves as well as emptying purses; disaffected elements were always ready to stimulate disorder, and the Communists to join in, or to lead. The strike of the butchers at Zaḥla in January lasted for two weeks, and was conducted with much violence. Due, it was said, to resentment at a meat-transport tax, it led to the forcible occupation of government offices, police counter-action, firing, wounds, and arrests. Communist participation was proved; peace was restored by priestly conciliation, and the ringleaders fled. The strike of Beirut taxi-drivers in March–April was based in part on legitimate grievances, but the intervention of politicians[2] aggravated the trouble and led to some sabotage after a first settlement had been dishonoured. The almost contemporary strike of advocates in Beirut, which involved the closure of all Courts, was directed against the terms of a draft law dealing with the organization of the Bar. This annoyed the lawyers by forbidding the joint practice of advocacy and teaching, and by permitting foreign barristers to plead; some revisions in its terms, made with the High Commissioner's agreement, rendered it more acceptable.

Of another feature of Lebanese life, the extreme public importance of the ecclesiastics, there were striking examples. The

[1] These included Emile Eddé, Dabbas himself, and Bishara al-Khuri.

[2] Notably Riyaḍh al-Ṣulḥ, who was in consequence banished for a period to the Upper Jazira.

Apostolic Delegate[1] in mid-1935 encountered severe, it would appear unjustified, criticism from the Jesuits, and found warm defenders; his health required his transfer elsewhere six months later. The Patriarch of the Syrian-Catholic community, Mgr Ignace Tappouni, by his elevation to the dignity of Cardinal, aroused bitter jealousy in Maronite circles devoted to their own Patriarch. And the obviously political visit to Lebanon and Syria of the ex-Mufti of Jerusalem, Ḥajj Amin al-Ḥusayni, in 1935 contributed to the revival of nationalist activity in Syria, and sectional feeling in the Lebanon. Finally, these months witnessed a remarkable *rapprochement* between the more extreme politicians of Damascus with no other than Mgr Arida who, pursuing his feud with the High Commissioner, easily found allies and admirers in the highest Muslim circles. His attitude was based in part upon irritation with French policy in general—its refusal of true independence,[2] its infinite range of interference, its failure to combat the economic crisis or to reduce taxes—, in part upon a pronounced mutual antipathy between himself and M. de Martel, and in part also upon a specific bone of contention, the Tobacco Monopoly. The decision to restore the latter system in an amended form, in supersession of the *banderole* method of securing tobacco revenues,[3] was taken by the Common Interests late in 1930. The announcement was greeted with alarm in some Lebanese circles as a threat to vested interests among the growers, manufacturers, capitalists, and workers, while the politicians claimed the need for discussion of such proposals in the Chamber. The system introduced by the mandatory authority as from 1 March 1935 was, in fact, conceived with ample safeguards for all local interests; the Monopoly was granted for a twenty-five-year tenure to a locally-formed Régie, suitably supervised, which took over the bulk of existing plant and labour. Nevertheless, strikes directed against it followed in a number of cities, petitions poured into Beirut and to Europe, and the Patriarch declared himself the Monopoly's most determined enemy, in the interests (as he conceived them) of Lebanese growers and owners. He telegraphed to Paris, received malcontent delegations, thanked strikers for their efforts, addressed letters to the Lebanese communities in five continents, joined forces with Syrian nationalist leaders in protest and agitation—and even, some alleged, in vague projects of Syro-Lebanese unity. With the far from unanimous support of his flock, he pursued his

[1] Mgr Frediano Giannini, an Italian, who had held this post since 1925.

[2] Mgr Arida, who had accompanied his predecessor to Paris in 1919, declared that such independence had been specifically promised by the French statesmen of that time.

[3] Tobacco was grown in about equal quantities in Lebanon and in the 'Alawi territory, with a lesser quantity in the Alexandretta sanjaq.

vendetta against M. de Martel, adding thereto sweeping political claims for Lebanon and a dozen connected grievances. His attitude to the Mandatory itself was for a time critical and fluctuating; he and the High Commissioner ceased to meet, and attempts at mediation by Bishops or senior functionaries had no success. It is noteworthy, because entirely typical,[1] that no pretence existed that the whole matter had any religious or spiritual content; Mgr Arida was acting, like every Middle Eastern community leader, solely as a politician.

The last weeks of 1935 were full of Presidential rumour and ambition, with either of the two Maronite party leaders as probable holders of that office. M. de Martel preferred this time not himself to make the nomination; by Decree of 3 January 1936 he gave that power to the Lebanese Chamber, while still insisting upon an unremoveable Secretary of State and still withholding the Chamber's other suspended prerogatives. Tenure, after election by secret ballot, would be for three years. Convened on 20 January, the Chamber elected M. Emile Eddé. Eyub (Ayyub) Tabet, a Protestant, assumed the post of Secretary in place of 'Abdullah Bayḥum.

Though events in Syria, including the revival of nationalist activity late in 1935, were as usual watched closely from Great Lebanon, and the latter's ever-discontented Muslims were still far from renouncing their claim for retransfer to Damascus, yet the fundamental institution of Lebanese separateness from Syria, and the continuance of the Mandate (which in Christian Lebanon had many sincere friends) were not seriously questioned during these years. Even for a Franco-Lebanese Treaty, to define their future relations, there was demand only in limited circles; indeed, the deterioration of the international situation in Europe, and the recent aggression of Italy against Ethiopia (a weak nation like themselves), seemed to many to give added reason for clinging to a close relation with France.

4. THE SPECIAL AREAS

While the long-drawn Syro-French political struggle persisted, certain areas of the country, no less Syrian than the rest, took little part in these polemics; they stood in administration, and to an uncertain extent in sentiment, apart from the country into which the Syrian nationalists were anxious to incorporate them. These areas were those of the 'Alawi Territory, with its mixed population:[2] the Jabal al-Duruz: the Arabo-Turkish sanjaq of Alexandretta–Antioch: the Christian-Kurdish-Arab province of Jazira:

[1] Such being the structure of the *millet* minority communities, and the duties of their recognized heads.

[2] French official figures of the period give the 'Alawis 69, the Sunnis 17, and the Christians 14 per cent. of the population.

and, lastly, the bedouin tribes of the Shamiya desert. All of these, save the last, were politically as well as socially important constituents of the country, and all were to see great changes in their status and fortunes in and after 1936.

The Jabal al-Duruz, for which a Constitution was provided by the Decree of 14 May 1930, was in effect directly governed by the French, with the use of Druze officials only in the lower grades. Frequently visited by the High Commissioner, a series of efficient military officers[1] held the governorship of the Mountain, and showed an almost excessive sympathy with Druze peculiarities:[2] no second Carbillet, and still less an administration on the feeble yet spasmodically truculent Turkish pattern, was likely again to rule the Jabal, where officers of the 'Special Services' were as ever active and pervasive. Under a new Statute of 1934, greater use was made of Druze officials, who under close supervision furnished the Directors of the headquarter Departments and the Qa'immaqams of qaḍhas. It was, of course, unthinkable that, for many years, the feudal Druze community would regard 'equality of all before the law' as in practice a possible way of life. In isolation from the rest of Syria (apart from normal hierarchical dependence on the French side) the compact administration of the successive Generals and Colonels, assisted by a nominated advisory Council, gave a rarely interrupted period of law and order, and this was aided by systematic arms collection, sympathetic taxation, and assistance to local agriculture, which formed the sole means of livelihood in spite of its frequent affliction by drought or low prices. Agricultural improvement was fostered by loans, and by the break-up of collective lands; other beneficent activities were the construction of wells, small barrages and canals for drinking water and irrigation, the repair of village war damage of 1925–6, and the provision of village schools and dispensaries. A moderate and acceptable rate of progress could thus be hoped for.

The relations of the Jabal to its neighbour, the Amirate of Transjordan, were peaceful. Small parties of exiled Druzes resident in that country, or returning from Sa'udi Arabia through it, regularly entered the Jabal to make their submission, while those still at Azraq or beyond[3] did nothing to disturb the peace. A frontier delimitation was carried out in 1931–2, not without creating alarm among the Druzes because it cut off some villages under Druze ownership, and left in Transjordan territory a part of the

[1] See p. 260, n. 2.

[2] The idealization of, and devotion to, Druze society (and separatism) was later called by M. Gabriel Puaux 'Drusitis', a disease which he found endemic among French functionaries there.

[3] Bitter quarrels were at this time (1929–32) dividing the Druzes settled in Najd. Some to whom amnesty was offered (1931) refused it.

nomad tribes whose obedience they claimed. The construction of the Kirkuk–Haifa oil pipeline across Transjordan in 1932–4 was ill regarded by the Druze landowners, as likely to seduce labour from their fields.

Internal politics followed familiar lines. The great Aṭrash clan was riven with the bitter discord which had ever characterized it: a discord partly personal, partly based on differences of political objective. A substantial minority were faithful to the policy of union with Syria, for which the rebellion had ostensibly been fought; others favoured separation from Damascus, with greater or less 'independence' for the Mountain. Since independence must involve unrestricted Aṭrash domination, many of those who would clamour for greater Druze authority were glad, nevertheless, of a substantial measure of French control. Indeed, a number of the lesser clans swung, by reaction against Aṭrash pretensions, to the formation in 1930 of a short-lived People's Party.[1] Majority opinion, which expressed itself in frequent public declarations, was for a protected but ostensibly autonomous State based on the de Caix Agreement of 1921. That such a State would never be viable or self-protecting, nor acceptable to pan-Syrian nationalism, but must on the contrary involve a perpetual Mandate or protectorate, mattered nothing to the Druze state-builders, and little to the Special Service officers—and perhaps the Governors—whose own views were not dissimilar. The course of treaty negotiations with Syria was closely watched from Suwayda, where the attitude of the men of religion was divided between a moderate and an extreme separatism.[2] Ḥasan Pasha al-Aṭrash, who returned to the territory in 1934, was recognized as the senior Chief and stood, like the great majority, for a degree of local autonomy unlikely to be compatible with the long-term settlement of Syria's political problems.

The 'Alawi Territory, which had narrowly avoided involvement in the troubles of 1925–7, enjoyed during the period 1927–35 an Administration no doubt superior to any they had known, although these were years of grave economic depression. M. Schoeffler retained the governorship throughout; French officials wielded all effective power; and the Representative Council—one half, and after 1930 three-quarters, elected—though full of confessional acerbities, did its work reasonably well. Interest in the elections to it grew markedly in this period as a field of inter-confessional

[1] Its chief strength was in Ṣalkhad area: much of its support, coming from malcontents and from abroad, was suspect in French eyes.

[2] The more extreme party, represented by a strong Aṭrash faction, stood for full internal independence, an elected Council, Druze executive officials, more and better schools (but without the Jesuit teachers) and a national Gendarmerie; some French advice was to be retained.

rivalry,[1] though the general public still ignored its proceedings. A judicial reorganization took place in 1934. The reintroduced Tobacco Monopoly was popular, after some years of overproduction and unsold crops. An inefficient Municipal Council at Ladhqiya was replaced by government officials. The slight use made of 'Alawi officials, as compared with Sunni or Christian, was resented by the small body of Nuṣayri intellectuals. Apart from the squabbles and rivalries of the Nuṣayri hill chiefs, and others involving their Sunni landlords or Isma'ili neighbours, the politics of the territory were unchanged in the alignment of the 'Alawi majority as separatist and pro-Mandate, and of the Sunnis with most (not all) of the Christians[2] as unionist and pan-Syrian. With marginal conversions and secessions, these two parties remained constant, and vied with each other in meetings, round-robins, and deputations to Beirut as occasion offered. French support for the separatist party was undisguised, and they regularly supported the half-sinister, half-ludicrous figure of the obese, illiterate, miracle-working 'god', Sulayman al-Murshid; yet any hopeful future for so small, backward, and scarcely viable a unit—and one so evidently a part of Syria—could be scarcely imaginable without an indefinitely continued French presence and support.

These differences did not, in general, prevent the collaboration of the sects in the Representative Council and elsewhere. One serious riot, born of a trivial market-place quarrel, disturbed Sunni-Nuṣayri relations at Ladhqiya in 1933, but in spite of alarms it had no sequel. A long-drawn disputation arose in 1935 between the same two communities regarding a purchase of village lands, and an alleged failure to pay for them. Episcopal quarrels in the Greek Orthodox community distracted the faithful, but without disorder other than of conscience; the crisis ended in 1932, though three years later further episcopal acrimony led to the temporary fragmentation of their Church. More serious were the efforts of Jesuit Fathers in the Ṣafita area to proselytize[3] among the ignorant 'Alawis; some scores of these accepted for a time, for whatever motives, a semblance of Christianity, and the resulting resentment among 'Alawis and Sunnis alike was conveyed to the High Commissioner. A protesting delegation was led to Beirut by Sulayman al-Murshid.

Residents of the Jabal and the 'Alawi Territory alike were (as the

[1] The seats were distributed as follows: to 'Alawis (Nuṣayris) 10, Orthodox, 2, Maronites 1, Sunnis 3, Isma'ilis 1.

[2] The small Maronite community, and the Jesuit missionaries, were strongly separatist.

[3] Local accusations that French officialdom supported such efforts were doubtless false; such a policy could do the Mandatory, as such, nothing but harm. The affair was the subject of comment in the Permanent Mandates Commission.

High Commissioner indicated at Geneva) 'Syrians' by nationality, but neither territory was, in his opinion, to be considered as integrally part of Syria. This position, M. Ponsot considered, would give no trouble—as long as the French were in direct control. Both Governments sent delegations to the Conference on Common Interests.

The problem which the mixed population of the Alexandretta sanjaq might one day pose was not presented in acute form during these years, nor was it yet necessary to compute the proportion of resident Turks, Turkomans, Turkish-speaking Armenians, Kurds, or Muslim and Christian Arabs. There existed, indeed, a clear or at times an ostentatious devotion to Turkey[1] in some circles, and open propaganda was conducted by these in mosque, diwan, and Assembly; many boys were dispatched from the sanjaq to school in Turkey; rumours of impending frontier change, which the interested passed on or originated, were provocative. Nevertheless the half-autonomous status of the sanjaq, within Syria, satisfied an undoubted majority. Such status was flattering to the people of the favoured area, except for a small pan-Syrian element among the Sunni Arabs, and general devotion to it was not shaken by the arguments of nationalist visitors from Damascus. It was confirmed more than once by the Syrian Premier and ministers; it could not, indeed, under the Franco-Turkish Agreements of 1921 and 1926, have given place to complete assimilation in Syria, while outright cession of the sanjaq to Turkey was never, at this period, even faintly suggested—unless by a few voices on the occasion of a visit to Antioch in April 1934 by the Wali of 'Ayntab, who was greeted by demonstrations.

The 'special régime' which was confirmed by the Constitution of 1930, and in which not only the confessionally-based Representative Council but also the whole Administration was dominated by the French Délégué,[2] provided satisfactory government, little disturbed by Syrian politics. Economic conditions were severely depressed and must render impossible, for the time, such favourite projects as the draining of the 'Amq lake. Taxation was collected without undue rigour, law and order were well maintained, the Turkish frontier increasingly peaceful though not innocent of occasional brigandage. Bedouin incursions occured at times in the summer months, and attacks on traffic on the Antioch–Alexandretta road were not unknown.

[1] It was noted that some of the Turks or Turcophiles belonged to the 'old school' of Ottoman Turkey, others to the modernized hat-wearing type of Kamal's republic.

[2] M. Durieux, throughout these years.

The sanjaq of the Jazira was constituted in 1932, before which date the area had been lightly administered by the Special Service officers and the Gendarmerie as part of the Euphrates province. The new sanjaq differed in no formal manner from the others, yet its remoteness, its composite racial content, its largely non-Arab character, its lack of loyalty to Syria, gave it a special complexion and peculiar difficulties. To its original nucleus of riverain and desert Arab and Kurdish tribesmen, the fertility and emptiness of the region had attracted, since 1926, a considerable further Kurdish population—including an element of self-conscious Kurd nationalists—in flight from Turkish reprisals[1] and yet more numerous Christian, mainly Catholic, communities equally seeking the safety of new homes. The process of settling these effervescent non-Syrian folk on the Khabur and its tributaries, along the railway, and in the better rainlands and nascent villages, devolved upon the French. These, accepting the charge, provided shelter and services, arranged defence against raids from Turkish territory, negotiated with the 'Iraqis for the settlement of Arab tribal vendettas,[2] and through the League of Nations took in hand the establishment of a final frontier with Turkey.

But the process of settlement was retarded by the nervous self-consciousness of the ill-assorted groups, and by the special pretension, as Francophile Catholics, of the Christians and their episcopal leaders. The intractable ferocity of the Kurds was eager to strike back at Turkey and assert a Kurdish nationality, heedless of the embarrassment thus caused to their new rulers; and it was matched by the disorderly penetrations of the Turks themselves, who viewed the area as improperly detached from Turkey. The French were compelled to increase their staffs in the district headquarters, to arrest Kurdish leaders guilty of disturbing the peace, and to restore order in Qamishli after a bout of rioting in 1932, to which Turkish irredentism was not a stranger. Bitter quarrels occurred among the Kurdish leaders themselves, some being wild tribesmen and some, like the Badr Khan family, cultivated intellectuals. A number of these had to be removed from the area. Movements were made by speech and writing at Ḥasaja and Qamishli, by temporarily united Arab and Kurdish elements, in favour of separation from Syria: movements which, supported by Catholic influences and often by French officers on the spot,[3] were rejected by French higher policy, in spite of the contrary accusations of Damascus nationalists, who claimed to

[1] After the suppression of the Kurdish rebellion under Shaykh Sa'id in 1925–6.

[2] Notably by conferences at Ḥasaja in February 1929, and at Niṣibin in 1934.

[3] Of such, M. Puaux writes that they 'résistaient mal à la tentation d'une politique personnelle' (p. 147).

see here a French intention to re-justify and prolong their Mandate.

A new element appeared late in 1933 with the entry from 'Iraq of Assyrian refugees, whose relations with their own Government had by now become intolerable.[1] To the relief of 'Iraq, and the dismay of Turkey who feared a new frontier menace, the French on humanitarian grounds accepted a substantial part of this hapless exiled community, which was increased to a number of some thousands by additional entries during 1934–6; and under League of Nations supervision, and at the expense of Great Britain, 'Iraq, and the League itself, it was gradually settled in new homes on the Khabur. Unwelcome to the Syrians, who raised outcry against yet another unwanted Christian minority, the Assyrians with their priest-led clans system and their extreme community exclusiveness became 'Syrians',[2] and added one more thankless embarrassment to the distractions of their new rulers.

Another type of community perennially difficult to accommodate to the scheme of modern government, or of modern society, was that of the *badu* of the wide Syrian desert, with their overflow into the cultivated fringe-lands and the neighbouring countries of 'Iraq, Turkey, Jordan, and Arabia. The supervision of the seasonal migrations of these nomads, the settlement of their disputes, their peaceful behaviour, their arms,[3] their relations with settled neighbours, and to some extent their welfare, were the concern of the French Contrôle Bédouin which, while necessarily in liaison with the Syrian district-authorities, remained under the close control of the Mandatory. A 'Tribal Section' of the High Commissioner's office considered problems arising from the tribes, and such measures for their benefit as dispensaries, travelling schools, and well-digging. Their taxation (by animal-count or by a lump sum levied on their herds) and such legal processes as involved them in the ordinary Courts,[4] were the concern of the Syrian officials of adjoining districts. A comprehensive tribal conference, representing all interests, was held at Ḥumṣ in 1927, another at Palmyra in October 1934. Outstanding disputes with Turkey had been settled by the Niṣibin Conference earlier in the same year, and a satisfactory agreement with 'Iraq on the mid-desert region resulted from a meeting at Mosul the year before. The *badu* enjoyed special representation in the Syrian Chamber.

[1] For the background of the 'Assyrian Question', see Longrigg, *'Iraq*, pp. 231–6 and elsewhere.

[2] British and League of Nations efforts to find other homes for the Assyrians failed. The Turks insisted upon their settlements being at least fifty kilometres from the frontier.

[3] The difficult task of disarming the *badu*, as they seasonally approached or entered cultivated land, was attempted every year.

[4] i.e. when one of the parties to a dispute was a bedouin, one a sedentary.

During these years desert security was satisfactory, inter-tribal fighting rare, attacks on motor convoys rarer. Grants continued to be paid to certain outstanding shaykhs, some of whom increasingly adopted modern ways. Sedentarization proceeded slowly on the desert fringes, encouraged by the promise of land, water, seed, and instruction for such as would attempt it. Unaffected by world economic conditions, the bedouin were sorely tried, especially in 1932, by drought and a consequent lack of grazing, which cost them many thousands of animals.

VII

LAST HOPES FRUSTRATED

I. TIME OF TROUBLE

THE pause in political activity from 1933 to late 1935 had been due to weariness and reaction, to the need of a period of reconciliation, to the strong interest felt by Syrians in the Italian adventure in Ethiopia and, in some measure, to the success of the High Commissioner's policy of economic endeavour. But it could not last; and the political outburst early in 1936 represented an eruption of stored energy. The occasion for the renewal of militancy was given by the death of Ibrahim Ḥananu in Aleppo, in November 1935: but beyond this and the mere 'swing of the pendulum' in political habit, these events were more deeply caused by a cumulative realization that passive acceptance of mandatory tutelage would never serve to end it: that economic advance lacked all the thrill of political campaigning: that their present Government failed to represent the most active and patriotic elements among the public: and that 'Iraq had now for three years made good its place as a sovereign State and League member. Moreover Egypt, late in 1935, was setting a precedent of renewed political effervescence after a similar period of quiet. At the turn of the year 1935–6 the stage was set for a strong nationalist revival: consultations in December 1935 had smoothed the way to closer unity in the National Bloc, plans had been made for the mission of delegates to Paris, telegrams had been sent to the High Commissioner demanding a revival of constitutional life, and emotional speeches in the mosques had commemorated the 'martyrs' who died in the election squabbles of December 1931. Nor was the cordiality visible between the Maronite Patriarch and nationalist leaders in Damascus without significance.

On the fortieth day after Ḥananu's death an imposing reception was given by the Nationalists, at which the National Pact was read and acclaimed. It demanded complete independence and effective union for Syria, the abrogation of Zionism, wide Arab unity, equality of rights for all communities, a higher living standard and, for the time, a ban on all political parties save the Bloc. There were, it was agreed, to be no talks with the Mandatory except on these bases.

A week later, fifty days of almost country-wide disturbance

and misery were ushered in by a dangerously emotional demonstration at a memorial service for Ḥananu on 11 January, a police raid on the Bloc headquarters, and the arrest of Fakhri al-Barudi. This was followed by the declaration of a general strike, by Bloc protests, and by distribution of leaflets and further arrests. The 'maisons Ḥananu' which had been opened as revolutionary centres were shut by the Police. The strong reaction of the Bloc showed its improved unity and discipline, its wide support, and its power for the first time to combine urban and rural movements. Telegrams of protest at police sternness, as well as on broader lines, were sent to Geneva and the Arab rulers. The public services were disorganized, shops shut, and business at a standstill; the schools were deserted by their pupils who, accompanied for the first time by women demonstrators, marched and sang in the streets. The assignment by M. Fain, the Délégué at Damascus, of responsibility to each town quarter for law and order was ignored, and the issue of new and devolutionary Regulations for the muḥafadhas was scarcely noticed. A Proclamation by M. de Martel, ordering students back to their desks, was unregarded; but his own visit to Damascus from 23 to 26 January gave the occasion for a full-scale meeting with Bloc leaders, who stated their demands—and received an uncompromising answer. Troops and tanks appeared in the main streets, lives were lost in actions of suppression. The number of arrests passed from individuals to scores and soon to hundreds. The same scenes of enthusiasm and mob action were seen, with the same toll of dead and wounded, in Aleppo, Ḥumṣ, Ḥamah, and Dayr al-Zur. A number of newspapers were suppressed.

From the last days of January the strike was substantially at an end in the provincial towns, though occasional demonstrations indicated pan-Syrian solidarity, especially in Ḥamah where a violent outbreak was sternly suppressed early in February. This had echoes in the Lebanon, where shops were shut in Beirut, demonstrations organized in Tripoli and Sidon, and messages of sympathy sent—by Mgr Arida himself—to arrested politicians of Damascus. A sympathetic strike was called at Ladhqiya. In the capital strong pressure was exercised by the merchants, teachers, divines, and many politicians for the restoration of normal conditions; but the students, ignoring warnings and the official closing of their schools, broke up such shops as timidly reopened, defied their teachers, disrupted communications, and spent their days in street parades and scuffles with the police. These conditions, acclaimed as heroic by leading nationalists (who were powerless to control them) continued throughout February, punctuated by violent deaths and provocatively ceremonial funerals. The forces of disorder were joined by dozens from the criminal underworld, and by villagers from outside. A lawyers' strike, which brought the Courts to a standstill, added to the current confusion. On 11 January Jamil Mardam Bey and Naṣib al-Bakri were arrested, and the usual protests and manifestos followed; nationalist university professors, the brothers Faris and Fa'iz al-Khuri, were dismissed; leaders in Aleppo—Sa'dullah al-Jabiri and Na'im Anṭaki—were arrested. The proclamation of a 'military régime' and curfew in the principal cities by General Huntziger brought no improvement; increased Gendarmerie recruitment, and the enrolling of Druze and other irregulars, did no more. Every day brought further suppressions of newspapers, episodes of demonstration and reprisal, shop looting and schoolboy violence, and emotional funerals of the 'martyrs'. The now sincere efforts of non-political circles to secure a return to normal life were stultified by student obduracy, and the outspoken comments of M. de Martel at interviews in mid-February were as ineffective as unpalatable. A group of 'Iraqi Senators contributed nothing helpful by a telegram from Baghdad to Geneva condemning the French.

Some hope was offered, at last, by the resignation of the Ministry of Shaykh Taj on 22 February by arrangement with the High Commissioner, the formation of another[1] in its place, as 'moderate' as the last but less unacceptable to the Bloc, and an early exchange of views between it and the Bloc leaders. It was headed by the respected ex-minister 'Aṭa al-Ayyubi. The High Commissioner addressed to it a conciliatory letter, restating his policy, calling for peace and confidence, and undertaking that arrested offenders, tried and untried, would be handled with clemency. He followed this by ordering a number of releases. The new Ministry in turn published a programme of normalization, transition, and return to parliamentary life. The first reactions of the Nationalists were unpromising; Hashim al-Atasi republished the National Pact, and declared the High Commissioner's promises to be vague and unsatisfactory. Further violent demonstrations occurred on 28 February in Damascus, where the French military commander declared that his troops would, if forced thereto, not hesitate to use their arms. But the way to real progress, in fact, now lay open; M. de Martel had obtained a new latitude from the Quai d'Orsay. He was able to call the new ministers to Beirut on 28 February, with M. Fain and the recognized Bloc leaders; and, after three days of conversations, substantial agreement

[1] Prime Minister and Minister of Interior, 'Aṭa al-Ayyubi: Justice, Sa'id al-Ghazzi: Education, Amir Muṣṭafa al-Shihabi: Finance, Edmond Homsi, an Aleppo Christian banker: Economics, Works, and Agriculture, Muṣṭafa al-Quṣayri of Antioch. al-Ghazzi and al-Shihabi represented the Nationalists.

was reached on 1 March on the essentials of a future treaty. The announcement that such progress had been made, and that a Syrian delegation would proceed at once to Paris to draft a treaty not inferior to the Anglo-'Iraqi, was followed by the release of eminent detained persons and the republication of newspapers. The now complacent tone of al-Atasi and other former irreconcilables created throughout Syria an atmosphere of hope and joy unknown since the days of the Constituent Assembly, and one which led to unusual expressions of Muslim-Christian fraternization. Moderate statesmen could either join the Bloc and hold their peace, or—like Shaykh Taj who remained in Paris till 1941—could leave the country. The delegation for Paris left Syria amid scenes of enthusiasm on 21 March. It consisted of Hashim al-Atasi as chairman, with Jamil Mardam Bey, Sa'dullah al-Jabiri, Faris al-Khuri, Edmond Homsi, and Muṣṭafa al-Shihabi. Edmond Rabbaṭ and Na'im Anṭaki were its secretaries.

2. THE TREATIES, 1936

The Syrian delegation, welcomed to Paris by M. Flandin on 2 April, soon found their task to be one of extreme difficulty. The French negotiators who, by this invitation to France, had obtained a respite from Syrian disorders, seemed little readier than before to yield the essential Syrian demands, and were indifferent to the pressures of Syro-Lebanese groups in Paris, telegrams from those at Geneva, or solidarity in Syria itself. In less than a month an apparent impasse had been reached, and a draft handed to al-Atasi late in April was in terms quite unacceptable. Agreement in fact would probably have been unattainable but for a 'god from the machine' in the French political field: that is, the supersession, after general elections, of the Government of Albert Sarraut (with Flandin as Minister of Foreign Affairs) by that of Léon Blum with Delbos. The new left-wing Cabinet was less traditionalist, and more appreciative of the Syrian viewpoint. The negative reply of the latter's delegation to the French proposals was intentionally delayed until the second week of June, and this permitted negotiations when resumed to proceed in a changed atmosphere. Much help was received from the liberal Under-Secretary, M. Viénot; the current Anglo-Egyptian negotiations, concluded in July, offered a parallel; and agreement was reached, and signatures exchanged, on 9 September, on terms which, reported with pride to Damascus, were received there with manifestations of joy. The delegates returned to their own country by way of Ankara, and were received by vast crowds, parades, and delegations from all parts.

In Syria and Lebanon the six months from March to September had been a period of uneasy waiting. To the latter, from which every move in the negotiations was closely watched, the High Commission gave early assurances that Lebanese integrity would be safeguarded, and urged his worried Maronite petitioners to patience. The Christian elements were concerned for their rights and majority status, the Muslims feared continuance of their present imposed and unwanted predicament, to perpetuate which, as a reward for his recent support of Syrian nationalism,[1] the Maronite Patriarch had bargained with the National Bloc in Damascus. Muslim views found full expression at a 'Conference of the Coast' convened on 10 January at Beirut, where, amid a variety of views and predilections, there was unanimity that the Muslim areas of Great Lebanon ought to be re-transferred to the Syrians. In succeeding weeks further Muslim initiative was shown in the form of deputations from the Biqa', from the slopes of Hermon, from the Shi'is of southern Lebanon, from Tyre and Sidon where strikes and rioting took place, and notably from Tripoli[2] where repeated demonstrations occurred. The similar action of the Syrian National Party (p. 225) was punished by its official suppression (which was, however, largely ineffective) and the temporary detention of its leaders; the party, considered an especial menace to Lebanese integrity, became in June the subject of a governmental Investigating Committee, which directed many arrests. Muslim meetings and ambitions at Beirut were countered by the formation, with the Patriarch's blessing, of a Party of Lebanese Unity, devoted to insisting on the *status quo*. To this the Muslim reply was to form a Muslim Consultative Council, under Sunni religious auspices. It was, at the same time, evident that a number of the Sunni notables, including their Deputies in the Lebanese Chamber, failed to support the pan-Syrian party, and earned odium by their attitude. The position of the Mutawalli Deputies was similar, and equally unrepresentative of the general attitude of their community. President Eddé's Administration remained watchful and in daily touch with M. Meyrier (the acting High Commissioner), the Maronite Patriarch, and the heads of communities.

In the Jabal al-Duruz, whose leaders knew themselves to be closely concerned in the Paris conversations, demonstrations were held both for and against union with Syria. The same

[1] The failure of the Patriarch to support Syrian claims to Tripoli was, however, disappointing to the nationalists, and the whole *rapprochement* proved short-lived. The Patriarch in April 1936 published a Green Book containing his views and complaints.

[2] The outstanding Muslim leaders here were 'Abd al-Ḥamid Karami (a future Prime Minister), Dr. 'Abd al-Laṭif Bissar, and Muṣṭafa al-Muqaddam.

occurred, for the same reasons, in the 'Alawi Territory. In the Alexandretta sanjaq the Turkish minority element began more openly to agitate for secession from Damascus in favour of Ankara.

To these causes of restlessness another was added by the action of the High Commissioner on 13 March in enacting new regulations (already discussed in draft with the heads of the Christian minorities, and rejected by them) regarding the personal status of the minority citizens. These regulations in no way met the wishes of the community heads, expressed repeatedly during 1930–5, for greater powers and independence: they were offensive also to the Muslim majority, as emphasizing the fragmentation of the body politic. The regulations officially delimited the communities, and prescribed their status, powers, and 'legal personality', and the procedure for authorized passage from one community to another. These provisions were rejected by a Congress of Christian dignitaries held at Bakurki, by the Greek Orthodox Synod, and by Muslim spokesmen: and the Lebanese Government itself demanded considerable modification of them. Agitation in this sense was to continue for the next two years.

The mid-year of 1936 in Syria was one of anxiety and anticipation, constant exchanges between the nationalists and their spokesmen in Paris, and distractions caused by the new-fashioned political organizations, of which more will be said. The return of the Syrian delegation in triumph, late in September, led to immediate steps for the holding of elections. The two stages of these were completed[1] on 14 and 30 November, undeterred by the apprehension visible in some Druze and 'Alawi circles, by a Circassian claim to autonomy, by Muslim-Christian clashes in Aleppo, and by an increasing, indeed a menacing, Turkish interest in the future of Alexandretta. The now all-powerful Bloc, secure of their over-all majority, wisely permitted moderate or non-political local magnates to be elected, as usual, in rural constituencies;[2] the election was, in fact, a plebiscite for or against the Treaty. After the elections, a change of Government was expected, and occurred: the President, Muḥammad 'Ali Bey al-'Abid, retired in favour of Hashim al-Atasi, and a new all-Bloc Cabinet was formed under Jamil Mardam Bey.[3] Faris al-Khuri became President of the Chamber. Parliamentary discussion of the Treaty

[1] Eighty-six deputies were elected, the population having increased. The usual protests were received from some communities, alleging under-representation.

[2] Where, as at Jarablus and the Jazira, they tried to impose outside candidates, they failed.

[3] The other ministers (with whom the present writer had occasion to spend long hours in 1937) were: Interior and Foreign Affairs, Sa'dullah al-Jabiri: Education and Justice, 'Abd al-Raḥman Kayyali: Finance and Defence, Shukri al-Quwatli. Jamil retained Economics, with the Premiership.

began on 26 December. Opposition to it was shown only by the League of National Action (p. 228) and by some schoolboy demonstrators; telegrams from Cairo told of the high disapproval of Dr. Shahbandar, still in exile there. The Treaty was ratified by eighty-one votes to none on the 27th. Ten days later the Chamber empowered the executive, for three months, to govern by decree-laws, and itself went into recess.

To permit peaceful introduction of the new status of the ʿAlawi and Druze provinces an official of the High Commission, M. Kieffer, had visited both areas to explain and conciliate, and joint conferences had been arranged during November. These brought together at Beirut the ʿAlawi, and later the Druze, Representative Councils with the Syrian negotiators who had signed in Paris. The latter, aware of the delicacy of the position, gave solemn assurances of their benevolent intentions. The reattachment of the two areas to the Government of Damascus was prescribed by Decrees of 5 and 2 December 1936, respectively. The Governors and certain other officials of the two muḥafadhas would be appointed by the President, the other officials by the Governors; the latter, with their elected councils, were given powers of local legislation. Each province was to have its own budget, each to contribute to the central treasury, each to send Deputies (16 from Ladhqiya, 5 from the Jabal) to the Syrian Chamber. French troops could, under the Treaty, remain in the two provinces for the first five years of its effective life. Mudhhir al-Raslan was appointed Muḥafidh of Ladhqiya, Naṣib al-Bakri of Jabal al-Duruz; both were keen Bloc supporters, and men of established position.

Events in the Lebanon had moved even more rapidly. It was inconceivable to the Lebanese Government and the majority elements that their republic should not acquire, by a similar treaty, an international status at least equal to Syria's; and this demand the French were happy to concede. A negotiating committee, appointed after the return of the High Commissioner from Paris, consisted of the Lebanese President, Secretary-General, president of the Chamber, and seven members of that body. No considerable difficulties were met, differences from the Syrian model being slight and a French guarantee of the *status quo* being, to the Lebanese, a greater desideratum than 'independence'. Additions suggested by the Maronite Patriarch, covering a stabilized currency, the abolition of the Mixed Courts, a reconsideration of foreign concessions, and other matters, were not pressed. The text placed before the Deputies on 13 November was passed unanimously; but a prolonged strike in Tripoli, a fierce encounter there between demonstrators and French troops, and an outbreak of anti-Christian rioting in country districts, showed that Muslim sentiment was unchanged. These were less serious than the Muslim-Christian clash at Beirut on 15 November, resulting in some scores of casualties who included four dead: a deplorable episode condemned not only by the High Commissioner but by many local Muslim leaders, and, in significant terms, by good friends of Syria–Lebanon in France itself. The Treaty was ratified on 17 November, and the Chamber proceeded to appoint a Commission to examine the administrative reforms which were prescribed in an annexure to the text.

Of these Treaties themselves, whatever their detailed merits or demerits, it must be felt that to all appearances they could with great advantage have been concluded between the same parties, on the same lines, ten or certainly five years earlier; it would, indeed, have been then an easier task since, before the Italian invasion of Ethiopia in 1935, or the massacre of Assyrian villagers in 'Iraq in 1933, negotiation would have been freer of tensions induced from outside, while within Syria precisely the same considerations, claims, and personalities had prevailed in 1931 as in 1936; and at the former date, as at the latter, the Anglo-'Iraqi Treaty of 1930 offered a ready precedent. There had, on the contrary, been intransigence on both sides, and damaging to both. As it was, the move forward from its earlier positions had been made, after May 1936, by a French Government hailed by the right wing as an 'experiment', and destined for a short life; and the failure of its successor to adopt as progressive or realistic an attitude is the tragedy of the succeeding years.

The Treaties attempted, by tact and compromise, to meet the clashing claims of Druze and 'Alawi separatism (dear to the French administrators) and of the Syrian nationalist demand for unification: to provide safeguards for the rights and individuality of the scattered minority communities in face of the centralizing and levelling attitude of the Syrian Government and intelligentsia: and to combine the advantages of an efficient Administration (such as the French could claim to have produced) with the necessity of handing it over unconditionally to Syrian and Lebanese hands. A mode was sought also for the disposal of the Common Interests, whose administration by the High Commissioner (future Ambassador) would henceforth be a clear anachronism. Time was to show how far the treaty-makers' efforts had been successful or would be sustained; the effort at the time, at least, was sincere and statesmanlike.

Both of the two Treaties,[1] closely modelled on the Anglo-

[1] Each was a complicated series of Treaty, attachments, protocols, and exchanges of letters. Text in R.I.I.A., *Documents on International Affairs, 1937*, and Hourani, *Syria and Lebanon*, App. A, pp. 314–40.

'Iraqi, were as between France and States which were henceforward to be independent and sovereign members of the League of Nations. They were treaties of alliance, peace, and friendship, under which there would be, in the field of defence, consultation in peacetime, and mutual help in case of war: help confined, however, on the side of Syria or Lebanon to the offering of its own land, air, and sea facilities as these existed. France was to enjoy in Syria the use of two (inconspicuously placed) air bases for the duration of the Treaty, and could also station, for five years only, ground troops in specified districts; but in Lebanon she could maintain forces of all kinds for periods to be mutually agreed. In each State a national army would be formed, with a French military mission and equipment. All advisers and technicians required would be obtained from France; the latter's diplomatic service throughout the world would watch the rights of Syrian or Lebanese subjects; the French Ambassador at Damascus or Beirut would take precedence over all others; parity of currency between the States and France would be maintained. Repayment to the latter of military or civil expenses incurred under the Mandate was waived. Foreign institutions, safe from molestation, would enjoy all their present privileges. A reliable judicial system would be installed to safeguard the rights of foreigners.

The foreign policies of the three parties were to be aligned, by consultation and action. The rights and obligations assumed by France during the mandatory period would all, on conclusion of the Mandate, devolve upon the two new League members. The States would thereafter assume all relevant French obligations and duties arising out of League action in the international field. The two Governments undertook responsibility for their own order and defence, and would safeguard French air routes across their territory. The Treaties were given an effective life of twenty-five years from the date of admission to the League—a date assumed (in an attached Protocol) to be not more than three years distant. Renewal, under the Syrian Treaty, would thereafter be arranged if both parties then desired it: under the Lebanese, it would be automatic unless specifically undesired. In the latter Treaty freedom, equality, and representation were assured for all communities, and a specific undertaking was given by the Lebanese to undertake a programme of administrative and financial reform. In both cases France would endeavour to release her new allies from the anachronistic burden of Ottoman Capitulations, which otherwise must (unless abjured by the privileged Powers) be recalled into existence at the end of the Mandate.

The documents attached to the Syrian Treaty contained provisions for the relations between the new State and the Druze and 'Alawi areas. These were to be annexed to the State of Syria, but with the enjoyment of a special administrative régime. The smaller minorities scattered throughout Syria would be safeguarded by effective use of the guarantees already provided in the Syrian Constitution. No change was intended for the status of Alexandretta. The Common Interests would be handed by France to whatever joint organization the two States might create or, alternatively, to the two States themselves.

The reception of the Treaties, which had very general though not universal support in Syria–Lebanon, was more mixed in France. Circles supporting the Blum Administration and its foreign policy believed that a happy restatement of the ancient Franco-Syrian relations had been achieved, a liberal and progressive gesture and régime substituted for mere authoritarianism, and French cultural (perhaps also economic) supremacy in the Levant preserved. Others saw with satisfaction the safeguards for minorities (in which Great Britain, in 'Iraq, was held to have failed), and felt that France was honourably freeing herself from mandatory burdens. To others, again, the prospect of genuine goodwill from the majority of Syrians, in place of the opposition and bitterness of the last sixteen years, was welcome as a probable element of real strategic and political strength.

But such views were not those of all, perhaps not of most, Frenchmen; and they were held by certainly no majority of the French officials in the territory, whose own careers, incidentally, were immediately threatened. The legend of a French unquestioned and popularly desired position in these territories died hard, and accorded ill with the terms of a bargained, compromising, and surrendering Treaty. To the missionaries, Jesuits, and military caste the Treaty was anathema, even though the régime of 1920–36 had been clearly imperfect. And to a wider French public, never fully aware of Syrian realities and living wishfully in the past, the Treaty as represented to them seemed a gesture of French weakness, extorted by agitators and mobs: a sacrifice of the efforts and expenses of so many years: and the imposition of a unitary régime upon an actually diverse territory. They regretted the failure to recover any part of the great sums spent by France during the Mandate; they foresaw an early probability of the oppression of Christians and the internecine strife of Muslims; and they feared that French withdrawal would give the signal for the entry of some other European Power—which could be, of course, no other than 'perfidious Albion'.

3. PARTIES AND GANGS

The history of our territories between Christmas 1936 and the outbreak of the Second World War is a saddening record. In Lebanon it is one of governmental failure to agree with its inland neighbour, to satisfy a large part of its own citizenry, or to rise, in the art of government, above petty and personal faction. In Syria, the hopes of country-wide territorial and political unity, with which the period opened, were disappointed: the nationalist movement lost much of its solidarity, the administration of the recovered provinces was unsuccessful, the Jazira was disloyal and distracted, and the Alexandretta province irretrievably lost to Turkey; and, behind all this, the new basis of Franco-Syrian relations provided by the Treaty never materialized, while most of the weaknesses and anachronisms of the mandatory régime persisted.

Of these matters, the following pages will offer a fuller record. But it will be convenient first to give some account of a characteristic phase of the period in both the States, the activity of political parties and paramilitary organizations of a novel type. The bodies concerned shared the characteristic, unknown before in local politics, of a fairly definite programme, a businesslike and widespread organization, the genuine enthusiasm of their members, the incorporation of the young and vigorous as distinct from the 'old gang' of local politicians, and an eager self-manifestation in the form of uniformed and disciplined squads or gangs. The fact that a number of such organizations came into prominence almost simultaneously in 1935–7 shows that they corresponded to a psychological need in the young men of the time, that they were mutually competitive, and that all were influenced by contemporary forms (and largely by the contemporary spirit) then prominent in Germany and Italy. These parties were all arrayed in protest, in some degree, against the delays and inefficiencies of existing government and diplomacy, against a sense of subjection, and against the older generation.

The first to be founded was the Syrian National Party, originally (from 1932 to 1935) a secret society, but after 1935 an open and widespread organization in the Lebanon, with branches in Syria, Palestine, and Egypt. It was founded at the American University by Anṭun Sa'ada, an unusually dynamic Lebanese Christian, then aged 32, who had been brought up in Brazil and educated partly in Germany. The party, composed mostly of young men, stood for a single Syrian nation within its 'natural boundaries', with the obliteration of all local separatism (including the Lebanese) and all confessionalism; it was non-Islamic, but was prepared for United Syria to lead the Arab world and to resist all foreign interference. The party on its emergence from secrecy already contained some 8,000 members, with a full regional organization rigidly hierarchical, under the absolute authority of its single leader. Headquarter departments, an Advisory Council, local executives in thirty-six zones and branches, all showed an organization of approved Nazi type.

The discovery of the party by the Government in 1935 led to efforts at its suppression; and these were increased when Sa'ada in March 1936 petitioned the High Commissioner for Syro-Lebanese union. He and some of his lieutenants were imprisoned for some weeks, and an official investigation into the party's activities led to renewed persecution. These were met with violent opposition by a membership still rapidly growing and by no means confined to Lebanese or Christians. Thereafter the history of the party, conspicuous with its leader worship, strict discipline, brown shirts, and rigid principles, was that of a vital, convinced but usually well-behaved body capable of organizing an impressive parade, and having its say, on all occasions. Nevertheless, it was weakened by the repressive hostility of both Governments, the secession in 1937–8 of some prominent members, and the frequent imprisonment of its leader. Sa'ada himself left the Lebanon late in 1938 (for Germany, said the Sûreté Générale) and the party passed into relative inaction; its premises were occupied, and its leaders arrested as pro-German, in the autumn of 1939. A persistent charge against it, that of receiving foreign subsidies, cannot be proved; its activity in gun-running into Palestine is highly probable.

Similar in organization, but professedly non-political, were the Phalanges Libanaises which, by origin an offshoot of the Party of Lebanese Unity, stood from late 1936 onwards for a purely Lebanese, and predominantly a Maronite, interest. The uniforms, drill, and paramilitary organization of the Phalanges gave their parades and squads more than the mere status in the world of social service and athletics which they claimed; led by an active and able young Maronite, Pierre Jumayyil, they became a considerable force in society and politics. The organization, with others, was suppressed by the High Commissioner in the autumn of 1939. Their counterpart in the cities of the Lebanon was the less efficient all-Muslim organization of the Najjada, or Muslim Scouts, whose political colouring, that of pure Arab nationalism, led to frequent clashes with the Phalanges.

The paramilitary organizations in Lebanon were simultaneously dissolved by governmental Decree in mid-November 1937, as having deserted the purely athletic character which alone the

Decree of July 1934 allowed them. The Phalanges offered a spirited resistance, and collected a mass demonstration in the streets of Beirut. This was scattered by police and French military action, with damage to property and loss of life. The Phalange members continued to meet in secret.

The orthodox or more old-fashioned Lebanese political parties, lacking the new features, have been or will be mentioned in their proper place, in so far as they deserve mention. One other party, unique in character and aims, was common to Syria and the Lebanon, and began in and after 1935 to gain considerable momentum: this was the Communist Party. It had been founded in Beirut in 1930 in supersession of less co-ordinated Communist action, its early members being nearly all Armenian; and it had already enjoyed some success in organizing industrial trouble[1] and in supporting political demonstrations. Highly intelligent Russian-trained leaders,[2] mostly from the educated class, assumed control, and a newspaper of some pretensions, the *Voice of the People*, was published in and after 1937. A constant output of leaflets and manifestos was assured, and Marxist works were translated. Branches were opened in all main cities. Relations between Armenians and Arabs in the party were strained, with the former gradually losing ground; and divided views were held as to collaboration with the nationalists until, in 1936, the party decision was temporarily to support them. The party took its place in all the disorders of the time, conducted demonstrations on its own, revealed its superior organization, and strove acceptably in Alexandretta for the Syrian cause; well controlled, it held its own as a national Communist Party (though detached from the Comintern after 1938), and was at endless loggerheads with the Phalanges, with Sa'ada's Party, and with all Catholic spokesmen. It was unsuccessful in parliamentary elections, but its members could keep on close terms with nationalist leaders and could wield decisive leadership in the trades unions. They inspired the Anti-Fascist League in Beirut in 1936, and conducted a Communist Congress in May 1939 to which leading Syrians sent friendly messages. The party had little proletarian following, but could use the period 1935–9 to establish its centres, cadres, and organization. Acutely embarrassed by the Russo-German Agreement of August 1939, it was suppressed by the High Commissioner soon after the outbreak of war, and disappeared from view, and from activity, for the next three years.

[1] A railway strike in 1932, a strike among the 'Iraq Petroleum Company's workers at Tripoli in the same year, and in 1934–5 a printers' strike.

[2] Notably Khalid Bakdash (a Kurd by origin), Farajullah al-Ḥilu, Muṣṭafa al-'Aris, Fu'ad Qazan, Nicola Shawi, Anṭun Thabit.

In Syria, the National Bloc, first consolidated in 1936 to the exclusion of all rivals, later yielded under the pressure of difficulties and ill fortune to the processes of disintegration. Such weakening was due to no superiority of rival policies, but to the impatience natural to Syrian politics, to the usual personal ambitions expressed in competitive extremism, and to the clear defects of the Bloc as a Government in power. It bore the burdens of the times, suffered for French tergiversation and Turkish acquisitiveness, and was distracted by internal faction, often unconscionable. The Statute of the party, which monopolized Cabinet and senior administrative posts during the period, was published late in 1937. It provided for a permanent office, a Council, and a Congress; organization was by regions and local headquarters, and efforts were made, never wholly successfully, to end the traditional rift between Aleppo and Damascus. The other political parties, except those to be next mentioned—and except also the group of Bloc dissidents who coalesced in 1939—played little part; those of the Moderates were in eclipse until in 1939, with the collapse of Nationalist hopes, they could re-enter the field. An element never absorbed by the Bloc, but highly characteristic of the times, was the League of National Action, founded in 1935 by a young lawyer (and future Prime Minister), Ṣabri al-'Asali. The League, designed mainly for the young, sought to extend its organization by a wide local devolution and, though it failed to operate seriously outside Syria, achieved there for some years a high level of publicity and vigour. Politically, it stood for an uncompromising nationalism and pan-Arabism, for total laicization of the Administration, and for energetic social reform on equalitarian but not Communist lines; and, never in a position of responsibility, it could press always for intransigent action. Its leader from 1935 to 1938 was 'Abd al-Razzaq al-Dandashi, whose death was a severe blow to it. Its strongest centre was at Ḥumṣ, and it played a notable part at Alexandretta in 1937–8. The League expressed itself by meetings, speeches, manifestos, and mass demonstrations, and by the creation of added difficulties for the Bloc Administration which it condemned as weak and temporizing. Its parades and meetings led continually to street brawls with the adherents of other organizations.

Among the latter, the most prominent were the Nationalist Youth movement, its affiliates and its rivals. The Nationalist Youth was founded early in 1936 under the aegis of the Bloc, to act as its agency among the young, to attract support away from rival formations, to offer a field in which the beginnings of the promised National Army could be sought, and to bring within the orbit of Bloc politics the paramilitary bodies which had come into being. The Statute of the movement, in which Munir al-'Ajlani[1] was a main organizer, provided the usual Nationalist objectives, with emphasis on discipline and sacrifice, sport, and military interests. The organization, which year by year rallied imposing Congresses at Damascus, sought to impose itself on all youth movements throughout the territory, but without success; its own Steel Shirt squads were in frequent conflict not only with those of National Action but also the orthodox Boy Scouts, the local National Guard companies, those of the Educated Youth, the Brotherhood of Ḥananu (the latter two specifically Aleppine), and the local troops or companies of boys which came into existence under various, including Druze and 'Alawi, auspices. The same was true of the vigorous but shortlived White Shirts, the paramilitary branch of the Christian 'White Badge' movement designed to express the anti-nationalist[2] feelings of north Syrian Christians, who professed to view their own future under the Treaty with apprehension, and, as they said, 'preferred a French to a Damascene Mandate'. Fights took place twice in the autumn of 1936 between White Shirts and Steel Shirts. The former did not survive the year 1938.

The Steel Shirts, in which Nationalist Youth found its chief outlet, and which ex-Turkish officers helped to train, proved as attractive to the young Syrians as did the Phalanges in Lebanon. Every city had its drilled and uniformed squads who, fully military in appearance, salute, and bearing, were in evidence on every public occasion, and were frequently in trouble with the police or the French. The latter, accused of favouring the Christian movements and fomenting anti-Bloc disunion, were in fact opposed to the whole current fashion which created these paramilitary and Nazi-fashioned forces, so fatal both to statesmanship and to tranquillity. The foundation of a Students Union in Damascus early in 1939 was likely to have similar results.

The years of Syrian history we are here considering called, more than most, for calm and firm statesmanship capable of proving to the world its ability in good government, and convincing the separatist provinces that it could handle them with acceptable sympathy. Such statesmanship was not forthcoming, in spite of the high qualities of many public men; in its place was effervescence, disunity, suspicion, and the least graceful phenomena of national adolescence. In particular, the contemporary type of political organization, with its squads and gangs, its leaders and salutes and narrow devotions, was a damaging obstacle to the sound

[1] Son-in-law (at that time) and supporter of Dr. Shahbandar.

[2] There was, however, also an important Christian element in the Nationalist Youth bodies, and in the League of National Action.

national development which the world would gladly have acclaimed.

4. LABOUR OF SISYPHUS

The French authorities, without waiting for Treaty ratification, were willing as a sign of goodwill (and to lessen their own burdens)[1] to treat 1 January 1937, without more ado, as the beginning of the three-year 'preparatory period'. To this end, in addition to installing the new arrangements for Ladhqiya and the Jabal, they instructed that French officials in the Syrian Government should henceforth limit themselves to advice on the more important matters, and should cease to exercise overt control over ministers and executives: that the State budget should be an affair for the Chamber and Cabinet alone: and that police work in the cities should be under Syrian authority. The High Commissioner himself proposed to abstain from vetoing acts of the Syrian legislature, though his services retained direct control of the Common Interests and of the bedouin tribes. Syrian attachés were posted to the French missions at Istanbul, Baghdad, and Cairo, and a diplomat with ministerial rank to Paris.

The transfer, or perhaps the division, of the Common Interests, as provided in the Treaties was of great importance, and had long been demanded by local patriots. But the willingness of the High Commissioner to proceed with this reform did not enable the Syrian and Lebanese authorities to agree on a new basis; joint meetings held from mid-1937 onwards reached no conclusion except, in general, to separate the services between the States; and, even so, no suggested basis for such separation could command agreement. Perforce, the Common Interests remained in the charge of the High Commissioner, assisted by the interstatal Conference, which rarely met.

No greater progress was made with the organization of a Syrian National Army. A Franco-Syrian Commission sat to consider the bases of the proposed force, but its conclusions could not, in the circumstances which declared themselves, be carried out. Unpopular as were the present arrangements, whereunder Syrian forces were merely an auxiliary part of the French Army, they remained in force, and the clamour of the Steel Shirts to be adopted as the core of the new Army was unavailing. Study of the future establishments continued, and the Syrian Ministry of Defence appointed a cadre of officials. Meanwhile ugly episodes

[1] It remained a usual Syrian nationalist accusation that the French relinquishment of control was insincere: that they deliberately created difficulties so as to prolong the Mandate. Though this is false, many French officials admittedly disliked the new or threatened régime.

showed the tension existing between the excitable and often truculent Steel Shirts or Nationalist Youth, and the French Army; one such occurred at Aleppo in February 1937, another at Ladhqiya some weeks later. These called for an inquiry, a trial of offenders, and severe sentences—which were, however, later remitted by General Huntziger.

In the Syrian-controlled services the years spent in opposition and the practical inexperience of the senior Bloc members were apparent in an inferior and much criticized level of administration. There was resolute opposition to any full implementation of the new Muḥafadha Regulations of early 1936 (p. 216), whereunder increased powers were to be given to provincial officials and locally-elected Councils. There was inefficiency, inordinate delay, nepotism on personal or community lines, and unwise selection of senior personnel. The level of administration was seen to decline in these years, with the increase of local (that is, Bloc) authority, in contrast to so many happy prophecies to the contrary. A Legislative Commission set up in June 1937 accomplished little.

The return of Syrian offenders of the 1925–6 period, and some others, from exile by permission of the French did nothing to help administration, or to preserve unity. The triumphant reappearance of Dr. Shahbandar and Sulṭan al-Aṭrash in May 1937 revived, in each case, movements contrary to Bloc policy. They were followed shortly by Iḥsan al-Jabiri, Shakib Arsalan, and others of lesser stature. None of these statesmen had ever been apostles of moderation or patience, none had had any part in treaty-making, and all expected a high place in political life. Their role, therefore, was likely to be purely destructive. Shahbandar from the first[1] showed himself a severe critic both of the Treaty itself, as too compromising, and of its non-ratification by France; and a group devoted to him was not slow in forming. Egoistic rancour was not absent from his anti-Bloc polemics, and his personal terms with Jamil Mardam Bey were bitter.[2] Signs accumulated from the spring of 1937 onwards that the Bloc's monopoly of nationalism, which the League for National Action and other groups had never accepted, was incomplete and precarious. A bread riot in Ḥumṣ in July had a political colouring, and arrest of anti-Bloc demonstrators in Aleppo in November led to a strike and to more arrests. Meetings of the (mainly Lebanese) Syrian National Party were forbidden in Syria, but still occurred.

Negotiations which the Government were called upon to conduct with influential foreign concerns—the 'Iraq Petroleum

[1] He left for Egypt some weeks after his return, but reappeared in Damascus in mid-1938.

[2] An attempt at reconciliation was made by Nuri al-Sa'id of 'Iraq early in 1938.

Company seeking an oil concession, and the Banque de Syrie whose rights were due for renewal—gave easy occasion for attacks on the ministers concerned. The absences of the Prime Minister in France and Turkey were a source of weakness. His and the Bloc's majority in the Chamber was not, at first, threatened, but its dominant position was already compromised.

The speedy Syrian ratification of the Treaty was not matched in Paris; with succeeding months in 1937 it became clear that opposition there was increasing. The Blum Administration ended in June 1937, and its successor contained strong anti-Treaty elements; moreover, the menace implicit in the developing European situation discouraged French statesmen from changes in the Levant. Jamil Mardam Bey visited Paris late in 1937,[1] reassured the Quai d'Orsay as best he could, and signed on 11 December a cordial exchange of letters which reiterated Syria's intention to respect minority rights (a point of special sensitiveness in the Chamber), his willingness to accept all experts and advisers whom the French should name, and his good intentions in provincial decentralization. Back in Damascus, he met the inevitable charges of weakness; but he found also active support in facing the politicians and press who were now uniting against him in the form of a so-called 'United' or 'Patriotic Front', led by Munir al-'Ajlani (chief spokesman for Shahbandar, who was in Egypt) and Zaki al-Khaṭib. These, strong in anti-Treaty manifestoes, arranged demonstrations (by no means one-sided) and violent street scenes in mid-February 1938, led to arrests and prison sentences. In April the same group issued a violent manifesto against all continuing French 'interference' or control, and all concessions made subsequent to the Treaty itself. The Prime Minister's position in the Chamber was still strong, but he preferred, in spite of the High Commissioner's insistence, not at present to seek ratification there of his recent Agreement in Paris; he himself believed that early French ratification was now certain. The resignation of Shukri al-Quwatli from his post in March was a blow due allegedly to illness but in fact also to Quwatli's reluctance to compromise, and to his leadership of the Istiqlal group within the Bloc. New ministers,[2] members of the Bloc, joined the Cabinet in July 1938. But the universal dismay at events at Alexandretta (pp. 237 ff.), which caused repeated strikes and demonstrations throughout the country, the disorders in the Jazira, the poor showing of Bloc Government among the 'Alawis and Druzes, and the endless distractions of political or paramilitary Youth, continued to afflict

[1] Simultaneous visitors to Paris were Riyadh al-Ṣulḥ, and the Communist leader Khalid Bakdash.

[2] Fa'iz al-Khuri (Economics), and Luṭfi al-Ḥaffar (Finance).

the nerves and hopes of Syrians as the summer of 1938 wore on. The local repercussions of the current Arab revolt in Palestine against British policy there led to heightened pan-Arab feeling; an interstatal Arab Conference was held at Bludan in September 1937, and communication with the Palestine rebels was maintained from Damascus. Deteriorating Syro-Lebanese relations added to the unease of the Bloc Government, thanks to continued squabbles over the Common Interests, the outcry of the still unsatisfied Tripolitanians, Lebanese sympathy for the Christian separatists of the Jazira, and the provocative tone of the press in each country.

In August, after a tour in northern Syria to restore public morale and Bloc supremacy, the Prime Minister felt bound again to visit Paris, to achieve at almost any cost the settlement now awaited for nearly two years. His conversations in Geneva and Paris with M. Bonnet, the Minister for Foreign Affairs, lasted for three months, and ended on 14 November with a Supplementary Agreement; this confirmed that of 11 December 1937, reaffirmed minority rights, denied all threat to the continuance of French teaching in schools, and undertook to meet French wishes in the matters of a Syrian oil concession and the Bank's tenure. The French Government on its side would—a considerable concession—treat 30 September 1939 (instead of 'three years after ratification') as the end of the transitional period. Both Governments were to expedite their ratifications of the amended Treaty.

The new Agreement was not published, but its contents leaked out. In spite of the sobering effect of the international situation, and the call for patience implicit in the appointment of a new High Commissioner, M. Gabriel Puaux,[1] and the paramount need to stabilize Franco-Syrian relations while this seemed still possible, the reception of the new terms was of the worst. The anti-Bloc 'Constitutional Group' found itself strengthened by many adhesions, and Shahbandar, now back in Damascus, assumed its leadership. Everywhere indignation at the French attitude prevailed over caution and hope alike. It was increased by a rumour that a French parliamentary mission was to visit the territory, and by anger that Syria had not been invited to the London Conference on Palestine, now assembling. Moreover, news that the French Chamber and Senate no longer intended ratification[2] was not slow to reach Damascus. For reasons of

[1] M. Puaux, a Protestant career diplomat, was appointed in October 1938 to succeed M. de Martel (who had reached the age for retirement), and reached Beirut in the first week of 1939.

[2] The reports of the Foreign Affairs Committees of both the Chamber and the Senate were flatly hostile to the Treaty, and on 14 December M. Bonnet admitted a reversal of his own position.

psychology and of international politics, a complete reaction in Paris had set in: there was to be, after all, no Franco-Syrian Treaty; the Mandate, unmodified, would continue. The French representative at the Permanent Mandates Commission, in January 1939, asked for time and could promise nothing.

Facing the facts, the Syrian Chamber on the last day of 1938 made clear its own position, to which even those who, with the Prime Minister, had persisted longest in hope and compromise at last fully subscribed. The Deputies demanded the 1936 Treaty, unaltered—or full independence without it! They blamed the French for delay and tergiversation, repudiated all concessions made by the Prime Minister, demanded full powers in every branch of government (including the Customs, diplomacy, and the Army), and called for the adoption of a firm policy in the three ungrateful provinces which still resisted central Government authority.

The French Government had indeed seemed, in the summer of 1936, to adopt a new course in its handling of the Syrian problem, away from its long record of hesitation and quasi-colonial control: a course consonant with the dominant political forces in the country, and one which could produce, even now, wide and genuine goodwill—the greatest by far of all advantages for which France could hope, and one which would by itself guarantee the safety of the French cultural effort. But the paramount benefit of such goodwill was unrecognized by French majority opinion which, in a period of international alarm and bitter political division at home, accepted instead the leadership of men of older-fashioned conceptions of strategy and of their country's 'rights' in the Levant. From the worst immediate consequences of this tragically mistaken reversal of policy, France was saved by the outbreak of war. But for that event, and failing another and very early attempt at more enlightened treaty-making, conditions in Syria must from later 1939 onwards have been those of national uprising, or of anarchy. This was, in the event, postponed by the series of political crises in Syria from February to July 1939, and by the menace of impending world war.

M. Puaux, well received by the Christian Lebanese, was welcomed in Damascus and the Syrian cities in icy silence, which his broadcast speeches,[1] by their remoteness from the spirit of 1936, did nothing to break. His very limited personal contacts were cordial, assisted by his own tact and good sense; but serious popular and students' demonstrations broke the public peace,

[1] He claimed a policy of 'neither violence nor illusions' but of a 'liberal and practical régime': France, a great Muslim and Christian Power, must stay in the Levant.

incendiary broadcasts were heard from a secret wireless station, a brief general strike occurred at Damascus and Ḥumṣ, and two Syrian ministers[1] resigned, but later resumed office. Many men of consequence left the Bloc, viewing with disfavour the retention of office by Jamil Mardam Bey, whose policy had come to nothing. The Bloc and its Shahbandarite rivals could find common ground in the formula of 'a Treaty not inferior to 'Iraq's'. The Government dispatched to the High Commissioner a memorial reciting its demands as formulated by the Chamber on 31 December 1938; and the Prime Minister, whose popularity had sunk low, asserted that their independence must be seized, not awaited. But the fall of his Ministry was at hand.

M. de Martel's Decree on personal status of 13 March 1936 (p. 220) had not ceased to be attacked, and its partial modification, by Decree of 23 November 1938, had reopened the issues. These could by politicians be represented as those of Sunni-Islamic rights against the minorities. A meeting of Sunni 'Ulama was held in Damascus in February 1939, emphasizing Muslim unity and, by implication, asserting the traditional identity of their community and the State. The Prime Minister declared by letter to the High Commissioner that, in the absence of a law of the Syrian Republic, a Decree of the French representative had no validity; and he forbade the Syrian courts to recognize it. This memorandum to Beirut, rejected, was handed back to him by the Délégué at Damascus. Reminded that a High Commissioner's decree could 'in present circumstances' be invalidated only by its author, Jamil and his Ministry resigned office on 18 February, followed by senior officials who shared their views. Demonstrations in the streets again broke out.

A new Ministry, which must be of the Bloc as long as al-Atasi remained President, proved hard to form. Mudhhir al-Raslan was invited, but failed. A senior judge, Muṣṭafa Barmada, failed equally. On 23 February a Ministry[2] under Luṭfi al-Ḥaffar was inducted, pledged to strive again for the 1936 Treaty unalloyed. As a beginning, a joint Franco-Syrian committee was appointed to study the personal status problem. Its work having been interrupted by student demonstrations, the report it produced was sent by M. Puaux to Paris. In an atmosphere of street parades and riots, and despair of an understanding with France, the Ḥaffar Ministry resigned after three weeks in office. French troops were involved to restore order after a week of violence, many newspapers were suppressed and politicians arrested, and the urban

[1] Luṭfi al-Ḥaffar and Fa'iz al-Khuri.

[2] Prime Minister and Minister of Education, Luṭfi al-Ḥaffar: Justice, Naṣib al-Bakri: Economics, Salim Janbart: Interior and Defence, Mudhhir al-Raslan: Finance and Foreign Affairs, Fa'iz al-Khuri.

police forces were re-transferred from Syrian to French command. Conditions of almost intolerable disorder prevailed in Aleppo and Damascus for three weeks of March and April.

Even after the High Commissioner had on 30 March agreed to suspend application of the 1938 Personal Status Decree to the Sunni community, no Bloc Ministry could be formed: indeed, its own membership was fast declining by defection even of its leading stalwarts. A non-party Ministry[1] under Naṣuḥ al-Bukhari was formed on 6 April, after difficult negotiations; but its survival would depend upon the French attitude, and M. Puaux was expected to reveal this on his return from France. There were those, meanwhile, who favoured the reforming of a genuine National Front,[2] while some suggested the invocation of the other Arab States. Dr. Shahbandar continued to urge the full Syrian demands.

The High Commissioner returned in May. His recommendations for a return to 'Alawi and Druze autonomy, and for the retention of French troops, had been accepted in Paris; his advocacy for the establishment of a Syrian monarchy had been rejected. His first speech on his return disappointed whatever hopes could have been formed, including those of the local Monarchists who included Dr. Shahbandar, a supporter of the Amir 'Abdullah. M. Puaux spoke in terms of a treaty to be ultimately agreed, but meanwhile of looser union between the various areas of Syria, and a needed 'reconsideration' of French military requirements. The Cabinet immediately resigned on 15 May and, though it stayed reluctantly in office for some weeks, no successor was forthcoming. The Premiership was offered in vain to 'Aṭa al-Ayyubi, and to Naṣib al-Bakri. The Chamber on 20 May, with the vainest of gestures, reasserted its insistence on the unamended 1936 Treaty. In contrast, new and half-separatist Statutes for the Ladhqiya, Druze, and Jazira provinces were issued by the High Commissioner on 7 July, reconfirming them in a status not far from that of before 1936. On the same day President Hashim al-Atasi telegraphed his protest to Paris, resigned his office, and went home to Ḥumṣ. The ministers ceased to attend their offices; the parliamentary session was already at an end. The High Commissioner, seeing no issue, published on 10 July Decrees suspending the Syrian Constitution, dissolving the Chamber, and appointing a Council of departmental directors-general under the moderate and experienced Bahij al-Khaṭib,

[1] Prime Minister and Interior, Naṣuḥ al-Bukhari: Economics and Education, Salim Janbart: Finance, Muḥammad Khalil al-Mudarris: Foreign Affairs, Khalid al-'Adhm: Awqaf, Ḥasan al-Ḥakim.

[2] From the remains of the Bloc, the 'Constitutional Group', the Shahbandar clique, the League of National Action, the Nationalist Youth, and various small groups and independents.

to govern[1] by Decrees countersigned in the Grand Sérail. The new position was accepted by politicians and the public with apparent calm. A brief inquiry and some arrests rendered harmless a plot said to have been discovered (apparently among the Ḥamah intelligentsia) to assassinate the chairman of the Council of Directors. Monarchist talk increased, stimulated by a visit of the child-king Fayṣal II to Lebanon. The old Moderate parties revived, especially in the north, and that of Shahbandar remained quietly active. The shadow of the impending war fell darkly over Syria, the serious effects of the recent devaluation of the franc occupied all business circles, and heads were shaken at the influx of Arab and Armenian refugees from the now lost province of Alexandretta.

Already signs of preparation and movement had been seen in the French forces in Syria. Land at strategic points had been acquired. The recruitment of irregulars had been increased in each of the Levant States. Regulations had been issued forbidding the export of certain goods, controlling movement of liquid fuels and vital stores, prohibiting the publication of military news or the use of cyphers, and empowering the Army to billet troops and to commandeer transport. Reinforcements, including units of the Foreign Legion, had arrived from France. Long consultations had been held between French civil and military officials; others were recalled from leave. The new Beirut airport had been opened in June. The local Governments began bulk-buying of grain. M. Puaux hurried back to Beirut after a one-day holiday in Switzerland. On 30 August General Weygand arrived to assume the post of Commander-in-Chief, Middle East Theatre of Operations, and to relieve the High Commissioner of his defence responsibilities.

5. TURKEY AND ALEXANDRETTA

The loss of the Alexandretta sanjaq, which occurred by stages between the autumn of 1936 and the summer of 1939, was a strange episode in international dealing. It can indeed be represented as a crude example of 'power politics' by Turkey, a regrettable yielding by France of another's rights in her own interest, and a resented blow to Syria whose claims were overridden and her weakness abused; yet such were the grim exigencies of the times, and such the value placed by French statesmen on the friendship of Turkey, that a mere sweeping moral condemnation

[1] The Directors were: in Interior, Bahij himself: in Finance, Ḥusni al-Bayṭar: in Justice, Khalil Rif'at: in Economics, Yusif 'Aṭa Allah. The Ministries of Foreign Affairs and Defence were abolished.

must seem too simple or inadequate a reaction. There are few nations in history whose statesmen would have acted, or would not have been condemned by their own countrymen for acting, otherwise than did the French in this matter. But its effect on Franco-Syrian, and Turco-Syrian, and indeed Turco-Arab relations has been long and sinister; and the contrast between the French action taken, or permitted, and the text[1] of their Syrian Mandate, cannot be ignored. French writers equally emphasize the loss of all the great and costly services rendered by France to the sanjaq in the preceding half-generation.

Previous pages have mentioned the Franco-Turkish agreements of 1921 and 1926 (pp. 119 and 172), regarding the special status of Alexandretta devised in the interests of its important Turkish minority, and the resulting régime maintained there for fifteen years to the general satisfaction. This was, on the whole, shared by the local Turks in spite of their racial consciousness, and in spite of occasional reminders, from Turkey, that the sanjaq had not been forgotten. Meanwhile, its status as an integral part of Syria was queried by none; the Franco-Syrian Treaty of September 1936 had no occasion to refer to it, except to indicate in an exchange of letters that the future status of the Druze and 'Alawi districts could well be based on the same convenient degree of decentralization as Alexandretta enjoyed.

The publication of the draft Treaty on 9 September was, nevertheless, followed immediately by a series of references by the Turkish representative at the League of Nations to their anxiety for their fellow Turks in Alexandretta. They maintained that whereas the 1921 and 1926 safeguards were adequate while the French remained Mandatory, they bore a very different look *vis-à-vis* an independent Syria; France must now sign a separate Treaty with the people of the sanjaq, 'the vast majority of whom are Turkish'.[2] Such a procedure was rejected by the French as a needless and unjustifiable dismemberment of Syria; the existing 'special status' met all rightful needs as well as conforming to a long-standing arrangement. No agreement having been produced by further Franco-Turkish exchanges during October and November, both agreed to refer the question to the League. The Council discussed it in mid-December, found no solution, but agreed to

[1] Article 4: 'The Mandatory shall be responsible for seeing that no part of the territory of Syria and the Lebanon is ceded or leased or in any way placed under the control of a foreign Power'.

[2] As to the precise strength of the communities in the sanjaq in 1936, certainty is impossible. The 1933 census gave (in thousands) Sunni Muslims 94·2: 'Alawis and Isma'ilis, 54·8: Christians, 37·9: Jews, ·5. By *race*, Arabs (Sunni) 20·4, ('Alawi-Isma'ili) 54·2, (Christian) 14·3, total 89·5: Turks 70·8: Armenians (Turkish-speaking) 23·5: Kurds 1·8: Circassians 1·1. In 1921 the French had estimated the Turks at 87,000 out of a total of 220,000.

send three neutral observers[1] to the sanjaq. Conversations between French and Turkish spokesmen at Paris and Ankara[2] continued during January 1937, without solving the problem; but the outline of a settlement appeared during talks at Geneva on 24–26 January, and on the 27th the League Council adopted the report of the *rapporteur* containing the terms. These provided for the transformation of the sanjaq into a separate demilitarized territory with its own Statute, internal autonomy, and a link with Syria only in the fields of Customs, currency, and foreign affairs; the League Council would itself be responsible for the application of the Statute, and for this purpose would rely on a French Resident with considerable powers. Turkish would be an official language, to which the Council might add another. Turkey would have special rights in the port of Alexandretta. The frontiers and the tranquillity of the region would be guaranteed by a Franco-Turco-Syrian Treaty. The Council followed acceptance of this compromise by appointing a drafting committee to produce a Statute. This when prepared included Arabic as the second language, and provided for a local forty-member Assembly to be elected proportionately from the various communities,[3] under a procedure to be established by a special League Commission which would assume charge on the spot. These proposals, and the agreement of 27 January, were all accepted by the Council on 29 May. The new régime was to come into force on 29 November.

These early weeks of the controversy in Europe were reflected by a sudden and emotional revival of national or sectarian feeling in the territory. The statesmen of Damascus heard with alarm of the claims of Turkish Deputies and journalists, of the journeys of President Ataturk himself in the frontier area, and of alleged Turkish troop movements. The Turks of the sanjaq demonstrated in October, boycotted and disturbed the elections (for the Syrian Chamber) in November, rioted and clashed with the police in December. In January strikes and processions of both Turkish and Arab partisans disturbed the peace, a bloody affray between them took place on the 12th, and further provocative exchanges followed. In view of past Turco-Armenian relations,[4] Armenian-Arab solidarity was firm, even though the Armenians spoke Turkish. The apprehension throughout Syria, and the threat—and fact—of violence of the sanjaq, grew day by day. In December

[1] In the event, a Dutchman, a Norwegian, and a Swiss.

[2] M. Ponsot was now (1936–9) French Ambassador to Turkey.

[3] These were, the Sunni-Arab, Turk, 'Alawi, Armenian, and other Christian (mainly Greek Orthodox): each was allotted a minimum of seats, but could obtain more if so voted.

[4] Almost all these Armenians were refugees from Cilicia in 1921 (pp. 76–7).

a Syrian delegation was named to assist the French mission at Geneva. In succeeding months, indeed for two years, the Alexandretta issue dominated Syrian political thinking and emotion, agitated the Youth movements and the League for National Action, gave cause for the bitterest attacks on the Bloc Ministry for alleged half-heartedness, and brought to birth a dozen Leagues or Committees for the Defence of Alexandretta. The Franco-Turkish Agreement of 27 January, welcomed in international (including British) circles and in Turkey, was almost universally condemned, with widespread strikes and visits to British Consulates;[1] and early in February the Prime Minister with two colleagues hurried to Paris. The argument that Syria's loss of Alexandretta (if such it was to be) should be balanced by the gain of Tripoli, was widely heard. The French were universally blamed for sacrificing Syrian interests. Turkish troop movements were daily rumoured. The three League observers returned from the sanjaq to Geneva. The acceptance by the League Council of the terms placed before it on 29 May occasioned further agitation and protests throughout Syria; and in the sanjaq itself violent Turco-Arab clashes at Alexandretta and Antioch involved the intervention of troops. This did not prevent further disorders in July and August involving the two main factions and their armed bands, and in places between rival elements among the Turks themselves; bitterness and violence throughout the sanjaq distracted a population who had for so many years lived together in great tranquillity. The Chamber in Damascus formally refused to recognize the Statute. The Franco-Turkish Treaty,[2] for which the Agreement of 29 May provided, was meanwhile signed and ratified, and an agreement[3] covering the inviolability of the frontier followed. Nothing was achieved by the visit of the Syrian President and Foreign Minister to Ankara late in June. The High Commissioner toured the sanjaq in July, and called vainly for peace and reconciliation. The French Délégué in the sanjaq, M. Durieux, was replaced by M. Garreau.

The League Commission intended to draft an Electoral Law, and then to supervise the elections, was named by the Council in October,[4] and arrived at Alexandretta on the 20th. It stayed for one month, visited Ankara, Damascus, and Beirut, and reported again to Geneva. Its recommendations were accepted, and the

[1] The present writer, in Damascus for the first half of 1937, was constantly appealed to by Syrian ministers to 'do something about it'.

[2] Text in the *League of Nations Official Journal*, November 1937, pp. 838–9.

[3] Ibid., pp. 839 ff.

[4] Great Britain supplied the Chairman, Mr. T. Reid, the other members being from Belgium, Holland, Norway, and Switzerland.

two-stage elections fixed for 28 March and 12 April. The Commission returned to the sanjaq and proceeded with the registration of electors.

Meanwhile, the proclamation of the new régime at Alexandretta on 29 November had been marked by violent dissensions, and some bloodshed. The Arab population boycotted the new Administration, which many officials refused to serve. In the absence of a Muḥafidh, a Secretary-General of the sanjaq was appointed under the Délégué, who himself became the subject of Turkish attacks. A substantial southward infiltration of Turks into the sanjaq was reported, a Turkish bank opened, a Turkish steamer docked. The repeated repudiation of the Statute by the Syrian Chamber was countered by a Turkish denunciation of the Bon Voisinage Agreement of 1926.

In December 1937 a further forward move appeared from the Turkish side, which had already gained so much. Their Foreign Minister protested at Geneva at the refusal of the registration authority in the sanjaq to accept, without further inquiry, the electors' own expressed choice of community. (The initial registrations were, in fact, showing the Turks so far as a minority.) Rüstü Aras insisted that declaration by the applicant should be the sole, unquestioned guide. The League Council referred the issue to an *ad hoc* committee,[1] which reported in the sense desired by Turkey—an important victory essential to their plans: whereupon the British chairman of the committee, foreseeing 'undue influence' upon electors, protested and resigned.[2] The new Election Regulations were issued on 19 March, and the Commission, on its return to the sanjaq, reopened registration. This continued during April and May in uneasy and sometimes stormy conditions, which showed the extent to which Turkish power and pretensions[3] in the sanjaq had now grown, in spite of the efforts of the Délégué to maintain peace and balance. Late in May, with current registration still showing the Turks in a minority, repeated disturbances led the authorities temporarily to discontinue it: and early in June the High Commissioner replaced Garreau (reputed Arabophile) by Colonel Collet (p. 308). The latter, appointing Turkish officers to posts of authority, showed a perceptibly pro-Turkish attitude, which telegrams to Paris from

[1] It consisted of a Turk, a Frenchman, and one member each from Sweden, Great Britain, and Belgium.

[2] He was replaced by Major A. P. Nicol. M. Puaux in his memoirs (p. 49) gives his authority to the fantastic allegation that Great Britain supported the Turks in order that France should not have a naval base at Alexandretta.

[3] Sunday instead of Friday had been proclaimed as the rest day, and celebration of Turkish national festivals was enforced. Ṣubḥi Barakat had thrown in his lot wholly with Turkey.

the despairing Syrian Government were powerless to modify. The tide was, indeed, running in favour of Turkey; confronted with perils in Europe, and forced to decide between alienating or gratifying Turkey, the French had by now chosen their path. Franco-Turkish talks in Europe—with the latter claiming to be the aggrieved party!—led to the admission of a Turkish military mission into the sanjaq, to participate in control. The news of this significant step was greeted in Damascus by a general strike, supported by the Communist and all other parties; 'French and Turkish imperialism' was everywhere assailed. Martial law having been proclaimed in the sanjaq on 3 June, the registration of voters was resumed under the novel control of a Franco-Turkish Committee. The League's own Commission, protesting specifically against the recent French attitude[1] of favouring Turkey, abandoned its work, and went home on 26 June; with it went the last possibility of honest electoral rolls, or unintimidated voting. Turkish troops, authorized by conversations[2] held in Antioch during June, entered the sanjaq in force on 5 July. A week later the results of electoral registration were announced as showing a 63 per cent. majority for the Turks, to whom accordingly 22 seats in the Chamber out of 40 were allotted. Of the rest, 9 would be given to the 'Alawis, 5 to the Armenians, 2 to the Greek Orthodox—and 2 to the Sunni Arabs.[3]

The Franco-Turkish Treaty of Friendship, for which Alexandretta was the price, was signed on 4 July.[4] It still contained no claim by the Turks to sovereignty over the sanjaq; the Statute of the latter was to be jointly supervised 'in the spirit of the agreement of 21 October 1921'. No progress could be made, thanks to Syrian disillusion and disgust, with talks begun in Ankara in July and designed to produce a Franco-Turco-Syrian Agreement. Discussion of the sanjaq in the Permanent Mandates Commission was, at French request, postponed.

The first meeting of the new Assembly, the sovereign body in the province (now renamed the Hatay), emphasized its wholly Turkish complexion. The Presidents of the State and the Assembly were both Turks, active in the politics of that country: the former exchanged telegrams with Kamal Ataturk.[5] The ministers chosen were Turks to a man. During September the Assembly passed a

[1] The High Commissioner declared his inability to intervene, since martial law was in force.

[2] This force, to keep order in the sanjaq until the new régime be established, was to consist of 2,500 men from each of the French and the Turks, and 1,000 local men, all under the control of the mandatory Power.

[3] This absurd result was due in part to the Arab boycott of the elections—and to Colonel Collet's outspoken advice, 'Call yourself a Turk'.

[4] It was never ratified.

[5] Ataturk died on 10 November 1938.

great body of legislation, covering the Gendarmerie, taxation, the Courts, the civil service, the new State flag, the wearing of hats, the schools, and much more. Antioch became the capital. Amnesty was granted to all political prisoners. Turkish officials controlled all departments. In January 1939 administrative absorption in Turkey was in effect completed by the enactment of Turkish penal and civil codes, and the adoption of their currency and fiscal procedures. Both the President and Premier of the Hatay were elected to the Turkish Chamber at Ankara in the elections held in March 1939.

To regularize the *fait accompli* of complete cession, the Foreign Minister at Ankara initiated conversations with the French Ambassador in January 1939. The latter was instructed by Paris to make no difficulties. Consulting M. Puaux at Beirut, he continued discussions in Ankara for four months, but had little to oppose to the now determined exigencies of the Turks, who indeed treated French pretensions—particularly for their own charitable institutions in the sanjaq—with little sign of respect. Turkish military manœuvres were held in the sanjaq, and a further concentration of their troops near the frontier led to the dispatch of a French warship; but no clash occured. On 23 June the long-sought Declaration of Mutual Assistance between Turkey and France was signed in Paris, and at the same time an agreement for the final relinquishment of the Hatay was signed at Ankara. It was ratified on 13 July. The Turks pledged themselves to respect the new frontier, and the integrity of Syria: Aleppo at least was safe! French troops withdrew during July. The Assembly of the Hatay held its last meeting on 29 June, whereafter the district became a normal wilayet of Turkey. The new Wali arrived, met and congratulated by the commander of the outgoing French forces. Protests poured as usual from Damascus to Paris and Geneva, and a bitter press campaign throughout Syria attacked the French betrayal of Syrian rights.

All foreign Christian institutions in the new wilayet were at once shut; the French missionary hospital was bought by the Turkish Government. A major exodus of the Armenians, to a number of some 14,000,[1] took place by land and sea; after a stay in camps near the new frontier, most were moved to Beirut, there to be supported by French funds. All citizens of the former sanjaq were given, under the agreement of 24 June, the right to opt for Syrian nationality, and could in that event move over the frontier with their goods or the proceeds of these. Some hundreds of Arabs loyal to Syria took advantage of these provisions; the rest became citizens of the Turkish Republic.

[1] Much higher figures are sometimes given.

6. THREE WAYWARD PROVINCES

An element in the general Syrian optimism of early 1937 was the apparently complacent acceptance by the 'Alawi district and the Jabal al-Duruz of their new status of merely local privilege under Syrian rule.

In the former of these provinces, the year 1936 had shown, as ever, the familiar cleavage of local opinion on unionist and separatist lines; the usual deputations had visited Beirut, begging for total or substantial union with Syria, or total or substantial independence from it. The solution by decentralization reached in Paris, and put forthwith into effect (p. 221), seemed for the moment to unite the clashing elements—Nuṣayri, Sunni, Isma'ili, Christian—even though the veteran Governor, M. Schoeffler, resigned in disgust. The new and happier atmosphere survived a serious incident at Ladhqiya on 25 February 1937, when a visiting party of uniformed Scouts clashed with Senegalese troops.

But the new Muḥafidh's task was not easy. He must avoid victimization of old anti-Nationalist separatists; he must if possible reward old supporters. He must find a middle way between the powerful faction leaders; he must persuade the Special Service officers to stop their support of the separatists; he must minimize the importation of officials from outside the muḥafadha; and, immediately and particularly, he must conduct general elections for the Syrian Chamber.

The rebirth of militant localism belongs to the early summer of 1937. It gained ground during the year, and was expressed at a Congress convened in September by its leader, Ibrahim al-Kanj, with emphasis on a local Muḥafidh and Gendarmerie force, more public posts for 'Alawis, improved social services. The efforts of Mudhhir al-Raslan to produce a single list for election purposes were continually thwarted, and even a visit by Jamil Mardam Bey failed to secure agreement. In the primary elections on 2 October, the Syrian Nationalist Party won easily, amid the usual outcry against improper interference; but for the secondary election, partly boycotted by the autonomists, an arrangement was made whereby they secured minority representation among the fifteen Deputies[1] to be returned. In November, Raslan was succeeded by Iḥsan al-Jabiri.

But partisanship was by now, and throughout 1938–9, running high. The complaint was heard that the 'full local autonomy' promised by the Treaty was withheld, centralized government had

[1] Representing the eight constituencies (Ladhqiya, Jabla, Ṭarṭus, Tall Kallakh, Safita, Maṣyaf, Ḥaffa, Banyas). Seats were reserved for 3 Sunnis, 9 'Alawis, 2 Greek Orthodox, 1 other minorities.

been imposed, 'Alawi rights ignored. The Muḥafidh now exploited existing divisions, now appealed to unifying Islam, and soon found his effective rule confined substantially to the coast towns. French officialdom seemed determinedly separatist, and gave little help to Iḥsan. The Jesuit press of Beirut wrote constantly against the Jabiri Administration, allegedly unfair to the Christian minorities; the demands of the Nuṣayri autonomists grew more insistent. More and more of the mountainous areas, and at times the main Ladhqiya–Tripoli road, passed out of official control to that of bandits and gang leaders, while the local quarrels of villagers and landlords were given each its political colouring. More than once an intervention by French troops was necessary. Iḥsan was removed, at the High Commissioner's suggestion, in March 1939, and a locally-born but Paris-educated successor was found in Shawkat 'Abbas.

With the failure to ratify the Treaty, the oncoming of the war (when tranquillity would be above all desirable), and the re-emergence of full autonomy as the claim of an important element in the province, the High Commissioner felt decreasing obligation to maintain the policy of 1936. Conditions in early 1939 were still deteriorating. M. Puaux's own visit in February, met by strikes and demonstrations, convinced him that the situation must be radically corrected. The Statute of 5 December 1936 was cancelled, another issued on 2 July 1939 restored a fuller autonomy: the 'Alawi and Syrian flags would both be flown, a Governor chosen by the local Council would be appointed by the Syrian President, the Council's own powers would be increased, judicial self-sufficiency established. With this régime, greeted on the usual divided lines, comparative peace descended on the area. Syrian unity had sustained another blow.

Events in Jabal al-Duruz were not dissimilar, though here the main elements of discord were all found in the single Druze body of the Aṭrash family and its followers; the cleavage was one of policy and personal[1] interest, not of community or faith. The more powerful Druze leaders resented the surrender of their personal authority, the lesser families, with the intelligentsia, supported a pan-Syrian régime. The Treaty, meanwhile, and the new Statute, were by apparent majority well accepted. Naṣib al-Bakri was generally tolerated as a temporary appointment, and visiting Damascus politicians and Steel Shirts conducted vigorous unionist propaganda. French officials on the spot were, as at Ladhqiya, accused of working against the spirit of the Statute.

Late in March 1937 agitation for a Druze Governor, and against

[1] Druze Amirs of the time represented, in fact, very varying stages of evolution, from the fully Europeanized to the primitive.

imported Syrian officials, had already led to worried consultations with the Syrian Government and the High Commissioner, and demonstrations both for and against the closer Damascus connexion took place in Suwayda. Visits of Druze and Syrian Nationalist spokesmen were exchanged between Suwayda and the capital, the shortcomings of al-Bakri exaggerated, pressure by the Bloc and its militant organizations increased. Naṣib wavered between clinging to, or abandoning, his post. In May a 'Group of National Defence', with parades and coloured shirts on the accepted pattern, was formed in the Jabal in the separatist interest, of which Ḥasan al-Aṭrash was now the acknowledged head. Sulṭan al-Aṭrash, still unionist as in 1925–6, was met at Ṣalkhad by strikes and shut doors, but held a monster meeting in his own village. Nationalists and their opponents raided each other's headquarters, and a movement was started for withholding all taxes until a Druze Governor be appointed. On 17 June, by the mediation of Dr. Shahbandar, an 'unconditional peace' was proclaimed between the factions; but the question of a successor to al-Bakri, whose six months expired in August, again divided them. The appointment by Damascus of Colonel Tawfiq al-Aṭrash as his successor was hailed as a defeat, and was made the occasion for angry demonstration, by the Nationalists of the Jabal; but the intervention of the religious chiefs again secured a precarious peace based on a promise of the ultimate appointment of Ḥasan al-Aṭrash. But the peace was soon again broken, Sulṭan refused to compromise, and in the autumn a Black Hand Association launched a campaign of intimidation against Syrian officials.

A temporary solution was found in the appointment of the competent non-political Damascene, Bahij al-Khaṭib, to the governorship for the period necessary to hold elections, after which a Druze would succeed him. He accomplished his task in December 1937, with great good sense; three unionist-nationalists and two autonomists were declared elected,[1] after voting peacefully conducted save in one instance. Bahij then withdrew, and the Bloc Government entrusted his post as Muḥafidh in February 1938 to Ḥasan al-Aṭrash: the last move in a long and harassing course of intrigue and violence.

But the separatists had not said their last word; indeed, even in peaceful neighbouring Ḥawran a move for local autonomy, with all-Ḥawrani officials, had to be met by postponement of taxes due, remissions of sentences, and the removal of the unpopular Muḥafidh. A year later (June 1939) came a similar demand by the Circassians. In the Jabal, organizations for full Druze autonomy persisted, Syrian officials were resented, and in August 1938 a

[1] The 5 Deputies for the Jabal were 3 Druzes, 1 Christian, 1 bedouin.

weighty petition was sent to the High Commissioner appealing for full release from Damascus, and tutelage by France alone; and a Druze delegate meeting was held in Beirut in the same month, with appeals for restoration of the 1922 Franco-Druze Agreement. In December, the Defence Party arrested the senior (Syrian) judge and dispatched him to Damascus, followed by a number of his colleagues. Ḥasan al-Aṭrash refused to go to the capital and explain, and permitted instead a demonstration in favour of complete autonomy. Syrian officials in the Jabal retaliated by striking, and it was necessary to replace Syrian judges by French. These events, and a further call by 'Abd al-Ghaffar al-Aṭrash for total separation from Syria and close links with France, were strongly condemned in the Syrian Chamber; but the Druzes went further and by a delegation assured the High Commissioner that they were now already *de facto* independent of Syria, their State and Governor deriving authority from the Druze community alone. M. Puaux visited the Jabal in January 1939 and met a strongly separatist welcome. Ḥasan al-Aṭrash resigned his office in February; the Délégué, Colonel Bouvier, succeeding him, allowed the French and the Druze flags to replace the Syrian on public buildings. His policy foreshadowed the decisive event of 2 July—the issue of a revised Statute for the Jabal on lines identical to that of the Ladhqiya province. It excited the usual extremes of satisfaction and dismay.

The French reversion, in both provinces, almost to the régime of before 1936 conduced, no doubt, to immediate peace, and might be justified by the exigencies of mid-1939; but it was a retrograde step which must in the future be inevitably again reversed. The failure to make good the 1936 decision in favour of unity in Syria was due to the strength of local autonomist feeling which, during sixteen years, an unhappy policy of planned fragmentation had allowed—or encouraged—to build up: to the resulting lack of confidence between these minorities and the main body of Syrian opinion: to the provocation on the spot by French officials with convinced localist preferences: and to the absence of firm French backing, at all levels, for the policy which their own new decisions and Statutes implied. To these causes of failure must be added a lack of tact in the Syrian officials directly concerned.

In the Jazira province, with its ill-stabilized non-Syrian population, the three-year period prior to the Second World War confronted these mutually suspicious Kurdish, Muslim Arab, and Christian Arab communities with the demands of a nationalist and centralizing Government in Damascus, alien to them all, and failed to find a solution to the problems thus provoked.

The essential issue was that of the extent to which normal

government by Damascus should, or could, be applied to the province. The Syrian Government essayed the application of a régime normal to the rest of the country, and was confident that it could, with French initial help (or even neutrality), apply it satisfactorily. Of the inhabitants,[1] the Christian elements almost unanimously demanded, at the least, specific local privilege and consideration or, at the most, complete autonomy under French protection; the Kurds and Arabs in large part concurred in some variety of these demands, though a considerable minority supported the claims of the central Government—which was at least Islamic! The French, on the higher level, were concerned to implement the 1936 Treaty, support Damascus, and urge the Jazira to obedience; but, on other levels, first a vocal part of the French public, then the missionaries in Syria, and finally many French local officials (always critical of the intelligentsia-politics of Damascus) sided strongly with the Jazira separatists. Moreover the protagonists of Jazira self-government, even though this was refused them, were sure of a welcome in Beirut or Paris, and French Catholic sentiment would, it was obvious, never tolerate the coercion which the situation would normally invite.

A further element was the tactless zeal of the incoming Damascene officials, whose appearance in the last weeks of 1936, with little appreciation of the prevailing localistic feeling, increased suspicion and antipathy. In the general elections, the Bloc unwisely produced their own candidates against those of the region itself; their defeat was resented in Damascus, and the validation of the Jazira Deputies was pointedly delayed. The Christian 'White Badge' movement (p. 229) made some progress in the Jazira, but was condemned by Government and not universally supported by Christians. Bahjat al-Shihabi, the incoming Muḥafidh, found himself surrounded by currents of crude Kurdish as well as Christian propaganda, and this was soon intensified by the unpopular dismissal of some local officials in favour of 'outsiders'.

The first half of 1937 was uneasy but not disastrous; although separatist leaders (notably Bishop Ḥibbi of the Syrian Catholics, and behind him Cardinal Tappouni himself) were organizing their forces, it seemed possible that, with unprovocative firmness and French support, the central Government could make good its position. But early in July violence broke out at Ḥasaja, the Muḥafidh and police officers were threatened, the Sarai attacked;

[1] The *Annual Report* for 1937 gives the population as 42,000 Muslim Arabs, 82,000 Kurds, 31,000 Christians, 2,000 Yazidis, and 1,000 each of Jews and Circassians. The Christians were Syrian Catholic, Armenian, Syrian Orthodox, and Assyrian. The Christians were by majority town-dwelling, the Kurds village-dwelling, the Arabs the same and partly nomadic.

and on the return of Bahjat from Damascus, his arrest of the (Christian) mayor of Ḥasaja restarted the trouble, and led to exchanges of shots, three deaths, and a critical situation. French troops occupied the town: but with both Christian and Kurdish involvement the trouble spread to Darbasiya, 'Amuda, and Qamishli, with angry demands for the withdrawal of the Muḥafidh and his officials, and with the climax at Qamishli of a two-hour street battle followed by the surrender and disarming of the gendarmes, flight of the Qa'immaqam, and intervention of French troops; and when the Nationalist faction invoked bedouin tribesmen to their help, these were evicted by the French only after some hours of shop looting. Telegrams flashed to Beirut begging the High Commissioner to enact a special Statute, and to rid the Jazira of Damascus officialdom. The Kurdish leaders, who had taken little part in the Ḥasaja or Qamishli troubles, declared themselves, by a hopeful reaction, to be in favour of the central Government; but they failed long to sustain that role. Most of the local headmen of all communities were called to Damascus, some unpopular officials were removed, and a Committee of Inquiry was sent to the spot. Consisting of the (Greek Orthodox) Muḥafidh of Dayr al-Zur, Tawfiq al-Shamiya, and two French officials, it was largely boycotted by the rebellious communities. These in turn sent deputations to Damascus to demand French protection, locally-chosen officials, and more schools, hospitals, and development. The Committee itself recommended a greater measure of devolution, and blamed the tactlessness of some officials. A number of local leaders, including the stormy Bishop Ḥibbi, were arrested and sent to Beirut as evident troublemakers.

But worse trouble was at hand. Even before the return to Damascus of the Committee of Inquiry a violent quarrel between Kurds (claiming for the moment, loyalty to Damascus) and Christians broke out at the village of 'Amuda. It was signalized by exchanges of rifle fire, looting of Christian shops, and loss of some twenty-five[1] lives. French aircraft bombed the rioters, troops occupied the village; but when Shamiya's committee ventured to start an investigation it was forced to retire. Two Damascus Deputies were wounded. Conditions were calmer when in August the Délégué from Damascus, Count Ostrorog, visited the area and heard the now familiar complaints and claims. French troops withdrew in October, deported headmen returned—but 'Committees of Resistance' multiplied. Even though the Deputies from the province still professed loyalty to the central Government, the local demand for an almost sovereign Government of their own was unabated, and the present Administration was

[1] Other accounts say 150 lives; the truth was and is unascertainable.

largely boycotted. Turkish propaganda was freely heard among the discontented. Cardinal Tappouni, visiting Paris, made the round of statesmen and dignitaries.

The new Assyrian settlements on the Khabur (p. 213) had since 1933 multiplied and consolidated.[1] The villagers, for whom the League of Nations provided funds, a Settlement Officer, and Trustees, remained as dissatisfied as they were unwelcome. They were denied access to the Lebanon, and a plan to settle them on the middle Orontes came to nothing. But at least they had found homes, and reasonable safety.

The next episode was the kidnapping, from his motor car in mid-desert, of the acting Muḥafiḏh—the same Tawfiq al-Shamiya—by the Christians of Ḥasaja. He was found unharmed after an intensive search and restored to his post; his captors were sent under arrest to Damascus. A visit by the Minister of Interior did nothing to improve relations; but a new Muḥafiḏh, Ḥaydar Mardam Bey, was appointed in March 1938, with instructions to adopt every form of tactful complaisance, and in fact he began well and acceptably. But neither he nor his superiors in Damascus could meet the wishes of the convinced separatists, and in mid-April he was himself assailed and compelled to relinquish his office. In the same month, the sentence of death passed on the leaders of the 'Amuda riot, and separatist demonstrations held (with unconcealed French support) on the occasion of a French Deputy's visit, kept the local temperature dangerously high, while spokesmen in Damascus blamed the crisis on French weakness or malice. In September 1938 a 'General Congress of the Jazira' was held at Ḥasaja, with the veteran Kurdish leader Ḥajo Agha (many times a turn-coat) in the chair; its deliberations ended in a telegram to the Quai d'Orsay demanding, once more, full Jazira self-government.

With no new appointment as Muḥafiḏh, and no line of conciliation apparent, the Délégué Adjoint (Colonel Marchant) continued to direct such administration as the public did not boycott. Feeling against Damascus did not diminish, and the first visit of M. Puaux was awaited with impatience. It was paid early in March, in an emotional and strongly secessionist atmosphere, with a conspicuous absence of Syrian flags[2] or apologists: only a few Kurds spoke for the Government and the Treaty. M. Puaux refused to countenance outright separatism, but temporized and pacified. But his implied attitude was similar to that to which

[1] In mid-1938, they numbered some 9,000 in sixteen villages astride the Khabur.

[2] In Qamishli, enthusiasts had seized and burnt the only supply of national flags.

events in the Druze and 'Alawi areas were simultaneously leading him; and widespread separatist demonstrations early in June, followed by the withdrawal of most of the non-local officials and the virtual cessation of government, forced him strongly in the same direction. Further demonstrations were forbidden, the nominal authority of Damascus remained: but on 2 July the High Commissioner decreed a 'special régime' for the Jazira, with the Délégué Adjoint in full military and civil control. With this, tranquillity returned to the province; but its problems, which a consistent French attitude from the first would have greatly lessened, remained all in being. The policy of the Mandatory had been in the Jazira, as too often elsewhere, unsure, vacillating, and acceptable to none.

7. LEBANESE TRIENNIUM

The Government of the Lebanese Republic, in the first days of its new (though unratified) independence, received from the High Commissioner a letter begging its statesmen to mend their ways: to abandon faction and intrigue, to simplify the machinery of the State, to be prudent in finance and disciplined in party organization. These warnings were unheeded; no efforts of the Mandatory availed to correct the weaknesses of Lebanese politics, so deeply rooted in the nation's civilization and its leaders' conception of public life.

Although the Constitution of 1926, even as later amended, had in its time given barely tolerable results, its restoration, to synchronize with the post-Treaty régime, was an ambition among the majority of statesmen. It was now conceded by M. de Martel, to avoid charges of obstructionism. He reintroduced the Constitution on 24 January 1937, with provision for a President with a four-year term, a Chamber with a three. At the same time the powers of French advisers were reduced, every encouragement was given to the Government to agree with Syria over the Common Interests, and a Franco-Lebanese committee sat to establish bases for a National Army. Though the small and restless State was full of problems, those of the Mandatory were, as ever, far slighter here than in Syria, and mutual resentment far less in evidence.

Amid the endless shifting of groups and personalities, hereinafter to be described, certain elements appear above or beside the mere play of ambition and bargaining. One of these was the persistence of confessionalism as the real basis of political, as social, division: division to which, however, deep rifts within the communities themselves were sometimes to be added. Another was the eminent part played by the ecclesiastics; violent speeches by the Maronite Archbishop of Beirut, the receptions and sometimes the fulminations of the Patriarch Arida[1] (as ever a party leader with the prerogatives of a monarch), the prestige of Cardinal Tappouni and his interventions for the Jazira Christians. Yet another was the prevalence of Youth movements and their squads, flags, parades, and harangues, elsewhere described (pp. 225 ff.).

The attitude of the Lebanese Muslims, among whom Tripoli had unquestioned leadership, was substantially unchanged; though most co-operated in public life, and some wearied of fighting the long-standing *fait accompli*, the majority were slow to reconcile themselves to perpetual inclusion in Lebanon. A demand for Tripoli in place of threatened Alexandretta was put forward by the Syrians to France in 1937, and a mission from Tripoli with the same request succeeded in visiting Paris and seeing M. Blum. But though the question was raised again by Jamil Mardam Bey in June, there was no real hope in this direction. Resentment continued, the President of Lebanon was greeted in Tripoli with stones, and partial 'autonomy' for Tripoli city was no radical cure.

If, behind the uneasy and futile range of politics, lay always the highly civilized, progressive social life of the Lebanese and their outstanding gifts in commerce, their prowess in statecraft, even under the spur of their new status, lagged far behind. Immediately after the restoration of the Constitution, and with the Chamber still on its (now constitutional) basis of two-thirds elected, one-third nominated, the formation of a Cabinet[2] was entrusted to a Sunni Muslim, Khayr al-Din al-Aḥdab. But the group led by Bishara al-Khuri refused to participate, and the Ministry found itself with command only of 13 votes against 12 in the Chamber. In spite of an initial vote of confidence, Khayr al-Din in his absurd position[3] could not govern, and on 13 March he re-formed his Cabinet as one of 'National Union':[4] that is, inclusive of the Khuri faction. But so precarious a harmony was soon interrupted by the death of the Minister of the Interior in June, and on the assumption of this office by the Prime Minister the Khuri party

[1] He visited Rome and Paris in the summer of 1937. His policy was generally pro-Zionist, anti-Communist, and entirely devoted to his own community.

[2] The Prime Minister kept also Interior and Justice: Finance, Khalid abu-Lam': Public Works and Agriculture, Ibrahim Ḥaydar: Education, Health, and Tourism, Ḥabib abu-Shala.

[3] The crucial margin in the Chamber was on occasion displaced three times in a day, and support of the Government must be secured by ever-renewed promises.

[4] In Justice and Finance, Khayr al-Din: in Interior, Michael Zukkur: in Education, Defence, and Economics, Ḥabib abu-Shahla: in Public Works and Agriculture, Aḥmad al-Ḥusayni.

withdrew its support, and the Cabinet was again reconstructed.[1] The Maronite Patriarch returned from Paris with a string of unrealizable proposals.

The later summer of 1937 was devoted to prolonged and hard-fought elections for the Chamber[2] which, under the Decree of July 1937, was now to consist of sixty deputies,[3] two-thirds being elected and all as usual representative of the communities in strict proportion. Street disorders and arrests marked the return of Bishara al-Khuri from abroad, and even the Muslims failed to agree on a single electoral list. Negotiations between the main factions—there were nearly 600 candidates—ended in an agreement (not reached without hard bargaining, and some corruption) whereby the Opposition were to be allowed twenty-five seats.

After elections held on 24 October, and after issue of the High Commissioner's Decree prolonging the Presidential tenure to six years as an aid to stability, the new Chamber met on 29 October. A new Cabinet, to which early opposition declared itself, was constituted from substantially the former personnel[4] and, with a programme containing a variety of interesting projects, secured its vote of confidence. If a violent political speech by the Maronite Archbishop was unhelpful, the dissolution of the paramilitary associations (p. 226), however unpopular, was greatly in the public interest. Patriarch Arida continued to hold meetings, press his objectives, and renew his criticisms of the new personal status proposals (p. 235).

The Aḥdab Ministry resigned on 18 March 1938, to avoid certain defeat on a vote of confidence. Its successor,[5] under the Amir Khalid Shihab, contained a majority of the Khuri party and called itself a Ministry of Concentration. A visible *détente* resulted; but the doubts of those who felt the whole scale of government to be too elaborate and costly did not diminish. Yet another Lebanese Nationalist Party was formed, by Musa Nammur. In

[1] Prime Minister (with Ministries of Economics and Justice) as before: Interior, Ḥabib abu-Shahla: Finance, Georges Tabet: Education, Health, Foreign Affairs, and Defence, the Amir Khalid abu-Lam'.

[2] It was dissolved on 24 July.

[3] The division of elected seats by provinces was: Beirut, 6: North Lebanon, 9: South Lebanon, 8: Mount Lebanon, 11: Biqa', 7: By communities it was: Sunnis, 9: Shi'is, 7: Druzes, 3: Maronites, 13: Greek Orthodox, 5: Armenians, 1: Greek Catholics, 2: other minorities, 1.

[4] The Prime Minister took also the Ministries of Justice and Foreign Affairs: Finance and Defence, Musa Nammur: Works, Salim Takla: Interior, Ḥabib abu-Shahla: Agriculture, Majid Arsalan: Health and Posts, Ibrahim Ḥaydar: Education and Economics, Georges Tabet.

[5] The Ministers were: Education, Camille Chamoun (Sham'un), a Maronite newcomer—and future President of the Republic: Public Works, Salim Takla: and in other Ministries Yusif Istifan, Aḥmad al-As'ad, Ḥikmat Janbulaṭ, Ḥabib abu-Shahla. The latter, late in March, gave way to Khalil Kusayb.

May an alleged conspiracy to restore direct French rule was discovered, with a Dr. Shalfun and some fifty associates as the named plotters. The Doctor was sentenced to two years imprisonment, then released: and, though French rule was admittedly the cherished dream of a small (Maronite) minority, it is doubtful whether this 'plot' had any seriousness. More significant was the resolution of loyalty to France passed by the Lebanese Chamber in the dark days of September 1938—a move which the Syrian Parliament did not emulate.

The Shihabi Cabinet, initially promising, survived for a bare eight months. Its successor, dropping the Constitutionalists, was headed by 'Abdullah al-Yafi.[1] But though correctly composed on confessional lines it neither commanded, nor deserved, greater respect than its predecessors; its factions and intrigues, absorbing to the Deputies and their clientèle, bore little relation to the main currents of Lebanese life and activity. The Administration, in which French officials continued to play an important part, was rather obstructed than aided by the legislature, and President Eddé secured at least some continuity and efficiency by his personal interpretation of his office as that of effective Chief Executive. The French non-ratification of the Franco-Lebanese Treaty was viewed by some with regret, by more with apathy, and by prevailing Maronite and Malkite opinion with satisfaction. In spite of evident warlike preparations by the local French forces (p. 237), and an ominous international outlook, there appeared internally, in July 1939, no reason why Lebanese government of the existing type, and the undetermined status of the territory, should not go on for ever. But the High Commissioner, and history itself, had other intentions.

8. NEIGHBOURING COUNTRIES

In the field of the foreign relations of the mandated territory, the two republics derived a general, if variously assessable, benefit from the régime of order and non-discrimination which it was a mandatory duty of France to sustain, and from their position within the orbit of League of Nations internationalism. Their *émigré* subjects throughout the world enjoyed French consular protection, and those domiciled in Turkey or Egypt were substantially helped by French intervention. It was by virtue of the Mandate alone that Capitulations were not still in force. Customs or exchange negotiations with Japan, Germany, or Russia were

[1] He took also the portfolio of Justice. In Interior and Defence was Khalil Kusayb: in Finance, Economics, and Foreign Affairs, Ḥamid Frangié (Franjiya): in Education and Health, Rukuz abu-Nadir: in Public Works and Agriculture, Ṣabri Ḥamada.

conducted by French experts. The internal conditions under the Mandate were considered by foreign capitalists as justifying enterprises in Syria and Lebanon which might otherwise have been withheld: such were oil exploration, the trans-desert pipelines and motor route, foreign banks and insurance companies, and archaeological missions. And the French presence offered a guarantee that no improper pressures or guile would avail to secure, for foreign interests, advantages which local officials, unadvised or unsupervised, might at times have accorded. These were partial compensation for the loss of experience, and perhaps of self-respect, felt by Syrians from their exclusion, under the Mandate, from the management of their own foreign affairs.[1]

Among neighbouring countries, Turkey gave rise to the most controversial issues. It could be hoped that, after the visit of M. de Jouvenel to Ankara (p. 173) and the signature of the Franco-Turkish Convention of May 1926, most of these would be soluble. The Convention provided for arbitration of disputes, for disposal of the goods of the absent, for quarantine, railway, Customs, and frontier matters. It provided also for a slight modification of the existing (1921) Turco-Syrian boundary, and for a Boundary Commission to demarcate it. Security in the border zone improved perceptibly after demarcation, though still leaving much to be desired: Turkish propaganda continued in the Upper Jazira, and Kurdish Aghas displaced by the upheaval in Anatolia in 1925–6 continued to raid in both directions. Liaison between frontier officials was variable; each party had its grievances. Frontier delimitation proved easy along the railway, but on the alignment between Niṣibin and the Tigris deadlock was reached for sixteen months. Further discussions between the Governments began in May 1929, and quickly evolved a compromise settlement[2] of the boundary, and of other matters, in a series of 'protocols'[3] signed by both at Ankara on 22 June 1929. These covered the security and traffic, the yearly animal taxation, the control of nomad tribesmen, and the right of the local inhabitants to opt for Turkish or Syrian nationality. The new frontier was demarcated in the winter of 1929. A detailed 'protocol' was signed in May 1930, in which year a Turkish garrison, which had been quite improperly in occupation, withdrew from the area. The Permanent Frontier Commission set up by the June 1929 protocols met later in that year and thereafter sat almost annually until 1938. Border security improved considerably, though

[1] Article 3 gave the French 'exclusive control' of these.

[2] The area in dispute was divided; about four-fifths of it fell to Syria, which gained 85 villages and 1,000 square kilometres of land.

[3] The protocols were followed by a general Franco-Turkish Treaty of Friendship and Conciliation, signed on 3 February 1930.

the Armenians on the Syrian side excited Turkish uneasiness, and the raids of Ḥajo Agha their resentment.

The operation of the railway,[1] which (itself on Turkish soil) formed the frontier for more than 200 miles, offered many occasions for mutual recrimination. Even after the 1926 Convention, and again after a further Railway Agreement of 27 October 1932, the Turks were still uneasy co-operators, who persistently refused various forms of joint working. Over Customs tariffs the position was not dissimilar; the temporary régime established in 1925, treating Turkey as equivalent to a League member, secured no corresponding benefits for Syria and lapsed in 1929. Thereafter, both before and after Turkey became a League member in 1932, her high Customs-rates against Syria and Lebanon were crippling to a market which before 1914 had been a main Syrian commercial outlet. The *modus vivendi* was ended in September 1933, and Syria had thereafter notably the worst of the exchanges, against which their representations availed nothing. Nor, in spite of French advocacy, was the position easier in the matter of the property of Syrian and Lebanese optants who had returned home from Turkey leaving belongings behind; the settlement of their affairs dragged on for years with reluctant or withheld co-operation—and failure, finally, to pay more than a fraction of the sums owed.

In Syria's relations with 'Iraq the community of Arab sentiment found little expression beyond cordial visits and messages and, in nationalist circles, mutual sympathy for their respective 'servitude' under Mandates. The 'Iraqis were envied for their greater and freer share in government, and for their emancipation and League membership won in 1932. On common Arab questions, such as Zionism, identical views were held. Diplomatic representatives were exchanged in and after 1938. Talk of 'Iraqi-Syrian union was not unknown, with the King of 'Iraq always a prominent candidate in monarchical circles.[2] Social relations, increased by the fashion of *estivage* in Lebanon, were of the closest. There was good liaison over locust control, the trans-desert motor convoys, and the long-projected junction of the 'Iraqi and the Syrian-Turkish sections of the Baghdad Railway, achieved in 1939. 'Iraqi officials, the Contrôle Bédouin, and French Intelligence officers worked together over the quarrels and migrations of the mid-desert tribes; joint conferences were held at 'Ana in 1927, Ḥasaja in 1929, and Palmyra in 1934, and an effective system

[1] That is, the sections of the Baghdad Railway east of Aleppo: Payas–Alexandretta, Maydan Akbas–Aleppo: Muslimiya–Choban Bey, and the prolongation beyond Niṣibin.

[2] The deaths of Kings Fayṣal (1933) and Ghazi (1939) made a deep impression in Syria.

of mutual help was established. The settlement of Assyrians from 'Iraq during 1933–8 has been separately described (p. 213). A satisfactory commercial agreement hung fire for some years, but was at last signed in Damascus on 24 April 1937. The settlement of the Syro-'Iraqi frontier, approximately indicated in December 1920, was a prolonged operation. The French and British authorities jointly asked the League Council in December 1931 to assist by appointing a Commission[1] of delimitation. This was done in the spring of 1932. Its recommendations were accepted by the Mandates Commission and Council, and demarcation on the ground was completed during 1933.

Official relations of the States with Palestine and Transjordan, both under British Mandate, were conducted always by the French High Commissioner, and were generally satisfactory. Customs and transit agreements were made and modified, and worked with little friction. Steps were taken, but inconclusively, to prevent the use of dual nationality by 'Syrian' ex-Turkish subjects. Extradition arrangements were made with both the British-mandated Administrations; in practice, however, each territory offered an easy refuge for fugitives, and fully effective control was not establishable. Joint conferences on tribal affairs were held on a number of occasions, as at Irbid in November 1929: those on the Transjordan–Syrian boundary, involving Druze elements, were the most delicate. A mixed Frontier Commission was set up early in 1930. The boundaries between French and British mandated territory were finally demarcated during this period; that of Palestine–Lebanon was confirmed by the League in 1934, while that of Syria–Jordan, left unsatisfactory in 1920, was revised by a protocol of 31 October 1931 and demarcated in the year following. It provided for a detailed frontier régime, of which the drafting was long protracted.

In the field of society and politics, both Palestine and Transjordan had much community of view and feeling, and an infinity of personal contacts, with the States of the Levant. On matters of Arab policy and unity, they were as one. The Amir 'Abdullah had his supporters as a candidate for the Syrian throne. Syrian statesmen accepted office repeatedly in the Cabinets of 'Amman. The progress of Jewish settlement in Palestine, with its threat to Arab supremacy and its frustration of self-governing institutions, was watched with full solidarity from Syria and Lebanon. The periodical outbreaks in Palestine of anti-Jewish—or anti-British—violence excited great sympathy, marked by demonstrations, public subscriptions, gun-running, and the departure of armed volunteers to Palestine. The attitude of the French authorities was,

[1] It had a Swiss chairman, and a Spanish and a Swedish member.

necessarily, restrictive; the High Commissioner at times uttered warning against the involvement of Syrians, and closed the frontier; but the Syrian and Lebanese authorities, at every level, gave all support within their power to Arab brothers.

The High Commissioner dealt with the authorities in Egypt regarding Customs and commercial agreements, which were discussed, concluded (in 1928 and 1930), lapsed (in 1929 and 1930) and gave way thereafter to a provisional *modus vivendi* which, with modifications, lasted from 1933 to 1939. Other inter-statal questions were those of the nationality and repatriation of Syro-Lebanese subjects long domiciled in Egypt, a field in which the French authorities laboured hard, but with limited success, to secure fair treatment for their mandated clients. With Sa'udi Arabia, there were fewer exchanges; an agreement of *Bon Voisinage* was concluded in November 1931. The annual French-made arrangements for the Syrian pilgrims to Mecca, involving the grant of a monopoly to a single supervised steamship contractor, were harshly criticized in Syria and Lebanon. Nothing came of the oft-mooted plan to reconstruct the Ḥijaz Railway.

VIII

APART FROM POLITICS

I. THE TASK OF GOVERNMENT

If most of the previous pages of this work have been devoted, as will be its concluding chapters, to the unhappy experience of the Mandatory in the political field, these cannot of themselves give other than a partial picture of the total French achievement in the territory. The duties of the Mandate, as its text prescribed, included a further range of efforts and interests conterminous with the national life, and operative in every field of administration, justice, security, the public services, agriculture, commerce, industry, communications, and all that could conduce to the better life of the public. How far can French efforts in this wide non-political field, pursued for more than twenty years, counterbalance by their merits the long-drawn political failure? The French themselves claimed and claim so wide a range of achievement as to amount to a transformation, on modern lines, of the life of the territory, with outstanding feats of elimination, improvement, enrichment, and modernization in every branch; anti-western Syrian publicists deny almost the entirety of this claim, and assert that a free, unmandated Syria (with perhaps some measure of invited foreign assistance) would have advanced more rapidly and more healthily. Between these extremes, moderate Syro-Lebanese opinion has enough of realism and discernment to appreciate in retrospect the scale and merit of the French effort in many fields, the indispensable functions of transition which it performed, and its part in creating the conditions for that further advance which (except in the political field) has been so notable since 1945. To agree with this view, as does the present writer, involves neither acceptance of the full uncritical measure of French self-praise, nor any belittling of the simultaneous contribution of the officialdom and public of the territory itself. It is, however tempting, futile to speculate on the comparative success which some other Power as Mandatory might have enjoyed, even while recognizing a great part of the French offering as specifically their own: nor can one assess the paramount contribution of time itself—twenty years of unprecedented rapid change, progress, development in every country in the world—and of all the new communications, influences, and aspirations to which even a Mandateless Levant would inevitably have been exposed.

It is convenient to examine this, the non-political, field of French endeavour at this point, around 1939, since war, invasion, and abnormal conditions were thereafter substantially to interrupt peaceful progress.

French influence—or compulsion—was exercised, as earlier pages have described (pp. 114–15), by the paramount power of the High Commissioner and his Délégués in legislation, regulation, control, veto, and appointment: by the important departments of Government—notably those of the Common Interests—directly administered under his orders: by the activity in planning, organization, advice, and inspection on the part of his own non-executive headquarter Services: by his sole control of the armed forces, and substantial monopoly of higher technical and financial functions: by the all-pervasive and authoritative officers of the Special Services: and by the network of French officials, mainly non-executive, throughout (and employed by) the States. That the total machinery of mandatory control was excessive, and in a large measure self-defeating, has been urged elsewhere in this work. The too-numerous body of French officialdom—it ranged from over 300 to over 400 functionaries during these twenty years, and at the close stood not far below its maximum—contained, with some indifferent and a few definitely unworthy[1] members, a majority of competent and vigorous servants of the State.[2] A

[1] It is surprising that these, who in the eyes of the local public and European visitors alike did serious damage to French prestige, were tolerated by their own superiors.

[2] Among holders of the post of Secretary-General, de Caix, de Reffye, Maugras, Tétreaux, Privat-Aubouard, Hoppenot, Helleu, Lagarde, Meyrier, and Lépissié are remembered; in the High Commissioner's Legal and Legislation Bureau, Aveilles and Mazas; in Financial Affairs, Abadie Gasquin, Roucolle, and Ehrhart; in Public Works, and Concessionary Companies, Vasselet; in Economic Services, Beriel and Reclus; in Education, Bounoure; in Land Services and Awqaf, Gennardi; in Public Health, Colonels Jude and Martin; in Customs, Merlenghi, Gombault, and Roux; in Posts and Telegraphs, Pain, Cianfarelli, and Pernot; in Antiquities, Seyrig; in the Sûreté Générale, Bouchède, Colombani, and Gautier; and in the Political Bureau, Hoppenot, Chauvel, Fain, Kieffer, Ostrorog, Conty, Baelen. Among Délégués at Beirut were Trabaud, Aubouard, Vandenberg, Cayla, Salomiac, Poupon, Reclus, Lafond (and, after 1939, Bart, Arlabosse, David). Some of the Advisers or Asst.-Délégués to the Lebanese Republic were du Paty de Clam, de Salins, Bart, Darche, Dumont, Demarçay, de Monjon, Martin, Tallec, Bahout, Thiebaut, Soule-Susbielle, Cointet, Dr. Lubert, Dr. Guillermo, Rendu; among Délégués at Damascus were Schoeffler, Aubouard, Fauconnier, Alype, Delelée-Desloges, Bruère, Salomiac, Lavastre, Weber, Fain, Ostrorog, de Hautecloque (and, later, Collet and Oliva-Roget). At Aleppo, Billotte, Reclus, Lavastre, David, and Fauquenot are remembered; at Alexandretta, Durieux, Garreau and Collet; at Dayr al-Zur, Colonels Callais, Goudouneix, Jacquot, Sarrade, Quilichini, Ardoint, Marchant, Brosset: among the 'Alawis, Billotte, Cayla, Schoeffler, Cahours, Bart, Malatre, and later Jourdan, 'Montclar', and des Essars: in the Jabal al-Duruz, following Carbillet, were Andréa, Henry,

number of outstanding orientalists, scholars, scientists, technologists, lawyers, and economists among them would have taken a distinguished place in any country. Important specific contributions by the French official element were the world-wide services rendered to Syro-Lebanese citizens and interests abroad, and the conduct of the foreign affairs of the territories, including all questions of nationality[1] and controversies and agreements with neighbouring States.

French residents and officers apart, each of the three great cities of Syria–Lebanon contained a small but active and sufficiently well-circumstanced European community—consular, commercial and industrial, and missionary or educational. These (that is, the industrialists) were notably increased in numbers from 1931 onwards by the multiplication of the resident staff of the 'Iraq Petroleum Company in the two territories: the British and American families who during years—sometimes a lifetime—of residence in the country had attained highly respected positions, and contributed much to the social and cultural wealth of the territory. International official life at the Consular and Consul-General[2] level was busy and amicable, though Italian activities were criticized as too evidentially designed to increase their national influence.

In the ranks of Syro-Lebanese officialdom the period witnessed a pronounced improvement in standards of competence, honesty, and capacity. Though commonly disparaged (not least by French residents), the body of local civil servants compared, by 1939, not unfavourably with that of other comparable countries, and contained at all levels scores or hundreds of honest, vigorous, and intelligent officials. These had, over twenty years, shed almost all the worst survivors of the Turkish period, and had, with a more enlightened (but still insufficient) comprehension of the nature of

Clément-Grandcourt, Massiet, Devic, Tarrit, Bouvier, and later Oliva-Roget. Among other Délégués-Adjoint and advisory staff in the State of Syria are remembered Berthelot, Regismanset, Fournier, Joubert, Valluy, Florimont, Burret, Bailly, Wendling, Achard, Pignarre, Colonels Prévot, Naudin, and Bringuier, and Laurentie, Thirion, Montagne. These are but a few of many scores of names remembered with credit, often with affection, in the territory: they do not include many senior, and often distinguished, departmental officers. Of all these a lengthier work than the present should, one day, offer a fuller account, from a French pen.

[1] Such 'nationality' questions were those of the status of Turks in Syria and Lebanon, and vice versa—a matter involving years of correspondence and negotiation—and that of the Syro-Lebanese colony in Egypt, which the statesmen of Beirut and Damascus were anxious to retain as their own nationals. The adhesion of the territories to international conventions was at the sole discretion of the French.

[2] Sir Harold Satow was British Consul-General at Beirut from 1920 to 1934, succeeded thereafter by Mr. (later Sir Godfrey) Havard, who held the post until 1941.

public service, incorporated representatives of the better-educated and promising younger men. Their faults were those sometimes of defective sympathy with the more backward public, sometimes of an admixture of politics or nepotism in their administration, sometimes of a shrinking from responsibility—a defect blamed, not without reason, on the excessive strictness of French tutelage. The structure, regulation, and discipline of the local civil services were carefully established, a pension system installed, reasonable salaries offered. That these were strikingly below French rates of remuneration was the subject of frequent comment, but was in practice scarcely avoidable.

Whatever the virtues of close French control, the independence and thereby the self-respect of the States which they served was as a consequence, in spite of the constitutional forms observed, notoriously incomplete. The States themselves had never (unless dubiously in Lebanon) approved their own status or Constitution; they applied laws which in many cases not they but the High Commissioner had enacted, and often after little consultation with them. Every act of their own Chamber required a French counter-signature; important departments—the armed forces, the Common Interests—were entirely outside their control, and whole provinces were directly French-administered. French cultural and charitable institutions were effectively untouchable; and throughout the State Administrations, French advice, inspection, and *de facto* control rendered local powers often no more than nominal. The provincial administrative scheme for the territories[1] was not fundamentally varied during the period, though changes in the status of units were made, new units created, and administrative regulations amended. Good efforts were made, with perceptible success, to improve current standards of daily government, and to define the powers conferred on district officials, on village headmen, and on local councils. The weight of French influence was cast usually on the side of decentralization, in which sense the Syrian Law of the Muḥafaḏhas, issued in January 1936, would if properly implemented have been an important step.

However effected, the body of legislation prepared and enacted during these two decades was voluminous. Forced to allow for the traditionalism of the public and for considerable local variations in past usage, French and local officials alike were anxious to modernize criminal, civil, and commercial codes, rules of judicial procedure, and the mass of administrative law. Although by 1940 certain fields of law remained still little improved since 1920, and other only imperfectly or confusedly covered by modern

[1] Tables of administrative units as in 1927 and in 1944 are given in Appendix A (ii) and (iii), pp. 370–1, below.

codes, an immense work of study, amendment, substitution, and codification had nevertheless been carried out. This work could have proceeded still more rapidly if the main body of the public had been more receptive to novelty, the officials better trained, or sectional interests less insistent, and if it had not at times suited the tactics of statesmen and their parties to oppose application of well-meaning and progressive measures which—or objection to which—lent themselves to political use. But in spite of phases of non-cooperation by the local authorities, or Bar, or Chamber, and occasional highhandedness by the French, the record in the field of law-making was on the whole more than respectable, and represented a major service by the Mandatory.

The same is generally true of the administration of justice. The system followed in the jurisdiction, status, and location of Courts has been elsewhere suggested (p. 135), and was altered between 1924 and 1940 only in detail. 'Fusion' in the Lebanese Courts (p. 136) was discontinued in 1927 as impracticable. The right of access to the still-resented Mixed Courts was in 1928 limited to subjects of the ex-capitulatory Powers, and the Japanese; the permission granted to local subjects to take their suits to these Courts was sparingly, in some areas never, exercised. The religious or community Courts, with their limited personal-status jurisdiction, were necessarily preserved intact as an inviolable legacy of Islam and the *millet* system; but they gave rise to widespread controversy, from which political motives were not absent, when repeated attempts were made by the High Commission to limit and modernize the range of community rights, to extend the jurisdiction of the ordinary (Nidhamiya) Courts, and to redress Christian disabilities at the cost of offending Muslim tradition. The right of community jurisdiction in personal status was extended between 1926 and 1939 to the Mutawila, Druzes, and 'Alawis. Special partly-French Courts were established in the States to deal, at the instance of the French or of the State President, with inter-community crimes and others involving violence or sedition. Offences of government officials were referred to one of three special judicial bodies,[1] and a Council of State dealt with suits involving government departments as such. The normal Courts, in their sequence of Peace, First-Instance, Appeal, and Cassation, were established, amended as to powers and status, or abolished, as current business or economy or changed circumstances might dictate. The courts of the 'Alawi province and the Jabal were separated from, or reintegrated with, the Syrian according to the interstatal constitutional position of the time;

[1] The Conseil Supérieur de la Magistrature (for judges): the Conseil de Discipline (for other officials): and the Tribunal Militaire (for gendarmes).

those of Syria and the Lebanon were mutually separate from the first.

In all the States great efforts were made, in accordance with the conviction and zeal of French lawyers, to raise judicial standards from the wretchedly low level prevailing in 1918–20 to one of higher efficiency and honesty. To this end judicial personnel were constantly reviewed, most (but never, in outstations, quite all) of the more dubious or uninstructed Turkish-type judges and magistrates were removed, and a professionally qualified personnel employed. Some efficiency was infused into Execution Departments. Courts everywhere were progressively better housed, equipped, and staffed than ever before, and could on the whole claim popular confidence. Relations between the French and local legal personnel were generally satisfactory, with some undercurrent of resentment at the numbers and higher status of the former, and their unlimited rights of inspection and tuition: rights which seemed, after 1936, to be in process of curtailment, with slightly diminishing numbers of Frenchmen employed and a lessened authority in the selection of personnel—and in combating political infiltration. If there was still by 1940 too much delay and obstruction, undue insistence on procedural niceties, and at times denial of justice through personal pressures or mere corruption, these defects do not deprive the system as a whole, and its practical working, of a claim to favourable judgement as a French contribution of fundamental value. The French judicial personnel employed by the States were generally of high quality.

Difficulties encountered over the administration of the Awqaf resembled those met in the field of personal-status jurisdiction: in effect, a clash between would-be increased efficiency and good sense on the one hand, and politically-infused traditionalism on the other. The system of Courts, Commissions, and Controller established in 1921 (p. 137) for the extremely widespread and important[1] Muslim Awqaf was in practice little obstructed by the background of resentment at ultimate non-Muslim control. It worked well, with excellent progress in administrative reform and the assertion of rights, and in safeguarding and restoring Awqaf properties—and building new—until the erection of the political units of Syria into separate States with their own Constitutions, in 1930, called for a revised system which would conform to the new statal basis. The Government of Lebanon accepted, that of Syria refused, new regulations tying the Waqf administration to

[1] In 1934 some 4,000 Waqfs existed, estimated to be worth 500 million francs: of these about one-fifth were directly administered by the established authority, the rest by supervised or unsupervised trustees. Mosque and connected staff numbered 5,000, total beneficiaries up to 80,000.

secular machinery; a four-year period of protest, and an uneasy temporary régime, revealed both the sensitive political implications of the situation and the vested interests involved. The National Bloc based strong nationalist propaganda on the alleged attempt by foreigners, or the secular state, to control the Awqaf, which they were eager to use as a political makeweight. Agitation against the new and seemingly unexceptionable law of 1934 continued, with refusal in Syria to set up the necessary regional Councils and repudiation of all government control, until the return of the Bloc to power in 1937. Thereafter it ceased, and the system of State control prevailed, in which the French had no part save one of making representations to the State as such. In spite of these controversies, and in spite of some sad cases of detected corruption, the two decades under review saw an immense improvement in the administration and finances of the Waqf properties, a more enlightened conception of the obligations involved, and a diversion of surplus funds to socially useful works of charity and teaching. Freedom was secured, for the first time, for the Druzes and Nuṣayris to administer their own Awqaf. The properties of the Christian communities remained in their own control without disturbance.

In the field of public finance the French contribution, based upon foundations laid in the earliest days of the Mandate (pp. 133 f.), was of fundamental value, but unspectacular and easily taken for granted. It took five forms. The first of these was the direct local expenditure by the French treasury on the Army, the High Commission and its services, certain educational work, refugee resettlement, and other items. Secondly, the financial and economic services of the High Commission busied themselves ceaselessly with the planning, co-ordination, and direction of all financial aspects of the States' administration, and with the preparation of financial legislation. Thirdly, the greatest of the revenue-producing departments, that of Customs, formed part of the French-administered Common Interests. Fourthly, the service and ultimate extinction of the Ottoman Public Debt owed much to French negotiation. And finally French advisers, inspectors, and experts employed by the States were able appreciably to raise standards in the collection of revenue, the control of expenditure, the higher accountancy and audit, the preparation of estimates and the like.

It was unfortunate that, in spite of all these services, the considerable cost of the Mandate to the French (a common theme for left-wing critics in Paris) was little calculated to win Syrian gratitude, since it largely represented money spent on French troops and the High Commission and its officials, from all of which it was the most earnest nationalist dream to be free. This expense meant nevertheless that the defence of the territory, and a substantial part of its officialdom, cost the local tax-payer nothing.[1] Of important French educational, cultural, and charitable institutions and works the same was true; but to pay for the normal civil government of the mandated territory neither was nor could be expected to be any part of French policy. The currency remained that whose institution an earlier page has described (p. 98), with the Banque de Syrie et du Grand Liban enjoying its note-issue monopoly.[2] The continued attachment of the Syro-Lebanese pound to the fluctuating and depreciating franc involved inconvenience and loss to the local States and public, and was among the commonest themes of criticism; but to the French finance (or political) authorities any loosening of this connexion was, rightly or wrongly, unthinkable.

The work of the numerous French financial and economic staffs, at Beirut or elsewhere, was necessarily carried out in closest collaboration with local colleagues, and the respective contributions of each are hardly assessable; in both Syria and Lebanon able finance officials were not uncommon,[3] and the improvement and modernization of the whole fiscal system was the objective of all. In effect, this ambition was, within limits, largely achieved; a fair machinery of control and supervision was instituted, abuses grew fewer, Turkish eccentricities were eliminated, and substantial uniformity was established between all areas, including the old Mount Lebanon. By constant, and in bad years intensified, economy the budgets of all States were kept in balance, at the cost of perpetuating some undesirable practices in the field of revenue assessment, and of firmly limiting the pace of possible development in beneficent State activity. A main contribution to revenue was that of the interstatal, French-administered Customs Department, whose net receipts[4] continued to be divided annually between the States, under carefully weighted formulae which no State thought just to itself.[5] Customs rates, which differentiated between members and non-members of the League of Nations,[6]

[1] The cost of the Armée du Levant ranged from fr. 160–325 m. a year, rising or falling according to the situation. The annual subvention to the *troupes spéciales* was, until 1937, fr. 15 m. The 'civil expenses of the Mandate', paid by the French Ministry of Foreign Affairs, ranged from fr. 10–15 m. a year.

[2] The note issue reached, in 1939, fr. 710 m. The royalty paid by the Bank to the local Governments was of the order of fr. 7 m. a year. The Bank had in 1920 eight, and in 1939 sixteen branches.

[3] Lebanese and Syrians had for years played a distinguished part in Egyptian and Sudanese finance administration, as well as in commerce.

[4] Customs net receipts, fr. 60 m. in 1921, reached 157 m. in 1936, 235 m. in 1938.

[5] Lebanon received 43 per cent., Syria with the lesser States 53 per cent. A proportion was retained by the Common Interests for possible later allocation.

[6] It was a subject of complaint that the lower Customs rates afforded by Syria and Lebanon to League member-states were not reciprocated. The United States ranked as a League member.

were raised at need to provide more revenue during the prolonged depression of 1929 to 1934, and to protect local industries; they were lowered in the case of necessary materials for the latter, and in that of essential foodstuffs. Specific rates were increasingly substituted for *ad valorem*, tariffs and procedure were simplified, Customs personnel more carefully chosen, corruption largely eliminated. Experts from the French Customs Service were imported, the organization was constantly reviewed, and 'Free Zones' at ports were instituted to encourage transit. Customs agreements were made, reviewed, discontinued, or renewed with Egypt, Turkey, 'Iraq, Transjordan, Palestine, and Najd. Smuggling was limited, with Gendarmerie and frontier guard assistance, but never wholly suppressed; ubiquitous sailing-craft and wide land frontiers prevented this. Syro-Lebanese discussions during 1937–8 on the institution of separate national Customs administrations, which the new Treaties would necessitate, were unproductive—and proved to be sadly premature.

The policy of the Customs Department, which was careful to give no preference to French merchandise as such, can fairly claim to have been inspired by the interests of the mandated territories, and was formed after some show of local consultation through the Conference of the Common Interests. The common complaint that Customs policy was insufficiently helpful to, or protective of, local manufactures was, under the terms of the Mandate, mainly beyond the power of the Administration to satisfy, and little better could have been done by a Syro-Lebanese combined department, the only feasible alternative—though not one ever seriously considered—to the complete French administration actually established. It remains, however, striking that the States were allowed so little voice in the management of one of their greatest sources of revenue, which they were by no means unqualified to administer. Certain other departments—those of the Control of Concessionary Companies, of Quarantine, and of Patents and Royalties—had their own budgets, and were entirely French-administered.

Direct taxation (pp. 134 f.) contributed even more to the States' budgets than did the Customs, even though reductions, especially in land-revenue demands, were commonly made in years of scarcity, and the whole system could not emerge in a day from the confusions, injustices, and ineptitudes of the Turkish régime; statistical data, a trained corps of officials, and a willing public were all lacking. Nevertheless, in default of a complete rebasing of direct taxation upon lines less regressive and less favourable to the rich, fair progress rather than revolutionary change was made throughout the field by elimination, adaptation, and modification of existing taxes. It included the substitution of fixed assessments for annual (and intolerably capricious) estimations, or tax-farming, as the basis of tithe collection: simplification and recasting of the tax on buildings: unification of rates and better administration of the animal tax: improved procedures in the trades' and professional tax (*tamattu'*), and the correction of abuses in the road tax. The important tobacco industry had since 1884 been the object of the Régie Co-intéressée monopoly (p. 134); and this, its relations with the Ottoman Public Debt and with the States themselves at last settled by a series of compromises, continued after 1926 to exercise its rights and to pay considerable sums to the State treasuries. The monopoly, lapsing in 1930, was succeeded by the *banderole* system whereby the growing and manufacture of tobacco were free but licensed, and a consumption tax was collected by the *banderole* (adhesive label) attached to the package in the factory. But the evils arising from unrestricted cultivation, unsaleable crops, and a glutted market forced a return in 1935 to the earlier system, and a new, locally-constituted Régie assumed the monopoly upon terms believed to safeguard the livelihood of those concerned in the industry, and beneficial to the States. It took over all existing factories and stores, employed the same workers, developed modern techniques, and weathered the storms of initial Maronite opposition.

The Public Debt itself, its incidence on the States fixed in final detail in 1929, proved far less of a burden than could be feared. Its allocated revenues (p. 18) considerably exceeded the amounts required for its own service, and the surplus was in part paid to the States, in part used for liquidating the debt itself by buying bonds[1] in the open market. The latter process was completed in 1933, when the States were able to free themselves[2] finally from its demands. They were burdened thereafter by no national Debt, and the valuable revenues of the Ottoman Debt became their own.

The system for providing armed forces for the territory, evolved in the early years of the Mandate (pp. 137–8), was applied with complete continuity. It was efficient, it stood for the security of the country, and it burdened the local treasuries with only part of the cost; nevertheless it was (like so much of the French effort) open to the charge that so complete a foreign control of the armed forces was damaging both to the *amour-propre* of the Syrians and to their chance of gaining experience in a field which must necessarily be theirs in post-mandatory days. That part of the French Army itself which it was found convenient[3] to station in the

1 An identical procedure was adopted in 'Iraq.
2 The equivalent of fr. 172 m. had been paid in all.
3 The cost was only marginally higher than in France or North Africa.

territory—the Armée du Levant—continued to be composed, trained, equipped, and commanded on the lines shown on an earlier page (pp. 137–8). Its strength, greatly increased for the crisis of 1925–7, was thereafter reduced, and again augmented in 1939. Military depots and workshops expanded, the discipline and appearance of units were generally creditable, and their equipment (not, usually, of the latest models) was progressively modernized. The important component of black colonial troops continued to be highly offensive to local feeling; at no time, indeed, did the military authorities—an element generally more powerful in French policy than, in corresponding circumstances, in British—show more than a minimum of sympathy towards Syrian susceptibilities or political aspirations, and they themselves were likely to gain from their own Regular Army *confrères*, the Special Service Officers, but a strange and partial picture of the local world. Nevertheless, and although in the period 1927–40 calls for local military support were few, the services of the Armée du Levant in providing an essential ultimate bulwark of law and order, are undeniable; and many officers and units of high quality, including those of the Aviation, served in Syria.

The locally-raised 'auxiliary troops' were reinforced during 1925–7 by various hastily-formed bodies of mobile or frontier guards and other *troupes supplétives* which, for fifteen years thereafter, were to form a characteristic element in the Army of the Levant. Recruitment was voluntary and derived largely from the Circassians, Armenians, and other minorities. The constituent units and Order of Battle were constantly reviewed, the equipment improved with increasing mechanization. The strength of the *troupes spéciales* varied from 9,500 in 1930 to some 14,000 in the middle 1930's. Discipline was, except under severe stresses, generally satisfactory, though the officer class was considered mediocre in quality and over-inclined to an interest in politics. The value of the Corps depended, it was considered, upon the completeness of its French *encadrement*. A considerable number of French officers and other ranks were employed, though the former were after 1931 outnumbered (never outranked) by local brother-officers;[1] the senior commands were French throughout. The cost was born by the surplus made available to the States by way of the Common Interests. Except for the Chasseurs Libanais, units were liable for service in any area and they were in fact frequently called to reinforce police action in civil disturbance, tribal or highway crime, frontier tension, or election disorder. The *troupes spéciales*

[1] In 1930, there were 141 French officers, and 295 other ranks: in 1936, 100 and 278 respectively. Syrian officers increased from 59 in 1927 to 201 in 1936.

seemed in 1937–8 likely to form the basis of the Syrian and Lebanese armies, of which the Treaties would permit the formation; their control was, in the last days of the Mandate, destined to provide a bone of bitter contention between France and the two republics.

Of the Gendarmerie, which except in military crisis remained at the disposal of the local Governments, little need be added to the account given earlier (p. 138). Their organization conformed strictly to that of the administrative units (State headquarters, sanjaqs, qaḍhas), within which French missions, inspectors, and executive officers worked to raise efficiency. In the bad days of 1925–6 the force proved unreliable, and was on other occasions doubtfully loyal; conscious of less devotion to the French, and closer ties with its own public, than the largely non-nationalist *troupes spéciales*, the Gendarmerie had also greater temptations to malpractice. Their duties, besides those connected with the suppression of crime and disorder, came to include also Customs and tobacco-monopoly work, care of the prisons, provision of semi-military mobile forces, and road-traffic duties otherwise than in main towns. Their duties were thus manifold, their activity incessant, their role vital to the maintenance of Government; and the part played by French personnel in their training and performance was responsible both for an important improvement in standard—a standard remote from that of Turkish days and, no doubt, from what any mandateless régime would have achieved—and for the misfortune of a divided loyalty.

The small urban Police forces (p. 138) retained an important or dominant French element. Apart from their other duties in the field of crime and administration, they formed the executive arm of the all-French Sûreté Générale (p. 138). Of the latter, many of the routine functions were a normal part of modern administration, and could not well, in some cases, have been left at this period to unaided Syrian or Lebanese hands; but many wholly innocent foreign residents in, or visitors to, Syria will recall also the almost morbid suspicion with which they felt themselves to be viewed by the Sûreté.[1] In the 1930's the latter kept careful watch on the increasing Communist propaganda, and on the persistent traffic in drugs and vice.

Typical of French inspiration and supervision at their best was the initial transformation, and the later continuous improvement, of a prisons service bequeathed by the Turks in conditions of sordid primitiveness. Although funds did not permit replacement

[1] The present writer, totally innocent of any anti-French conduct or attitude, notes that according to Kirk (*The Middle East in the War*, p. 104), 'an extensive and imaginative dossier of Brigadier Longrigg's activities over many years' was found in the Beirut archives in 1941.

of all, or nearly all, old and unsuitable premises, it was possible to build a number of new jails, to improve others, and to develop the administration on modern lines by segregation of the sexes, suitable discipline, care of juvenile offenders, regularized feeding and equipment, sanitary measures, and, in the large central jails, selected prison industries. In the Lebanon in 1930, and in Syria in 1933, all prison duties were assured by the Gendarmerie.

2. ECONOMICS UNDER THE MANDATE

It has been fashionable, in the xenophobic Syria of the 1950's to belittle or traduce the part played by France in the economic and material development of the territory during the two inter-war decades: an attitude based largely, however, on misrepresentation, or ignorance, of the facts. No conceivable Mandatory could, in a few years, have endowed the country with non-existent sources of wealth; no statal authority can, with whatever goodwill, control all economic forces (least of all those of world-wide extension) nor the fiscal policies of foreign countries; and grandiose schemes for immediate development by French agency, or for basic changes in local society, would have been more condemned than applauded, as sure signs of 'imperialist' policy, while France herself was far from being a rich country, whose gifts or loans to her mandated territories could be limitless. But such part as her representatives were able, by prudent guidance of economic policy, to play in increasing prosperity was by any standards a creditable part, and foundations laid during this period were used with great advantage by—were, indeed, indispensable to—the independent States of Syria and Lebanon after 1945. Though local politicians and officials, and the public, had evidently a share in framing and executing economic policy, the closeness of French control compels the observer to ascribe to the latter the dominant share of resulting credit or discredit.

The territory, incurring no foreign or domestic debt, remained humbly and sometimes precariously viable, and was capable of supporting a generally, though but slightly, higher standard of life than in the preceding period. Its sources of wealth remained those traditional to it—agriculture, with stockbreeding, fish, forests, and minor natural resources: small-scale industry: commerce and commercial services: and a variety of valuable 'invisibles'. In connexion with each of these the mandatory Power, in consultation with the more prudent local opinion, took such progressive or ameliorative steps as seemed possible.

Foreign trade, which showed yearly a persistent if fluctuating visible adverse balance, was aided by such measures as could be devised. Agreements covering Customs rates, transit, and conditions of trade were made with foreign neighbours. A background of banking,[1] insurance, and (not very effective) Chambers of Commerce was provided, modernizing thereby the long-traditional financial equipment of the country. The disadvantage of the territories' fragmented structure was minimized by a single currency, Customs system, and commercial code, and the absence of internal barriers; the impediment to the old trade routes (to Anatolia, southern Syria, Arabia, Egypt, 'Iraq) must be faced as an abiding handicap. Harbours, roads, and telecommunications were everywhere improved, 'free zones' demarcated at ports, desert routes developed, transit facilities[2] offered. The metric system was introduced, as effectively as local conservatism allowed. The Customs tariff was almost annually amended as an instrument to assist trade and protect industry. New outlets for local exports were continuously sought, whether in the countries which had traditionally traded with the Levant—Great Britain, France, Italy, the United States, Belgium, Germany, Egypt, Greece, Persia, Rumania—or in those, notably Turkey, Palestine, Transjordan, Najd, and 'Iraq, which had but recently become foreign countries, or in such newcomers to the scene as Japan; but most of those named preferred the role of supplier to that of purchaser. Imports covered, as they had always done, the whole range of commodities which the country needed but could not produce, and these were increased by new needs grown from changing times, such as motor cars, machinery, and modern-type clothing. Exports were mainly those long familiar—animals and animal products (skins and wool), grain, fruit, silk, olive oil, vegetables, cotton, and some contribution of local manufactures. The processes of import-export survived creditably the disturbed period of 1925–6, the long-drawn depression of 1928 to 1935 (in which Syria–Lebanon fared less badly than countries with a greater industrial and economic superstructure), the lowered purchasing power of, and the adverse restrictions applied by, other countries, the frequent political disorders, and the damaging devaluation of the franc. It was possible to claim in 1939 that the value of exports had been 70 million francs in 1921, and 892 million in 1938: and of imports, 600 million in 1921 and 1,687 million in 1938. Hopes for a diminution of the adverse balances (partially realized from 1931 to 1937) were based on greater local self-sufficiency in manufactured

[1] Besides numerous local 'banks', discount houses, and money-lenders, there were in 1936 three French banks in addition to the official Banque de Syrie, one Italian, and one Egypto-Syrian.

[2] During the 1930's fully one-third of all foreign trade of Syria–Lebanon was transit trade, notably outwards in carpets, silk, and fruit, and inwards in cotton goods, vehicles, and machinery.

goods, and a greater export of these and of agricultural produce.

The 'invisible exports'[1] which, and which alone, meanwhile rendered the territory viable, were the remittances from *émigrés* (of which the decrease during the early 1930's was serious), the local expenditure by French civil and military personnel and departments, foreign funds received for refugee relief and settlement, foreign missions and educational institutions, the tourist and pilgrim trade, the disbursements by industrial concerns which operated in but took no profit from the territory,[2] the credits granted (sometimes too optimistically) by foreign concerns or Governments,[3] and the receipts from local commercial agencies and services. All of these items, except the first and last mentioned, were substantially assisted by the French presence.

In the industrial field, the humble cottage or workshop industries of the early nineteenth century were far from satisfying the modern-minded among local planners and men of business, even after the partial recovery of these crafts from their near-destruction in the period 1914–18. Increasing and modernized industrialization appeared to many progressive citizens a desirable goal on grounds of national *amour-propre*, of greater economic self-sufficiency, of an improved trade balance—and of potential personal fortunes to be made; and the movement was supported, within the limits of prudence, by French policy. The period witnessed first a revival, then a serious decline, than a slight recovery, of the old-type industries, and notably those of silk growing, spinning, and weaving. This typically Lebanese activity was the object of every care by the French, at each stage from mulberry planting to marketing the finished products; preferential rates were allowed in Customs and taxation, and improved methods advocated and demonstrated in each branch of sericulture by a special service under the High Commission;[4] but the competition of foreign goods (including artificial silk) and modern factories was too strong, prices ran unfavourably, tastes had changed. The output dropped year by year, mulberry trees were uprooted; and by the end of the period, when a slight recovery occurred, Lebanese and 'Alawi silk production, and the cottage industry dependent on it, had to the general (including the French) regret found but the humblest local level of survival. The same was true in large measure of the other traditional folk industries of the territory—leather-work, distilling, metal work,

[1] They were believed in 1935 to amount to some fr. 350 m. a year.

[2] Notably, of course, the construction, transit, and loading operations of the 'Iraq Petroleum Company.

[3] For instance, by Italian concerns, for political reasons, in the 1930's.

[4] The not uncommon charge that 'the French killed the Lebanese industry in the interests of that of Lyons' is grossly untrue.

tanning, tile and brick-making, woodwork, milling, soap making, handloom weaving, carpets, and lace-work; thanks to the new trade-barriers, to changes of fashion and to higher costs, these could maintain themselves only as providing a living, or part of one, to persons otherwise unemployed, but could no longer fill more than a lowly economic function, nor hope to compete with modern mechanized and capitalized production. The old workshops and presses of the inland Syrian towns diminished year by year in activity and output. Their export market was no more, their present outlets were to the poor and rustic, or to tourists; and it seemed in 1939 that no brighter future awaited them.

In compensation, however, the period witnessed another and more vigorous growth, that of the modern-type industry which has since 1945 developed so rapidly that its foundations and careful fostering in the period 1928–40 are often forgotten. It took three forms: the partial modernizing (usually with mechanical power) and extension of older workshops, the erection of new factories to produce the same or similar articles[1] better and more cheaply, and the initiation, on modern or semi-modern lines, of industries[2] new to the territory. In each case the local Governments, under French prompting, legislated for assistance to the infant enterprises by Customs franchise on their plant and necessities, and often (within permissible limits) by higher duties on rival foreign products. Thus, with little co-ordination as between the two[3] States, and with a number of failures due to imprudence or error, but well assisted by the cheapness of labour and of such raw materials as existed and by the capital available to rich returned *émigrés*, there came into existence a considerable variety of not unpromising semi-modern—and at times entirely modern—industry, using local raw materials where these existed (olive oil, silk, cotton, leather, fruits, barley), or importing where they did not. If the body of industrial workers thus employed was numerically small, the capital relatively trifling, and the output capable of supplying but a fraction of local needs and a still more exiguous share of exports, yet an important beginning had been made, much thought and planning shrewdly devoted, and experience gained of both positive and negative value. Nothing could be less true than the common belief that Syro-Lebanese modern industry dates only from the post-Mandate period, or that

[1] For instance, in weaving (with power-looms, and to foreign designs), tanning, rope making, distilling, soap making, silk spinning, flour milling, shoemaking, and asphalt working.

[2] Cotton spinning, cement, matches, hosiery, and knitted goods, machine-made cigarettes, beer, canned fruits and other foods, sweets, brushes, perfumes, cloths and fabrics in silk, cotton, and wool.

[3] There was no industry of this type (except one ginnery) in the 'Alawi sanjaq, none in the Jabal al-Duruz.

the French, even though their own nationals took little part in such investment, failed to give its earliest days careful and effective fostering.[1] The direct contribution of refugee Armenian artisans, and the indirect influence of Jewish-immigrant example in Palestine, was not negligible; and many of the founders and directors of the new industries were men of great capacity and enterprise.

Electrical and mechanical power for industry, as well as for the public services, was substantially but still inadequately developed in this period. Hydro-electric power was used at certain points, though less than the favourable contour of water-courses (notably in the Lebanon) might have indicated; elsewhere—that is, over nine-tenths of the field—Diesel plant was installed. Pre-existing installations at main cities were modernized and extended; small new plants were established and could serve industry at a score of towns and even villages hitherto lacking this resource. But the cost of installation and connected works was high, cheap fuel unavailable, the consuming public limited, profits doubtful; and progress was correspondingly slow.

Apart from agricultural products, the raw materials for industry or produce for export could not by any efforts be brought to a considerable level. In spite of modernized mining legislation, and the issue impartially to French, foreign, or local concerns[2] of licences to explore and exploit a wide variety of minerals, no deposits even of minor importance were discovered; as the sole exception, a concession was given for the interesting asphalt deposits in the Ladhqiya area, and these, under French enterprise,[3] were made to contribute to road-making, building, and export. Sea fishing and the recovery of sponges, though they attracted a slight foreign (Italian and Greek) interest and a half-dozen of modern craft, and though experts were brought from France to study and advise, were prosecuted on a small and barely profitable scale, and supported but a few score of workers; the profits, it was alleged, went mainly to middlemen. The forests of the territory (p. 35), an ancient and still a potential source of wealth, lacked all important improvement or exploitation in these years, and this in spite of vigorous French propaganda and some

[1] The Davidson Mission of April–May 1946, records (p. 33 of its *Report*) that it had been informed that 'one of the principal reasons for the bitterness of feeling against France . . . was the alleged suppression of Syrian industry . . . by the French authorities in order to reduce competition with the industries of France'. This suppression did not occur.

[2] Application for mining rights were made directly to, and scrutinized by, the concerned service in the High Commission, but the licences were issued by the States.

[3] Control of the Asphalt Company was later acquired by the 'Iraq Petroleum Company, but its French management and personnel persisted.

tangible efforts.[1] The forests, long deteriorated to the point of ruin, were at least demarcated, the planting of small areas was carried out, and 'natural reafforestation' encouraged elsewhere with the establishment of nurseries, and the formation of a small corps of forest guards. A comprehensive Forest Code was issued in 1935, rules were made (but little observed) for fire precaution and the prohibition of charcoal-making and goat grazing, and the foundation was announced of a benevolent society of 'Friends of the Trees'. But for major operations there was little capital, scanty public interest, no hope of immediate profit, and a resentful conservatism among the local villagers. Only in the 'Alawi country, part of Lebanon, and the Alexandretta sanjaq was anything visible accomplished, and there not much; but without a strong executive intervention and large capital expenditure the Mandatory could scarcely have done more.

The search for mineral oil, in terms of a new Mining Law of 1933 (revised in 1936) was carried out by the 'Iraq Petroleum Company[2] in and after 1933, and covered wide areas of Syria, the Alexandretta sanjaq, and Lebanon. After early geological exploration and test-drilling a 'blanket' concession for five-sixths of Syria was granted in 1938:[3] but a prolonged and costly drilling campaign failed, then or later, to reveal commercial deposits.[4] The need for overland transit of 'Iraqi oil from Kirkuk to the Mediterranean led, however, to the construction in 1932–4 by the same Company (with its nearly one-quarter French shareholding) of a 12-inch pipeline across Syria and Lebanon to a terminal tank farm, loading point, and operating base at Tripoli. Three main pumping-stations and a stores depot were in Syrian territory, the terminal and management in Lebanon. Construction of this, by far the greatest industrial and engineering work in the territory, employed for a time some 5,000 men of all grades and skills: its subsequent maintenance, about half that number. Although the Company's transit concessions, dating from 1931,[5] provided for

[1] It is unhappily characteristic that a Syrian Government spokesman, writing in 1954, can speak of 'the intentional negligence of forestry by the French mandatory authorities, who did not protect forest trees' (*Syria,* vol. II, p. 48). It was, on the contrary, the local public which resisted control, and the local Governments which showed scant interest.

[2] In the guise, after July 1936, of Petroleum Concessions (Syria and Lebanon) Ltd.; later, a separate company was formed for each State. The concession for Syria was held, accordingly, by the Syria Petroleum Company.

[3] Ratified in 1940. Alexandretta was excluded, and the licences obtained there in 1933–7 lapsed in 1939. In Lebanon, licences were obtained but no 'blanket' concession.

[4] Details of oil operations in Syria and Lebanon, and of the Concessionaires, is available in the present writer's *Oil in the Middle East* (London, 1954), pp. 76 ff.

[5] But for French pressure *ad hoc,* the line would no doubt, like its southern twin, have been designed to traverse Transjordan and Palestine, and avoid Syria–Lebanon altogether.

no cash payments to the local Governments, the economic benefits of the enterprise in employment, land purchase, local contracts, and expenditure were important, and the opening up of desert routes, water points, and telecommunications was notably advanced. The contribution by French geologists to the study of the Levant States, and of French military cartographers from 1925 onwards to its mapping, was of high value.

The work of the Mandatory at its best is exemplified by the important development of communications during these years, with all that these signified in the fields of industry, trade, agriculture, and society. The sea ports of the territory, whose administration and staffing involved the specialized services of the High Commission, the local authorities, and the original concessionaire companies (pp. 32 f.), were all, to a greater or less degree, enlarged and modernized. At Beirut a major improvement scheme involving a wider and deeper anchorage area, improved jetty space, sheds, and facilities, was achieved in 1937, and a further phase initiated; at Tripoli its natural advantages were enhanced by breakwater protection works; at Ladhqiya a minor work of dredging and construction, and at Alexandretta one of reclamation, were carried out. At lesser ports, heavily sand-silted, protection for small craft was improved. The lighthouses were maintained under their original concessionaire, and new lights were added. The considerable local sailing fleet, of which half was based on Arwad Island, presented many problems of discipline and of safety, especially after the introduction of motor craft, and called for regulations which the illiterate captains habitually ignored. Steamship traffic, in which the lines of French, Italian, British, and many lesser owners (but no local enterprises) participated, was distributed between the four ports already mentioned, Beirut taking by far the largest share.

The road system was, as far as skill and goodwill could prevail over the chronic shortage of funds, brought to a level of excellence entirely new to the territory, and well in advance of any of its neighbours. The phenomenal increase of wheeled traffic[1] was met by hundreds of miles[2] of newly-constructed and usually asphalted roads of high standard, scores of passable tracks, and many greater or smaller bridges. Many areas were given road access for the first time, and the importance of omnibus and lorry traffic was recognized. Reliable highways joined all main centres, and local and village authorities were helped in their parochial plans by grants, and by the permitted use of volunteer labour. The

[1] Motor vehicles increased between 1919 and 1939 from 100 to 11,000.

[2] It was claimed that 2,900 km. of 'made' roads existed in 1939, against 700 in 1920: and 6,800 km. of passable tracks, against 600.

most spectacular achievement, that of the trans-desert Damascus–Baghdad motor service, was due first to the initiative of two New Zealanders (the Nairn brothers), aided by the practical support of the High Commissioner and of the Syrian and 'Iraqi Governments. Established in 1923, the British-registered Nairn Company absorbed a local imitator three years later, survived the bad days of the Druze rebellion with a temporary change of route, built a mid-desert hotel and depot at Ruṭba (in 'Iraq) in 1927, developed full maintenance services for its specially-designed vehicles, and easily retained the primacy among rival local companies which sprang up. The service represented a new element in Middle Eastern travel and mail carrying.

The railway system of the territory was extended after 1918 only by a single addition—the prolongation in 1935, by the use of funds of the Common Interests, of the Baghdad Railway from Niṣibin (in Turkey) to the 'Iraq frontier. The main line east of Adana was rehabilitated after 1921 by Franco-Turkish agency, the sections within Syria being entrusted by the High Commissioner to a French company (Cilicie-Nord-Syrie), which restored and operated them for ten years in collaboration with the Turkish state-owned B.A.N.P. (Bozanti-Adana-Niṣibin et Prolongements). After a comprehensive agreement with the Turks in October 1932, a new *modus vivendi* was reached, with the hope (not always realized) of better collaboration; the Syrian sections were thereafter placed under the management of the D.H.P. Company (p. 33), as had been (p. 145) the Ḥijaz Railway since 1924. The coastal line from Palestine to Tripoli, often advocated, was never built, nor those sometimes projected to link Syria with 'Iraq and Persia. The short line Beirut–Ma'malatayn was unextended. All existing lines were maintained, improved, modernized; rail-cars were added, and a complementary road service[1] established. Wagons-lit facilities became available and a through-service from Europe to Aleppo, Rayaq, and the 'Iraq frontier was introduced; from the latter a road service took passengers to join the 'Iraq Railways system at Mosul.[2] The Syro-Lebanese railway system managed, except in years of scantiest harvests, to make a modest profit, sustaining serious competition from road traffic and perforce varying its own freight rates accordingly.

The telegraph and postal services called not for re-erection on Turkish foundations, but for entire reinitiation. This was done, under French guidance and largely French execution. Each State had its own department for these communications, the whole

[1] The Société Autoroutière du Levant. It was controlled after 1931 by the Régie Générale, which also controlled the railway companies.
[2] The section Tall Kochek–Mosul was completed in 1939.

being co-ordinated and directed by an Inspectorate General under the High Commission. Syria and Lebanon both became members of the Postal Union. Posts both internal and external reached and maintained a reasonable standard,[1] with notable development towards 'Iraq, Persia, and the East by way of the desert motor route, and to the Far East by air. A telegraph and telephone system of modern construction was erected to cover the territory, and yearly increased its foreign connexions.[2] The need for wireless communication was met by a seventy-five-year concession given to, and the station erected near Beirut in 1922 by, the Radio-Orient Company. Civil aviation, a phenomenon of limitless future, appeared in the early 1930's, and could be linked with the construction of military airports at Nayrab (Aleppo), Mazza (Damascus), and Rayaq, and a sea-plane station and landing ground at Tripoli. To these the first Beirut airport was added in 1939. Upper-class Lebanese and Syrians showed an immediate air-mindedness, and were conscious of possessing a territory centrally placed for the air routes of the hemisphere. Meanwhile, all air enterprise was French.

The last place in the present section has been kept for the most widespread and most productive of all the territory's resources in this or any age, that of agriculture: the occupation and the livelihood of the great majority of the inhabitants, and one in which progress, or stagnation, must have the greatest social and economic effects. That this resource was, for easily assignable reasons, underdeveloped in extent, method, quality, and productivity in the early years of the century, has been indicated on previous pages (pp. 35–7); what, if anything, was to be the contribution of the French Mandatory in so all-important a field?

The task of improvement involved factors of climate and natural conditions, of basis economics, of deep-rooted vested interests, and of present conservatism.[3] It was not possible for French goodwill, science, or persistence, fundamentally to alter the rainfall or the soil of Syria, the minds of its inhabitants, or the structure of its society or land system; the latter, indeed, was intimately connected with the ascendancy of the social and political classes on which any local Government must, at that stage, depend. No effort made in the territory could offset falls in world prices, nor adverse currency fluctuations, nor the attitudes of foreign countries towards the purchase of Syrian produce. French or other foreign capital could not (even if openings awaited it) be easily

[1] In 1919, 68 post offices existed, in 1939, 411.

[2] A submarine line Beirut–Tunis–Marseilles was completed by the French Government in 1938.

[3] Admirably summarized by Weulersse, p. 313, as 'cet immobilisme agressif des campagnes, accrochées au passé'.

attracted to a country so insecure, and the catastrophic error (as it would have been) of settling French *colons* in the territory was not seriously considered. It was, therefore, within a strictly local and limited sphere that the improvement of agriculture was possible or was attempted. The activity deployed belonged to the fields of land tenure, of rural poverty, of irrigation (sole solution for the problem of precarious, inadequate rainfall), of crop types and qualities, and of farming methods and facilities.

In the cadastral settlement of the territory which the French initiated, by contract with a privately-owned Régie de Cadastre,[1] their objectives were the bestowal of greater security of tenure, the avoidance of land disputes, the provision of pledgeable assets upon which agricultural credit could be based, the consolidation of viable units of holding, and an improved basis for land taxation. The Cadastre itself proceeded by triangulation, topographical and then cadastral survey, delimitation of plots, definition of ownership (aided by special Commissions, followed by *juges immobiliers*), and registration; and on this basis new land registers, a new Land Code (in 1930), and a new system of title replacing the old Tapu system and the qadha *daftarkhanas*, were established. This work, fundamental in importance, represented an immense stride forward from the morass of previous usage: and it had, by 1939, been completed for a high proportion of the cultivable areas.[2] It did not, indeed, abolish the evils of absentee landlordism, nor of crop-sharing, nor of maldistribution; but it established a precise background of rights and delimitation such as to make major reforms ultimately possible, and meanwhile it was accompanied by a considerable break-up of State Domain land to individual ownership (under a hire-purchase system), the regrouping of unworkable plots, and the division into private holdings of *musha'a* (undivided) village lands.

The problem of rural poverty and indebtedness, a fatal obstacle to progress—at times to life itself—in Syrian agriculture, was attacked in various ways, but effectively solved by none. The Agricultural Banks set up in each State in the early 1920's were perennially short of funds, as were the would-be borrowers of security-providing assets, and they could make no really substantial contribution to the provision of much-needed capital. Rural Co-operative Societies were mooted, but made little progress. The commercial banks could lend only to the rich.

[1] Under M. Duraffourd, throughout the period; the High Commission's Services Fonciers provided guidance and co-ordination. The States employed the Duraffourd organization to work within their own boundaries.

[2] By 1939, some 3¼ million hectares had been covered though, for financial reasons, progress had slackened in 1937–9. No part of the Jabal al-Duruz had been cadastrally surveyed.

Loans of cash and seed by the States to the needy were made not uncommonly, but rather as famine relief than as a step in progressive economics. The same was true of occasional indulgences in agricultural taxation or helpful amendments to Customs tariff.

In irrigation, the progress made in the period 1920–40 was on the whole disappointing; yet, with available funds limited always to derisory proportions, and with no basis of hydrographical knowledge until it could be slowly and laboriously acquired, this could scarcely be otherwise. Water rights, which were vested in the States by law in 1926, remained ill ascertained and still productive of frustrating disputes; but a Régie des Études Hydrauliques, set up in 1929 at the expense of the Common Interests, did excellent work for five years in collecting basic data and formulating projects. Substantial improvements were made in certain existing irrigation-systems—those, for instance, of the Damascus oasis, of the Quwayq river at Aleppo, and of the Liṭani. Water-lift on the Orontes and the Euphrates was partly modernized by the introduction of hundreds of mechanical pumps and oil engines. Among larger schemes, the drainage of the 'Amq marshes at Alexandretta was uncompleted, the important Ghab irrigation project on the middle Orontes was mooted but not initiated, the reclamation of Biqa' lands by water from Lake Yamuna was expensively and arduously attempted but could not be brought to completion. The heightening of the Ḥumṣ Lake barrage, and initial canalization from it, was completed in its first phase in 1938, with promise of considerable later development. But no comprehensive plans and (save at Ḥumṣ) no individual works comparable with those carried out in the 'Iraq of the same period were in question.

Much was done, on the other hand, towards the improvement of crops and produce. By import from abroad, by experiment and plant-breeding, in the field of grains, pulses, and fruit crops, attempts were made to find new or improved crop types capable of giving higher quality and yields. Pyrethrum, hemp, sugar-cane, castor, potatoes, buckwheat, and Jerusalem artichokes were among new crops or varieties introduced, and tobacco culture was the subject of close study. Expert investigations on various aspects of rural life were made.[1] A meteorological service was among the activities of the High Commissioner's office. The introduction of American-type (Lone Star) cotton and, in spite of bad years and commercial handicaps, the important extension of this crop were features of great promise; indeed Syria became, in a few years, a

[1] An Institute of Rural Life was founded by the (American) Near East Foundation, and attracted the interest of the American University. Valuable studies were made also by French scholars based on their Institute at Damascus.

considerable cotton grower, to her great profit and the rapid development of the connected industry. A system of grading and improved packing was introduced to aid citrus export. Every encouragement was given, by lightened or remitted Customs duty, to the import of tractors and agricultural machinery, the use of which notably increased. The war on pests and parasites was waged by every means of science and organization. Chambers of Agriculture were founded in the principal cities. If these and similar experiments and achievements, hopeful as they were, could make as yet no great impact on the broadest areas of still primitive and unprogressive Syrian agriculture, the French could claim to have brought benefit to the rural population by better security in desert-fringe areas, by village roads and water-supplies, and by successful war on malaria and eye disease.

In the sphere of stock-breeding and animal products, geographically conterminous with the territory itself, the local Governments and public had the help of a specialized service under the High Commission, of the Veterinary Corps of the French Army, and of such interested private bodies as the Union Ovine Coloniale. There was, as ever, little money to spend, nor could any form of organization have prevailed against the basic obstacles to immediate and major improvement in a sphere of, nevertheless, great potentiality: the obstacles of unforeseeable and ruinous droughts, of a backward and apathetic public, of uncertain demands, tastes, and prices in the export-receiving countries, and of the decline of camel transport. Bedouin and village breeders were helped over bad times, and their own conditions of life ameliorated. Desert and village security gave confidence against raiders and thieves. Commercial diplomacy made the best of foreign marketing. The taxation of animals (whether by direct count or by lump sum) was regulated, and at need remitted. Animal movement, including transit, was controlled. Steps were taken against epidemics of cattle plague, foot-and-mouth disease and other afflictions, and prophylactic measures were enforced. Mechanical shearing was demonstrated. New stock was introduced experimentally to improve strains. The trade in Arab horses was fostered, but it amounted to little.

In the whole of this field of economics, mass livelihood, and communications the French performed, it has been seen, no miracles; such were precluded by lack of money and of time, by the limited co-operation of the educated classes, and the depressing apathy of the masses. How far the Syria and Lebanon of 1939 differed from what might have been their condition if no French or other Mandate had been imposed, is debatable only in the void of hypothesis and imagination; but it is not questionable that in spite of all phases of unpopularity and resistance, continued political unquietness, and defects real or alleged in the French attitude or organization, the good intentions, the higher standards, and the mature experience of the Mandatory had in twenty years contributed in an important degree to the security services, to the administration of justice, to day-to-day administration, to public finance and its many problems, to the land and its products, and to modern forms of communication and industry. In many parts of this wide field the French of a later day can, amid many disappointments, look back with reasonable satisfaction at excellent work accomplished for the Syrians and Lebanese, and the latter can, if they will, recognize in that work the beginnings of much which has persisted, unquestioned and still developing, in the material and governmental life of their independent Statehood.

3. LIFE AND SOCIETY

The striking phenomena of change, modernization, acceleration which marked Syrian society between the world wars—phases of transition far from being uniformly beneficent, and ascribable evidently to many other besides direct French influences—were of necessity far less conspicuous in the tribes and villages of the country than in the larger towns. Village life indeed, except for some visible beginnings of social services, better accessibility, and less capricious or arbitrary acts of the local authorities, was not greatly changed from its traditional appearance, tempo, and atmosphere. Standards of living improved but little, feudal or landlord dominance still prevailed, peasant life remained penurious and unhopeful. In the nomadic and half-settled tribes the sense of changed times was even fainter. The Contrôle Bédouin—with, indeed, desert lore in general—was an especial pride of the Mandatory who, organizing it directly under the Délégué at Damascus, withheld all executive part in it from the Syrian authorities. It managed by its posts, patrols, and in later years its mechanized armament to maintain good order in the desert; the taxation of the tribesmen was at the same time rebased, their direct representation in the Chamber assured, their quarrels composed, their arms controlled, desert water wells dug, seasonal mid-desert schools opened (though but ill supported), and dispensaries made available. But these well-meant measures, of which many would scarce survive the Mandate, could not deeply affect the character, the risks, or the precariousness of desert life. The settlement of nomads in villages made little progress, and the attitude of the intelligentsia and Syrian officialdom to nomadic tribal life and needs remained unsympathetic if not contemptuous.

Rare individuals among the wealthier shaykhs adopted modern ways and succumbed, regrettably, to city attractions.

Though influences even now radiating from the towns and government offices might be destined one day to transform the conditions of rural life, it was meanwhile in the cities themselves that change was already apparent. The medieval vagaries or apathies of municipal government were no longer tolerated; in more than half the townships of the territory an inefficient or corrupt elected town council were deposed in favour of direct rule by government officials, municipal law was recast, local taxation overhauled, and the performance of a wide variety of urban duties was exacted, with varying measures of success. Governmental loans for urban projects were not uncommon. Municipal pride was encouraged, but controlled. Special forms of town council were devised for the *centres d'estivage* and for the capital cities. Largely but not exclusively under French initiative, and always under French control, much was accomplished in town planning, the creation or improvement of streets, parks, and avenues, drainage systems, the control of slaughtering, and in the provision (often by locally-given concession) of town water-supplies, public transport by tramway or bus service, and electric light and power. Such steps, and contributions made by municipalities to school buildings, dispensaries, and orphanages, and more rarely such direct enterprise as the erection of an hotel, combined to transform the material living conditions of some dozens of townships in the Levant States, from the great cities of Aleppo, Damascus, and Beirut to the larger villages newly promoted (as were some dozens during this period) to municipal status. Private enterprise, using but a negligible proportion of funds other than Syrian or Lebanese, was responsible for much house, shop, and hotel building, for industrial and office premises, and for a number of schools and hospital buildings. The Syro-Lebanese cities of 1939 represented—as in varying proportions they were still to do half a generation later—a striking juxtaposition of the ancient traditional fashions and aspects of the Islamic East with those of the most modern West.

The development of tourism and *estivage* by foreign visitors, to an extent far exceeding the scale of before 1914 (p. 33), was an economically as well as a culturally interesting feature of the time. The States themselves, and travel associations formed *ad hoc*, and the agencies of the Mandatory abroad, combined to encourage exploitation of the territories' great natural beauties and interest by wide advertisement, by improving or sometimes creating hotels and access roads, and by the provision of transport and 'attractions'. These efforts were successful; some thousands of tourists from America, Great Britain, Germany, Egypt, France, and elsewhere, from the later 1920's onwards, spent their money annually in the territory. Winter sports in the Lebanon, Anti-Lebanon, Amanus, and the 'Alawi hills attained the scope of a considerable local industry. The benefit of this to the mandated territory was matched by the satisfaction of the *estivants* escaping from the summer heat of Egypt or 'Iraq; and the later years of our present period showed that even world-wide depression, and local disturbances in Palestine, could not seriously affect the profitable traffic.[1]

The age-long movement of emigration from the territory, a movement involving perhaps two-thirds Lebanese, one-third Syrians in terms of the personnel concerned, continued throughout the 1920's, mainly as ever to the United States, Argentina, Brazil, and West Africa. But economic depression in the receiving countries, and the partial closing of their doors, diminished the stream of emigration in the 1930's, and added volume to that of the exiles returning to their original homes; in some years the arrivals well outnumbered the departures. Of those domiciled abroad (estimated at between 300,000 and 500,000 souls, and by great majority Christian) some nine-tenths had taken the nationality of their adopted country. The sharp decrease in the *émigré* remittances homeward—in normal times a substantial invisible export—was serious in the later years of this period. A multitude of personal questions involving the nationality, status, or claims of the *émigré*s throughout the world called for the services of the mandatory Power.

The outward drain of Lebanese-Syrian manpower and talent represented, for a century past, by the persistent emigration movement, which was rendered inevitable by the narrowness of Lebanese conditions, was compensated in some measure during this period by the influx of refugees from Turkey, whose reception and settlement was a substantial task for the mandatory Power and for local resources. To the main influx of Armenians from Cilicia (p. 119) were later added the arrival of Catholic-Christian elements from Turkey to the northern Jazira in the later 1920's, that of the hapless Assyrians from 'Iraq from 1933 to 1938, and of more Armenians from the Alexandretta sanjaq in 1938–9. Funds for the necessary operations of relief for these new (but widely unpopular) citizens were provided by the French Government, by the Refugee Office of the League of Nations, by American, British, and Armenian charitable funds, and by the

[1] From almost negligible beginnings in 1920 (100 tourists, 500 *estivants*) the traffic had by 1939 reached some 16,000 tourists in a year, 19,000 *estivants*, and 1,000 (foreign) skiers.

local States themselves; the main tasks of organization, and the policy of settlement, devolved upon the High Commission. Assyrian settlement, to which 'Iraqi as well as British funds contributed, involved some 12,000 souls; it was arranged by village communities on the Khabur, on lines faithful to their own clan system. Schemes for a new Assyrian home on the middle Orontes, or abroad, came to nothing. In the settlement of Armenians, involving little short of 100,000 immigrants between 1920 and 1940, their establishment in farming villages was an attempted small-scale expedient, and a few hundred could make their way to South America; but the main and protracted task was one of urban housing within Syria–Lebanon, the provision of water, sanitation, food, schools, dispensaries, and orphanages, and the means of employment. With the assistance of devoted charitable workers, mainly French and American (of the Near East Relief Organization), it involved, over ten years, the progressive replacement of sordid shanty-towns by new streets and dwellings, and the absorption of many thousands in the cities of Beirut and Aleppo[1] and, in lesser numbers, the other principal towns. Obstacles lay in the limited finance available, the physical difficulties of settlement, the precarious co-operation of the Armenians themselves, the dislike excited locally by their cheaply offered but highly skilled labour, and by such serious episodes as the attacks on Armenian camps at Damascus in 1925, and the ruinous fire in Beirut in 1933; but by 1939 the back of the task had been broken, and a considerable social work achieved.

In the local industrial world, into which most of the refugees were absorbed, little could, or needed to, be done at this stage towards regulation by law of the conditions of work. Whole-time, part-time, seasonal, or occasional labour was, on the contrary, provided in every field of activity in town or country according to traditional ways impossible to codify or, in practice, to alter. The proportion of workers employed in modern-type factories was negligibly small; and no more was attempted by the Governments or urged by the Mandatory (in spite of some prompting by the Permanent Mandates Commission) than the issue (followed by little practical application) of rudimentary labour codes covering female and child labour, accidents and dismissals. The former and notorious abuses of the system of road-service labour were seen no more after the days of Captain Carbillet. An attempt by the Syrian Government in 1938 to regulate industry from the employers' side led to the formation of professional associations

[1] Figures given in 1937 were of 43,000 settled in Aleppo, 32,000 in Beirut, 8,000 in Damascus, and a few hundred each in Tripoli, Ḥumṣ, Ḥamah, and Sidon.

which, however, proved purely partisan and self-seeking, and made no social contribution of value. The earliest trade unions were those of clerical or commercial workers, or were based on the traditional guilds of the skilled artisans. Certain 'syndicates' formed anew in the early 1930's had little policy but one of crudest strike action, without grasp of the true functions of labour organization.

Far more for the public weal could be achieved by a group of State services which the period saw greatly extended and modernized, and which afforded a strong contrast to those of Turkish times. In this field, that of Health, Quarantine, and Public Assistance, the over-all direction, setting of standards, and inspection were French; the High Commissioner through his Health Service (of which the senior Army medical officer was *ex-officio* the head) controlled the improved and developed Quarantine Service and its sea, air, and land frontier posts, supervised (against strong local opposition) the pilgrim shipping to the Ḥijaz, provided funds from those of the Common Interests for interstatal medical institutions, and supervised refugee movements and their dangers to public health. This service organized the main campaigns against malaria, venereal disease, trachoma, leprosy, and the drug traffic, offered subventions to works or institutions initiated by the local communities and to the medical colleges, co-ordinated charitable works, and gave assistance and direction at many points to the Medical Services of the States.[1] The latter, always frustrated by lack of adequate funds—and in part by the frequent refusal of local doctors to leave the cities—advanced in these years from almost non-existence to respectable proportions and efficiency. They provided a growing number of hospitals, asylums, and dispensaries, supported the Medical School in Damascus University, collaborated with non-governmental institutes and (on payment) shared in their facilities, combated epidemics, and carried out the inspection of water-supplies, bazaars, butcheries, and sanitation. Nevertheless, the sum of such services must have remained quite inadequate to public needs had they not been supplemented in providing hospitals, dispensaries, and orphanages by an important body of private (that is, local community) effort,[2] and by that of French, American, British, Danish, Swiss, Greek, and Italian charitable bodies.[3] Many such institutions reached a high standard, as did

[1] Those of the Jabal al-Duruz were wholly, those of the 'Alawi Territory almost wholly, French administered.

[2] The Syro-Lebanese communities were in 1934 supporting 16 hospitals, 11 dispensaries, 2 sanatoria, 18 orphanages, 4 old peoples' homes.

[3] French charities were in 1934, supporting 39 institutions of the types mentioned in n. 2 above, American 11, British 3, Danish 4, Swiss 3, Italian 8, German 2. The French Red Cross, with local participation, provided in some areas country-side nursing services, and the kindly 'Goutte de Lait' organization for infants.

the well-respected medical school of the American University and that of St. Joseph. In general the dependence of the population upon extra-statal clinical and allied institutions was a striking feature of the territory, and one which, however inevitable at the time, was not without its dangers of impermanence and even of political disruption.

The same was true, in a yet higher degree, of the educational services, a field of high and sensitive interest to public and Mandatory alike. Here also the High Commissioner's specialized Service had an important role to play; it included the direct supervision of all French schools, the authorization of all new foreign-directed schools (in the face of a keen nationalist desire to substitute their own control), and the assurance of free scope and non-interference for all units of the great body of non-governmental educational effort. The task involved the setting of standards, the organization of examinations for degrees and certificates, the correlation of programmes and methods in the various States, the varied connexions with parent bodies in France, and the supervision of Syrian students abroad. French teachers were provided, many local-community institutions were directly subsidized, advice was given on university and professional matters, a specialized monthly publication was issued, and inspection, advice, and criticism were freely dispensed to the statal education services. Even the humble and barely tolerated Qur'an schools of the villages and town quarters were kept under supervision. The efforts of the States to extend their own services within their cramping financial limits were continuously pressed, and the rise in numbers of schools and pupils during the period was striking and creditable; it was achieved in the face of grave difficulties in personnel, buildings, and equipment, a wide popular misconception of the true objectives of education, and, among the educated classes, a general aversion from the technical or agricultural training[1] for which in fact the need was paramount and was rightly urged by the Mandatory. Nevertheless, at every level —kindergarten, primary, higher-primary, secondary, professional, and even (at Damascus[2] only) university—expansion was steady or rapid,[3] and the results obtained were incomparably superior to those of any previous age, even though but limited ground could

[1] It proved impossible to maintain even such Agricultural Colleges as existed: Salimiya was closed, Buka handed to missionary enterprise.

[2] All teaching at the (State) University of Damascus, including medical, was in Arabic; its academic standards and discipline were variable, being probably at their lowest in the Law faculty. The connected Arab Academy rapidly achieved a distinguished position, was adorned by some reputable scholars, and produced interesting work of high cultural value.

[3] Accusations made after 1945 that 'the French deliberately starved governmental education', in order to preserve their own monopoly, are baseless.

still be gained from the prevailing mass of popular illiteracy. Girls' schools had for the first time their full and increasing place. Teacher-training was wisely given a high priority, though often sadly mediocre standards must be accepted. Government secondary education, still (for differing reasons) non-existent in Lebanon, the Jabal or the 'Alawi province, became well established in Syria. Boy-scouting and sports were encouraged, though it proved difficult to prevent the infusion of the former by 'political' colouring. In neither extent nor in standards, however, could the State educational services compare with the long established and, throughout the period, still increasing body of foreign or community effort. Two out of the three universities,[1] by far the greatest part of normal, secondary and professional education, and a clear majority even of the primary schools, were those of French or (on a lesser scale) of other foreign educational or charitable bodies, or were those of the Christian (more rarely Muslim or Jewish) communities. In sum, far more children received their education from non-statal[2] than from statal schools—and this, normally, with higher standards and better conditions, and with an interesting admixture of children attracted to these schools from neighbouring countries. The complete picture of educational activity in the territory was one of imperfect balance and distribution as well as politically open to criticism; it resulted from long historical processes, and above all from a century of earlier French effort which had become a matter of sensitive pride and a major vested interest of France, so that a clash between these feelings and the militant local nationalism of the times, was in 1939 not difficult to foresee.[3] But the magnitude of the French contribution over the whole field was, meanwhile, beyond denial.

This contribution extended, less conspicuously but with high value, into the sphere of higher study and research in the fields of art, sociology, religion, history, and science carried on among the books and archives of the Institut des Lettres Orientales at the University of St. Joseph, at the (Jesuit) Observatory of Kasara, at

[1] For many years of the period covered by this book Dr. Bayard Dodge, of the American University, was among the outstanding personalities in the territory.

[2] In 1935 there were (excluding Qur'an schools) 703 government schools in the territory, with 75,000 pupils, against 1,214 'community' schools with 95,000 pupils, 618 foreign schools (of which 450 French, 99 American, 36 British, 20 Italian, 9 Danish, 2 German, 1 Swiss, 1 Greek) with 59,000 pupils. The community schools (in some cases assisted from government funds) were those of the Greek Catholics (149), Maronites (334), Syrian Catholics (28), Armenian Catholics (20), Greek Orthodox (212), Syrian Orthodox (29), Armenian Orthodox (194), 'various' (32), Muslim (157), and Druzes (59). In 1939 the contrast could be drawn between the availability of 2,800 schools (with 271,000 pupils) of all types and provenance, against 670 schools with 50,000 pupils in 1919.

[3] It took effect notably in 1944–6.

the justly famous French Institute of Damascus with its outstanding orientalists and its range of specialized Islamic studies, and at the School of Modern Arab Arts, also at Damascus. To these institutions, and not these alone, and to their publications is due a considerable body of knowledge highly esteemed by those able to value it. The foundation of public libraries, unknown before 1918, was fostered though not in all cases initiated by the French, and led to valuable collections and handsome premises at Beirut, Damascus, and Aleppo. The museums founded during the period, at the same cities and at Antioch, Ladhqiya, and Suwayda were on a scale of some pretension and could display articles of high archaeological value; they were a visible outgrowth of the Antiquities Service, itself an all-French administration placed in 1919 directly under the High Commissioner. This was a field of particular appeal to French scholarship and sentiment, and one for which, as of international interest, the Mandate had made specific provision (pp. 111, 379). Suitable legislation covering the obligations and dangers of this activity was passed in 1926, re-codified in 1933. The sphere of the Antiquities Service, working in part through the Permanent Archaeological Mission created in Syria in 1921 by General Gouraud, was the record and, through agencies provided by the States, the physical preservation of all discovered antiquities and sites: contacts with learned bodies abroad: the control of excavation and distribution of the spoils (normally on a half-and-half basis) between the 'expedition' concerned and the State: the foundation and upkeep of museums: and the publication of a specialized journal, *Syria*. Excavation at a dozen ancient and medieval sites[1] was carried out, season by season, by expeditions from universities or funds of France, America, Great Britain, Denmark, or Belgium, and on occasion by the Lebanese Government itself. In a single case, that of Krak des Chevaliers, the French Government itself acquired the site by purchase, before undertaking restoration. The archaeological work carried out during these twenty years, and the scrupulous handling of all connected interests, aroused indeed little interest (but rather mistrust) among the public; but it was of great benefit to the country in the spheres of prestige and scholarship, and even of immediate economics.

In the wide field of social life the period under review was one

[1] The great diversity of sites and interest included Hittite fortesses, Phoenician sanctuaries and cemeteries, Greek or Graeco-Roman cities and temples, Byzantine fortifications, Greek-Christian and Roman churches, mosques, Crusader and Arab castles. The principal monuments restored between 1919 and 1939 were those at Ba'lbek, Palmyra, Aleppo (citadel), St. Simeon Stylites, the Krak des Chevaliers, and Ṭarṭus (cathedral). Principal 'digs' had been at Jubayl, Sidon, Dura Europos, Antioch, Ḥamah, Bosra, Apamiya, Shakir Bazar, and Ras al-'Ayn.

of rapid but fitful and unplanned evolution towards the ways of the West and of modernity. In this the part played by the Mandatory as such cannot easily be assessed, but was certainly less than that of the sum of modernizing influences which must in any case have played freely on the territory, and had indeed been so playing for many years past. There were fields in which, between the two wars, these influences made little visible headway: for instance, in the continued dominance of sectarian loyalties, wherein the period, in spite of isolated voices preaching laicism and 'enlightenment', saw little fundamental change. The hold of regionalism and of the minority Islamic religious groups diminished little; the general characteristic structure of society was substantially unmodified; the backwardness, the relative isolation, the scarcely shaken conservatism of main sections of the population remained. Nevertheless, there were perceptible changes in the diminishing power of some of the old 'great families', in the visible growth of a middle class (future victorious candidate for political power) in numbers and self-consciousness, in a new though still imperfect sense of social obligation among the rich, and (the political consequence of this) the first appearance of social reform as a desideratum of statesmanship—or sometimes, less fortunately, as a weapon in irresponsible agitation.

In the social field, the larger towns could show in these decades abundant signs in their streets and better quarters, though few in the poorer sections and bazaars, of the revulsion of their inhabitants from the age-long ways of Eastern town life. In the fashion of clothing (from Eastern to European), of food, of household equipment and habit, of modern-type or intermediate-type shops and hotels, in the exchanges and distractions of social intercourse, in sport and travel, the adoption of some form or degree of Western ways was with various inconsistencies and compromises ever on the increase, year by year, to the chagrin of traditionalists and of considerable old-type Muslim elements. Such tendencies changed in some measure the character and appearance of all but the poor and backward sections of town life: whether on the whole for better or worse, for happier or less happy, it cannot here be pronounced! The unveiling of women made some, but so far limited progress; but its wide and early increase[1] was clearly presaged by the articulate feminism of small groups in the greater cities, and by ladies' participation in secondary and higher education, literary output, clubs, charitable work, and even politics. Traditional marriage customs, the last citadel of traditionalism, were still mainly retained, but individual departures

[1] This, in effect, belonged to the period immediately following 1944, to a very striking extent.

from them slowly multiplied and future tendencies were easy to foresee. Polygamy among Muslims grew ever rarer.

The superabundant daily and periodical press, mainly but far from exclusively[1] political, seemed to the Mandatory to call more for discipline, and often for repression, than for encouragement, and, for all its clever and forceful writing, it failed, with the exception of a few well-established papers, to maintain a reputable standard of journalism. Otherwise, the literary output of the territory in Arabic was not great in volume, was cramped by primitive methods of publishing and production, and, with some honourable exceptions, was not often better than mediocre in quality;[2] the exceptionally high level of ability in speech and exposition attained in Syria and the Lebanon, and the literary tradition already well established by their citizens or ex-citizens abroad, might well have led to higher expectations, had not politics in these years absorbed the energies of the educated class. The arts of painting, sculpture, or decoration, had few creative followers, though the beginnings of some interesting work could be found;[3] in occidental music the record was similar, though this was in the Lebanon the subject of university teaching. Any considerable work in other media—broadcasting, the cinema—lay still in the future. The tradition of pure scholarship, largely in oriental subjects, kept some of its old vitality in small circles of both territories.

[1] Of the large number of literary, scientific, and specialized periodicals few achieved a viable circulation, or lasted for many months.

[2] A few writers attained a respectable standard of historical, economic, legal, or miscellaneous writing. Those who, in Europe or America, wrote in French or English are not here considered, though some were well known and their influence extended into their country of origin. More and better work saw the light in Syria and Lebanon after 1945.

[3] The Lebanese Academy of Fine Arts was founded in 1943.

IX

TWILIGHT OF THE MANDATE

I. WAR AND ARMISTICE

THE late summer of 1939, though it marks no 'end of the Mandate' in Syria–Lebanon, was the last period in which the French could hope to do more than hold their position. Their own grave embarrassments, soon to culminate in the tragic catastrophe of their country, left their representatives in the Levant no time, resources, or power of initiative to attempt political or economic progress in those countries. The economics of these must, from then onwards, be at the mercy of wartime exigencies, while political advance was to be scarcely less subject to war-dictated policy or impolicy, and abnormal in its vicissitudes. France in Syria, from 1939 to 1945, must be judged less as a Mandatory endeavouring to carry out its functions as it conceives these, than as the weak and (latterly) dissident outpost of an enemy-occupied Power intent above all on survival, highly conscious of its position *vis-à-vis* metropolitan France, and deprived locally both of resources and of prestige to control the territory and retain its own 'rights' intact.

The Lebanese and Syrian States shared, in mid-1939, a depressed and unhopeful economic situation, a recent history of frustration in their dealings with the French Government, and the world-wide apprehension, or near-certainty, of a European war sure to include them. They had together witnessed the influx of refugees from the lost province of Alexandretta, and the French activity in military preparations, decrees, expropriations, recruitment, and reinforcement. They diverged widely, however, in their own immediate political situation; in Lebanon this was one of characteristically unstable and ruthless play of sectarian and personal faction, which seemed to have learned nothing and forgotten nothing in the last twenty years; in Syria, the suppression of constitutional life by the French, and their institution of a temporary non-political régime which left Syrian claims unsatisfied and her statesmen resentful, must lead probably to further disorders unless the conditions of war should lay upon the public and their policies a burden heavy enough to discourage them. For both territories, in the event, the period from the outbreak of war (3 September 1939) until after the Franco-German

Armistice (22 June 1940) was one of tranquillity little disturbed by the vicissitudes of the world outside or by the inevitable restrictions of wartime.

The latter proved, in fact, not severe. The State of Emergency proclaimed by M. Puaux took the form of a strengthened French control of police activities, an embryonic organization for first-aid posts, black-out and air-raid shelters, a strict censorship which included a prohibition to listen to German broadcasts. To these were added unconvincing attempts to control the major industries,[1] to stabilize prices, and to secure an adequate supply and distribution of foodstuffs. Some military requisitioning was proclaimed, civilian supplies from overseas diminished, and shortages were suffered due largely to hoarding and speculation. Exchange-control and financial regulations were issued in December 1939.[2] But the sum of all this as yet little incommoded the public. Testimonies of friendship to France were not lacking in Lebanese and even in some Syrian circles, though these did not reflect the prevailing apathy or puzzled anxiety of the general public, on whose ears propaganda from all sources fell with no great effect. There was little increase in rates of recruitment for the *troupes spéciales*, though this might be encouraged by the country-wide tours of General Weygand and his high prestige.

To ensure control and to correct the tiresome distractions of Lebanese politics the High Commissioner on 21 September took the step to which he had, by different reasons, been driven in Damascus on 8 July; he suspended the Lebanese Constitution, dismissed the Ministry and Chamber, and, while retaining Émile Eddé as President, placed full executive powers in the hands of a Secretary of State, ('Abdullah Bayhum) with a French Adviser and a Council of senior officials. Legislation was by Presidential Decree, with the counter-signature of the High Commissioner and, as usual, over a wide field, by the latter himself. A simplified and reasonably efficient administration[3] was produced by these changes, and by subsequent reductions among the redundant hundreds of officials. The suppression of constitutional life was deplored, indeed, mainly by the losers of posts and the players of the political game; the essential background of political life, the restless intrigues for employment, power, and preferment, and the rivalries of sects and parties in which the Christian priesthoods

[1] Those of soap, metal work, textiles, cement, and chemicals.

[2] The Anglo-French Monetary Agreement of 17 February 1940 was extended to Syria–Lebanon early in March.

[3] The resulting departments were those of Interior (including Health and Justice), Finance, Works (including Posts and Telegraphs) and Education, and National Economy (including Agriculture). The Director of Interior was Adib Naḥḥas: of Works, Yusif Sham'un: of Economics, Rafiq Arsalan.

were as ever prominent, went on scarcely diminished. M. Puaux continued to sigh, but hopelessly, for a simple, authoritarian Government under a Christian prince,[1] preferably (like himself) a Protestant. Meanwhile, he ordered the suppression of the Communist Party and its newspaper (*Ṣawt al-ʻArab*) and the arrest of its leaders. Conspicuous members of the Syrian National Party of Anṭun Saʻada (himself abroad) were also detained as probable trouble-makers; the belief that their activities were in part German-inspired and German-paid was persistent. A Decree condemning membership of 'foreign associations' was understood to be aimed at the Communists and the Syrian National Party. The rabidly Anglophobe Mufti of Jerusalem, Amin al-Ḥusayni, removed himself from Beirut to Baghdad, while a number of his supporters were arrested and sentenced for smuggling arms into Palestine. The continuity of the usual full French control over all departments of government was ensured by the retention of all save a few French officials serving in the two Republics (wearing in many cases their uniform of Army reservists), as well as of all the High Commission services.

In Syria it was considered safe to leave to their own devices the former Francophobe elements of the Bloc National and the Shahbandar group; but action similar to that taken in the Lebanon was directed at the Communists and the Syrian National Party. Severe sentences were passed on politicians already under arrest for their misdoings of some months back, and leaders of the League of National Action (pp. 228 f.) were condemned, on unpublished evidence, to death[2] or to long prison sentences. The hotly nationalist Arab Club in Damascus was closed. But the High Commissioner was able to maintain terms of outward cordiality with leading nationalists,[3] even though Dr. Shahbandar in and after December 1939 was already suggesting a *quid pro quo* for Syrian good behaviour; and the formation of the new Provincial Councils—the only elected bodies likely for some time to appear in Syria—was accomplished without incident, and might offer some acceptable outlet for effort in the field of public service. The fire which destroyed the offices of the Délégué at Damascus, in January 1940, seemed without political significance. A definitive Franco-Turkish agreement on the Syro-Turkish frontier, made in March 1940, secured Syria from one possible menace; it covered transfrontier passage and contraband, veterinary and health services, security and Customs. A number of Russian

[1] Puaux, *Deux Années*, p. 68.

[2] These sentences were later quashed.

[3] The ex-President, Muḥammad ʻAli al-ʻAbid, died in October 1939: M. de Martel in January 1940.

residents were expelled from Beirut and the Syrian cities. Syro-Lebanese relations were cordial, with exchange of ministerial visits and decorations, and mutual privileges in taxation. Syrian relations with other neighbours were normal: M. Puaux exchanged friendly visits with the High Commissioner of Palestine, and went to Ankara. No ill news reached Damascus from the former Druze or 'Alawi malcontents or from the Jazira province, where a number of new villages were established.

This period of calm ended with the rapid deterioration of the war situation in Europe from the spring of 1940.[1] After some weeks of anxiety intensified by the German advance in Europe, General Weygand was recalled to France on 17 May as Commander-in-Chief. He was succeeded in the Levant by the elderly and prudent General Mittelhauser. Military precautions were increased, full black-out imposed. The Army of the Levant, equivalent now to some three full divisions of colonial and metropolitan troops, with Corps and Army units, was prepared for all eventualities. Gas-masks were distributed, first-aid and disinfection posts were multiplied, air defence practised, transfrontier travel restricted. The High Commissioner called in his broadcasts for discipline and calm. All except skeleton staffs of his headquarter services, and his own office, were moved out of the Grand Sérail.

The news from Europe passed from bad to grave, from alarming to desperate; Italy entered the war on 10 June, and a week later the news arrived that Marshal Pétain had asked for an Armistice. This was signed in the forest of Compiègne on 21 June, and metropolitan France, its Government and resources, passed under German control. This left uncertain, but evidently threatened, the position of French dependent or mandated territories overseas. M. Puaux, who refused to consider a suggestion by the British Commander-in-Chief, Middle East (conveyed to him by the Consul-General[2] in Beirut) that the Turks should be allowed to occupy the north Syrian air-fields, had no doubt that the French position in Syria–Lebanon must be firmly maintained, her 'mission' pursued: and General Mittelhauser, in close touch with General Wavell in Cairo, proclaimed that the Army of the Levant would continue the struggle with its British allies. But no support for such an attitude was forthcoming from Paris or from French authorities similarly situated in North Africa; and before the month ended the General and his forces, and the High Commission itself, had accepted the effective withdrawal from the war

[1] German invasion of Norway, 9 April: of Holland and Belgium, 10 May: Dunkirk, 29 May: Italian declaration of war, 10 June: Germans in Paris, 14 June: Franco-German armistice, 21 June, announced on 23rd.

[2] Mr. (later Sir) Godfrey Havard.

of the French Army and authority in the Levant. One or two senior French officers,[1] having struggled in vain against this decision, succeeded in leaving the country; the Polish brigade[2] managed, with Mittelhauser's reluctant agreement, to cross into Transjordan without its heavy arms, but units of the Foreign Legion were forbidden to do the same. Had permission been given openly or tacitly at this stage to all French and French-colonial officers and men freely to leave the country and join the British forces in Palestine or Egypt, a far greater number (but doubtless still a minority) would have so acted. The British attitude was to leave any such movement to find its own level, and to hope for a stable Syria garrisoned by a not unfriendly army.

This French attitude of bowing perforce to events in Europe, unaccompanied at first (save in a small minority) by specifically anti-British sentiment, was not for the moment threatened by the call to continued resistance—resistance to Germany, and to the defeated and prostrate French Government[3]—itself so soon to be heard from the Free French movement[4] initiated by General de Gaulle; it was taken for granted, as having little alternative, by nine-tenths of the French in Syria. Nor was this attitude modified by the British Government's declaration on 1 July to the effect that, in face of a possible future German or Italian threat to Syria–Lebanon, it 'could not allow' these territories 'to be occupied by any hostile Power, or to be used as a base for attacks upon those countries in the Middle East which they (the British) are pledged to defend, or to become the scene of such disorder as to constitute a danger to those countries'; such action as the British might, in this sense, be compelled to take would, however, be 'entirely without prejudice to the future status of the territories now under French Mandate'. If such words could well appear ominous to French ears, ever suspicious of British interest in Syria, they did no damage to Anglo-French relations comparable to that caused two days later by the British attack on the French fleet at Oran, which led the Vichy Government directly to the rupture of diplomatic relations with Great Britain. Even so, if the French civil and military authority in the Levant had found it possible to refuse[5] the orders of Paris to 'cease hostilities', and had accepted

[1] Notably Colonel (later General) de Larminat.

[2] Composed of Poles who had escaped from their country in 1939 by way of Turkey.

[3] It moved from Paris to Vichy on 1 July 1940.

[4] General Charles de Gaulle's first appeal (from London) for continued French resistance was made on 18 June; he was cashiered by General Weygand on the 23rd, formulated his resistance plans on the 26th, and two days later was recognized by Great Britain as leader of the Free French. But the possibilities of his movement were not quickly apparent in Syria.

[5] As was the case in certain French Central African colonies, and was later to be also in North Africa.

the proffered help of Great Britain[1] in such refusal, many of the painful events of later years would have been avoided; the British armed intervention of 1941 would have been unneeded (and indeed unthinkable), and the cause of France far better served. Instead, the Syria–Palestine frontier was partly closed as from 30 June, and local as well as higher-level relations deteriorated. The trans-Syrian branch of the 'Iraq Petroleum Company's pipelines from 'Iraq ceased, under British Government orders, to operate; British subjects in Lebanon and Syria were placed by French authority under restraint and were forbidden to leave the country, and the Consul-General was ordered out of Beirut to a hill station. General Mittelhauser, recalled suddenly to Europe as unreliable, was succeeded by General Fougère, whose attitude was one of unquestioning loyalty to Vichy, and of distrust of the British ex-allies.

2. GENERAL DENTZ

The period following the Armistice, with its profound change in the status of the French authority and forces in the Levant, was for these one of extreme embarrassment. It witnessed a persistent *malaise* within the French community itself, a deterioration of Syrian and Lebanese feeling towards France, an economic crisis easily used for political (that is, for Nationalist) purposes, public disorders reminiscent of the early weeks of 1936, and a dangerous and humiliating infiltration of German and Italian agents.

M. Puaux survived the Armistice by five months, his policy one of ostensibly correct but actually minimal obedience to Vichy, of sincere efforts to unify and placate his own divided staff and community, of polite obstruction to General de Giorgis and the Italian officers of the Armistice Commission (which landed in Beirut in July 1940) and of the maintenance of fair though not cloudless relations with the British, whose Consuls could remain in Syria and the Lebanon until May 1941. Help in supplies was accepted from Palestine, the inactive trans-Syrian pipelines were protected from sabotage, and British arms were permitted, in spite of protests by the Armistice Commission, to pass through Syria to Turkey. Wireless broadcasts from London were allowed to be heard in public places not less freely than the German. A lenient view was taken of a conspiracy, in September 1940, by senior and other French officers to depose the High Commissioner himself in favour of General Georges Catroux who,

[1] General Wavell visited Beirut in person on 20 June and again on the 29th. Against acceptance of British aid was ranged, as usual, suspicion of Great Britain and her alleged ambitions in the Levant (Puaux, *Deux Années*, pp. 201–2).

with his high seniority and status, had passed through Syria[1] in August: a conspiracy of which the British in London had been aware, but which in the event was betrayed by local indiscretion and came to nothing. Even after the fiasco of Dakar (21–25 September), so damaging to Anglo-French relations, M. Puaux though hardened in his attitude remained tolerant of his British neighbour, and at heart tepid towards Vichy policy; but he felt bound to reject the broadcasts as well as the personal blandishments of the Free French, on whose behalf General Catroux was, late in September, stationed at Cairo. The High Commissioner's attitude was, however, found inadequate by the Vichy Cabinet, and he was ordered to relinquish his office on 24 November. He remained in Syria for a further three weeks before leaving, amid military parades and multiplied official farewells, on 14 December.[2] M. Puaux, who was thereafter to serve the Gaullist cause in high positions, had shown in Syria the best qualities of a French diplomat, to whom adverse events had denied success. His designated successor, the notorious collaborator Jean Chiappe, was inadvertently shot down by Italians over the Mediterranean on 27 November, while flying to his new post; and the succession fell to the uninspired but respected Alsatian, General Henri Dentz, a loyal Vichy follower and conscientious defeatist. His tenure of office was destined to be uniformly unfortunate.

The world of French officialdom in Syria and Lebanon, though devoted to maintaining or even increasing its own powers in the local administrations, did so henceforth with lowered morale and the consciousness of divided opinions. A fair proportion of civil as of military officers (and those often the most active and vital) were attracted by the possibilities of Gaullism and resistance. Some dozens of this party, after the leakage of their abortive plans of September 1940, were repatriated to France, with a serious loss to administrative efficiency; others were uneasy and hesitant, others yielded more easily to the *fait accompli* of Vichy authority, and, especially after Dakar, expressed towards their former allies a detestation composed of many elements of old rancour[3] and present envy. The French armed forces were reduced by the repatriation of a considerable proportion of the colonial element, including most officers and men of the Reserve. These sailed homewards with evident satisfaction; and the remaining force at the disposal of

[1] On his way to join de Gaulle (to whom he was far senior) in London, from Indo-China of which he had been Governor.

[2] He declined, on 29 November, a British last-minute suggestion that he should abandon his Vichy allegiance.

[3] The usual stories of 'British agents' in Syria were in circulation and widely believed; such agents, ubiquitous and diabolical, were said to be bent on alienating the affections of the local public from the French.

General Dentz, and his subordinate, General Fougère, was by great majority loyal to the Marshal and anti-Gaulliste.

Local Syro-Lebanese political circles could not but be deeply affected by the French debacle, however resolutely they were informed that the French 'mission', Mandate, and policy were still intact—and whatever signs might be visible (and these were not wholly lacking) of the continued loyalty to France of Catholic and limited other elements. To many or most Syrians the war was over, France defeated, her Mandate effectively extinguished both by this fact and, more specifically, by her own withdrawal from the mandate-giving League of Nations in the spring of 1941; it remained now to find means of achieving the twenty-year-old but still withheld aims of Syrian nationalism from an ex-Mandatory now clearly weakened, doubtful in status, and profoundly mistrusted. Nuri al-Sa'id Pasha of 'Iraq, in the course of a tour of neighbouring countries, gave the impression that little could now stand between Syria and its full independence; and local nationalists were encouraged to assert themselves and petition for the amnesty and release of imprisoned friends, in which they were partly gratified. The forces of nationalism sustained at this time a strange and unexpected blow by the assassination of Dr. 'Abd al-Raḥman Shahbandar on 7 July 1940. His murderers were revealed, four months later, as obscure fanatics who were duly executed for their crime; but suspicion, totally false, rested for a time on the French themselves[1] (as anxious to remove an extreme opponent) or on 'British agents' (on unspecified grounds), or on the leaders of the Bloc, with whom Shahbandar had been chronically at loggerheads. Three of these—Jamil Mardam Bey, Luṭfi al-Ḥaffar, Sa'dullah al-Jabiri—even fled from Syria to 'Iraq, and could return only in 1941 when officially exculpated. The tragic disappearance of Shahbandar, a man of character and honesty, was nevertheless a probable gain for the present tranquillity of the territory, and for the unity of its political front.

To the general probability of a revival of political militancy, in spite of the current prohibition of demonstrations and meetings, were added two specific elements. The first of these was the grave, at times almost desperate, plight of the population in face of shortages of food and goods, and rising prices. With the endemic evils of hoarding and the selfish manipulation of supplies and black markets went the actual deficiency of many imported necessaries (due in large part to the British blockade), the inefficiency of attempts at control, price-fixing, or rationing, the early exhaustion of grain stocks from the 1940 harvest, deteriorated transport and distribution facilities, and a depreciated currency.

[1] More specifically, on the unpopular chief of the Sûreté, Colombani.

These factors produced, in the early weeks of 1941, conditions in which the misery of the town populations could afford strong or violent aid to the demands of politicians.

A further element, besides the scant respect in which Bahij al-Khaṭib's Cabinet of Directors was held by the out-of-office nationalist leaders, was now present to play its part in encouraging demands of the familiar type: that is, the further blows struck at French authority by incoming German agents. The Italian Armistice Commission had, indeed, accomplished little, and was treated as of no great account by the French themselves; but a succession of German visitors, chosen for their knowledge and contacts in the Levant, reinforced from September 1940 onwards the now liberated German residents of Lebanon and Syria, and their local admirers. A network of German connexions was established throughout the country, and their more prominent spokesmen[1] placed themselves in touch with leading Nationalists,[2] gained favour by proclaiming anti-Zionist and pan-Arab conceptions, toured the country, and did much to depress French prestige and to encourage nationalist ambitions which they would be happy to serve. It was not surprising that an element in the more extreme nationalism of Damascus—as simultaneously in Baghdad—looked increasingly for a German victory as the outcome which, besides its clear probability, would suit them best;[3] cordial interviews took place, films of the German victories in Europe were appreciated, and coteries of outspoken German sympathizers were formed.

The economic misery created among the poor by unconscionable prices, acute shortages—notably of kerosene, bread, and sugar—and unemployment[4] came first into the open in the early days of January 1941. It took visible form in hunger marches in Damascus and Aleppo, with banner-carrying crowds in ugly mood; and the French prohibition against such parades led to the shutting of shops, intimidation, and arrests of the organizers. Weeks of smouldering discontent ended with a further outbreak late in February, when shops and bakeries were rushed and police counter-action led to the proclamation of a general strike. The appearance of French troops and armoured vehicles in the streets served only to emphasize the scale of the movement, of which the leaders of the National Bloc had now assumed the direction.

[1] Notably Otto von Hentig, a veteran of Middle Eastern intrigue; he held ministerial rank.

[2] Including Shukri al-Quwatli and other Bloc leaders.

[3] One may compare the attitude of certain Syrian political leaders in 1919–20 towards the Turks.

[4] Raw materials for local (especially the textile) industry were scarce and available only at black-market prices.

Some hundreds of arrests were made, but could not stop the strike movement from spreading to most of the cities of Syria. The accepted leader of the movement, now recognizable as predominantly political, was Shukri al-Quwatli. In the second week of March he put forward the demands of his group to the Délégué at Damascus. Based on the assumption that French authority had no longer a legal basis, the demands were for the dismissal of the unrepresentative Khaṭib Administration, the formation of a National Government, and ratification of the abortive 1936 Treaty in its original form: and, as further items, were added the abolition of press censorship, a general amnesty, and the surrender by the French advisers of most of their powers. Disorder continued throughout the country, and spread also into Lebanon, in the second week of March. The resignation of Bahij and his colleagues on the 15th did not, however, lead to fulfilment of the rest of the programme; General Dentz, a puzzled and unsure negotiator, offered unacceptable compromises, while French troops—most prominently, as usual, the resented Senegalese—were busy in suppressing demonstrators, with loss of life, in the Syrian cities. It was only after some days of disorder, with wide disruption of communications and the public services, that the High Commissioner, having failed to agree to terms with the real leaders of nationalism, could announce a settlement. On 1 April he proclaimed that, though a definitive establishment of Franco-Syrian relations was not possible in war conditions, a new Cabinet under a Head of State (Khalid al-'A<u>dh</u>m) would be formed, supported by a widely-based Consultative Assembly including Druze and 'Alawi members and ready to announce a programme of immediate economic improvement, public works, and better supplies. The Cabinet of al-'A<u>dh</u>m, formed on 4 April from personnel[1] who excluded the Bloc and other leading politicians, was to govern by Decree, subject as ever to the High Commissioner's countersignature. The ministerial programme as announced spoke of administrative reforms, the development of trade, social services, and the welfare of youth and the workers. It professed political neutrality; and an early effort by al-Quwatli to convene an all-Syrian political congress at Damascus was forbidden by the French authorities. A Council of State, charged with the preparation of new legislation, was placed under 'Abd al-Qadir al-'A<u>dh</u>m.

The Syrian disorders, which spread for some days to Beirut, Sidon, and Tripoli, produced in Lebanon less violent scenes

[1] With Khalid as Premier and Minister of Interior, were Ṣafwat al-Qaṭraghasi (an Appeal Court judge, of Aleppo) in Justice, Ḥanin Ṣaḥnawi (a wealthy merchant) in Finance, Muḥsin al-Barazi (a young French-educated lawyer) in Education, and Naṣib al-Bakri in Economics and Works. Bahij al-Khaṭib reverted to the Inspectorate-General of Interior.

because, apart from the mere instinct of emulation, they were inspired by a less rancorous political discontent. The Lebanese public nevertheless, was almost equally ready for a change of government. Muslim circles were complaining of too small a share of public appointments, the Phalanges and Najjada both cried out for more honesty and major reforms, many unemployed politicians would welcome a change, and the dissatisfactions of material life were scarcely less acute on the coast than in the inland districts. It was natural that the period of strikes and demonstrations late in March should be followed by a gesture of reform, though this had little significance. The enforced resignation of President Eddé and his Secretary-General permitted their powers to be exercised for a few days by General Arlabosse, before their transfer to a new Administration placed under a Head of State (no longer President) on 5 April. For this post the choice fell on Alfred Naqqash, a middle-aged Maronite writer and Appeal Judge; he was supported by an Under-Secretary in the Ministry of Interior (which he himself retained) and by four ministers.[1] These, all non-political, accepted guidance from Arlabosse, who for a time dominated the Administration.

The efforts made by the new Administrations, and by the French, better to meet the difficulties of the time were generally ineffective. The slightly greater authority permitted to the Syrian Government and its officials failed to placate the nationalists. Conferences of the Muḥafidhs of provinces could not improve the hard facts of life. An Economic Congress summoned at Damascus could debate and form its busy sub-committees, but could neither increase supplies nor facilitate distribution; an ambitious programme of public health measures made hopeful reading, but a new interstatal Rationing Committee, to meet alternately at Beirut and Damascus, made but a slow start. Increases of pay for public-service workers failed to keep abreast with rising prices. The local press and political parties remained unsatisfied, bread riots broke out sporadically, French prestige and popularity were never lower—nor German activity more evident and seductive.

The last-mentioned, moreover, under pressure of the eastward development of the war, and of events in 'Iraq,[2] was soon to play

[1] In the Ministries of Finance and Supply was Joseph Najjar, an engineer and senior official: in Public Works and Posts, Aḥmad al-Da'uq, a Sunni official and leading Beirut citizen: in Education and 'Youth movements', Philippe Bulos, a young judge: in Health and Economics, Fu'ad 'Uṣayran, a Shi'i doctor.

[2] Events in 'Iraq, where the leading Generals (the 'Golden Square') and some politicians led by Rashid 'Ali al-Gaylani were openly Germanophile, moved during April towards a situation in which 'Iraqi invocation of German military help was probable. Hostilities against the British broke out on 2 May and were to last for thirty days; they ended in the restoration of the legal 'Iraqi Government and its Regent (Longrigg, *'Iraq*, pp. 288 ff.).

a very different part in the affairs of the territory; the occasion in which a pro-German attitude of the public (and, still more, of the Mandatory) would be valuable to Hitler, was no longer remote or potential, but immediate. The danger of a German domination of Syria, to which the British Government had on 1 July 1940 referred as a dangerous possibility, became alarmingly imminent with their advance in North Africa, their conquest of Greece and assault on Crete, and their now overt efforts at subversion in the Levant itself; nor, even if these plans were delayed, was the likelihood of a move so fatal to the Allied position in Egypt and the Middle East the less menacing, if and when it should please the Reich to initiate it. The Levant States assumed a new importance in general war strategy, and this at a moment when the policy of their Vichy-ruled Mandatory was ranging from the dubious to the specifically Anglophobe.

While messages exploratory of this position passed, late in April, between London and the British Command in Cairo, the Consul-General in Beirut was instructed to ask General Dentz for an indication of his attitude. The Vichy Government, where Admiral Darlan was deep in negotiations involving the hope of immediate advantages to metropolitan France,[1] directed their High Commissioner in Syria that if Germany should seek to use Syrian airfields, then France would be 'not in the position of a neutral Power' towards Hitler's officers, who 'could not be considered as hostile', whereas the British, seeking to intervene, should be 'opposed with force'. No instructions could have been clearer. For General Dentz, though he professed bewilderment as to their scope and local application, they were amply sufficient: and an authoritative Vichy representative, accompanied by a senior German official, reinforced them by a visit to Beirut on 10 May. Herr Rahn[2] sought the High Commissioner's agreement to landing and refuelling facilities for German aircraft in Syria, hastening to aid the usurping Government in 'Iraq; he demanded also a supply of munitions for the 'Iraqi rebel forces, to be taken from those stored under Armistice arrangements in Syria. Dentz, whose conception of his own position and sense of military discipline left him no alternative, was generally if unenthusiastically compliant. He offered Palmyra airfield, but was ordered by Vichy to provide also that of Nayrab, near Aleppo. His instructions from Darlan, and from the Marshal himself, were for the grant of full facilities to German forces in transit, and for firm resistance to

[1] Such were the surrender of considerable areas of occupied France, the release of prisoners and a reduction of the war indemnity: all matters of much greater immediate appeal to Vichy than correctness or otherwise in distant Syria.

[2] He adopted the name of Renoir for the occasion.

British intervention: and the former in fact used Syrian resources freely during the three weeks following mid-May, while substantial quantities of munitions[1] were forwarded, by railway to 'Iraq. The Protocol of 21 May between France and the Reich specifically confirmed the giving in Syria of such assistance to German forces. The limited but perceptible movement of distaste for these proceedings among French officers in the Levant was met by broadcasts by the High Commissioner, by the strongly Anglophobe utterances of the military commander, General Fougère, and by the repatriation of a number of those thought to be opposed to the now official policy of frank (if still reluctant) collaboration with Germany. British Consuls and the Consul-General were ordered to leave the country, and the Government in London repeated significantly that, in face of open French 'collaboration', it must hold itself free to 'attack the enemy wherever he may be found'.

The Syrian public, largely ignorant of these developments and threats, continued to find its chief preoccupation in watching the course and nearer approach of the war, with every variety of hope or apprehension: and in struggling day by day with economic conditions in which hunger or even perhaps famine might again (as, they well remembered, in 1915–18) make their appearance. A definitive German victory, with its expected consequence of the liberation of their country, was the hope of some politicians, the terror of others, while to many the future seemed most likely to hold the same succession of French domination and local protest, strikes and riots, negotiations and concessions, as in the last twenty years. Few, a year after the Armistice, foresaw a decisive British armed intervention, with an initially most hopeful change in the French attitude; yet this, with the succeeding weeks of May 1941, lay in the immediate future.

3. THE FREE FRENCH

The British decision to intervene in Syria and end its militarily dangerous Vichy-French control was, though long foreseen as a grim possibility, taken finally with the utmost reluctance. It was from March 1941 onwards opposed by the British Commander-in-Chief at Cairo as an impracticable addition to his existing commitments (in Libya, Crete, 'Iraq, Ethiopia) which left him no adequate margin of troops available, and as an operation in which the defenders in Syria would start with great advantages of numbers, armament, interior lines, good defensive positions, and

[1] General Dentz, in his own later defence, stressed that these were of low value, largely defective, and would anyhow probably never reach the 'Iraqis.

local knowledge. But to the higher direction of the war in London it appeared impossible to leave the Syrian door wide open for German entry, with all the strategic and political consequences of this. If General Dentz and his superiors in France had based their policy firmly on the terms of the Franco-German Armistice, and had felt able to refuse all entry or facilities for Axis forces in Syria, it is most unlikely that the invasion by Anglo-French forces would ever have occurred.[1] Neither the British Minister of State[2] in Cairo, nor General Wavell, nor the High Commissioner in Palestine,[3] asked more than a clear assurance that the States of the Levant would remain neutral and defended; such had been in fact their policy for the eleven months following the Armistice, and such also in other parts of the French Empire.

The Free French, whose movement under General de Gaulle had by now been organized as that of an Ally, and to whom the widest British[4] help had been extended in supplies, money, and facilities, had enjoyed varying fortunes in French overseas territories; they could count on reliable bases in a number of these, and on limited military forces; and they were anxious, on every ground, to extend their authority and scope, and to establish their position as the authentic vehicle of the authority of France. To de Gaulle, and to Catroux who now represented him in Cairo, no more welcome accession to the Gaullist movement could be imagined than Syria–Lebanon, with its accessibility, its range of French and French-trained forces and installations, and its unique position in French sentiment. Its strategic importance was obvious, the immediate accession of strength to be obtained from it was considerable, its transfer from Vichy (that is, German-dominated) control to Gaullist would be an outstanding stroke and an inspiring precedent for other territories. And the clear collaboration of General Dentz with the Germans gave a pretext of great validity for action, not otherwise acceptable, against French forces. At the same time, since de Gaulle and his advisers shared in a notable degree the obsessive myth of 'British designs in Syria', they would be the last to tolerate British action against that country (to be followed, doubtless, by its occupation) otherwise than in their own company.

An all-British operation on this occasion would almost certainly have avoided many tiresome difficulties and disunities, and would

[1] The view of some French writers, that the British would *in any event* have invaded Syria, is contrary to all indications and probabilities; e.g. Fabre-Luce, *Deuil au Levant*, p. 182.

[2] Captain Oliver Lyttelton, from the spring of 1941. He was a member of the War Cabinet.

[3] Sir Harold MacMichael, throughout the war.

[4] A military agreement with General de Gaulle had been made on 7 August 1940.

have met with a less bitter resistance from the Vichy forces; but the relations of Great Britain with the Gaullist movement, and the strength of Gaullist (and all French) feelings about the time-honoured 'France of the East', and the useful battalions now available under General Legentilhomme[1] to help in the operation, rendered it clearly undesirable to refuse French participation in the campaign. Nevertheless, introducing as it did considerable differences of method, training, and even policy, the Gaullist participation was to prove sadly productive of future bitterness between the Allies. An added complication, sometimes embarrassment and sometimes asset, was the persistent Gaullist identification of their own authority and forces with those of France itself, and the claim that Syrians and British alike should accept this status without reserve.

The project for an invasion of Syria–Lebanon was under contemplation in British circles in London, and those of Free France in Cairo and Brazzaville, in middle and later April 1941. General de Gaulle was resolute in his aversion from British unilateral action, and at the same time so impatient of British hesitancy that he threatened brusquely to withdraw his spokesmen and troops entirely from the Middle East. General Wavell, in reply to the Chiefs of Staff preliminary inquiry, protested his sheer inability to find forces[2] for such an expedition. General Catroux in Cairo, urged by de Gaulle and replying upon information (later shown to be false) of a coastward withdrawal of French forces in Syria, was for a time the advocate of decisive Free French action to be aided only by borrowed British artillery and transport: but, after talks with deserter officers from Syria, he was forced to admit that no cordial welcome across the border would await the Gaullist forces, and that action without major forces of the British was unthinkable. To these conflicting projects was added the tentative idea of Mr. Churchill that even a militarily inadequate force could perhaps succeed in the enterprise, if all advantage were taken of the expected hesitations of Vichy troops and the political and psychological possibilities of the situation. But by 25 May General Wavell, yielding to the orders of his superiors, had formed a plan for joint Anglo-Free French[3] invasion, could count on General Sir Henry Maitland Wilson to command it, and could proceed to the detailed planning of the operation, for which he was still gravely under-equipped. His

[1] Ex-Governor of French Somaliland; he had rallied to de Gaulle when that territory was overrun by the Italians late in 1940.

[2] The required force was, in his opinion, of the order of two infantry and one armoured division.

[3] He admitted his dislike of using Free French forces, as being certain to increase opposition, but had no alternative troops to use.

forces, including some made recently available from other fronts, were to consist of two brigades of the 7th Australian Division (from Tobruq), part of the 1st cavalry division (now partly mechanized), the 5th Indian brigade (from Eritrea), a squadron of armoured cars, a Commando force, some miscellaneous artillery,[1] and General Legentilhomme's six battalions of Free French. The Royal Navy had 2 cruisers and 10 destroyers off the coast of Lebanon. About 70 aircraft were, at the beginning, available. The forces of Vichy France in Syria and the Lebanon (in addition to the *troupes spéciales*), after the post-armistice repatriation of a large part, amounted to some 35,000 men in all, including 18 infantry battalions,[2] 120 guns, 90 tanks and 90 aircraft, with 2 destroyers and 3 submarines in Lebanese waters.

The date for launching the operation was fixed for 8 June—a week after the liquidation of the position in 'Iraq (from which troops could, therefore, shortly be made available), a week also after the withdrawal from Crete, two weeks after the failure at Sallum and Capuzzo in the North African campaign, and three weeks after the final Italian surrender at Amba Alagi in Ethiopia.

In the days immediately preceding the invasion, of which the probability was now well realized in Beirut, the Vichy French Command moved its troops to positions on the Syria–Jordan and Lebanon–Palestine borders, and improved its defences. Increased recruitment to the locally-raised forces had been in progress for some months. In spite of General Catroux's appeals, and to his great disappointment, little or no desertion southward across the frontiers occurred; an exception was the outstanding case of Colonel Collet, an officer of distinction in the auxiliary (mostly Circassian) forces, who had been for some weeks in touch with Catroux and on 22 May led a force of his devoted cavalry to join Legentilhomme. For the rest, the normal motives of loyalty and discipline among the garrison of Syria, the persisting *mystique* of the Marshal, a prevailing sentiment of hostility to de Gaulle and Gaullism—and the unfailing Vichy propaganda that the British were, under Gaullist cover, seeking dominion in Syria—were effective in holding the great majority, and caused the Gaullist leaders to revise their earlier hopes of a landslide of adherents in their direction. The attitude, indeed, of Dentz's army and civil service during as well as after the invasion period was such as in all the circumstances could be anticipated; nor, in the moral crisis

[1] The most notable British shortages were in tanks, AA guns, transport and signal equipment.

[2] General Dentz, in his subsequent defence, urged that British battalions were double the strength of French, the British 20 being equivalent to 40 French. Also the British had (he stated) 38 against his 21 squadrons, and 74 batteries against his 11. These figures are questionable (*Or. Mod.*, June 1942).

with which they (and notably their High Commissioner) found themselves confronted, can blame be reasonably attached to either side.

The action taken, from 12 May onwards, by the Royal Air Force against aerodromes in Syria used by German aircraft—Palmyra, Damascus, Rayaq—aroused keen resentment among officers of the French Aviation (especially when accompanied by the dropping of Catroux's leaflets) and was taken as indicating the closer probability of other British action; but no retaliatory sorties were made over British-held territory. On 25 May the Palestine frontier was finally closed, telegraphic communication across it ceased, and the Intelligence Departments in Beirut could report ominous British troop movements. A last hope of the High Commissioner that invasion could be averted, and the morale of his own forces strengthened, by the accelerated departure of all Germans from the territory was to prove abortive; all save a dozen aircraft (and these largely damaged) had in fact left Syria by 6 June (a week after the collapse of the 'Iraq campaign) and the fact was urgently reported to the American Consul-General. But the broad strategic danger remained and German re-occupation could at any time be expected. The allegation published in Vichy that 'nothing could now explain or excuse' an invasion fell necessarily on deaf ears, and was strategically fatuous.

Towards the public and politicians of the Levant, still dissatisfied and apprehensive, still anxious to secure maximum gains from war conditions and from their harassed Mandatory, it was clearly prudent for the invaders to make some striking gesture calculated to secure goodwill and to mark a decisive turn of events; the Syrians could not be expected to provide a battle-ground, suffer the dangers inseparable from war, and yet gain nothing save a change of masters. A promise of independence, dearest of all their political goals, must be given. The terms of the Proclamation which heralded the invasion had, accordingly, been carefully considered between the Free French and British. The latter, against de Gaulle's opposition, insisted upon adding their own guarantee to that of the French; but they confirmed, by letter to de Gaulle, that Britain had no ambitions for herself in Syria–Lebanon, sought no advantages, and hoped for the fullest French restoration. The British motive was both to add conviction to a promise which would come, after all, not from the Government of metropolitan France but from a dissident movement denounced by France itself as disloyal and illegal, and at the same time to show the Arab world—the more desirably in view of recent events in 'Iraq, their repercussions in Syrian sentiment,[1] and the need

[1] The windows of the British Consulate in Damascus were broken by demonstrators during May.

for Egyptian goodwill—that Britain was actively sympathetic to Arab aspirations.

The intention of General de Gaulle, in face of the extreme delicacy of the position *vis-à-vis* the French public, was to proclaim for Syria and the Lebanon an independence conditional for its realization upon the conclusion of such treaties with these states as would secure the 'rights and special interests' of France; but the instructions which in their final form reached Catroux—himself destined to be not High Commissioner but Délégué-Général—led him to employ in his Proclamation, dropped in thousands of leaflets over the mandated territory on 8 June, expressions of unequivocal clarity.[1]

In the name of Free France, which is the traditional and authentic France, I come [he announced] to put an end to the Mandate and to proclaim you free and independent. You will therefore be from henceforth (*désormais*) sovereign and independent peoples. . . . Your independent and sovereign status will be guaranteed by a treaty in which our mutual relations will be defined. The treaty will be negotiated as soon as possible between your representatives and myself . . .

The war aims of the Free French were rehearsed, Hitler denounced, a promise given of freer commercial facilities; and, though reference was made to the 'age-long interests of France' as needing rescue from German hands, the final words of the Proclamation were again specific: '. . . a great hour in your history has struck: France declares you independent by the voice of her sons who are fighting for her life and for the liberty of the world'. The unconditional nature of this promise of immediate 'independence and sovereignty', made with the fullest claim to authority, will be found to contrast strangely with the later Free French assertion (which formed the basis of their policy for the next two years), that the Mandate was still in existence and that effective independence was to *follow* the conclusion of such treaties (which must not be hastened) as would ensure all French rights, privileges, and defence requirements. Though the latter sequence was doubtless at the outset the intention of General de Gaulle, the former was in fact proclaimed, and in these terms was supported by His Majesty's Government. The British guarantee, issued simultaneously by the British Ambassador in Cairo, referred to the Catroux proclamation as 'declaring the liberty and independence of Syria and Lebanon' and 'undertaking to negotiate a treaty to ensure those objects'; it expressed the support of the United Kingdom for the French assurance, and looked forward to the

[1] Catroux, pp. 137–9.

lifting of the blockade in the Levant and its admission to the sterling bloc.

The terms of the Free French promise, even though received with not unnatural scepticism by Syrian statesmen long disillusioned, could not but become, nevertheless, a substantial factor in the political pattern, and meanwhile ensured (as was intended) popular goodwill and a welcome for the Gaullist newcomers and the gifts they promised.

British, Free French, Australian, and Indian troops crossed the border northwards before dawn on Sunday, 8 June. The campaign, known as Operation Exporter, was to last for thirty-four days between forces of approximately equal strength. No more undesired campaign has ever been fought by a British Army than one thus directed against the allies of yesterday now consorting with the enemy. The forces of General Dentz[1] offered throughout a resistance far more stubborn than optimists on the Gaullist side had predicted; they showed on many occasions extreme bitterness to the invading 'rebel' Frenchmen and, apart from the claims of their professional pride and duty, were concerned to prove to the Axis Powers (who might otherwise retaliate in French North Africa, or elsewhere) that their resistance was authentic.[2] The initial entry was made at three points, towards the three areas clearly indicated as objectives—the coastal strip and Beirut, the Biqa', and the Damascus oasis. Columns advanced, therefore, by way of the main coastal road, which was soon found to be blockaded at defensible points: by way of Maṭulla, in the extreme inland north of Palestine: and east of Jordan, by way of Dar'a. Progress on all fronts was moderate, nowhere unopposed, everywhere conditioned by the need to avoid lateral thrusts and the cutting of communications, to which the broken terrain admirably lent itself. After a week of contested advance[3] the coastal column had taken Tyre and moved beyond it, with great profit from the supporting fire of the two warships; but it had been, for the moment, halted. The inland forces had taken Marj'uyun and villages and positions surrounding it, had captured Dar'a on the railway and Qunayṭara, and had occupied Kiswa not far from Damascus itself. But increasing opposition at this stage temporarily checked the momentum of advance, and the Commander-in-Chief realized the need to reinforce the invading army. He

[1] He was promoted Général d'Armée during the fighting. Forces in the field were commanded by General de Verdilhac.

[2] This was constantly in the mind of General Dentz. Even so, the Italians (General de Giorgis, of the Armistice Commission) could later claim that Vichy resistance had been inadequate; he himself had pressed for the blowing up of the oil pipelines and pumping stations.

[3] This included a gallant, but costly and only partly successful, Commando raid at the mouth of the Liṭani river, on 10 June.

managed to make available one brigade of the 6th (British) Division, followed a fortnight later by another, and at the same time was enabled by the restored position in ‘Iraq to draw on light forces released from that campaign. A brigade-group of the 1st Cavalry Division moved from Baghdad towards Palmyra (where it met stiff opposition lasting for some days), and two brigades of the 10th Indian Division moved up the Euphrates towards Dayr al-Zur and Aleppo. But in mid-June the outcome of the campaign was still uncertain; on the 16th indeed the Vichy forces were able to launch local counter-attacks and, with great benefit to their morale, to reoccupy Marj‘uyun. At sea, a series of minor and indecisive engagements occurred. Three British destroyers were damaged, a French destroyer was sunk. British naval fire at shore installations was effective. Throughout the mandated territory a state of siege had been proclaimed, all Gendarmerie and Police came under Army command, strict control of movement and assembly was enforced, schools were shut, British subjects interned, labour requisitioned. Black-out against air-raid attack was instituted at Beirut, not at Damascus. The city authorities of the former insisted that the town should be declared ‘open’. Villages within the zone of operations were largely evacuated. Political *détenus* were in many cases released.

The High Commissioner, meanwhile, was passing through agonies of embarrassment and indecision. Early offers of German and Italian help were distasteful to him, and were fortunately refused by the Vichy Government. But the demands of his forward troops for air support, especially on the coast road, could be met only by invoking German air squadrons, which were known to be available and more than willing; and to this course General Dentz was urged by senior members of his staff and by Admiral Gouton. He realized the political dangers of a conspicuous German participation, and was in sentiment opposed to it; but under stress of events he twice, once before and once after his successful counter-attack of 16 June, allowed himself to apply to Vichy for Stuka intervention, but each time changed his mind and countermanded it. Other forms of assistance could hardly be expected; the Turkish Government refused to allow French troops and military supplies to pass through its country, and direct aid from metropolitan France was, in the event, limited to a few aircraft and a few aircraft loads of specialists and stores. A French ship carrying men and supplies from Salonika for Syria was sunk by British aircraft off the Turkish coast. There were signs also that the Germans, who invaded Soviet Russia on 22 June, had for the moment lost their interest in Syria; this, however, in no way applied to the zealous German officers by whom the distracted Dentz was surrounded.

Help for the High Commissioner from outside, it was now apparent, was unavailable or inadmissible, and the Vichy forces, particularly their tanks and aircraft, were already diminished by serious losses. The invading columns, now strengthened, had regained the initiative and could press their advance from the deserts of the east and north-east as well as on the southern fronts. The conclusion of the British 'Battleaxe' offensive in North Africa (15 June) released more aircraft for 'Exporter'. On 21 June, after severe local fighting, Damascus was entered by the forces of General Legentilhomme[1] and the Indian brigade, and columns detached therefrom could move freely to the north and west. The Syrian capital was at once visited by General Catroux, who installed Colonel (later General) Collet[2] as his Délégué with the Syrian Government. Three days later the position in and around Marj'uyun was restored. The threat offered by forces from 'Iraq to Ḥumṣ by way of Palmyra, and to northern Syria from the Upper Euphrates, could not be further opposed.[3] The column moving on Beirut gained one position after another, not without difficulty and loss, and threatened Damur a bare ten miles from the capital. The High Commissioner had already, on 20 June, asked the American Consul-General to ascertain the British terms for an armistice, and was assured that they would be favourable. On the 26th he sent officers by air to Vichy to propose that an armistice be requested. Authority in this sense was delayed, however, mainly by the intransigence of Admiral Darlan, until 7 July when all hope of successful resistance was at an end. On the 8th General Dentz, again through Mr. Van Enghert, proposed a cease-fire to the British Commander, General Wilson,[4] and received his terms on the following day. These, which were reasonable and not ungenerous, were later to be embodied in the Armistice Agreement on 14 July: but the reaction of Vichy, to which Dentz immediately referred them, was stubbornly unfavourable. A promise of Syrian independence, it was asserted, must belong solely to the legitimate Government of France, and in the form now offered (and guaranteed by the British) must be null and void;

[1] He was himself wounded but continued in command. His force included Collet's Circassians and part of the (British) Transjordan Frontier Force.

[2] He died in 1945.

[3] The local struggle for Palmyra by 'Habforce' from 'Iraq was long and severe. It fell to the British forces on 3 July. An interesting episode was the fight, near Sukhna, of a detachment of the Arab Legion (that is, of the Transjordan Army, under Brigadier J. B. Glubb) against mechanized Syrian *méharistes*.

[4] General Wilson's own superior Commander in Cairo, General Wavell, on 5 July exchanged commands with the Commander-in-Chief in India, General Sir C. Auchinleck.

the other terms suggested were 'contrary to the interests and dignity' of the Vichy Government, and were unacceptable; and no help was offered to the High Commissioner more effective than instructions to 'take measures appropriate to the *de facto* situation'. To these unrealistic and face-saving objections, the High Commissioner, now at the point of complete military collapse,[1] could give little weight. The Australians were only six miles from Beirut, General de Verdilhac's force everywhere exhausted and defenceless. Dentz had British officer prisoners flown to Europe, dispatched his remaining aircraft to other destinations, sank a captured (British) steamer in the Beirut harbour entrance, caused his own ships of war to be interned by the Turks at Alexandretta, and arranged for a spy service in Syria to supply information later to the Axis. Meanwhile a cease-fire was offered and accepted[2] as from midnight 11–12 July, and Dentz sent his envoys to the British (Australian) outposts on the coast road in the early morning of the 12th. Headed by de Verdilhac[3] they were driven to Acre, where discussions between them and the British representatives[4] lasted all day. Free French representatives[5] were present, but in the face of the attitude of the Vichy spokesmen could not participate nor sign—to the chagrin of General Catroux, who accused Wilson of a 'Pontius Pilate' attitude in his lack of interest in these French dissensions.

The terms agreed and signed on 14 July were those, in substance, already proposed by the British Command. They contained no surprises. Syria and Lebanon were to be occupied forthwith by British and Free French forces, those of Vichy having been accorded the full honours of war. The latter troops would keep their personal arms (but not their ammunition), and would hand over all heavier equipment undamaged,[6] and all ports and ships, installations, aircraft, fuel stocks, and public services. Troops were, for the moment, to withdraw to embarcation bases. No reprisals would be taken, on any pretext, against any Syrian or Lebanese subject who might have been involved. Prisoners of war would be exchanged, selected Vichy officers being retained until

[1] Vichy losses had been 222 officers and 6,130 men killed, wounded, or prisoners (and a few deserters). Allied casualties were in all some 4,700, of whom 1,300 were Free French.

[2] The cease-fire was violated by Vichy troops in a number of sectors, probably through delay in communication of the order to advanced troops.

[3] Accompanied by General Jennequin (of the Aviation) and MM. Conty and Chambard of the High Commissioner's political office.

[4] These were General Wilson and senior Naval and Air Force officers.

[5] General Catroux with two staff officers.

[6] Considerable quantities of equipment had been hurriedly transferred to Turkey, and some destroyed.

all British prisoners were produced and handed over.[1] The rights of French cultural institutions in the territory (hospitals, schools, and missions) were to be respected. Among Vichy troops a free choice was to be given as between repatriation or adherence to the Gaullist authority. Civilians in the local government, and officers of the Special Services, would remain at their posts as long as might be necessary to secure the continuity of the Administration; they could, if they so wished, be thereafter repatriated.

The exclusion of the Free French from the armistice negotiations, painful to Catroux and his officers but forced by circumstances upon General Wilson, was a symptom of the bitter feeling of the Vichy party towards them; indeed, the extent to which Frenchmen of the winning side found themselves cold-shouldered in Syria, and even excluded by their compatriots from the better quarters and amenities, was much remarked. The execution of the armistice terms devolved upon a mixed Commission, which consisted of a British chairman (Brigadier Chrystall) and two British and two Vichy (but no Gaullist) officers. It sat till 10 October. Its proceedings were viewed by the Free French as too indulgent to Vichy feelings, and in this (in so far as true) it reflected the unembittered view taken by the British of the recent strife, and their desire above all to liquidate the position, and the ex-enemy forces, as rapidly as might be.

The terms,[2] communicated to General de Gaulle at Brazzaville, excited his instant wrath.[3] He found them 'incompatible with the political and military interests of France' in their willingness to let the Vichy army return home in formed units and in French ships: in their failure to provide sufficiently specific procedures to facilitate pro-Gaullist propaganda among the Vichy personnel: and in their failure to specify that all ex-Vichy arms should be handed to the Gaullist authorities and that the *troupes spéciales* be placed under these and not under the British. Hastening to Cairo on 21 July and there declaring himself in no way bound by the armistice agreement, de Gaulle threatened Captain Lyttelton with a complete dissociation of his forces from the British. Three days later a British-Free French 'Interpretative Agreement'[4] was

[1] In fact, British officer prisoners had been sent by air to Europe both immediately before *and after* the signing of the Armistice, and, some in German some in Italian keeping, had been confined in improper and humiliating conditions. They were restored to their own forces in Syria only when senior Vichy-French officers (including General Dentz himself) had been held for a period under General Wilson's orders.

[2] They had been the subject of exchanges between de Gaulle and the British Prime Minister since mid-June.

[3] He describes the agreement in his *Mémoires de Guerre* (i. 164) as 'une transmission pure et simple de la Syrie et du Liban aux Britanniques'.

[4] It was negotiated between de Larminat and Major-General E. L. Spears, at the time head of the 'Spears Mission' to the Gaullist movement in all countries.

signed, after long parleys: it gave wider scope for Gaullist officers to explain their case to the Vichy forces and provided that the transferred armaments, and the *troupes spéciales*, would be placed under Catroux's command. A day later a formal Agreement between de Gaulle and Lyttelton prescribed the details of the military collaboration to be practised thereafter in the Levant, as regarded command, consultation, defence, and joint operations. The military command would be exercised by a British or a French officer according as these or those had the preponderating forces in the country at the time. The 'territorial command' (public services and security, the civil governmental machine, and the exploitation of local resources) was to be strictly the French prerogative. It was agreed that a section of the British Security Service should be attached to the Sûreté-Générale.

In the event, a modest proportion only of the Vichy forces—metropolitan, colonial, and Foreign Legion—could be persuaded to rally to the Gaullist cause; a greater measure of adhesion was precluded by reasons of existing loyalty, of devotion to their own Vichy officers and to the Marshal, of professional hopes or fears, of aversion from the 'rebel' Catroux and the British intruder, of war-weariness, and of personal or family circumstance. About one-fifth of the Vichy forces, or 127 officers and about 2,500 rank and file,[1] could be incorporated in the French forces under General Catroux. Twenty-five thousand sailed home, in a succession of convoys of French ships, to the chagrin of the Gaullists and, on the whole, to the considerable relief of General Wilson. The last contingent left for Marseilles in late August. General Dentz, released from his detention (in Jerusalem) when the British officer prisoners were at length produced, sailed on 4 September. Arrived in France, he refused further employment, and passed into private life, but was arrested and tried in April 1945. He was sentenced to death but reprieved, and died miserably in prison in December 1945. By any but a partisan judgement, he must be felt to have ill deserved so pitiless a fate, for this was a brave and conscientious officer placed by his superiors, to whom he chose to remain loyal, in a position from which there was, within his powers and qualities, no issue.

Meanwhile the objects of the joint invasion of Syria–Lebanon, now concluded, had been achieved. Any easy reoccupation by the German power, soon or later, had been precluded. The defence of Egypt and the Suez Canal was aided by the removal of bases of attack some 250 miles farther away. Turkey was notably strengthened against assaults on her neutrality, and must be felt all the

[1] General de Gaulle himself claims about double that number, but his figure is unsupported.

more likely some day to join the Allies now established as her neighbours. And the authority now dominant in Syria could henceforward, if it would, carry out a policy likely to secure another major war asset, the goodwill of the Arab States.

It remained to be seen what use the incoming French would make of this opportunity—their last—to bring the Mandate painlessly and acceptably to an end, as they professed always to have intended, and were now bound by recent and specific promise, to do.

4. GENERAL CATROUX

The date for the 'end of the Mandate' may be variously assigned. It was officially announced by the Proclamation made by the Free French, and guaranteed by the British, on 8 June 1941. It was implicit in the authoritative Declaration of the Independence of each of the mandated States, in September and November of the same year. It was expressed again in the constitutional changes made in 1943 by the concerned Governments, and, more practically, by the long-delayed but at last convincing transfer of powers by the Délégué-Général in the first weeks of 1944. Yet even so the obligations of the Mandate could still be invoked by the French in the protracted and painful discussions which preceded the withdrawal of their troops in 1945–6. In each of the histories of 'Iraq, of Transjordan, of Palestine, there was a moment when it could be said that 'this day the Mandate ceased to be', and such a pronouncement was true in theory and in practice. In Syria and Lebanon there was no such moment; the Mandate, long impaired and increasingly unreal, disappeared with graceless reluctance.

The earliest political contacts of the Free French with the world of Syria and Lebanon were cordial and hopeful. The reception of Generals Catroux and de Gaulle at Damascus on 21 June, and at Beirut in mid-July, satisfied them that French prestige was intact, the change of régime acceptable, collaboration assured. New and better times were the theme of letters exchanged between Catroux and the ex-President of Syria; notables and politicians thronged his receptions. In his progress through Lebanon and Syria in July and August de Gaulle could feel that he was accepted at his own valuation as the supreme spokesman of France (as he was explicit in asserting) and of the only Power concerned in state-building in the Levant, even if willing for the moment to accept British military help. The Maronites and their Patriarch showed all their old *empressement*; the Muslims, to whom de Gaulle gave gracious audience in all the municipalities he visited, were cautiously expansive.

The transfer of powers from Vichy to Free French officials,

following the entry of Generals Wilson and Catroux to Beirut on 16 July, was uneventful, though Catroux declined to deal on equal terms with his predecessors.[1] The Free French flag appeared on public buildings, duties were everywhere assumed by officials under Catroux's orders. Immediate shortages of food and drugs were met by accelerated imports, inevitably through British channels. The promise of a boom in military employment and purchasing (which however could not wholly ameliorate the adverse economic conditions of wartime) was already apparent. Soreness arising from episodes[2] in the recent campaign was already yielding to time and treatment. The press, with minimum suspensions, reappeared in its multitudinous sheets. The Beirut wireless station was repaired. Roads became safe and normal. The martial law imposed for a few days in and around Beirut was soon lifted. German and Italian subjects were safely re-interned. A great part of the civilian 'French Colony' left for France, handing their interests to local agents. The personnel of the Catholic missions were by great majority favourers of Vichy, and many left the country; the Sisters (except those of the Hôpital de Damas), and the Apostolic Delegate, were Gaullist. Many senior officials of the High Commission and the local Governments elected to sail homewards, and were replaced in their functions by such more or less suitable officers as Catroux could find among his own adherents; the loss of efficiency was considerable. Of the technical and lower ranks of French officialdom, most remained in Syria and the Vichy sympathies of many were ignored—or were, in many cases, converted. It was stated that, of the total body of French functionaries as of before July 1941, a third left for France, a third adopted or retained Free French loyalties, and a third, criticized severely by local Free French opinion, remained without pretence of loyalty[3] in the service of the Governments. Of the officers of the Services Spéciaux a number continued to serve though known to be Vichy followers, while some were replaced by officers of, admittedly, no special qualifications for such work. But, with all difficulties and shortages, a not unsuccessful show could be made in filling all posts and maintaining the Administration, on the strict lines of the régime of 1920 to 1939.

[1] General Dentz had removed himself from Beirut to a village, leaving Admiral Gouton to hand over. Catroux refused to accept authority at the latter's hands.

[2] In particular, some shots had been fired at or in Damascus, which Vichy officers, and some Syrians, imputed to the British. At Beirut, bombs from aircraft had been dropped in the city on the night of 2–3 July, and were hailed maliciously as British 'deliberate bombing of residential quarters'; they were subsequently traced to German aircraft (e.g. A. Laffargue, *Dentz*, p. 158).

[3] These were the '*ralliés alimentaires*', who were accused of following the dictates of their material interest in staying in the Levant.

The British military Command, anxious above all to avoid involvement in local affairs, was generally benign, nor was there reason to expect any other attitude from General Spears who, already on close personal terms with Catroux as well as with de Gaulle,[1] assumed charge of liaison between the Army—or British interests in general—and the Délégué-Général; and the Minister of State in Cairo, by his exchange of letters with de Gaulle[2] and his personal visit to Beirut in August, showed an attitude such as to reassure de Gaulle himself, though only after some days of an almost critically strained attitude on the part of the irascible and intolerant French leader.

The latter, though profoundly suspicious of British intrusion into French affairs, and seeing a British plot or malice in every petty indiscretion or *obiter dictum* of a British officer,[3] could leave Syria for Brazzaville in August fairly satisfied with the prospects of Free France, and not least in the political sphere. A request from Cairo that Spears should be admitted to the expected Franco-Syrian negotiations had been firmly rejected: and the misunderstandings or improprieties which the zeal of isolated and imperfectly instructed British officers had produced in episodes in the Jabal al-Duruz, the Jazira, and the Euphrates province during the campaign or in the first days of the occupation—episodes which could be naïvely or maliciously interpreted to signify sinister British ambitions in this or that region of Syria—were soon at an end, thanks to vigorous French reaction, and could be dismissed as of solely local importance.

Far more serious, though not yet fully apparent, were the more fundamental difficulties which now confronted the French. One of

[1] Himself bilingual, Spears had served in France in highest-level liaison duties in 1939–40, and had personally brought de Gaulle to London, by air, after the fall of France.

[2] The Minister of State repeated, in the letter forwarding to de Gaulle the Agreement of 25 July (Catroux, pp. 168–71), the total lack of British selfish or territorial ambitions in the area ('except to win the war'), and added that 'both Free France and Great Britain are pledged to the independence of Syria and the Lebanon. When this essential step has been taken, and without prejudice to it, we freely admit that France should have the dominant privileged position in the Levant among all European nations.' The same viewpoint was to be expressed by Mr. Churchill in the House of Commons six weeks later (9 September); he gave it as agreed British and Gaullist policy that the Syrians should be enabled to 'assume at the earliest possible moment their independent sovereign rights', and not have to wait until the end of the war. He added 'There is no question of France maintaining the same position which she exercised in Syria before the war. . . . There must be no question, even in wartime, of a mere substitution of Free French interests for Vichy French interests. . . . This is fully recognized in the documents which have been exchanged between the Minister of State and the representative of the Free French.'

[3] General Wilson, who moved his H.Q. from Beirut to Brumana to avoid local entanglements, records (*Eight Years*, p. 120) how '*incidents graves* and *incidents très graves* came to be regarded as a part of one's daily ration'.

these, never admitted, was the character of the great and dominating figure who had created the Free French movement and now presided over the destinies of Syria and the Lebanon. For all his genuine elements of greatness, General de Gaulle, who, with his stiff angularity of character, when French interests (as he saw them) was concerned knew no compromise[1] and allowed for no other facts or feelings, was, by ill-fortune, the least likely of French leaders to conduct an evidently difficult and ill-balanced task of Franco-British collaboration; he was instead, as events proved, the most certain to damage both Franco-British and still more Franco-Arab relations by his exclusive and anachronistic conception of French 'rights', prestige, and advantages, and his profound non-comprehension of the political and psychological facts of the Arab world. By contrast, Catroux, within the limits set by Free French policy (and especially in the earlier months of his office), was moderate[2] and comparatively realistic.

Personalities apart, the French task in Syria from 1941 to 1943 was one of peculiar difficulty. Wartime exigencies would urge them to adopt a policy of waiting, suspension; but Syrian feeling would never accept this, and specific promises had in fact been made of immediate independence and sovereignty. Grave or dangerous discontent must accompany all failure to honour these; and the harsh realities of close control must be all the less tolerable to Syrians in the new hopeful though soon disillusioned atmosphere, just when such control seemed, in mid-war, all the less easy to relax. French prestige, moreover, had suffered grievous damage in 1940; and the events of midsummer 1941, when before watching Syrian eyes they were defeated on their own ground by British forces and those of their own dissidents, had done nothing to re-establish it. At present the military power which since July 1941 imposed French dominance in the Levant—and which, under no compulsion, had restored to them their old authority—was British power. Even so the Free French, for all their claim uniquely to represent the real and continuing France, were optimistic in expecting their words or acts to be accepted for the moment by realistic Syrian statesmen as those of a Great Power; the Gaullist authority was, in those years, clearly far from this. On the contrary, Gaullist policy must act constantly in terms of what metropolitan France, with its strong sense of tradition, or almost of empire, in Syria, would accept—and the events of 1936–9 had shown the limits of this. General de Gaulle could not

[1] In his own words (*Mémoires*, i. 175) 'notre grandeur et notre force consistent uniquement dans l'intransigeance pour ce qui concerne les droits de la France'.

[2] Nevertheless, in his own full account of this period (*Dans la bataille de Méditerranée, passim*) he allows himself to write with great bitterness of Anglo-French relations, and particularly of General Spears.

afford to give easy pretexts for the charge that he was 'sacrificing the interests of France'; he had been bold even to speak, as did his proclamation of 8 June, of an 'end of the Mandate'. It was for this reason more than any other that a unique (and the last) opportunity for strengthening France's moral position in the Levant, and acquiring a new fund of goodwill, was missed.

In spite of the agreed French assumption of 'territorial command', the divergence of French and British conceptions of present policy was deep, and must be embarrassing. The policy of the French was, in effect, to offer the very minimum towards honouring their promise of independence: to retain all essential control: to hold, and to secure for the future, all that existed of French rights, institutions, privileges: and to postpone until after the war the settlement which must be made to safeguard all these, and even then to make the reality of 'independence' conditional upon it. To considerations other or wider than these the French authorities or policy-makers gave scanty heed; they had little part in over-all world-wide war strategy, and 'Arabophile' was to them a pejorative term to be hurled at the British.[1] The latter, with far less commitments (sentimental or practical) in Syria–Lebanon, and thereby far greater objectivity, took less interest in the niceties of the local world, and far more in the requirements of regional security and, as part of this, in the conciliation of Arab sentiment in all this group of countries. A clear condition of military safety was reasonable popular contentment, which must include political satisfaction, or absence of extreme dissatisfaction, not less in 'Iraq and Egypt than in the Levant. The British concern with defence and security, and their commitment to a Syrian-Lebanese independence which, with wider Arab sentiment also in view, they had themselves guaranteed, necessarily led them towards a politically progressive policy which the French in Syria (and in Algeria) viewed as indicating all the old bugbears of British interference, designs to extrude and replace the French, and the rest. At no time was any part of such fears justified, nor did British policy on the spot deviate in any essential from the declared aims of the British Government at home. But this was never believed by the Délégué-Général and his officers, and if believed would have consoled them little for the authentic, and in the circumstances particularly embarrassing, difference in policy which in fact existed, as between Great Britain and France, towards Syria and the Arab world.

In the administrative field, it was clear from July 1941 onwards that, whatever had been or might be said of independence, the Délégué-Général was departing by little or nothing from the

[1] e.g. de Gaulle, *Mémoires*, i. 169.

control exercised in earlier years. All former French posts were filled, advice and inspection, control and veto were as ever ubiquitous. The Délégué-Général could and did continue to legislate by Decree, beside or above the local Governments. French judges still sat in the Courts of the Lebanon. The French Sûreté-Générale was as powerful as ever, press censorship as strict, the all-important Common Interests still French-administered, and a Commission under the Délégué-Général and the Commander-in-Chief assumed charge of all railways. The Contrôle Bédouin was still solely a French concern, as was the control of all frontiers. The principle was, in fact, now and from now onwards adopted, both by predilection and by specific orders from de Gaulle, that the Mandate (from which, it was at this stage discovered, only the League of Nations had the power of release) was still in existence, and that whatever had been promised, independence must follow, not precede, the signature of satisfactory treaties.

The *troupes spéciales*, still under exclusively French command, were re-formed wherever events had disbanded them, and were augmented; it became French policy, which they carried out to good effect, to minimize their own colonial forces in the territory and to use these instead as self-sufficient brigades for active service in Africa.

But the claims of independence were, even so, not wholly ignored. In Syria the Cabinet of Khalid al-'Adhm, which had survived the campaign and the Free French occupation, was asked in September 1941 to make way for a Ministry under which the suspended Constitution would be restored and independence proclaimed. Conversations with Hashim al-Atasi and the real leaders of political life had proved fruitless; they refused to lend themselves to the execution of General Catroux's policy as a puppet Government who would gratefully sign a treaty on the now re-offered 1936 model, with its heavy quota of French privileges. The General turned, as a *pis aller*, to Shaykh Taj al-Din, who seemed capable once again of serving French interests and carrying at least some moderate opinion with him. He appointed a 'neutral', Ḥasan al-Ḥakim,[1] as Prime Minister and allowed the latter to form a Cabinet[2] excluding all National Bloc representation, but including an 'Alawi and a Druze. The new Premier, assuming such of the limited functions of President as the times allowed, witnessed on 27 September the formal

[1] An economic expert, he was an ex-collaborator with Dr. Shahbandar.

[2] Prime Minister and Minister of Finance, Ḥasan al-Ḥakim: Justice, Zaki al-Khaṭib: Foreign Affairs, Fa'iz al-Khuri: Education, Fa'iz al-Atasi: Defence, 'Abd al-Ghaffar al-Aṭrash: Economics, Muḥammad al-'Ayyash: Works, Munir al-'Abbas: Supplies, Ḥikmat al-Ḥaraki. Bahij al-Khaṭib remained as Under-Secretary for Interior.

proclamation of 'Syrian independence': an independence which, though carrying in name the enjoyment of 'the rights and prerogatives of an independent Sovereign State', and guaranteeing that the State should form 'politically and territorially an indivisible unit', involved, specifically, none the less, a strict alignment of policy with that of France, and (at least for the war period) excluded all Syrian control of the armed or police forces, or the public services, or economic affairs, or communications. With all these limitations and with the machinery of the Délégation-Générale intact, with British military control unquestioned and officers of a British Security Mission and Field Security Service and the Spears Mission in widespread evidence, there could be, obviously, no effective freedom for the Government of Damascus—and no façade, even, which could long satisfy the restless and suspicious Syrian leaders.

In the Lebanon it was decided to administer the same dose, with Alfred Naqqash to remain as President. Late in November a Cabinet[1] of scarcely representative personalities was appointed under Aḥmad al-Da'uq, on the usual confessional lines, to constitute the Lebanese Government whose independence was duly proclaimed on the 26 November. The Proclamation contained references, which some elements could not but find disquieting, to the continuing French 'mission' in the country, to the integrity of Lebanese territory,[2] and to the Treaty of 1936 as the basis of future relations; but though reception was on the whole unenthusiastic (as in Syria it had been cold), the Lebanese were thought unlikely to give trouble. In both territories the hope was to postpone all effective change until 'after the war' the Mandatory, freed from British garrisons on the spot and strengthened by an undivided authority in France, could obtain her objectives by favourable treaties.

Such as it was, the independence of Syria and the Lebanon was at once recognized by Great Britain, who in February 1942 appointed General Spears as Minister to both Governments. It was accepted by a number of (largely nominal, because exiled) Governments of European countries. The State Department at Washington, though entirely benevolent, was still in relations with

[1] Prime Minister and Finance, Aḥmad al-Da'uq: Justice, Philippe Bulos: Interior, Aḥmad al-Ḥusayni: Works, Amin al-Sa'd: Foreign Affairs, Ḥamid Franjiya: Defence, Ḥikmat Janbulaṭ (who died in April 1943): Supplies, Waṣif 'Izz al-Din: Agriculture, Aḥmad al-As'ad: Communications, Alfred Saqqaf: Education and Health, Ramiz Sarkis.

[2] The Proclamation of 8 June, addressing 'inhabitants of Syria and Lebanon' had said: 'you will be able either to form yourselves into two distinct States, or to unite into a single State.' There was, however, after the Free French occupation, no word or occasion of reopening the subject of Lebanese status, or its boundaries.

Vichy, and remained unconvinced by French claims to a superior position in the Levant; it therefore withheld formal recognition, but a year later posted a Diplomatic Agent and Consul-General (Mr. George Wadsworth, of long Middle Eastern experience) to the two territories. Turkey took no such step. Of the Arab States, Egypt gave a guarded, and Sa'udi Arabia a formal, recognition to Syria only; 'Iraq deferred its attitude; to none did the new 'independence' suggest a reality. The two Governments recognized each other, implying (it was hoped in Beirut) an end to Syrian claims to the Muslim qaḍhas of Lebanon. General de Gaulle lost no time in informing the League of Nations (which Vichy had long repudiated), and thereby invited all Governments to recognize the new States.

Of the economic difficulties and dislocations of the period, in the field of supplies, prices, and employment, more will be said on later pages; here is to be noticed their effect on public morale, on the administrations and on local politics, to all of which the abnormal conditions provided a disturbing background. At the same time, the political parties reformed their ranks and could come into the open. In both territories occurred a marked increase in Communist organization and activity (including that of their newspaper), though this was, for the moment, mainly on lines favourable to nationalism and to the Allied war effort. The Anti-Fascist League held meetings, the first for some years. In both territories pan-Arab feeling notably gained ground, though never among the Christians of Lebanon; in both, the parties of outspoken nationalism coalesced, gained confidence, and realized that if real independence were in question the true struggle still lay ahead. The desire for their own National Army, as promised in the Proclamation of Independence, was lively in both countries, and in each the inevitable but happily rare cases of quarrelling between troops and local inhabitants did not fail to occur—at Ḥumṣ, Aleppo, Beirut—and these were given at times a political complexion. In Syria the National Bloc and the survivors of the Shahbandar group found common ground, and in the spring of 1942 Shukri al-Quwatli returned, with reluctant French agreement, from self-imposed exile. The task of Shaykh Taj grew monthly more difficult as discontent increased at the ubiquity (and sometimes the indifferent or low quality) of French officialdom, the deteriorating supply position, and the failure of the Délégué-Général to restore the Constitution as the basis of a normal State. Signs of a revival of Islamic self-consciousness, shown in congresses of 'Ulama and projects for a Shar'iya University, were no doubt a reaction against renewed foreign occupation. The Druze and 'Alawi territories were in February

1942 retransferred to Syrian authority, on the same cautious terms as in 1936; and this time the step was not, for once, to be subsequently reversed.

The Cabinet of Ḥasan al-Ḥakim, after losing its Druze Minister of Defence by death in March 1942, and its Minister of Communications a month later, resigned in mid-April. Its successor[1] was formed under the Kurdish-descended notable of Ḥumṣ, Ḥusni al-Barazi, and again included a Druze War Minister. The change signified little more than the failure of the outgoing ministers to deal with the troubles of administration, and especially with supply and rationing questions. But the new Cabinet could do no better, and after an uneasy half-year al-Barazi resigned in December 1942. He was succeeded on 10 January 1943 by Jamil al-Ulshi and a team of ministers[2] largely identical. It was destined for the briefest of lives.

In the Lebanon, where the Uniate element still cherished a lingering if cooler affection for France, and the Maronite Patriarch, strengthened now by a new-formed Maronite Council, remained its political head, President Naqqash himself gave the French all support, but his own personality carried little influence. Some useful judicial reforms were made, the Council of State was re-instituted, a few French judges were replaced. The Da'uq Ministry resigned in late June 1942, and was replaced a month later by another,[3] under a leading Sunni nationalist, Sami al-Ṣulḥ, a cousin of Riyaḍh; it showed considerable vigour in planning schemes of development and in combating, as best it could, the economic difficulties of the time. Many references were made, with pride, to the numbers of Lebanese now serving in the Allied, especially the American, forces.

To the nationalists, the French and the British alike, however, widely different as were their views, the question of normalizing the constitutional position of the Governments and, for that purpose, holding general elections transcended all others in importance, and provided a major battle-ground as between French and British conceptions. Other current controversies between them, exacerbated as ever by the profoundly differing

[1] The Prime Minister acted also in Interior: in Finance and Foreign Affairs, Fa'iz al-Khuri: in Economics, Muḥammad al-'Ayyash: in Supplies, Ḥikmat al-Ḥaraki: in Press, Propaganda, and Youth Movements, Munir al-'Ajlani: in Works, Munir al-'Abbas: in Defence, the Amir Ḥasan al-Aṭrash. The portfolio of Education was transferred in July 1942 to Khalil Mardam Bey, a poet.

[2] Prime Minister and Interior, Jamil al-Ulshi: Finance, Amir Muṣṭafa al-Shihabi: Justice and Works, Munir al-'Abbas: Education, Khalil Mardam Bey: Economics, Muḥammad al-'Ayyash: Supplies, Ḥikmat al-Ḥaraki: Defence, Ḥasan al-Aṭrash: Social Services, Munir al-'Ajlani.

[3] Interior, Ḥikmat Janbulaṭ: Finance, Supplies, and Communications, Musa Nammur: Health and Defence, Aḥmad al-Ḥusayni: Justice and Agriculture, Philippe Bulos: Education, Georges Kafusi.

minds and emotions of the two nations, concerned the numbers, authority, and alleged interferences of the numerous British economic and liaison officials:[1] the two opposed attitudes towards local nationalism and its leaders, such as Quwatli: and a differing interpretation of the proper limits of 'territorial' authority.[2] Episodes more acutely irritant occurred in the Jazira and at Dayr al-Zur, in which (for whatever reasons) British officers had taken action displeasing to the highly sensitive Mandatory. The setting up, after considerable acrimony, of a joint Grain-procurement Office (p. 337) did not end the daily friction to which its working gave rise. The occasional suggestions of General Wilson that martial law (which would supersede French 'territorial' authority) might at times and places be desirable, and that the Levant was still, after all, a vital military base, were infuriating to General Catroux, who complained that, for all the much-emphasized need for comprehensive defence plans, he was never consulted about them. More antipathetic still was the frank desire of the British Minister, admitted with great freedom in conversation with local notables and statesmen, for the initiation of such political steps by the Délégué-Général as would satisfy the public and their leaders: and to this end he claimed a finger—or a whole hand—in the pie of political decisions, of which the connexion with Allied security and strategy General Spears felt to be of the closest.

It followed that the question of holding general elections became, from April 1942 when it was first urged by Spears, one of great sensitivity, the more so since it was clear to all that these, if conducted with real freedom, could not but result in nationalist victory—with unpredictable consequences to the French position. The French authority rejected the alternative of merely recalling the Chambers dismissed in 1939, and under further and personal pressure from the new British Minister of State in Cairo—Mr. Richard Casey, successor to Lyttelton—General Catroux in May recommended, with great reluctance, that election procedures should be set in motion the following month. But allied reverses in North Africa provided reasons for a postponement *sine die*: and General de Gaulle, in the course of a month-long visit to the Levant in August and September 1942, proclaimed instead a policy of extreme caution and conservatism, curiously remote from the spirit, or words, of the Proclamation of June 1941. Warning

[1] It had been the original wish and request of de Gaulle that all British agencies should be concentrated into a single body, with a single channel of approach to the French authority.

[2] General Wilson (*Eight Years*, p. 122) found this 'a continuous source of friction' as it 'seemed to include every authority in the country'. The French reply was, in effect, 'So it does!'

the British to keep clear of such matters,[1] as being the sole concern of France, he declared that the two States of the Levant might for years to come be still unready for their independence, and that all talk of elections was premature; France was still bent on 'civilizing' them, and she alone controlled the situation. The General's attitude throughout his tour was, indeed, one which seemed designed to impress the public and Franco-British officialdom with his quasi-sovereign status,[2] the tenacity of his *idées fixes*, and an Anglophobia verging at times on the pathological. Following his return to London, his conversations there with British ministers produced the curious suggestion of a standing Anglo-French consultative machinery to cover all (including Egyptian) Middle Eastern matters; this however was rejected at sight by General Catroux, to whom it was referred, as a British trap crippling to French prestige if she fell into it. French pressure for the removal of the British Minister, now the favourite *bête noire* of de Gaulle—and indeed also of Catroux[3] and his staff—continued strong, but was ungratified. On lower levels the relations of British and French officers and functionaries were normally correct and usually friendly, though during 1942 a few of the Délégué-Général's officers were removed, by his orders, for blatant non-cooperation.

A marked improvement in the war situation in the autumn of 1942 led the French authorities, nevertheless, to adopt a less negative attitude. In November Catroux obtained from his National Committee at Algiers preliminary permission to envisage a restoration of the two Constitutions, followed by general elections, in the following year: elections for which other Arab Governments—'Iraq and Egypt—were by this time eagerly watching, and which, as was everywhere known, for months past the French had been postponing, the British advocating. An announcement in this sense was made accordingly in Beirut during January 1943, a few days after the sudden death of Shaykh Taj. It was issued by M. Jean Helleu, an official of ambassadorial rank (and formerly Secretary-General in Beirut) who had lately joined General de Gaulle from his diplomatic post at Ankara, and was now Catroux's senior subordinate and destined *remplaçant*. It remained

[1] De Gaulle claimed also, during his visit, that the supreme military command in the Levant ought now to belong to France, whose forces there (including the Syro-Lebanese regiments) outnumbered the British. The latter, figures in hand, did not agree.

[2] An admittedly critical British eye-witness of General de Gaulle's tour in these weeks speaks of his 'conducting himself like a monarch', of his 'icy arrogance', and his 'fantastic assumption of sovereign power when he possessed no such thing, his persistent will to repel and refuse all friendly (British) gestures' (M. Borden [Lady Spears], *Journey Down a Blind Alley*, p. 187).

[3] Nothing could exceed the bitterness with which General Catroux in his memoirs writes of General Spears.

to take the administrative steps which would make possible the holding of elections, and to arrange, as far as possible, to control them: a task the more difficult in a period when impatience and unrest in northern Syria were leading to scuffles in Aleppo, bread riots occurred in Damascus in February, severe measures of control and repression were called for in April, and press restrictions were being tightened.

5. THE STATECRAFT OF M. HELLEU

The course of events in the latter half of 1943 was among the unhappiest, as also the last, of the whole mandatory period. It threw into full evidence the curious unreality of surviving French conceptions of the Levant situation, and the contrast between their pretensions—to authority, popularity, and an acceptable statecraft—and the actual weakness and low prestige to which events from 1939 to 1943 had reduced them; and in particular it showed a curious blindness, after twenty years of local experience, to the true force and direction of public opinion. Justifying, in a sense, the fears of General Catroux and his staff of what might result from the free elections so long avoided, it was to demonstrate also the barely credible maladroitness of which an experienced French diplomat could be capable. The conclusion of '*les événements*' of Beirut in November 1943 marked the effective end of the tenacious mandatory régime.

It was the first concern of General Catroux, on his return from Algiers in February 1943, to consider with what separate and carefully formulated appeals the electorate of the two States should be wooed by the formidable corps of his advisers, Délégués, Special Service officers, and devoted local Catholic followers. He then issued, on 25 March, Decrees cancelling those of July and September 1939 and restoring the Syrian and Lebanese Constitutions as of before that year, with effect from the date of the opening of the new Chambers. Power in each Government was to be transferred, for not more than three months, to a Head of State served (in the Lebanon) by two or (in Syria) by three ministers, whose task was to conduct the elections. The Délégué-Général then arranged for the resignations of the existing Presidents and Cabinets, whereafter the provisional functionaries assumed their duties. This skeleton Administration[1] was headed in Lebanon by Eyub Tabet; in Syria, after the failure of Catroux to persuade Hashim al-Atasi or Shukri al-Quwatli to accept office, it was

[1] Other than the (temporary) Heads of State, ministers (each responsible for a number of portfolios) were, in Lebanon, Khalid al-Shihabi and Juwad Bulos: and in Syria, Fa'iz al-Atasi, Na'im Anṭaki, and Muṣṭafa al-Shihabi.

placed under 'Aṭa al-Ayyubi. Political parties and factions everywhere rallied their followers—Uniates, Lebanese Muslims, Communists, ·National Bloc adherents, splinter parties, pan-Arabists in touch with 'Iraq and Egypt, and groups of mixed aims and content. The British Minister issued a statement welcoming the elections, and hoping that they would be free and fruitful: to secure which he used, during the following weeks, all his influence.[1] On 3 June, while electioneering was in full swing, the appointment of M. Helleu as Délégué-Général in succession to General Catroux, now transferred to Algiers,[2] was announced, and the new incumbent broadcast to the population in terms of unconvincing banality.

In Lebanon, Dr. Tabet began with the unwisely partisan step of enfranchising by Decree the whole body of Lebanese *émigrés* who had not adopted foreign nationality. The effect of this would have been to increase Christian representation in the Chamber by 50 per cent.[3] Muslim indignation—that of Sunni, Mutawalli, and Druze alike—led these to threaten a boycott of the elections, and instant protests by Syria, 'Iraq, and Egypt showed the keenness with which the elections were being watched. No step less than the removal of Tabet, and his replacement by Pierre Trad (Butros Turad) was considered adequate; urged by General Catroux (then, early in July, visiting the Levant), this step was taken[4] and the British Minister lent his aid in securing Muslim agreement to a redivision of the seats as between Christians and non-Christians, with 30 and 25 respectively. General Spears, at M. Helleu's suggestion, again appealed publicly for freedom and loyal co-operation in the elections. After a period of keen electioneering, in which all available means of French influence was brought to bear upon the electorate in town and country, the results of the voting were to give success to supporters of the French in the Maronite strongholds and in Beirut city, but large majorities to their opponents elsewhere. The new Chamber met on 21 September, elected Bishara al-Khuri as President of the Republic, and thus extinguished the hopes of his inveterate and whole-heartedly Francophile Maronite rival, Émile Eddé. The premiership in the

[1] No justification can be found for accusations of 'tampering with the electors' against General Spears or his or the Army Commander's staff; it is certain, however, that these saw no need to disguise from friends and inquirers that (since Great Britain was, unlike the French, without local ambitions or commitments) the full freedom of democratic elections could and should, in their view, be practised. That this attitude should be construed as 'anti-French', or 'pro-Arab' was, no doubt, inevitable.

[2] As Commissioner for Islamic Affairs.

[3] That is, from 22 seats (against the Muslims' 20–32).

[4] The two new Ministers, replacing those of Tabet, were 'Abdullah Bayhum and Tawfiq 'Awwad.

first Cabinet[1] under the restored régime went to Riyadh al-Ṣulḥ, a Muslim from Sidon with a long record of pan-Arab and anti-Mandate nationalism.

In Syria, where outward signs of partisanship were less, and the results a foregone conclusion, the primary and secondary elections were held in July. As in the Lebanon, a minority of electors[2] turned out to vote; but the return of the Bloc to power was never in doubt, and the Chamber, meeting on 17 August, elected Shukri al-Quwatli as President of the Republic. His first Cabinet,[3] under his old associate, Sa'dullah al-Jabiri, contained a strong majority of veteran Nationalists.

Once installed, the two Governments entered upon active consultations. Eager in both capitals to assume full and sole legislative powers, to form their national armies (based initially on the *troupes spéciales*), to take control of the Common Interests and of security and the Contrôle Bédouin, and to free their administrations from the omnipresence of French intervention, they addressed, late in October, identical notes to M. Helleu. In these each Government gave notice of its intention to amend the Constitution so as to eliminate mandatory restrictions, and asked not only for the transfer of full legislative and administrative powers, but also for the early conversion of the Délégation-Générale into an Embassy of normal type. M. Helleu replied in discouraging terms, especially as regards constitutional change, which he felt to be untimely; and on 28 October, leaving M. Yves Chataigneau, in charge, he left Beirut for Algiers to consult the French National Committee. The latter, affirming its own status as the representative of French sovereignty, declined to consider any transfer of powers or services to the Levant States otherwise than as the outcome of a treaty; a treaty which would be, in effect, that of 1936, with the possibility of later amendment. The contrast between this attitude and the terms of the Proclamation of 8 June 1941 is striking, but represents the essence of Gaullist policy, or impolicy, in this field.

A message, drafted by the National Committee on this basis and telegraphed on 5 November by Helleu to President Bishara,

[1] The Cabinet was: Premier and Minister of Finance, Riyadh al-Ṣulḥ: Justice and Education, Ḥabib abu-Shahla: Foreign Affairs and Works, Salim Takla: Interior and Defence, the Amir Majid Arsalan: Agriculture and Communications, 'Adil Uṣayran. The Sunni, Orthodox, Maronite, Druze, and Shi'i communities were thus respectively represented.

[2] General Catroux (p. 402) says 35 per cent.; but for the Lebanon his figure, 25 per cent., is (presumably for propaganda purposes) less than half that officially given by the Lebanese authorities, 53 per cent.

[3] In Foreign Affairs, Jamil Mardam Bey: Interior, Luṭfi al-Ḥaffar: Defence and Education, Naṣuḥ al-Bukhari: Justice, 'Abd al-Raḥman al-Kayyali: Agriculture and Communications, Tawfiq al-Shamiya: Finance, Khalid al-'Adhm: Works and Supplies, Mudhhir al-Raslan.

announced that the French could not admit unilateral changes made by the Lebanese in a Constitution which itself 'resulted from obligations . . . undertaken by France, and still in operation'. The President's advice, that this letter should not at present be published, was ignored; and the Lebanese Chamber, rather provoked than restrained by it, proceeded to debate the proposed constitutional amendments on the afternoon of 8 November. A telephoned message from Helleu in Cairo strongly urging postponement, in default of which he must 'reserve his complete freedom of action', was no more effective. The Bill containing the objectionable provisions[1] was presented, its delaying reference to a Committee for study was refused, and its terms were accepted with no dissentient vote. Helleu, arriving at Beirut on the 9th, referred ominously to 'the act of defiance'; and, influenced by certain embittered and conspicuously Anglophobe members of his staff, made decisive plans: plans of which M. Chataigneau, his deputy, was, it would appear, not informed.

At a dinner-party given by the British Minister in honour of the King of Yugoslavia, on the evening of the 10th, M. Helleu gave his host a specific verbal undertaking to take no such action as could be disturbing to public order. At four o'clock on the following morning the Lebanese President, all but two ministers, and certain Deputies were arrested in their beds by French Marines, or in some cases by French colonial (including Senegalese) troops, and were hurried without ceremony to captivity at the inland village of Rashaya. An hour later Decrees appeared on the house walls of Beirut announcing the nullification of the constitutional amendments, the suspension of the Constitution itself, the dissolution of the Chamber, and the appointment of Émile Eddé as Chief of State.

The public reaction was immediate and powerful. A general strike spread throughout Beirut and other towns of the Lebanon, angry demonstrations were followed by rioting and by counter-firing by French troops. A rigid curfew was imposed. Portraits of General de Gaulle were everywhere torn down. City life was paralysed, streets were deserted, the British Legation was besieged by visitors. In the days following, Eddé, sitting almost alone in an empty building, failed to establish a Government. The two ministers[2] who had avoided arrest directed, from a mountain village, a Government claiming sole legitimacy, with the open support of the Maronite Patriarch and almost the entirety, including the Catholic section, of the population. Druze warriors in

[1] These were, briefly, the removal of all references to the Mandate, emphasis on Lebanon's sovereign status, omission of all functions, obligations or rights of the ex-Mandatory, and the discontinuance of French as an official language.

[2] Ḥabib abu-Shahla and Majid Arsalan.

hundreds rallied in the mountains, prepared for any measure of defence or offence, and part of the dismissed Chamber met, outside Beirut, under the protection of these.

Not only in Syria, where noisy demonstrations occurred, but in 'Iraq and Egypt and Muslim Palestine the strongest of protests were issued. The British Minister of State in Cairo, Mr. Casey, flew to Beirut for consultations with General Spears and with the French. In Algiers, the French National Committee was divided; though it announced on 13 November that the action taken in Beirut had not had its authority,[1] General de Gaulle applauded Helleu and his action[2] (and seems never to have revised that view), while realizing that it could not be fully sustained; to General Catroux it appeared indefensible in law, expediency, and morality alike. The (acting) British Minister at Algiers handed to the National Committee a note couched in grave terms demanding, in the interests of essential tranquillity in the Levant, the immediate recall of Helleu and the liberation of the President and ministers, and, in default of this, envisaging the probability of a British military intervention to be followed, perhaps, by a shared inter-Allied control of the Levant States for the rest of the war period. A simultaneous message from the United States demanded, no less frankly, the reversal of recent measures in Beirut, under pain of American 'complete disapproval'. General Catroux was deputed by de Gaulle to proceed urgently to Beirut and to deal with the situation.

He reached Cairo on the 15th, pointedly declined to call upon Naḥḥas Pasha, and in his conversations with Casey insisted on the continued vitality of the French Mandate, the sole competence of the French authorities in the matter, and the iniquities of General Spears, who must certainly be recalled *pari passu* with Helleu. In Beirut, where he wisely avoided the Résidence des Pins, he found strong support for Helleu among 'diehard' French elements,[3] but elsewhere a universal popular indignation which now covered the whole of the ex-mandated territories, and was likely soon to take forms rendering British intervention—at all costs to be avoided—more than probable. Helleu's act, he was forced to recognize,[4] had

[1] M. Helleu claimed, publicly in Beirut, the exact reverse: he had acted in strict accord with General de Gaulle's instructions. It is probable that *general* authority (in part verbal) had been given to him to sustain the French mandatory position 'by whatever means might be necessary' (or some equivalent phrase), but that the *particular* step taken was M. Helleu's own—or that of his more extremist staff.

[2] cf. his *Mémoires*, ii. 197: 'Tout en jugeant parfaitement justifiables les mesures prises par notre délégué et, surtout, les sentiments qui les lui avaient dictées.'

[3] General Catroux (p. 414) reflects that 'tous ces hommes gardaient la nostalgie du Mandat et de l'autorité. . . . Leur jugement était obscurci par cet état d'esprit passionnel qui leur voilait les réalités et les nécessités.'

[4] Catroux, p. 414.

unified the entire Lebanese nation against France in a single night.

On the 18th he telegraphed to Algiers his recommendation for the release of the President and ministers and, lest worse befall, the reinstatement of the former with a new Cabinet. Bishara al-Khuri, although not unamenable when visited in his captivity by Catroux, declined to abandon his colleagues; the Prime Minister, Riyadh al-Ṣulḥ, insisted that public opinion would scarcely accept his own eviction from office: and Catroux, under insistent pressure by Spears, by the Damascus Government, and on the 19th by an impatient ultimatum from Casey with a three-day time-limit, realized that his attitude of free and independent arbiter of the situation could not be sustained. The recall of Helleu was no longer doubtful, and no more was to be heard of this French representative who, patently inadequate to his functions, and dominated by a staff no wiser than himself, must vie with General Sarrail for the distinction of having done most, as High Commissioner, to damage the French position in the Levant. A half-dozen of his leading advisers and executives followed him from Beirut a week later.

On the 20th General Catroux was constrained to advocate the reinstatement of all the imprisoned ministers. A last-minute attempt of the National Committee in Algiers to 'save face' by limiting reinstatement to the President could not be effective; and on the 23rd amid great popular enthusiasm, and a conspicuous absence of French troops, the released and jubilant ministers were escorted to their offices. M. Eddé retired. The new national flag of Lebanon fluttered from public buildings, replacing the Tricolour and its cedar. '*Les événements*' were over; the Délégué-Général's Decrees of 11 November were cancelled, except the one which nullified the constitutional changes. A bitter blow to French prestige had been sustained. It had been invited by her weakness, her disproportionate pretensions, and a particular act of gross impolicy, and there was to be, this time, not even a façade of recovery from it: for all of which it was found possible by General Catroux, and by many less moderate and less intelligent than him, once more to blame British malignity! General Catroux, visiting the Sarai through vast crowds, and installing M. Chataigneau as acting Délégué-Général, could in a broadcast speech claim for France a gesture of 'liberation and nobility', and ask that the Lebanese in their turn should respect thenceforward the French 'moral patrimony and her position'. Of these claims, it was true, the last had not yet been heard; but, in the immediate position of France in the Levant, changes which the past twenty years had failed to achieve were to be made within the next few weeks.

X

END AND BEGINNING

I. LIFE IN WARTIME, 1940–45

THE effects of the events of December 1943 upon the position of France in the Levant were immediate and permanent; they involved, in a very real sense, the effective end of the Mandate. But before these are described some attention should be given to a less dramatic but not irrelevant subject, the economic and by consequence the social fortunes of the territory during the war period. The conditions which supervened in the two States between 1940 and 1945 contained, indeed, few elements unforeseeable or surprising; they were of a type scarcely avoidable in a society and economy never self-sufficient, and now for nearly six years to be largely isolated from the economics (themselves abnormal) of the world outside, and to be occupied for that period by foreign armies on a war footing. The resulting phenomena were those never of widespread (though of intermittent and local) unemployment, nor of famine, nor of national bankruptcy; but they included serious shortages in supplies and inequalities in distribution, the development of severe inflation, the loss of the main 'invisible exports' with the substitution of others, and the partial paralysis of commerce. At the same time great but indifferently successful efforts were made not only to control the uncontrollable situation but simultaneously to increase national output. A social background shaped and dominated by these features, which were all-pervasive for half a decade, could not but greatly affect public tranquillity and morale, and offer to the politicians new weapons as well as new embarrassments. It may at the same time be felt that the main course of political events would have been not dissimilar even in the absence of these stresses; and it is remarkable that even in the economic field certain wartime lines of progress were achieved—in industry, power supply, and agricultural method—which were to outlast the years of abnormality.

The pages here following deal, in no strict chronological order, with the period from the spring of 1940—since the earliest months of the war affected the Levant but little—until the middle of 1945.

The essential desideratum of the territory was to continue or to improve its normal economic life, based as this was on an active commerce, a moderate level of export, the indispensable import of some necessities, a humble volume of local manufactures, considerable 'invisible exports', and a primitive agriculture nearly but never quite able to ensure national self-sufficiency in food. Each of these elements was, in the event, deeply disturbed, in some cases destroyed, by war conditions. The exports of the territory—barley, citrus fruits, lentils, onions, chick-peas, wool, cement—fell heavily in quantity through lack of shipping space and of marine security; but this was compensated by the stimulated and increased ability of the country to feed both its own population and the occupying armies. The purchasing agencies of the Allies were able to buy large quantities of local silk (for parachutes), and their armies clamoured for all that they could obtain of foodstuffs as well as industrial products. Local manufacturers, though in places handicapped by shortage of the raw materials normally imported, were able considerably to augment their output, notably, in cotton yarn, flour, soap, jams, canned fruit, beer, tobacco, cotton piece-goods, and silk cocoons; the demands of the armies, and the shortage (or stoppage) of imported goods, were encouraging to the achievement of such increases, capital was available on the spot from the high level of wartime profits, and much expert advice was provided by specialists in the Middle East Supply Centre,[1] an agency founded with Anglo-American management and personnel in 1941 with headquarters in Cairo, and represented in Syria and Lebanon by officers of the Spears Mission.[2] The textile industry in particular achieved remarkable progress, notably in northern Syria. Care was taken to avoid lines of development which, however immediately attractive, after-war conditions would render uneconomic.

Shortages of petroleum products led in 1940 to the rapid improvisation of a small refinery at Tripoli by French engineers; using crude oil from the 'Iraq Petroleum Company's tanks, it came into production at the end of 1940 and passed its products to a consortium of distributors. Elsewhere, the oil industry in the wartime Levant had varying fortunes. The 'Iraq Petroleum Company (or Syria Petroleum Company) 'blanket' concession for four-fifths of Syria was confirmed in 1940, but exploratory drilling could not be maintained. The trans-desert pipeline from 'Iraq was interrupted from mid-1940 till late 1941, then gradually

[1] It was originally a branch of G.H.Q., Middle East, but became by evolution a semi-independent agency under the Minister of State in Cairo. Its British and American elements were, until 1945, closely integrated, its primary function being to secure all essential supplies to the Middle Eastern countries with minimum calls on Allied resources, factories, or shipping. M.E.S.C. was always an advising and co-ordinating, not an executive body.

[2] A separate Anglo-American branch office for Syria–Lebanon was opened in 1945.

restored to normal with great advantage to the Allied navies. The Company's depots, telecommunications, and landing grounds were largely used by the Army. Before the end of the war applications were made by two American companies to erect refineries on the coast of Lebanon; these were granted (not without criticism on political lines), but the projects were in each case unfulfilled.

Local activity did not preclude the necessity of placing a rigid limitation on imports[1]—notably those of sugar, rice, tea, coffee, and cotton piece-goods—since these occupied shipping space, economy in which, as the greatest of all Allied shortages, was a main *raison d'être* of the M.E.S.C.; and from this followed both the comprehensive efforts made by all concerned in 1942 and thereafter first to increase every form of local output, and secondly to secure fair distribution of essentials among the public. The former of these objectives led, in and after 1942, to a close survey by British experts of such steps to improve local agriculture as could be immediately feasible.[2] Such steps included the import of tractors, the provision of increased transport for agricultural labourers, intensified war on pests, minor irrigation schemes, improved water-lifting plant, and the introduction of new crop types, especially potatoes. The increase of cotton growing, from 1944 onwards, was indeed remarkable. The second objective led to elaborate arrangements by M.E.S.C. (largely outside the cognizance of the local governments and publics, and indeed of the French authorities also) for the import of carefully controlled[3] minima of essential commodities, and to arrangements within Syria and Lebanon to offer these, as well as the materials locally produced, to the public by procedures aiming to secure fair shares for all.

Rationing machinery, administered by an *ad hoc* Ministry in each of the two States from 1940 onwards, could not be expected to be, and was not, efficient. It applied to some only of the materials liable to shortage, and not to identical commodities in each territory. Divided and sometimes clashing authority, administrative

[1] The objective of M.E.S.C. was to cut Middle Eastern civilian imports by 80 per cent. In 1939 such imports were calculated to about 5½ million tons, and in 1942 and 1943 were reduced to 1¼ million; even so, the military-civil congestion at sea ports was among the least tractable problems of the time.

[2] Monographs by agricultural and other experts, written after local research at this period, were published and are of permanent value.

[3] The M.E.S.C. adopted a carefully-evolved procedure for ascertaining minimum local needs (in consultation with Governments) and for providing these by permitting purchase under strict control by licensed trading concerns in Great Britain or the U.S.A., followed by the allocation of shipping space. The 'executive arm' of M.E.S.C. for handling certain of the commodities (sugar, tea, cereals, coffee, edible oil) was the United Kingdom Commercial Corporation (U.K.C.C.), which held and distributed stocks. Drugs, and iron and steel. were handed to the local Governments for distribution.

inexperience at the top, an indifferent and in places corrupt civil service, and strong personal and local pressures, were inimical to sound administration; and, throughout the public, inveterate habits of speculation and hoarding, constantly changing conditions and price levels, the forgery of ration-cards, and the certainty that easy abuses (such as the improper traffic in import licences) could quickly produce large fortunes, all militated against reliable results in distribution.

In the Lebanon, all had ration-cards; in Syria, fewer commodities were rationed, and distribution to villages was by block allowances. Each Government had a Ministry of Rationing, or Supply, and frequent improvements in organization were made, or attempted. Scandals, inclusive even of Cabinet Ministers, were not unknown, and over wide areas of the territory the prescribed procedures were in fact barely operative. Actual shortage, or maldistribution, of grain produced bread riots on many occasions —usually with some political exploitation—and other deficiencies or inequalities led to the frustration and resentment of industrialist and housewife alike. Various interstatal committees of joint control were set up, with indifferent success.

The fixing of prices for essential commodities was attempted by both Governments with no great measure of effectiveness, and a flourishing black-market existed at all times beside that of the law-abiding salesman. Wholesale prices rose by the end of the war to eight or nine times those of 1939, black-market prices exceeded the authorized level by three to five times. Rents were controlled, but increases up to 100 per cent. were permitted. Co-operative selling was attempted in Beirut, but failed. 'Corners' in essential articles were organized, with varying success. Government 'advisory boards' for each of a number of necessaries (vehicles, iron, steel, textiles, paper) were on the whole ineffective.

The locally-operating agency most in view was the Office des Céréales Panifiables or O.C.P., known locally as M.I.R.A. Its object was to obtain, by close supervision and the offer of good prices, the utmost disposable surplus of grain from farmers, whereby to feed the town populations and to obviate the need for import. Import, however, organized by the British from Australian sources, was unavoidable in 1941–2—a year of disastrous harvests —and reached some 100,000 tons. The institution of the agency, on a quadripartite (Anglo-French-Syro-Lebanese) basis, gave occasion for one of the sharper exchanges between General Catroux and the British Minister. The former resented the intrusion of others into any part of his 'territorial command', the latter desired efficiency, and the Syrian Government felt unhappy at the prospect of the establishment in their country of so important an all-French organization; but, though the many British officers so employed all over Syria[1] were denounced by the more implacable French critics as spies or propagandists, in fact the improvised joint organization established its monopoly of purchase, collection, transporting, milling, and finally allotment and distribution of grain so successfully that, aided by better harvests and an increased sown acreage, imports could after 1942 be entirely discontinued, and all civil needs met. Grain was, instead, exported to other theatres of war.[2]

The high prices obtained by farmers[3] resulted in their ability to pay off, as never before, their age-long debts, and to increase their hoards of gold coins:[4] but their greater effect, in conjunction with shortage of consumer goods, was to magnify inflation. This, in spite of the lesser remittances from *émigrés*, was further increased by high military expenditure, which was in 1943 (at £23 million) more than three times its 1940 level. Inflation prevailed to an exaggerated degree,[5] and little attempt was made to diminish it by heightened rates of taxation or by forced loans. The cultivator was complacent, as the main recipient of the vastly increased sums in circulation; many urban dealers or middlemen reaped a rich harvest in the difference between the bulk prices charged for controlled imported goods and the bazaar rates obtainable; but the town worker, his pay at best only doubled—or, if an oil-company worker, trebled or quadrupled—enjoyed a lower real income than before the war, and was the worst sufferer. Employment under the Army absorbed available manpower, up to a figure of 30,000 men directly employed late in 1943, but was insufficient to hamper industry or agriculture.

The later months of the war saw already the gradual relaxation both of controls imposed by the M.E.S.C. organization—from which, with considerable though undeserved loss to her prestige, France was excluded as being able to produce, in present circumstances, neither goods nor shipping—and of those devised by the local Governments and their advisers. To reopen full freedom of trade and competition at the earliest moment was an object of

[1] cf. J. Soustelle, *Envers et contre tout*, i. 347: 'les deux États partout pénétrés et sapés par les *political officers* de Spears'.

[2] A very important saving of shipping space resulted. Other means to increase such saving (in the sphere of food supply) were a diminution in the tonnage of nitrates imported, adulteration of bread by coarser local grains, and increased grain acreages.

[3] From pre-war rates of £4·5 per ton, to £39 in 1942 (when the price of imported grain was £24), and £54 in 1943.

[4] The British authorities in 1943–4 offered gold, to an extent of £5 million, on the local market, in order to convert spending power into hoarding and thereby diminish inflation. The effect was negligible.

[5] Notes in circulation rose from £LS 43 m. in 1939 to £LS 367 m. in mid-1945; that is, by 8½ times. Bank deposits rose from £LS 19 m. to 202 m. (£LS 8·83 = £1 sterling).

American policy, and precluded any longer extension of joint control; and it was not less that of the local Governments, eager to assert their full independence, and of local merchants anxious to spend accumulated funds and to plunge into the profitable business of supplying the shortages in all types of importable goods. The year 1945 and thereafter formed, therefore, a period of return to conditions of *laisser-faire*.

Certain features developed during the war were to prove permanent. Some industries, and notably the textile, had already begun a serious development which was to progress rapidly: the impulse to industrialization in general had been notably strengthened by wartime experience and perspectives. Individual fortunes acquired by contracting, supplying, or producing had contributed new men, perhaps a new type of man, to public life. Co-operative forms of organization, especially in agriculture, had been attempted under foreign inspiration, and these would not entirely disappear.[1] Experience had been gained by local officialdom in such difficult fields of organization as census-taking, rationing, and price-fixing. The possibility of regional economic planning, well exemplified in M.E.S.C. itself, had become clear to some of the broader minds, though the intense nationalism of the Middle East was to prove too strong for its development. A wartime atmosphere had encouraged, in the upper and middle ranks of society, movements towards extended cultural institutions, modern town-planning, social service, and feminism; the last-named inspired a number of enthusiastic conferences, and some genuine progress towards the social and political emancipation of women. A number of public works had been carried out, roads extended, and a Haifa–Tripoli railway completed by the British Army. In the field of labour organization the trade unions, however crude in their conceptions and largely Communist-dominated, had improved their organization and shown their power, while in both States the Labour Code was redrafted and extended—and even, in the still narrow industrial field where the organization and supervision of labour was possible, began to be applied.

Public finance was no more likely than private, or than society itself, to return after the war to the ideas or scale of 1939. To an extent which did not represent, evidently, any real proportionate progress, the figures at which the State budgets of the two republics were balanced[2] in and after the war years, left far behind them those of earlier days. This, reflecting mainly higher prices

[1] M.I.R.A. itself was continued in existence by the Syrian Government for a time after the war.

[2] In thousands of £LS, and for Syria and the Lebanon respectively, the budgets balanced in 1933 at 6,700 and 4,500: in 1939, at 11,800 and 6,300: in 1944, at 69,400 and 34,000: and in 1946 at 129,700 and 60,000.

and taxable values, and the increased costs of government, was due in part also to better procedures in taxation, a richer field for its incidence, and an increase in the functions assumed by Government.

A census taken at the end of the period showed substantial increases in population since the previous census. The population of the Lebanon was now approaching $1\frac{1}{4}$ million, against little more than the three-quarters of a million recorded (however approximately), fourteen years earlier; that of Syria was now shown as exceeding 3 million, against $2\frac{1}{2}$ million less than a decade before. In the Lebanon, the Christians maintained their small majority over all others, with some 53 per cent. of the population; in Syria the Muslims (more than four-fifths Sunni) formed 82 or, with the Druzes, 85 per cent.

2. TRANSFER OF POWERS

Onwards from the last day of November 1943 the French authorities ceased to challenge such constitutional changes as the Governments of the Lebanon and Syria saw fit to make. The Syrian Prime Minister declared early in December that no Mandate was now recognized and that all powers of government were their own, or must forthwith be made so, without further bargaining or an imposed Treaty; and six weeks later members of the Chamber in Damascus took their oath of allegiance to a Constitution which ignored all mandatory ties. In Beirut equally the Chamber's resolutions of 8 November were treated as in force, in spite of M. Chataigneau's proviso (p. 330), which was ignored.

General Catroux, after a short visit to Algiers, returned on 16 December to negotiate the transfer of powers to the local Governments: a transfer clearly overdue, of which the long denial had been, not unforeseeably, disastrous. On 22 December a Franco-Syrian-Lebanese tripartite Agreement was reached without difficulty, and provided a manageable first instalment. It covered, in five protocols, the transfer to the States, as from 1 January 1944, of the Customs administration, the Tobacco Monopoly, the Lighthouse Service, and the control of the concessionary companies with their important share in the urban public services and the country's oil development. The future management of the Common Interests was prescribed by a Syro-Lebanese Convention of 27 January, which *inter alia* set up a joint Higher Council to control such services as must remain interstatal.

The announcement of the transfers was well, though not uncritically, received; but a correspondingly bad impression was made by Catroux's refusal to consider cession of the Syro-Lebanese *troupes spéciales*, who were recruited largely from the minorities and were claimed as predominantly loyal to France. The control of French schools and philanthropic institutions remained also a valued and powerful weapon in French hands. Later in the year 1944 further protocols were agreed, transferring to Syrian and Lebanese hands the Departments of Antiquities and of Trade Marks and Royalties, and the Inspectorates of Quarantine, the Veterinary Service, and Posts and Telegraphs. Control of the railways was, after some period of 'further study', vested in the local Governments before the winter of 1944–5. The Sûreté-Générale, the press censorship, and the Contrôle Bédouin were all made over during the year. In most departments, including the last-named, a number of formerly executive French officers remained in advisory capacities, but these were gradually reduced. The smoothness of the transfer, and the degree to which working efficiency was lost, varied widely between departments; the partition between the two States of economic and other previously combined services of the High Commission was not without problems, nor was the division of the spoils always amiable. But by the end of 1944 few important government services, except that of the *troupes spéciales*, remained in other than local hands, and these (civil airports, geological survey, the Ḥijaz Railway,[1] the port of Beirut, the hydrological, astronomical, and cartographic services—and, with much significance, the Grand Sérail itself) would follow without incident during 1945. Legislation was, for the first time, entirely their own; French officials survived on sufferance, and even in the Courts were fewer and less dominant; and an Anglo-French financial[2] agreement made on 8 February 1944 had ostensibly stabilized the currency in terms of the franc and of sterling, and within limits guaranteed its stability for the future. Some nationalist satisfaction greeted the assertion that the national currencies were no longer 'tied to' that of the ex-Mandatory.

In the retention by France of the *troupes spéciales*, and her unconcealed justification in that these formed the last remaining weapon whereby a favourable treaty could be obtained and the territory dominated (or 'protected') in the meanwhile, there were too evidently the seeds of trouble. The two republics demanded the right to form national armies, as had been specifically promised

[1] For this, a separate administration was formed, directly under the Prime Minister's office.

[2] The franc rate was fixed at 200 to £1 sterling. In Syria and Lebanon the £LS would be valued at 22·65 francs (in place of the existing 20), and £LS 8·83 would remain equivalent to £1 sterling. The agreement covered also the reserves of the Banque de Syrie. The two States did not become (as the declaration of 8 June 1941 had indicated) full members of the sterling bloc, and this was resented.

to them three years ago as part of their independence; they resented the command of their subjects by foreign officers, and the bad effect of this on their own authority; and they required the services of these forces (which had in the past, on well-remembered occasions, been used by the Mandatory against them) for their own security functions as well as their *amour-propre*. But negotiations on the subject dragged throughout 1944, the authorities in Algiers (or, after August, in Paris) were intransigent, and local statesmen refused to accept a connexion between the fate of the *troupes spéciales* and the conclusion of a treaty, to which they were avoiding all commitment; and though both Governments made budgetary provision for an army, and the Syrians in January 1945, amid riotous student demonstrations which had their counterpart in Beirut, announced its imminent formation, no army could in fact be set on foot, and no greater satisfaction was given to local feeling than by a slight increase in Gendarmerie strength, for which the British, on request, supplied small-arms. The early months of 1945 found the position unresolved. Nor had General Beynet, brought from Washington in February 1944 as Délégué-Général and Commander-in-Chief, been able to make progress towards the conclusion of the much-desired treaty: a treaty (for which, in spite of wishful thoughts, the 1936 model could clearly no longer serve) destined legally to end the Mandate, as had been the case of 'Iraq, to secure French assets and interests, and to confirm their primacy among European Powers in the Levant. But the Governments of Syria and Lebanon, rejecting all pretensions that 'the Mandate still exists', could not be brought, in the face of strong public opinion, to contemplate negotiations at this stage for a treaty which could not but detract from their now realized independence, and was likely to tie them to considerable survivals of mandatory restriction. They went further than this; the Syrian Chamber resolved that the French language should no longer be taught in government primary schools and should be alternative to English in secondary, and that all official correspondence should thenceforward be in Arabic only. In the Lebanon the use of French was limited to specific offices and purposes.

The reinstated Ministry of Riyaḍh al-Ṣulḥ faced a task of government complicated by mid-war economic and supply difficulties, and by the painful stresses still felt between the administration and the French. The latter had lost, inevitably, much even of their Maronite support, and bitterness between 'patriots' (among whom the Phalanges Libanaises of Pierre Jumayyil regained their old place) and 'traitors' sympathetic to the French showed itself in many episodes. The most serious of these arose in Beirut, in the last days of April 1945, from a scuffle and shooting outside the Chamber. The occasion was the induction of a new and ostentatiously Francophile Deputy, and the episode was followed by extended disorder in which fatal casualties occurred, and which was with difficulty pacified by combined French, British, and Lebanese efforts. An attempt was made on the life of the Muslim leader of Tripoli, ‘Abd al-Ḥamid Karami, a victim of the November 1943 arrests and imprisonment. Communism gained substantial ground, aided by Russia's admired place in the Allied war effort. Other political parties, no more considerable than usual, formed and re-formed their ephemeral coteries. M. Eddé was for a year no more seen. November 22 was acclaimed as the new Independence Day.

If the basis of Lebanese nationalism had been broadened by recent events, and Muslim opinion decreasingly inclined to question (except, upon occasion, for tactical reasons) the permanence of Greater Lebanon itself, the stability of political life seemed after November 1943 to have increased but little. Good work was done, indeed, in minor administrative and judicial reform, in fiscal improvements, plans for an Arab Academy, preparations for a census, the suppression of gambling houses; but political instability still prevailed, Cabinets still changed easily and unregretted. That of Riyaḍh al-Ṣulḥ needed to be re-formed[1] in early July 1944, when the Minister of Interior, Camille Chamoun (Sham‘un) left for London; and it fell, to be replaced by another[2] under ‘Abd al-Ḥamid Karami, early in January 1945 and by yet another[3] late in August, headed this time by Sami al-Ṣulḥ. The President, Bishara al-Khuri, was forced by mental illness to retire to Palestine for treatment in February and March 1945, but could return thereafter to resume his duties. These weeks were, in his absence and after his return, filled with meetings of Lebanese with Syrian ministers at Shatura; with the late spring of 1945, another crisis with the French authority was approaching.

In Syria, the same preoccupations faced the Government, which

[1] Riyaḍh retained the Premiership and held also the Ministries of Interior and Supply: Ḥabib abu-Shahla took Justice and Education: Ḥamid Franjiya, Finance: Salim Takla, Foreign Affairs and Works: Amir Majid Arsalan, Health, Agriculture, and Defence: and Muḥammad al-Fadḥl, Industry and Communications.

[2] The Prime Minister took also the Ministry of Defence: Nicolas Ghuṣn, Industry and Communications: Salim Takla, Foreign Affairs and Justice: Ḥamid al-As‘ad, Works and Health: Wadi Na‘im, Interior and Education: Dr. Jamil Talḥuq, Agriculture and Supply. Takla died a few days later, and was succeeded by Henri Pharaon (Far‘un).

[3] Prime Minister, and Minister of Supply and Communications, Sami al-Ṣulḥ: Interior, Yusif Salim: Works, Gabriel Murr: Health, Dr. Talḥuq: Justice, Sa‘di al-Munla: Foreign Affairs and Education: Ḥamid Franjiya: Defence and Agriculture, Aḥmad al-As‘ad.

on all issues concerned with France and foreign affairs was in friendly solidarity with its neighbour. The atmosphere was one of triumph at the successful acquisition of real self-government, pride in its exercise, but impatience with such continued limitations as were implied by the still separated *troupes spéciales* and the presence of foreign armies. Both Communism (always strong among the Syrian intelligentsia) and a certain revival of militant Islamic conservatism, as well as the spiritual and economic abnormalities of wartime, played their part in keeping society nervous and unsettled; nor was the comparatively moderate Ministry of the time always in accord with mob and student elements which found true patriotism only in street rioting. Such episodes occurred at Ḥamah in February 1942 and at Damascus (with an anti-Christian colouring) three months later, and a strike of printers in the capital brought the press to a temporary standstill. The assumption of direct Syrian control of the bedouin tribes[1] passed peacefully. In the 'Alawi sanjaq, which provisionally kept its special status on the lines of 1936, the non-cooperation or flat disobedience of the obese and half-shrewd, half-crazy 'god', Sulayman al-Murshid, led to his detention in Damascus; he was a Deputy, but no nationalist. A Syrian Gendarmerie expedition was launched against his followers, whom French forces—and in a measure the French Délégué of the province also, General 'Montclar' (alias the zealous Colonel Magrin-Verneret)—hastened to support. Hard pressed, Sulayman later renounced his isolationism—but not his private army—and became for a time a pan-Syrian patriot. (He was hanged in November 1946, with excellent effect upon 'Alawi tranquillity.) The Jabal al-Duruz province was, by Decree, finally absorbed in the Syrian State in December 1944, without immediate protest by its traditional separatists; not many months passed, however, before faction in the Jabal again raised its head, the old divisions reappeared, and a visit of the Prime Minister, in November 1946, was necessary to stabilize loyalty to the Syrian State in face not only of the time-honoured local separatism but of an abortive movement to secede to Transjordan.

The Cabinet, without change of programme and without appeal to the electorate, changed twice during these months. In October the Jabiri Ministry, weakened by internal discords, was replaced by another[2] under the veteran Protestant statesman, Faris

[1] A contemporary census of these showed figures of 23,200 in Damascus sanjaq, 45,200 in those of Ḥumṣ and Aleppo, 21,200 in the Palmyra area, 11,000 in Euphrates, 31,300 in Jazira, 8,700 in Jabal al-Duruz.

[2] The Prime Minister took also the portfolios of Interior and Works: Jamil Mardam Bey, those of Foreign Affairs, Defence, and Economics: Khalid al-'Adhm, Finance and Supply: 'Abd al-Raḥman Kayyali, Justice and Education (and the Awqaf, which had previously been under the Prime Minister's office). Sa'dullah al-Jabiri became President of the Chamber.

al-Khuri. This Cabinet was joined in March 1945 by two new ministers,[1] with the portfolios of Interior and Education; but a month later (9 April) it gave place, without significance, to a re-formed Ministry[2] under the same Premier. Its four months of life were to be marked by violent events which showed—what was already implicit when it took office—how far apart, even at this late stage, were French and Syrian conceptions of 'independence', and how strained were nerves on both sides.

3. FINAL CLASH

By the mid-spring of 1945 almost all the powers and functions of government had been transferred from French into Syrian and Lebanese hands and, with whatever loss of the specifically French contribution of specialized experience, had been absorbed[3] into their Administration. But, apart from the endemic difficulties of 'godly and quietly' governing so unquiet a territory, there was still, and ever more clearly as the explosion of November 1943 receded, one serious remaining exigency of the French—that of a treaty with each State assuming French primacy, privilege, and advantage; and one immediate grievance against them, their refusal to transfer the *troupes spéciales*. And, though in the Allied military view the Middle East continued to be a vital base and transit area whose tranquillity was all-important, the lingering presence of foreign garrisons was viewed with impatient disfavour by all political elements, and in particular that of the French forces, since there could be no question of the British Army being other than a wartime phenomenon.[4]

The poised and conciliatory attitude of General Beynet, who managed at least initially to combine popularity in the local world with the approbation of General de Gaulle,[5] could not disguise the

[1] Respectively Ṣabri al-'Asali and Aḥmad al-Sharabati.

[2] Ministers now were: in Foreign Affairs and Defence, Jamil Mardam Bey: in Justice, Awqaf, and Supply, Sa'id al-Ghazzi: in Finance, Na'im Anṭaki: in Interior, Ṣabri al-'Asali: in Education, Aḥmad al-Sharabati: in works: Ḥikmat al-Ḥakim.

[3] Those sections of the Common Interests which were unavoidably interstatal were, in each Republic, grouped under their Ministries of Finance: Security, Passive Defence, and the Explosives Office came under Interior: public-service and mineral concessions, Geological Survey, and the (wartime) control of vehicles and spare parts, under Works and Communications: Economic Affairs (as grouped in the former High Commission), Trade Marks and Royalties, Maritime Interests and Excise, under Economics, or in some cases under Finance: Broadcasting, Antiquities, Foreign Schools, and cultural institutions, under Education: Finance, Defence, and Posts under the Ministries so named.

[4] This distinction was drawn specifically by the Syrian Premier, Sa'dullah al-Jabiri, and by his President, later in 1945.

[5] *Mémoires*, ii. 199: 'beaucoup d'habilité et de fermeté'.

close connexion envisaged by the French between the strength of their own garrisons (and of the *troupes spéciales*) and the desired treaties. They claimed, moreover, that existing agreements gave them the right to retain such garrisons in the Republics, at least until the end of the war; and, amid continued assertions of the interferences or sinister ambitions of the British officers variously employed in the country,[1] they refused to consider a withdrawal or weakening of their own forces while British or British-commanded[2] units remained.

From the end of 1944, following measures taken by the Syrian Government in the field of education which were hailed as hostile to France, relations in Damascus and Paris grew more evidently strained. On 25 January 1945 demonstrations against the French were held in the Syrian capital and other cities, to which the French reply took the form of military parades accompanied by heavy armour, to prevent (but in fact more likely to create) clashes and casualties. Feeling in France ran high, French ministers and General de Gaulle himself admitted no compromise on their indispensable right to a 'pre-eminent position' in the Levant; the British, in the press and the Commons, hoped in their perplexity that direct Franco-Syrian negotiations could begin and somehow succeed. Mr. Churchill himself gave moderating advice in this sense to the Syrian President, al-Quwatli, when these statesmen met[3] on 17 February 1945. Americans and Russians, less directly concerned, specifically rejected French claims to a special position.

Early in March, General Beynet was summoned to Paris for instructions on the opening of negotiations for the treaties, of which the safeguarding of the French 'cultural mission' was, as the Délégué-Général asserted, the prime objective. Syrian opinion remained nervous and hostile, and little inclined to acquiesce in any policy of compromise. The expected negotiations were given, in the event, no chance of success, thanks to French action of a curious and self-defeating perversity: action in which they would doubtless have been less insistent had not General de Gaulle been, once more, the victim of his obsessive Anglophobia. During April Franco-Syrian personal relations deteriorated; the Délégué

[1] The leading *bête noire* of the French, Sir E. L. Spears, the British Minister, left his post (at his own insistence) in December 1944 after three years of a dynamic championship of the British (and American) viewpoint which, while admittedly transcending normal diplomatic usage, could be justified by the strong Allied interest in the territories as a war base, and by the specific British guarantees of 8 June 1941. He continued in the House of Commons, and with much publicity, to sustain the two republics as against French policy. His successor at Beirut was Mr. (Sir) Terence Shone, a career diplomatist.

[2] The Ninth Army included, at various periods, Polish, Czech, and Greek units.

[3] On Mr. Churchill's return journey from the Yalta meeting.

in Damascus, General Oliva-Roget, was already on the worst of terms with local ministers; and, more significantly, rumours were abroad in the country of a French intention to reinforce their garrisons. These proved only too accurate, in spite of the clear unwisdom of provocative action at this juncture, and in spite also of a personal *démarche* made by the British Prime Minister to de Gaulle on 4 May, begging him to abstain; they were, moreover, by the most unfortunate of choices, none other than Senegalese troops who disembarked from a French cruiser in Beirut harbour on 7 May. Though announced by the French as mere replacements, the arrival of these, in numbers which popular or malicious report was quick to exaggerate, was greeted by an ill-tempered demonstration in Beirut. This involved tumultuous bodies of troops and civilians waving French and Arab[1] flags and—as was alleged, but not established—a Nazi emblem, amid disorders of which, inevitably, conflicting accounts were subsequently given.

General Beynet returned to Beirut a week later. On 18 May, three days after the Syrian Chamber had voted a Law for the Protection of Independence, with severe penalties for 'serving a foreign Power', he revealed to representatives of the two Governments the proposed bases of the treaties. The *troupes spéciales* were to remain under French command until some future date, unspecified but certainly subsequent to the end of the war; cultural matters would be covered by a special Convention, another (designed to ensure her communications) would deal with French military bases, and yet another would prescribe economic and diplomatic relations. In fact, all the French desiderata were to be unequivocally secured, and only thereafter would the objectives dearest to Syro-Lebanese feelings—the transfer of local forces, the evacuation of foreign troops—be considered. Both the local Governments, after a decisive consultation at Shatura on the 19th, refused categorically to negotiate on such lines, or on any others while military reinforcements[2] were continuing to arrive. On 19 May shops were shut and a strike proclaimed in Damascus, Beirut, and elsewhere; demonstrations and some aimless firing occurred. Next day, a more truculent demonstration in Aleppo, organized by extremist political elements[3] and backed (it was said) by Syrian Gendarmerie, led to French counter-action, with armoured cars. Some dozens of

[1] Part of an Arab company of the Palestine Regiment, Arab nationalist in sentiment, took part, but without authority.

[2] The French, both in France and in the Levant, asserted that the British had also been reinforcing their garrisons in Syria. This (for which it would be difficult to imagine a motive) was authoritatively and circumstantially denied by the British.

[3] Led, according to French sources, by the incorrigible Iḥsan al-Jabiri.

casualties occurred, and strict military control of the city was enforced for some days. French troops were evacuated from the Citadel at Aleppo on the 24th. An anti-French revulsion of feeling showed itself even in the Druze, Ḥawran, and 'Alawi districts. A number of casualties resulted from street fighting at Dayr al-Zur; there, and elsewhere, mutual violence was stopped only by British intervention. In other principal cities a general strike paralysed business for three days, and Franco-Syrian relations were strained to breaking-point at main centres of nationalist feeling (Ḥamah and Ḥumṣ), where street fighting broke out; this led on 28 and 29 May to a complete breakdown of law and order and, in a confused atmosphere of mutual recrimination and attacks, to sporadic shelling by French guns. In Damascus the same or more dangerous excitement prevailed, and unruly mob demonstrations occurred with the loss of all semblance of normal order. The French, severely provoked by insulting or aggressive acts by the Syrian street mob (or even the Gendarmerie), sought to persuade the world that all was the work of 'British agents', who had been arming the mob and intentionally provoking bloodshed.[1] Their own military commanders, provoked by shots fired (it was alleged) at French headquarters, and directed by the bitter and unstable Oliva-Roget,[2] shelled and air-bombed the city on and from the evening of 29 May, and persisted until noon on the 30th. Vigorous ground operations cleared a number of public buildings, and bombs from the air destroyed houses, a mosque, and much of the Parliament building. In the afternoon of the 30th the bombardment slackened, though, in spite of efforts by British staff officers to arrange a truce, some artillery and mortar fire continued for a further thirty-six hours. Looting and mob violence occurred as usual under cover of the French bombardment, French institutions were attacked, and *méhariste* officers were killed by their own men. On the morning of 1 June the senior British officer in Damascus area handed to Oliva-Roget (whom instructions from France[3] on the 30th, to cease fire, had seemingly failed to reach) a written order from the Commander-in-Chief, Middle East, directing him to stop all firing immediately, to withdraw all posts

[1] These absurdities (including a story of an assault by the British on a French nunnery) are faithfully repeated by, for example, Fabre-Luce (*Deuil au Levant*, pp. 230 f.). This writer (p. 233) adds that General Beynet blankly refused to 'continue resistance to the British' when so ordered by General de Gaulle.

[2] This officer, a severe critic of the British, against whom he alleged or credulously repeated fantastic calumnies, had served with distinction in earlier years (in the Jabal al-Duruz and elsewhere), and was highly valued by General Catroux, until he became (as the latter asserts) the victim of a nervous unbalance. The bombing of Damascus was unequivocally condemned by Catroux (p. 211).

[3] These had resulted from urgent (and keenly resented) pressure exercised on the French Government by the British.

and armoured patrols, and to confine his forces rigidly to their barracks. French troops and civilians were then escorted from the city to camps outside, a step strictly necessary, for their personal safety. British military control was established for a few days, before the Syrian authorities could resume normal administration. Charge of the M.I.R.A. Office (p. 337) was temporarily assumed by the British, to ensure food supplies and to deal with the collection of the now ripening harvest. The casualties incurred among Syrians in the course of the Damascus bombardment and street fighting were given variously as 400 dead, with double that number of wounded and missing, or at considerably greater numbers. Such figures may well be exaggerated; the truth was not, and is not, ascertainable.

Feeling against the French in Syria surpassed, at this juncture, all previous levels of bitterness; it was unsafe to utter a word of that language in the streets. The British, thanked by the Cabinet in Damascus for their intervention, enjoyed a brief moment of popularity; Syrian hopes rested indeed, for the moment, mainly on British and American support. Vigorous protests were made by all Arab Governments, by their new-founded League (p. 351), and by the Arab delegates now in session at San Francisco. French troops were removed from hinterland Syria to the 'Alawi province, civil officials disappeared from their offices and, a blow which horrified French opinion at home, the French missionary and lay schools were closed. In Lebanon a general strike significant of solidarity with Syria was, at government request, called off soon after the crisis was at an end; but even before these events a 'National Congress' at Bakurki had aligned its policy strictly with Syria's and refused all negotiations with France unless on a basis of 'strict equality'. The two Governments on 21 June announced their joint resolve to refuse a 'special position' to any European Power, to dismiss French officials, abolish the Mixed Courts, take over the *troupes spéciales*, and continue pressure for the total withdrawal of French troops. The Délégation-Générale found itself, as never before, morally isolated, and General Beynet could but await instructions from Paris. These arrived early in July. They contained permission to the Délégué-Général to transfer forthwith the long-debated *troupes spéciales*, under the timely pretext that the war situation now at last made this possible. In the process of transfer no time was lost. Arrangements for the consignment of barracks and depots to Syrian and Lebanese control were announced a fortnight later and in August a beginning was made by handing 1,000 Lebanese troops to the Ministry of Defence in Beirut. Experts and committees in both States studied anew their projected military organization. The Lebanese planned provisionally for an army of 5,000 men, the Syrians for one of 20,000. An agreement made between the British military Command and General Beynet on 25 July provided for details of the withdrawal.

Political life in Syria during these months pursued its normal course. Reproaches of weakness against the Cabinet of Faris al-Khuri led late in August 1945 to its replacement by another[1] under the same Premier. This was itself soon to be weakened by three ministerial resignations,[2] and it was superseded in October by a new team[3] under Sa'dullah al-Jabiri, which in turn was destined to last a bare half-year. All the ability and goodwill at Syria's disposal could not, it seemed, avail to produce a régime more stable, or less ephemeral administrations.

Meanwhile it could not be long, after the midsummer of 1945, before the full and final evacuation of foreign troops became the next Syrian and Lebanese objective; indeed, scarcely any other sign now remained of the mandatory régime. Internally, no word of French advice, far less of direction, could again be acceptably proffered to the two republics; unsecured by any agreement or undertaking—less secured, even, than in Turkish days—the historic French cultural institutions must survive as best they could. Externally, the invitation of the Levant States' representatives to the San Francisco Conference of April–June 1945 set the seal upon their entrance to the comity of sovereign nations. This status, pronounced by Free France as already theirs in June 1941, had been in fact achieved four years later, after a melancholy series of tenacious misjudgements and reluctant concessions.

The invitation to San Francisco, which some diplomatic pressure had been exercised to secure, followed the nominal declaration of war by the two States against Germany and Japan on 27 February 1945. Their right of attendance at other international meetings was not, thereafter, disputed: that, for instance, on civil aviation, and that held at Washington to prepare a project for the International Court of Justice. Both the republics adhered in due course to the Charter of the United Nations, both in 1947 joined the International Monetary Fund and the International Bank. The United States gave formal recognition of their independence

[1] Prime Minister, Faris al-Khuri: Interior, Luṭfi al-Ḥaffar: Supply, Ḥasan Jabbara: Works, Ḥikmat al-Ḥakim: Foreign Affairs, Mikha'il Liyan: Finance, Khalid al-'Adhm: Justice, Ṣabri al-'Asali: Economics and Education, Aḥmad al-Sharabati.

[2] Sharabati, Ḥaffar, and 'Asali.

[3] Premier, Defence and Foreign Affairs, al-Jabiri: Justice and Education, Ṣabri al-'Asali: Works and Finance, Na'im Anṭaki (who resigned after a few weeks): Interior, Luṭfi al-Ḥaffar.

by promoting Mr. Wadsworth[1] (p. 324) as Minister in the autumn of 1944. Soviet Russia had narrowly anticipated this action; but neither of the latter countries, unlike Great Britain, admitted any French claim to special privilege in the Levant. The Arab States and Iran all extended their unqualified recognitions during 1944. Turkey alone was longer in withholding it; her relations with the Levant States were still in some measure equivocal, while in Syria persistent claims were reiterated, and were emphasized by street demonstrations and press articles, to the sanjaq of Alexandretta, now the Turkish wilayet of Iskenderon, or Hatay. The Ankara Government gave, however, its unconditional recognition to the two States in March 1946, and the President of Lebanon visited Ankara. Other nations, in every continent, opened normal diplomatic relations. The Syrian and Lebanese diplomats posted to various capitals, where they took a creditable place, included some of their leading public men. Throughout 1945–6 more and more recognitions by foreign countries were announced, and Syro-Lebanese representation was extended accordingly. The cadres for their foreign services were fixed in mid-1946. The engagement of foreign experts and consultants—British, Egyptian, Belgian—by both republics was an encouraging feature of their attitude.

A particular and on the whole (as it then appeared) a strengthening status was given to the young States by their membership of the League of Arab States[2] which, mainly on ʿIraqi and Egyptian initiative, was formed at Alexandria by a Protocol on 7 October 1944, and established with a formal and final Charter at Cairo on 22 March 1945.[3] In these prolonged discussions Syria and Lebanon through their delegations took their full part, and the adherence of each was ratified by their respective Chambers.[4] The Charter, which provided for the adhesion of other Arab States if and when free and sovereign, struck a careful balance between, on the one hand, interstatal consultation, co-operation, co-ordinated policies, arbitration, and mutual help, and, on the other hand, the unfettered independence and integrity of every member. The latter insistence envisaged in particular the case of Lebanon, of whose population an important section was known to be opposed to

[1] He was succeeded by Mr. Pinkerton late in 1946, at which period Mr. Shone (p. 346 n.) was succeeded by Mr. (Sir) W. E. Houstoun-Boswall as British Minister.

[2] Founder-members were Egypt, ʿIraq, Syria, Lebanon, Transjordan, and Saʿudi Arabia. The Yemen joined soon afterwards. Arab Palestine, not being a State, was represented only by an observer.

[3] Great Britain, frequently accused of (or complimented on) being the true founder of the Arab League, played in fact no such part; she did no more than 'view with favour' this or any other spontaneous Arab effort towards greater unity *inter se*. The prime movers were Nuri al-Saʿid and Muṣṭafa al-Naḥḥas, acting at a time when Arab opinion was favourable and receptive.

[4] By Syria on 31 March 1945, by Lebanon on 7 April.

pan-Arabism and tepid towards the Muslim world; in order to secure Lebanese adhesion, therefore, a clause was deliberately inserted in the Protocol affirming the general 'respect for the independence and sovereignty of Lebanon within its present frontiers'. The republics of Syria and Lebanon have in fact acted, throughout the first decade of the League's existence, as loyal and active members. They were also the first to call for its moral support, which was forthcoming, when in May 1945 the crisis of Franco-Syrian relations occurred only three months after signature of the Pact of the League and the establishment of its Council.

Both states subscribed to the funds of the Arab Offices founded to conduct propaganda (particularly as against the Zionist threat) in London, Paris, and Washington. Both witnessed occasional demonstrations against Jewish immigration into Palestine,[1] whose fortunes were of close interest as ever to neighbours and former fellow countrymen. General strikes in the two territories greeted the publication of the 1946 Anglo-American report on Palestine, and some 'repatriation' of local Jews was carried out, though Jewish communities of Syria and Lebanon were loud in their anti-Zionism; the Mufti of Jerusalem, though at that time in Germany, retained the support of many Arab nationalists in Syria, and cases of gun-running from southern Lebanon into Palestine were brought to Court. Varying attitudes, but by large majority those of rejection, were adopted in Syria and Lebanon towards a project initiated in 1945 by the Amir 'Abdullah of Transjordan: the project of Greater Syria. This was to unify Syria, Lebanon, Palestine, and Transjordan into a single State, to be ruled by the Amir himself and closely linked to 'Iraq. The plan, mistakenly supposed to enjoy British sponsorship, was approved by a minority in Syrian political circles, which for a time included the Syrian National Party and the League of National Action; but it was rejected by many more in the other political parties on the ground that the too Anglophile Amir was himself neither 'free' nor democratic. The project was anathema to nearly all, and particularly to the Christian elements, in the Lebanon.[2] The idea remained in being for some years, with decreasing probability of realization. The Amir's own position in Syria was insufficiently strong, and his unpopularity in Egypt and Sa'udi Arabia was reflected in Syrian opinion, with which those countries had a close traditional connexion. Syrian and Lebanese representatives attended the first meeting, in Cairo in October 1945, of a body destined to play thenceforward an often sinister part in Middle

[1] There was nevertheless some Maronite support for Zionism, led, *inter alios*, by Archbishop Mubarak.

[2] One version of the Greater Syria plan, however, admitted the exclusion of Lebanon from it.

Eastern affairs, the Muslim Brotherhood. The Anglo-Jordanian Treaty of 22 March 1946 was considered to be too 'imperialistic' by the students in Damascus, who expressed their feelings by deserting their classrooms and parading the streets.

4. LAST PHASE: WITHDRAWAL

The period of eighteen months which followed the clash of May 1945 is for our present purpose made significant by the final withdrawal of foreign troops from the soil of the Levant States: by the French renunciation of coercion, or of further hope, for favourable treaties with the two republics in the foreseeable future: and by the beginning of a settlement, *tant bien que mal*, of such matters as the withdrawal left in suspense, and the renewal of pacific relations. At the same time future Syro-Lebanese relations began to take shape, and each of the two neighbours showed already, in the phenomena of its now unguided, post-mandatory Government, most of the features which would prevail throughout the next decade.

Since the British Government had at no time envisaged the retention of troops in the Levant after the war, and their temporary presence there was not, or was little, resented by the local authorities, their withdrawal could not be a disputed issue; but with the French, whose military occupation had endured for a quarter-century, and who had repeatedly indicated that a *quid pro quo* for evacuation was demanded, the case was far otherwise. Feeling ran high. While the Governments of Damascus and Paris were still without official contact, Syrian statesmen and publicists repeated their demand for the immediate evacuation of the French forces, and a series of ugly episodes occurred between the Syrian public (including the Gendarmerie) and French troops or institutions. Such were reported from Banyas, Ladhqiya, Aleppo, and Qamishli in July 1945, and from Ṭarṭus in September. With the end of the war, less was heard from the French side of the requirements of regional security, and meanwhile national forces based on the *troupes spéciales* were coming into existence; barracks were transferred to them (on payment later agreed), cadres were fixed, recruitment was pressed forward, staff and higher training were instituted, and an Air Force and an Aviation School were founded in Syria. Military supplies were obtained from America and Great Britain, as well as from the surpluses of French depots. Such was the birth of the Syrian and Lebanese Armies, whose 'baptism of fire' against Israeli forces in 1948 was to prove humiliating, their later value doubtful, their upkeep and equipment a burden which barely-viable States could ill afford;

but as pressure groups in domestic politics, and as an ultimate repository of power in the State, they were to play, especially in Syria, a persistent and a sinister part.

An Anglo-French Agreement on military evacuation was reached in Europe, after reluctant French realization of its inevitability, and was signed on 13 December. It provided for an early joint meeting of experts at Beirut to arrange for the military regrouping preliminary to a withdrawal by stages; Syria would be simultaneously evacuated by both Powers, but the French would retain forces in the Lebanon 'until the United Nations has decided on the organization of collective security in this zone'. This Agreement, however, far from satisfying the Lebanese and Syrians (whose Governments had at no stage been consulted), was greeted with angry demonstrations; and while the French and British officers met for talks on 21 December—and failed to agree on the meaning of the text before them—Lebanese statesmen demanded in Paris and New York early and unconditional withdrawal. In the new year, 1946, demonstrations and strikes spread to the Syrian cities; they were directed against the landing of military reinforcements or replacements (on 31 December) at Beirut, and against a reported reappearance[1] of General Oliva-Roget at Damascus.

A joint protest to the United Nations, at the first meeting of its General Assembly in London, was made by the two Governments on 10 January 1946. It produced, on and after 15 February a prolonged debate in that body. The delegates from the Levant pressed as before for withdrawal without further negotiation or conditions: an attitude in face of which the British were complacent, the Russians in full support, the French finally acquiescent. The meeting, though for procedural reasons it failed to achieve an agreed resolution, ended with the promise of the earliest feasible evacuation. The lingering fear that this would, after all, be made conditional upon cultural or economic or strategic privileges proved unfounded; there were those who connected the more accommodating French attitude with the recent disappearance of General de Gaulle[2] from the headship of their Government. The decision reached at United Nations was in any event, promptly carried out; Franco-British discussions began in Paris on 1 March, and reached agreement to begin final withdrawal from Syria forthwith and to complete it within seven weeks. Movement out of Syria was indeed already in progress; telegraph lines and airports were handed over to the Syrian Government, and regrouping of forces in coastal areas was

[1] This was actually a brief visit on purely personal business.
[2] He ceased to be President of the Council on 20 January 1946.

complete by mid-April, the 17th day of which was hailed in Syria as a day of national thanksgiving. The French found greater practical difficulty in moving all troops and stores out of Lebanon, and asked for a year more for completion; their installations were, after all, extensive and long-established—and Marseilles was 2,000 miles away. This request was unacceptable to the Lebanese, but an intermediate date, 31 August 1946, was agreed; and on that day it could be announced that all French troops were clear of Lebanese territory, as British troops had been eight weeks earlier. Only a small civilian 'liquidation staff' remained. These left at the end of the year, after settling with the local Governments (not without some bitterness at Lebanese demands for the free or indulgent transfer of valuable assets) almost all outstanding questions affecting French-owned lands,[1] buildings, telegraph lines, and military stores. The last units of the French Navy left Beirut in the autumn of 1946. General Beynet had departed 'for duties elsewhere' on 6 July. A French Minister, M. Armand du Chayla, was accredited to the Government of Lebanon in the same week; and less than a month later new hopes of improved and normalized relations were implied by the appointment of M. Jean-Charles Serre to Damascus. The Apostolic Delegate, Mgr Rémy Leprêtre, a warm supporter of Free France throughout the war, left at the same period. French Consulates were opened in October at Tripoli, Sidon, and Zaḥla.

The question of the French schools in Syria was more delicate. The Damascus Government, refusing agreements based on privilege or procedure as these existed in Turkish times, declared them to have no different status from other foreign and local-community schools, all of which must expose to the Ministry of Education their incomes, teachers, and syllabus, must accept inspection and regulation, and must employ Arabic as, in the lower grades, the language of instruction. On this basis a number of French schools were allowed to reopen in October 1946; the rest would follow. Although French educational and cultural enterprise, so long and so fruitfully dominant in the Levant, was still to play a highly important part, the restrictive provisions now enforced, and the nationalistic spirit which prompted them, showed the beginnings of that substantial transference of educational effort and control from foreign and missionary hands into those of the State, which was to mark the period of Syrian and Lebanese history now opening.

The Department of Enemy Property, or Sequestration, was

[1] The Government at Beirut acquired from the British Army, for a derisory payment, the Naqura–Tripoli coastal railway, built in 1941–2. A British commercial mission under Lord Davidson visited Syria and Lebanon in 1946.

among the last to be transferred by the French authorities; and before the transfer a large sum was consigned from it to the Italian Vice-Consul at Jerusalem, representing the value of seized property of Italian subjects. This procedure, disappointing to the Lebanese Government, which had hoped itself to handle these properties, was the subject of vigorous protest. They disapproved scarcely less of the continuance of the long-traditional Consular Masses, celebrated by Maronite prelates in the presence of the French diplomat or Consul of the time; but the feeling was met by a transfer of the ceremony from its usual scene, the Maronite Cathedral, to the Patriarch's private chapel at Bakurki. In another field, of wider interest, the settlement of intergovernmental currency matters was not easy to achieve, and was not attempted till late in 1947. As backing for the bank-note issue in the two territories (controlled by the Banque de Syrie) the French offered to transfer funds, bonds, or properties to cover most of the issue, and to guarantee the rest for ten years against devaluation of the franc. The Lebanese accepted, the Syrians refused these offers; the latter, accordingly, early in 1948 left the 'franc bloc', while the former remained in it, encouraged by other commercial concessions helpful to their chronically adverse trade balance. Demands by France for fair payment for certain of her property in the Levant States, and for refund of part of her military expenditure incurred in the war years, led after some dismay to a settlement early in 1948 with the Lebanese (who paid 1,000 million francs for French property in their country), but to none at present with Syria.

Upon all this range of delicate questions, which called for friendly liquidation on and after the French withdrawal, willing agreement could hardly be hoped. Nerves were still frayed, suspicion and rancour active, twenty-five years of political struggle unforgotten; and the young sovereign States were bound to be zealous in asserting their own rights and decrying those of the French. In Lebanon, indeed, much of the traditional devotion of the Uniate Catholics to France was, even after *les événements*, not slow to reassert itself, led by the Maronite Patriarch to whom after all French-supported Christian supremacy must remain a paramount objective; but Syria continued, for further years, unwilling to relinquish her attitude of bitterness.

5. THE TWO REPUBLICS, 1946

Within the two States both domestic and foreign affairs, which fell from mid-1945 onwards into the patterns they would retain for the ensuing decade, showed less and less conscious traces of the recently extinguished Mandate. Between themselves as Governments, in spite of a wealth of shared experience and continued close consulation as the most intimate of partners, they were to find, from the very outset of their effective independence, many fields of disagreement. Their financial relations with the French differed; over the less tractable parts of the Common Interests, and especially in Customs policy and organization, they quickly fell apart; neither early nor later could they attain the unified conception and machinery for which the situation evidently called.[1] Economically, the two States felt themselves to be not so much complementary as of differing and even clashing orientation, and with but little sympathy for each other's needs. Among personalities and political factions there were jealousies and antipathies as well as cordiality and fraternity. The common outlook of Sunni Muslim thought at most levels in both the territories did not preclude a narrower national self-consciousness in ruling circles and in the press. And the contrast between the wholehearted Arabism of Syria and the divided attitude (springing from a divided heart) in a Lebanon hesitant between Christianity and Islam, between Europe and Asia, was destined to be an operative element in Middle Eastern politics for years to come.

Nevertheless, there was a wide community of demeanour and action between the States. Their attitude to the Greater Syria project and towards Palestine (as later towards Israel) was similar, to Egypt (then and later in controversy with Great Britain) was one of cordial support for an Arab brother. Towards other foreign countries and interests they differed little. Both States generally intended, and in the event achieved, an active participation in international life, where their spokesmen made a distinguished personal showing. Memories of mandated status were fast fading or already forgotten. The Arab League was a constant, though in its practical results a disappointing, scene of their diplomacy and an outlet for warm Syrian and cautious Lebanese Arabism. The shared loyalties of Arabism or pan-Arabism were taken as the justification of their brotherly concern with, and willing intervention in, events in all other Arab-speaking countries;[2] interventions which were to create at times a pattern of international behaviour embarrassing to Powers, notably France and Great Britain,

[1] Disagreement began in February 1948, a short-lived agreement reached in July 1949 soon ceased to operate, and in March 1950, after Lebanon had rejected a proposal for full financial union, the Customs Union between the two (and with it the joint Conseil Supérieur des Intérêts Communs) was dissolved. Both States, but particularly the Lebanon, continued to show unfavourable visible trade balances; this for Syria, but not for Lebanon, was a curable phenomenon.

[2] For instance, French North Africa, the Aden Protectorate, the Persian Gulf States, as well as (obviously) Palestine.

accustomed to the older world of exclusive sovereign States. More broadly, the frequent signs of intolerance or defective realism, or even violence, in Arab national attitudes (of which Syria for the ensuing decade was to offer characteristic examples) made these States, each in their degree, not always comfortable members of the international comity. Towards the West in particular, against which many past and present sources of resentment were discovered, and which was to offend bitterly by its creation and support of the State of Israel, the Arab attitude was to vary from coolness or suspicion to hostility and rancour.

In both countries retrenchment and reform were in and after 1946 the order of the day; economies in the administration were made, and staffs reduced. The level of administrative efficiency and honesty appeared neither to improve nor sharply to decline. No striking but many minor reforms were made in the governmental machine, laws (including the electoral laws) were modernized; in Syria, single-stage voting was introduced in 1947 and a limited right of women's suffrage in 1949. There were in that year 55 constituencies in the Lebanon, 135 in Syria, including those allotted to the minority communities.[1] Military organization, recruitment, and supply were pressed forward. The departure of thousands of Armenians from Lebanon and Syria to settle in Soviet Armenia was a welcome relief, if industrially a loss; the Polish colony in Lebanon also left the country. Plans for works of development, and for civilian air enterprises, took shape. Agreements were made, or revised, with the international or American oil companies for transit of their pipelines across the territory. The 'Iraq Petroleum Company agreed *ex gratia* to payments to the Governments for protective services and facilities for its pipelines. Trans-Arabian Pipelines (Tapline), which was all-American, secured ready agreement from Lebanon for its pipeline transit and for a terminal and refinery near Sidon, but had greater difficulty in satisfying Syria. The country-wide search for oil deposits was resumed, but none were located. The French Government's refinery at Tripoli was acquired by the 'Iraq Petroleum Company, and was used thereafter to supply Lebanon and Syria with oil products. Harbour and irrigation projects were formulated, British consultants engaged (by the Syrian Government), and in the industrial field expansion and modernization were planned, and sometimes achieved, by the progressive, the war-enriched, or the returned *émigré*.

The formation of new political parties remained, as ever, of

[1] The allotment of seats in Syria was: Muslims 113, Druzes 3, Christians 18, Jews 1. In the Lebanon, Sunnis 11, Shi'is 10, Druzes 4, Greek Orthodox 6, Armenians 2, Maronites 18, Greek Catholics 3, other Christians 1.

limited value. In Lebanon, the Syrian National Party of Anṭun Sa'ada (who returned from South America in 1947)[1] dropped 'Syrian' from its name but retained its programme. The Phalanges, with their exclusively Lebanese loyalty, were as ever well organized and popular. The Constitutional Party of the President, Bishara al-Khuri, represented moderate nationalism. Émile Eddé returned to politics to re-form his National Bloc, but it remained weak: he himself died in 1949. The National Appeal Party of Kadhim al-Ṣulḥ was incorporated in 1945, and stood for an approach blending Lebanese with pan-Arab feeling. The Muslim Najjada lacked the dynamism of their rival, the Phalanges. A Progressive Socialist Party, under the youthful Kamil Janbulaṭ, aimed at a socialist régime and sought support from the intellectuals; it took its official place as a party only in 1949. The Mediterranean Party, of Henri Pharaon, stood for a European, non-Arab orientation. In Syria, two National Parties and a People's Party (founded in 1948) divided the members of the now disintegrating National Bloc, while the Renaissance[2] Party inspired and led by Akram Ḥawrani, stood both for active socialism (to be obtained by revolution if necessary) and for universal, anti-western Arab brotherhood. The programme of the less dynamic Arab Socialist[3] Party was more modest but fundamentally similar. The Communists, under able leadership, were active in both republics and willing to work with the strangest of allies. The division of the Syro-Lebanese Communist Party into two, one for each republic, dated from 1944; that of the Lebanon was to be officially proscribed in 1948, but its members continued highly influential in trade union circles. The Liberation Bloc, a clandestine group, worked in both States for the re-Arabization of Palestine. In both Syria and Lebanon much real power still lay with 'Independents', usually representing a landed or monied interest and at heart non-political.

The frequent strikes of industrial workers (and even of government officials, barristers, and judges) were a sign that a labour movement, accompanied in both Damascus and Beirut by new labour legislation, had come vigorously to life, and was closely connected with left-wing, and especially Communist, activity. Incessant demonstrations by students in every city, for or against political events or proposals of every kind, continued to be a Middle Eastern phenomenon both ruinous to education and discipline, and contributory to the distressing instability of local politics. The city mob, equally, was too often and too easily

[1] He was put to death in 1949.
[2] This (the Ba'th Party) joined forces with the Socialists in 1953.
[3] Led by the ex-Communist Mikha'il Aflaq.

mobilized by hot-headed politicians, with strikes and shop shutting, stone-throwing, and violence as the frequent results. It became yearly clearer, indeed, that the mob, the students, and the intelligentsia acting usually through these, were the true repositories of power, and as such were to be joined shortly by the Army.[1] The press, as ever ephemeral, irresponsible, and all-too copious, cried out for fullest liberty, and habitually abused it; and politicians who, out of office, most praised its efforts were the first to suppress its licence when themselves attacked. No legislative event, in either country, was commoner (or more certainly followed by indignant outcry) than a revision of the Press Law of the time. No daily paper could boast of a greater circulation than 3,000, at most 4,000, copies; most were limited to a few hundred and to brief lives. All races, communities, sects, and interests had their paper or papers. State broadcasting stations were operating in both countries after 1946.

Ministries came and went. In Syria, after all the changes in 1945, further Cabinet upheavals occurred in 1946, the first in April with another Ministry under Sa'dullah al-Jabiri—whose last office this was; he died, greatly regretted, in 1947—and yet again in December with a team of ministers headed by Jamil Mardam Bey. Such changes, which the ensuing years were to see endlessly repeated except during periods of dictatorship, signified little alteration of policy, standard or method. In the Lebanon, the same year 1946 witnessed changes of Ministry in May and in October. In the first-named month a Cabinet under Sami al-Ṣulḥ could maintain itself a bare two weeks, and was recast under Sa'di al-Munla, to obtain its vote of confidence on 25 May. In October, Riyaḍh al-Ṣulḥ formed an Administration containing largely the same personalities or others from the small, ever-moving, restless circle of the *ministrables*.

Apart from the frequency of ministerial changes, and the pettiness and faction which too often lay behind them, it was to be faced in 1946, as it is today, that in both republics the greatest of their true needs, stability, seemed to be rendered almost unobtainable, for the foreseeable future, by those persisting factors in the local world, with which these pages have made the reader all too familiar. Chief among them were the abiding heterogeneity of the body politic with its disparate levels of evolution, knowledge, and wealth: the division by confessions and sects, as well as by regional loyalties: and the lack of a tradition of law-abiding—or, put otherwise, the prevalent popular resentment against government

[1] Notably in the three Syrian military dictatorships of 1949–54, and in the intervention of the Lebanese Army, to produce a change of Administrations and President, in August 1952.

itself and its restraints. Behind and exacerbating these, was the excitable and unquiet national character, ill-adjusted to the compromises and disciplines of maturer politics. By reason of the still early stage of its corporate development, the doubtful suitability (as many must feel) of the so-called democratic form of government adopted, the limited experience of the governing class, the shifting and ill-rooted political parties, the dominance of personal ambitions, the wide penetration of the army officer-corps by militant politics, and the multiform particular problems offered by the territory to its administrators, the task of future governments of Syria and the Lebanon, left now wholly to their own devices, could not but prove difficult. Future years were to show them that the long-prayed-for departure of the French had been, after all, far from ushering in a period of quietness and prosperity, or from solving the problems which, in many cases, the presence of the Mandatory had itself concealed or mitigated.

Nevertheless, great progress was to be made by both the republics during the ensuing years, in national education with increasing emphasis on government schools and new faculties added to the seats of higher learning: in the public services, notably that of Health, which developed rapidly: in industry and its background of banking, insurance, and communications: in a less primitive, and sometimes fully modernized, agriculture: in building, town-planning,[1] and the provision of mid-twentieth-century amenities. The tone and tempo of urban life approximated, year by year, more and more to that of Europe; this included family life, amusements, clothes, and the domestic scene. The mass of rural, and in part urban conservatism suffered increasing penetration; village and tribal life grew less remote, increasing tourism and sport played their part in opening up rural areas. Such advance has been remarkable, is rightly the theme of much national self-congratulation, and is entitled to all due credit. The extent to which such building has been on foundations laid by the French between 1920 and 1940 varies, evidently, from one branch of activity to another, and can be very variously assessed. In the broader field, on the other hand, of the firmer structure and integration of the State, and the development of a sound political life based on an educated electorate, well-organized political parties inspired by principles, honestly conducted elections, and an altruistic spirit of public service, there is markedly less advance to be discovered. Progress since 1946 towards the adoption of realistic national policies, genuinely adapted to the two countries'

[1] The scale of the principal cities in 1946 is shown by the following figures of population (in thousands): Aleppo 339, Damascus 303, Beirut 247, Ḥumṣ 106, Tripoli 78, Ḥamah 75, Dayr al-Zur 65, Ladhqiya 39.

needs, or even towards the preservation of nation-wide order and tranquillity, may well be felt as disappointing. In the political field, indeed the Syria and the Lebanon of 1957, in spite of—perhaps because of—the upheavals and vicissitudes of the latest decade, appeared to friendly observers to offer most of the same causes of dismay or bewilderment as had afflicted them ten years earlier.

6. THE FRENCH MANDATE

Leaving the new-born sovereign states of Syria and Lebanon to face the exigencies and dangers of unprotected independence, the French Mandate, granted by the Principal Allied Powers and confirmed by the League of Nations a quarter-century earlier, passed into history. Although the French had many times declared that, as deriving from the authority of the League, it could (like the Mandate over 'Iraq) be extinguished only by that body, it was in fact terminated by no other process than the practical cessation of its exercise, and this in an atmosphere of almost unrelieved ill-feeling as between the parties concerned. One element in the Lebanon could indeed still regret, if not the Mandate itself, at least the protection and comfort of an intimate French connexion; but such a view was alien to the vast majority in both the republics, by whom, in their harsh judgement of the mandatory record, the disappearance of French authority and withdrawal of their troops were hailed not as the end of a valuable or valued association but as a triumph of Francophobe nationalism.

Among other nations, not often kindly judges of their neighbours' fortunes, the French career in Syria has been on the whole condemned; but the severe emphasis on the faults imputed has rarely been based on objective study of the record, has given no adequate credit for the excellent work achieved in diverse fields of action, and has ill appreciated the magnitude of the difficulties which the French encountered. This, certainly true of Arab criticism, is not untrue of British, Italian, and American observers.

In France, where a minority was always critical of the Mandate and of alleged illiberality in its administration, public opinion as a whole viewed its abandonment with dismay, as it had watched its uneasy exercise for twenty years with feelings of disillusion or bitterness. With reason, they felt the French performance to have been disappointing; whether to idealist or to practical man, the desired goal had appeared attainable, but had not been attained; and there was no recourse but to blame unfavourable times, world events, the intractability of the local publics—and, according to the familiar myth, British interference or ambition. The French Mandate in Syria and Lebanon, now a completed episode of the past, will never rank as one which brought glory or gratification to France; its history will seem rather to illustrate an undoubted, probably a fundamental, defect in French psychological equipment for dealing with subject or subjected peoples, and to have foreshadowed their handling of not dissimilar problems in the French Union and its dependencies in later years.

It is unlikely that an international experiment on lines similar to those of the early 1920's will again be attempted. But the mandatory conception was itself humanitarian and anti-colonialist in origin; it had, ideally, much to recommend it; it seemed at its inception, to many of the most enlightened minds of the time, to be not merely a progressive and valuable international device, but one also in practice as well as in theory realizable. It might well be so, if and when applied to a primitive people still too little evolved to be conscious of political aspiration; but it must obviously face its greatest difficulties when applied to a community whose own political programme was already developed, and whose spokesmen specifically rejected such a relationship from the outset. Nevertheless, it was not impossible in 1920 to hope for a fair measure of success, even in the presence of these difficulties as between the French and the Syrians. The former were beyond question a leading nation of the world in culture, enlightenment, and statecraft; they had experience of Arabs and of Islam; they were sentimentally devoted to the Levant and claimed close knowledge of it; and they commanded the services of first-class diplomats and administrators. The Syrians on their side possessed a highly intelligent and well educated (largely French-educated) class ready to hand, had seen French interest in the past confined to the beneficent spheres of education and charity, and could not but be conscious of the real need for the constitutional, administrative and economic help which a great nation could offer to their backwardness and poverty.

What, then, could constitute 'success' in the mandatory experiment? Its first and indispensable feature must be a cordial goodwill between Mandatory and mandated. The second would be the effective and fairly rapid consolidation, by a graduated preparatory period, of full self-government and self-reliance, this to include a suitable Constitution (if possible self-evolved), sound political institutions and methods, a competent administration, a viable economy. With these must come a general improvement in standard of life and happiness throughout the population, with improved public services, better health, enlightenment, security, and justice, all to be achieved by the benevolent precept and example of the agents of the Mandatory, with full local cooperation. And the final stage would occur, not too remotely—

and certainly before the funds of goodwill were exhausted—in the passing of the mandatory charge, the entry of the ex-mandated into the free fellowship of nations on terms of gratitude, perhaps of alliance, towards its friend and supporter.

These are ideals of which time, place, and the imperfections of humanity must preclude the full realization. But how far in fact could the French claim, when all was over, a measure of success? Less than they could have hoped, but more than harsh critics have allowed. There is exaggeration, often malice, in the charges commonly brought against the French effort. It is untrue that their system was one of colonization, and that they were insincere in accepting the burdens of a system specifically intended as altruistic. It is untrue that their long persistence in fragmentation of the territory was based *solely* on a cynical policy of 'divide and rule'. It is untrue that in economic matters French interests were habitually given undue preference. It is untrue that no steps were taken to train Syrian officials, or that any but a low proportion of French officials were corrupt, inefficient, or ill-behaved. In each of these and similar accusations there is, thanks to individual lapses or occasional aberrations, a certain element of truth; but they are, in the large, overstated, misleading, and unjust. For other defects, such as the frontier barriers between the mandated territory and its once-united neighbours, or the fall in the value of the franc-based currency, by no means all the blame can attach to France.

The acerbities of the political scene were by no means pervasive over the sphere of social or even of administrative life. Many French officials were highly valued by their Syrian friends for the excellence of their work and character, and many happy personal relationships existed. The great network of French educational work could pursue its activities under good conditions, and continued to make an outstanding contribution to local enlightenment. Their scientists, doctors, archaeologists, scholars, engineers, contributed to the fabric of the Levant States a quality and volume of effort which no local abilities could hope to match. In almost every department of Government French planning, co-ordination, and constructive control helped to raise standards and to prepare for tomorrow. Public finance was, under close French guidance, prudently administered. The forces of law and order, and the administration of justice, were so improved as to bear little relation to those of the Turkish period. Throughout the world French diplomatic and consular services were at the disposal of Syrian and Lebanese interests. Internally, the territories were enriched by a new system of roads, telegraphs, aerodromes, harbours, and public works; the extension of these, as of the public services in general, were limited solely by lack of funds which the country could not supply and which France could not reasonably be expected to expend from her own resources. In the whole non-political sphere the accusation, if any, against the French should be rather that they over-emphasized their own contribution and assumed excessive control, than that they did too little.

In the constitutional and political sphere, on the other hand, by which they have been mainly judged, their failure was, over more than two decades, persistent and almost unrelieved. For this three main reasons can be isolated: the circumstances in which the Mandate was imposed, the Syrian attitude, and the shortcomings of France herself.

The period in which the mandatory experiment was attempted was one in which the principle and the emotions of political nationalism had already obtained possession of the Arab world; and such aspirations in a mandated territory cannot but rudely conflict, in essence and in tempo, with the policies of a cautious Mandatory. The third and later decades of the century followed a period of significant 'Arab awakening', with a deeply-felt impulse to Arab unity; and the Mandate as applied was inimical to both. Specific promises of Arab independence were believed to have been given by Great Britain, with whom France was closely associated, during the war of 1914–18; France herself in 1916 had agreed to the formation of Arab States with a suggestion of tutelage only in specified areas; she was a signatory, moreover, of the outspoken Anglo-French Declaration of November 1918. The imposition of a Mandate after these and, by implication, other undertakings of Syrian independent status was the more deeply unwelcome. And the manner of its imposition, by armed force on the ruins of a National Government and Arab monarchy evocative of the strongest local pride, and after an emphatic Syrian rejection of mandates in general and that of France in particular, was the most unfortunate imaginable. The régime was (save in certain minority circles) from first to last unwanted and resented by the Syrian public.

The resulting attitude of the latter was incompatible with co-operation between France and the mandated. The political leaders, men of force and intelligence, refused from the first to curb or postpone their nationalist aspirations. They were impatient of mandatory delays and restraints, resented the suggestion of inferior national status, regarded anti-French militancy by the mob, the tribes or the students as heroic virtue, and treated political objectives as invariably entitled to take precedence over economic or social. The masses, whose interests were by no means identical with those of the intelligentsia, had no channel of expression independently of the latter; it followed that the elements who would benefit most from the efforts of an enlightened mandate had the least power to facilitate its working. The French, who desired to act in the interests of the masses, were unable to rally them as a political force in their support. The political leaders, meanwhile, who for the most part partook of the hasty, emotional, uncompromising, national character, were deficient in political and constitutional experience, and excelled in criticism and opposition but were new to responsibility. Their errors of procedure, their ready calls to violence, created too often the appearance of irresponsible immaturity and unfitness for the sober tasks of governing, and disinclined the French to entrust them with power. Finally, they spoke with no single voice; not only various parties, various degrees of moderation or extremism confronted the Mandatory, as was natural, but various communities and enclaves throughout the territory insistently claimed special treatment and refused assimilation. It was therefore from the first impossible to devise a policy which would not dissatisfy, at least temporarily, protesting minorities. It would have been no less impossible to attempt the application of any constitutional system other than the parliamentary democracy which (however ill-suited to actual Syrian conditions) all local publicists assumed as desirable; indeed the denial of this form of government would have aroused bitter outcry, all the stronger because, behind its façade, could operate the 'oligarchy of the intelligentsia' which was in effect the 'democracy' advocated by the articulate classes.

If many of the charges brought against France are ill-based, and if her unavoidable difficulties were grave, yet there remain faults on her own side which must be held responsible for a main part of her political failure. The mandatory conception was never more than doubtfully welcomed by the French, who (even while loyally trying to apply it) would always have preferred a frankly protectorate or colonial system. They failed, in the event, to establish the sort of governmental régime for which a Mandate calls: a régime fully utilizing local talent, careful to give (and to be seen to give) priority to local needs, and safeguarding local self-respect by allowing the maximum exercise of visible powers. The true desideratum was not a French Government using some Syrian staff as powerless subordinates or as an official façade; it was a Syrian Government supported and guided by the French. Because the French element was excessive, perfectionist, and endlessly active in negation and interference, and because Syrian pride was thus belittled, the co-operation of many of the best minds and powers in the territory was never secured; they remained in opposition. Indeed, as the French today appreciate with retrospective clearness, the strength of the nationalist movement was habitually underestimated, and undue reliance was placed on the anti-nationalist minorities, on puppets, and on 'neutral' administrators.

The dependence of the régime in the Levant upon the politics of Paris was clear and damaging. Not only were changes of High Commissioner (three times, for instance, between 1924 and 1926) politically inspired and undesirably frequent, but the appeal to French strategic needs (such as killed the 1936 Treaties, and ceded Alexandretta), and the devotion to time-honoured French 'rights' in the territory, and the anxious need to avoid policies which could react dangerously in North Africa, were all elements inconsistent with considering Syrian interests as paramount.

In the territory itself no error of policy was more persistent than that of emphasizing the distinctness, and minimizing the essential unity, of the religious and geographical enclaves. Though defensible by some strictly local considerations, it was a policy without prospect of long-term success, damaging in the end to the populations concerned, and opposed consistently by the widest and dominant political forces. The separate statehood of Great Lebanon, augmented by non-Lebanese Muslim districts, is the outstanding example; the segregation or repeatedly confirmed 'special status' of the Druzes and 'Alawis are others. The adoption in 1920 of a unitary Syria (containing, no doubt, a mildly priviledged Mount Lebanon) would have saved a whole multitude of later troubles, and if, at the time of writing (1957), it may be felt that Lebanon was lucky in its freedom from Syrian foreign policies of the mid-1950's, with their leaning to Russia, it may equally be believed that a Syria strengthened by a more westward-looking Lebanon, with a stronger sense of political (and commercial) realities, might well have been saved from courses thought by many of her friends to be gravely dangerous to her.

Other cases of misjudgement or insensitivity or mistaken psychology by the French formed in aggregate a formidable obstacle to success. Such were the early reversal of policy towards the Druzes: the placing of the religiously-oriented Ḥijaz Railway under a French concessionary company: the attitude of General Sarrail to the Maronites, and to the Druze emissaries: the impenitent use of black colonial troops; the permitted presence of some inadequate, and a few corrupt, French officials; the attachment of the local currency to a fluctuating or sinking franc. These are no more than random examples; far more serious were the acts of impolicy directed by General de Gaulle—the refusal of all but a faint and nominal independence after June 1941, the *bêtises* of M. Helleu, the bombardment of Damascus and, at the eleventh hour, the continued demand for a favourable treaty as a price of transferring services and withdrawing troops.

After every proper allowance has been made for the intrinsic unease of the mandatory relationship, the particular difficulties of—and resistance by—Syria itself, and the unfavourable period and circumstances, the French effort, so eagerly undertaken, so tenaciously pursued, was destined to an outcome which has been assessed by the world as one of unhappy failure in the most conspicuous sphere, that of state-building and politics. Minor or personal shortcomings apart, this failure was due to the Mandatory's refusal to appreciate the true static or dynamic forces of the territory: to an excessive concern with the prestige, claims, and strategy of France: to too uncertain a hand in selecting and controlling her local agents; and to a deficiency in sympathy and adaptability in handling people and conditions remote from the clarity, logic, and standards of the French themselves. A quarter-century of effort, expense, and sacrifice had been spent; many brave deeds, many devoted labours had been recorded: the end was sad and humiliating. Nevertheless, the rise and fall of the Mandate offers a picture full of interest, perhaps of instruction, and it has clear relevance to problems with which, years later, the same French were confronted, and to which they seemed at times to show not dissimilar attitudes. Meanwhile, the beautiful and attractive territory in which the Mandate was exercised had received from it, positively and negatively, visibly and invisibly, a contribution fundamental to its present status, form and characteristics; and its people will be fortunate if the future holds for them no worse days than those which they passed, so reluctantly, under the French Mandate.

APPENDIX A

(i) Administrative Units in Turkish Syria, 1914

Wilayet	*Sanjaqs*	*Qadhas*
Aleppo (Halab)	‘Ayntab	‘Ayntab, Rum Qal‘a.
	Aleppo	Alexandretta (Iskenderon), Baylan, Antioch (Anṭaqiya), Killis, Ḥarim, Aleppo, Idlib, Jisr al-Shaghur, Ma‘arrat al-Nu‘man, al-Bab, Manbij.
	Mar‘ash	(Transferred to Diyarbakr, 1915).
Damascus (al-Sham)	Ḥamah	Ḥamidiya, Salimiya, Ḥumṣ, Ḥamah.
	Damascus	Ba‘lbek, Biqa‘, Ḥasbaya, Nabq, Qunayṭara, Zabdani, Rashaya, Duma, Damascus, Wadi al-‘Ajam.
	Ḥawran	Shaykh Sa‘d, ‘Ajlun (Irbid), Musmiya, Azra‘ (Mazra‘a), Dar‘a (Ḥawran), al-Aḥira, Suwayda (Jabal al-Duruz), Ṣalkhad, al-Salṭ, Karak,
	Karak	Ṭafila, Ma‘an.
Beirut (Bayrut)	Ladhqiya (Latakiya)	Ladhqiya, Ṣaḥyun, Jabala, Baniyas (Marqab).
	Tripoli (Ṭarabulus)	Tripoli, ‘Akkar, Ṣafiṭa, Huṣn al-Akrad (al-Ḥuṣn).
	Beirut (Bayrut)	Beirut, Sidon (Ṣayda), Tyre (al-Ṣur) Marj‘uyun.
	Acre (‘Akka)	Acre, Haifa, Ṣafad, Nazareth (Naṣira), Tiberias (Ṭubariya).
	Nablus (or Balqa)	Nablus, Janin, Ṭul Karam.
NIL	Dayr al-Zur	Dayr al-Zur, Albu Kamal, Ras al-‘Ayn, ‘Ashara.
NIL	Jerusalem (al-Quds).	Yafa (Jaffa), Ghazza (Gaza), Khalil al-Raḥman (Hebron), Bir al-Saba‘ (Beersheba).
NIL	Autonomous Lebanon	Batrun, Kasrawan, Matn, Shuf, Jazzin, al-Kura, Zaḥla, Dayr al-Qamr.

(ii) Administrative Units, 1927

STATE OF SYRIA

Sanjaq	*Qadhas* (and headquarters)
Aleppo (wilayet)	Kurd Dagh (Mabadli), 'Azaz, Ḥarim, Idlib: Jabal Sam'an (Aleppo), Jisr al-Shaghur, Ma'arrat al-Nu'man, Bab, Manbij, Jarablus.
Alexandretta (Iskendaron)	Alexandretta, Kirik Khan, Antioch (Anṭaqiya).
Ḥamah	Ḥamah, Salimiya.
Ḥumṣ	Ḥumṣ, Qariyatayn.
Damascus	Nabq, Zabdani, Damascus, Wadi al-'Ajam, Qunaytara, Zuwiya (Fiq), Duma, Jarud.
Hawran	Musmiya, Azra', Dar'a.
Dayr al-Zur	Dayr al-Zur, Raqqa, Ḥasaja, Tall Cholek, Mayadin, Albu Kamal.

STATE OF THE 'ALAWIS

Ladhqiya	Ladhqiya, Ṣaḥyun (Babana), Jabala, Banyas, 'Umraniya (Maṣyaf).
Ṭarṭus	Ṭarṭus, Ṣafita, Tall Kallakh.

JABAL AL-DURUZ

Suwayda	Suwayda, Ṣalkhad, Shahba.

LEBANON

(No sanjaqs)	Beirut, Tripoli, Kasrawan (Juniya), Ba'lbek, Matn (Baḥannes), Zaḥla, Shuf (Ba'aqlin), Ṣayda, Ṣur, Marj'uyun.

(iii) Administrative Units, 1914

SYRIA

Muḥafidha	*Qadhas*
Damascus	Damascus (city), Mazza, Ghuṭa, Duma, Nabq, Wadi al-'Ajam, Qunaytara, Zabdani.
Aleppo	Aleppo (city), Jabal Sam'an, Idlib, Manbij, Bab, Ḥarim, Jarabulus, Ma'arrat al-Nu'man, Jisr al-Shaghur, 'Ayn al-'Arab, Jabal al-Akrad.
Ḥumṣ	
Ḥamah	Ḥamah, Salimiya.
Ḥawran	Dar'a, Azra', Zuwiya.
Euphrates	Dayr al-Zur, Raqqa, Mayadin, Albu Kamal.
Jazira	Ḥasaja, Qamishli, Dijla
Jabal al-Duruz	Suwayda, Ṣalkhad, Shahba.
Ladhqiya	Ladhqiya, Ḥaffa, Jabala, Banyas, Ṭarṭus and Arwad Is., Ṣafita, Maṣyaf, Tall Kallakh.

LEBANON

Districts	*Sub-districts*
Beirut	—
Biqa'	Zaḥla, Ba'lbek, Harmal, Rashaya.
North Lebanon	Tripoli, 'Akkar, Zaghurta, Batrun, Kura.
South Lebanon	Ṣayda, Ṣur, Marj'uyun, Jazzin.
Mount Lebanon	Ba'abda, Matn, Kasrawan, Shuf, 'Aliya (Aley).

APPENDIX B

Presidents, Prime Ministers, and Foreign Ministers of France, 1917–46

Presidents

17 January 1913	Raymond Poincaré	
17 January 1920	Paul Deschanel	
23 September 1920	Alexandre Millerand	
13 June 1924	Gaston Doumergue	
13 May 1931	Paul Doumer	
10 May 1932	Albert Lebrun	
5 April 1939	" "	(re-elected)

		Prime Ministers	*Foreign Ministers*
1917	November	Georges Clemenceau	Stephen Pichon
1920	January	Alexandre Millerand	Alexandre Millerand
	September	Georges Leygues	Georges Leygues
1921	January	Aristide Briand	Aristide Briand
1922	January	Raymond Poincaré	Raymond Poincaré
1924	June	Édouard Herriot	Édouard Herriot
1925	April	Paul Painlevé	Aristide Briand
	November	Aristide Briand	" "
1926	July	Édouard Herriot	Édouard Herriot
	July	Raymond Poincaré	Aristide Briand
1929	July	Aristide Briand	" "
	November	André Tardieu	" "
1930	February	Camille Chautemps	" "
	March	André Tardieu	" "
	December	Théodore Stieg	" "
1931	January	Pierre Laval	" "
		January 1932	Pierre Laval
1932	February	André Tardieu	André Tardieu
	June	Édouard Herriot	Édouard Herriot
	December	Joseph Paul-Boncour	Joseph Paul-Boncour
1933	January	Édouard Daladier	" "
	October	Albert Sarraut	" "
	November	Camille Chautemps	" "
1934	January	Édouard Daladier	Édouard Daladier
	February	Gaston Doumergue	Louis Barthou
		October 1934	Pierre Laval
	November	Pierre-Étienne Flandin	" "
1935	May	Fernand Bouissin	" "
	June	Pierre Laval	" "
1936	January	Albert Sarraut	Pierre-Étienne Flandin
	June	Léon Blum	Yvon Delbos

		Prime Ministers	*Foreign Ministers*
1937	June	Camille Chautemps	Yvon Delbos
1938	March	Léon Blum	Joseph Paul-Boncour
	April	Édouard Daladier	Georges Bonnet
1940	March	Paul Reynaud	Paul Reynaud
1940	June	Marshal Pétain	Paul Baudouin
		October 1940	Pierre Laval
		December 1940	Pierre-Étienne Flandin
		February 1941	Admiral Darlan
1942	April	Pierre Laval	Pierre Laval

[25 September 1941 *French National Committee* formed.
President: General de Gaulle. Foreign Affairs: Maurice Dejean
February 1942: René Massigli
3 June 1943 French *Committee for National Liberation* formed.
Presidents: General Giraud and General de Gaulle
November 1943 General Giraud resigned.
President: General de Gaulle. Foreign Affairs: René Massigli.]

		Prime Ministers	*Foreign Ministers*
1944	September	General de Gaulle	Georges Bidault
1946	January	Félix Gouin	,, ,,
	June	Georges Bidault	,, ,,
	December	Léon Blum	Léon Blum

APPENDIX C

Covenant of the League of Nations[1]

Article 22

1. To those colonies and territories which as a consequence of the late war have ceased to be under the sovereignty of the States which formerly governed them, and which are inhabited by peoples not yet able to stand by themselves under the strenuous conditions of the modern world, there should be applied the principle that the well-being and development of such peoples form a sacred trust of civilisation, and that securities for the performance of this trust should be embodied in this Covenant.

2. The best method of giving practical effect to this principle is that the tutelage of such peoples should be entrusted to advanced nations who, by reason of their resources, their experience, or their geographical position, can best undertake this responsibility, and who are willing to accept it, and that this tutelage should be exercised by them as Mandatories on behalf of the League.

3. The character of the Mandate must differ according to the stage of the development of the people, the geographical situation of the territory, its economic conditions and other similar circumstances.

4. Certain communities formerly belonging to the Turkish Empire have reached a stage of development where their existence as independent nations can be provisionally recognised subject to the rendering of administrative advice and assistance by a Mandatory until such time as they are able to stand alone. The wishes of these communities must be a principal consideration in the selection of the Mandatory.

5. Other peoples, especially those of Central Africa, are at such a stage that the Mandatory must be responsible for the administration of the territory under conditions which will guarantee freedom of conscience and religion, subject only to the maintenance of public order and morals, the prohibition of abuses such as the slave trade, the arms traffic and the liquor traffic, and the prevention of the establishment of fortifications or military and naval bases, and of military training of the natives for other than police purposes and the defence of territory, and will also secure equal opportunities for the trade and commerce of other Members of the League.

6. There are territories, such as South-West Africa and certain of the South Pacific Islands, which, owing to the sparseness of their population, or their small size, or their remoteness from the centres of civilisation, or their geographical contiguity to the territory of the Mandatory, and other circumstances, can be best administered under the laws of the Mandatory as integral portions of its territory, subject

[1] G.B., Foreign Office, *The Covenant of the League of Nations* (H.M.S.O., 1935).

to the safeguards above mentioned in the interests of the indigenous population.

7. In every case of Mandate, the Mandatory shall render to the Council an annual report in reference to the territory committed to its charge.

8. The degree of authority, control, or administration to be exercised by the Mandatory shall, if not previously agreed upon by the Members of the League, be explicitly defined in each case by the Council.

9. A permanent Commission shall be constituted to receive and examine the annual reports of the Mandatories and to advise the Council on all matters relating to the observance of the Mandates.

APPENDIX D

THE MANDATE FOR SYRIA AND LEBANON, 24 JULY 1922[1]

The Council of the League of Nations,

Whereas the Principal Allied Powers have agreed that the territory of Syria and the Lebanon, which formerly belonged to the Turkish Empire, shall, within such boundaries as may be fixed by the said Powers, be entrusted to a Mandatory charged with the duty of rendering administrative advice and assistance to the population, in accordance with the provisions of Article 22 (paragraph 4) of the Covenant of the League of Nations; and

Whereas the Principal Allied Powers have decided that the mandate for the territory referred to above should be conferred on the Government of the French Republic, which has accepted it; and

Whereas the terms of this mandate, which are defined in the articles below, have also been accepted by the Government of the French Republic and submitted to the Council of the League for approval; and

Whereas the Government of the French Republic has undertaken to exercise this mandate on behalf of the League of Nations, in conformity with the following provisions; and

Whereas by the aforementioned Article 22 (paragraph 8), it is provided that the degree of authority, control or administration to be exercised by the Mandatory, not having been previously agreed upon by the members of the League, shall be explicitly defined by the Council of the League of Nations;

Confirming the same mandate, defines its terms as follows:

Article 1: The Mandatory shall frame, within a period of three years from the coming into force of this mandate, an organic law for Syria and the Lebanon.

This organic law shall be framed in agreement with the native authorities and shall take into account the rights, interests and wishes of all the population inhabiting the said territory. The Mandatory shall further enact measures to facilitate the progressive development of Syria and the Lebanon as independent states. Pending the coming into effect of the organic law, the Government of Syria and the Lebanon shall be conducted in accordance with the spirit of this mandate.

The Mandatory shall, as far as circumstances permit, encourage local autonomy.

Article 2: The Mandatory may maintain its troops in the said territory for its defence. It shall further be empowered, until the entry into force of the organic law and the re-establishment of public security, to organise such local militia as may be necessary for the defence of the territory and to employ this militia for defence and also for the maintenance of order. These local forces may only be recruited from the inhabitants of the said territory.

[1] *League of Nations Official Journal*, August 1922, pp. 1013–17.

The said militia shall thereafter be under the local authorities, subject to the authority and the control which the Mandatory shall retain over these forces. It shall not be used for purposes other than those above specified save with the consent of the Mandatory.

Nothing shall preclude Syria and the Lebanon from contributing to the cost of the maintenance of the forces of the Mandatory stationed in the territory.

The Mandatory shall at all times possess the right to make use of the ports, railways and means of communication of Syria and the Lebanon for the passage of its troops and of all materials, supplies and fuel.

Article 3: The Mandatory shall be entrusted with the exclusive control of the foreign relations of Syria and the Lebanon and with the right to issue exequaturs to the consuls appointed by foreign Powers. Nationals of Syria and the Lebanon living outside the limits of the territory shall be under the diplomatic and consular protection of the Mandatory.

Article 4: The Mandatory shall be responsible for seeing that no part of the territory of Syria and the Lebanon is ceded or leased or in any way placed under the control of a foreign Power.

Article 5: The privileges and immunities of foreigners, including the benefits of consular jurisdiction and protection as formerly enjoyed by capitulation or usage in the Ottoman Empire, shall not be applicable in Syria and the Lebanon. Foreign consular tribunals shall, however, continue to perform their duties until the coming into force of the new legal organisation provided for in Article 6.

Unless the Powers whose nationals enjoyed the aforementioned privileges and immunities on August 1st, 1914, shall have previously renounced the right to their re-establishment, or shall have agreed to their non-application during a specified period, these privileges and immunities shall at the expiration of the mandate be immediately re-established in their entirety or with such modifications as may have been agreed upon between the Powers concerned.

Article 6: The Mandatory shall establish in Syria and the Lebanon a judicial system which shall ensure to natives as well as to foreigners a complete guarantee of their rights.

Respect for the personal status of the various peoples and for their religious interests shall be fully guaranteed. In particular, the control and administration of Wakfs shall be exercised in complete accordance with religious law and the dispositions of the founders.

Article 7: Pending the conclusion of special extradition agreements, the extradition treaties at present in force between foreign Powers and the Mandatory shall apply within the territory of Syria and the Lebanon.

Article 8: The Mandatory shall ensure to all complete freedom of conscience and the free exercise of all forms of worship which are consonant with public order and morality. No discrimination of any kind shall be made between the inhabitants of Syria and the Lebanon on the ground of differences in race, religion or language.

The Mandatory shall encourage public instruction, which shall be given through the medium of the native languages in use in the territory of Syria and the Lebanon.

The right of each community to maintain its own schools for the instruction and education of its own members in its own language, while conforming to such requirements of a general nature as the administration may impose, shall not be denied or impaired.

Article 9: The Mandatory shall refrain from all interference in the administration of the Councils of management (Conseils de fabrique) or in the management of religious communities and sacred shrines belonging to the various religions, the immunity of which has been expressly guaranteed.

Article 10: The supervision exercised by the Mandatory over the religious missions in Syria and the Lebanon shall be limited to the maintenance of public order and good government; the activities of these religious missions shall in no way be restricted, nor shall their members be subjected to any restrictive measures on the ground of nationality, provided that their activities are confined to the domain of religion.

The religious missions may also concern themselves with education and relief, subject to the general right of regulation and control by the Mandatory or the local government, in regard to education, public instruction and charitable relief.

Article 11: The Mandatory shall see that there is no discrimination in Syria or the Lebanon against the nationals, including societies and associations, of any State Member of the League of Nations as compared with its own nationals, including societies and associations, or with the nationals of any other foreign State in matters concerning taxation or commerce, the exercise of professions or industries, or navigation, or in the treatment of ships or aircraft. Similarly, there shall be no discrimination in Syria or the Lebanon against goods originating in or destined for any of the said States; there shall be freedom of transit, under equitable conditions, across the said territory.

Subject to the above, the Mandatory may impose or cause to be imposed by the local governments such taxes and customs duties as it may consider necessary. The Mandatory, or the local governments acting under its advice, may also conclude on grounds of contiguity any special customs arrangements with an adjoining country.

The Mandatory may take or cause to be taken, subject to the provisions of paragraph 1 of this article, such steps as it may think best to ensure the development of the natural resources of the said territory and to safeguard the interests of the local population.

Concessions for the development of these natural resources shall be granted without distinction of nationality between the nationals of all States Members of the League of Nations, but on condition that they do not infringe upon the authority of the local government. Concessions in the nature of a general monopoly shall not be granted. This clause shall in no way limit the right of the Mandatory to create monopolies of a purely fiscal character in the interest of the territory of Syria and the Lebanon, and with a view to assuring to the territory the fiscal resources which would appear best adapted to the local needs, or, in certain cases, with a view to developing the natural resources either directly by the State or through an organisation under its control, provided that this does not involve either directly or indirectly the creation of a monopoly of the natural resources in favour of the Mandatory or its nationals, nor involve any preferential treatment which would be incompatible with the economic, commercial and industrial equality guaranteed above.

Article 12: The Mandatory shall adhere, on behalf of Syria and the Lebanon, to any general international agreements already existing, or which may be concluded hereafter with the approval of the League of Nations, in respect of the following: the slave trade, the traffic in drugs, the traffic in arms and ammunition, commercial equality, freedom of transit and navigation, aerial navigation, postal, telegraphic or wireless communications, and measures for the protection of literature, art or industries.

Article 13: The Mandatory shall secure the adhesion of Syria and the Lebanon, so far as social, religious and other conditions permit, to such measures of common utility as may be adopted by the League of Nations for preventing and combating disease, including diseases of animals and plants.

Article 14: The Mandatory shall draw up and put into force within twelve months from this date a law of antiquities in conformity with the following provisions. This law shall ensure equality of treatment in the matter of excavations and archaeological research to the nationals of all States Members of the League of Nations.

(1) 'Antiquity' means any construction or any product of human activity earlier than the year 1700 A.D.

(2) The law for the protection of antiquities shall proceed by encouragement rather than by threat.

Any person who, having discovered an antiquity without being furnished with the authorisation referred to in paragraph 5, reports the same to an official of the competent Department, shall be rewarded according to the value of the discovery.

(3) No antiquity may be disposed of except to the competent Department, unless this Department renounces the acquisition of any such antiquity.

No antiquity may leave the country without an export licence from the said Department.

(4) Any person who maliciously or negligently destroys or damages an antiquity shall be liable to a penalty to be fixed.

(5) No clearing of ground or digging with the object of finding antiquities shall be permitted, under penalty of fine, except to persons authorised by the competent Department.

(6) Equitable terms shall be fixed for expropriation, temporary or permanent, of lands which might be of historical or archaeological interest.

(7) Authorisation to excavate shall only be granted to persons who show sufficient guarantees of archaeological experience. The Mandatory

shall not, in granting these authorisations, act in such a way as to exclude scholars of any nation without good grounds.

(8) The proceeds of excavations may be divided between the excavator and the competent department in a proportion fixed by that department. If division seems impossible for scientific reasons, the excavator shall receive a fair indemnity in lieu of a part of the find.

Article 15: Upon the coming into force of the organic law referred to in Article 1, an arrangement shall be made between the Mandatory and the local governments for reimbursement by the latter of all expenses incurred by the Mandatory in organising the administration, developing local resources, and carrying out permanent public works, of which the country retains the benefit. Such arrangement shall be communicated to the Council of the League of Nations.

Article 16: French and Arabic shall be the official languages of Syria and the Lebanon.

Article 17: The Mandatory shall make to the Council of the League of Nations an annual report to the satisfaction of the Council as to the measures taken during the year to carry out the provisions of this mandate. Copies of all laws and regulations promulgated during the year shall be attached to the said report.

Article 18: The consent of the Council of the League of Nations is required for any modification of the terms of this mandate.

Article 19: On the termination of the mandate, the Council of the League of Nations shall use its influence to safeguard for the future the fulfilment by the Government of Syria and the Lebanon of the financial obligations, including pensions and allowances, regularly assumed by the administration of Syria or of the Lebanon during the period of the mandate.

Article 20: The Mandatory agrees that, if any dispute whatever should arise between the Mandatory and another Member of the League of Nations relating to the interpretation or the application of the provisions of the mandate, such dispute, if it cannot be settled by negotiation, shall be submitted to the Permanent Court of International Justice provided for by Article 14 of the Covenant of the League of Nations.

The present instrument shall be deposited in original in the archives of the League of Nations and certified copies shall be forwarded by the Secretary-General of the League of Nations to all members of the League.

Done at London on the twenty-fourth day of July, one thousand nine hundred and twenty-two.

APPENDIX E

Bibliographical Note

*(Works in Arabic are marked *)*

The following lists are misleading inasmuch as they mention, on apparently equal terms, the most valuable sources and others of far less importance; this however is neither unusual nor avoidable. Very few works of general or diplomatic history are mentioned, and still fewer of primarily religious or topographical interest. It has been necessary to ignore most of the travellers who make only a slight contribution, many departmental and specialist reports and brochures (of which the writer's knowledge is quite incomplete), and works dealing (other than retrospectively) with the Syria–Lebanon of the period following 1946.

(I) PERIODICALS AND REPORTS

(*a*) A large quantity of daily-press material for the whole period covered, from English, European, and American papers, was available in the admirable Press Library of Chatham House. The total contribution of this is highly important.

(*b*) The monthly and quarterly periodicals most used were *Oriente Moderno*—a unique and most valuable publication, not least for its copious extracts and summaries of the Syro-Lebanese press—*Correspondance d'Orient* (till May 1940), *Cahiers de l'Orient Contemporain* (from 1944), *L'Asie française* (from 1920), *International Affairs*, the *Bulletin of International News* (Chatham House), *The Economist*, *The World Today*, *The Middle East Journal*, *Foreign Affairs*, the *Journal of the Royal Central Asian Society*; and many others for occasional articles. Also the '*Notes et études documentaires*' of the Documentation Française.

(*c*) Reference has been made at times to *Hansard*, the *Journal Officiel* of the debates of the French Chamber, and, more frequently, to the Proceedings of the Council of the League of Nations, of the Permanent Mandates Commission, and (from 1945) of the United Nations Security Council.

(*d*) Use has been made of the (annual) *Statesman's Yearbook* and the *Annual Register*.

(II) PERIOD ANTECEDENT TO THE FIRST WORLD WAR

Azoury Beg, Najib. *Le Réveil de la nation arabe dans l'Asie turque.* Paris, 1905.
Baedeker. *Guide to Syria*, 1912.
Bell, G. M. L. *Amurath to Amurath.* London, 1911.
—— *The Desert and the Sown.* London, 1907.
Bernard, A. *La Syrie et les Syriens.* Paris, 1919.
Blyth, Estelle. *When We Lived in Jerusalem.* London, 1927.
Charles-Roux, F. *France et Chrétiens d'Orient.* Paris, 1939.

Chéradame, A. *La Question d'Orient; la Macédoine, le chemin de fer de Bagdad*. Paris, 1903.
Cressaty, R. J. M., *Count. Les Intérêts de la France en Syrie*. Paris, 1915.
—— *La Syrie française*. Paris, 1915.
Cuinet, V. *Syrie, Liban, Palestine*. Paris, 1886.
—— *La Turquie d'Asie*. 4 vols. Paris, 1890–1900.
Duboscq, A. *Syrie, Tripolitanie, Albanie*. Paris, 1914.
Earle, E. M. *Turkey, the Great Powers and the Bagdad Railway*. London, 1923.
Ghalib, P. *Le Protéctorat religieux de la France en Orient*. Avignon, 1920.
Great Britain, Admiralty, Naval Intelligence Division. *A Handbook of Syria, including Palestine*. London, 1920.
—— Board of Trade. *Report on British Trade in Syria*. London, 1911.
—— Foreign Office, Historical Section. *France and the Levant*. London, 1920. (Peace Handbooks, No. 66.)
—— *Syria and Palestine*. London, 1920. (Peace Handbooks, No. 60.)
Jouplain, M. *La Question du Liban; étude d'histoire diplomatique et de droit international*. Paris, 1908.
Jung, E. *Les Puissances devant la révolte arabe*. Paris, 1906.
Lammens, H. *L'Évolution historique de la nationalité syrienne*. Alexandria, 1919.
Lamy, E. *La France du Levant*. Paris, 1900.
Madelin, L. 'La Syrie Française', *Revue de Deux Mondes*, June 1917.
Moutran, N. *La Syrie de demain*. Paris, 1916.
*Naṣir, 'Umar abu'l-. *Suriya wa Lubnan fi'l Qarn al-tasi' 'ashar*. Beirut, 1926.
Oppenheim, M. von. *Vom Mittelmeer zum Persischen Golf*. 2 vols. Berlin, 1899–1900.
Richard, H. *La Syrie et la guerre*. Paris, 1916.
Ristelhueber, R. *Traditions françaises au Liban*. Paris, 1918.
Roederer, C. and P. *La Syrie et la France*. Paris, 1917.
Ruppin, A. *Syria; an Economic Survey*. Trans. 1918.
Samné, G. *La Syrie*. Paris, 1920.
Smith, Sir G. A. *Syria and the Holy Land*. London, 1918.
Sykes, Sir M. *The Caliph's Last Heritage; a Short History of the Turkish Empire*. London, 1915.
Tyan, E. *France et Liban*. Paris, 1917.
Verney, N. and G. Dambmann. *Les Puissances étrangères dans le Levant, en Syrie et en Palestine*. Paris, 1900.

(III) PERIOD 1914 TO 1921: WAR, POST-WAR SETTLEMENT, AND FRENCH INSTALLATION IN SYRIA

Abdallah Sfer [Sufair] Pacha. *Le Mandat français et les traditions françaises en Syrie et au Liban*. Paris, 1922.
Achcar, J. *Études sur la Syrie et la Cilicie*. Paris, 1922.
*Adib Pasha, Auguste. *al-Lubnan ba'd el ḥarb*. Beirut, 1919.
Ahmad Djemal Pasha. *Memoirs of a Turkish Statesman, 1913–19*. London, 1922.

Baker, R. S. *Woodrow Wilson and World Settlement*. Vol. 3. London, 1923.
Brémond, E., Général. *La Cilicie en 1919–20*. Paris, 1921.
—— *Le Hedjaz dan la guerre mondiale*. Paris, 1931.
Cherif [Sharif], Ihsan el-. *Le Statut international de la Syrie*. Paris, 1920.
Congrès français de la Syrie. *Séances et travaux*. Marseilles, 1919.
Cozé, É. *La Syrie et le Liban*. Étampes, 1922.
Cumming, H. H. *Franco-British Rivalry in the Post-War Near East; the Decline of French Influence*. London, 1936.
*Daghir, As'ad. *Thawrat al Arab*. Cairo, 1916.
David, P. *Un Gouvernement arabe à Damas; le Congrès syrien*. Paris, 1923.
Deygas, F. *L'Armée de l'Orient dans la guerre mondiale*. Paris, 1932.
Du Véou, P. *La Passion de la Cilicie*. Paris, 1938.
Falls, C. B. *Military Operations, Egypt and Palestine*. Vol. 2: *June 1917 to end of the War*. London, H.M.S.O., 1930.
France, Ministère des Affaires Etrangères. *La Syrie et le Liban en 1922*. Paris, 1922.
Frischwasser Ra'anan, H. F. *Frontiers of a Nation; a Re-examination of the Forces which created the Palestine Mandate and Determined its Territorial Shape*. London, 1955.
Gaillard, G. *Les Turcs et l'Europe*. Paris, 1920.
Gautherot, G. *La France en Syrie et en Cilicie*. Courbevoie, 1920.
Georges-Gaulis, Berthe. *Angora, Constantinople, Londres*. Paris, 1922.
Gontaut-Biron, R., *Comte* de. *Comment la France s'est installée en Syrie*. Paris, 1923.
Great Britain, Foreign Office. *Franco-British Convention of 23 December 1920*. Cmd. 1195.
House, E. M. and C. Seymour. *What Really Happened at Paris; Peace Conference 1918–19*. New York, 1921.
*Ḥuṣri, Saṭi' al-. *Yawm Maysalun*. Beirut, 1947.
Huvelin, P. 'Que Veut la Syrie?', *L'Asie Française*, December 1921.
Khairallah, K. T. *Le Problème du Levant; les régions arabes libérées*. Paris, 1919.
Kheduri, E. *England and the Middle East*. London, 1956.
*Khuri, A. Yamin al. *Lubnan fi'l ḥarb*. Beirut, 1919.
Lammens, H. *La Syrie: précis historique*. Vol. 2. Beirut, 1921.
Lawrence, T. E. *The Seven Pillars of Wisdom*. London, 1935.
Leslie, Shane. *Mark Sykes; His Life and Letters*. London, 1923.
Liman von Sanders, O. K. V., General. *Fünf Jahre Türkei*. Berlin, 1919.
Lloyd George, D. *The Truth about the Peace Treaties*. Vol. 2. London, 1938.
Loder, J. de V. *The Truth About Mesopotamia, Palestine and Syria*. London, 1923.
Lyautey, P. *La Syrie et le Liban*. Paris (originally Cairo), 1922.
MacGilvary, Margaret. *The Dawn of a New Era in Syria*. New York, 1920.
McMunn, Sir G. and C. Falls. *Military Operations, Egypt and Palestine*. Vol. 1: *To June 1917*. London, H.M.S.O., 1928.

Miller, D. Hunter. *My Diary at the Peace Conference of Paris*. 21 vols. New York, 1924–6.
Nicolson, Harold. *Curzon, the Last Phase, 1919–25*. London, 1934.
—— *Peacemaking, 1919*. London, 1933.
Poincaré, R. *Au Service de la France*. 4 vols. Paris, 1926–7.
Redan, P. *La Cilicie et le problème ottoman*. Paris, 1921.
Remusat, P. de. 'Les Cent Jours du Roi de Syrie', *Revue des Études Historiques*, June 1924.
*Sa'id, Amin. *al-thawrat al-'Arabiya al Kubra*. 3 vols. Cairo, 1934.
*Sa'id, Nuri al-. *Lectures on Military Operations of the Arab Army in the Hijaz, 1916–18*. Baghdad, 1947.
Shotwell, J. T. *At the Paris Conference*. New York, 1937.
Sixtus Ferdinand, M.I.B.A., *Prince of Parma. La Syrie et la France*. Paris, 1919.
Temperley, H. W. V., *ed. History of the Peace Conference of Paris*. Vol. 6. London, 1924.
'Testis'. *pseud*. 'L'Œuvre de la France au Levant', *Revue de Deux Mondes*, 1921.
The Times. *History of the War*.
La Vérité sur la question Syrienne. Istanbul, [Headquarters, Turkish 4th Army], 1916.
Wavell, A. P., *1st earl. Allenby; a Study in Greatness*. London, 1940.
Zeine, Z. N. *Syria and the Lebanon, 1918–20*. [Unpublished thesis, 1956.]

(IV) PERIOD 1922 TO 1939: MAIN PERIOD OF THE MANDATE

Aboussouan, B. *Le Problème politique syrien*. Paris, 1924.
Achcar, J. *La France et l'Angleterre dans le Proche-Orient; l'Évolution politique de la Syrie et du Liban, de la Palestine et de l'Irak*. Lyons, 1937.
Andréa, C. J. E., Général. *La Révolte druse et l'insurrection de Damas, 1925-6*. Paris, 1937.
*Armanazi, Najib. *Muḥadḥarat 'an Suriya*. Cairo, 1954.
Armellini, A. *La Francia in Siria*. Lanciano, 1934.
Armstrong, H. *Turkey and Syria Reborn*. London, 1930.
Barrès, M. *Une Enquête aux pays du Levant*. Paris, 1923.
Beauplan, R. de. *Où va la Syrie? le mandat sous les cedres*. Paris, 1929.
Benoit, P. *La Châtelaine du Liban*. Paris, 1924.
Bonardi, P. *L'Imbroglio syrien*. Paris, 1927.
Bordeaux, P. H. *Dans la montagne des Druses*. Paris, 1926.
Bouron, N. *Les Druses; histoire du Liban et de la Montagne haouranaise*. 2nd ed. Paris, 1930.
Bulletin Officiel des Actes du Haut Commissariat (Beirut), 1919–.
Burckhard, C. *Le Mandat français en Syrie et au Liban*. Nîmes, 1925.
Capdejelle and Cheikh 'Aziz el Hachem. *La Question syrienne*. Beirut, 1927.
Carbillet, G. *Au Djebel Druse*. Paris, 1927.
Cardahi, C. 'Le Mandat de la France sur la Syrie et le Liban', *Bull. de l'Académie de Droit International*, 1936.

Censoni, D. *La Politica francese nel vicino oriente*. Bologna, 1948.
Collet, Anne. *Collet des Tcherkesses*. Trans. Correa, 1952.
Desjardins, R. *Avec les Sénégalais par delà l'Euphrate*. Paris, 1925.
Dix ans de mandat: l'œuvre française en Syrie et au Liban. Paris, 1931.
Djabry [Jabiri], O. *La Syrie sous le régime du mandat*. Toulouse, 1934.
Doris, J. *La Syrie aux Syriens*. Paris, 1926.
Du Véou, P. *Le Désastre d'Alexandrette, 1934–8; rapport sur les causes, les préliminaires et les conséquences de l'Acte du 29 Mai 1937*. Paris, 1938.
Europe Nouvelle. *La Syrie sous mandat français, 1920–6*. (Collection of articles.)
Farhat, Adib. *La France, puissance mandataire en Syrie et au Liban*. Paris, 1926.
Fidès, P. 'La France et les États du Levant', *Europe Nouvelle*, 1930.
France, Ministère des Affaires Étrangères. *La Syrie et le Liban 1919–1927*. Paris, 1929.
—— *Rapport sur la situation de la Syrie et du Liban, 1922–3* to *1938*.
Gamelin, M. G., Général. *Servir*. 3 vols. Paris, 1946–7.
Georges-Gaulis, Berthe. *La Question arabe*. Paris, 1930.
Gontaut-Biron, R., Comte de. *Sur les routes de Syrie après neuf ans de mandat*. Paris, 1928.
Gordon, Helen C. *Syria As It Is*. London, 1939.
Gouraud, H. J. E., Général. *La France en Syrie*. Corbeil, 1922.
Great Britain, Foreign Office. *Boundary line between Syria and Palestine from the Mediterranean to El Hamme. Agreement between H.M. Government and the French Government*. Cmd. 1910. (Treaty series no. 131, 1923.)
—— *Palestine and Syria and the Lebanon. Agreement to facilitate relations in connexion with frontier questions. Signed at Jerusalem, February 2, 1926*. Cmd. 2919. (Treaty series 1927, no. 19.)
Gruvel, A. *Les États de Syrie*. Paris, 1931.
Henry-Haye, G. and P. Viénot. *Les Relations de la France et de la Syrie*. Paris, 1939.
Homet, M. *L'Histoire secrète du traité franco-syrien*. Paris, 1938.
Jalalbert, L. 'L'Insurrection du Djebel Druse', *Études*, May 1926.
Joffre, A. *Le Mandat de la France sur la Syrie et le Grand-Liban*. Lyons, 1924.
Jones, J. M. *La Fin du mandat français en Syrie et au Liban*. Paris, 1938.
Kayyali [Keyyali], A. *Réponse à Ponsot, Haut Commissiare de la République Française en Syrie et au Liban*. Aleppo, 1933. (Arabic and French.)
Kessel, J. *En Syrie*. Paris, 1927.
Kuzbari, Nadir. *La Question de la cessation du mandat française sur la Syrie*. Paris, 1937.
Lapierre, J. *Le Mandat français en Syrie*. Paris, 1937.
Laurent-Vibert, R. *Ce que j'ai vu en Orient*. Paris, 1924.
Lepine, P. *En Mésopotamie syrienne*. Paris, 1927.
Le Livre d'or des troupes du Levant, 1918–1936. Beirut, Bureau typographique des troupes du Levant, 1936.

Le Mazière, P. *Partant pour la Syrie*. Paris, 1926.
L'Œuvre française en Syrie et au Liban, 1919–1939. Paris, 1939.
Longrigg, S. H. *'Iraq, 1900 to 1950*. London, 1953.
Luquet, J. *La Politique des mandats dans le Levant*. Paris, 1923.
Lyautey, P. *Gouraud*. Paris, 1949.
MacCallum, E. P. *The Nationalist Crusade in Syria*. New York, 1928.
Maestracci, N. F. *La Syrie contemporaine*. Paris, 1930.
Maronite Patriarchate (Mgr Aride). *Le Liban et la France*. Beirut, 1939.
*Mas'ud, Paulus. *Lubnan wa Suriya qabl al-intidab wa ba'duh*. Cairo, 1929.
Moreau, A. *Sur les Routes de Syrie*. Paris, 1924.
Na'im, E. *La Syrie et ses frontières*. Paris, 1934.
Nava, Santi. *Il Mandato francese in Siria dalle sue origini al 1929*. Padua, 1930.
—— *La Questione del Hatay (Alesandretta) et la sua soluzione*. Florence, 1939.
O'Zoux, R. *Les États du Levant sous mandat français*. Paris, 1931.
Pic, P. *Syrie et Palestine; mandats français et anglais dans la Proche-Orient*. Paris, 1924 (and Supplement, 1931).
Poulleau, Alice. *Damas sous les bombes; journal d'une Française pendant la révolte syrienne, 1924–6*. Paris, 1928.
Rabbath, E. *L'Évolution politique de la Syrie sous mandat*. Paris, 1928.
—— *Unité syrienne et devenir arabe*. Paris, 1937.
*Rashid, Ḥanna abu-. *Jabal al-Duruz*. Cairo, 1925.
Roux, G. *La Ratification du traité syrien*. Paris, 1938.
Russell, H. C., *see* Gordon, H. C.
Saint-Point, V. de, *pseud*. *La Vérité sur la Syrie*. Paris, 1929.
Samy, G. 'I Partiti e le associazioni politiche in Siria', *Oriente Moderno*, vol. 20, 1940.
Sandiford, R. *La Siria sotto il mandato della Francia*. Rome, 1925.
*Shahbandar, A. R. *Mudhakkarat*. Cairo, 1939.
Sloan, A. *Wanderings in the Middle East*. London, 1925.
Sorel, J. A. *Le Mandat français et l'expansion économique de la Syrie et du Liban*. Paris, 1929.
Stark, Freya. *Letters from Syria*. London. 1942.
Stein, L. *Syria*. London, 1926.
Tajeddin [Taj al-Din], Cheikh. *Trois ans de gouvernement en Syrie, 1928–31*. Damascus, 1932.
Tharaud, J. and J. *Alerte en Syrie*. Paris, 1937.
—— *Le Chemin de Damas*. Paris, 1923.
—— 'Syrie, 1938', *Revue de Deux Mondes*, 1938.
Toynbee, A. J., *ed*. *Survey of International Affairs, 1925* (pp. 346–466); *1928* (pp. 328–38); *1930* (pp. 304–16); *1934* (pp. 284–305); *1936* (pp. 748–82); *1938* (pp. 479 ff.).
Tritoni, R. *La Fase attuale del problema siriano*. Rome, 1934.
—— *L'Unità della Siria e l'indivisibilità del suo mandato*. Rome, 1934.
Viénot, P. *Le Traité franco-syrien*. Paris, 1939.
Wetterlé, E., *Abbé*. *En Syrie avec le général Gouraud*. Paris, 1924.
Woods, H. C. 'The French in Syria', *Fortnightly Review*, 1925.

Wright, Q. 'The Bombardment of Damascus', *American Journal of International Law*, April 1926.
—— 'Syrian Grievances against French Rule', *Current History*, February 1926.

(V) SECOND WORLD WAR AND LAST YEARS OF THE MANDATE

Abuchidid [abu-Shadid], E. E. *Thirty Years of the Lebanon and Syria*. Beirut, 1948.
Auchinleck, Sir C., General. *Despatches on Operations in the Middle East from November 1941 to August 1942*. (Supplement to *London Gazette*, 1 January 1948.)
—— *Despatches on Operations in the Middle East from July 1941 to October 1941*. (Supplement to *London Gazette*, 21 August 1946.)
Buckley, Christopher. *Five Ventures; Iraq, Syria, Persia*, &c. London, H.M.S.O., 1954.
Borden, Mary [Lady Spears]. *Journey Down a Blind Alley*. London, 1946.
Catroux, G., Général. *Dans la Bataille de Méditerranée; Egypte, Levant, Afrique du Nord, 1940-4*. Paris, 1949.
Charles-Roux, F. *Cinq mois tragiques aux Affaires Étrangères*. Paris, 1949.
Churchill, Sir W. S. *The Second World War*. 6 vols. London, 1948–54.
Collins, R. J., General. *Lord Wavell, 1883–1941*. London, 1947.
Fabre-Luce, A. *Deuil au Levant*. Paris, 1950.
France Combattante, la. *Les Allemands en Syrie sous le gouvernement de Vichy*. London, 1942.
Gaulle, C. A. M. J. de, Général. *Mémoires de guerre*. 2 vols. Paris, 1954–6.
Glubb, *Sir* J. B. *Story of the Arab Legion*. London, 1948.
Goold-Adams, R. J. M. *Middle East Journey*. London, 1947.
Great Britain, Foreign Office. *Statements of Policy in respect of Syria and the Lebanon, 8th June-9th September, 1941*. Cmd. 6600.
Khadduri, M. 'The Franco-Lebanese Dispute of November 1943', *American Journal of International Law*, October 1944.
Kirk, G. *The Middle East in the War*. London, 1952.
—— *The Middle East, 1945–50*. London, 1954.
Laffargue, A. *Le Général Dentz: Paris 1940–Syrie 1941*. Paris, 1954.
Livre jaune de la Correspondance d'Orient sur la crise syrienne et libanaise. Paris, Correspondance d'Orient, 1945.
Lloyd, E. M. E. *Food and Inflation in the Middle East*. Stanford, 1956.
London, G. *L'Amiral Esteva et le général Dentz devant la Haute cour de justice*. Lyons, 1945.
Muselier, E. H., Vice-Amiral. *De Gaulle contre le Gaullisme*. Paris, 1946.
Playfair, I. S. O. *and others*. *The Mediterranean and the Middle East*. 2 vols. London, 1954–6. (*History of the Second World War*, U.K. military series.)
Prest, A. R. *War Economics of Primary Producing Countries*. Cambridge, 1948.
Puaux, G. *Deux années au Levant; souvenirs de Syrie et du Liban*. Paris, 1952.
Soustelle, J. *Envers et contre tout*. 2 vols. Paris, 1947–50.

Spears, Sir E. L. 'British Policy in the Middle East', *Royal Central Asian Society Journal*, 1945.
*Taj al-Din, Munir. *Birth of Independence*. Beirut, 1953.
Wavell, A. P., 1st Vicount, Field-Marshal. *Despatch on Operations in the Middle East from 7th February, 1941 to 15th July, 1941*. (Supplement to *London Gazette*, 3 July 1946.)
—— *Despatch on Operations in Iraq, East Syria and Iran, from 10th April, 1941 to 12th January, 1942*. (Supplement to *London Gazette*, 14 August 1946.)
Weygand, M., Général. *Mémoires; vol. 3: Rappelé au Service*. Paris, 1950.
Wilson, H. M., 1st Baron, Field-Marshal. *Despatches on Operations in the Middle East from 16th February, 1943 to 8th January, 1944*. (Supplement to *London Gazette*, 12 November 1944.)
—— *Despatches on the Persian and Iraq Command covering the period 21st August, 1942 to 17th February, 1943*. (Supplement to *London Gazette*, 27 August 1946.)
—— *Eight Years Overseas, 1939–47*. London, 1950.

(VI) GENERAL WORKS

(A) HISTORICAL, POLITICAL, CONSTITUTIONAL

*'Abdullah, King. *Transjordan White Book* (*Greater Syria*). Jerusalem, 1947.
—— *Memoirs*. Jerusalem, 1945.
Ambrosini, G. *Paese sotto mandato*. Rome, 1932.
Antonius, G. *The Arab Awakening*. London, 1938.
Ayoub, C. *Les Mandats orientaux*. Paris, 1924.
Bentwich, N. *The Mandates System*. London, 1930.
Bruneau, A. *Traditions et politique de la France au Levant*. Paris, 1932.
Bullard, Sir R. W. *Britain and the Middle East*. London, 1951.
Caix, R. de. *Histoire des colonies françaises*. Vol. 3. Paris, 1931.
Cataluccio, F. *Storia del nazionalismo arabo*. Milan, 1939.
Chamoun, C. *Les Mémoires de Camille Chamoun*. Beirut, 1949.
Coke, R. *The Arab's Place in the Sun*. London, 1920.
Dareste, F. R. and P. *Les Constitutions modernes*. 6 vols. Paris, 1928–34.
Davis, Helen M. *Constitutions, Electoral Laws, Treaties &c. in the Middle East*. North Carolina, 1948.
Driault, E. *La Question d'Orient, 1918–1937*. Paris, 1938.
Giannini, A. *Le Costituzione degli stati del Vicino Oriente*. Rome, 1931.
—— *L'Ultima fase della questione orientale, 1913–1932*. Milan, 1941.
Hitti, P. K. *History of Syria, including Lebanon and Palestine*. London, 1951.
Hourani, A. H. *Syria and Lebanon*. London, 1946.
Howard, H. N. *The Partition of Turkey; a Diplomatic History*. Oklahoma, 1931.
Jung, E. *L'Islam et l'Asie devant l'impérialisme*. Paris, 1927.
Khadduri, M. 'Constitutional Development in Syria', *Middle East Journal*, April 1951.

Kirk, G. *Short History of the Middle East*. London, 1948.
Kohn, H. *Nationalism and Imperialism in the Hither East*. London, 1932.
—— *Western Civilization in the Near East*. New York, 1936.
*Kurd 'Ali, Muhammad. *History of Damascus*. Vol. 6. Damascus, 1925.
Laqueur, W. Z. *Communism and Nationalism in the Middle East*. London, 1956.
Lenczowski, G. *The Middle East in World Affairs*. New York, 1952.
Majzoub, Mohammed. *Le Liban et l'Orient arabe, 1943–56*. Aix-en-Provence, 1956.
Nava, Santi. *Il Problema dell'espansione italiana ed il Levante islamico*. Rome, 1931.
Pernot, M. *L'Inquiétude de l'Orient sur la route de l'Inde*. Paris, 1927.
Pichon, J. *Les Origines orientales de la guerre mondiale*. Paris, 1937.
—— *La Partage du Proche-Orient*. Paris, 1938.
*Rayḥani, Amin. *Muluk al-'Arab*. Beirut, 1924.
Rondot, P. 'L'Expérience du Mandat Français en Syrie', *Revue Générale de Droit International Publique*, 1948.
—— *Les Institutions politiques du Liban*. Paris, 1947.
Sa'id, Nuri al-. *Arab Independence and Unity*. Baghdad, 1943.
Syria, Direction Générale de l'Information. *Syria*. 2 vols. Damascus, 1955.
Tarazi, Salah al-Din. *Les Services publics Libano-Syriens*. Beirut, 1946.
Van Rees, D. F. W. *Les Mandats internationaux*. Paris, 1927.
White, Freda. *Mandates*. London, 1926.
Wright, Q. *Mandates under the League of Nations*. Chicago, 1930.
Ziyadeh, N. A. *Syria and Lebanon*. London, 1957.

(B) TOPOGRAPHICAL AND SOCIOLOGICAL

Birot, P. and J. Dresch. *La Méditérranée et le Moyen-Orient*. Vol. 2. Paris, 1956.
Castle, W. T. F. *Syrian Pageant; History of Syria and Palestine*. London, 1947.
Cayla, L. *Terres d'Outre-mer*. Paris, 1948.
Chiha, M. *Le Liban d'aujourd'hui*. Beirut, 1949.
Dodd, S. C. *Social Relations in the Middle East*. Beirut, 1946.
Eddé, J. *Géographie Liban-Syrie*. Beirut. 1941.
Fedden, H. R. *Syria; an Historical Appreciation*. London, 1946.
Fisher, W. B. *The Middle East*. London, 1950.
Grant, Christina P. *The Syrian Desert*. London, 1937.
Les Guides bleu. *Syrie &c*. Paris, 1932.
Haddad, G. *Fifty Years of Modern Syria and Lebanon*. Beirut, 1947.
Hourani, A. H. *Minorities in the Arab World*. London, 1947.
Izzidin, F. abu- and G. Hakim. 'Labour Conditions in the Lebanon', *I.L.O. Review*, November 1933.
Jacquot, P., Colonel. *Antioch, Beirut, 1931; l'État des Alaouites*. Beirut, 1929. (Guides touristiques.)
Latron, A. *La Vie rurale en Syrie et au Liban*. Beirut, 1936.
Luke, Sir H. C. *Prophets, Priests and Patriarchs; Sketches of the Sects of Palestine and Syria*. London, 1927.

Matthew, R. D. and M. Akrawi. *Education in Arab Countries of the Near East*. Washington, D.C., 1949.
*Min Huwa: *Who's Who, for Syria*. Damascus, 1949.
Moran, V. P. *La Route des Indes*. Paris, 1936.
Mueller, V. *En Syrie avec les bédouins*. Paris, 1931.
Pearse, R. *Three Years in the Levant*. London, 1949.
Penrose, S. B. L. *That They May Have Life; the Story of the American University of Beirut, 1866–1941*. Princeton, 1941.
Pernot, M. *En Asie musulmane*. Paris, 1927.
Ross, F. A. *and others*. *The Near East in American Philanthropy*. New York, 1929.
Rouhi, Jamil. *Beirut and Lebanon*. Beirut, 1948. (Green Guides.)
—— *Damascus, Palmyra and Ba'albek*. Beirut, 1945.
*Sayeg, Salma. *Quelques aspects d'humanisme au Liban*. Beirut, 1949. (French and Arabic.)
Stark, Freya. *Letters from Syria, 1927–9*. London, 1942.
Steimatzky's Guides. *Syria and Lebanon*. Jerusalem, 1942.
Weulersse, J. *Les Pays des Alaouites*. 2 vols. Tours, 1940.
—— *Paysans de Syrie et du Proche-Orient*. Paris, 1946.

(c) ECONOMIC

*Badré, A. *Economics of Lebanon*. Cairo, 1955.
Bonné, A. *Economic Development of the Middle East*. London, 1943 (and revisions).
Great Britain, Board of Trade, Dept. of Overseas Trade. *Iraq, Syria, the Lebanon, Cyprus, British Goodwill Trade Mission* [Davidson Mission], *Report, August 31, 1946*. London, 1946.
—— *Report on Economic Conditions in Syria and the Lebanon*, June 1936. London, 1936.
—— *Report on the Trade, Industry and Finanace of Syria, May 1925*. London, 1925.
Himadeh, S. B., *ed*. *Economic Organization of Syria*. Beirut, 1936.
—— *The Monetary and Banking System of Syria*. Beirut, 1935.
International Bank for Reconstruction and Development. *The Economic Development of Syria*. Baltimore, 1955.
Keen, B. A. *Agricultural Development of the Middle East*. London, 1946.
Longrigg, S. H. *Oil in the Middle East*. London, 1954.
Mousalli, N. *Études économiques sur la Syrie et le Liban*. Harissa (Leb.) 1933.
*Samman, Aḥmad. *Economics of Syria*. Cairo, 1955.
Vecchia, Vaglieri, L. 'La Situazione Economica della Siria', *Oriente Moderno*, 1936.
Warriner, Doreen. *Land and Poverty in the Middle East*. London, 1948.
—— *Land Reform and Development in the Middle East*. London, 1957.
Worthington, E. B. *Middle East Science*. London, 1946.

INDEX

This Index contains only proper names. Certain place names of very common occurrence (Beirut, Paris, Asia Minor, Damascus, Aleppo, &c.) are designated as ‘passim’, or are omitted. Names in the tables which form Appendixes A and B are not mentioned if they do not occur elsewhere. Authors of source-books are indexed *only* if quoted in footnotes to the text; they are listed in alphabetical order in the various sections of Appendix E.

Some alternative, usually French, spellings of place-names are inserted.

Pisani, Capt., 64n.
Poincaré, M. R., 56n.
Poland, Poles, 297, 346n., 358
Ponsot, M. Henri, 176-95, 203, 211, 239n.
Pope, the, 150
Port Said, 53, 76
Poupon, M., 260n.
Presbyterians, 12, 40
Prévot, Col., 261n.
Privat-Aubouard, M., 123n., 131n., 149n., 204, 260n.
Progressive Party, 150
Progressive Socialist Party, 359
Protestants, 12, 41, 53, 91
Puaux, M. Gabriel, 82n., 208n., 212n., 233ff., 237, 243, 245, 247, 250f., 294ff.
Public Debt, *see* Ottoman Public Debt.

Qabbani, Najib al-, 170n.
Qadhamani, 'Awni al-, 183n.
Qadri, Dr. Ahmad, 86n.
Qadri, Tahsin, 86n.
Qahtaniya (Society), 28
Qa'im, al-, 142
Qal'at al-Jindal, 158
Qaltaqchi, 'Abd al-Hamid Pasha, al-, 51n., 98n.
Qamishli (Kamechliyé), 212, 249, 353
Qanawat, 126
Qardahi, Shukri (Shakir), al-, 178n., 201n.
Qasim, Mulhim, 122
Qassab, Kamil, al-, 98
Qatraghasi, Safwat al-, 302n.
Qawuqchi, Fawzi al-, 165, 167
Qazan, Fu'ad, 227n.
Qudsi, Kamil Pasha al-, 126
Quilichini, Col., 260n.
Qunaytara (Qouneitra), 123, 157, 165, 311
Quraya, 131
Qusayri, Mustafa al-, 217n.
Quwatli, Shukri al-, 51n., 104n., 220n., 232, 301n., 302, 324, 326, 328f., 346
Quwayq (river), 174n., 281

Rabbath (Rabbat), M. E., 49n., 73n., 115n., 218
Radio-Orient (Company), 129n., 279
Rafah, 62
Rahn, Herr, 304
Ras al-'Ayn (Ras El Aïn), 290n.
Rashaya, 75n., 100, 161, 202n., 331
Raslan, Mudhhir al-, 27n., 192n., 194, 221, 235, 244, 330n.
Rayaq, 33, 96, 101, 157f., 278f., 309
Raynaud, Capt., 153f.
Reclus, M., 260n.
Reffye, M. de, 260n.
Reform Party, *see* Syrian Reform Party.
Régie Co-interessée de Tabacs, 18n., 34, 36, 42, 129n., 134f., 146, 150, 268; monopoly, after 1930, 198, 206, 210, 268, 340
Régie de Cadastre, 280
Régie des Études Hydrauliques, 281
Régie Générale des Chemins de Fer, 32n., 33, 278n.
Regismanset, M., 261n.
Renaissance (Ba'th) Party, 359
Republican Reform Party, 203f.
Reid, T., 240n., 241
Rendu, M., 260n.
'Renoir', 304n.
Ridha, Shaykh Rashid, 28n., 142
Rif, the, 152
Rif'at, Khalil, 237n.
Rikabi, 'Ali Ridha Pasha al-, 52n., 64, 67, 83, 95, 98, 100, 187
Rizqullah, George, 100n.
Romans, Rome, 1, 3, 39, 252n., 290n., *see also* Italy, Italians.
Rothschild, Lord, 60
Roucolle, M., 260n.
Roux, M., 260n.
Royal Air Force, 168n., 309
Rumania(ns), 32n., 272
Rum Qal'a, 119
Rural Life, Institute of, 281
Russians: before 1914, 13, 15n., 19, 31n., 32, 40f., 46f.; 1914–20, 49, 53, 58, 67n., 71; period 1920–46, 227, 254, 312, 346, 351, 354, 367
Rutba, 157n., 278

Sa'ada, Antun, 225ff., 295, 359
Sa'd, Amin al-, 323n.
Sa'd, Habib Pasha al-, 66n., 76n., 128, 201, 203, 205
Safad, 67n.
Safita, 125n., 210, 244n.
St. Joseph, University of, 43, 77, 288; Sisters of, 431
St. Petersburg, 56
St. Simeon Stylites, 290n.
St. Vincent de Paul, Sisters of, 43
Sahnawi, Hanin, 302n.
Sa'id, Shaykh (Kurdish leader), 212n.
Sa'id Nuri Pasha al-, 63, 84n., 86n., 101, 103, 300, 351n.
Sa'id, Ridha al-, 151n.
Salefka, 75n.
Salesians, 43
Salih al-'Ali, Shaykh, 80
Salim, Fu'ad, 104n.
Salim, the Grim (Sultan), 2
Salim, Yusif, 343n.
Salimiya (Agricultural College), 288n.
Salins, M. de, 260n.

Wilson, F.M. Lord, 307ff., 313ff., 319n., 326
Wilson, President Woodrow, 71f., 87, 92n., 97, 128
Wingate, Sir R., 54n.

Yafi, 'Abdullah al-, 254
Yalta, 346n.
Yaman (Yemen), 351n.
Yamuna, Lake, 281
Yasin Pasha, *see* Hashimi, Yasin Pasha al-.
Yazidis, 10, 182n., 248n.
Yenija, 118
Young Arabs Society, *see* Fatat, al-.
Young Turks, 20, 28. *See also* Union and Progress, Committee of.
Yugoslavia, King Peter of, 331
Yusif, 'Abd al-Raḥman al-, 103n., 104

Zaghurta, 202
Zaḥla (Zahlé), 102n., 150n., 202n., 205, 355
Zawiya, Jabal al-, 165
Zayd bin Ḥusayn, the Amir, 95, 187
Zion, Priests of, 43
Zionism, Zionists, 46, 54, 59ff., 67n., 71, 88f., 90n., 97f., 107, 109, 141, 151, 186, 215, 252n., 256, 301, 352. *See also* Jews, Palestine.
Ziyadeh, N. A., 170n.
Zuhdi, Jalal al-, 98n., 100n., 103n., 151n.
Zukkur, Michael, 252n.

Printed in Great Britain by
The Camelot Press Ltd., London and Southampton